Dictionary of Literary Biography

Documentary Series

1 *Sherwood Anderson, Willa Cather, John Dos Passos, Theodore Dreiser, F. Scott Fitzgerald, Ernest Hemingway, Sinclair Lewis,* edited by Margaret A. Van Antwerp (1982)

2 *James Gould Cozzens, James T. Farrell, William Faulkner, John O'Hara, John Steinbeck, Thomas Wolfe, Richard Wright,* edited by Margaret A. Van Antwerp (1982)

3 *Saul Bellow, Jack Kerouac, Norman Mailer, Vladimir Nabokov, John Updike, Kurt Vonnegut,* edited by Mary Bruccoli (1983)

4 *Tennessee Williams,* edited by Margaret A. Van Antwerp and Sally Johns (1984)

5 *American Transcendentalists,* edited by Joel Myerson (1988)

6 *Hardboiled Mystery Writers: Raymond Chandler, Dashiell Hammett, Ross Macdonald,* edited by Matthew J. Bruccoli and Richard Layman (1989)

7 *Modern American Poets: James Dickey, Robert Frost, Marianne Moore,* edited by Karen L. Rood (1989)

8 *The Black Aesthetic Movement,* edited by Jeffrey Louis Decker (1991)

9 *American Writers of the Vietnam War: W. D. Ehrhart, Larry Heinemann, Tim O'Brien, Walter McDonald, John M. Del Vecchio,* edited by Ronald Baughman (1991)

10 *The Bloomsbury Group,* edited by Edward L. Bishop (1992)

11 *American Proletarian Culture: The Twenties and The Thirties,* edited by Jon Christian Suggs (1993)

12 *Southern Women Writers: Flannery O'Connor, Katherine Anne Porter, Eudora Welty,* edited by Mary Ann Wimsatt and Karen L. Rood (1994)

13 *The House of Scribner, 1846–1904,* edited by John Delaney (1996)

14 *Four Women Writers for Children, 1868–1918,* edited by Caroline C. Hunt (1996)

Yearbooks

1980 edited by Karen L. Rood, Jean W. Ross, and Richard Ziegfeld (1981)

1981 edited by Karen L. Rood, Jean W. Ross, and Richard Ziegfeld (1982)

1982 edited by Richard Ziegfeld; associate editors: Jean W. Ross and Lynne C. Zeigler (1983)

1983 edited by Mary Bruccoli and Jean W. Ross; associate editor: Richard Ziegfeld (1984)

1984 edited by Jean W. Ross (1985)

1985 edited by Jean W. Ross (1986)

1986 edited by J. M. Brook (1987)

1987 edited by J. M. Brook (1988)

1988 edited by J. M. Brook (1989)

1989 edited by J. M. Brook (1990)

1990 edited by James W. Hipp (1991)

1991 edited by James W. Hipp (1992)

1992 edited by James W. Hipp (1993)

1993 edited by James W. Hipp, contributing editor George Garrett (1994)

1994 edited by James W. Hipp, contributing editor George Garrett (1995)

1995 edited by James W. Hipp, contributing editor George Garrett (1996)

Concise Series

Concise Dictionary of American Literary Biography, 6 volumes (1988-1989): *The New Consciousness, 1941-1968; Colonization to the American Renaissance, 1640-1865; Realism, Naturalism, and Local Color, 1865-1917; The Twenties, 1917-1929; The Age of Maturity, 1929-1941; Broadening Views, 1968-1988.*

Concise Dictionary of British Literary Biography, 8 volumes (1991-1992): *Writers of the Middle Ages and Renaissance Before 1660; Writers of the Restoration and Eighteenth Century, 1660-1789; Writers of the Romantic Period, 1789-1832; Victorian Writers, 1832-1890; Late Victorian and Edwardian Writers, 1890-1914; Modern Writers, 1914-1945; Writers After World War II, 1945-1960; Contemporary Writers, 1960 to Present.*

Dictionary of Literary Biography® • Volume One Hundred Seventy

The British Literary Book Trade, 1475–1700

Dictionary of Literary Biography® • Volume One Hundred Seventy

The British Literary Book Trade, 1475–1700

Edited by
James K. Bracken
Ohio State University
and
Joel Silver
Lilly Library, Indiana University

A Bruccoli Clark Layman Book
Gale Research
Detroit, Washington, D.C., London

The paper used in this publication meets the minimum requirements
of American National Standard for Information Sciences–Permanence
Paper for Printed Library Materials, ANSI Z39.48-1984. ∞ ™

Library of Congress Cataloging-in-Publication Data

British literary booktrade, 1475–1700 / edited by James K. Bracken and Joel Silver.
   p. cm. – (Dictionary of literary biography; v. 170)
"A Bruccoli Clark Layman book."
Includes bibliographical references and index.
ISBN 0-8103-9933-4 (alk. paper)
1. Booksellers and bookselling – Great Britain – Biography. 2. Publishers and publishing – Great Britain – Biography. 3. Printers – Great Britain – Biography. 4. Book industries and trade – Great Britain – History – Bibliography. 5. Literature publishing – Great Britain – History – Bibliography. 6. English literature – Early modern, 1500–1700 – Publishing – Bibliography. 7. English literature – Middle English, 1100–1500 – Publishing – Bibliography. I. Bracken, James K., 1952- . II. Silver, Joel, 1951- . III. Series.
Z325.B74 1996
016.381'45002'0942 – dc20
[B]

96–31977
CIP

10 9 8 7 6 5 4 3 2 1

Contents

Plan of the Series

. . . Almost the most prodigious asset of a country, and perhaps its most precious possession, is its native literary product — when that product is fine and noble and enduring.

Mark Twain*

The advisory board, the editors, and the publisher of the *Dictionary of Literary Biography* are joined in endorsing Mark Twain's declaration. The literature of a nation provides an inexhaustible resource of permanent worth. We intend to make literature and its creators better understood and more accessible to students and the reading public, while satisfying the standards of teachers and scholars.

To meet these requirements, *literary biography* has been construed in terms of the author's achievement. The most important thing about a writer is his writing. Accordingly, the entries in *DLB* are career biographies, tracing the development of the author's canon and the evolution of his reputation.

The purpose of *DLB* is not only to provide reliable information in a convenient format but also to place the figures in the larger perspective of literary history and to offer appraisals of their accomplishments by qualified scholars.

The publication plan for *DLB* resulted from two years of preparation. The project was proposed to Bruccoli Clark by Frederick C. Ruffner, president of the Gale Research Company, in November 1975. After specimen entries were prepared and typeset, an advisory board was formed to refine the entry format and develop the series rationale. In meetings held during 1976, the publisher, series editors, and advisory board approved the scheme for a comprehensive biographical dictionary of persons who contributed to North American literature. Editorial work on the first volume began in January 1977, and it was published in 1978. In order to make *DLB* more than a reference tool and to compile volumes that individually have claim to status as literary history, it was decided to organize volumes by topic, period, or genre. Each of these free-standing volumes provides a biographical-bibliographical guide and overview for a particular area of literature. We are convinced that this organization — as opposed to a single alphabet method — constitutes a valuable innovation in the presentation of reference material. The volume plan necessarily requires many decisions for the placement and treatment of authors who might properly be included in two or three volumes. In some instances a major figure will be included in separate volumes, but with different entries emphasizing the aspect of his career appropriate to each volume. Ernest Hemingway, for example, is represented in *American Writers in Paris, 1920–1939* by an entry focusing on his expatriate apprenticeship; he is also in *American Novelists, 1910–1945* with an entry surveying his entire career. Each volume includes a cumulative index of the subject authors and articles. Comprehensive indexes to the entire series are planned.

With volume ten in 1982 it was decided to enlarge the scope of *DLB*. By the end of 1986 twenty-one volumes treating British literature had been published, and volumes for Commonwealth and Modern European literature were in progress. The series has been further augmented by the *DLB Yearbooks* (since 1981) which update published entries and add new entries to keep the *DLB* current with contemporary activity. There have also been *DLB Documentary Series* volumes which provide biographical and critical source materials for figures whose work is judged to have particular interest for students. One of these companion volumes is entirely devoted to Tennessee Williams.

We define literature as the *intellectual commerce of a nation:* not merely as belles lettres but as that ample and complex process by which ideas are generated, shaped, and transmitted. *DLB* entries are not limited to "creative writers" but extend to other figures who in their time and in their way influenced the mind of a people. Thus the series encompasses historians, journalists, publishers, and screenwriters. By this means readers of *DLB* may be aided to perceive literature not as cult scripture in the keeping of intellectual high priests but firmly positioned at the center of a nation's life.

---

*From an unpublished section of Mark Twain's autobiography, copyright by the Mark Twain Company

DLB includes the major writers appropriate to each volume and those standing in the ranks immediately behind them. Scholarly and critical counsel has been sought in deciding which minor figures to include and how full their entries should be. Wherever possible, useful references are made to figures who do not warrant separate entries.

Each *DLB* volume has a volume editor responsible for planning the volume, selecting the figures for inclusion, and assigning the entries. Volume editors are also responsible for preparing, where appropriate, appendices surveying the major periodicals and literary and intellectual movements for their volumes, as well as lists of further readings. Work on the series as a whole is coordinated at the Bruccoli Clark Layman editorial center in Columbia, South Carolina, where the editorial staff is responsible for accuracy of the published volumes.

One feature that distinguishes *DLB* is the illustration policy – its concern with the iconography of literature. Just as an author is influenced by his surroundings, so is the reader's understanding of the author enhanced by a knowledge of his environment. Therefore *DLB* volumes include not only drawings, paintings, and photographs of authors, often depicting them at various stages in their careers, but also illustrations of their families and places where they lived. Title pages are regularly reproduced in facsimile along with dust jackets for modern authors. The dust jackets are a special feature of *DLB* because they often document better than anything else the way in which an author's work was perceived in its own time. Specimens of the writers' manuscripts are included when feasible.

Samuel Johnson rightly decreed that "The chief glory of every people arises from its authors." The purpose of the *Dictionary of Literary Biography* is to compile literary history in the surest way available to us – by accurate and comprehensive treatment of the lives and work of those who contributed to it.

The *DLB* Advisory Board

Introduction

This volume of the *Dictionary of Literary Biography* covers the literary book trade in Britain from 1475 to 1700, a span of two and a quarter centuries that began with the introduction of the handpress and printing into the British Isles and ended within a century of the revolution that widespread mechanization would bring to book production. As the fourth volume of the *Dictionary of Literary Biography* to treat British literary publishers, it joins volumes 106 and 112, which cover the years from 1820 to 1965, and volume 154, which covers the period from 1700 to 1820.

Like its predecessors, volume 170 of the *Dictionary of Literary Biography* adopts a broad definition of *literary,* including figures who are known primarily for works in fields other than poetry, drama, and prose. This volume includes, for example, William Cooper, a specialist in alchemy and science; John Playford, a publisher of music books; and Nathaniel Butter and Nicholas Bourne, publishers of news books and newspapers. It also follows the general selection practices of those previous volumes on the book trade by including studies of some individuals and presses (for example, Jacob Tonson, Christopher Bateman, Barnaby B. Lintot, and the university presses at Oxford and Cambridge) whose initial book-trade activities occurred between the designated years (1475–1700) but whose greatest productivity and significance came after those years.

The developments in the British book trade described in this volume occurred against a backdrop of religious, political, and social upheaval including the Reformation of the sixteenth century, with its legacy of tension and enmity between Protestants and Catholics, and the struggles between the Crown and Parliament, leading to the Civil War of the 1640s and the Glorious Revolution of the 1680s. As the products of the press reveal, this was an age of great intellectual vitality. Along with pamphlets of factional and doctrinal religious strife and political unrest, the plays of William Shakespeare and Ben Jonson; the poetry of Geoffrey Chaucer, Edmund Spenser, and John Milton; the music of William Byrd and Henry Purcell; and the scientific works of Robert Boyle, Robert Hooke, and Sir Isaac Newton distinguished the period.

The British book trade from 1475 to 1700 was an age of firsts on native soil. This volume includes many notable firsts, although one must also recognize that printing came late to England and that throughout the period it developed more slowly than on the Continent and was often practiced less artfully by English printers than by some Continental tradesmen. It is characteristic of this relatively slow development by the English book trade that, although William Caxton was the first British printer and the first printer in England, he printed the first English book in 1473 not in England but on the Continent at Bruges.

When Caxton returned to England in 1476 to establish the first native press, he discovered a thriving and organized trade in manuscripts that had been centered in London since the end of the fourteenth century. In London Caxton also saw trade in new and secondhand books – fine illuminated works bound in vellum and printed on commission for specific patrons as well as cheaper popular titles copied quickly by entrepreneurial scribes to fit prepackaged paper-and-vellum booklets for an audience of literate bourgeoisie, an audience of uncertain size. That Caxton set up his press at Westminster, outside the existing London manuscript trade, and commenced printing with royal encouragement and the patronage of Anthony Woodville, second earl Rivers and brother-in-law of Edward IV perhaps reveals some apprehensions he had about the popular market. It was left to John Lettou, an alien, to set up the first press in London in 1480; another alien, William Faques of Normandy, would become the first printer to the king in 1503.

A significant feature in the careers of many of the earliest British printers and publishers (with the notable exception of Caxton) was their seeking to create and expand a viable popular market for their printed productions and to reduce their dependence on royal or aristocratic patronage. For example, Wynkyn de Worde – Caxton's successor, who lacked Caxton's aristocratic contacts – moved his predecessor's press in 1501 to London, where he relied far less on patronage than Caxton had. The period is marked by many individuals like Caxton, whose activities combined some of the responsibilities of author, editor, translator, printer, publisher, and bookseller, but shortly after the introduction of printing to England increasingly complex production arrangements evolved. These reflected the development of trade specializations such as those that had appeared in the British manuscript trade, developments resulting in partnerships and the distribution of risks associated with competition and market demands. Another later by-product of this movement from economic dependence on patronage to dependence on a wider market was the development of professional authorship. The formation of great publishing syndicates, or congers, in the eighteenth century was anticipated during the period 1475–1700 by temporary alliances of individuals in publishing specific books – alliances such as that of William and Isaac Jaggard, John Smethwicke, and William Aspley for Shakespeare's First Folio of 1623 – as well as by more formal alliances such as those among the printers of the Eliot's Court Press.

The publication of the first English Bible affords another example of the relatively slow development of the British book trade. In an age of religious fervor Bibles were among the first printed books on the Continent, and they continued to be a staple of early European book production. But Caxton and his most notable successors, Wynkyn de Worde and Richard Pynson, printed no vernacular Bibles, and only after Henry VIII broke with Rome in the 1530s did Bible production in England begin. Like Caxton's first book printed in English, the first Bibles in the English language were printed not in England but on the Continent. William Tyndale's English New Testament was first printed at Cologne in 1525, and his translation of the Pentateuch appeared in Marburg in 1530. The Coverdale Bible, the first complete Bible in English, was printed at Cologne or Marburg in 1535, and not until 1537 was a Bible printed in England. Bible printing came so late to England partly because its printing was controlled by royal patent, but also because the book trade suffered from native weaknesses: printing of the Bible required extensive technical skills and resources lacking in most early British printing houses. Although some thirty complete Bibles and fifty New Testaments were to appear by 1557, when compared with Bible printing on the Continent, the printing of Bibles was slow to develop in England.

Other notable firsts included in this volume also reflect the slower development of the print trade in England than that which had evolved on the Continent. While the first volume of mensural music had been printed in Paris in 1496, William Rastell printed the first such English volume in 1527. The first use of italic type was in Venice in 1500; the first use of italic type in England was by Wynkyn de Worde in 1528. Whereas the first work printed fully in Greek had appeared in Milan in 1476, Reyner Wolfe was to produce the first such work in England only in 1543. On the other hand, several other English firsts show the increasing sophistication of the British book trade: John Windet printed the first trade catalogue for Andrew Maunsell in 1595. William Jaggard in 1617 produced the first book to be sold by subscription; Nathaniel Butter and Nicholas Bourne produced the first newspaper in 1621; William Cooper conducted the first book auction in 1676; and Joseph Moxon wrote the first book on printing in 1683.

In the early sixteenth century the momentous events of the Reformation in England – followed in the seventeenth century by the Civil War, Commonwealth, Restoration, and Glorious Revolution periods – are directly reflected in the civil regulation of the early book trade. The craft that Caxton introduced into England in 1476 was essentially dependent on foreign technology, materials, and skills. Many English printing houses obtained their fonts from the Continent until William Caslon's designs became popular during the second quarter of the eighteenth century. Likewise, until the late seventeenth century English printers depended largely on foreign sources of paper to supply their presses.

On the other hand, legislation intended to develop skilled native talent in the book trade was rapidly instituted, and a series of regulations culminating in the Act of 1534, which prohibited aliens from setting up new presses as well as from retailing foreign books, put the conduct of the British book trade firmly under the control of native craftsmen. This authority was in turn both centralized and consolidated by the incorporation of the Stationers' Company of London on 4 May 1557. Under the terms of the company's royal charter, company members were given a monopoly on both printing and bookselling, except for stationers at the universities of Cambridge and Oxford. In addition to recounting this history of the London Stationers' Company, this volume includes entries on several individuals prominent in the consolidation of the company's power – figures such as John Day, Henry Denham, and William Seres – as well as others such as John Wolfe and Richard Waldegrave, who challenged the limits of state and trade regulation.

If the Reformation in England brought more restrictive government and trade control of the press and the book trade, then the events of the Civil War and its aftermath deregulated the conduct of the press and the book trade. Under Charles I the court of the Star Chamber had illegally extended its own powers and served, through its decrees and prosecutions, to control the English press. Abolition of the Star Chamber court in 1641 and of the monarchy following the Civil War brought the possibility of free trade and allowed the reestablishment of the press outside London. These events also permitted challenges to the accepted notions and methods of copyright and invited increases in copyright infringement and piracy violations. Among the more prominent figures in efforts to liberate the press from traditional controls was Michael Sparke, whose *Scintilla* (1641) condemned the trade's accepted practice of monopolies. Under these monopolies, which were popular with those individuals or groups who held them, the rights to print a title or a particular class of book, such as Bibles or music, were granted to those fortunate recipients for long periods of time. Other figures who participated in the politically charged debates of the period include the Whig publishers Richard and Anne Baldwin, the Royalists Joseph Hindmarsh and Richard Royston, and Quaker printer Tace Sowle.

Perhaps the most studied works of the age, often regarded as the "golden age" of English literature, are those of William Shakespeare. Because of the pioneering bibliographical work of such scholars as Ronald B. McKerrow, W. W. Greg, Fredson Bowers, Charlton Hinman, and more recently Peter Blayney, perhaps more is known about the particular working conditions of Shakespeare's printers, publishers, and booksellers than of any of their contemporaries. Indeed, much of what was discovered about the production of Shakespeare's works has been taken as normative; more recently, as D. F. McKenzie has demonstrated in "Printers of the Mind," his important article on printing practices in the period, those "norms" often conceal far greater variety than was previously thought.

This volume includes about one-third of the London bookmen associated with the publication of Shakespeare's quartos – bookmen such as Thomas Creede, John Danter, George Eld, Nicholas Okes, Peter Short, and Valentine Simmes, as well as the printers of the 1623 First Folio, William and Isaac Jaggard. But the period from 1475 to 1700 was also the age of Sir Philip Sidney, Edmund Spenser, Francis Bacon, Ben Jonson, John Milton, and John Dryden, and certainly the activities of their printers and publishers, although not as thoroughly studied as those of Shakespeare, also merit attention. This volume includes only a few: John Wolfe and William Ponsonby were the printer and publisher of Spenser's *The Faerie Queene* (1590); John Windet printed Bacon's *Essays* (1597); William Stansby was printer and publisher of Jonson's Folio *Workes*

(1616); Humphrey Moseley published the works of Milton; and Jacob Tonson published the works of Dryden.

Recent book-trade research that has focused on the operations in individual early British printing houses – most notably on compositor and business practices, sources and uses of type fonts, and shared printing – has discovered far more variation within and differences among printing houses as well as far more cooperation and collaboration across the trade than earlier research had suggested. Many of the entries in this volume emphasize such discoveries. Much more research remains to be accomplished, of course, on other fundamental matters of early printing and publishing – particularly on matters such as the uses and the expense of standing type (for the common practice was to distribute and reuse type after a forme had been printed) and marketing decisions and practices related to various edition formats (folio, quarto, octavo, and others), edition sizes (the number of copies of a book to be printed), and copy pricing.

About this last matter, as with other aspects of the print trade in Britain during the handpress period, much remains unknown, but some information is available. Printers appear to have set retail prices of their books based on rules of thumb derived from their own experience, but the Stationers' Company also adopted rules to prevent excessive wholesale charges for works. A company regulation of 1599 limited such prices that one company member could charge another for various kinds of books. This rule specified that a book set in pica or English type could sell at a wholesale price of one halfpence per sheet, which limited such a price for a typical quarto play requiring ten to twelve sheets (eighty to ninety-six pages) to five or six pence. At a bookseller's markup of 50 percent or so, such an unbound quarto would have retailed at a price of seven to nine pence – approximately the average daily wage for a London journeyman of the 1580s, and many times the cost of a one-pound loaf of bread, which sold for one pence.

Details for the production and sale of Shakespeare's First Folio of 1623 have been studied more intensely than those for any other book of this period, and in *The First Folio of Shakespeare* (1991) Peter Blayney has written that the wholesale price of a First Folio was probably about ten shillings, with a retail price for an unbound copy likely to have been about fifteen shillings. If a customer wished to have a bound copy (a likely situation for the purchase of a large book such as the Folio, but far less likely for that of a single quarto play), then the price would have been higher, depending on the binding selected. A First Folio would have cost about sixteen or seventeen shillings in limp forel (parchment made to resemble vellum), from seventeen to eighteen shillings and sixpence in forel-covered boards, or about one pound in plain calf. These costs of both books and binding might vary somewhat, especially outside London.

The nearly complete absence of business records for early British printing houses makes it almost impossible to generalize about these and many other aspects of the book trade. Yet many of the entries in this volume identify much of what now is and can readily be known about some of the most rare and important books ever published in our language.

— *James K. Bracken and Joel Silver*

Acknowledgments

This book was produced by Bruccoli Clark Layman, Inc. Karen L. Rood is senior editor for the *Dictionary of Literary Biography* series. Denis Thomas was the in-house editor.

Production manager is Samuel W. Bruce. Photography editors are Julie E. Frick and Margaret Meriwether. Photographic copy work was performed by Joseph M. Bruccoli. Layout and graphics supervisor is Emily Ruth Sharpe. Copyediting supervisor is Jeff Miller. Typesetting supervisor is Kathleen M. Flanagan. Systems manager is Chris Elmore. Laura Pleicones and L. Kay Webster are editorial associates. The production staff includes Phyllis A. Avant, Ann M. Cheschi, Melody W. Clegg, Patricia Coate, Joyce Fowler, Brenda A. Gillie, Stephanie C. Hatchell, Penelope M. Hope, Kathy Lawler Merlette, Pamela D. Norton, Delores Plastow, William L. Thomas Jr., and Allison Trussell.

Walter W. Ross and Steven Gross did library research. They were assisted by the following librarians at the Thomas Cooper Library of the University of South Carolina: Linda Holderfield and the interlibrary-loan staff; reference-department head Virginia Weathers; reference librarians Marilee Birchfield, Stefanie Buck, Stefanie DuBose, Rebecca Feind, Karen Joseph, Donna Lehman, Charlene Loope, Anthony McKissick, Jean Rhyne, Kwamine Simpson, and Virginia Weathers; circulation-department head Caroline Taylor; and acquisitions-searching supervisor David Haggard.

Dictionary of Literary Biography® • Volume One Hundred Seventy

The British Literary Book Trade, 1475–1700

Dictionary of Literary Biography

Richard and Anne Baldwin

(London: circa 1680 – 1713)

From 1680 to 1713 the Baldwins, Richard and Anne, championed through their press the cause of English political freedom. Representing the great English Third Estate, they scored Stuart tyranny, Bourbon imperialism, and Vatican intrigue. They welcomed the resolute purpose of William of Orange. Occasionally muzzled by the opposition, their books, newspapers, and periodicals doggedly upheld liberalism in a period of political uncertainty and personal danger.

Richard Baldwin, son of Thomas, was born in High Wycombe, Buckinghamshire, circa 1653. Fifteen years later Richard traveled to London, where he was bound apprentice to George Eversden at the Atlas and Eve, St. John's Lane, a printer specializing in the publication and sale of theological texts. Having served the customary seven years, Baldwin was admitted on 25 August 1675 to the freedom of the Stationers' Company. Although no Baldwin imprint appears to have been recorded prior to 1680, he was engaged in the sale of books as early as 1677 and had in his employ two apprentices, Joseph Rydale and John Bowen. The year 1680 marks the publication of the earliest Baldwin imprints: *Animadversions . . . upon the Last Speech of William, Viscount Strafford* and *The Popish Damnable Plot against Our Religion.* At his premises in Ball Court, Old Bailey, Baldwin was also engaged in bookbinding and counted among his customers the garrulous John Dunton, who characterized him as "a man of a generous temper. . . . His purse and his heart were open to all men that he thought were honest; and his conversation was very diverting."

The honesty to which Dunton refers is clearly evident in many Baldwin publications. From 1680 through 1688, the year of the Glorious Revolution, he published approximately forty-four books, twenty-seven of which are of a political nature: anti-Stuart and anti-French. In his de-

votion to the Whig cause and his animosity to James II and the French king Louis XIV, Baldwin had encountered Stuart restraint of the press and of his person. Yet when William III was safely ensconced on the English throne in 1689, Baldwin published during that one year some forty-two books.

As early as October 1681 Baldwin – along with Richard Janeway, Thomas Vile, and others – was summoned before the Privy Council "for publishing severall scandalous and seditious pamphlets against the government." Baldwin pleaded ignorance of the work that he was specifically accused of having published: he declared that the manuscript had been sent to him in a letter "from an unknown hand, and if there were anything in it of dangerous Consequence, it was more than he knew, having never read the said Book." Assuring the court that he had published it for no other reason "than to get money in the way of his trade," he was nevertheless obliged to give bail and to appear later at the term court.

This early encounter with royal magistrates whetted Baldwin's appetite to antagonize the authorities. In December 1681 he either printed or bound for John Kidgell a new edition of John Sadler's *Rights of the Kingdom or Customs of Our Ancestors.* The work, written by an ardent Cromwellian, produced a round of fisticuffs between Baldwin's apprentices, Rydale and Bowen, and a local surgeon and draper. Following custom, Baldwin's boys had posted on Saturday, 31 December, the titles of books that were to be bound for their employer during the ensuing week, and among those listed had been Sadler's *Rights of the Kingdom.* According to a vivid report in *The Impartial . . . Protestant Mercury,* a surgeon named Tallman, incensed by Baldwin's publication of Sadler's work, had torn the posted title down and, with the aid of a local draper, flung it at Rydale and Bowen.

One of Richard Baldwin's Whig and Protestant news sheets

In May 1682 Baldwin became not the mere protagonist of local indignation but a defendant charged with municipal libel. On 4 May the grand jury of Bristol declared that Baldwin had grossly misrepresented its political and religious convictions in his *Protestant Courant*. Bristol, long a royal stronghold, had been denounced as a papist lair, a charge vehemently denied by the Bristol authorities. In response to Baldwin's accusation the beadle of common execution was ordered to burn several libels publicly.

A few weeks later Baldwin received additional publicity for participating in the cause of the much-discussed earl of Shaftesbury. In December 1681 Anthony Cooper, first earl of Shaftesbury, had been tried for treason and released. In connec-

tion with Shaftesbury's trial and anomalous political position Baldwin published two tracts, *The Proceedings of the Right Honourable the Earl of Shaftesbury* and *A Modest Account of the Present Posture of Affairs in Particular Reference to the Earl of Shaftesbury's Case*. In May 1682 Shaftesbury was again seriously confronted by a packed Tory judge and jury. Quick to observe the earl's predicament, Baldwin published in his *Protestant Courant* a scathing indictment of the court's prejudice and attacked the judges and several peers. He was promptly brought to court and arraigned before the reactionary justice George Jeffries, "who severely checked him[,] . . . made a sharp complaint and moved that all the news pamphlet publishers be severely punished." Jeffries demanded that

Baldwin be committed, but the defendant "pleaded that he had good bail ready and prayed they might be accepted." There is no evidence that the undaunted publisher was imprisoned, and in all likelihood his "good bail" was accepted and his release eventuallyeffected.

Baldwin again soon confronted the opposition, this time the unpopular licenser of the press, Sir Roger L'Estrange, an ardent Royalist. Aware of Baldwin's support of anti-Stuart publications, L'Estrange wrote to the diplomat Sir Leoline Jenkins in January 1683,

> Had my importunities to have had the sifting of Baldwyn prevailed, he should have either delivered up some persons more considerable than himself or not have been in a condition at this day to do more mischief. To-day is published by him a libel entitled *A Defence of the Charter and municipal rights of the City of London,* written by Hunt, of venemous malice against the King and the Duke, so far as I can judge by dipping into it.

Having abrogated the privileges granted by the charter of London, Charles II had antagonized the local populace and aroused considerable criticism. Among the principal assailants of Stuart policy was Thomas Hunt, known as "Postscript Hunt," whose *Defence of the Charter and Municipal Rights of the City of London, and the Rights of Other Municipal Cities and Towns of England* was published by Baldwin in 1682. Its appearance incensed the Royalist Party, and copies of the work were seized at Baldwin's shop. The case remained unsettled until July 1683 when the attorney general rendered his verdict that "the books in Baldwin's hands may be seized by warrant from any judge of the King's Bench and be detained till the matter is determined." Although the work had been taken into custody six months earlier, Robert Stephens, a messenger of the press, reported on 1 August 1683 that Baldwin still possessed copies of the Hunt book. Stephens immediately received a warrant to apprehend "all copies thereof that he shall find in the warehouse, shop or keeping of the said Baldwyn or any other . . . as having copies thereof to vend or dispose."

Although Baldwin was a strong supporter of William III, the candor of his publications nonetheless aroused official ire. Narcissus Luttrell writes that in 1690 he was sentenced to Newgate for "misprision of treason," for having "publish'd a sticht book entitled A modest Enquiry, &c., which reflects upon the dissenting bishops, and other bold passages." Copies of the book were

seized by Stephens, but Baldwin, ever ready with bail, was released from custody.

From 1689 through 1698 Baldwin published approximately 240 books – 150 of which were political texts, while the rest concerned theology, belles lettres, and miscellanea. Of particular interest are Baldwin's political publications, about 75 of which are anti-French. The principal butt of the Baldwin libels and lampoons was the aging Louis XIV, whose limitless passions for war and territorial aggrandizement had rendered France bankrupt and destroyed its manhood. Growing fear of a French invasion and English contempt for the monarch at Versailles are manifest in Baldwin's publications: *The Great Bastard Louis XIV Protector of the Little One* [James II] (1689), *King Lewis of France The Hector of Europe* (1690), *The Present French King Drawn to the Life* (1690), *The Fate of France* (1690), *The Royal Cuckold* (1693), and many others were designed to arouse English ire and militant spirits.

Along with hearty contempt for the Sun King, many readers displayed undisguised antipathy toward James Stuart. During this same period Baldwin published about thirty works attacking James and linking his name with Jesuit cabal. These include *The True Spirit of Popery* (1688), *An Address to King James in Which Popish Designs upon the Kingdom Are Discovered* (1690), *The Anatomy of a Jacobite Tory* (1690), *The Character of a Bigoted Prince* (1691), and others, all of which were intended to expose the wiles and treachery of James Stuart.

The anti-Jacobite Baldwin supported the Whig Party and attacked "all who traduce . . . those that have been in the worst of times the only true assertors of the ancient Monarchy." Baldwin's enthusiasm for King William and Queen Mary caused the licenser of the press, Edmund Bohun, to forfeit his position, for Bohun had licensed Baldwin's publication of Charles Blount's *King William and Queen Mary Conquerors* (1693). Although Bohun believed the work to be "full of reason," it proved highly distasteful to the king, for it argued that William had won his English throne through force, and the House of Commons pronounced it "a rascally book." Bohun's licensing of the book led to his removal from his position, and copies of the work were burnt by the hangman.

Although many readers were attracted to political texts bearing the Baldwin imprint, many were likewise interested in the news sheets and periodicals published by Baldwin, who ranks high

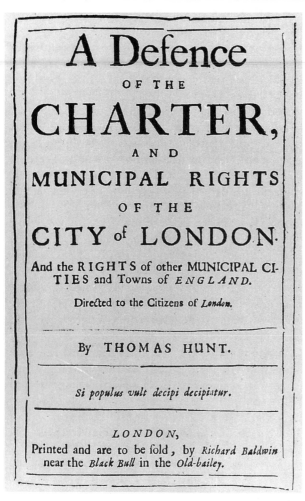

A Defence
OF THE
CHARTER,
AND
MUNICIPAL RIGHTS
OF THE
CITY of LONDON.

And the RIGHTS of other MUNICIPAL CI-
TIES and Towns of ENGLAND.

Directed to the Citizens of London.

By THOMAS HUNT.

Si populus vult decipi decipiatur.

LONDON,
Printed and are to be sold, by *Richard Baldwin*
near the *Black Bull* in the *Old-bailey.*

*Title page for an early Baldwin publication that offended
Royalist authorities, who seized copies of it at Baldwin's
shop when it first appeared in January 1683*

after Empire," and other issues. Having questioned Parliament's prosecution of the War of the Grand Alliance with France, Baldwin was summoned before the House of Commons. Shortly after his appearance the *Mercurius Reformatus* suspended publication.

A third venture, the most successful and enduring of Baldwin's newspapers, proved to be *The Postman,* which, despite its vilification from rival sheets and occasional government intervention, outlived its founder. *The Postman* had begun modestly as *An Account of the Publick Transactions in Christendom* on 11 August 1694. Despite Baldwin's obdurate dislike for the France of Louis XIV, he naturally supported the harassed Huguenots and hence enthusiastically selected as editor of *The Postman* the able Huguenot writer Jean de Fonvive.

De Fonvive shared with Baldwin a hearty contempt for the Stuarts and their kinsmen at Versailles. He considered the former English government a "cabal of rascals and tricksters" who had engaged "weekly libellers to impose upon the people." The candor of his observations brought him and Baldwin before the king's justice in November 1692 for their reflections upon "the dauphin and the crooked disposition and body of his eldest son the Duke of Burgundy." Again, Baldwin and his editor were bailed out.

Despite the political animosities of *The Postman,* Baldwin and Welwood produced one of the principal London newspapers of the age. It appeared regularly each Tuesday, Thursday, and Saturday, and Stanley Morison notes that the reader of the *London Gazette,* at little expense, could be "acquainted with all the Publick Transactions in Christendom." For the most recent news *The Postman* retained correspondents in Italy, Spain, Portugal, Flanders, Holland, and elsewhere, and it provided Baldwin an annual income of £600. Its renown was such that the duke of Marlborough insisted that it alone carry his frontline dispatches. Following Baldwin's death *The Postman* was continued by his widow, Anne, until 1700, when she sold it to Francis Leach of Elliot's Court. Its popularity remained such that in 1704 a French translation of the paper was published for distribution among Huguenots exiled in London and for foreign consumption.

From 1691 to 1695 Baldwin was associated with two literary periodicals – the first of which was *The Gentleman's Journal; or, The Monthly Miscellany,* edited by Peter Anthony Motteux, a fellow exile of de Fonvive. Motteux, a native of Rouen, had arrived in London after the revocation of the

among late-seventeenth-century publishers of newspapers and periodicals, most of which signal his Whig allegiance. These include the *Mercurius Anglicus,* consisting of three issues published in 1681; the *London Mercury,* circulating from April to October 1682; and the short-lived antipapist *Protestant Courant,* published in spring 1682.

The Pacquet of Advice from France was a short-lived enterprise of six months that Baldwin sponsored in 1691. It discussed with fervor the political machinations of France and "the progress of French intrigue towards the enslaving of Europe." A second dialogue sheet, *Mercurius Reformatus; or, The New Observator,* was edited by James Welwood and bore the Baldwin imprint from April until November of 1691. Printed on both sides of a folio sheet, this latter considered various domestic and foreign problems – "The French King's Conduct toward the Irish," "The French King's Thirst

Edict of Nantes; there he had entered business as owner of an East India warehouse on Leadenhall Street. Dissatisfied with commerce, he abandoned trade for literary pursuits, and in Baldwin he found a sympathetic champion for exiled Huguenot readers.

The editorial policy of *The Gentleman's Journal* appears not to have been too discriminating, and Baldwin and Motteux were deluged with various materials from known and unknown authors. Among the contributions were John Dryden's *Cleomenes* (1692), songs by Henry Purcell, scientific discourses, stately essays, a book-review section, and an assortment of novels and reports: "Love's Alchymy; or, A Wife Got Out of the Fire, A Novel"; "A Letter from Moscow"; "An Account of a Painted Indian"; "The Jealous Husband"; and other selections.

Although *The Gentleman's Journal* was well advertised in *The London Gazette,* it ran into publication difficulties and monthly issues were postponed, although the publisher claimed that such delays were to be ascribed merely to the "rigor of the weather and the author's indisposition." Motteux informed subscribers that the December 1692 copies had been completely "sold off" and that former issues were being reprinted, but Baldwin did not share his editor's confidence and welcomed Richard Parker as a partner in January 1693. Under their aegis *The Gentleman's Journal* continued until December 1693, when it was sold to Henry Rhodes at the Star.

A year after Baldwin had sold *The Gentleman's Journal* he became associated with a new literary periodical, *Miscellaneous Letters,* founded in October 1694 by William Lindsey of the Angel, near Lincoln's Inn. Its design was "to give an account of the Works of the Learned, both at Home and Abroad," and the publishers planned to produce it as a weekly digest of the most recent books — both "English Books Printed in London" and foreign books. Individual issues sold for sixpence, and Lindsey and Baldwin eagerly solicited advertisements of current and forthcoming books. Although the two assured the public in January 1695 that their journal had met with general approval, they rescheduled its publication from weekly to monthly issues, and in April Baldwin sold his interest to Henry Rhodes, who two years earlier had purchased *The Gentleman's Journal* from him.

As a publisher of books, tracts, news sheets, and periodicals, Baldwin carried a large and diverse stock. In addition to his own publications, he sold

THE
Great Bastard,
PROTECTOR
OF THE
Little One.

Done out of French.

And for which, a PROCLAMATION, with a Reward of 5000 Lewedores, to Discover the Author, was Publish'd.

Printed at *Cologne,* M DC LXXXIX.

Title page of an anonymously published anti-Bourbon work, one of many through which the Baldwins voiced their contempt for Louis XIV

various books published by different London and provincial dealers. These, like many of his own imprints, reflect contemporary political and religious concerns, and Baldwin's readers could find an occasional play, novel, scientific report, or historical memoir at his office. His inventory included Richard Ames's *Pleasures of Love and Marriage* (1691), William Fulke's *A Full Account of the Late Earthquake in Jamaica* (1692), Jean Le Clerc's *Memoirs of Emeric Count of Teckely* (1693), Aphra Behn's *The Younger Brother, or Amorous Jilt* (1696), and many other works.

There can be little doubt that Baldwin prospered. In 1683 Baldwin had owned or rented a warehouse for his large stock, and he was admitted in December 1692 to the livery of the Stationers' Company. Dunton's statement that Baldwin "printed a great deal but got as little by it as I" must be measured against Dunton's contrary remark that Baldwin's "fame for publishing spread so fast, he

Advertisement in Baldwin's 24 October 1691 news sheet, Mercurius Reformatus; or, The New Observator, *which focused on religious and political affairs in Britain and on the Continent*

grew too big to handle his small tools. Mr. Baldwin having got acquainted with persons of quality, he was now for taking a shop in Fleet Street."

In fact Baldwin never took a shop in Fleet Street; he remained at the Oxford Arms near Warwick Lane, where he had moved in 1690. There he continued to publish and sell books, pamphlets, and newspapers advancing the cause of English nationalism. And Dunton reported that there in 1698, after twenty-one years of incessant activity, Baldwin was "flattered into the grave by a long consumption." He was interred in the graveyard of High Wycombe parish.

Baldwin's passion for English "rights and liberties" passed to his wife, Anne, whom Dunton described as "an help meet of her husband" who "eased him of all his publishing work. Since she has

been a widow [she] might vie with all in Europe for accuracy in keeping accompts." Anne Baldwin kept her accounts and sold her tracts and periodicals from her late husband's shop from 1699 to 1713, the year either of her retirement from the book trade or of her death. During this period she published about 237 works. One-half of these concern domestic and foreign issues; one-fourth are of a theological character; and the rest are works of literature, science, and miscellaneous matters.

Her activity recalls that of her husband, as his influence is manifest in her strong Whiggish sympathies and her anti-Bourbon vituperations. At home England endured a succession of governmental changes and abroad still faced the aggressive challenge of the monarch at Versailles, who was to witness the victories of the English army and the tri-

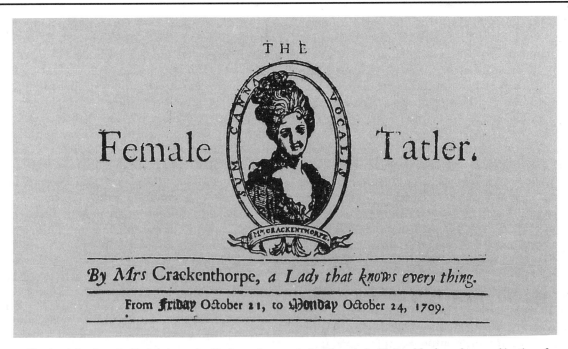

Masthead for Anne Baldwin's journal, edited pseudonymously by Mary de la Rivière Manley, whose combination of advice and gossip made the journal popular until its editor and publisher were indicted

umphant allied peace treaty at the Congress of Utrecht. Such domestic shifts, battle reports of the English forces, and glowing successes of John Churchill, duke of Marlborough, were grist for the press, as the latest rumor of government intrigue and foreign misalliance was transmuted into a two- or three-penny tract. With the abolition of the Licensing Act of 1695, the English book trade received a greater stimulus for self-expression, and Grub Street became the Eden of the pamphleteer and news vendor. A deluge of tracts, lampoons, squibs, pamphlets, postscripts, and penny sheets rained down upon the coffeehouses and political clubs.

Against this background of an almost unrestrained press Anne Baldwin published her many political tracts – supporting the Whigs, criticizing the Tories, reporting and celebrating English victories abroad, and calumniating Louis XIV of France. Among her important publications addressing domestic issues were the writings of Whig authors such as Daniel Defoe, Robert Harley, Matthew Prior, and Francis Hare. From 1700 to 1710 Anne Baldwin published nine Defoe pamphlets, among which were *Villainy of Stock-Jobbers Detected* (1701); *The Present State of Jacobitism Considered* (1701); *Tempus Adest; or, A War Inevitable* (1702); and *A Speech without Doors* (1710). In 1711 she published five editions of *The Management of the War* by Hare, a Whig clergyman, and three issues of his *Letter to a Member of the October Club.*

Although Anne Baldwin's political publications did not reflect the opinions of a united England, her anti-French tracts expressed general national sentiment. In response to Louis XIV's claim to the Spanish throne, she published an important refutation, the anonymous *The Duke of Anjou's Succession, Parts I & II* (1701), and James Methuen, English foreign minister, brought the publication to the attention of a member of the Foreign Office. Other tracts reflecting English hostility toward the French and issued from the Oxford Arms were *Aesop in Spain* (1701), *The Dangers of Europe from the Growing Power of France* (1702), *The Old French Way of Managing Treaties* (1711), and *The Offers of France Explained* (1712).

Of unusual interest among Anne Baldwin's publications are those championing social welfare. The abuse suffered by English seamen had been the subject of controversy in the press, and she joined the fray in 1699 by publishing four works demanding navy reform: *A Letter to a Member of Parliament Concerning the Four Regiments Called Mariners, A Short Vindication of Marine Regiments, The State of the Navy Considered in Relating to Victualling,* and *The Seaman's Opinion of a Standing Army in England.* These last two sold for threepence and fourpence respectively, and they contained lists of current books relating to such issues, including "Books Written against a Standing Army, sold by A. Baldwin." From her Oxford Arms shop one could purchase for twopence *Present State of the Prison of Ludgate* (1710) or *The Rates of the Hackney*

Coaches and Chairs (1711), the latter work offering some compromise on the regulation of wages for London coachmen.

To advertise her stock she employed media similar to those used by her husband. Forthcoming books were announced in her own publications, newspapers, and periodicals, as well as in current issues of *The London Gazette, The Spectator, The Tatler,* and *The Monthly Register.* The price range of her political pamphlets was similar to that established by her husband. Hare's diatribes varied from twopence to a shilling, while Defoe's *Villainy of Stock-Jobbers* could be purchased for sixpence and his *Speech without Doors* for twopence. The anti-French tracts ranged from threepence to a shilling, and religious works retailed at approximately the same prices.

Her income, like that of her husband, depended not only on the sale of books of her own and of her colleagues' but on the publication and distribution of various political and literary journals. She acted as a distributing agent for several political journals — *The New State of Europe* and *The Politick Spy,* both published in 1701. *The Monthly Register,* edited and printed by that "Linguist of Wit," Samuel Buckley, was sold for sixpence an issue.

As an independent publisher she sponsored *The Medley,* the Whig counterpart to *The Examiner,* the mouthpiece of the Tory ministry. Published from 1710 to 1712, *The Medley* was issued semiweekly, appearing on Mondays and Fridays, and was edited by Arthur Maynwaring, a member of the Kit-Kat Club, with the assistance of Sir Richard Steele, Anthony Henley, and John Oldmixon. It continued publication until passage of the Stamp Act in 1712.

Anne Baldwin ably gauged not only the political temperament of the London reader but also the literary inclinations of many householders. While the *British Apollo* appealed to the literary and sartorial tastes of the London beau, her *Female Tatler* — with its tales of romance (rich in aristocratic and flowery background), advertisements of Peptycon for weak digestion, and omniscient editor's sage comments — proved equally attractive to the housewife. Making its first appearance on Friday, 8 July 1709, *The Female Tatler* was edited by one Mrs. Crackenthorpe, who described herself as "A Lady that knows everything." Its masthead bore an oval portrait of this journalistic Minerva with her motto, "Sum Canna Vocalis." Although Mrs. Crackenthorpe strove to conceal her name, she has been identified as the well-known author Mary de la Rivière Manley, described by Jonathan Swift as "about forty, very homely and very fat."

The Female Tatler was published by Anne Baldwin from August 1709 to March 1710. Twenty-six issues were edited by Mrs. Crackenthorpe, dubbed "Scandalosissima Scoundrelia" by her enemies. The characterization was appropriate, for the editor used this folio sheet to supply subscribers with sugarcoated slander and malicious gossip. Nor was Mrs. Crackenthorpe above compiling a blacklist of malefactors that included "any clergyman guilty of spiritual Lingeridge, that is taking a Nap or Smoaking a Pipe in the Vestry, at Prayer Time and then mount [*sic,* mounting] the Pulpit."

With her infinite wisdom Mrs. Crackenthorpe gave frequent advice on every problem to readers young and old. In October 1709

> the young lady in the Parish of St. Laurence near Guild Hall, that lately went to the Coffee House in Man's Cloathes with two 'Prentices, called for a Dish of Bohee, smoak'd her Pipe, and gave herself an abundance of Stroddling Masculine Airs, is desir'd to do so no more.

At the same time "the Gentleman that gave Mrs. Crackenthorpe an Invitation per Penny Post to come to his Lodgings at Ham to have her throat cut, was to expect an answer to his Letter shortly."

It is quite possible that "the Lady who knows everything" knew too much. By October 1709 too many subscribers to *The Female Tatler* had been victimized by Madame "Scandalosissima Scoundrelia," and Mrs. Crackenthorpe found her paper, her publisher, and herself indicted by the grand jury of Middlesex, which declared that

> A Great Number of printed papers are continually dispersed under the name of the Female Tatler sold by A. Baldwin and other papers under other Titles . . . which . . . reflect on and scandalously abuse several persons of honour and quality, many of the magistrates and abundance of citizens and all sorts of people . . . which practise we conceive to be a great nuisance. We therefore humbly hope this honourable Court will take effectual care to prevent these abuses as their wisdom shall see fit.

On 1 November 1709 Anne Baldwin saw fit to remove her omniscient editor. Mrs. Crackenthorpe regretfully announced her retirement, and *The Female Tatler* was now edited by "A Society of Ladies" until it ceased publication in March 1710.

Although she had been compelled to relinquish *The Female Tatler* in 1710, Baldwin did not abandon her interest in distributing literary magazines. She acted as agent for the sale of *Memoirs of Literature,* edited by the Huguenot exile Michel de la Roche, and she was also associated with one of the foremost eighteenth-century literary periodicals, *The Spectator,* which she sold and used as an advertising medium.

In disseminating *Memoirs of Literature* and several other publications she became associated with John Roberts, a printer who in 1713 replaced her at the Oxford Arms. After fifteen years as sole proprietor of the shop near Warwick Lane, Anne Baldwin either died or retired.

Through their careers in the book trade the Baldwins had influenced a larger commonwealth. English political ideology was reflected in their publications, from the interests of the middle class to the anti-French attitudes of John Bull. A man of uncompromising convictions and unrelenting political prejudice, Richard Baldwin persisted in actions that invoked legal hazard and social ostracism. He faced the power of the King's Bench and met the disapproval of his guild. He admitted that he "published to get money by way of his trade," but the sincerity of his patriotism cannot be questioned. As his successor, Anne Baldwin continued her husband's example and helped achieve English victory abroad and at home through the polemic influence of her press.

The careers of the Baldwins reflect a unity of spirit and a dedication to good causes. While English armies fought a foreign enemy to safeguard the realm with musket and pike, Richard and Anne Baldwin helped rally the domestic English with journal and tract. With an unflagging devotion to the "rights and liberties" of their fellows, Richard and Anne Baldwin hold places among the champions of English political freedom.

References:
John Dunton, *The Life and Errors of John Dunton, Citizen of London, with the Lives and Characters of More Than a Thousand Contemporary Divines and Other Persons of Literary Eminence, to Which Are Added Dunton's Conversation in Ireland, Selections from His Other Genuine Works, and a Faithful Portrait of the Author,* 2 volumes (New York: Franklin, 1969);

Narcissus Luttrell, *Brief Historical Relation, 1678–1714* (Oxford: Oxford University Press, 1857);

William Morgan, *A Bibliography of British History (1700–1715), with Special Reference to the Reign of Queen Anne* (Bloomington: Indiana University Press, 1934–1942);

Stanley Morison, *The English Newspaper* (Cambridge: Cambridge University Press, 1932);

Leona Rostenberg, *Literary, Political, Scientific, Religious & Legal Publishing, Printing & Bookselling in England, 1551–1700: Twelve Studies,* 2 volumes (New York: Franklin, 1965).

– Leona Rostenberg

Christopher Bateman

(London: 1684–1731)

Christopher Bateman was the most distinguished antiquarian bookseller of his generation. At the peak of his career his shop in Paternoster Row was larger than any surrounding property except Newgate Market, and it became a meeting place for scholars, bibliographers, antiquaries, and book collectors. Among them were men such as Thomas Hearne, the Oxford antiquary, and Michael Maittaire, the expatriate French bibliographer, and when Bateman occasionally published new books, they were books by such writers and for such customers.

Bateman began life with fewer advantages than John Dunton suggests when he remarks that Bateman was "the Son of that famous Bateman who got an Alderman's estate by Bookselling," for Bateman's father was neither an alderman nor a bookseller. When Bateman was bound as an apprentice on 7 August 1676, his father was named as Robert, a "sheereman" (shearer of woolen cloth) from Kendal in Westmoreland. His master and future father-in-law was Stephen Bateman, who was probably the "famous Bateman" to whom Dunton refers and who was possibly a relative of Christopher. Stephen Bateman's birthplace at the time of his own binding as an apprentice in 1657 was given as Strickland Kettle in Westmoreland, barely three miles northwest of Christopher's home in Kendal. Christopher Bateman was freed on 3 November 1684 and by the next year was in business at the Bible and Crown in Middle Row, Holborn. With Gray's Inn to the north, Lincoln's Inn to the south, and Staple's, Furnival's, and Barnard's Inns to the west, Bateman's shop was well located for the trade in old books, for as sale catalogues of the period reveal, only physicians and clergymen could rival lawyers as book collectors.

His first surviving catalogue of books for sale appeared circa 1685: *A Catalogue, of Philogical and Historical Greek Books* included about equal numbers of sixteenth- and seventeenth-century books, mainly Greek and Latin, with smaller sections of manuscripts and medical books. Bateman was from the first primarily a dealer in old books. He is known to have issued four catalogues from his Holborn address and only one book, an edition of *The Travels of Sir John Chardin into Persia,* that was published in 1691. Within two years of setting up in business he had prospered sufficiently to marry, and in October 1687, at the age of about twenty-seven, he married Stephen Bateman's seventeen-year-old daughter, Elizabeth.

Bateman preferred to sell by retail and to advertise the arrival of new stock in the shop by means of printed catalogues, and in only a few cases did he auction acquisitions. One auction involved the sale of the library of Sir Charles Scarburgh in 1695. That young Bateman had been able to secure this important library of some two thousand items, rich in the classics and in medical and mathematical works, is a measure of his success as a bookseller. He published a catalogue of the whole Scarburgh collection to be sold by retail on 8 February 1695, but virtually all of the items listed in the second half of the catalogue, mainly the relatively less salable mathematical and medical books, were sold at auction on 18 February.

Bateman followed this pattern of selling the best books in a collection by retail and the rest by auction not only in the Scarburgh sales of February 1695 but also in his sale of the library of Dr. John Tillotson, archbishop of Canterbury, who had died on 22 November 1694. The sale of Tillotson's books was advertised to start on the following 9 April, only seven weeks after the Scarburgh auction of 18 February. Although titled *Bibliotheca Tillotsoniana: or a Catalogue of the Curious Library of Dr. John Tillotson,* Bateman's retail catalogue contained only about half of the late Archbishop's collection, with the rump of cheaper books to be auctioned by John Nicholson at "Mrs. Bourn's Coffee-House adjoyning to St. Laurence's Church near Guild-hall" on 23 April. It seems likely that Bateman — having purchased the whole collection, taken what he wanted, and commissioned Nicholson to auction the remainder — was the consignor of the second sale.

The underlying assumption that medical and scientific books, together with most books in English, were less salable at retail than certain other categories of books seems borne out by Bateman's decision to sell the earl of Clarendon's largely historical collection, which he announced in *A Catalogue of the Library of a Person of Honour* (circa 1701) by fixed prices, and Sergeant-Surgeon Charles Bernard's largely scientific library by auction in 1711. Bernard's colleague, Dr. Mead, wrote the preface to the Bernard collection for Bateman; the catalogue was compiled by bookseller Jacob Hooke, and the bidding was conducted by auctioneer Thomas Ballard. The owner of the collection was almost certainly Bateman, who would have hired the services of Hooke and Ballard. The sale attracted considerable attention: the earl of Sunderland purchased 151 lots, including some antiquarian medical works, but mainly history and classics. Jonathan Swift made four or five visits to the sale, and Thomas Rawlinson found the collection so interesting that he transcribed Bernard's bibliographical notes into his own copy of the catalogue, now in the Bodleian Library.

These sales of four personal libraries – Scarburgh's, Tillotson's, Clarendon's, and Bernard's – together with two sales of stock comprise the whole of Bateman's known catalogues in the years from 1685 through 1713. Thereafter he published no more catalogues until near the end of his life, when circumstances dictated a change of direction. That Bateman's surviving sale catalogues are so few and that four of the six include libraries of important men may indicate that he chose to make it his policy to issue a catalogue only when the name of the owner was likely to attract enough attention to make it worth his effort. Sufficient available space and confidence in a regular clientele made it unnecessary for Bateman to advertise his recent acquisitions. This sharply contrasts to the long series of catalogues of stock and miscellaneous small collections issued by Franch booksellers on the Strand, sellers such as de Varennes and Levy, for whom regular advertisement was crucial.

That Bateman did absorb into stock at least one collection of some note is known from Thomas Hearne's remarks on the disposal of the library of Dr. Thomas Smith in the summer of 1710. Hearne felt strongly that Smith's books should have gone to the Bodleian Library, but virtually the whole collection was sold to Bateman for "but £150." As Hearne rather sourly observed, Bateman "often buys good Bargains and makes a great deal of Money of them." The collection was sold piecemeal through the shop and thus dispersed, one of the purchasers being Hearne's London friend Thomas Rawlinson.

Some collections were, however, bought and resold in toto. According to the antiquary Richard Gough, for eighty guineas Bateman bought the three hundred volumes of Archbishop William

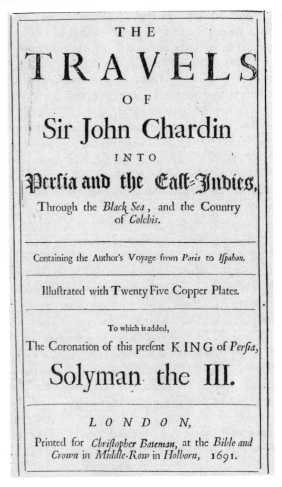

THE
TRAVELS
OF
Sir John Chardin
INTO
Perſia and the Eaſt-Indies,
Through the *Black Sea*, and the Country of *Colchis*.

Containing the Author's Voyage from *Paris* to *Iſpahan*.

Illuſtrated with Twenty Five Copper Plates.

To which is added,

The Coronation of this preſent K I N G of *Perſia*,
Solyman the III.

L O N D O N,
Printed for *Chriſtopher Bateman*, at the *Bible and
Crown* in *Middle-Row* in *Holborn*, 1691.

*Title page for the only book that Christopher Bateman
published from his Holborn address (courtesy of the
Lilly Library, Indiana University)*

Sancroft's manuscripts from Sancroft's nephews and then resold the collection to Bishop Tanner, who bequeathed them to the Bodleian Library upon his death in 1736. In October or November 1716 Bateman also sold in their entirety the collections of book dealer and antiquary John Bagford, who had died on 15 May 1716. The purchaser was Edward Harley, who had been especially eager to secure Bagford's collections on the history of printing – as had Thomas Hearne, who intended to publish a book based on them. When Hearne later learned of Humfrey Wanley's machinations to obtain them for Harley, Hearne wrote in his diary, "This was Roguery. For they were most certainly design'd for me." He was silent upon the part played by Bateman in selling this collection, which is now among the Harleian manuscripts in the British Library.

By 1697 Bateman was clearly enjoying enough success in selling old books to be able to move from Holborn to a large shop on the corner of Paternoster Row, and on 5 July 1697 he entered his first (and only) copy in the registers at Stationers' Hall: "A new discovery of a very great inhabited country in America scituate betwixt New Mexico and the Frozen Sea, with a naturall and morall history of the place, &c., by Father Hennepin now made English." Of the few known works that involved Bateman in their publication between 1697 and 1717, in all but three Bateman's role was that of wholesale distributor, in which he ran little risk but probably stood to gain correspondingly little profit. They are scholarly books, often bibliographical or antiquarian. Clearly the economic foundation of Bateman's business lay elsewhere.

This side of Bateman's business amounted to scarcely more than an occasional service rendered to a favored or eminent customer. He testified in June 1695 to "a long experience and acquaintance" with Hadrian Reverland, the compulsive book collector who had earlier sold his library to the earl of Sunderland and for whom Bateman in 1697 published his *De Fornicatione Cavenda Admonito*. In the preface to Maittaire's *Stephanorum Historia* (1709) Maittaire gracefully complimented Bateman as "Amicus . . . meus & familiaris Christophorus Bateman, vir in re literaria juvanda impiger, dignusque Stephanis Typographis Bibliopola." Both the *Stephanorum Historia* and a second work by Maittaire, *Historia Typographorum Aliquot Parisiensium* (1717), appeared under Bateman's own imprint and at his expense.

Bateman also acted for James Petiver, whose many botanical works Bateman published during the period from 1700 to 1713, although in his dealings with Petiver the extent of Bateman's responsibilities and his likely financial stake are not always entirely clear. It seems likely that most or perhaps all of Petiver's works were, despite their various forms of imprint, published at his own expense. Among Bateman's more celebrated customers were probably Sir Hans Sloane and Richard Bentley, for both of whom he acted as publisher. Sloane chose Bateman in 1707 as one of the distributors of the first volume of his substantial folio, *A Voyage to the Islands Madera, Barbados, Nieves, S. Christophers and Jamaica,* and Bentley in 1713 chose Bateman as distributor of the second edition of Sir Isaac Newton's *Principia,* which Bentley had printed at his own expense by the Cambridge University Press.

Knowledge of Bateman's circle of scholarly friends and customers probably prompted the curators of the Cambridge University Press in 1705 to choose Bateman as the sole London publisher of their ill-fated three-volume folio *Suidae Lexicon*. The arrangement was not successful, and the press still held unsold copies of it in 1752. Yet much of the blame for this must be attributed to the inexperience of the curators, who for the first time were acting as booksellers of the work. The high retail price they insisted on (£3 in quires, or £4 10s. for large paper copies), their decision not to allow a trade discount on single copies, and the unusually large number of copies printed (a very optimistic fifteen hundred) all conspired to make Bateman's task insurmountably difficult. He was constrained moreover by stipulations that he was not to sell copies to subscribers, nor to supply booksellers prepared to purchase more than one copy (such booksellers were to deal directly with the curators). For any copy he did manage to sell under these far from favorable conditions Bateman was to be allowed £1.

Aside from his entrepreneurial activities as a bookseller and his wholesaling activities as a publisher, Bateman occasionally also acted as wholesale distributor to the London trade, and he included a few new books in his stock on a retail basis. He bought 160 volumes of remainders of books from the Oxford University Press in 1705–1706 at reduced prices: the titles included editions of Homer and Xenophon, Edward Bernard's *Catalogi Librorum manuscriptorum Angliae et Hiberniae* (1697), and Heinrich Wilhelm Ludolf's *Grammatica Russica* (1696). He also collected subscriptions for the publications of Thomas Hearne, and Bateman's name appears in the subscription lists of many London publications between 1708 and 1724, including Mattaire's *Opera et Fragmenta Veterum Poetarum* (1713), John Strype's new edition of John Stow's *A Survey of the Cities of London and Westminster* (1720), and Anthony Wood's *Athenae Oxonienses* (1721). Whether these were destined for the shelves of his own library or those of his shop cannot always be determined, because the number of copies for which Bateman subscribed is not always given. Yet some of the eight copies of Ulrick Rourke's *Memoirs of . . . the Marquis of Claricarde* (1722) must have been destined for the shop. Such titles — classical texts as well as works of bibliographical or antiquarian scholarship — would clearly have interested both Bateman and his customers. In or just after 1713 he also issued a catalogue of stock "tam Antiquorum quam Recentium Librorum" with the imprint "Prostant Venales apud Chr. Bateman in Vico vulgo dicto Pater-noster-row." This sixteen-page catalogue of 681 mainly Greek, Latin, Italian, and some French titles contains a high proportion of recent books, leavened with a sprinkling of about a dozen fifteenth-century and many sixteenth-century books, all described in the enticing catchphrase of the old Latin trade booksellers, "ex variis Europae Partibus advectorum."

Following the end of his apprenticeship in November 1684, Bateman rose rapidly in his profession: being admitted to the Stationers' Company within five years, moving to prestigious premises in Paternoster Row in 1697, and serving in 1702 as one of the two renter wardens of the Stationers' Company, the necessary qualification for election to the court of assistants, a position that he attained in 1719. Dunton described him by 1705 as "a man of great reputation and honesty" and claimed that "there are very few Booksellers in England (if any) that understand Books better better than Mr. Bateman; nor does his diligence and industry come short of his knowledge."

Soon his fame was more than merely local. J. E. B. Mayor recounts how Zacharias Conrad von Uffenbach, visiting England from Germany in 1710, found "Radman's [sic] store of old bound books . . . the best in England. Elsewhere you find a few Latin books, but here there were two shops full, and the floors piled up with books." A country correspondent in search of a scarce book in June 1712 was advised by Hearne in Oxford that "The most likely Person to furnish you with such Books is Mr. Bateman in Pater Noster Row London." During his stay in London from 1710 to 1714, Jonathan Swift spent a total of £5 2s. at the Bernard sale of March 1711 and recorded making regular visits to Bateman's shop. He bought "three little volumes of Lucian in French" on 4 January 1711, a Strabo and an Aristophanes on 31 January 1711, and a Plutarch and others on 12 January 1713, and on each occasion he ruefully noted for Stella Johnson the extent of his extravagance: 48s. on the first occasion, 25s. on the second, and on the third, "I layd out 4ll like a fool, and we dined at a hedge alehouse for 2sh and 2 pence like Emperors." On 9 July 1711 he recorded,

I was at Bateman's the booksellers's, to see a fine old library he has bought; and my fingers itched, as yours would do at a china shop; but I resisted, and found every thing too dear, and I have fooled away too much money that way already.

By this time Bateman was quite clearly the major antiquarian bookseller in London.

His position conferred a measure of independence from powerful private collectors such as the earl of Sunderland and Edward Harley. Bateman's name occurs infrequently in the archives of such collections, and the reason is clear from the diary of Harley's librarian, Humfrey Wanley: such collectors expected any lesser bookseller, as a condition of dealing with them, to give them first choice of any books. That Bateman would give no such consideration is equally clear from Harley's wish at the time of Lord Somers' death in 1716 that "Noel could buy Lord Somers' things, if Bateman buys them, I shall not have my choice."

Earlier in November 1714 Harley had made a revealing remark about Bateman's interest in the library of John Moore, bishop of Ely. The collection contained more than thirty thousand volumes, and the price asked was £8,000, which Harley thought was "impracticable." He believed that "the best way is to let Bateman love it or to let it come to auction and get the valuable books, and those that I have a mind for, without the trouble of all the rubish and Duplicates." The collection was ultimately purchased by King George I and presented to the University of Cambridge in 1715. That Harley should suppose Bateman capable of finding £8,000 when he could not do so is revealing. Bateman had no aristocratic patron and relied instead on the book-buying public at large, which, at least in the case of antiquarians, comprised primarily members of the professional classes — the doctors, lawyers, clergymen, and minor government officials who frequented his shop in Paternoster Row. The libraries of these book fanciers were augmented by (and at their deaths augmented) the astonishing number of auctions and fixed-price sales held at this time. Bateman's ability not only to survive but clearly to prosper thus may parallel the growing ability of contemporary writers to subsist without aristocratic patronage by appealing directly to the literate classes for support.

The years between 1708 and 1720 comprise the high point of Bateman's career. As early as 1707 he first appears in the rate books as one of the local commissioners, a position in which he appeared intermittently for many years in supervising the assessments and the collections. The commissioners were drawn from the most substantial men in the ward — which, in the case of Castlebaynard, included the entire bookselling area north and south of St. Paul's, for some distance beyond. In 1708 Bateman took extra premises behind Paternoster Row. At first he let these to a tenant, but from 1714 Bateman occupied them, as he expanded his already large corner shop into the "backhouses" behind. With a rated value of £64 Bateman's premises were the second largest to Newgate Market in the parish of St. Faith's. In 1720 he was a substantial buyer at the sale of the copyrights of Awnsham Churchill,

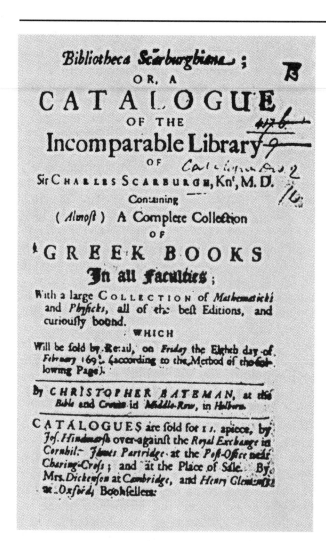
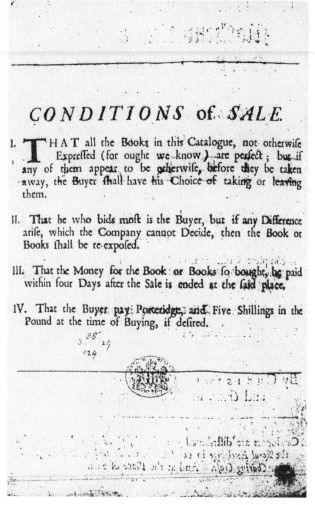

Title page (left) from Bateman's catalogue of more than two thousand books that had belonged to Sir Charles Scarburgh, and catalogue page (right) outlining Bateman's procedures in selling these books (Lilly Library, Indiana University)

where he spent £51 on one twenty-fourth share of Adam Littleton's *Linguae Latinae liber dictionarius quadripartitus* (1678). When his long-standing customer Rawlinson was being pressed by creditors that same year, Bateman was able to lend him £420. Bateman's name is frequent throughout this time in Hearne's diary and letters, not only in connection with Hearne's own publications (for which Bateman acted as a subscription agent) but also as a source of information about books and their prices. After 1721 Bateman's name disappears for a time, and when it reappears in 1726 Bateman was in very different circumstances.

On 24 August 1726 he was in Oxford, probably in connection with a manuscript that he was then preparing for the press. This was an unpublished description of Cornwall by Elizabethan topographer John Norden, a manuscript for which Bateman had paid £20. Hearne recorded on 8 Sep-

tember 1726 that "Kit, being in but bad Circumstances, would print it, to raise some Money, and had been at the charges of engraving the Draughts in it, of wch Proofs lay in the Book, tho' I found the Engravings wrong in many particulars." After some delay the book appeared in 1728 and received further criticism from Hearne: in May he recorded that "Norden's Chorographical Description of Cornwall is printed pompously at London in 4to. Four were printed on Vellom, one for the Earl of Oxford, the Patron, who gave 50 libs. to poor Christopher Bateman under the notion of Editor, another Dr. Rawlinson hath, and two others are in private hands."

What had happened in the interval between Bateman's proposal to print the Norden manuscript in 1726 and the time that it was published in 1728 is made clear in the records of the Stationers' Company: a commission of bankruptcy had been issued against Bateman, and he had been forced to give up his Paternoster Row shop. He attended the court of assistants as usual on 6 December 1726 and was still occupying his shop in January 1727, when he was listed as one of the booksellers responsible for taking subscriptions for Abraham Gronovius's edition of Claudius Aelianus, *De Natura Animalium*. The commission of bankruptcy was issued by 7 February 1727, when it was reported to the court of assistants, and Bateman was forbidden to attend future meetings of the court. On 7 November 1727 Bateman attempted to take his seat again but was reluctantly excluded on the grounds that he had still not satisfied his creditors, although the court was "greatly Inclined to favour Mr. Bateman." By 27 February 1728 Bateman's shop was in the hands of Charles Davis, who on that day opened the Lowthorn and Carew sale "at his Shop (lately Mr. Bateman's) in Pater-noster-Row, next to Warwick-Lane." Although the exact location of Davis's new shop is not made explicit until the Lowthorn and Carew sale, the changeover must have occurred between May and August 1727, when Davis first left his Hatton Garden premises and moved to Paternoster Row.

Without the legal papers relating to the case it is idle to speculate about the circumstances of a Bateman bankruptcy. In Hearne's opinion it had been "in some measure occasioned by an ill, undutiful son, and a faithless servant." The son was probably Stephen Bateman, presumably named after his grandfather. Stephen had been bound to his father on 6 October 1707, but he did not follow his father and grandfather into the book trade. No record has been found of his completing his apprenticeship, no publications identified with his name, and no apprentices known to have been bound to him. Lacking an heir to the business, Bateman as he grew older may have come increasingly to rely upon his shopman, who dealt less than honestly with him. The identity of the shopman is uncertain, although the most likely candidate perhaps would be John Atkinson, Bateman's last apprentice, who had been turned over to Bateman in 1714 and apparently never made free. Charles Davis, although found at Bateman's address by August 1727 and not known for his honesty (according to both Hearne and Rawlinson), seems not to have been the man: he had been apprenticed to Nathaniel Noel and by 1721 was working for or with James Woodman before beginning business for himself in Hatton Gardens circa 1723.

While Davis conducted fixed-price sales in Bateman's old shop, Bateman seems to have been temporarily without premises of his own. Hearne reports that Bateman "gave off his Trade, but afterwards took to it again," and this may well be the period to which he refers. Not until November 1729 did he find new premises "on the South side of St. Pauls Church Yard," the address to which Harley wrote on 23 November 1729 to engage Bateman to bid for him at the fourteenth Rawlinson sale, due to begin on the following day. As Harley instructed Bateman, "I desire my name may not be made use of. . . . I do not limit you for I should be glad of the Books."

No doubt Bateman was glad to have this commission, and Harley was continuing by this means the patronage of "poor Kit" that he had demonstrated earlier with publication of the Norden volume. The new shop was considerably smaller. Whereas in his Paternoster Row shop Bateman had conducted essentially a retail business, relying on a regular clientele and a large stock and issuing only occasional fixed-price catalogues, he was now obliged to adapt his methods to his changed circumstances. He turned to auctioneering as a livelihood: from having only once, so far as is known, himself conducted the bidding in an auction (in the second Scarburgh sale of 1685), Bateman now conducted at least ten auctions between November 1728 and May 1731. With one exception these were auctions of named private libraries or the stock of named booksellers, and it is clear that Bateman now acted on commission and did not own the books he sold.

The most important of these were two sales of the stock of booksellers James Woodman and David Lyon (on 4 May 1730) and Harmen Noorthhouck (on 2 July 1730). Woodman and Lyon had been among the most important antiquarian booksellers in London for the past decade, as they had imported the libraries of many eminent Continental collectors for sale in London. Woodman was dead at the time of the sale, and Lyon, who commissioned Bateman to auction their remaining stock, had decided to retire. Marked with both shop and auction prices (the former perhaps included as a guide toward which Bateman should aim the bidding), a copy of the auction catalogue survives in Yale University Library. It is significant that the auction prices averaged one-third lower than the retail prices. Noorthhouck was also a dealer in old books but one who, like Bateman himself, had gone bankrupt. Bateman's instructions were to sell Noorthhouck's entire stock and all his household goods (right down to the "Pepper-Box, two Sash-Weights, [and] four old Locks") "for the Benefit of the Creditors, without any Reserve."

Bateman's fortunes were not restored by his new career as an auctioneer, however. His will, made on 29 June 1731 and proved on 23 July, was a simple one that left mourning rings to a few close friends and the rest of his estate to his wife, Elizabeth. As Hearne said, "the second setting up would not do," and

On Thursday last, being the 22nd inst., died Mr. Christopher Bateman of Paternoster Rowe, London, bookseller, and was buried on Monday night, July 26, at the church of St. Gregory near St. Paul's. He had been a most noted Bookseller and was looked upon as a very honest man. He understood Books incomparably well, and always was so fair in selling that a child might purchase as easily as a man of skill. As he used to buy Whole Studies, so 'twas his way to put a reasonable or moderate Price upon each, wch as it produced a quick sale, so it made him much esteemed, and people were sure that they were not cheated. I knew him for near thirty years, and ever found him an open, single-hearted, chearfull man, above the world, and so regardless of money, that tho' he might have acquired a great Estate, yet he died but poor.

References:
Harry Carter, *A History of the Oxford University Press* (Oxford: Clarendon Press, 1975-);
John Dunton, *The Life and Errors of John Dunton Citizen of London with Lives and Characters of More than a Thousand Contemporary Divines and Other Persons of Literary Eminence,* 2 volumes (London: Malthus, 1705; New York: Franklin, 1969);
Richard Gough, *Anecdotes of British Topography* (London: Richardson & Clark, 1768);
Thomas Hearne, *Remarks and Collections of Thomas Hearne,* 11 volumes, edited by C. E. Doble, D. H. Rannie, and H. E. Salter (Oxford: Clarendon Press, 1885–1921);
William Dunn Macray, *Annals of the Bodleian* (Oxford: Rivingtons, 1890);
J. E. B. Mayor, *Cambridge under Queen Anne: Illustrated by Memoirs of Ambrose Bonwicke and Diaries of Francis Burman and Zacharias Conrad von Uffenbach* (Cambridge: Deighton, Bell, 1911);
D. F. McKenzie, *The Cambridge University Press 1696–1712,* 2 volumes (Cambridge: Cambridge University Press, 1966);
Jonathan Swift, *Journal to Stella,* 2 volumes, edited by Harold Williams (Oxford: Clarendon Press, 1948);
Humfrey Wanley, *The Diary of Humfrey Wanley 1715–1726,* 2 volumes, edited by C. E. Wright and R. C. Wright (London: Bibliographical Society, 1966).

– Katherine Swift

John Bellamy

(London: 1620 – 1651)

If John Bellamy were to be remembered for one achievement, it would be for the roughly 150 religious tracts that comprise approximately two-thirds of all his publications. While Bellamy published various materials – sermons, descriptive accounts of American plantations, many political writings of Parliament-controlled England in the 1640s, treatises on women and Indians, and even a *Seamans Dictionary* (1643) – his primary interest was in theological matters. The strength of his religious conviction is clear in the conclusion to *A Justification of the City Remonstrance and its Vindication* (1646), in which he writes, "I esteem it no shame to be conquered, when Christ proves the Victor, nor no losse to bee vanquished when the Truth prevailes, for it's verity, not victory that shall be my comfort." As a Christian, Bellamy was determined to discover and live that "Truth"; as a publisher, bookseller, and author, he set out to disseminate and defend it.

Given his later professional connections with the New England colonies, it is fitting that John Bellamy shared his year of birth, circa 1596, with Richard Mather, the famous Puritan divine. Bellamy was born to a family of comfortable means in Oundle, Northamptonshire. The details of his will do not mention that he had any wife or children, but they indicate that he had brothers and sisters to whom he could leave his property and belongings.

In 1611 Bellamy was apprenticed in the shop of London stationer Nicholas Bourne, located near the Royal Exchange, where he assisted in publishing many texts, theological writings among them. During his apprenticeship he also became a member of Henry Jacob's Southwark congregation, which was heavily influenced by principles of the Separatist centers of Amsterdam and Leiden, headed respectively by Henry Ainsworth and John Robinson. Many Protestants had begun to fight changes in their churches that they saw as signs of a return to Catholicism. Unlike their non-Separatist Puritan counterparts who worked to reform the church from within, the more radical Separatists called for a complete separation from the contemporary Protestant church. Although Bellamy left the Southwark church shortly before the age of thirty, his introduction to religion early in his life and career had a profound effect on him.

Bellamy received his freedom from Bourne on 17 February 1620 but continued occasionally to publish some works in conjunction with him. One such publication – a series of five sermons titled *Christs Last Supper, or The Doctrines of the Sacraments of Christes Supper* (1620) – appears as his first in the registers of the Stationers' Company. Several of Bellamy's early publications include writings by Separatists from Leiden. In the spring and summer of 1621 he published two sermons by William Teelinck, who was originally from Leiden but had been preaching in Middleborough, England; the first was *Paule His Complaint against his Naturall Corruption* and the second, *The Forceable Power of Love of Christ.*

It is likely that Teelinck had read the ideas of his colleague Henry Ainsworth. John Bellamy, working temporarily as a partner with Benjamin Fisher, published the first English edition of Ainsworth's *A Commentarie on the Five Books of Moses, and the Psalmes* (1622) and later published by himself a second edition under the title *Annotations upon the Five Books of Moses* (1624). Bellamy also published other Ainsworth tracts, such as *Solomon's Song of Songs in English* (1624) and *The Communion of Saints* (1641). In 1626 registration of the first English publication of John Robinson's *Observations Divine and Morall* appeared among Bellamy's entries in the rolls of the Stationers' Company.

By 1622 Bellamy had moved from Bourne's shop and opened his own, called the Two Greyhounds, in Cornhill, London. Here and at his last location in Cornhill, the Three Golden Lyons, Bellamy published all the material he was to receive in his career relating to the American colonies. The date of his separation from his master Bourne roughly coincided with that of the first immigration of Puritans to New England. Having bid farewell to his Leiden congregation that sailed 5 August 1620 on the *Mayflower,* John Robinson remained behind. A little more than a year later Robert Cushman, who had been instrumental in preparing for the departure of the Leiden congregation, visited the colonists at Plymouth plantation, where he gave his sermon "The Sin and Danger of Self Love and the Sweetness of True Friendship" to commemorate the first anniversary of their settlement. In March of the following year Bellamy published that work, the first of any from Plymouth, ti-

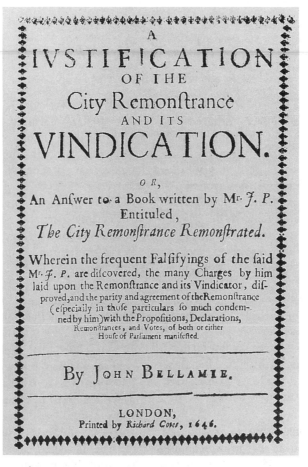

A
IVSTIFICATION
OF THE
City Remonſtrance
AND ITS
VINDICATION.

O R,

An Anſwer to a Book written by Mᵣ. J. P.
Entituled,

The City Remonſtrance Remonſtrated.

Wherein the frequent Falſifyings of the ſaid
Mᵣ. J. P. are diſcovered, the many Charges by him
laid upon the Remonſtrance and its Vindicator, diſ-
proved, and the parity and agreement of the Remonſtrance
(eſpecially in thoſe particulars ſo much condemned by him) with the Propoſitions, Declarations,
Remonſtrances, and Votes, of both or either
Houſe of Parliament manifeſted.

By JOHN BELLAMIE.

LONDON,
Printed by *Richard Cotes*, 1646.

*Title page for one of publisher John Bellamy's writings, a
religious treatise in which he acknowledges his early
membership in the Separatist congregation
of Henry Jacob*

tled *Sermon Preached at Plimmoth in Nevv England December 9. 1621* (1622).

While writings from the Plymouth and later Massachusetts Bay Colonies comprised most of his publications, Bellamy did have the opportunity to publish one work relating to the Virginia Company. To raise money for a school in Virginia, Patrick Copeland, who served as minister of Bowe Church in Cheapside, delivered a sermon that Bellamy published as *Virginia's God Be Thanked* (1622). He copublished this piece with William Sheffard, with whom Bellamy had also published John Forbes's *An Exhortation* (1622) and *The Saintes* (1622) only a few weeks earlier.

Bellamy's printing of New England documents was especially prolific throughout 1622. When Cushman returned to England on the *Fortune* that year, the ship also carried descriptions of the Plymouth area written by William Bradford, the governor of the plantation, and Edward Winslow, who was later to be its governor twice in the 1630s

and once in 1644. A French vessel under the command of Captain Fontenau de Pennart intercepted the *Fortune* near the English Channel, and de Pennart rifled through and stole some of the writings on board. Yet Bellamy received at least part of these documents before 29 June, when he published them with the simple title *Newes from newe England* (1622).

He also published further accounts written by Bradford and Winslow under the title *Relation or Iournall of the beginning and proceedings of the English Plantation setled at Plimoth in New England, by certaine English Aduenturers both Merchants and others* (1622). Attributed to George Morton, a York merchant and agent for the Leiden congregation, this material is commonly known as Mourt's *Relation,* for Morton was to have received the accounts in England and is thought to have embellished the original material with some of his own remarks. Exactly how Bellamy obtained the manuscripts is unclear, but *Relation* remains an important piece of writing because it is the first historical rather than strictly theological document written in the colonies and published in England.

Working with publisher William Bladen, Bellamy printed a third account by Winslow after the author had delivered the work while on a brief trip to England. Published as *Good Nevvs from New England or A true Relation of things very remarkable at the Plantation of Plimoth in Nevv-England* (1624), the narrative continues Winslow's observations begun in *Relation*. Some twenty years later Bellamy published and sold more of Winslow's writings, but of a very different nature. The descriptions and historical narratives of life in the colonies were then replaced by strong defenses of American theocracy, defenses aroused by those who dared to challenge it.

Even before Bellamy became embroiled in the politics of the 1640s, he had published various histories and religious materials about both the Plymouth settlement and the Massachusetts Bay Colony, the latter established in 1628. Often giving details of the natural history of a place, such works were particularly crucial, because they served as advertisements to English readers who might emigrate. William Morrell's *New England or a Briefe Ennaration of the Ayre, Earth, water, fish and fowle of that country* (1625) was one such narrative that Bellamy published. A polished verse style and an enthusiasm for nature (although the native people were excluded from such treatment) made the work an ideal seventeenth-century travel brochure. Two years later Bellamy published Morrell's writing and Mourt's *Relation* as part of *An Historicall Discoverie and Relation of the English Plantations in Nevv England* (1627). In 1634 Bellamy issued yet another work of this kind by William Wood, who came to the Boston area during the Great Migration, from the late 1620s through the early 1640s. Unlike Morrell, who offered an almost too-perfect picture of the plantations, Wood intended his *Nevv Englands Prospect* (1634) to be realistic, to meet the expectations of future planters. Bellamy reprinted it twice, in 1635 and again in 1639.

Several works by John Winthrop and John Cotton, famous leaders of the Massachusetts Bay Colony, received Bellamy's imprint in the 1630s. Bidding a final goodbye to his brethren of the Old World as he and his brethren were about to embark on an adventure to the New, Winthrop wrote *The Hvmble Reqvest Of His Maiesties lyall Subjects, the Governour and the Company late gone to Nevv-England; To the rest of their Brethren, in and of the Church of England* (1630). In 1630 and 1634 Bellamy also published editions of *Gods Promise to His Plantation*, John Cotton's farewell sermon to Winthrop's group, and

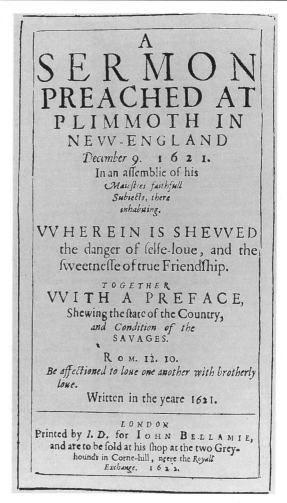

A
SERMON
PREACHED AT
PLIMMOTH IN
NEVV-ENGLAND
December 9. 1 6 2 1.
In an aſſemblie of his
Maieſties faithfull
Subiects, there
inhabiting.

VVHEREIN IS SHEVVED
the danger of ſelfe-loue, and the
ſweetneſſe of true Friendſhip.

TOGETHER
VVITH A PREFACE,
Shewing the ſtate of the Country,
and Condition of the
SAVAGES.

R o M. 1̇2. 10.
Be affectioned to loue one another with brotherly
loue.

Written in the yeare 1621.

LONDON
Printed by *I. D.* for I o H N B E L L A M I E,
and are to be ſold at his ſhop at the two Greyhounds in Corne-hill, neere the *Royall*
Exchange. 1 6 2 2.

Title page for the first published work relating to the Pilgrim settlement at Plymouth, a book Bellamy published in March 1622

more than fifteen years later, when Cotton had become one of the great religious leaders in Boston, Bellamy published Cotton's *The Way of Congregational Churches Cleared in Two Treatises* as well as Thomas Hooker's *Survey of the summe of Church Discipline* in 1648.

Until the late 1640s Bellamy had published no work solely concerned with Native Americans in Massachusetts, although Edward Winslow's *Good Nevves From New England* (1624) had studied them in part. Its title page announces an intention to describe the planters *Together with a Relation of such religious and civill Lawes and Customes, as are in practice amongst the Indians, adjoyning to them at this day.* The Pequot War in 1637 also gave Bellamy and Nathaniel Butter, formerly associated with Nicholas Bourne, a later opportunity to provide the public with three printings of Philip Vincent's sobering *True Relation of the Late Batell fought in New England, between the English and the Salvages* [sic]; *With the pres-*

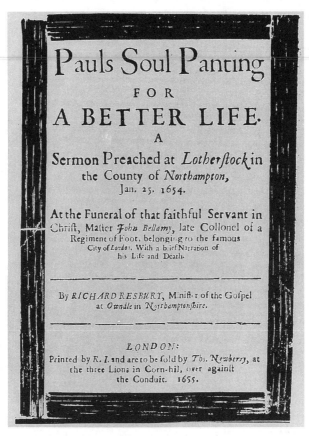

Title page for Bellamy's funeral sermon, delivered at Oundle,
Northamptonshire, his place of birth

ent state of things there (1637, 1638). In 1648 Bellamy published Thomas Shepard I's *Clear Sunshine of The Gospell Breaking Forth upon the Indians in New England*, describing the Puritans' efforts to convert those Native Americans.

In the late 1640s John Bellamy's interests turned increasingly from descriptive narratives to political concerns that were inextricably tied to theological issues. With the arrival of each new group of settlers in New England, there were more who challenged the tenets that the original planters had established. Controversies ultimately increased, several of which involved Winslow. He launched attacks against Samuel Gorton, Robert Child, and Samuel Maverick, who had questioned the character and authority of church government. *Hipocricie Unmasked* (1646), Winslow's diatribe against Gorton, was released again in 1649 by Bellamy as *The Danger of Tolerating Levellers in a Civill State*. Bellamy also published *New England's Salamander* (1647), a subsequent response by Winslow to these opponents. Given the fact that Bellamy had published the works of some of the staunchest Puritan divines, it is ironic that his final publication of American colonial writing was *Jewes Synagogue* (1652) by William Pyncheon, whose ideas about atonement ultimately were rejected by the colonists as being too revolutionary.

Increasing tensions between the Crown and Parliament as well as factions developing within the latter gave a predominantly political tone to John Bellamy's publications during the 1640s in England. Initially Bellamy aligned himself with the Presbyterian and controlling majority of Parliament and published, among many ordinances, *A Declaration of the reasons for assisting the Parliament of England* (1643). When civil war broke out, Bellamy became a colonel in the parliamentary forces and served as a ward of Cornhill on London's Common Council. In 1644 he challenged the authority of the mayor of London, who canceled the court of the council. Bellamy first attacked the actions of the mayor in a speech before the council on 24 February 1644, and he subsequently published his arguments in *A Plea for Commonalty of London* (1645). In this document and a sequel, *Lysimachus Enervatus, Bellamius Reparatus: or a Reply* (1645), Bellamy called for the mayor and council to hold equal authority.

He continued to support the parliamentary cause in *A Justification of the City Remonstrance and its Vindication,* in which he reminded readers that God's authority must finally prevail over its earthly counterparts and encouraged his compatriots to understand the strength to be found in a unified government. Speaking of the two houses of Parliament and the monarchy, Bellamy insisted that "to the upholding & continuance of this so excellent a Constitution, there is such a *Politique necessary* of every one of the three Estates in this Commonweath, for the preservation of the whole." Several years after the Presbyterian majority gave way to the Independents in 1648, Bellamy retired from publishing, leased his printing shop to stationer Philemon Stephens, and ceased his political writing. Leaving most of his books to the Cotherstock Library and his property and other possessions to various family members, John Bellamy died on 20 January 1653/54.

Throughout his life Bellamy dedicated himself to the Word of God in two ways: first, in publishing the views of the Leiden and Amsterdam Separatists as well as the differing accounts of the colonial settlements given by members of the Plymouth, Virginia, and Massachusetts Bay communities; and second, in composing and publishing his own responses to the parliamentary politics of his time. He provided a valuable and vital link between the American colonies and England, as his publications helped the Protestant intellectual community remain abreast of the latest theological issues and reforms.

References:

John Bellamy, *A Ivstification of the City Remonstrance and its Vindication* (London: Cotes, 1646);

Bellamy, *Lysimachus Enervatus, Bellamius Reparatus: or, a Reply* (London: Miller, 1645);

Bellamy, *A Plea for the Commonalty of London* (London: Miller, 1645);

Bellamy, *A Vindication of the Humble Remonstrance and Petition of the Lord Major, Aldermen and Commons of the City of London, in Common-Councell Assembled* (London: Cotes, 1646);

William Haller, ed., *Tracts on Liberty in the Puritan Revolution: 1638–1647* (New York: Octagon, 1965);

Leona Rostenberg, *Literary, Political, Scientific, Religious & Legal Publishing, Printing, and Bookselling in England 1551–1700: Twelve Studies* (New York: Franklin, 1965).

– Julie Whitman-Zai

Thomas Berthelet

(London: c.irca 1524? – 1555)

The more than 150 editions that Thomas Berthelet published between 1524 and 1555 make him a prolific early-sixteenth-century printer, but bibliographers since the late nineteenth century have also considered him one of the most important figures in the early English book trade. As an independent artisan and, between 1530 and 1547, printer to King Henry VIII, Berthelet was responsible for publishing or reprinting many of the most important works of the period: Thomas Paynell's translation of *Regimen Sanitatis Salerni* (1528), all the works of Thomas Elyot (1531–1545), most of Juan Vives's works, Bartholomew Glanville's *De proprietatibus rerum* (1535), William Lily's grammars *Institutio compendiara totius grammaticae* (1540) and *Introduction of the Eyght Partes of Speche* (1542), William Thomas's *The Historie of Italie* (1549) and his Italian grammar (1550), as well as many other classical and humanist texts, Bibles, legal statutes, primers, and devotional and theological works. He was also responsible for printing many historically important statutes and proclamations of the period and for making many innovations in bookbinding design.

As with many other early-sixteenth-century printers, binders, and booksellers, some facts of Berthelet's life and works are subject to uncertainty and open to dispute. Though his imprint typically lists his name as *Berthelet* or gives a Latin variant of this form, his coat of arms is recorded in the College of Arms under the name *Berthelot,* and several colophons record the name as *Berthelette.* Both variations probably indicate French ancestry and quite possibly some relation to Jacques Berthelot, bookseller and printer at Caen and later Rennes. On other colophons, however, his name is spelled *Barthelet* or *Barthlet* – suggestions that his name was probably pronounced *Bartlett.* This fact might identify him as one Thomas Bartellet, a London draper who in 1517 is noted among state papers cited by E. Gordon Duff as entering the service of Sir Richard Wingfield, deputy of Calais.

More mysterious, however, is a possible link to one Thomas Bercula (or Bercleus), with whom many bibliographers since William Blades have attempted to identify him. Since Bercula was in the service of John Ratsell and was a self-styled "lectori" and "typographus" to Richard Pynson, the king's printer until Pynson's death in 1529, soon after which Berthelet succeeded him, strong circumstantial evidence supports such an identification. Duff speculates that Bercula was responsible for making typographical improvements in Pynson's house and for overseeing the editing of contemporary Latin texts. Yet it is also true that neither Bercula nor Berthelet is mentioned in Pynson's will, though Berthelet did use some of his predecessor's

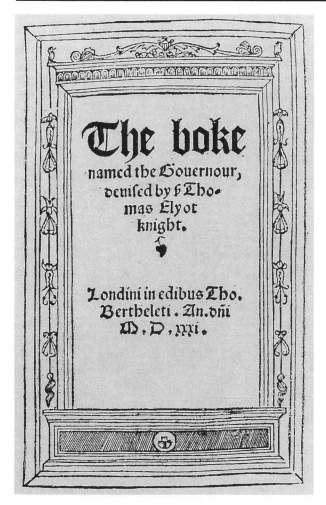
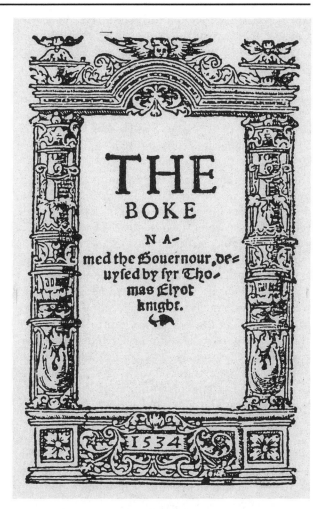

Title pages for Berthelet's first edition of Sir Thomas Elyot's The boke named the Gouernour *(1531) and for the second edition, with a border printed from new metal type that Berthelet continued to use as late as 1624*

decorative borders after his death. A case has also been made that the elusive Bercula was in fact Thomas Barclay, who accompanied John Ratsell to the New Found Lands in 1517.

Details of Berthelet's life are somewhat better documented from about 1524, the year of his first extant publication under his own name of the extremely rare *Opus sane de decorum dearumque* by Galfredus Petrus, monk of Bayeaux. Also in 1524 Berthelet married his first wife, Agnes Langwyth. In March 1526 he and about thirty other London printers were questioned by the vicar-general for not having obtained ecclesiastical licensing for three works, but the printers apparently never faced charges. Pynson died on 15 November 1529, and his will was proved on 18 February of the next year, the same month in which Berthelet was named as his successor. His appointment as king's printer on 2 February 1530 granted him a life income of four pounds per annum, the same sum that Pynson had

received fifteen years before. Unlike his predecessor, who might simply have assumed the title "Printer unto the King's noble grace" without official sanction, Berthelet was formally granted the office in a document dated 13 February 1530. According to W. W. Greg's *Some Aspects and Problems of London Publishing between 1550 and 1650* (1956), this nomination marks an important milestone in the prehistory of copyright, as suggested in the way that Berthelet employed his royal monopoly to protect his 1538 edition of Elyot's dictionary.

Berthelet enjoyed his privilege as king's printer from 1530 until the accession of Edward VI in 1547. Some years before being granted this position, he had set up his own shop in the conduit district of Fleet Street, southeast of Shoe Lane and just a few steps from St. Bride's Church. At this time he adopted the sign of The Roman Lucretia. He kept both the address and the sign throughout his career, though the ways in which they are noted in his works vary. By locating in Fleet Street, Berthelet was among those at the center of the new and rapidly expanding publishing industry. From about 1500, when three principal printers relocated there, Fleet Street had been the hub of most of the printing and trades directly related to printing in London. Berthelet's shop was in the immediate vicinity of the premises of such contemporaries as Wynkyn de Worde, William Ratsell, John Byddell, and Edward Whitchurch.

While serving as king's printer, though not necessarily in that official capacity, Berthelet produced most of his important works. These include reprinted classical and contemporary texts in their original languages and in translation; religious works such as prayer books, Psalters, and sermons; Bibles; historical, moral, legal, and lexicographical texts; conduct literature; and some imaginative writing. Particularly significant among Berthelet's projects during this period are reprinted works of classical authors such as Plutarch, Xenophon, Marcus Aurelius Antoninus, Livy, and Terence, and important medieval writers such as the poet John Gower, the theologians William of Ockham and Bartholomew Glanville, and the fifteenth-century legal historian Thomas Littleton.

In many ways Berthelet was also engaged with the intellectual, political, and spiritual trends of his own day. His publishing of living writers tended toward a practical and political humanism perhaps best represented in the writings of philosophers and educators such as Desiderius Erasmus, Vives, Elyot, John Fitzherbert, and Thomas. The works of such writers touched on the weighty social and educational issues of the first half of the century, issues (in the cases of Erasmus, Vives, and Elyot) ranging from the correct conduct of men and women to the legal and economic duties of the nobility, as in Fitzherbert's influential *The Boke of Husbandry* (1523) and *The Boke of Surveyinge and Improvements* (1523). These authors were elegantly represented, often in multiple editions, by Berthelet, and many of their works were reprinted long after Berthelet's death and remained standard texts throughout the sixteenth and seventeenth centuries. Several of the texts were published in both Latin and English editions.

To what extent these projects indicate Berthelet's conscious editorial policy to advance the causes of humanism is difficult to say with certainty. His reprints of classical and late-medieval authors do seem to indicate a pattern, even if that pattern may not necessarily imply such a conscious intention. Contemporary authors such as Elyot, Vives, and

Thomas might have sought out Berthelet because they perceived that a certain status was attached to works published by the king's printer, especially when those works were carefully produced – as indeed Berthelet's best works were. For whatever reasons, Berthelet clearly was able to publish many of the period's most significant humanist writings.

Berthelet was also at the center of religious and political reforms in the heady years of the 1530s and 1540s. As the king's printer, he was responsible for publishing the proclamations and new statutes that have helped historians define the last two decades of the reign of Henry VIII. These are catalogued in a short but useful study by Robert Proctor. Part of Berthelet's role also involved being trustworthy and loyal: Cyril Davenport cites instances in which Berthelet was entrusted with secret or volatile information as it went to press. In addition, Berthelet printed both a revised "Matthew" Bible in 1539 and the Great Bible the following year, although in both cases he subcontracted with other London printers in producing these. In the 1540s he also printed two of the most influential devotional tracts of the period: the so-called King's Psalms, titled *Psalms or Prayers, Taken out of Holye Scripture* (1544); and the Queen's Prayers, titled *Prayers Stirryng the Mynd vnto Heauenlye Meditacions* (1545) and *Prayers or Meditations, wherin the Mynde is Styrred Paciently to Suffre All Afflictions Here* (1545). These works were often bound together during the period and were reprinted many times, even a generation later by Henry Wykes, who eventually took on Berthelet's business after he had left it to Thomas Powell. These were not the only works directly associated with the royal family that Berthelet produced, however: in 1543 he printed an ABC titled *Alphabetum Latino-Anglicum* that was designated for Prince Edward's use.

At about the same time that he assumed the office of printer to the king, Berthelet began experimenting seriously with the techniques of bookbinding. As the importance of printing grew during the sixteenth century, specialization in the book trade increased, a development that Berthelet seems to have resisted by remaining printer, bookseller, and binder. At the same time, however, the period was characterized by an increasing nationalism in printing and binding techniques, a movement to which Berthelet contributed significantly. Davenport, whose study of Berthelet as bookbinder is extensive and detailed, notes that many of his designs show an Italian influence, though it is not known how direct his association with Italian binders might have been. It is not certain whether Berthelet studied with, commissioned, or hired these artisans. He was apparently the first English binder to employ gold-tooling techniques in producing some books by using tools identical to those of contemporary Italian binders. Certain book bills of Catherine Parr reveal that Berthelet worked in vellum and satin and that he also worked with embroidered binding, his experiments with calf bindings were an innovation in England: he modified and nationalized techniques that he borrowed from Italian models, and he consistently adapted designs to satisfy English tastes while setting an elegant domestic standard.

Berthelet's experiments in binding were conducted in an increasingly protectionist atmosphere. In 1533 a statute in force from the time of Richard III was repealed and a new tax of 6s. 8d. was levied on books bound outside England and imported into the country – a measure designed to insulate from foreign competitors "a greate nombre of the kynges subiectes within this realme, whiche lyve by the crafte and mysterye of byndynge of books." He worked also against a backdrop of increasing specialization (in such roles as editing, printing, binding, and retailing) in the book trade. To what extent Berthelet was also active as an editor is difficult to ascertain, although one signed dedicatory poem attached to the 1544 edition of *Anniball and Scipio* and earlier prefatory materials seem to suggest that he had some significant editorial role in at least some of the publications.

Berthelet's typefaces, borders, ornaments, and patterns of design were the subjects of a 1907 study by Greg, who isolated some forty types, at least thirteen different borders, and some sixteen ornaments used by the printer. Greg determined that many of Berthelet's early borders probably came directly from Pynson, while others that Berthelet used late in his career appear in works printed by Powell, his nephew and successor in the business. Greg also surmised that several of these borders were cut from metal blocks, as they do not show the patterns of stress and deterioration associated with wooden ones. One of these borders was still in use as late as 1624. Berthelet's borders include architectural, arabesque, and window-frame styles, and their designs range from the rather subdued to the highly ornamental. Several appear only once in Berthelet's oeuvre, an observation that led Greg to speculate that some borders might have been borrowed. Others often used by Berthelet – such as that used in the 1530 *Italiae et Galliae academiarum censurae* and many subsequent works – were lent to other printers.

The distinctive Lucrece or "Lucrecia Romana" device was used beginning in 1535 and contin-

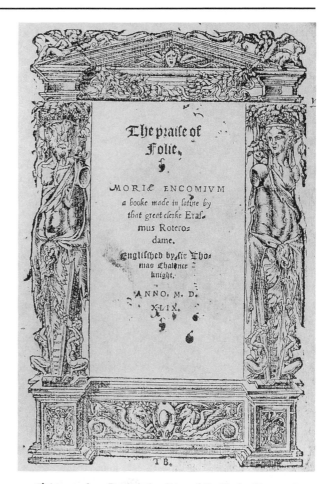

Title page from Berthelet's edition of Desiderius Erasmus's The Praise of Folie *(1549), the first edition to appear in English, translated by Sir Thomas Chaloner*

ued to be the only one associated with Berthelet's house until 1549, after which time no device appears. If, as Greg surmised, by mid 1548 Powell was responsible for the daily running of the shop, he might have been the one who abandoned the practice of using the device. Like the sign, the location of Berthelet's house did not change during this time, although several variations do occur in the ways that both address and device are presented in the publications: after 1536 neither of the phrases "at the sign of Lucrece" nor "near the conduit" appears. Before this date, however, the Lucrece device is commonly accompanied by some version of the address in Latin or English, along with some indication that the shop can be found at this sign. Taken together, this evidence may suggest that by the mid 1530s Berthelet's shop was sufficiently well known for the name alone to identify the business. Certainly his status as king's printer made his business a most important one in the conduit district during most of the thirty-one years that he was located

Page from The Bishop's Book *(1537), printed in Berthelet's black-letter font, the type he used most often*

there, and it seems reasonable to conclude that his shop was among the best known in London.

The various typefaces used by Berthelet are actually limited to a few commonly used fonts, generally black letter. His most commonly used font was a ninety-five-millimeter black letter, which probably came directly from Pynson and was recast at least once during Berthelet's independent career. Although it was used for books, statutes, and proclamations until 1546, after that date its use was restricted to official publications. Berthelet used other fonts as well, some of them only occasionally in his career — such as the elegant ninety-five-millimeter italic of *Acta Curiae Romanae in causa matrimoniali cum Catharina Regina* (1530), which also appears in prefaces and the like. He employed an equally elegant series of Roman typefaces occasionally during his career, usually for printing works or sections in Latin. Of the forty that Greg identified, only about fifteen typefaces were used with any frequency dur-

ing Berthelet's long career, and among these, the most common were black-letter designs. The other twenty-five were probably not complete fonts and were used for title pages, colophons, headings, and similar applications.

As Stanley Morison and Kenneth Day point out, the standard of elegance in book design against which all European printers would have measured themselves in the mid sixteenth century no longer came from Italian artisans, but from Paris houses of leading printers such as Geofroy Tory and Robert Estienne. Compared to their work of the 1530s and 1540s, Berthelet's seems humble enough, especially in its northern European predilection for black letter and mixed typefaces. That said, however, among English printers of the period his works stand out for their usually elegant, decorous designs. As many bibliographers have noted, the use of black-letter typeface was a regional characteristic and not necessarily a sign of inferior skill in design.

Upon the accession of Edward VI, Richard Grafton, who had served as the prince's printer, was given the privilege enjoyed by Berthelet since 1530. Although many explanations for the change might be given, one of the more compelling is that, unlike Grafton, Berthelet never showed radical leanings in his professional work, but rather a safe and centrist humanism. His displacement in favor of Grafton reflects a significant shift toward radical reform in religious politics that followed the death of Henry VIII in 1547, a change all the more interesting because Henry himself had appointed Grafton as his son's printer in 1540. Despite losing his privilege, Berthelet continued to publish *cum priviligio* for most of that year. Greg speculates that about this time Berthelet handed over the daily running of his house to Powell. Certainly the annual production of the business decreased sharply, to a rate of about ten editions per year, following Grafton's new assumption of duties as printer to the king.

Berthelet died on 26 September 1555 and was buried in St. Bride's Church, Fleet Street, where he had been first married more than thirty years before. According to Frank Isaac, he left a well-stocked printing house accustomed to working "in a high state of efficiency." Certainly he died a well-to-do man who held numerous properties in London, its suburbs, and the provinces and whose income exceeded £125 per annum. His will (in which his name is spelled *Barthelett,* incidentally) divided his holdings and goods among his two sons and Margaret, his second wife of some five years, and was proved 9 November of the same year. In it Berthelet directed twenty shillings to St. Bride's Church, £4 to each of his apprentices, Richard Hudson and Henry Wykes, and £10 to Christ's Hospital. Of special interest to scholars of the printing trade is the fact that he also left £20 in goods to Thomas Powell, along with the reversion of that portion left to his younger son, Anthony. The London merchant tailor and funeral supplier Henry Machyn, an eyewitness to Berthelet's funeral, described a lavish ceremony and many mourners, among whom were "all the craftes of prynters, boke-sellers and all the stassyoners."

Powell seems not to have made any radical changes to the business in the years before about 1563, at which time the company passed to Wykes. In fact, several works printed after 1555 do not acknowledge Berthelet's death, as the colophons state only that the works were printed by him. Others, however, capitalize on his obvious prestige by using formulae such as "in the late house of Thomas Barthelet."

Given his importance in many aspects of the early book trade, Thomas Berthelet has regrettably received little scholarly attention. His works, while not always innovative, are consistently of high quality, both as technical achievements and as literary, political, or moral texts. His books are marked by a stately conservatism in design and typography and by a consistently professional approach to typesetting, layout, and proofreading. By insisting on care in all facets of book production, Berthelet set a standard for subsequent generations, even though that standard was often honored in the breach more than in the observance. As a bookbinder he clearly was an innovator whose influence continued to be felt for many decades after his death.

Of the many editions published by Berthelet or his shop, many remain today among the most important texts of the early sixteenth century: reprints of works by classical writers, classical and contemporary translations, theological writings, and a range of works by several influential native writers whose subjects included many different interests. In addition, he was responsible for publishing proclamations, statutes, and other official documents that concretely signal important changes that occurred during the reign of Henry VIII. Berthelet's works remain significant as models of elegance, quality, and professionalism. These facts made him the object of many excellent early twentieth-century bibliographic studies by leading authorities such as Davenport, Duff, and Greg. Even before that generation of scholars began their studies, however, Joseph Ames concluded of Berthelet in his *Typographical Antiquities* (1816) that "it may be questioned whether there be any British printer who has stronger claims upon the gratitude of posterity."

References:

Joseph Ames, *Typographical Antiquities: Or, the History of Printing,* volume 3, revised edition, augmented by William Herbert (London: John Murray, 1816);

William Blades, "Who Was Bercula?," *Bibliographer,* 1 (1882): 13–15;

Charles C. Butterworth, *The English Primers (1529–1545)* (Philadelphia: University of Pennsylvania Press, 1953);

Colin Clair, "Thomas Berthelet, Royal Printer," *Gutenberg Jahrbuch* (1966): 177–181;

Cyril Davenport, *Thomas Berthelet: Royal Printer and Bookbinder to Henry VIII, King of England* (Chicago: Caxton Club, 1901);

E. Gordon Duff, *A Century of the English Book Trade* (London: Bibliographical Society, 1905);

Duff, "Richard Pynson and Thomas Bercula," *Library,* new series 8 (July 1907): 298–303;

Duff, Henry R. Plomer, and Robert Proctor, *Handlists of English Printers, 1501–1556,* part 3 (London: Bibliographical Society, 1905);

Strickland Gibson, "The Protocollum of Thomas Berthelet," *Library,* fifth series 1 (June 1946): 47–49;

W. W. Greg, "Notes on the Types, Borders, Etc. Used By Thomas Berthelet," *Transactions of the Bibliographical Society,* 8 (October 1907): 187–220;

Greg, *Some Aspects and Problems of London Publishing between 1550 and 1650* (Oxford: Clarendon Press, 1956);

Frank Isaac, *English Printers' Types of the Sixteenth Century* (Oxford: Oxford University Press, 1936);

R. B. McKerrow, *Printers' and Publishers' Devices in England and Scotland, 1485–1640* (London: Bibliographical Society, 1913);

McKerrow and F. S. Ferguson, *Title-Page Borders Used in England and Scotland, 1485–1640* (London: Bibliographical Society, 1932);

Stanley Morison and Kenneth Day, *The Typographic Book, 1450–1935* (Chicago: University of Chicago Press, 1963);

Marjorie Plant, *The English Book Trade: An Economic History of the Making and Sale of Books* (London: Allen & Unwin, 1939);

Henry R. Plomer, *Abstracts from the Wills of English Printers and Stationers from 1492 to 1630* (London: Bibliographical Society, 1903);

Robert Proctor, "A Short View of Berthelet's Editions of the Statutes of Henry VIII," *Transactions of the Bibliographical Society,* 5 (December 1899): 256–262;

F. Rose-Troup, "Two Book Bills of Catherine Parr," *Library,* third series 2 (January 1911): 40–48.

                        – Thomas G. Olsen

Nathaniel Butter

(London: 1604 – 1663/1664)

Nicholas Bourne

(London: 1608 – 1660)

In December 1604 Nathaniel Butter entered his first publication in the register of the Stationers' Company: *The Life and Death of Cavaliero Dick Boyer*. Perhaps in memory of his beginnings Butter in 1660 affixed his name to his last known imprint, *The Cavalier's Complaint*. During the first six decades of the seventeenth century Nathaniel Butter emerged not as the publisher of romances but as an astute stationer who, with his associate Nicholas Bourne, launched and maintained English journalism with a host of news sheets. Of the two quasi partners, each maintaining his own establishment, Butter remained the greater specialist, publishing domestic and foreign news almost until his death.

Nathaniel Butter was born into the trade. His father Thomas, a London stationer, was active from 1576 to 1590 with premises at the Pied Bull, St. Paul's Churchyard. Thomas Butter was among those who petitioned William Cecil, Lord Burghley in 1582 for action against the monopolists. When he died in 1590 his business was continued, as was customary, by his widow Johanna, who soon married another London stationer, John Newberry, but still maintained her own business.

Born circa 1583 and educated from childhood in the trade, Nathaniel doubtless served as an apprentice under the guidance of his mother and stepfather. On 20 February 1604 he was admitted to the Stationers' Company as a freeman "per patrimonium," and he could thereafter occupy with confidence the original premises of his father at the Sign of the Pied Bull. He appears to have been well established by 1614, when he lent thirty-six pounds to London bookseller Ralph Mabbe. Two years later he joined the London Stationers' stock company as a second-class member responsible for a capital investment of fifty pounds. By 1622 he had trained four apprentices – Philemon Stephens, George Glascocke, Robert Salmon, and John Cooper – the first of whom was to enjoy esteem in the London book trade.

Butter's success was such that he became the butt of Ben Jonson's satire "Staple of News." Despite his gibes of Butter, Jonson offers a lively portrait of the bustle and activity that enlivened the premises of the Pied Bull. There Butter's office consisted of several rooms in a large house, well furnished with carpets, desks, and tables heaped with manuscripts, rolls, and files. Apprentices occupied the outer chambers, while Butter sat within, "the decay'd Stationer ... true Paules bred, i' the Church-yard." In fact, Butter was not "decay'd." A knowledgeable dealer, he was well aware of those reader interests that induced him to specialize not in theological tomes but in various sensational texts, the latest news items, and foreign relations.

Following his first publication of *The Life and Death of Cavaliero Dick Boyer* Butter issued in 1605 an anonymously written, bloody, and violent tract, *Two most vnnatvrall and blovdie Murthers: The one by Maister Caluereley, a Yorkshire gentleman, practised vpon his wife . . . the other, by Mistris Browne and her servant vpon her hvsband*. Public interest in the butchery of his wife by Walter Calvereley, lord of the manor of Calvereley and Pudsey, was great, and Butter hastened to gratify a large, morbid readership. Obviously pleased with sales of the recounting of this double murder, Butler published a sequel: *The Araignment Condempnacion Execucion of Maister Calverley at Yorke in August 1605* (1605).

With an expanding overseas dominion, the British reader longed for reports of distant lands and peoples. He was also curious about the Continental events — its rulers, mores, and wars. Butter provided sensational news in the tradition of the Calverley pamphlets through such items as *Newes from sea . . . of two Notorious Pyrats, Ward and Danseker* (1609) and *The Life, Confession and Repentance of Francis Cartwright Gentleman: for his bloudie Sinne in killing Master Storr* (1621). For the less bloodthirsty reader who preferred narratives of faraway places, the master of the Pied Bull published *An Houre Glasse of Indian Newes* (1607), the tale of John Nicholl, who had sustained "most lamentable miseries" in his voyage to Guiana; Sir Thomas Smith's *Voiage and Entertainment in Rushia* (1605); Sir Anthony Sherley's

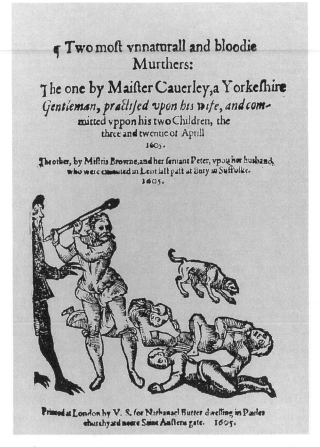

Title page for one of Butter's early tracts appealing to public interest in sensational news

Relation of his Travels to Persia (1613); and two narratives of the brutal treachery of Sir Cahir O'Dogherty, the Irish rebel, in 1608: *Newes from Loughffoyle in Ireland* (1608) and *Newes from Ireland* (1608).

Catering to English patriotism, Butter in 1621 published *A Trve Relation of a wonderfull Sea Fight betweene two great and well appointed Spanish ships or Men of Warre. And a small and not very well prouided English Ship*. Nationalism was further fired by Turkish insolence and cruelty, and Butter fed this interest by publishing *Relation Strange and Trve of a Ship of Bristol named the Jacob which was taken by the Tvrkish Pirates* (1622).

The political unrest throughout the Hapsburg Empire that culminated in the Thirty Years' War keenly interested many English readers, and *Articles of peace between the Archduke Mathias and the Lord Botzkay* relating to religious and domestic problems of the Holy Roman Empire bears a 1607 Butter imprint. He also examined the growing aggression of Sweden in publishing works of English pamphleteer Anthony Nixon – *Warres of Swethland* (1609) and *Swethland and Poland Warres* (1610). Butter further

acquainted his readers with international affairs in such publications as *News from Spaine* (1611), *Good Newes from Florence* (1614), M. Du Tertre's *News from France* (1616), and Lodovico Cortano's *Good Newes to Christendome: Sent to a Venetian in Ligorne, from a Merchant in Alexandria* (1620).

Butter was interested in disseminating reports from the many parts of the known and unknown world, yet his reputation was also enhanced by his publication of the first edition of one of the greatest English dramas. On 26 November 1607 Butter and stationer John Busby entered in the company's register "A booke called. Mr William Shakespeare his historye of Kynge Lear as yt was played before the kinges maiestie at Whitehall vppon St Stephans night at xpistmas Last by his maities servantes playinge vsually at the globe on the Banksyde." The second edition of *King Lear* bearing the Butter imprint appeared in 1619, three years after the poet's death.

Writings of other Elizabethan authors also carry the Butter imprint: Thomas Heywood's *If You Know Not Me, You Know No Bodie* (1605), and Thomas Dekker's *The Whore of Babylon* (1607) and his brilliant prose satire, *The Belman of London* (1608), published in four editions. One of Butter's most significant publications is the first edition of George Chapman's translation of Homer, *The Whole Works of Homer* (1616), made up from unsold sheets of *The Iliad* and *The Odyssey,* both of which Butter had published separately.

To some extent Butter's assessment of public tastes was shared by his fellow stationer Nicholas Bourne. Bourne, Butter's junior by three years, was the son of Henry Bourne, a cordwainer of London. Nicholas had been apprenticed at age fifteen to stationer Cuthbert Burby of Cornhill, near the Royal Exchange, and in 1607 Burby died during Bourne's term of apprenticeship. In his will Burby remembered his apprentice "in respect of his true and faithfull service" and left him "the lease estate . . . in my said Shopp scituate in Cornehill."

Thus through the generosity of Burby young Bourne was set up in his own business. Rising to prominence in his company, Bourne occupied those Cornhill premises for almost fifty years. In 1608 he published his first work, a religious treatise, in collaboration with John Bache. In time he employed three apprentices – John Bellamy, Hugh Grafton, and John Hope, the first of whom was to become the outstanding London publisher of works relating to New England.

From 1608 to 1622 Bourne published approximately seventy-eight books and pamphlets on various subjects, his productivity being less than that of Butter. His interest in the circulation of news is reflected in 50 percent of Bourne's output. In 1609 he published *Articles of a treatie of truce, made in Antwerp, the 9 of April, 1609.* In the genre of sensational works are his publications *A true Relation of travailes and most miserable captivities of William Davies barber surgeon of London under the Duke of Florence* (1614), *The true narracon of the Confession of 2 murthers by John De Paris and John de la Vigne* (1616), and *A True Relation of strange accidents in the kingdom of the great Magor* (1622). Circa 1620 Bourne entered into partnership with Thomas Archer – an established dealer in news sheets, jestbooks, and plays – with premises in Pope's Head Palace near the Royal Exchange. Archer was unfortunately in jail by midsummer of 1621, guilty of having published unlicensed news sheets concerning the war in the Palatinate.

By 1622 Butter and Bourne were collaborating in the publication and circulation of news sheets. Their sources included many foreign accounts (many treating the Thirty Years' War), the correspondence of merchants, and reports from Englishmen living abroad. Commencing in 1622, the news

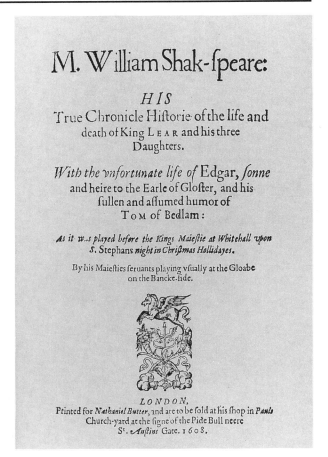

Title page for the first edition of William Shakespeare's King Lear *(1608)*

sheets issued by Butter and Bourne were usually weeklies. Unlike the seven news sheets that Butter alone had printed in folio in 1621, these appeared in quarto and ranged in length from four to twenty-four pages. The two printers continued to publish these news sheets, which appeared in various series, until 1632. The early ones were edited by Capt. Thomas Gainsford, a friend of Butter and the author of *Letters of Newes* (1616). The series concerned only foreign news, because the Crown tightly restricted the circulation of domestic news.

More than once the authorities were tempted to harass the press for having published offensive news items, and finally in October 1632 a Star Chamber decree ordered that the gazettes and news pamphlets "be supprest and inhibited. And that as well Nathaniell Butter and Nicholas Bourne . . . presume not from henceforth to print publish or sell any of the said Pamphletts, &c." Having printed more than three hundred numbers since September 1624, Butter and Bourne ceased publication with number 1 of their ninth series of periodical news sheets in October 1632.

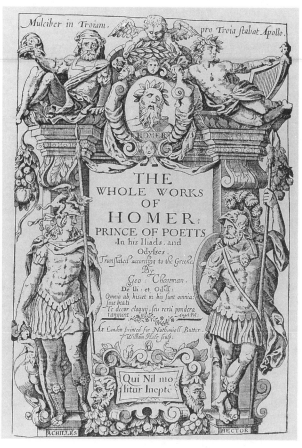

*Title page for the first edition of George Chapman's translation
of the works of Homer, which Butter published in 1616.
William Hole was the engraver.*

Yet Butter did not accept this official ban without protest. By November 1632 he had visited Secretary Edward Coke to plead his case, but he had little success. In all likelihood, according to geographer John Pory, the ban had been occasioned by "the importunity of the Spanish and Archduchess's agents, who were vexed at the soul to see so many losses and crosses, so many dishonours and disasters, betide the house of Austria." The following October 1633 Butter and Bourne jointly petitioned King Charles I and asserted that they had "received some benefit and a great part of the King's subjects content by the Gazettes and weekly news." They promised that "nothing dishonourable to princes in amity with his Majesty should pass the press." The matter was referred to the secretaries of state for further consideration.

In the meantime Butter and Bourne published one of their outstanding gazettes in several parts — *The Swedish Intelligencer,* an account of the European conflict and of the career of Gustavus Adolphus. Not until December 1638 did Butter and Bourne re-ceive Royal Letters Patent permitting them to publish news books, depending upon their annual payment of ten pounds toward the repair of St. Paul's, for a term of twenty-one years. The first number of their new series is dated 20 December 1638, and this series lasted until July 1639; the two publishers then followed this with another short-lived periodical, which concluded in March 1640. During this last series Butter and Bourne dissolved their association.

Butter's career from 1640 until his death in 1669 was downhill. He still retained his interest in publishing news books, although the quality of their paper and type declined. Until his last known publication in 1660 Butter published about fifteen works treating foreign and some domestic events. Among these were such titles as *A little forraine newes* (1641–1642), James Gibbes's *Good and bad news from Ireland* (1641), Eleazar Gilbert's *Newes from Poland* (1641), *The continuation of our forraine occurrences* (1642), *Divers remarkable occurrences that have hapned in the Tower* (1642), *A cruel and blovdy battaile betwixt the Weymarish* (1642), and Alonso Cardenas's *A speech or complaint*

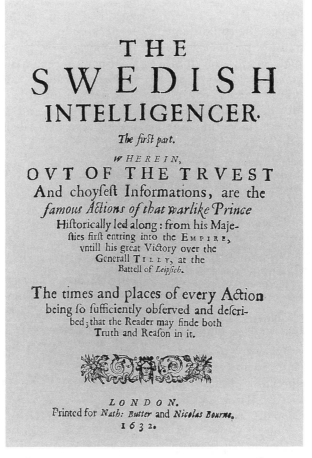

THE
SWEDISH
INTELLIGENCER.
The first part.
WHEREIN,
OVT OF THE TRVEST
And choyfeft Informations, are the
famous Actions of that warlike Prince
Hiftorically led along : from his Maje-
fties firft entring into the EMPIRE,
vntill his great Victory over the
Generall TILLY, at the
Battell of *Leipfich.*

The times and places of every Action
being fo fufficiently obferved and defcri-
bed; that the Reader may finde both
Truth and Reafon in it.

LONDON.
Printed for *Nath: Butter* and *Nicolas Bourne,*
1 6 3 2.

Title page for a collection of newsletters in which Butter and
Bourne recounted recent events of the Thirty Years War

lately made by the Spanish ambassadour (1643). Butter supplemented his income during his latter years by circulating the religious polemics of Joseph Hall and others.

Prior to 1639 he had trained six apprentices, but during his declining years he appears to have conducted his business alone. He encountered serious problems in January 1643 when he was arrested and taken as a prisoner to the Fleet. On 26 January Parliament ordered that he be removed "to Windsore; to be tried by the Council of War, for an Intelligencer." As he was later tried by martial law as an "Intelligencer and Spy," his news publications had apparently aroused suspicion. The term of his imprisonment and the nature of his offense remain unknown. It appears that he was released at some time in 1644, when he published a single work, Bishop Joseph Hall's *The Devout Soul.*

In 1649 the once-successful occupant of the Pied Bull moved to far less prestigious quarters in Cursiters Alley. The final appearance of the name of Nathaniel Butter in the register of the Stationers'

Company is dated 3 December 1663, when "by . . . an assignment bering date the 9 day of October last past under the hand and seale of Nathaniel Butter," Thomas Rookes entered "a booke or coppy intituled Doctor Hollidayes Sermons." Shortly thereafter, on 22 February 1664 "Nath. Butter, an old stationer, died very poore."

Unlike Butter, his former associate Nicholas Bourne prospered, accumulating esteem and wealth. Bourne was a perspicacious man who recognized the shifting moods of the public, a changing kingdom with an expanding overseas traffic, and a growing economy. Hence, his publishing list during his latter years reflects to some extent the mercantile needs of the age.

Bourne's publications include several significant works in economic theory and practice: Lewes Roberts's *The Treasure of Traffike* (1641); the anonymously written *A Short and True Relation concerning the Soap-business* (1641); Simon Smith's *The Herring Busse Trade* (1641); John Webster's *Tables for Interest* (1649); John Marius's *Advice concerning Bills of*

Exchange (1651); Richard Hodges's *Enchiridion Arithmeticon, or, a Manual of Millions* (1651), which was "to be sold by Richard Hodges the author; and by N. Bourn" and others; W. B. A.'s *Free Ports, the Nature and Necessitie of Them Stated* (1652); and John Collins's *An Introduction to Merchants Accounts* (1653).

Of particular commercial value are the ephemera that Bourne carried: "Bills of Lading [in] English, French, Italian [and] Dutch, Indentures for Virginia, Saint Christophers, the Somer Islands and Bills of Debt for Moneys [and] for Tobacco." Additional indentures were "for Apprentices for England, Virginia, Barbadoes and Somer Island being cutt in copper." At the shop in the Royal Exchange the customer could acquire various engravings – "mapps of both houses of Parliament. The mapp of all the armes of the Companies of the citty of London. . . . The picture of Gustavus Adolphus king of Sweden. The picture of Sr Francis Drake." He also offered licenses for alehouses.

Bourne's activity was such that during the years 1621–1657 he engaged nine apprentices, among whom the most competent was Robert Horne, future master of the Turk's Head and eventual successor to Bourne's premises. Bourne enjoyed high repute as member of the Stationers' Company, which he served as master twice (in 1643 and 1651) and as warden three times.

Bourne died during the early months of 1660, and in his will he left thirty-five bequests amounting to £776. One of those bequests – in the amount of five pounds – was to the Stationers' Company. Yet both Bourne and his associate Butter had bequeathed far more than monetary wealth to their readership. In the years before the Restoration they had informed the public of events abroad. Through their news sheets they had enlightened readers and brought events in remote kingdoms to England. The publications that carried their imprint helped to link England and the Continent and thereby to broaden the political and social horizons of their nation.

Bibliography:

Folke Dahl, *A Bibliography of English Corantos and Periodical Newsbooks, 1620–1642* (London: Bibliographical Society, 1952).

References:

Joseph Frank, *The Beginnings of the English Newspaper, 1620–1660* (Cambridge, Mass.: Harvard University Press, 1961);

Laurence Hanson, "English Newsbooks, 1620–1641," *Library,* fourth series 18 (March 1938): 355–384;

Leona Rostenberg, *Literary, Political, Scientific, Religious & Legal Publishing, Printing & Bookselling in England, 1551–1700: Twelve Studies,* 2 volumes (New York: Franklin, 1965);

Matthias A. Shaaber, *Some Forerunners of the Newspaper in England, 1476–1622* (Philadelphia: University of Pennsylvania Press, 1929).

– Leona Rostenberg

Henry Bynneman

(London: 1566 – 1583)

As an apprentice to Richard Harrison, stationer and printer in White Cross Street, Cripplegate, Henry Bynneman (also spelled Benneyman, Binneman, or Binnman) on 24 June 1559 began what would become his career as a London bookseller and printer. When Harrison died in 1562, Bynneman completed his apprenticeship with Reyner Wolfe, father-in-law to Harrison's son, John. Bynneman became a freeman of the Stationers' Company in 1566, as he began printing in Paternoster Row and at the sign of the Black Boy.

He set up a printing house in Knightrider Street at the Mermaid in 1567, and Bynneman's business was sufficient by 1572 to support both his primary establishment and a bookseller's shed known as The Three Wells in St. Paul's Churchyard. In 1574 he acquired a fine set of printing devices, ornaments, and letters from the estate of Reyner Wolfe, and on 30 June 1578 he was admitted to the Stationers' Company livery. On 10 March 1579 he leased a messuage in Thames Street, near Baynard's Castle, and while there he served as constable to the parish of St. Bennet, Paul's Wharf.

At the time of his death in 1583, in addition to his dwelling in Thames Street, Bynneman maintained the shop in St. Paul's and another in St. Gregory's. Both his bookselling and printing enterprises at the time of his death were substantial. He maintained three presses, and before his death a 1583 entry in the Stationers' Register indicates that he intended to print all of Aristotle's works in Latin, Homer's in Greek and Latin, and a Greek New Testament. Mark Eccles reports that an inventory of Bynneman's books and property shows that at his death he held more than twenty-four thousand copies of more than seventy-five titles. During his lifetime Bynneman had printed nearly two hundred different titles, many of which were published in multiple editions. Following his death Bynemann's printing materials were passed to the Eliot's Court Press, some partners of which – Ninian Newton, Arnold Hatfield, and Edmond Bollifant – may have worked as journeymen for him in 1583 and continued working together following his death. One of Bynneman's sons, Christopher, was in 1600 apprenticed for seven years to Thomas Dawson.

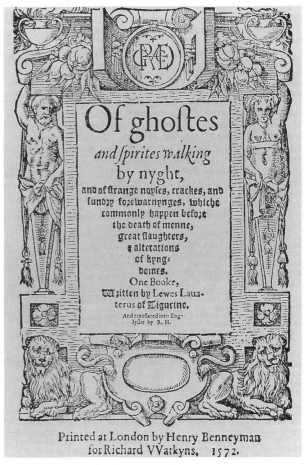

Title page for one of Lewis Lavater's works on ghosts and spirits, topics of interest to sixteenth-century readers. Bynneman's name appears on this title page in one of its variant spellings.

Henry R. Plomer identifies Bynneman as a member of a small group of printers of excellent craftsmanship "to whom Archbishop Parker extended his patronage and encouragement between 1560 and 1575." At least twice in 1578 Bynneman styled himself as "servant to the right hon. Sir Christopher Hatton," and, according to Eccles, Robert Dudley, earl of Leicester, and Hatton secured for Bynemann a privilege granted on 28 April 1580 to print "all Dictionaries in all tongues, all Chronicles and histories whatsoever."

Throughout his career Bynneman printed various official documents, including episcopal visitation articles (*Articles to be Ministered by the Right*

Title page for the first edition of John Polmon's All the
famous Battels *(circa 1586), one of many histories to
which Bynneman had secured a broad
privilege in 1580*

Reuerend Father in Christ, Robert [Horne] . . . *in His Visitation, to be Kept and Holden thorow His Sayd Dioces of Winchester,* 1570, and *Articles to Be Inquired of, by the Reuerende Father in God, Richarde by Gods Prouidence Bishop of Elye,* 1573); two proclamations, one by the Privy Council (*Proclamation: A Very Rich Lotterie Generall,* 1567) and one by the queen (*Proclamation: Whereas the Queenes Most Excellent Maiestie by Her Highnesse Proclamation in Nouember Last, Did Appoint and Limit the Reading of the Lotterie within Her Citie of London This X. of Ianuarie,* 1569); and a special liturgy, *The Order of Prayer vpon Wednesdayes and Frydayes, to Auert and Turne Gods Wrath from Vs, Threatned by the Late Terrible Earthquake* (1580).

He also printed quasi-official propaganda, including Thomas Norton's *To the Quenes Maiesties Poore Deceyued Subiectes of the North Countrey, Drawen into Rebellion by the Earles of Northumberland and Westmorland* (1569) and John Bridges's *The Supremacie of Christian Princes* (1573). Ralph Newbery and Bynneman printed Christopher Ockland's historical poem *Anglorum Praelia* (1580), which was ordered to be read in the schools by royal proclamation. Bynneman also printed the report of the queen's progress

to Norwich, as well as Thomas Churchyard's reports of her entertainments in Norfolk and Suffolk.

In a related but less official capacity Bynneman frequently printed for Humphrey Toy on the side of the church in religious controversy, as in his publication of Alexander Nowell's *A Confutation, as Wel of M. Dormans Last Boke Entituled a Disproufe. & c. as also of D. Sander His Causes of Transubstatiation* (1567) and Henry Howard, earl of Northampton's *A Defense of the Ecclesiasticall Regiment in Englande, Defaced by T. C. in His Replie agaynst D. Whitgifte* (1574). Most notably he printed John Whitgift's answers in the Admonition Controversy in the early 1570s — *The Defense of the Aunswere to the Admonition, against the Replie of T. C.* (1574) and *A Godlie Sermon Preached before the Queenes Maiestie at Greenwiche, the 26 of March Last Past* (1574).

In one respect Bynneman was a "printer's printer," doing nearly one-third of his printing either for or in partnership with other printers and publishers. He printed poetry, including the writings of George Gascoigne — *A Hundreth Sundrie Flowres Bounde vp in One Small Poesie* (1573), *The Poesies* (1575), and *The Steele Glas* (1576) — for Richard

Smith. His most sustained relationships, however, were with George Bishop, Lucas Harrison, and Ralph Newbery. Bishop and Harrison had been associated with Reyner Wolfe, as Bynneman had been, and for them he printed works that looked to the interests of Continental Protestantism – theological discourses, confessions, and sermons, along with contemporary histories and reports of contemporary political events affecting the faithful. These include Niels Hemmingsen's *A Postill, or Exposition of the Gospels That Are Vsually Red in the Churches of God, vpon the Sundayes and Feast Dayes of Saints* (1569), Heinrich Bullinger's *Questions of Religion Cast Abroad in Helvetia by the Aduersaries of the Same: and Aunswered by M. H. Bullinger* (1572), Rudolf Gwalther's *Certaine Godlie Homelies or Sermons vpon the Prophets Abdias and Ionas* (1573), John Calvin's *Sermons of Master Iohn Caluin, vpon the Booke of Iob* (1574), Martin Luther's *A Treatise, Touching the Libertie of a Christian* (1575), Innocent Gentillet's *A Declaration concerning the Needfulnesse of Peace to Be Made in Fraunce* (1575) and Charles IX's *Edict for Appeasing of Troubles in His Kingdome* (1570), and Jean de Serres's *A Discourse of the Ciuile Warres and Late Troubles in Fraunce* (1570).

After Harrison's death Bynneman continued to print such material for Ralph Newbery. It might be tempting to assume that Bynneman's interests were merely commercial, except for two things. First, around 1580 Bynneman and Newbery appeared to be working as partners, with the name of the latter (as Bynneman's assignee) appearing as that of the printer on title pages, even though Bynneman appears to have been doing most of the printing. Indeed, Newbery and Henry Denham acted as Bynneman's deputies in company matters shortly after his death, because his wife, Brigide, forfeited her rights to Bynneman's copies by remarrying outside the company. On 8 January 1584 Denham and Newbery yielded fourteen of Bynneman's copyrights to the company to be printed by its poorer printers. On 30 December 1584 Denham and Newbery clearly entered in the Stationers' Register their rights as Bynneman's deputies to the dictionary, chronicle, and history patent. Second, Bynneman's surreptitious printing of a history of the St. Bartholomew's Day Massacre of French Protestants (the English version of François Hotman's *De Furiobus, Gallicus,* 1573), with its clear appeal in the printer's prologue for Queen Elizabeth I to support the French Protestant cause, clearly signals how aligned Bynneman's own interests were with those of Harrison and Newbery.

Plomer and Ronald B. McKerrow both comment on the high quality of Bynneman's printing.

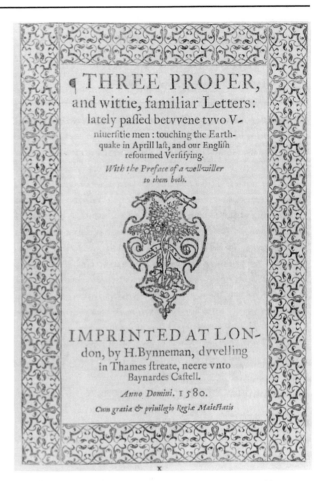

Title page for Bynneman's edition of an exchange of letters between Edmund Spenser and Gabriel Harvey, discussing, in part, the difficulties that poets faced in trying to write English poetry in classical meters

He possessed fine italic, roman, and black letter fonts. His 1577 edition of Raphael Holinshed's *Chronicles,* an edition consisting of 2,835 small folio pages, usually bound in two volumes and containing woodcut illustrations, is an excellent example of fine printing: the black letter font is clear and even, the printing careful and clean.

More remarkable than the quality of his printing is the learned output of his press. Bynneman printed in Latin (John Caius's *De antiquitate Cantabrigiensis Academia libri duo,* 1568), Dutch (Pierre Viret's *De cautelen (dat is te segghen, de waershouwinghe ofte onderwijsinghe) met het canon ende ceremonien vander Misse,* 1568), French (*A Dictionarie French and English,* 1571), and English, and he intended to print Homer in Greek. Besides printing in the original languages, much of Bynneman's output included Continental writers and classical writers in translation. From Bynneman's print shop came published works of the most important Christian humanist, Desiderius

Erasmus (*Familiarium colloquiorum,* 1571), and Continental writers – including Giovanni Boccacio's *Filococo* (1569), Baldassare Castiglione's *Comitis de curiali siue aulico libri quatuor* (The Book of the Courtier, 1577), and Thomas Paynell's translation of *The Treasurie of Amadis of Fraunce: Conteyning Eloquente Orations, Pythie Epistles, Learned Letters, and Feruent Complayntes* (1572).

Classical authors join the most learned men in England on Bynneman's list: Plutarch (*Amorous and Tragicall Tales,* 1567), Cicero (*Ad Familiares,* 1571), Ovid (*His Invective against Ibis,* 1577), Aristotle (*Ethicorum ad Nicomachum,* 1581), Virgil (*The First Foure Bookes of Virgils Aeneis,* translated by Richard Stanyhurst, 1583), John Colet (*A Right Fruitfull Admonition, concerning the Order of a Good Christian Mans Life,* 1577), Roger Ascham (*Disertissimi viri Rogeri Aschami,* 1581), Gabriel Harvey and Edmund Spenser (*Three Proper, and Wittie, Familiar Letters: Lately Passed betweene Two Vniuersitie Men: Touching the Earthquake in Aprill Last, and Our English Refourmed Versifying,* 1580), and William Painter (*The Palace of Pleasure,* volume 2, 1567).

Continental religious reformers (Theodore Beza, John Calvin, Martin Luther, and Heinrich Bullinger) appeared with the most important English religious apologists (John Jewel, John Whitgift, Robert Crowley, and John Bridges). Rhet-oricians such as Gabriel Harvey (*Rhetor . . . de natura, arte, & exercitatione rhetorica,* 1577), Petrus Ramus (*Rudimenta Gracae P. Rami grammaticis pracipue collecta,* 1581), and Ralph Lever (*The Arte of Reason, Rightly Termed, Witcraft,* 1573) appear alongside mathematicians such as Leonard Digges (*Stratioticos,* 1579) and natural philosophers such as Pierre Boaistuau (*Certaine Secrete Wonders of Nature,* 1569). Works of voyage literature – *A Shorte and Briefe Narration of the Two Nauigations and Discoueries to the Northweast Partes Called Newe Fraunce* (1580), by Jacques Cartier, and Marco Polo's *The Most Noble and Famous Trauels of Marcus Paulus* (1579) – are listed along with practical guides to the sea such as William Bourne's *A Regiment for the Sea* (1574). Guides to English country pleasures such as gardening, hawking, and hunting accompany political propaganda. In short, the nearly 200 books printed by Bynneman epitomize the world of English letters during the English Renaissance.

References:

Mark Eccles, "Bynneman's Books," *Library,* fifth series 12 (June 1957): 81–92;

Henry R. Plomer, "Henry Bynneman, Printer, 1566–83," *Library,* new series 9 (July 1908): 225–244.

– Cyndia Susan Clegg

Cambridge University Press

(Cambridge: 1583 –)

The University of Cambridge was given the right to print books by King Henry VIII in 1534. Before that date Johann Lair (usually known as John Siberch) of Siegburg, near Cologne, had been the only printer in Cambridge. He was a member of a family with extensive interests in the book trade, a family including Franz and Arnold Birckmann of Cologne and Johannes Graphaeus of Antwerp. Between 1521 and 1523 John Siberch printed in Cambridge about a dozen books, all of modest size, among which were works by Galen, Desiderius Erasmus, and the English humanists Henry Bullock, John Fisher, and Sir Thomas Linacre. But his business did not prosper, and he was obliged to return to the Continent.

Henry VIII granted a charter to the university a decade later to protect its right to publish from legislation directed more generally against foreign workmen. Granting the charter acknowledged the authority of the university as a reliable support in political and religious matters, and it tacitly admitted British reliance on foreign books, on consequently close links with the foreign book trade, and on skills that could not necessarily be found among British printers at that time. The first stationers and printers to be named were Nicholas Spierinck, Garrett Godfrey, and Segar Nicholson: all were from the Low Countries.

But in fact none of these established a press, and no press followed that of Siberch in Cambridge until 1583. In that year a fellow of King's College, Thomas Thomas, married Anne Sheres, the widow of a wealthy local bookseller and bookbinder, John

Sheres, and established a press in a house near the university church. From the time that rumor of his plans reached London, his enterprise was treated with suspicion and jealousy by London printers, who sought (but found only moderate sympathy in) the support of Queen Elizabeth's chief minister, William Cecil, Lord Burghley. Relations between the Cambridge press of Thomas and John Legate, his assistant and successor, and the London trade were strained and frequently litigious for a century: the Stationers' Company, for instance, had been granted its own charter in 1557 (after the date at which the university had received its charter), and the company disliked having its monopoly challenged by Thomas and Legate. The Cambridge printers eventually and reluctantly were reconciled, however, with the London trade.

Thomas began with the intention of printing works that would aid in teaching. Only a fragment survives of his first book, a text from Pliny (1583) that was probably never completed. Thomas's selection from Ovid (1584) was among his first books, and his Latin dictionary, first published in 1587, was republished twelve times before 1631. Many of the other books that he printed reveal his Puritan religious inclinations, and he kept close ties with Continental theology in this respect.

From the beginning each of his books had to be licensed by the university's vice chancellor, who thus introduced a degree of censorship that in effect varied with the individual work to be published. Printing in Cambridge was thus controlled (as it was in Oxford) by an arrangement parallel to that

Letters Patent by which Henry VIII in 1534 granted the University of Cambridge the right to appoint three stationers as printers (Cambridge University Archives)

established in London, where the power of the Stationers' Company could be censoriously exercised. For most of the seventeenth century (except for the civil war), printing in England remained legally restricted to London and the two universities. With varying attentiveness, the vice chancellor for long periods was also expected to set prices at which books could be sold and thus to mediate between the interests of the printers and the needs of the university population, to whom many of their books were directed.

Because the university, set in a small town and amid a local population that had little spare money, could not absorb all that was printed and because the university also required books from London (many of which had been in turn imported), much of the stock of the early university printers was traded directly with London booksellers and also with local booksellers who used Cambridge-printed books as exchange for stock acquired in London or Oxford. Thus, as most business was conducted by credit, comparatively little money had to change

hands between London and Cambridge. This remained the practice at least until the late seventeenth century. Thomas's main early trading partner was London bookseller Thomas Chard. John Legate, who bought Thomas's stock and equipment after his death in 1588, had been trained in London – as Thomas had not. Legate found the London market easier than Thomas had, and he succeeded in building up a trade that included several of the most popular contemporary religious writers, most especially William Perkins, a fellow of Christ's College in Cambridge and one of the most celebrated preachers of his generation.

Both Thomas and Legate, though licensed to print by the university (and hence legally protected against claims of the Stationers' Company), were independent printers rather than successors in a corporate university press. Their stock, equipment, and rights to print individual books therefore remained their own. As a consequence, when Legate left Cambridge for London circa 1608, his successor as university printer, Cantrell Legge, had little on

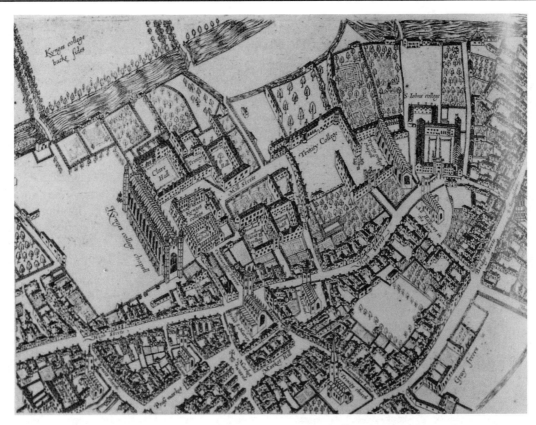

Cambridge in 1592; Thomas Thomas maintained premises in University Street, near its intersection with High Street

which to build. Legge died impoverished in 1622, and his successor, Leonard Greene, fared little better.

In 1625 change came with the appointment of two brothers, Thomas and John Buck, both members of the university, and they were joined briefly by their brother Francis. None of the Bucks was a printer or bookseller, but they were ambitious for the press – and for profits. Then in 1632 the university appointed Roger Daniel, a London printer with close connections to the trade in engravings, after he had been at Cambridge for some time. By joining Daniel's practical skills and connections to the scholarly interests of the university, the vice chancellor hoped to reinvigorate a privilege that threatened to become a burden rather than an advantage: the legal costs of repeatedly defending the privilege were substantial.

Thomas Buck, a fellow of St. Catharine's College and one whose wealth seems to have commanded respect, sought and clearly expected to dominate Daniel, the practical printer who also had excellent connections in the London trade. Nonetheless, the Buck and Daniel partnership enjoyed some of the most fruitful years in the early history

of the Cambridge University Press. Their authors included George Herbert, whose first edition of *The Temple. Sacred Poems and Private Ejaculations* was published in 1633, and John Milton, whose "Lycidas" was published in a 1638 volume of verses in memory of Edward King, a member of Christ's College. A major new edition of Bede's *Ecclesiastical history,* based principally on an eleventh-century manuscript given to the university library by Matthew Parker, archbishop of Canterbury, in 1574 and edited by Abraham Whelock, the university librarian, remained the standard Old English text from 1643 until a new edition appeared in 1722. Thomas Fuller's *Historie of the holy warre* appeared in 1639, and his *Holy state* in 1642.

Although the Cambridge imprint and Daniel's work became increasingly respected in the eyes of the London trade, these books were nonetheless produced amid increasing acrimony between Thomas Buck and Daniel. Their arguments were complicated, but their bases lay in the division of profits and property as well as on the means whereby the press could become most profitable. Arrangements with the Stationers' Company and with other London publishers brought lucrative

43

Title page for Thomas Fuller's history of the Crusades, with an engraving by William Marshall

thus had to be transported both to and from Cambridge, before and after printing. Paper was also heavy to transport. As a result, London stationers found little inducement to print at Cambridge – unless substantial local sales could be anticipated or a particularly forceful local author was involved, or unless printing costs could be saved by using cheaper Cambridge labor, or unless a shortage of presses in London (particularly at a time when the amount of printing required in England was increasing) made printing at Cambridge viable.

Partly because of such considerations, authors found much advantage in having their works printed and published in London. Moreover, if their work was directed at European, rather than British, audiences, a few London booksellers maintained some presence at the principal book fairs in Frankfurt and (later) Leipzig, and London thus offered at least limited access to such Continental markets. William Harvey, whose work on the circulation of the blood was completed in London, well after he had left Cambridge, arranged for his *De motu cordis* (1628) to be published in Frankfurt, at the center of the European trade, rather than in London. But when civil war brought turmoil to his own life as well as to the book trade, his next book, *Exercitatio anatomica de circulatione sanguinis,* was printed in 1649 by Roger Daniel – in Cambridge and for a London bookseller.

Buck and Daniel's disagreements had partly centered on ownership of title to publish particular books. These difficulties were compounded by Daniel's departure to London, and in the 1650s the university sought to administer its printers' affairs more closely. In 1622 it had stipulated that books it licensed should not be alienated, assigned, or sold to printers other than those of the university. This was strengthened by further orders intended to provide a financial foundation upon which each university printer could freely build, rather than having gradually to start building up new titles and new stock again. In making such stipulations the university was edging toward a concept finally realized only in the 1690s, with the foundation of a university press in the modern sense – one owned and controlled by the university as a part of its educational function.

From the time of Thomas Thomas the press had printed Bibles, and the first complete Bible to be printed at Cambridge was a pocket-sized octavo edition of the Geneva text in 1591. It was designed in conscious imitation of similar cheap editions printed in London, since in the highly competitive market of Bibles for private use the retail cost was

contracts, particularly for almanac printing and for schoolbooks, including cheap editions of elementary Latin texts. But during the civil war Daniel printed several books and pamphlets sympathetic to the Royalist cause. As a result, Buck had a chance to arrange for the removal of Daniel, and the university found an excuse to dismiss the latter in 1650. He was the victim partly of professional and financial jealousy, and partly of the university's search for a scapegoat to protect itself at a time when its future was threatened.

Geographical difficulties posed by Cambridge generally added to those of the press as well. The town lay slightly more than fifty miles from London, accessible in the seventeenth century either by a long river and sea voyage via King's Lynn or by roads that were often difficult to use in winter. Paper, for which England relied almost wholly on imports, was shipped mostly through London and all-important. But to print the Bible was to challenge the king's printer, and there was a world of difference between insisting on the right to print by concentrating mainly on books of short or moderate length and printing popular books whose sale was guaranteed by the investing booksellers or publishers. The Bible was a long book requiring commensurate investment in large quantities of paper, and the risks involved in printing it were as much economic as political.

It is not surprising, therefore, that only after Charles I and the Privy Council had confirmed the university's privileges and provided for a modus vivendi with the king's printer and with the Stationers' Company – actions that effectively gave the university limited but clearly protected rights – did the university printers again become determined to print the Bible. In 1629 Daniel printed the first Cambridge edition of the King James, or Authorised Version (first published in London in 1611); editions in octavo and quarto followed, and in 1638 a carefully revised edition was printed. Both the 1629 and the 1638 editions were in folio, for lectern or library, rather than for the cheap or middling market. The 1638 text remained the touchstone of accuracy until the mid eighteenth century.

Although the university dismissed Daniel (and he continued to print in London), his reputation as Bible printer lived on, and his name was used in thousands of copies of English Bibles printed with false imprints in Amsterdam in the late seventeenth century. But when John Field, a London printer who would eventually become one of Daniel's successors at the university press in 1655, printed the Bible in 1648, his work was quickly castigated for its inaccuracy. Following his appointment as university printer, Field continued to print Bibles, some of the folio editions being provided with lavish engravings bought from the print trade. The Bible remained one of the economic mainstays of the Cambridge University Press for the next two generations.

Thomas's premises had been in converted rooms in a private house, but after he died the presses used by his successors – John Legate, Cantrell Legge, and Leonard Greene – were moved around the center of Cambridge to several successive addresses, more or less cramped, until Thomas Buck, with more money than his predecessors, first leased and then bought the remaining buildings of the old house of the Augustinian friars. There the books that so distinguished the history of printing in Cambridge for two decades were printed by Daniel, in surroundings that, probably for the first time,

William Marshall's engraved title page for the Cambridge University Press Bible of 1638. This edition, a revision of Roger Daniel's first Cambridge edition of the King James Version, was the authoritative text for the next two centuries.

were adequate. But following Field's appointment as printer in 1655 new premises were again established – opposite the gate of his landlord, Queen's College, an institution that influenced considerably the course of the subsequent history of the press. Field's house adjoined a large workshop that was to be much admired by visitors for the quality of its lighting. When in 1697–1698 the new arrangements for a university press were introduced, the adjoining premises (used formerly in connection with plays put on by Queen's College) were acquired for the university printer, and, following the death of John Hayes, Field's successor, his premises were taken over by the new, and now corporate, university press.

Both Field and Hayes (the latter of whom was appointed in 1669) reached accommodation with the Stationers' Company. By a series of open (and more-controversial secret) agreements Hayes be-

Frontispiece for the first complete edition of Euripedes in English (1694) published in Great Britain

of several books printed by the press have both been acknowledged. These included John Ray's *Catalogus Plantarum circa Cantabrigiam nascentium* (1660–1663) on the flora of Cambridgeshire, the first local catalogue of the flora of any part of the British Isles, and his *Collection of English Proverbs* (1670). Both of these works were published by local booksellers, who showed increasing interest in financing books printed at the press. Some of the most ambitious works of these years came from the Greek scholar Joshua Barnes, who wrote and published at his own expense *The History of That Most Victorious Monarch Edward III^d King of England and France* (1688) and followed this in 1694 with the first complete edition of Euripides to be printed in England. But while mathematics and natural philosophy began increasingly to interest some members of the university, the university printers and local booksellers contributed comparatively little to this development. There was never any serious question about Sir Isaac Newton's *Philosophiae naturalis principia mathematica* (1687) being published anywhere in England other than in London. Instead, as Hayes became hampered by lack of investment and concentrated on business that was most lucrative, some minds found cause for concern in the university's printing. "Cambridge Press should be busied about something better than Almanacks, and books for children," exclaimed one member of the university in 1668.

The position did not essentially change until in 1696 the classical scholar and royal librarian Richard Bentley, with the encouragement of the duke of Somerset, chancellor of the university, proposed a new university press. Thus ended the old arrangement whereby the university licensed and appointed printers who were then able to use their skills (subject to the vice chancellor's license) according to whatever agreement they pleased. Bentley's proposals, which were largely adopted by the university, envisaged a university press controlled by a committee, or syndicate, drawn from professors, heads of colleges, and other senior members. Printing was to be done under the aegis of another senior member who was sympathetic to scholarship but not necessarily himself a trained printer. With this fresh beginning the university established a press that until the death of Hayes in 1705 existed alongside his. New type was imported from Holland; new presses were bought in 1697; and a new printing shop was established. In 1697 a Dutchman, Cornelius Crownfield, was put in charge, and in August 1698 the new curators (or syndics, as they soon came to be called) agreed on the first books –

came the salaried servant of the company. The Stationers' Company controlled, directly or indirectly, virtually all that he printed, and it owned his equipment as well. In this way the English stock of the company – that is, its principal publishing arm – could take advantage of low manufacturing costs (many of which it could set for itself) in Cambridge to provide schoolbooks, almanacs, and other cheap publications continually required in new editions and in exceptionally large numbers that were always more easily salable than the academic works expected from a university press. Competition, which had been the bane of relationships between Cambridge and the Stationers' Company since the 1580s, was thus removed, and the company could also enjoy the privileges of a printer for the university.

Against this background after the restoration of the monarchy in 1660, the importance and fame a series of quarto Latin poets to be published by London bookseller Jacob Tonson. A new edition of Horace was published in the following year.

Following the death of Hayes, whose own business had meanwhile contracted, Crownfield was also appointed university printer. Bentley, who had become master of Trinity College in 1700, and his associates had given thought to printing, but they had not considered how books were to be published or marketed. Having published four volumes of Latin poets, Tonson's connection with the Cambridge Press virtually ceased. Other London booksellers were persuaded to have their books printed in Cambridge, but financing of major work remained a continuing problem. The publication by subscription of an ambitious new edition of the *Suidas* (1705), a Greek lexicon, proved a financial embarrassment, as remaining copies were not sold until the residue was finally disposed at a low price almost fifty years later. A revised second edition of Newton's *Principia* was published in 1713 at Bentley's expense, and Bentley's own editions of Horace (1711) and Terence (1726) were but the most prominent of a series of editions of Latin classics in particular. In 1722 the press published (again by subscription) the first edition of Bede to be based on an eighth-century Northumbrian manuscript, the earliest then known, which had been discovered in the 1690s and presented to Cambridge University Library in 1715.

Crownfield remained university printer until 1740, and he died in 1743. Only after his retirement did the Cambridge University Press resume a strong commitment to Bible printing and so establish the solid financial foundations that also allowed other scholarly publishing. Bible publication generally remained the financial mainstay until in the late twentieth century the growth of English as an international language provided new and seemingly ever-increasing markets.

Since the 1690s all decisions on editorial and publishing policy have remained in the hands of the syndics appointed by the university. In 1949 the press opened a branch in New York, in 1969 another in Australia, and in 1995 yet another in South Africa. Having been in the center of Cambridge for almost four centuries, the press needed more space and specialist buildings, and decisions were made to remove first the printing and then the publishing to a new site on the outskirts of the town. The new printing house was opened in 1963 and the Edinburgh publishing building in 1981, although the Pitt Building (opened in 1833) has been retained for some purposes. Cambridge University Press now publishes about fifteen hundred titles per year, making it one of the largest publishers in the United Kingdom.

Bibliography:

D. F. McKenzie, *The Cambridge University Press, 1696–1712: A Bibliographical Study,* 2 volumes (Cambridge: Cambridge University Press, 1966).

References:

M. H. Black, *Cambridge University Press, 1584–1984* (Cambridge: Cambridge University Press, 1984);

E. P. Goldschmidt, *The First Cambridge Press in Its European Setting* (Cambridge: Cambridge University Press, 1955);

George J. Gray, *The Earlier Cambridge Stationers and Bookbinders and the First Cambridge Printer* (London: Bibliographical Society, 1904);

Gray and W. M. Palmer, *Abstracts from the Wills and Testamentary Documents of Printers, Binders, and Stationers of Cambridge from 1504 to 1699* (London: Bibliographical Society, 1915);

David McKitterick, *Printing and the Book Trade in Cambridge, 1534–1698,* volume 1 of *A History of Cambridge University Press* (Cambridge: Cambridge University Press, 1992);

Otto Treptow, *John Siberch, Johann Lair von Siegburg* (Cambridge: Cambridge Bibliographical Society, 1970).

                          – David McKitterick

William Caxton

(Bruges: 1474? – 1476; London: 1476 – 1491?)

To William Caxton belongs the distinction of being the first English printer. He was born of a family that may have been connected with the Caxtons or Caustons, who owned a manor in Hadlow near Kent in the thirteenth century. Some biographers have argued that he was the grandson of William de Causton, a well-to-do fourteenth-century London mercer, an argument based on the fact that William Caxton was apprenticed in this trade. Speculation has tied him to an Oliver Causton (d. 1474) and to a William Caxton (d. 1478), both of whom are buried at St. Margaret's Church, Westminster. (This latter figure may have been his father, but the facts are not ascertainable.) Even the date of William Caxton's birth is disputed. The archives of the Mercers' Company record his apprenticeship to Robert Large on 24 June 1438. If he were sixteen at the time of his apprenticeship, he would have been born in 1422. However, arguments have been made for other dates, even one as early as 1411.

The place of his birth is known, as the printer tells us in the preface to his first book: "I was born and lerned myn Englissh in Kents in Quanta in the Weeld where I doubte not is speken as brode and rude Englissh as is in ony place of Englond." In the introduction to Fierabras's *The Lyf of the Noble and Crysten Prynce Charles the Grete* (1485) Caxton comments on his education as he explains his translation: "I hope that it shal be vnderstonden, & to that entente I haue specyally reduced it after the symple connyng that god hath lente to me, wherof I humbly & wyth al my herte thanke hym, & also am bounden to praye for my fader and moders soules that in my youthe sette me to scole, by whyche, by the suffraunce of god, I gete my lyuyng I hope truly."

Caxton's apprenticeship ended with his master's death on 24 April 1441. Having received a bequest in the will of Large, the young Caxton went to Bruges, an important commercial center for English mercers, where he continued his apprenticeship until 1446. He then went into business on his own. The records of this time give some indication of his progress. In 1450 he became surety for a debt owed by a fellow merchant, John Granton, in the amount of £150, a considerable sum and clear evidence that Caxton was becoming financially well off. In 1453 he returned to England and was admitted to the Livery of the Mercers' Company, a fact indicating that he was by this time a freeman of the guild.

During the next several years Caxton apparently throve, for in the early 1460s he became governor of the Merchant Adventurers, a company created to guard the interests of merchants engaged in trade abroad. Caxton held this position until 1469. His duties included arbitrating disputes arising among the merchants engaged in trade in the Low Countries. As trade representative for the English government, he directed imports and exports of En-

Thus ende I this book whyche I haue translated, aftir myn Auctor as nyghe as god hath gyuen me connyng to whom be gyuen the laude and
preysyng / And for as moche as in the wrytyng of the
same my penne is worn / myn hande wery and not stedfast
myn eyen dimed with ouermoche lokyng on the whit
paper / and my corage not so prone and redy to laboure
as hit hath ben / and that age crepeth on me daily and
febleth all the bodye / and also be cause I haue promysid
to dyuerce gentilmen and to my frendes to adresse to hem
as hastely as I myght this sayd book / Therfore I haue
practysed and lerned at my grete charge and dispense to
ordeyne this said book in prynte after the maner and forme
as ye may here see / and is not wreton with penne and
ynke as other bokes ben / to thende that euery man may
haue them attones / ffor all the bookes of this storye named the recule of the historyes of troyes thus enpryntid
as ye here see were begonne in oon day / and also fynys-
shid in oon day / whiche book I haue presented to my
sayd redoubtid lady as a fore is sayd . And she hath
well acceptid hit / and largely rewarded me / wherfore
I beseche almyghty god to rewarde her euerlastyng blisse
after this lyf . Prayng her said grace and all them that
shall rede this book not to desdaigne the symple and rude
werke . nether to replye agaynst the sayng of the ma-
tres towchyd in this book / thauwh hyt acorde not vnto the translacon of other whiche haue wreton hit / ffor
dyuerce men haue made dyuerce bookes / whiche in all
poyntes acorde not as Dictes . Dares . and Homerus
ffor dictes and homerus as grekes sayn and wryten fauo-
rably for the grekes / and gyue to them more worship

Page from William Caxton's epilogue to his translation of La recueil des histoires de Troye *(circa 1474), his first book and the first book printed in the English language. The initial T was added in pen by a seventeenth-century owner (British Library).*

For I Wote Wel, of What someuer condicion Women ben in Grece, the Women of this contre ben right good, Wyse, plaisant, humble, discrete, sobre, chast, obedient to their husbondis, treWe, secrete, stedfast, euer besy, z neuer ydle, Attemperat in spekimg, and vertuous in alle their Werkis, or atte leste sholde be soo, For Whiche causes so euydent my sayd lord as I suppose thoughte it Was not of necessite to sette in his book the saiengis of his Auctor socrates touchyng Women But for as moche as I had comandemet of my sayd lord to correcte and amende Where as I sholde fynde faulte, and other fynde I none sauf that he hath left out these dictes z saynges of the Women of Grece, Therfore in accomplisshig his comandement for as moche as I am not in certayn Weder it Was in my lordis coppe or not, or ellis perauenture that the Wynde had bloWe ouer the leef, at the tyme of translacion of his booke, I purpose to Wryte tho same saynges of that Greke Socrates, Whiche Wrote of tho Women of grece and nothyng of them of this Royame, Whom I suppose he neuer kneWe, For if he had I dar plainly saye that he Wold haue reserued them inespeciall in his sayd dictes AlWay not presumyng to put z sette them in my sayd lordes book, but inthende aparte in the rehersayll of the Werkis humbly requiryng al them that shal rede this lityl rehersayll that yf they fynde ony faulte, tarette it to Socrates and not to me Whiche Wryteth as here after foloWeth

Socrates sayde That Women ben thapparaylles to cacche men, but they take none but them that Wil be poure, or els them that knoWe hem not And he saye that ther is none so grete empeshement vnto aman

Page from The dictes or sayengis of the Philosophres *(1477), the first book that Caxton printed in England*

The first known book advertisement, Caxton's Advertisement for the Sarum Ordinal *(1479)*

glish goods, and during this period Caxton became involved in a trade war when the duke of Burgundy, Philip the Good, banned the importation of cloth made in England. In retaliation the English Parliament passed an act prohibiting the entry of Flemish goods. As a consequence, Caxton was simply unable to conduct his business, but, fortunately, Philip died in 1467 and was succeeded by Charles the Bold. With the marriage of Charles to Margaret, the sister of Edward IV, on 9 July 1468, trade relations between the two countries returned to normal.

Perhaps still during the suspension of trade in the late 1460s Caxton found himself with idle time and began to translate into English the popular romance *La recueil des histoires de troye* by Raoul LeFèvre. The last record of his duties as governor of the Merchant Adventurers is 1469; by 1471 he had entered the service of the duchess of Burgundy. Whether he was weary of the difficulties he had encountered in trade or simply developed new interests that he felt he must pursue can never be known. Whatever the case, he used his new leisure to complete his translation of *La recueil des histoires de troye* at Ghent and published it at Cologne circa 1474. He explains in the epilogue that hand-copying the manuscript was too laborious and that he resorted to the newly invented process of printing:

> Thus ende I this book whyche I have translated after myn Auctor as nyghe as god hath gyven me connyng to whom be gyven the laude and preysyng. And for as moche as in the wrytyng of the same my penne is worn, myn hande wery and not stedfast, myn eyen dimmed

with overmoche lokyng on the whit paper, and my corage not so prone and redy to laboure as hit hath ben, and that age crepeth on me dayly and febleth all the bodye, and also because I have promysid to dyverce gentilmen and to my frendes to addresse to hem as hastely as I myght this sayd book. Therefore I have practysed and lerned at my grete charge and dispense to ordeyne this said booke in prynte after the maner and forme as ye may here see. And it is not wreton with penne and ynke as other bokes ben to thende that every man may have them attones. For all the bookes of this storye named the recule of the historyes of troyes thus enprynted as ye here see were begonne in oon day, and also fynysshed in oon day.

Thus, Caxton became a printer.

Precisely where, when, and from whom Caxton learned printing is not known. In 1471 he did visit Cologne, where a press had been established, and he may have learned printing there. That Cologne was the likely place of Caxton's tutelage is based on the statement of his successor, Wynkyn de Worde, in de Worde's prologue to the translation of Bartholomaeus Anglicus's *De proprietatibus rerum* (1472):

> And also of your charyte call to remembraunce,
> The soule of William Caxton, the fyrste prynter of this book,
> In Laten at Coleyn, hymself to avaunce,
> That every well disposed man may thereon look.

John P. A. Madden presents a theory, much disputed, that Caxton learned printing at the Weidenbach monastery near Cologne. However, William Blades argues that a press had been set up

So hote he loued that by nyghter tale
He slepte nomore than a nyghtyngale
Curteys he was lowly and seruysable
He carf beforn hys fader at the table

Yeman hadde he and seruauntis nomo
At that tyme for he lyst to ryde so
And he was clad in cote & hood of grene
A sheef of pecok arwes bryght and shene
Under hys belt he bare ful thryftyly
Wel coude he dresse hys takyl yomanly
Hys arwes drouped not wyth fetherys lowe
And in hys hond he bare a myghty bowe
A not hed he had wyth a brown vysage
Of wodemannes craft coude he al the vsage
Vp on hys arme he bare a gay bracer
And by hys syde a swerd and a bokeler
And on that other syde a gay daggar
Harneysed wel and sharpe as poynt of spere

*Woodcut of Geoffrey Chaucer's yeoman in Caxton's second
edition of* The Canterbury Tales *(1485?)*

in Bruges circa 1470 by Colard Mansion, that Caxton paid for the press, and that Mansion trained him. Apparently Caxton returned from Cologne around 1474 and printed *Recuyell of the Historyes of Troye,* the first book in English, on Mansion's press, although the volume identifies no date or place. When Caxton set up his press in Bruges, Mansion was his assistant or possibly his partner. Based on Caxton's use of typeface identical to that of John Veldener of Louvain, the thesis has also been advanced that Veldener assisted Caxton in setting up his Bruges press.

While other printers were publishing works in classical languages, Caxton set out to produce printed volumes in his native English. This practice he continued in a second translation published in 1475 from the Bruges press. This was *The Game and Play of the Chesse* by Jacobus de Cessolis. Caxton worked from two French translations that had been made by Jean Faron and Jean de Vignay. At Bruges probably in 1476 Caxton produced one last book,

Quatres derrenieres choses, the "four last things" being death, judgment, heaven, and hell. This volume is distinctive because it marks the first appearance of what has come to be called Caxton's type No. 2 and because it has some red print produced not by putting sheets through the press twice, but by applying red ink to some typeface and black to others.

Caxton set out for England with his new type around 1476, leaving Mansion to publish on his own with the type employed in Caxton's first three books, a fact that has caused some to attribute to Caxton books that were probably printed by Mansion. Two of these are LeFèvre's *Les fais et proesses du noble et vaillant cheualier Iason* (1476) and Cardinal Pierre d'Ailly's *Meditacions sur les sept pseaulmes* (1475). Caxton settled in Westminster, where on 18 November 1477 he printed *The dictes or sayengis of the philosophres* – the first book printed in England, although in the eighteenth century some argued that, rather than Caxton, a German printer, Corsellis, had introduced printing in England by establishing a press at Oxford in 1464. *The dictes* is also the first of Caxton's books to contain a colophon giving the publisher's name, place of publication, and date.

In his first book published in England, Caxton identified the place of publication simply as Westminster, yet in *The Chronicles of England* (1480) he stated specifically that the work was "emprynted by me, Wyllyam Caxton, in thabbey of Westmynstre by london." Caxton rented his shop from the sacristan of Westminster Abbey, John Esteney, a man whose power and influence must have been useful as Caxton introduced his new process into the country. He also made an excellent choice of location, for having his shop within the precincts of the Abbey gave him easy access to monks with extensive backgrounds in ancient texts, men who could be consulted for problems in translation.

Robert Copland in a translation of *King Apolyn of Tyre* (1510) states that Caxton began his career in England "with small storyes and pamfletes and so on to other." Just how many pamphlets he printed is unknown, but some have survived; the best collection is in University Library, Cambridge. Caxton followed *The dictes* with another dated book, Christine de Pisan's *Morale Proverbes,* on 20 February 1478, which contains the earliest specimen of his attempts at poetry:

Go thou litil quayer and recommaund me
Unto the good grace of my special lorde
Therle Ryveris, fir I have enprinted the
At his commandment, followyng eury worde
His copye, as his secretaire can recorde

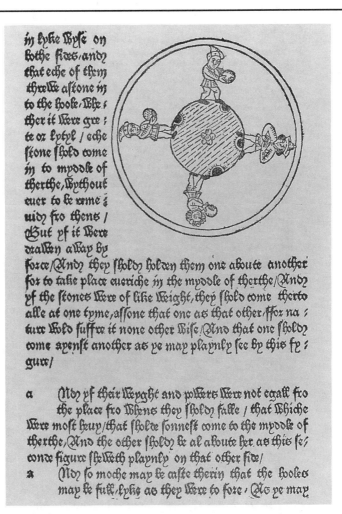

Page from Caxton's translation of The Mirror of the World
(1481), his first book to include illustrations

At Westmestre, of feuerer the xx daye
And of kynd Edward the xvjj yere vraye.

The earliest known example of a book advertisement is Caxton's. It was posted on walls and reads:

If it plese any man spirituel or temporel to bye ony [co]pyes of two and thre comemoracions of salisburi use enpryntid after the forme of this present lettre whiche ben wel and truly correct, late hym come to westmonester in to the almonesrye at the reed pale and he shal have them good chepe. Supplico stet cedula.

One particularly interesting item, because it deals with contemporary affairs, is the *Propositio Clarissimi Oratoris Magistri Iohannis Russell* (1476). This presents the speech of the bishop of Lincoln, John Russell, upon the investiture of the duke of Burgundy with the Order of the Garter.

The well-known criticism of Edward Gibbon that Caxton printed no classics is quoted by every biographer. Yet Gibbon has ignored the translation of Cato, *Paruus Cato and Magnus Cato* (1477), and a translation of Cicero into English from the French, *De senectute* (1481). Plenty of other printers became available to assure the perpetuation of the classics. Caxton's great contribution was the printing of works by native English writers, particularly Geoffrey Chaucer. These include his translation of Boethius's *Consolation of Philosophy* (1478?, published as *Boecius de consolacione*) as well as Chaucer's *The Parliament of Fowls* (1477, published as *The temple of bras*), *Troilus and Criseyde* (1483, published as *tThe [sic] double sorrow of Troylus to telle*), and *The House of Fame* (1483, published as *The book of Fame made by Geoffrey Chaucer*), but most important of all is *The Canterbury Tales* (1477, published as *wHan that Apprill with his shouris sote*). In his 1485(?) prologue to the second

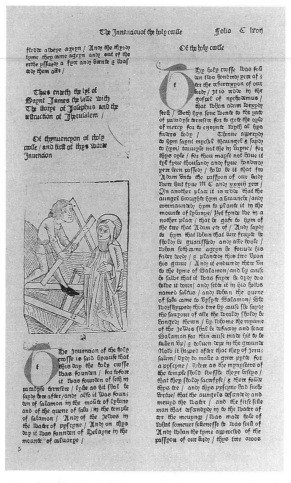

Page from Jacobus de Voragine's Golden Legend *(1483),
the most extensive and expensive translation that
Caxton printed*

edition of *The Canterbury Tales* Caxton explains how he came to correct the text:

[O]ne gentylman cam to me and said that this book was not accordyng in many places unto the book that Gefferey Chaucer had made. To whom I answered that I had made it accordyng to my copye and by me was nothyng added ne mynusshyd. Thenne he sayd he knewe a book whyche hys fader had and moche lovyd that was very trewe and accordyng unto hys owen first book by hym made; and sayd more, yf I wold enprynte it agayn he wold gete me the same book for a copye, how be it he wyst wel that hys fader wold not gladly departe fro it. To whom I said, in caas that he could gete me suche a book trewe and correcte yet I wold ones endevoyre me to enprynte it agayn. And thus we fyll at accord. And he ful gentylly gate of hys fader the said book and delyverd it to me, by whiche I have corrected my book.

In addition to providing a corrected text Caxton included twenty-four illustrations. He was a shrewd businessman and knew that there was a desire for "joyous and pleyausant romaunce" that he could supply by printing the work of his fellow Englishmen.

Other English works Caxton published include various writings of John Lydgate – including *The Hors, the Shepe, and the Ghoos* (1479?), *Stans puer ad mensam* (1477?, translated from Sulpitius's *Carmen Juvenile de Moribus Puerorum*), *Curia Sapientiae, or the Court of Sapience* (1481), and *Life of Our Lady* (1484?) – and Sir Thomas Malory's *The Noble History of King Arthur and of Certain of His Knights* (1485) as well as John Gower's *Confessio Amantis* (1483).

Having come to realize in 1480 how labor could be saved by not putting signatures in each gathering by hand, Caxton began including printed signatures in his books. About this time he also introduced what for him was an innovation, the use of illustrations, in his translation of *The Mirror of the World*. In the prologue to this work he explains that

no dreð ne fere no thynge/ For I ſhalle not accuſe the/ For I
ſhalle ſhelve to hym another way/ And as the hunter came/
he demaunded of the ſheepherd yf he had ſene the wulf paſ-
ſe/ And the ſheepherd both with the heed and of the eyen ſhewed to the hunter the place whern the wulf was / & with the
hand and the tongue ſhewed alle the contrarye / And ins
contynent the hunter vnderſtood hym wel / But the wulf
whiche perceyued wel alle the fayned maners of the ſhepherd
fledde awey/ ¶ And within a lytyl whyle after the ſhepherd
encountred and mette with the wulf/ to whome he ſayd/ paye
me of that I haue kepte the ſecrete/ ¶ And thenne the wulf
anſuerd to hym in this manere / I thanke thyn handes and
thy tongue/ and not thyn hede ne thyn eyen / For by them I
ſholde haue ben betrayd/ yf I had not fledde awey/ ¶ And
therfore men muſt not truſte in hym that hath two faces and
two tongues/ for ſuche folke is lyke and ſemblable to the ſcor
pion/ the whiche enoynteth with his tongue/ and prycketh ſo-
re with his taylle

Page from Caxton's edition of Aesop's Fables *(1484)*

the text could not be easily understood without the illustrations, but the appearance of a competitor, John Lettou, the first London printer, may have encouraged Caxton to make his books more attractive. When Caxton had been learning his trade in the early 1470s, the importance of book decoration to publishing was not yet apparent. His customers did not at first demand ornament, and his concern was with the text. His broadside *Indulgence,* printed in 1480, is the first known example in England of the use of a woodcut initial.

The *Golden Legend* of Jacobus de Voragine is dated 20 November 1483. It is a particularly lengthy book (894 pages of double columns), and Caxton records that he was overwhelmed with the task of translation and strained by the expense. When only halfway through, he was preparing to put it aside when the earl of Arundel saved the project by agreeing to buy copies and also promising to supply Caxton with a buck each summer and a doe each winter.

Perhaps the finest piece of Caxton's work is his *Fables of Aesop,* dated 26 March 1484. Caxton translated it from the French, used a full-page frontispiece of Aesop, and followed it with 185 woodcut illustrations. He also used a large ornamental letter *A* in printing this book and the *Book of the ordre of chyualry or knyghthode* (1484).

In 1487 Caxton published *Legenda secundum usum sarum,* which was printed for him by Guillaume Maynial, a Parisian printer. The book presents the first appearance of Caxton's famous device, which consists of his initials on either side of his merchant's mark, plus a small *S* and *C* that stand for "Sancta Colonia," perhaps a tribute to the place where he had learned to print. Some have argued that the merchant's mark is, in fact, an elaborate "74" and comprises Caxton's continuing statement that he printed the first English book in 1474. Whether the device has any significance of the sort, Caxton clearly used it to identify his work and attached it to a dozen subsequent books.

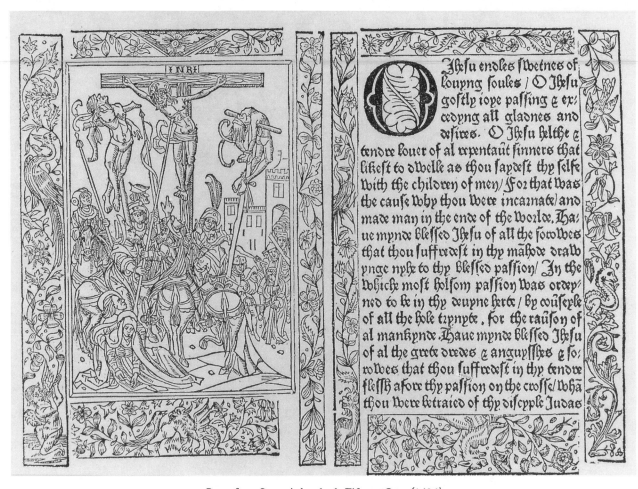

Pages from Caxton's last book, Fifteen Oes *(1491)*

Early biographers gave 1493 as the date of Caxton's death, probably because the colophon of the 1493 edition of the *Golden Legend* gives his name. Although the exact date of his death cannot be confirmed, most biographers have settled on 1491 because of this entry from the account book of St. Margaret's Church, Westminster, for 1491–1492:

> Atte bureyng of William Caxton for
>   iiij torches   vjs   viiid
>   Item for the belle at same bureyng   vjd

As one can see from the foregoing account, very little is known of Caxton's life. The fact that he had a daughter is confirmed, because a party to a lawsuit in 1496 is identified as Elizabeth Croppe, the wife of a tailor at Westminster and the daughter of William Caxton. As part of the settlement, the husband, Gerard Croppe, was to receive twenty books from the estate of Caxton. A Mawde Caxston, whose funeral in 1490 is mentioned in an account book of St. Margaret's Church, Westminster,

may have been William Caxton's wife. The fact that Caxton's assistant, Wynkyn de Worde, acquired the Caxton workshop suggests that Caxton left no son.

Because de Worde began printing with his master's font from the Caxton shop immediately after Caxton's death, it is impossible to determine who printed some of the books issued in 1491. In this group are *The Chastising of God's Children, A Treatise of Love, The Life of St. Katherine of Senis,* and *The Siege of Rhodes.* Most critics aver that de Worde was the printer, but there is no unanimity on this. Clearly Caxton printed a prodigious number of works in the fourteen or fifteen years he worked in England. His production there has been estimated as exceeding eighteen thousand pages and comprising about eighty books, many in more than one edition. Although Caxton never received a title such as "Printer to the King," he had the patronage of both Edward IV and Richard III.

The history of the discovery of previously unknown works by Caxton comprises a fascinating

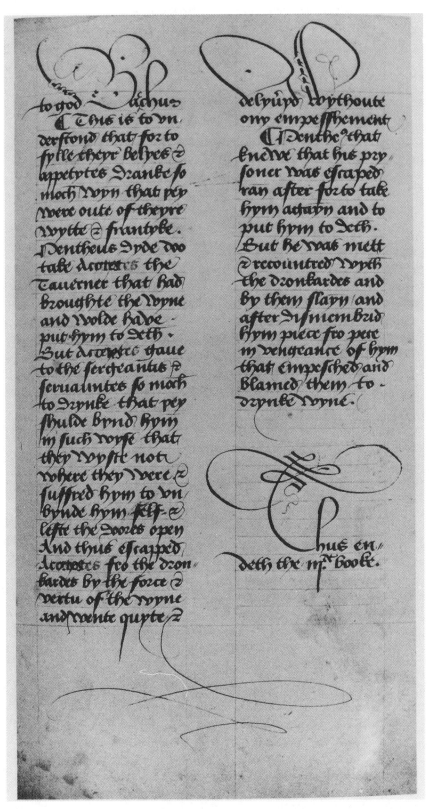

Last page of the manuscript for the third book of what was to be Caxton's translation of
Ovid (Magdalene College, Cambridge)

body of literature. One of the most frequently quoted incidents is that of William Blades finding a volume in the grammar school library at St. Albans:

> After examining a few interesting books, I pulled out one which was lying flat upon the top of others. It was in a most deplorable state, covered thickly with a damp, sticky dust, and with a considerable portion of the back rotted away by wet. The white decay fell in lumps on the floor as the unappreciated volume was opened. It proved to be Geoffrey Chaucer's English translation of *Boecius de Consolatione Philosophiae*, printed by Caxton, in the original binding, as issued from Caxton's workshop, and uncut!

What was more interesting than the text between the covers was the material he found in the composition of the covers: "On dissecting the covers they were found to be composed entirely of waste sheets from Caxton's press, two or three being printed on one side only. The two covers yielded no less than fifty-six half-sheets of printed paper, proving the existence of three works from Caxton's press quite unknown before."

Estimates of the total number of books actually printed by Caxton continue to increase, and, of course, some are disputed. The most recent bibliography by N. F. Blake lists ninety-seven works printed and published by Caxton, ten additional works printed by him, three works translated by Caxton but printed by others, and four works published by him but printed by others. Some titles have certainly disappeared. In his introduction to the *Golden Legend* Caxton lists various titles of books that he had printed, one of which is "the XV bookes of Metamorpheseos"; however, no edition of Ovid by Caxton has survived. As was the practice of the time, Caxton employed a bookbinder in his shop and issued books ready-bound. These bindings were in brown calf and were ornamented with dyes, the design usually forming a frame divided into diamond shapes with the figure of a dragon or monster in the center of each diamond.

Caxton provided a great service to his native country in bringing printing to England, in insisting on printing books in English, and in popularizing English authors.

Bibliography:

N. F. Blake, *William Caxton: A Bibliographical Guide* (New York & London: Garland, 1985).

Biographies:

Charles Knight, *William Caxton: First English Printer, A Biography* (London: Knight, 1844);

John P. A. Madden, *Lettres d'un bibliographe, 4e série, William Caxton* (Paris: Tross, 1875);

William Blades, *The Biography and Typography of William Caxton* (London: Trubner, 1877);

Madden, *Lettres d'un bibliographe, 5e série, lettre 15: Caxton et son apprentissage* (Paris: Tross, 1878);

Susan Cunningham, *The Story of William Caxton* (London: Harrap, 1917);

Henry R. Plomer, *William Caxton* (London: Parsons / Boston: Small, Maynard, 1925);

N. F. Blake, *Caxton: England's First Publisher* (Totowa, N.J.: Barnes & Noble, 1976);

Richard Deacon, *A Biography of William Caxton, The First English Editor, Printer, Merchant and Translator* (London: Muller, 1976);

George D. Painter, *William Caxton: A Biography* (New York: Putnam, 1977).

References:

Joseph Ames and William Herbert, *Typographical Antiquities, or an Historical Account of the Origin and Progress of Printing in Great Britain and Ireland*, 3 volumes (London: Printed for the editor, 1785–1790);

Nellie Slayton Aurner, *Caxton: Mirrour of Fifteenth-Century Letters. A Study of the Literature of the First English Press* (Boston & New York: Houghton Mifflin, 1926);

N. F. Blake, *Caxton and His World* (London: Deutsch, 1969);

William Caxton, *The Lyf of the Noble and Crysten Prynce Charles the Grete* (London: Oxford University Press, 1880);

Caxton, *The Prologues and Epilogues of William Caxton*, edited, with an introduction, by Walter J. B. Crotch (London: Oxford University Press, 1928);

John P. A. Madden, *Lettres d'un bibliophile, 2e série, lettre 7: William Caxton a-t-il imprimé le De proprietatibus rerum?* (Paris: Tross, 1873).

– *J. Don Vann*

William Cooper

(London: circa 1669 – 1689)

In the annals of the seventeenth-century English book trade William Cooper, proprietor of the Pelican, Little Britain, can claim two firsts. He is the first English stationer to specialize exclusively in alchemy-related texts and the first member of his company to conduct a public auction sale in England.

Cooper's introduction to his *Philosophical Epitaph* (1672) offers a glimpse into the years before he entered the book trade. Apparently he had undergone a violent spiritual crisis and had transferred his faith to astrology. Either he had been ill or in some difficulties with the authorities, since he refers to the year 1652 as "a living grave." Antiquary Elias Ashmole appears to have rescued him from his troubles in 1662. Ashmole, whom Cooper called "the greatest virtuoso and curioso that ever was known and read in England before his time," was deeply interested in astrology, alchemy, and chemistry. He obviously much influenced a kindred spirit in Cooper, who doubtless had perused Ashmole's *Theatrum Chemicum Britannicum* (1652) and emerged in 1669 as a specialist dealer in alchemy and chemistry. During that year Cooper also published two works bearing identical titles, *Secrets Reveal'd* — one by the high priest of alchemy, George Starkey, and the other by a fellow adept, Eirenaeus Philalethes. In addition to his many auction catalogues, Cooper was to publish until his death in 1689 a total of forty-four books.

He was familiar with the masters of alchemy at home. In the introduction to his *Catalogue of Chymicall Books* (1675), the first bibliography of alchemical and chemical works in English, he boasts that he had perused all but nine of the two hundred listed therein. If this were true, Cooper's knowledge of his subject was extensive. His expertise is further evidenced by his having translated and edited several alchemical texts. A 1670 English edition of Johann Friedrich Helvetius's *A Briefe of the Golden Calfe, or the World's Idol* is attributed to Cooper, and the works of Philalethes and Starkey include Latin texts by Cooper. Other works by Starkey that Cooper published include *Exposition upon Sir George Ripley's Preface* (1677), *Exposition upon . . . Ripley's Epistle* (1677), *Enerratio Methodica* (1678), *Opus Tri-*

partitum (1678), *An Exposition upon Sir George Ripley's Vision* (1678), *A Breviary of Alchemy* (1678), and *The secret of the immortal liquor calld Alkahest* (1683).

Other Cooper imprints in alchemy include a collection of fifteen treatises, among which are *Aurifontina Chymica* (1680) by John Frederick Houpreght, edited by Cooper; *Chymicall Secrets* (1685) by Sir Kenelm Digby, "published [edited] since his death by George Hartmann Chymist and Steward to the aforesaid Sir Kenelm"; and *Collecteana Chymica* (1684) as well as the *Works* (1678) of Jabir Ibn Haiyan, known as Geber. In 1658 Cooper published the celebrated Franciscus Mercurius van Helmont's *One Hundred Fifty Three Aphorisms,* translated into English by Christopher Packe, who styled himself a "Philo-Chymicus-Medicus." The work, which sold for twenty shillings, was offered on fairly attractive terms: the customer was expected to pay ten shillings following delivery, and subscribers for six copies were given one gratis. Metallurgy, an adjunct of alchemy, is also represented in the Cooper trade list: Thomas Houghton's *Rara avis in terris* (1681); Gabriel Platte's *Discovery of Subterraneal Treasure* (1684); the anonymous *The ancient Laws, Customs and Orders of the Miners in Mendipp Forest* (1687); and *Two Ephemerides for the year 1687* (1687), by the great astronomer Edmond Halley.

Although Cooper rarely ventured outside his special field, he published in 1674 Paul Festeau's *A French Grammar . . . how to Read and Write it perfectly . . . both in French and English.* "Published by the Academy for the Reformation of the French Tongue," the work sold for one shilling. In 1685 Cooper again evinced an interest in philology and issued *Minerva, The High Dutch Grammar,* "teaching the Englishman perfectly easily and exactly the Dialect of the High German Tongue."

Cooper's *Catalogue of Chymicall Books* remains his most important contribution to publishing history. It reveals not only his predilection for alchemy and allied subjects but also his awareness of public demand: in his preface he "take[s] the boldness to inform the Reader that most of the Books contained in these Catalogues (with many others of this Subject in Latine . . .) are to be sold by Will. Cooper at the Sign of the Pelican in Little

Frontispiece for William Cooper's Philosophical Epitaph
(1672), which includes an early catalogue of chemistry books

Britain, London." The first two parts include six-teenth- and seventeenth-century books published in England, many of which had been translated from other languages into English. Its third part lists titles of articles from the preceding ten-year run of the *Philosophical Transactions,* the monthly periodical of the Royal Society of London. Hence, the *Catalogue* remains a substantial guide to the *materia alchymica et chymica* that appeared in England prior to 1675.

It cites writings of various specialists: the *Secrets* (1558) of Alexander of Piedmont, the *Mirror of Alchemy* (1597) of Roger Bacon, and the *Three Books of Occult Philosophy* (1651) of Henry Cornelius Agrippa. *Of Natural and Supernatural Things,* by the popular Basil Valentine, bore the imprint of Moses Pitt. Having been translated into English by Richard Russell, the first English edition of the *Tyrocinium-chymicum,* by Jean Beguin of Lorraine, appeared in London in 1669. A work of some rarity is the *Aurora*

chymica (1665) by the English physician Edward Bolnest, as part of the impression had been destroyed in the great fire of London in 1666, and copies of it were therefore scarce when Cooper's *Catalogue* was published. Other items include Samuel Boulton's *Magical but Natural Physick with a Description of the very Excellent Cordial of Gold* (1656) and the *Basilica Chymica & Praxis* (1670) of Oswald Crull, a follower of Paracelsus. Robert Hooke may have purchased his copies of Marcus Vipsanius Agrippa, Jean Beguin, and Oswald Croll from Cooper.

Other works by Englishmen enjoyed a ready market: *The Treatise of Aurum Potabile* (1656) of Nicholas Culpepper, Digby's *Discourse touching the Cure of Wounds by the Powder of Sympathy* (1658) and his *Choice and Experimental Receipts* (1668), as well as the *Mosaicall Philosophy* (1659) of the physician, astrologer, and alchemist Robert Fludd. Rosicrucians, who believed they possessed the deepest knowledge of the transmutation of metals, were among many of Cooper's customers. Although John Heydon, the astrologer, denied that he was closely affiliated with the English Rosicrucians, he averred that his writings interpreted their philosophy, and many Heydon works appear in Cooper's lists: *Wise-man's Crown or the Glory of the Rosie Cross* (1664), *Hammegulah Hampaaneah or Rosi Crucian Crown* (1664), *Theomagia or the temple of wisdome* (1664), *Harmony of the world* (1662), and *El havarevna or the English Physitians tutor in the Astrobolisms of Metals* (1665). Cooper also listed *Unlearned Alchymist, his Antidote* (1660), by Richard Mathews, who sold his composition "at his house by the Lyons Den at the Tower, next Gate to the By-Ward" — and with the text customers could obtain a potion made by the author, who supplied directions for using it.

Paracelsians found their master's *Key of Philosophy, Chymical Transmutations,* and *Archidoxes* in Cooper's listings. His *Catalogue* also cites many works by the alchemist Thomas Vaughan, who adopted the pseudonym Eugenius Philalethes (not to be confused with Eirenaeus Philalethes): *Anthroposophia Theomagica* (1650), *Magia Adamica* (1650), *Euphrates or Waters of the East* (1655), *Lumen de Lumine* (1651), *Man-Mouse taken in a trap* (1650), *Aulae lucis* (1652), and others. Significant studies were those of Joachim Poleman, *Novum lumen medium* (1662), Michael Sendivogius, *New Light of alchymie* (1650), and the miscellaneous contributions of George Ripley.

Cooper's *Catalogue* achieved additional distinction by including the writings of the greatest and most popular English scientist, Robert Boyle, many of whose works appeared there in first editions: *New Experiments Physico-Mechanicall Touching the Spring of*

Air (1660), *The Sceptical Chymist* (1661), *Certain Physiological Essays* (1661), *Hydrostatical Paradoxes* (1661), *Experiments and Considerations touching Colours* (1664), *Experimental History of Gold* (1665), *An Essay about the Origine & Virtue of Gems* (1672), *The Origine & Forme of Qualities* (1666), *Essay of Effluviums* (1673), and others.

For his specialist client seeking gold and the great alkahest, Cooper cited several metallurgical treatises: *The Booke of the Art of Metals* (1674), the first complete edition of Alvaro Alonso Barba that had been translated into English by the earl of Sandwich and that was of importance for its reference to America; *Foedinae Regales* (1670), by Sir John Pettus; and several others. Medical texts, pharmacopoeiae, treatises on balneology, and the articles from *Philosophical Transactions* complete Cooper's *Catalogue of Chymicall Books*.

As an innovator Cooper realized the value of advertising new as well as old publications. A list of thirty-five titles that is appended to Houpreght's *Aurofontina Chymica. A Caveat for the Protestant Clergy, if Popery be restored* (1680) scarcely reflects Cooper's alchemical predilection; it does indicate English fear of the return of the Roman church to the realm. The Houpreght appendix includes Edmund Spenser's *View of Ireland* in folio, a work first published inaccurately by Irish historian James Ware as an appendix to Ware's *Historie of Ireland* (1633). No other edition of Spenser's *View of Ireland* had been published at the time of Cooper's advertisement; apparently the *View* had been detached from Ware's *History* and sold separately.

Cooper's income from the sale of books in alchemy and chemistry cannot be determined. Hooke mentions few outright purchases that he made from Cooper, but on 8 August 1679 he records having acquired "Scheiner's Opticks 4s. and Snellius Observations Hassicae 1 ½s. paid." The auction catalogue of Hooke's library also includes a few items that Cooper had for sale: the treatises of Christoph Scheiner, Thomas Houghton's *The Compleat Miner* (1687–1688), and Libert Froidmont's *Meteorologicae libri 6* (1655).

Cooper's role as a specialist bookseller in alchemical and chemical texts was augmented by his career as the first English auctioneer. He introduced this method of bookselling in England and thus encouraged a host of imitators. This innovative system may have appealed to Cooper for a couple of reasons. The pace of the transactions it invited was far more spirited than the occasional visit of a customer to the shop in Little Britain, and a public auc-

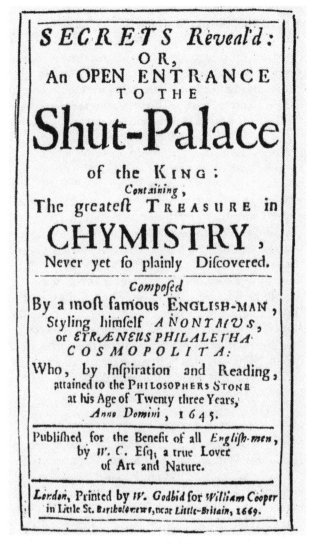

Title page for one of Cooper's earliest publications dealing with chemistry and alchemy (courtesy of the Lilly Library, Indiana University)

tion sale also provided Cooper with additional income.

On 31 October 1676 he conducted his first auction at Coxes Court, Paternoster Row, the home of Lazarus Seaman, a deceased collector. For the occasion he issued the first known English book auction catalogue, *Catalogus Variorum et Insignium Librorum instructissime Bibliothecae Clarissimi Doctissimique Viri Lazari Seaman.* The catalogue announces the place and date of the sale, held jointly with London bookseller Edward Brewster of the Crane. An entry in Hooke's diary reads, "The auction began at Dr. Seamans in Coxes court. The books yeld £800 for which the booksellers proferd £400." In a short time Hooke became an inveterate auction devotee. In his crabbed hand Hooke left a memorandum of fifty-six book sales held between August 1686 and August 1689, many of which he attended.

In introducing this new transaction Cooper declared that "it hath not been usual here in England to make Sale of books by way of Auction . . . but it having been practised in other Countreys to the Advantage both of Buyers and Sellers; it was therefore conceivd (for the encouragement of learning)." Cooper believed that having specific editions listed in the catalogue would thereby permit prospective bidders to become acquainted with the material in advance. Customers might then "depute any one to buy such books . . . as they shall desire," and "if any manifest difference should arise that then the same Book or Books shall be forthwith exposed again for sale and the highest bidder to have the same." Cooper averred that all books were perfect and were sold as such, "but if any of them appear to be otherwise before they be taken away, the Buyer shall have his Choice of taking or leaving the same." Payment was to be made upon delivery or "within one month's time after the auction is ended." The sale was to begin at 9 A.M. and again at 2 P.M., "and this was to continue daily until all the books be sold."

The contents of the Seaman catalogue of approximately five thousand books bear little resemblance to the *Catalogue of Chymicall Books* compiled by auctioneer William Cooper. Seaman had been a Puritan divine, master of Peterhouse, "a learned nonconformist" who had erected a chapel in Meetinghouse Yard, Silver Street, Holborn. His library included major works of the church fathers, Bibles and psalters, some classics, and a few items of American interest. The Bible – "translated into the Indian Language . . . Turn[ed] by the servant of Christ who is called John Eliot" and published at Cambridge in 1661 by Samuel Green and Marmaduke Johnson – fetched eighteen shillings. Johann Huttich's *Novus Orbis Regionum Insularum Veteribus Incogniti Scriptores* (1555), a copy of which enhanced the Hooke collection, brought five shillings. A first edition of Homer's *Works,* published at Florence in 1488, was sold for nine shillings. Buyers could acquire these and other items during a period of eight days, excluding the intervening Sunday.

The Seaman sale concluded on 8 November 1676, and thus about seven hundred lots had been sold daily – an exhausting feat for both auctioneer and bidders. Yet it was apparently extremely successful, as Cooper wrote that "the first attempt of this kind by the sale of Dr. Seaman's Library [gave] great Content and Satisfaction to the Gentlemen who were Buyers and no great discouragement to

the Sellers." Cooper was encouraged to conduct a second auction, that of the library of the late Reverend Thomas Kidner of Hitchins, Hertfordshire.

The Kidner sale began on 16 February 1677 at the King's Head, Little Britain. Despite Cooper's optimistic endorsement of the auction process, some opposition to this method of bookselling had been growing. In his introduction to the Kidner catalogue he states that "in the hopes of receiving such encouragement from the learned, as may prevent the Stifling of this manner of Sale, the benefit (if rightly considered . . . [is] equally balanced between Buyer and Seller.)" Despite the grumbling of the opposition – probably of those booksellers who saw the auction as some threat to their own business – it was mutually beneficial. The conditions of sale for the Kidner auction were identical to those of the Seaman sale, except for one innovation – books might be viewed before the auction commenced. Cooper also introduced an attractive device still favored by auctioneers today in selling works of great rarity: such a special item was set in small capitals – for example, ROBERT ABBOT, DEFENCE OF WILL. PERKINS AGAINST THE CALUMNIATIONS OF DR. BISHOP, London 1606. The Kidner sale consisted of nearly fourteen hundred lots comprising texts similar to those sold at the Seaman auction.

Cooper conducted at least twenty auctions alone or with Edward Millington, the stellar auctioneer who outshone Cooper as a man of wit and eloquence. For the average sale Cooper issued a catalogue – either at his own expense or that of the consignee – for distribution among the trade. At the time of his fourth sale – that of the library of admiralty lawyer Dr. John Godolphin and others on 11 November 1678 – Cooper reviewed the general acceptance of the auction as a modus operandi. The preface to the 6 June 1681 sale catalogue of the holdings of Phillip de Cardonell, a sycophant of King Charles II, indicates that Cooper had begun to use his own premises at the Pelican for auction sites, and he became quite arbitrary about hours of sale and the necessity of punctuality. Bidding was to begin at 8 A.M., even "if there be but twenty Gentlemen present." He advised prospective buyers to arrive in time, "since many have confessed they have lost the opportunity of buying for themselves by coming or sending too late, and afterwards would have given double what they sold for if they could have had them."

His sale of the library of Dr. Nathan Paget, held 4 July 1681 at the auctioneer's premises, reflects Cooper's interests: books on alchemy and chemistry, the writings of Jerome Cardan, Paracelsus, Agrippa, Fludd, Van Helmont, Raymond Lull, Basil Valentine, and others. The *Catalogue* of the Walter Rea sale held at the Pelican on 19 June 1682 is of interest for its list of previous auctions held in London by Cooper and other dealers. Cooper states in his introduction to this sale that he had wished "to gratifie the curious whose genius may lead [them] to make perfect their Collection." Therefore he had caused "to be printed the names of those persons whose Libraries have been sold by Auction, and the series of the time when." For the late-seventeenth-century English bibliophile and for an appreciative posterity Cooper lists thirty sales, including the Rea auction sale.

He was surely aware of the acquisitive instinct and collecting passion of the bibliophile. He repeated the list of auction sales in a catalogue of 14 February 1687, informing prospective bidders that he wished "to gratifie those Gentlemen, whose Curiosities may lead them to make perfect their Collections. . . . I have caused to be printed those Persons whose Libraries have been sold by Auction and the Series of the time when." His list records seventy-four sales, beginning with his first (that of Lazarus Seaman) and concluding with the one at hand.

The largest auction sale of books conducted by Cooper and Millington was that of the stock of Oxford publisher and bookseller Richard Davis. Davis had been one of the most active stationers of the time and interim publisher of the *Philosophical Transactions*. He had published many of Boyle's works and other notable texts. By 1688 the competition of younger, more-active dealers had apparently caused Davis's business to decline. In need of money, he put up his stock at auction, the first to be held in Oxford. Cooper again announced this in a catalogue – *Catalogus variorum in quavis Lingva et facultate insignium tam antiquorum quam recentium Librorum Richardi Davis Bibliopolae* – which was apparently published at Davis's expense. Copies of this catalogue were available gratis in London not only at the Pelican but also at the premises of colleagues and at coffee shops: the Queens Arms in Pall Mall, the Acorn, St. Paul's Churchyard, the Blackboy in Fleet Street, the Three Pigeons near the Royal Exchange, the Posthouse in Russell Street, Covent Garden, Davis's own house in Oxford, and Cambridge coffee houses. Approximately eighty thousand books were sold during the three sales, comprising most of Davis's holdings.

Davis, rather than Cooper, wrote the preface to the first sale catalogue, in which he somewhat speciously declared that the auction was being held for "the benefit of the University of Oxford." He ac-

Title page engraved by Robert Vaughan for alchemist George Starkey's Ripley Reviv'd *(1678)*

knowledged the favors that had been bestowed upon him by "the worthy heads of that famous and celebrated Body of Learning" who he hoped "will further, and promote the sale . . . by . . . Auction." Following his analysis of the various kinds of books to be sold, Davis "leaves all persons to judge for themselves" and concludes with the promise that the auction

shall be managed with all fairness . . . and though I am extremely sensible, that let my friends be as kind as they please, I must be a considerable loser in the disposal, yet the single consideration that my books will be dispersed amongst you, and are sold for your advantage, perfectly expiates the sense of it, and makes me cheerfully subscribe myself as I really am, your humble servant Richard Davis.

The sale began at 8 A.M., lasted until 11 A.M., and resumed at 1 P.M.; it ended at 5 P.M. on 22 April 1686 at "Mr. Newman's house over against St.

Michael's Church." Conditions of sale were as usual, but "all Gentlemen buyers [were] requested to give in their names and the Colleges or Halls they belong to, to the end that every Person respectively may have Justice done him in the buying and the delivery of the Books." The catalogue of the first Davis sale contained 10,168 lots, or apparently thirty thousand books encompassing various subjects from "Libri Theologici" to "Libri Mathematici," romances, novels, and the common law of England. The sale lasted approximately two weeks, Sunday excluded.

The second Davis sale, 4 October 1686, was again conducted by Cooper and Millington at Dorman Newman's house in Oxford. Hoping once again that his books would be dispersed among members of the university, Davis flatters the university body in his introduction, where he ingratiatingly states that he would not "willingly expose any of them elsewhere, so long as I find your favorable acceptance." He trusts that "this way of sale by auction" would give them "the greatest Content and Satisfaction." There is every reason to believe that the faculty and students found great "satisfaction" from a selection of 8,534 lots, approximately twenty-five thousand books.

After a lapse of more than a year and a half, Cooper and Millington conducted the third sale of the Davis stock. Probably during this lengthy interval Davis had hoped to recoup his fortune – which his introduction to this catalogue, in referring to his recent misfortunes, indicates had continued to dwindle. The materials offered were similar to those of the preceding sales, and Davis hoped that customers would find items not "much inferior." This collection consisted of 7,071 lots, approximately twenty-five thousand books. It is quite possible that Davis had not consigned all of his stock to auction but had reserved some of his rarer materials to offer to special customers. The Davis sale catalogues, nonetheless, are an index to the size of the holdings of a formerly prosperous university bookseller who had either overextended himself or grown unable to meet competition.

William Cooper had conducted his last sale, the third of the Davis collection, on 25 June 1686. He was shortly thereafter to disappear from the auction rooms and the world of the alchemical books he so loved. As the pioneer of the auction system and the first stationer to specialize in the sale of *materia scientifica,* he has earned a double tribute as an auctioneer and specialist bookseller. He died before 6 November 1688, as an auction held that day at Popes Head Alley states that copies of the catalogue could be obtained from various dealers – among them the Widow Cooper, Little Britain.

References:

William Cooper, *The Philosophical Epitaph* (London: Cooper, 1673);

Denis Duveen, *Bibliotheca Alchemica et Chemica* (London: Weil, 1949);

John Ferguson, *Bibliotheca Chemica,* 2 volumes (Glasgow: Maclehose, 1906);

John Lawler, *Book Auctions in England in the Seventeenth Century (1676–1700)* (London: Stock, 1898);

Leona Rostenberg, *The Library of Robert Hooke: The Scientific Book Trade of Restoration England* (Santa Monica, Cal.: Modoc, 1989).

– *Leona Rostenberg*

Thomas Creede

(London: 1593 – 1619?)

Thomas Creede's birthplace is unknown, but the date of his birth could not have been after autumn 1554: an apprentice could not be freed, unless by patrimony, before the age of twenty-four, and Creede was made a freeman of the Stationers' Company by printer Thomas East on 7 October 1578. He appears to have remained a journeyman for a decade and a half, living for at least some time in the parish of St. Giles, Cripplegate. By his first marriage he had two daughters, Jane and Thomasin, who did not live long and were buried, respectively, on 18 April and 23 November 1585. His son, John, was christened at St. Giles, Cripplegate, on 8 April 1587. About nine months later on 18 January 1588 his first wife, Dorothy, died, and he took Margery King as his second wife on 7 July that year.

Little more is known of Thomas Creede until 1593, when at the age of about thirty-nine he opened his own printing house at the sign of the Catherine Wheele near the Old Swan in Thames Street, where he produced the first books bearing his imprint. These were Robert Greene's *Gwydonius: The Carde of Fancie* and *Mamillia*, both printed for the well-known publisher William Ponsonby. Creede's business appears to have begun well: he produced nine titles in his second year and at least twelve every year thereafter until the end of the sixteenth century. Among the books he printed are some forty plays of Elizabethan dramatists – a fact that betokens his importance in this volume. Among the dramatic works he printed are the first quartos of William Shakespeare's *The First Part of the Contention betwixt the two famous Houses of Yorke and Lancaster* (an abridged text of *Henry VI*, part 2, published in 1594), *The Cronicle History of Henry the fift* (1600), and *A Most pleasaunt and excellent conceited Comedie, of Syr John Falstaffe, and the merrie Wives of Windsor* (*The Merry Wives of Windsor*, 1602) – all being the so-called bad quartos – as well as the second bad quarto of *Henry V* (1602), the second good quarto of *The Most Excellent and lamentable Tragedie of Romeo and Juliet* (1599), and the second, third, fourth, and fifth doubtful quartos of *The Tragedie of King Richard the third* (1598, 1602, 1603, and 1612).

His business began well enough for him to take an apprentice, John Wilkinson, on 31 March

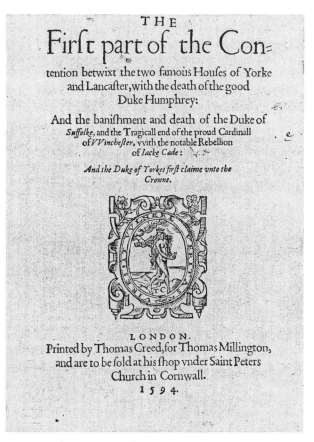

Title page, bearing Creede's device, for the 1594 first quarto edition of an abridged and corrupt text of William Shakespeare's Henry VI, part 2

1594. About a year later, on 2 February 1595, he took another apprentice, Daniel Duxfeild, but how long this apprentice actually worked under Creede is unknown – the absence of any record of Duxfeild's freedom may suggest that his apprenticeship did not last long. Within only five months of having taken on Duxfeild (and probably because the apprenticeship was discontinued), Creede decided to take a third apprentice, Henry Vawse. Thus by the summer of 1595, two years after opening his business, Creede appears to have had at least two apprentices in his shop.

Taking more than one apprentice was an offense, according to the Star Chamber decree of 1586. Creede knowingly neglected his duty to present his last apprentice to the court of the Stationers'

Company, and on 7 July 1595 he was fined five shillings for this. But Edward Arber's *Transcript of the Stationers' Registers* records that Creede was allowed "to enioye the service of the apprentize whose name is Henrye Vawse," presumably in exchange for Creede's promise to the court "not to teach John Wilkynson the arte of pryntinge."

As Wilkinson had already served for more than a year, the way in which the matter was settled appears to have been rather unusual. Creede may have thought the new apprentice to be better gifted and easier to train. In any case both Wilkinson and Vawse worked together under their master until the time of their freedom, respectively, on 19 April and 28 June 1602. Meantime Creede's fourth apprentice, John Mason, began his term on 25 March of that year, but his apprenticeship, like that of Duxfeild, also appears to have been discontinued, as the absence of any record of his freedom suggests.

By the end of the summer of 1600 Creede had moved about half a mile from his first address in Thames Street to the Old Exchange near Old Fish Street, where he set up a new office at the sign of the Eagle and Child, within a short distance from St. Paul's Churchyard. In 1600, as the imprint of Henry Roberts's *Haigh for Devonshire* implies, Creede had a bookshop in Watling Street near Friday Street, two or three hundred yards from his new printing house, but apparently he had to close it soon. His new printing office in the Old Exchange, which stood only about two hundred yards from the Stationers' Hall, must have been conveniently located and undoubtedly attracted more customers. He was still flourishing at his address in the Old Exchange in 1610 when he prepared his signed epistle "To the Readers in General" and printed it in Nicolas de Montreux's *Honours Academie,* which has a colophon with Creede's Old Exchange address. He maintained business connections with more than seventy booksellers – including William Barley, Arthur Johnson, Thomas Man, Thomas Pavier, William Ponsonby, and William Welby – and he was probably active there until the end of his career.

One of the early ordeals Creede had to encounter was condemnation by episcopal authority on 4 June 1599. A public announcement was made at the Stationers' Hall that the London Stationers' Company had received the archbishop's order to burn books of satires and epigrams. Creede's name appeared beside those of thirteen other condemned printers such as John Windet, Edward Allde, and Valentine Simmes – all to be his close associates in sharing printing jobs in years to come. Two of the books that Creede printed that year, T. M.'s *Micro-Cynicon* and Torquato Tasso's *Of Mariage and Wiuing,* were actually burned in the hall. Two other books, Joseph Hall's *Virgidemiarum* (1597) and Thomas Cutwode's *Caltha Poetarum* (1599) were likewise mentioned in the announcement at the Stationers' Hall but not burned in the hall. These condemned books, with the exception of *Micro-Cynicon,* had been all duly entered in the Stationers' Register not as copies belonging to Creede but to his fellow booksellers. Yet perhaps, as W. W. Greg suggests, Creede was one of those printers "whom the Court thought most likely to meddle with forbidden wares." Besides the actual financial loss imposed on the printer and the booksellers, some blemish on Creede's reputation must have resulted.

Another somewhat curious event in Creede's career is the disappearance of his name from the Stationers' Register for eighteen months from July 1600 through December 1601. Since October 1593 he had been more or less regular in entering titles as his copies in the register and had no serious problems until early in 1600. But on 25 February of that year, when Creede applied for a license to print Thomas Becon's *The Pomander of Prayer,* his registration fee of sixpence was invalidated because, Arber records, "it [was] in Controuersye." Less than a week later on 3 March his registration of *Christes Sermon [on the Road] to Emaus* was likewise canceled, but on 11 March and 10 June Creede entered more books, Quintus Curtius Rufus's *The Historie of Quintus Curcius* and Robert Cawdrey's *A Treasurie or Store-House of Similes.*

Shortly after these two books had been registered, something appears to have happened to the copyright of Virgil's *Aeneid,* which Creede had printed for himself in 1596. To Creede's original entry on 23 February of that year was appended a later note reading "*vacat quoad* VIRGILIS *Aeneados/* VIRGILIS *Aeneados* is master Knightes Copie. 26 *Junij.* 1600." Clement Knight, a member of the Drapers' Company, was transferred to the Stationers' Company on 3 June 1600, only a few weeks before the date of the nullifying additional note. Whether Creede lawfully transferred his copyright to Knight is not clear, but it is most likely that, if such a transfer had occurred, some arrangement must have been made between them, because Creede printed for himself two further editions of the book in 1600 and in 1607. For whatever reason, following this additional note of 26 June 1600 Creede's name does not appear again in the Stationers' Register until 28 December 1601, when he

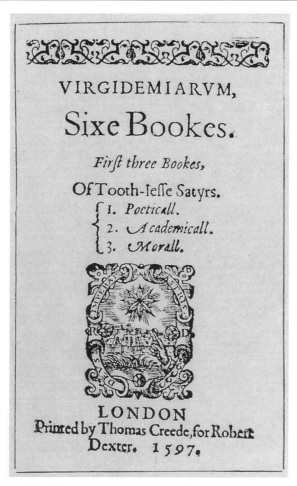

*Title page for one of four books published by Creede and
condemned by episcopal authorities in 1599*

entered his registration of William Whately's *A Godlie
Treatise, intituled the View of Pride* as his own copy.

Perhaps the most mysterious event related to
his disappearance from the Stationers' Register is a
sudden recession in what had been his increasing
business in 1601. Creede produced that year only
seven small books – including I. B.'s *The Hope for
Peace,* George Blackwell's *Relatio Compendiosa
Turbarum quas Iesuitae Angli Vna cum D. G. Blackwello
Sacerdotibus Seminariorum Côciuere,* an anonymous
author's *The Copies of Certaine Discourses,* and a play –
less than seven hundred pages in all. Three of the
seven books carry various enigmatic imprints. One
reads "Imprinted at Franckford by the heires of D.
Turner"; another, "Rothomagi, per Iacobum
Molaeum sub signo Phaenicis"; and yet another,
"Imprinted at Roane by the heires of Ia. Walker."
Ornaments and typeface in these three books confirm that Thomas Creede was the printer.

These publications were only a part of some
sixteen tracts, or pamphlets, that started to appear

early in 1601 as a result of disturbances within the
Catholic clergy in England – the so-called Appellant
controversy that had originated with the appointment in 1598 of George Blackwell, a friend of the
Jesuits, as archpriest of all the English Catholic
priests. Because the Jesuits were being attacked by a
group of seminary priests who criticized their political involvement, English authorities were eager to
know what was happening between these two
Roman Catholic parties and to have their works
published by the London stationers under the disguise of false imprints. The three books Creede
printed were by the seminary priests known as Ap-
pellants, and the mysterious imprints were sensible
fabrications that the printer, rather than the writers,
can be presumed to have incorporated – in order to
accord with the customary practice of some papist
books at the time. Yet Creede was daring enough to
use on the title page of the book by Blackwell one of
the ornaments that he had used before. This was a
risky gesture, for authorities warily watched the ac-

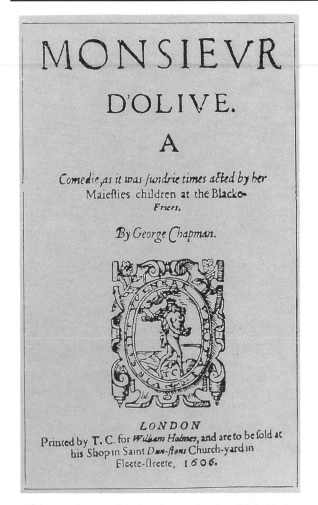

MONSIEVR D'OLIVE.

A

Comedie, as it was sundrie times acted by her
Maiesties children at the Blacke-
Friers.

By George Chapman.

LONDON
Printed by T. C. for William Holmes, and are to be sold at
his Shop in Saint Dun-stons Church-yard in
Fleete-streete, 1606.

*Title page for one of the last dramas Creede published before
the annual production levels of his print shop
began to diminish*

tivities of printers — whose ornament stocks, well known to those authorities, permitted them to identify the printers whom they wished to suppress as easily as they identified and watched recusant Nonconformists. Whether the sudden recession of his business in 1601 resulted from his involvement with printing such recusant works is not known.

Creede's reduced production in 1601 corresponds to the infrequent appearance of his name in the Stationers' Register, but he soon recovered from this diminution of business. In the following year he printed twenty-three titles, the largest number he had ever undertaken, and on 2 August 1602 he paid six shillings (as he had done until February 1600) for the poor of the company, as his "sixpence-in-the-pound" duty, for printing *The Historie of Quintus Curcius,* a sizable book on the life of Alexander the Great.

This recovery from the drastic recession of 1601 may have been helped by Creede's policy of

sharing with other printers. So far as is known, he had shared printing duties only once before his recession: with Valentine Simmes in printing Raoul Le Fèvre's *The Auncient Historie of the Destruction of Troy* (1596). But after 1601 he shared printing tasks during several years with other printers such as Allde, Thomas East, George Eld, William Jaggard, Humphrey Lownes, Thomas Purfoot, James Roberts, Simmes, Simon Stafford, William White, and Windet. The amount of Creede's shared printing was relatively small, but he maintained business connections with booksellers such as Cuthbert Burby, Thomas Bushell, Nathaniel Butter, William Cotton, William Holmes, Matthew Law, Nathaniel Ling, Man, Pavier, George Potter, Henrie Tomes (and Richard Ockould), Simon Waterson, Welby, and Edward White. As owners of the rights to the shared titles, they all must have had some practical control over the printing trade, and a possible change in Creede's managerial attitude toward his fellow printers and booksellers may thus have favorably affected his business.

For more than a dozen years from the beginning of his career Creede had printed the dramatic works of Shakespeare and his contemporaries such as Greene, Thomas Dekker, John Marston, and George Chapman. But for some reason after 1606 he printed none for four years, and his annual output of nondramatic works also diminished drastically in 1607, 1608, and 1610. His busiest years were probably past.

The nature of his business around this stage of his career was beginning to change. For many years Creede had constantly been printing books for himself as well as for others, sometimes more for himself than for others. But the general decline in his output starting in 1607 seems to signal his decision to print no more than one or two books for himself and a manageable number for others. This is certainly true of the years 1610–1613, when he had already passed the age of fifty-five. An elderly printer-bookseller, whose son could not succeed him in business, was becoming a trade printer, wishing probably just to maintain his business and to avoid having to worry too much about the market for copies to be sold in bulk.

Creede's situation at this stage appears to be reflected in the diminishing number of his apprentices. In 1611 at least three apprentices were working together in his shop from 25 March to 17 June, when one of them, Parys Vandien (or Vandewe), was freed. The other two remained working until December, when one of them, Robert Gerrard, after three years of service to Creede, was transferred to a new master, Felix Kingston. Only one apprentice, Richard Reade, remained after that date. Some months later on 7 September 1612 Creede was fined by the court of the Stationers' Company for having bound this last apprentice at a scrivener's, contrary to ordinances, but the apprentice was able to work with Creede, who was still among the nineteen master printers of London in 1615.

Sometime in 1613 Creede could not resist a temptation to make money by printing a pirated edition of George Wither's popular satire in verse, *Abuses Stript, and Whipt; or, Satirical Essayes,* which had been printed earlier that year by Eld. The initiative probably came from a few booksellers, including Ralph Mabb, for whom Creede had two years earlier printed John Seller's small book, *A Sermon against Halting betweene Two Opinions.* In order to make his fraudulent edition look genuine, Creede decided to cut anew several ornaments and decorative initials that had appeared in Eld's original edition. Skillful craftsmen copied the blocks exquisitely, but the piracy was disclosed several months after their efforts. When Creede succeeded in concealing his connection with the printing, only the booksellers were fined by the court of the Stationers. Even after this incident Creede continued to do business with at least one of them, William Bladon, for the following two years.

Probably from the beginning of his career Creede was allowed officially to have only one press, but it is possible that he also maintained a spare one. His stock of ornaments and decorative initials was comparatively small. In addition to a near-complete set of decorative initials, he had only a few odd initials, two of which he had added in perpetrating his piracy in 1613. Besides laces or flowers he possessed some twenty blocks of ornaments, six of which he had acquired during that same incident in 1613. It is surprising that he had only two or three headpieces of his own before the time that he made these other additions. In fact, the majority of the books from his shop contained few ornaments, and the appearance of his printed pages was rather bleak. In or after 1613, however, the printing style of his shop seemed to change, and ornaments began to appear more frequently in many of the books that Creede printed thereafter. They were to appear also in nearly all the books that Creede and Bernard Alsop printed jointly in 1616 and 1617.

Creede printed solely only two of the seventeen books that appeared from his press in 1616 – Thomas Gainsford's *The Secretaries Studie* and Richard Webb's *The Lott* – and they were both entered

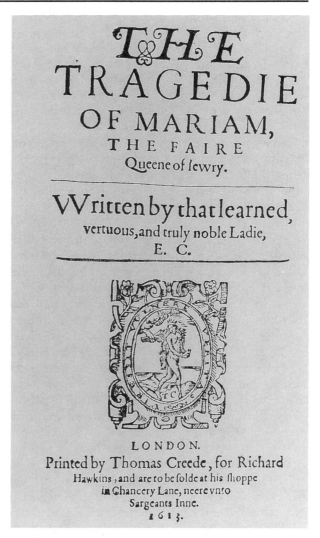

Title page for Creede's edition of a play by Lady Elizabeth Carew, a kinswoman of Edmund Spenser and patroness to many Elizabethan writers

as Roger Jackson's copies in the Stationers' Register on 9 October 1615. Seven weeks later on 26 November *A Select Second Husband for Sir T. Overburies Wife, now a Matchlesse Widow* by John Davies was entered as another bookseller's copy, and for the first time Creede and Alsop collaborated in printing it. Two other books were registered in December 1615 and three more in January 1616, all of which were printed jointly. This seems to imply that by this time Creede and Alsop had agreed to share the business. Their joint work, however, did not last long, as in 1617 they collaborated on no more than one book – William Cecil's *Certaine Precepts or Directions –* and Alsop in that year printed more than a dozen books without Creede's assistance. For whatever the reason, their joint work must have become impractical early in 1617.

One can surmise that Alsop had been helping Creede for some time, for Alsop had been a journeyman for several years after William White made him a freeman on 7 February 1610. On 16 May 1613 Alsop joined a group of fifty-three journeymen printers (one of whom was Parys Vandien, Creede's former apprentice) in signing a petition in which they described themselves as being "beggared by want of employment." At the end of the collaboration between Creede and Alsop in 1617, when the former retired from business, Alsop acquired Creede's printing materials. Creede's last apprentice, Reade, was transferred to the new master on 2 June 1617.

The fortunes of Creede's son, John, are rather obscure. Stationers' records provide no information about his apprenticeship or freedom, but his name appears in the Poor Book of the Stationers' Company: he received payments in the third and the fourth quarters of 1617, after his father had retired. Because John Creede was not entitled to such charity, he must have received it on behalf of his father, who was not able to collect it. During the next eight or nine months Thomas Creede appears to have managed to get along without help from the company, until he received benefactions in the third quarter of 1618 and again, after a short break, in the first quarter of 1619. No further records of him exist after this: he must have died at the age of sixty-four, after he received his last payment, but the exact date or place of his death is not known.

Creede's significance in the history of the British book trade is twofold. His primary importance lies in the fact that, although he never held any major office in the London Stationers' Company, his long career as master printer provides a good picture of the rise and fall of a London printing house at a time when printers generally were under growing managerial pressures imposed by booksellers who had found the book trade for members of that to be more rewarding and profitable than it was for the printers. Creede dwindled from an ambitious printer-bookseller to a mere trade printer. Of secondary significance is the fact that among the books Creede produced are many that never fail to attract modern readers, especially historians and literary students. In addition to many religious writings that occupy nearly half of his total production, he printed a total of forty-two editions of thirty-four different contemporary plays, twenty-eight of which were first editions of new works. These are of great importance to British literary history, and no serious students of Elizabethan and Jacobean drama can ignore them.

References:

W. Craig Ferguson, "Thomas Creede's Pica Roman," *Studies in Bibliography,* 23 (1970): 148–153;

G. M. Pinciss, "Thomas Creede and the Repertory of the Queen's Men, 1583–1592," *Modern Philology,* 67 (May 1970): 321–330;

Akihiro Yamada, *Thomas Creede: Printer to Shakespeare and His Contemporaries* (Matsumoto, Japan: Shinshu University, 1981; revised and enlarged, Tokyo: Meisei University Press, 1994).

                                                                                 – Akihiro Yamada

John Danter

(London: circa 1586 – 1599)

John Danter published various significant works in his London print shop during the 1590s, including the first of William Shakespeare's plays to appear in print, *The Most Lamentable Romaine Tragedie of Titus Andronicus* (1594). He also printed the first half of Shakespeare's *An Excellent conceited Tragedie of Romeo and Juliet* (1597), a job he shared with Edward Allde. In addition, Danter printed Sir Philip Sidney's *Astrophel and Stella* (1591), Arthur Golding's translation of Ovid's *Metamorphosis* (1593), and works by Robert Greene, Thomas Lodge, Thomas Nashe, George Peele, Henry Smith, and many others. His productions include literature, sermons, advice books, and contemporary news items – an impressive variety, much of which might have been lost had it not been for this particular master printer.

Danter was born in 1565 in Eynsham, Oxfordshire, a small village a few kilometers from Oxford. Danter's father, also named John, was a weaver whose administration letter (dated 1574) in the Oxfordshire Record Office mentions the young Danter along with his mother, Alice, and three brothers – Abraham, Walter, and Robert. While at least one of the brothers, Abraham, followed his father's trade by becoming a weaver in the nearby village of Woodstock, John chose to try his fortunes in London. As was customary, arrangements were probably made in advance for the typically seven-year apprenticeship. In 1582 at the age of seventeen John Danter was apprenticed to John Day, the well-known London master printer.

Day died 23 July 1584, and the Stationers' Register shows that on 15 April 1588 Danter was transferred from "mistres Day *Alias* Stone" to Robert Robinson. Before obtaining his freedom, Danter was caught (probably around 1586) pirating two schoolbooks – printing the privileged property of another stationer – a rather bold adventure for a young apprentice. However, such pirating was in fact quite common among the master printers who were teaching the book trade to apprentices.

After obtaining his freedom on 30 September 1589, Danter entered into partnership with William

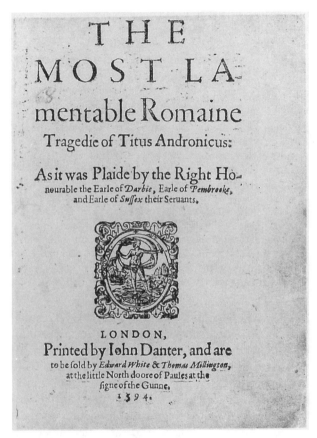

Title page for one of the earliest published plays by William Shakespeare, with one of Danter's familiar ornaments

Hoskins and Henry Chettle, and, according to the title page of Nicholas Ayer's *The English Phlebotomy: Or, Method and way of healing by letting of blood* (1592) he lived with Hoskins in Fetter Lane. By the end of 1592 Danter had moved to Duck Lane near Smithfield, as shown on the title page of Robert Wilson's *A Right excellent and famous Comedy called The Three Ladies of London* (1592). He then moved again to Hosier Lane near Holborn Conduit, and, having finally settled, Danter notes – perhaps with some pride – on his title page for Richard Barnfield's *Greenes Funeralls* (1594) that it is "his house." As a householder (generally the status one achieved upon becoming a freeman of a company or guild), Danter's living quarters would have been located above his print shop, the work being shared by his wife and children. Unfortunately this arrangement did not last long, as Danter died five years later at the age of thirty-four. Yet despite the brevity of his life and career he managed to print many interesting books during the 1590s.

Beginning with Henry R. Plomer in 1906, however, a series of critical commentaries has kept Danter and his work from receiving much appreciation. Apparently deploring the particular typeface Danter had used in *An Excellent conceited Tragedie of Romeo and Juliet,* Plomer attacked him and his printing house, unaware that the play had been printed in part by Danter and in part by Edward Allde. Plomer claimed that

> never was a masterpiece ushered into the world in a worse manner. The printer started with a type which, in spite of its worn condition, was fairly readable, but before he had half finished the work, he substituted a very much smaller and even more worn fount. The compositors' work was of the worst description, reversed letters and mis-readings being sprinkled over every page. And with this we part thankfully with John Danter. He disappears in a whirlwind of official indignation and Star Chamber shrieks for daring to print those sacred volumes, the "Grammar" and "Accidence," and in less than three years afterwards he died.

Plomer's exaggerated reaction most likely results from a difference in perspective. In the twentieth century *Romeo and Juliet* is a known masterpiece; in the sixteenth century it was not. As Charlton Hinman has emphasized, work on the First Folio proceeded only when there was nothing "better" to print. It is therefore conceivable that a printer would not use his best type to set a mere play but would save his best for the printing of sermons or instruction books.

The shared printing of *Romeo and Juliet* – a common business arrangement for this period – also explains the use of two type fonts, as well as some of the other features that Plomer notes. Yet the damage done by Plomer has proven to be nearly irreversible. Citing Plomer and subsequent references to Plomer, scholars have created a John Danter who never actually existed. Unfortunately those early-twentieth-century scholars – Ronald B. McKerrow, Alfred W. Pollard, and Walter W. Greg – were and still are particularly prominent ones in analytic bibliography and textual criticism.

Standard reference sources published during the early twentieth century have also helped create a fictive John Danter. For example, the *Cambridge History of English Literature* (1919) notes that "Henry Chettle entered into partnership with two not very reputable stationers, William Hoskins and John Danter," and McKerrow, in his *Dictionary of Printers and Booksellers* (1910), finds Danter's 1597 *Romeo and Juliet* to be "like all his work ... very badly printed." McKerrow, like Plomer, singles out the printing of *Romeo and Juliet* as particularly poor and then leaps to a conclusion that condemns all of Danter's work. Edmund K. Chambers's influential reference work *The Elizabethan Stage* (1923) also characterizes Danter as "a stationer of the worst reputation," a comment perhaps even more damning than those that group Danter with a whole class of irresponsible printers.

Pollard sounds much like his contemporaries – Plomer, Greg, and McKerrow. After briefly and nonjudgmentally mentioning Danter's printing of *Titus Andronicus,* Pollard emphasizes Danter's printing of *Romeo and Juliet* and notes that he "had in the intervening three years gone down in the world (his press had been seized in 1596)." Danter, according to Pollard, had printed the pirated edition of *Romeo and Juliet* and probably one of *Love's Labour's Lost,* thus causing the players concern over their rights to the plays. Pollard claims that the players then attempted to protect their rights by giving to Cuthbert Burby and James Roberts ("the first of their confidential publishers") good texts of *Romeo and Juliet* and *Love's Labour's Lost.* They did this "on Danter's death, or possibly a little earlier on his damning himself past redemption by pirating the *Grammar and Accidence.*" (In fact, the pirating had occurred while Danter was an apprentice.)

Besides condemning John Danter as usual, Pollard here distinguishes between two groups of stationers – the good ones such as Burby and Roberts and the bad ones such as Danter. From Plomer (eleven years earlier) to Pollard, scholarship moved from condemning all printers to dividing the good from the bad. Pollard's index clearly distinguishes the two categories: "Danter, John, driven to literary piracy by need" versus "Roberts, James, enters plays on Stationers' Register to defeat pirates." Before the 1930s, then, Danter was pegged – by scholars who had examined neither his whole career nor more than a few of his books – as disreputable in his business affairs and unreliable in his production of books.

Subsequent scholarship continues this particular characterization of Danter and his work. Cyril B. Judge claims that "Danter was unable to keep out of trouble." Likewise, F. E. Halliday states that Danter was "active as a printer of poor quality and dubious reputation," and his press was seized by wardens of

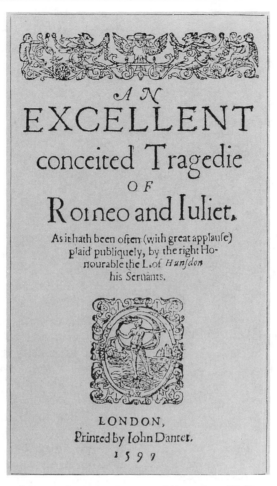

Title page for the 1597 quarto of Romeo and Juliet,
which Danter printed with Edward Allde

the Stationers' Company *during* the printing of
Romeo and Juliet. Four years before Halliday, Harry
R. Hoppe had noted this seizure also, as did Greg a
few years later in 1956. As would be expected, all
made similar character judgments regarding Danter.

In 1974 G. M. Pinciss repeats Greg's fifty-one-
year-old denigration that all of Danter's work is suspect. In discussing the order of acting companies
listed on the title page of the first quarto of *Titus Andronicus,* Pinciss notes that Danter probably chose
the particular order not for chronological but for
sales reasons, and Pinciss concludes (illogically)
that "for this reason [Danter's] works, like his editions, are never very reliable." On the other hand,
according to Pinciss, James Roberts, printer of the
second quarto of *Titus Andronicus,* used a different
order for the acting companies on *his* title page of
Titus. The inference is of course similar to Pollard's
distinction between the good and the bad. Moreover, Pinciss fails to note that the second quarto

was set from printed copy (of the first quarto) while
the first quarto had been set from manuscript copy.
Not only was Roberts's copy easier to read than
Danter's had been, but Roberts could very well
have been the printer who altered the chronological
order of companies on the title page. Furthermore,
Roberts's compositors had set type from a damaged
copy of Danter's first quarto, and either they or
someone else in the printing house had simply made
up text for the unreadable portions.

Despite our increasingly better understanding
of the Elizabethan book trade, negative criticism of
Danter continues in some recent work. Charles
Boyce, for example, states that Danter was constantly pirating other stationers' property and that
"all of his surviving work is sloppily done." The
1992 *Encyclopedia Britannica* refers to Danter as a "notorious pirate." David Bevington, in his discussion
of *Romeo and Juliet,* refers to Danter's 1597 quarto as
"a pirated edition issued by an unscrupulous publisher, no doubt to capitalize on the play's great pop-

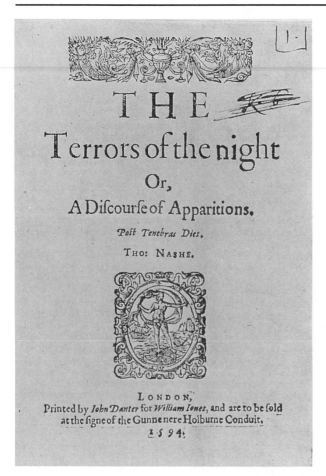

THE

Terrors of the night

Or,

A Difcourfe of Apparitions.

Poft Tenebras Dies.

THO: NASHE.

LONDON,
Printed by *Iohn Danter* for *William Iones,* and are to be fold
at the figne of the Gunne nere Holburne Conduit.
1594.

*Title page for Thomas Nashe's work on dreams and nightmares,
a book dedicated to Lady Elizabeth Carew*

ularity," and he repeats the charge that "Danter's unauthorized publication in 1597 [sought] to exploit a popular new play." And in discussing John Wolfe and Danter as printers, D. Allen Carroll says of the latter that "everyone knows of the odor which attaches itself to the name of Danter."

A much smaller body of scholarship attempts to correct this characterization of Danter. Despite some of his questionable conclusions, Hoppe is one of these few who suggest that the printing of *Romeo and Juliet* is not extraordinarily poor but rather typical for its era. Likewise, Leo Kirschbaum notes in *Shakespeare and the Stationers* (1955) that Danter has been unduly singled out as a troublemaker and that "Pollard, Greg, and Judge have followed Plomer in denouncing Danter." In an appendix Kirschbaum summarizes Danter's "criminal" career and concludes that he "was neither more nor less unscrupulous than many another stationer." Unfortunately this absolution appears not until the end of the book, and in an appendix as well. Kirschbaum's partial exculpation of Danter appears to reiterate those earlier claims by Plomer and others that *all* the printers were somehow less than ideal.

J. A. Lavin offers another attempt to correct some of those earlier studies, but his article also makes corrections with reservations. Even though Lavin adds nineteen books to the Danter canon through a study of ornament stock, for example, he also finds Danter to be somehow less than an ideal printer: "In Danter's case the general picture of him as a marginal jobbing printer is hardly altered by these additions, but similar large increases in the canons of other printers might appreciably alter our estimation of their importance." (Hoppe had used the term *marginal* twenty-two years earlier to describe Danter's career.) In one way or another virtually all scholars have perpetuated exaggerated notions associated with John Danter; one must therefore use caution when referring to their assessments of Danter's life and career.

Despite false assumptions that underlie much of the criticism of Danter, examination of Stationers' Company records and of Danter's output reveals a stationer not of dubious reputation but rather of ability and intelligence. Plomer, for instance, notes that Danter used two different type fonts. Such an obvious difference does appear between signatures D and E in *Romeo and Juliet,* but it is not true that Danter printed the second half of the play nor that his presses were seized at that moment in its printing. As Lavin points out, "It seems inconceivable that the Stationers' raid on Danter should have occurred at precisely the moment when all the sheets of the D gathering had been perfected, rather than, say, half-way through the composing or printing of one or other of the formes." In fact, Danter was raided not while printing *Romeo and Juliet* (for which there are no grounds for seizure), but rather while printing *The Jesus Psalter,* an illegal Catholic text for which there were grounds for seizure. Because Plomer assumed that a change in font suggested sloppy workmanship and because Hoppe and Halliday, for example, assumed that this same change suggested a raid by the Stationers' Company, Danter's reputation suffered greatly. It was not at all uncommon for printers to participate in shared printing; signatures A through D of *Romeo and Juliet* were printed by Danter, and signatures E through K were printed by Edward Allde.

Another false assumption surrounding Danter's printing of the first quarto of *Romeo and Juliet* is based on the unfortunate terms "good" and "bad" quartos. Pollard used such terms in distinguishing a few bad quartos from the many good quartos of the Shakespeare canon. *Romeo and Juliet,* considered a piracy by Pollard, was one of the bad quartos. Pollard assumed that some stenography had been used to reproduce the text of the play from a performance or, as later scholars suggested, from memory, usually by the actors. These reconstructions were then often sold to a printer or publisher.

Pollard's terminology of "good" and "bad" traditionally denotes those plays printed from an author's foul papers or a subsequent edition – the good quartos – and those plays printed from manuscripts or subsequent editions reconstructed by memory – the bad quartos. Such terms, however, do not apply to the nature of the printing: Danter's compositor may have produced a reliable text (one that faithfully follows the copy) of a manuscript reconstructed from memory. Yet at the same time a compositor might have produced a very unreliable text (with many variations) from a reliable and/or good copy. As studies of Danter reveal, this distinction is often blurred because the good texts/bad texts dichotomy apparently transfers readily to a good printer/bad printer assessment.

Another important clarification needs to be made. Studies regarding Danter's reputation frequently refer to his pirating of the work popularly known as "Lily's *Grammar"* (1543). Queen Elizabeth had granted the privilege to print this schoolbook to Francis Flower for the duration of his life. In 1585 Thomas Dunn and Robert Robinson, who had allegedly printed twenty-five hundred copies of it, were brought before the court of the Star Chamber for infringing upon Flower's privilege. In 1586 three more printers (Robert Bourne, Henry Jefferson, and Edward Smythe) were accused of printing two thousand copies of the same book. Bourne and Jefferson responded formally to the accusation by emphasizing, in their defense, the problems caused by monopolies in rights to print works – problems such as high prices and low-quality products. The argument, however, did not convince the wardens of the Stationers' Court, who made the following decision (quoted in part) that

> yt is ordered and decreed that the said Robert Bourne Henrye Iefferson & Iohn danter Gilbert Lee & Thomas dunne and all others that wroughte vpon thimpression of the said booke, shall from henceforth be Dyshabled to prynte.

John Danter and Gilbert Lee, who had not been named in Flower's original complaint to the court, were added to this list of offenders. Why Plomer and Pollard would single out Danter as being partic-

ularly offensive in printing William Lily's "Grammar" is difficult to determine.

That this printer pirated or disregarded Flower's royal privilege to print Lily's "Grammar" was not an isolated case. Many stationers disapproved of the granting of royal privileges and enunciated that disapproval not only through disregard but also through written responses to the Stationers' court. The owner of a royal grant had to protect his rights by constantly filing complaints, and those who were named in the complaints were not necessarily "bad" printers. Many were simply reputable printers questioning the value and legitimacy of the royal privilege or monopoly system.

John Danter seems therefore to have been in no more trouble with the Stationers' Company than were his contemporaries. Furthermore, according to the Stationers' Company records, the order for the seizure and defacement of Danter's property in 1597 did not have anything to do with piracy of any kind. The only book named in the court record was that of an illegal Catholic text, not the property of someone else whose printing rights Danter had violated.

An examination of Danter's production affords a more positive picture of this printer. Seventy-nine extant editions are attributed to Danter today, and these books are competently produced, their "errors" being common among works printed during the handpress period: an occasional slipped letter, an upside-down factotum, irregular pagination, and so on. Danter's literature, sermons, and contemporary news items, as well as advice and how-to manuals, consist of various type fonts and format sizes; the font and size are generally chosen rather artistically.

Although not of the same level of subject matter as the sermons by Henry Smith or John Calvin or the literary works by Shakespeare, Sir Philip Sidney, or Robert Greene, the contemporary news items that Danter frequently printed were nevertheless probably quite popular and profitable, particularly in an age before newspapers and other mass media. For example, the content and format of *A Merrie pleasant and delectable Historie, betweene King Edward the fourth, and a Tanner of Tamworth* (1596) make it an easily read and interestingly illustrated text, consisting of six leaves and containing three block prints. Also of general interest is *The Famous Historie of Chinon of England* (1597), and to feel the excitement of the news flash one can turn to *Strange Signes seen in the Aire, strange Monsters behelde on the Land, and wonderfull Prodigies both by Land and Sea, ouer, in, and about the Citie of Rosenberge in high Germany the ninteenth*

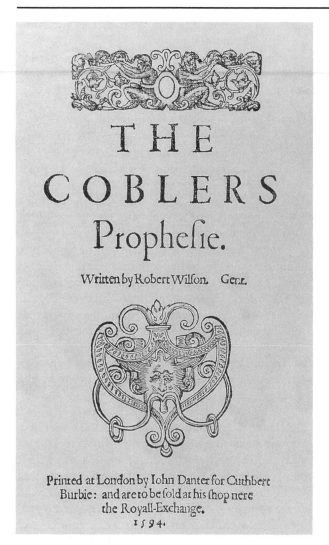

Danter's title page for Robert Wilson's allegorical interlude

of Ianuare last past (1594). Such wonders include that of a woman who gave birth to a male child who was "without a head, hauing his eyes, eares, nose and mouth placed in his breast, his eyes especially being of meruailous bignes." Interesting "news," indeed, and most likely printed, sold, and read rather quickly. Despite their ephemeral nature, these modest books are rather nicely printed.

By contrast, the how-to and advice books would have been discarded only after having been consulted many times. They instruct one in learning how to play the lute, orpharion, or bandore; or in learning new patterns for needlework; or even in learning how to control a troublesome child, as in *The Schoole of Good Manners* (1595). Self-help was also available from Danter's printing shop in the *Instruction of a Christian Woman* (1592). The physically afflicted could consult, for example, *Present Remedies against the Plague* (1592), an apparently popular

book, for Danter printed a second edition of it in 1594. Coming from a printer of reportedly ill repute, these varieties of subject matter, format, and typeface are thus quite impressive.

Such a variety and quality of work are not unusual for a London printer of that time, but John Danter was unusual among his fellow stationers in that his name appeared in print on three separate occasions. First, in I.iii. of the anonymously written popular play *Part Two of The Return from Parnassus; or The Scourge of Simony* (which was acted between 1598 and 1603 at St. John's College, Cambridge, and printed in 1606), one finds an interesting stage direction: "*Enter Danter the printer.*" A brief dialogue follows between the character, Danter, and the writer, Ingenioso. Danter complains that he lost money on the last printing he completed for Ingenioso, but Ingenioso argues that his *new* manuscript, "A Chronicle of Cambridge Cuckolds," will be profitable for Danter. The two strike a deal.

Secondly, Danter's name appeared in connection with the Gabriel Harvey and Thomas Nashe controversy. Having been Nashe's printer, Danter received a biting slander (that also included Danter's wife) from Harvey. Nashe pointedly defended his printer and Mrs. Danter in the ensuing controversy.

Thirdly, Danter also wrote several dedications to his readers. These include, for example, his dedications to the reader of Richard Barnfield's *Greenes funeralls* (1594) or to Edward Stanley in Christopher Middleton's *The Famous Historie of Chinon of England*. Although a printer who wrote dedications during this period is not that unusual, Danter's rhetorical flourishes are unusual, and his repeated references to himself as a printer convey a sense of pride in his trade. In addition, a reading of these dedications reveals a printer of some competence and intelligence. For example, Danter's address in "To the Gentlemen Readers Health," another dedication, states that one cup of pure wine will quicken fine wits, but many cups will dull them; likewise, a little poetry will be good for the mind, whereas large volumes "would but cloy and weary you." Danter's approach is particularly effective, for he is trying to sell a small twelve-leaf quarto of poetry. He has provided a healthy reason to purchase the modest book.

In Henry Smith's *God's Arrow against Atheists* (1593) the ingenuity of Danter's dedication to "the Godly Ladie Katherine Hayward, wife to Syr Rowland Hayward" has likewise gone relatively unnoticed. To have such a prestigious lady as one's patroness or, at least, to flatter her could only help during those difficult times with Stationers' Hall. While the dedication of the book is to Lady Hayward (and there is much praise of her), Danter also includes her very influential husband, the Lord Mayor of London: Danter says that he has waited for the appropriate time to show his "bounden dutie to the Graue Fathers and auntient Gouernours of this famous Citie of London, but especially to the right worshipfull Sir Rowland Hayward your reuerent Husband."

Although John Danter has been the victim of very negative critical commentary, the physical evidence – each extant book published from his house – suggests the opposite. The workmanship, subject matter, and Danter's dedications provide evidence of a relatively competent and intelligent master printer. He steadily progressed from being an Eynsham weaver's son (1565–1582) and apprentice (1582–1589) to become a householder – a relatively high status in society – and a master printer – a high status in the powerful and prestigious Stationers' Company (1589–1599). His literary pieces and sermons, the advice books, and the shorter news items must have provided him with various marketable works and with at least some success.

In addition, and perhaps of most importance, Danter appears to have had some strong personal connections to London's literary world, not only because he printed so many works by popular contemporary authors, but also because he specifically was incorporated, as a character, in a popular academic play. Furthermore, both Nashe and Harvey included Danter in their lengthy and popular controversy. To characterize John Danter as a stationer "unable to keep out of trouble" or as a stationer "of the worst reputation" is worse than misleading. It is wrong.

References:
David Bevington, ed., *The Complete Works of Shakespeare* (New York: HarperCollins, 1992);

Charles Boyce, *Shakespeare A to Z* (New York: Dell, 1990);

D. Allen Carroll, "Who Wrote *Greenes Groats-worth of Witte* (1592)?," in *Renaissance Papers 1992,* edited by George Walton Williams and Barbara J. Baines (Durham, N.C.: Southeastern Renaissance Conference, 1993), pp. 69–77;

Edmund K. Chambers, *Elizabethan Stage,* 4 volumes (Oxford: Clarendon Press, 1923);

Walter W. Greg, *Some Aspects and Problems of London Publishing Between 1550 and 1650* (Oxford: Clarendon Press, 1956);

Greg, *Two Elizabethan Stage Abridgements: The Battle of Alcazar and Orlando Furioso. An Essay in Critical Bibliography* (Oxford: Clarendon Press, 1923);

Greg and E. Boswell, eds., *The Records of the Court of the Stationers' Company 1576–1602 from Register B,* volume 1 (London: Bibliographical Society, 1930);

F. E. Halliday, *A Shakespeare Companion 1550–1950* (London: Duckworth, 1952);

Harry R. Hoppe, *The Bad Quarto of "Romeo and Juliet," A Bibliographical and Textual Study* (Ithaca, N.Y.: Cornell University Press, 1948);

Cyril B. Judge, *Elizabethan Book-Pirates* (Cambridge, Mass.: Harvard University Press, 1934);

Leo Kirschbaum, *Shakespeare and the Stationers* (Columbus: Ohio State University Press, 1955);

J. A. Lavin, "John Danter's Ornament Stock," *Studies in Bibliography,* 23 (1970): 21–44;

William E. Miller, "Printers and Stationers in the Parish of St. Giles Cripplegate 1561–1640," *Studies in Bibliography,* 19 (1966): 15–38;

G. M. Pinciss, "Shakespeare, Her Majesty's Players, and Pembroke's Men," *Shakespeare Survey,* 27 (1974): 129–136;

Henry R. Plomer, "The Printers of Shakespeare's Plays and Poems," *Library,* second series 7 (April 1906): 149–166;

Alfred W. Pollard, *Shakespeare's Fight with the Pirates* (London: Moring, 1917; revised, London: Cambridge University Press, 1920);

G. W. Prothero, *Select Statutes and Other Constitutional Documents* (Oxford: Clarendon Press, 1894).

                                        – Judith K. Rogers

John Day

(London: 1546? – 23 July 1584)

Heere lies the Daye that darknes could not blynd
When popish fogges had ouer cast the sunne
This Daye the cruell night did leaue behynd
To view and shew what bloudi Actes weare donne
He set a Fox to wright how Martyrs runne
By death to lyfe: Fox ventured paynes & health
To giue them light; Daye spent in print his wealth
But God with gayn retornd his wealth agayne
And gaue to him: as he gaue to the poore
Tow wyues he had pertakers of his payne
Each wyfe twelve babes and each of them one more
Als was the last encrease of his stoore
Who mourning long for being left alone
Set upp this toombe her self bond to a Stone

obijt 23 Iulii. 84

The epitaph on the brass memorial plate erected by John Day's widow in the parish church at Little Bradley, Suffolk, sketches his career in broad outline. Throughout his career as a stationer Day zealously supported religious reform. His zeal was so well known that in *Beware the Cat* (1570) William Baldwin's allusion to Day's print shop over Aldersgate signaled to readers the religious leanings of his fictional guests. According to his epitaph Day lived through two periods of light – the reigns of Edward VI and Elizabeth I – which surrounded a period of "darknes," the reign of Mary I. Following that darkness Day published John Foxe's *The Actes and Monuments* (1563), a book that publicly recon-

firmed Day's Protestant beliefs and assured his place in history. The claim that God gave to Day as he gave to the poor is problematic. While Day gave some alms, the poorer members of the Stationers' Company would have disputed the veracity of this claim.

Day's epitaph is as interesting for what it does not say about him as for what it reveals. In restoring Day's wealth to him, God's collaborators – the episcopal hierarchy of the Church of England and the earl of Leicester – are not mentioned. Day's association with John Ponet, the bishop of Winchester, was partially responsible for his patent on *The ABC with Little Catechism* (1553). This royal grant originated during the tenure of John Dudley, earl of Northumberland, as protector of Edward VI. Northumberland's son, Robert Dudley, earl of Leicester, was instrumental in reinstating Day's privilege after the accession of Elizabeth I, and John Dudley was one of the patrons of Thomas Sternhold, whose metrical version of the Psalms was another of Day's exclusive printing privileges. The popularity of both *The ABC* and *The Metrical Psalter* (1560) formed the basis of Day's wealth. Furthermore, the English episcopacy abetted the popularity of *The Actes and Monuments* by ordering that a copy of that work be chained in a public place in all English cathedrals. With official encouragement the books that John Day printed shaped the ways members of the Church of England worshiped and the ways they saw the history of their church and country.

If Day were not remembered as the publisher of Foxe's great work, he would nonetheless be remembered as an innovator in the marketing of print. He published Roger Ascham's *The Scholemaster* (1570), the first English translation of Euclid (1570), and the first authorized edition of *The Tragidie of Ferrex and Porrex,* or *Gorboduc* (1570), by Thomas Norton and Thomas Sackville. He was one of the first printers to mix roman and black letter types in his books, and he was the first to print books in Anglo-Saxon type. He also printed books in Latin, Greek, French, and Dutch. Day had a large stock of printer's tools, including a wide variety of types, ornaments, and woodcut illustrations with which he made even the most modest of his books visually appealing. He marketed *The Metrical Psalter* and the works of Thomas Becon in every format from folio to thirty-twomo, thereby offering those books to the widest possible audience. Day should also be remembered as a printer of Christian humanist texts and as an innovator in the marketing of print.

The year of Day's birth is established by a woodcut device that he used in his deluxe folios. The device features a right-facing profile portrait of Day with the date 1562 floating in the background. "Ætatis suæ XXXX" (his age, forty) appears inside the border surrounding the portrait. The earliest accounts of Day's life assert that he was born at Dunwich, Suffolk. C. F. Oastler is inclined to accept the theory of Day's Suffolk origins, since a history of the area by the famous chronicler John Stow is addressed to a Master Day, its supposed commissioner. Oastler has been unable to find conclusive evidence among Dunwich church records or Suffolk subsidy and muster lists that any Day family lived in the area, however, and Day's origins are therefore uncertain.

When he once took up the vocation of stationer, Day quickly became prominent. As with his origins, his training in the art of printing is obscure. He is thought to have been apprenticed to Thomas Gibson, since he used a device that once belonged to Gibson. Yet the device, which depicts a man bending over a prone sleeper and admonishing him to "Arise, for it is Day," would have been appropriate for John Day regardless of whether he had ever been apprenticed to Gibson. The dates of the earliest books attributed to Day were printed around 1546, when he was not yet a member of the Stationers' Company. He was, however, a free citizen of London circa 1546. He could not have served a full apprenticeship, as he would have been only twenty-four years old at that date, but he was translated from the Stringers' Company to the Stationers' Company in 1550. Unfortunately the records of the Stringers' Company for this era are not extant, so it is not known how Day achieved his freedom. By 1548 he was producing many books both alone and in partnership with William Seres, and the majority of these aimed to dispel the "popish fogges" of earlier times.

Day and Seres were partners in Protestant belief as well as in finances. Together they produced inexpensive octavos that addressed the most pressing religious issues of their time, and they consistently supported Protestant positions. Whether or not *The tragical death of David Beaton bisshoppe of sainct Andrews* (1548) by Sir David Lindsay was actually their first book together, as Henry Richard Tedder asserts, it is consistent ideologically with the rest of the Day-Seres catalogue. The book is a modest octavo in which the tragedy is a matter of Protestant interpretation. Lindsay transforms the story of Cardinal Beaton's death into a cautionary tale aimed at stubborn Catholic clergy reluctant to give up their temporal power. More frequently Day and Seres weighed into the controversy surrounding the Mass and the Eucharist. During 1548 ten of the twenty books that they jointly issued addressed these subjects. The authors whom they published on eucharistic matters included John Calvin, Luke Shepherd, Thomas Broke, Robert Crowley, and William Turner, all of whom were staunchly anti-Catholic. Day and Seres also participated in the Protestant project of disseminating Scripture in the vernacular. In 1548 they published an octavo edition of William Tyndale's English New Testament and his commentary on Matthew. Only one of their 1548 books, William Turner's *The Names of herbes in Greke Latin Englishe Duche & Frenche,* treats a nonreligious subject. Day and Seres exerted the power of their presses strenuously in support of religious reform.

During his partnership with Seres, Day published similar religious books under his own imprint. Of the eight books that Day published alone during 1548, only one was not on a religious subject. Among those issued under Day's imprint in 1548 were *A myrroure or lokynge glasse wherin you may beholde the sacramente of baptisme described,* by John Frith, and *A breue cronycle of the bysshope of Romes blessynge & his prelates rewardes from the tyme of kynge Heralde,* both of which echo the anti-Catholic themes found in Day's work with Seres. Day's 1548 edition of *Wyclif's Wicket* includes the testimony of

Brass memorial plaque to John Day in Little Bradley Church, Suffolk

John Lassels and William Tracy, considered martyrs by many Protestants, and it was edited by Miles Coverdale, the future bishop of Exeter and translator of the Bible. Day's individual work as a printer contributed to the current of religious reform in England.

The events precipitated by Day and Seres's publication of Shepherd's *Jon Bon and the Mast Parson* (1548) illustrate the nature of their partnership. This satiric poem aims its abuse at the Catholic clergy and lampoons superstitions surrounding the Eucharist. Publication of the poem nearly resulted in Day's imprisonment, since it offended the Catholics among London's aldermen. However, Edward Underhill, the gentleman pensioner who was a confidant of Bishop Hooper and John Dudley, defused the controversy by stressing the "pythe and mery" nature of Shepherd's work. Why Day should have been considered more responsible for the book than Seres is not clear, but the punishment of Day would make more sense if he were the printer of the book. Since Day's name always appeared first in their joint imprints and often in a larger type font, Day may perhaps have been the printing member of the partnership and Seres primarily a bookseller and source of capital.

The two continued to publish books under joint imprint until 1550, and their books continued to espouse a Protestant ideology. In his *Survey of London* (1598) Stow says that Day's first place of business was "in Sepulchres parishe, a little above Holburne Conduit." He shared these premises with Seres at the sign of the Resurrection from 1547 through 1549, after which time Day moved to rooms built upon the city wall near Aldersgate. These premises were Day's principal place of business and residence until his death. At about this same time Seres moved to Peter's College at the west end of St. Paul's Churchyard. Imprints from this period indicate that the partners sold books at the sign of the Resurrection in Cheapside near the Little Conduit as well as from their individual establishments. Their business must have been very remunerative to have required or allowed them to maintain three separate shops.

Among the more important items published under Day and Seres's imprint were their editions of the Holy Scriptures. In 1549 and 1550 they published a complete edition of the Bible, including the Apocrypha, in a series of five modest octavo volumes; the fifth of these volumes containing the Pentateuch was issued under Day's individual imprint in 1551. In 1549 they also participated in producing an elaborate five-part folio edition of the Bible. This edition, often attributed to its translator, Thomas Becke, had a main title page printed in two colors and contained many intricate woodcut illustrations and decorated initial letters. Becke's Bible was a deluxe product clearly intended for wealthy buyers, as the octavos were intended for an audience of more modest means.

The contrast between the Day-Seres folio and octavo editions of the Bible reveals the contrast between the different market conceptions of the two men. While Day produced inexpensive books in small formats throughout his career, he consistently produced large deluxe volumes as well. Except for the odd bit of single-sheet folio ephemera, Seres printed only one folio-sized item after 1549. By reinvesting a portion of his profits Day built a large stock of printers' tools, which enabled him to print in any format from the elaborate folio to the most modest thirty-twomo and for any market from the deluxe to the cheap and popular. Seres was not inclined to print for the deluxe market, as he was instead satisfied with printing primarily for the cheap and popular market. Many patterns of doing business that Day established during his collaboration with Seres remained consistent throughout his career.

When Day found that one of his properties was popular, he exploited its profitability by packaging in it a wide variety of formats. Some of the works that he printed originally with Seres as individual editions in small formats Day eventually reprinted as elaborate collections in larger formats. The partners first printed an octavo edition of Hugh Latimer's *Sermon of the Plow* in 1548, and it proved popular enough to warrant another edition in that same year. In 1549 they printed four octavo editions of *The fyrste sermon of Mayster Hugh Latimer, whiche he preached before the kynges grace* and three of *The seconde sermon of Master Hugh Latimer, which he preached before the kinges grace,* also in octavo.

One indication that the partnership between Day and Seres was dissolving is the fact that Day began printing Latimer's sermons under Day's own imprint in 1550. In that year he issued two editions of *A most faithfull sermon preached before the kynges most excellente maiestye and hys most honorable Councell M.D.L.* and one of *A sermon of Master Latimer, preached at Stamford the ix day of october. Anno M.CCCCC. and fyftie,* all in octavo. In 1562 Day issued *27 Sermons preached by the ryght reverende father, and constant Martyr of Jesus Christ Maister Hugh Latimer,* the first of his multipart quarto collections of Latimer's sermons. He contin-

ued to print and expand these collections thereafter, issuing editions in 1571, 1572, 1575, 1578, and 1582.

Day's handling of the works of Thomas Becon shows a similar pattern. Day and Seres together published Becon's *The castell of comforte* (1549), *The fortresse of the faythfull* (1550, two editions), and *The iewel of ioye* (1550) in modest octavo editions. After his split with Seres, Day issued so many editions of Becon's works in small formats that forty separate editions from the period 1551–1584 are extant. In fact, in 1564 Day completed publication of *The Worckes of Thomas Becon,* an elaborate, three-volume folio edition that collected everything Day had already printed by Becon as well as some works that had not appeared in print before. Day had begun printing the works of Latimer and Becon in partnership with Seres, and they were among the properties that Day retained when the partnership dissolved in 1550. Day's treatment of the works of both writers was characteristic of his marketing techniques.

Barely thirty years old when he secured his first royal license for the exclusive printing of specific books, Day succeeded in protecting his most lucrative products by obtaining royal patents to print them. In 1553 he was granted a patent covering the works of Becon and of John Ponet, the bishop of Winchester. Bishop Ponet's *Brevis Catechismus* (known in English translation as *The Little Catechism*) proved to be lucrative for Day when it was appended to *The ABC.* However, because Ponet's *Brevis Catechismus* was originally written in Latin, Day became embroiled in a dispute with Raynold Wolfe, who already held a patent on all Latin books. The dispute was settled when Wolfe agreed to allow Day to print the *Brevis Catechismus* in English, while Wolfe retained the rights to print it in Latin. On 25 March 1553 Day was granted a royal patent on *The Little Catechism,* as well as on all other works of Ponet and of Becon without limit of time. Day moved to exploit this privilege immediately, printing *The A.B.C. with the Lords praier, the .xii. articles of the Christen fayth* and *A short catechisme, or playn instruction* before 1553 ended. Eventually Day was able to protect all his most lucrative properties in the same way that he protected *The Little Catechism* and Becon's works.

Generally Day's books are visually appealing and technically proficient. His works were not on the cutting edge of technology when compared with those produced in Paris, but many were more sophisticated than those of the average English printer. Day was among the first of the English printers to use italic and roman types in the same

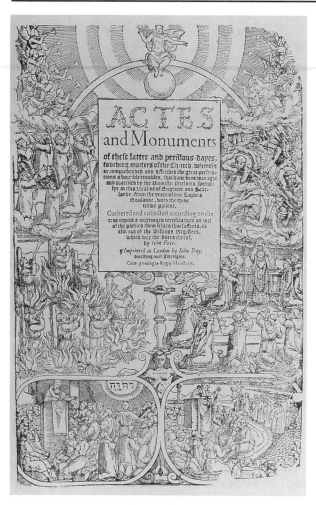

*Day's title page for Foxe's 1563 history of the Christian Church
and the sufferings of its martyrs*

book. He used decorated initials and woodcut illustrations more routinely than the average Elizabethan printer, especially in books printed in small formats, and he was one of the earliest English printers of musical notation. The high quality of many of Day's books stems from his early years as a printer.

During the late 1540s Day developed alliances with Protestant members of the print trade from the Continent, in the Low Countries, and among the Dutch community in London. His association with Continental tradesmen was part of the reason that his books were more sophisticated than those generally comprising the English book trade. As early as 1548 Day employed Stephen Mierdmann, a Dutchman living in London, to print some of his books, and in a 1549 roll of foreign workmen living in London such men as Gysberd Geyson, John Hollinder, Henry Fleteman, and Mychell van Lendon were all listed as servants of Day's dwelling at his premises

under Aldersgate. A similar inventory from 1550 lists Jacob Pieter as a printer working with Day. The punches for many of his most attractive types were cut by François Guyot, a French Protestant who lived in Antwerp. Day's association with the Guyot family was apparently a close one, as François's sons Gabriel and Christopher lodged with him in 1576. The constant tide of Protestant immigrants to England during the mid sixteenth century allowed Day to stay in close touch with the development of print technology.

By 1553 many of the bases of Day's later success as a stationer were already established. He had become known as a zealous voice for Protestantism. His zeal had recommended him to John Dudley's government as a reliable printer of *The Little Catechism,* and the royal patent he was granted on that work included a claim to Becon's works. He had begun to cultivate connections within the Dutch printing community that provided him with access to more-sophisticated printing technology, particularly in typefounding. Early in 1553 Day's future was promising, but by the end of the year the reign of Mary I interrupted his future.

Accounts of Day's activities during the reign of Mary agree on several points. He is said to have been imprisoned and then to have fled abroad. Several books attributed to Day during the years 1553 and 1554 bear false imprints. The government of Mary was moving during October 1554 to stem the torrent of anti-Catholic propaganda flooding England, and that Day was imprisoned for printing subversive books is indisputable. Whether he printed any of the extant books with false imprints and whether he spent any time in exile are more-dubious propositions.

Two contemporaries briefly recount Day's troubles during the reign of Mary. In *The Actes and Monuments* Foxe relates that Day spoke with John Rogers in the Tower of London while Rogers was awaiting execution there. Henry Machyn, a Catholic sympathizer, states in his diary that John Day, one of Day's servants, an unspecified priest, and another printer were committed to the Tower on 16 October 1554 for having printed "noythy" (naughty) books. Since John Rogers was in the Tower at this time awaiting his execution (which occurred on 4 February 1555), Day was in prison during the latter part of 1554. How long he was in prison is not known, but he was certainly released sometime during 1555.

Most subversive books were issued under false imprints, two of which are often associated with Day: N. Dorcaster of Wittenberg and M.

Wood of Rouen. The aim of using a false imprint is concealment, of course, and therefore it is hard to establish the veracity of such attributions. Typographical evidence is often adduced as the best available, but such evidence is not reliable especially because subversive printers were careful to limit themselves to the most generic types.

One of the last Dorcaster books to be published, *The humble unfained confession of belefe of certain poor banished men* (1554), was the work of Ponet. The exiled bishop could have been expected to choose someone like Day to print his confession, for Day was both zealously Protestant and already known to him. Nonetheless, the attribution of the Dorcaster books to Day must be considered tentative.

The attribution of the Wood books to Day rests on a marginally firmer basis. In the 1563 edition of *The Actes and Monuments* John Foxe says that William Cooke induced "this oure printer" to produce an English translation of Stephen Gardiner's Latin tract, *De vera obediencia* (of true obedience). This tract, which bears the imprint "Roane, M wood," would have been embarrassing to Gardiner, bishop of Winchester and lord chancellor under Mary, for it advocates royal supremacy over the church and argues against papal supremacy. What had been an expedient position when Gardiner wrote the tract during the reign of Henry VIII had become inexpedient under the Catholic Mary. Gardiner would certainly have considered the printing of this book naughty.

Furthermore, Gardiner held the see from which Day's associate Ponet had been ejected, and in his secular capacity as lord chancellor, Gardiner approved the suspension of Day's royal patents. Day had reason enough to embarrass Gardiner. The evidence that Day printed at least one of the Wood books is circumstantially sound, and if one rejects all of the 1554 books attributed to Day that do not bear his imprint, one can only conclude that Day printed no books that year. Why Day should have been imprisoned for subversive printing during a year in which he printed no books is difficult to understand. It is true that no books have been attributed to Day's press during 1555, but his imprisonment in the autumn of 1554 for having printed books odious to the government of Mary would make this understandable. Day's release from prison is the time at which most of his biographers report that he went into exile on the Continent.

John Foxe is the primary source for the belief that Day spent some time in exile, but for this belief Foxe seems less reliable than for others: his account of Day's exile lacks the corroboration that exists for accounts of Day's imprisonment. It could be argued that Day's printing for the Dutch church in London after 1560 was a result of bonds he formed while living as an exile in the Low Countries. However, such an argument must be balanced against the facts that Day had worked with Dutch printer Stephen Mierdmann in 1548 and had employed Dutch workmen in his own house as early as 1549. William Whittingham vaguely suggests that a message entrusted to Day by Rogers reached the Continent. As Oastler points out, the delivery of a message does not necessarily betoken Day's physical presence in Frankfurt. This is especially true, because printers still in England smuggled propaganda back and forth from the Continent as a matter of course. Foxe's claim that Day fled to the Continent after his release from the Tower cannot be confirmed.

Certainly Day could not have spent much time in exile, for he was printing again by 1556 – although his fortunes had clearly diminished. His Protestant sympathies had caused his royal patents to be canceled, and most of his religious patrons were either dead or in exile. Many of the books that Day printed during 1556 and 1557 were executed for other bookmen; he was no longer in a position to act as his own publisher. For instance, he printed *The epistles and gospels of every Sonday and holy daye throughoute the whole yeare. After the vse of the catholicke church* (1556) for booksellers Thomas Petit and Abraham Veale. This is an interesting book to have been printed by a noted Protestant, and it is not the only orthodox liturgical book that Day printed during the reign of Mary. He also produced *The prymer in English for children after the vse of Salisburye* (1556) and *The primer in Latine* (1557).

No matter how wealthy he had been in 1553, Day had not worked profitably for the better part of two years, and he had a growing family: his oldest son, Richard, had been born in 1552. Apparently Day simply needed work, and his need made him reliable in the eyes of booksellers who hired him. Day printed ephemera such as William Cunningham's *Almanack* (1557) at this time, and he was printing a greater percentage of nonreligious books, such as Thomas Elyot's *The bankette of sapience* (1557). Conspicuously absent from his production during 1556–1557 are religious books with Protestant ideology or controversial subject matter. As a result of his diminished circumstances, Day was forced to work as a job printer. However, he was still a person of some note in the printing community.

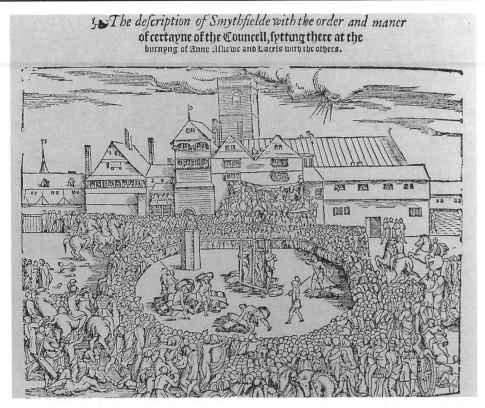

Illustration of "The Burning of Anne Askew at Smithfield" from Day's edition of John Foxe's Actes
and Monuments *(1563)*

When the Stationers' Company was granted a royal charter in 1557, John Day was fifty-seventh on the list of free printers whose names were appended to the charter. Since Mary was still queen, Day's appearance on the charter testifies to his rehabilitation in the eyes of the government. His position on the list also bespeaks his diminished position within the company, but Day was recovering, and he never completely lost his technical resources as a printer.

This is amply demonstrated by Leonard Digges's *A boke named Tectonicon* (1556), which Day printed for Thomas Gemini. This carefully printed octavo volume required a large amount of type: five type fonts and a woodcut illustration were used on its title page, and *Tectonicon* contains many ornamental initials. Most of the capital for the volume certainly came from Gemini, whom the imprint describes as "dwellyng within the blacke Friers: who is there ready exactly to make all the Insturments appertaynyng to this booke." Day had retained his stock of tools and expertise to produce an elaborately printed book, but he did not have the capital to finance such an enterprise.

The second item in the Stationers' Register for 1557–1558 is an entry to John Day for a proclamation from the lord mayor setting the legal prices of bread and ale in London. This entry is the earliest evidence of Day's activity as printer to the city of London, and because no reliable register records the printing of books by particular stationers for the years preceding the grant of the royal charter, it is impossible to know how long Day had held this office before 1557. Proclamations and orders printed for the city government seem to have been part of the ephemeral work that kept Day financially afloat during the latter years of the reign of Mary. In 1558 he printed thirteen books – his highest production since 1551, if one discounts the dubious attributions of 1554. Even before the death of Queen Mary, Day was reestablishing himself slowly, and he moved quickly to better his position after the accession of Elizabeth I.

Elizabeth's accession marked the beginning of John Day's renaissance as one of the most influential stationers. Exiled members of the church hierarchy returned from the Continent or from rustication to resume their places as bishops, deans, and canons. Nobles such as Robert Dudley, who had been merely tolerated under Mary, began to wield influence in the Privy Council, and Day began to work toward restoring his privileges. On 11 November 1559 Day was granted an exclusive license under the Privy Seal to print William Cunningham's *The Cosmographical Glasse* for life and to produce any other books at his own expense for the next seven years. Christopher Barker, the queen's printer, states in a 1582 report to the Privy Council that Day had his patents at the urging of the earl of Leicester. In their separate spheres, the influence of both men was growing and would continue to do so.

Perhaps the most interesting thing about Day's 1559 license is its ambiguity. With only minor qualification he is granted the exclusive privilege to print any books that are "compiled at Daye's expense." He is enjoined not to print any books that are the subjects of other patents or any that are "repugnant to Holy Scripture or the law." The locution "compiled at Daye's expense" is crucial, because it grants him property rights to anything that he takes the trouble to set in type. Day's patent was among those that established the precedent of intellectual property in the publishing business, and it was also the basis on which he was able to establish ownership of his most lucrative and contested properties.

While Day's patent explicitly mentions neither *The ABC with Little Catechism* nor *The Metrical Psalter,* it implicitly mentions both of these, which were to be his most profitable books. All that Day needed to do to establish a claim to either was set them in type and print them at his own expense. His publication of *The psalmes of Dauid in Englishe metre by T Sterneholde and others* (1560) demonstrates this aptly, for, comprising only 87 of the requisite 151, the work is not a complete psalter. Day moved quickly to establish a claim to the Psalms in English meter with musical notation, and he was then free to print a complete version at his leisure. In fact, Day published two additional incomplete editions of the metrical psalter in 1561 before he finally printed a complete version in 1562. In the same year that he published *The whole booke of psalmes, collected into Englysh metre by T Sternehold, J Hopkins, & others: with apt notes to synge them withall* (1562), he also published *The residue of all Dauids psalmes in metre made by J Hopkins and others, Now fyrst imprinted and sette forth in this fourme for such as haue bookes already.* It was crucial that Day establish his claim to the metrical psalms as quickly as possible, but he was not about to lose customers who had one of the earlier volumes and who might have been loath to pay twice for some psalms.

All of these editions of the Psalter were printed "Cum gratia et priuilegio Regiæ Maiestatis

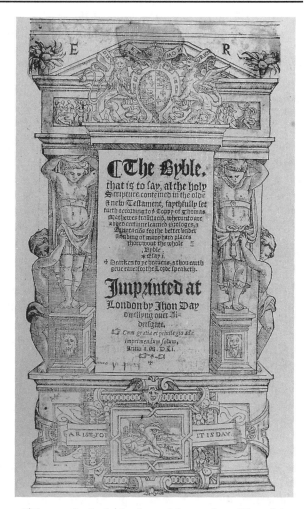

Title page for the final volume of the complete edition of the Bible, which Day and William Seres began printing in 1549 and which Day completed in 1551

per septennium" – that is, by the grace and privilege of her royal majesty for seven years. When this patent expired, Day was granted another more specific one. The license of 2 June 1567 granted him the right "to print the Psalms of David in English metre with notes, the A.B.C. with the little catechism . . . , and all such books and works as he has printed or shall print which are compiled or translated by any learned man at the costs of Daye only" for a period of ten years and with the same minor qualifications as the patent of 1559 had specified. By means of this two-stage strategy Day acquired the exclusive right to the metrical psalms and assured himself that they were indeed worth the trouble. From 1560 until 1584 seventy-three editions of *The Metrical Psalms* that survive were issued under Day's imprint. They were issued in every format from folio to thirty-twomo, including a 1563 quarto set of four-part books, each presenting one of the parts of the harmony. *The Metrical Psalms* became one of the staples of Day's profitable business. Like the position of Robert Dudley, Day's position was stronger in 1567 than it had been in 1559. The phrase, "or translated by any learned man," opened possibilities that Day had come to appreciate by 1567.

The Actes and Monuments was a book produced precisely as Day's 1567 patent was to specify, a book compiled by a learned man at Day's expense. John Foxe, the compiler of that weighty tome, was by any measure a learned man. Educated at Magdalene College, Oxford, where he completed both B.A. and M.A., Foxe there formed friendships with Latimer, Tynsdale, and Richard Bertie, who were fervent Protestants and whose deaths or persecutions *The Actes and Monuments* eventually was to chronicle. Although Foxe was a popular preacher and a respected writer, he never achieved material success, and his means were so modest that he had to be supported while compiling his Protestant saints' legend.

While working on the first edition of *The Actes and Monuments,* Foxe split his time between the Aldgate residence of his former pupil Thomas Howard, duke of Norfolk, and Day's printing shop. From the time of his return to England in 1559 until the publication of this work in 1563, Foxe labored primarily, but not entirely, on it. Day helped support Foxe by employing him as both a proofreader and as an editor, and the latter worked intermittently for Day in various capacities. They collaborated on three subsequent editions of *The Actes and Monuments* that appeared during Day's lifetime, and its success can be attributed largely to Day's skillful printing and marketing of it.

Day and Foxe had apparently conceived this work almost immediately after Foxe's return to England in October 1559. *The Freindly Farewell* by Nicholas Ridley, a popular Edwardian bishop who had been burned as a heretic by Mary, was published by Day on 10 November 1559 with a preface by Foxe, who calls Ridley's farewell letter a "monument" to Ridley's faith, a monument left by God for the living. This book was the first monument to the persecutions under Mary that Day published, and, as if it were an appetizer to a sumptuous main course, the work took its place among the acts and other monuments that fill Foxe's martyrology.

Comprising more than eighteen hundred folio pages, the first edition of *The Actes and Monuments* was truly massive, and subsequent editions in 1570, 1576, and 1583 exceeded more than two thousand pages, as Foxe revised and added material that filled two folio volumes. The first edition was printed predominantly in black letter type and contained many full-page woodcut illustrations that were crafted specifically for that book. Preliminaries to the volume included four dedicatory epistles, a preface, and a massive calendar of martyrs similar to that which the Catholic Church used for its saints. This calendar did double duty as a table of contents. The edition also included marginal subject guides and scores of decorative initials. This 1563 *Acts and Monuments* resembled his 1551 Bible, and it rivaled in lavishness anything that Day had produced until that date. The expense of producing the book can be appreciated from the payment that Day received from Magdalene College, Oxford, to which Day sent a copy: £6 13s. 4d. Even if it had been a specially printed version of the text using superior quality paper or parchment, this sum is enormous for the period. Subsequent editions of the book were more elaborate than the first.

The 1570 edition of *The Actes and Monuments* marked the culmination of Day's activities as a printer and a Protestant. The title page for the volume offers an elaborately engraved visual representation of the church of reformers and the damned church of Rome. The engraving neatly divides the sheep from the goats by depicting the church of elect Englishmen on the right and the damned church of Catholics on the left. The initial *C* cut for the dedicatory epistle to Queen Elizabeth in the 1570 edition is one of the finest, most elaborate initials produced in sixteenth-century England. Within the compass of the letter Day, Foxe, and another figure stand to the right of the queen, who sits enthroned and holding sword and orb while she crushes underfoot the serpent and the Pope with his keys. The ideology born by the initial is obvious and is expressed explicitly in the epistle following the initial.

In the second edition of the book the dedicatory epistle was completely rewritten to serve as a justification for that second run, for

> the blustryng and styrryng was then against that poore booke through all quarters in England, euen to the gates of Louaine: so that no English Papist almost in all the Realme thought him selfe a perfect Catholicke, vnless he had cast out some word or other, to geve the booke a blow.

Additional material was also added to the narrative throughout the text, and the marginalia were greatly expanded. Furthermore, the two columns of text were enclosed within thin lines of ruling, and a wider range of types and fonts was used. The print-

Letter from one of the sets of initials used by Day, whose artist, possibly John Bettes, may have cut this series of letters specially for use in William Cunningham's Cosmographical Glasse *(1559)*

ing of this edition was so technically demanding that Foxe sued William Cecil, Lord Burghley, to allow Day to employ more than the legal maximum of four foreign workmen in producing it. The shape of the narrative was recast to emphasize the triumph of God's providence embodied in the figure of Elizabeth, whose story of persecution and enthronement concludes the book. Subsequent editions of *The Actes and Monuments* in 1576 and 1583 were as lavish as the second edition, and in minor ways their texts were revised, but the providential design of the 1570 narrative remained intact. Day created the demand for these subsequent editions by skillfully taking advantage of events in 1570.

The year 1570 was crucial in the history of England and in the career of John Day. One reason that he needed so many workmen in producing the second edition of *The Actes and Monuments* was to ensure that it would be finished before the convocation of English bishops in that year. When they perused the book, the English episcopacy concluded that Foxe's historical vision was fit reading for their flock and moved to make it available to those who could not afford the expensive folio. On 3 April 1570 the convocation issued an order requiring that a copy of Foxe's book be chained in every English cathedral and in the homes of bishops and other ecclesiastical officials. While this order was never confirmed by Parliament, it was nonetheless common to find the book chained next to the Bible in English churches for a long time thereafter.

On 1 February 1571 Matthew Parker, archbishop of Canterbury; Edwin Sandys, bishop of London; and Richard Cox, bishop of Ely, wrote letters enjoining the municipal government of London to provide for the public display of *The Actes and Monuments*. The Aldermen eventually ordered that a copy should be chained in a public place in the city orphanage and in the halls of all guilds with the means to afford the book. Of course, 1570 was also the year of the papal bull excommunicating Queen Elizabeth and relieving her subjects of their duties to her. Day published three treatises by Thomas Norton in response – *A Bull granted by the pope* (1570, two editions), *An addition declaratorie to the bulles* (1570), and *A disclosing of the greate Bull* (1570). Day shared this support of the queen against the Pope with the majority of Englishmen, and the pa-

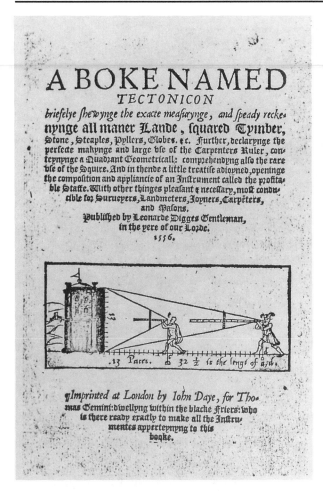

*Title page with five different type fonts and a woodcut,
illustrating Day's technical skill and resources as
a printer*

triotic religious vision he published in *The Actes and Monuments* was both a symptom of and a partial cause for Elizabeth's popularity.

Day had a long-standing reciprocal relationship with Matthew Parker, who was Elizabeth's archbishop of Canterbury and who, both as an archbishop and as a private citizen, employed Day as a printer. In a letter to Cecil dated 13 December 1572 Parker indicated that he had made provisions to answer Nicholas Sander's book, *De visibili monarchia ecclesiæ* (1571), by commissioning Day "to caste a new Italian letter" with which to print the reply. Bartholomew Clerke's *Fidelis serui infideli responsio* (Faithful response to an unfaithful servant) was published by the Day press in 1573. Although it was not printed in the italic type mentioned by Parker, presumably Parker had paid for the new type that Day had cut. Quid pro quo was the rule of Day and Parker's relations, and in this case Parker received the services of a reliable printer to answer

Sander's polemic, while Day added to his printing stock.

In his leisure time Parker was an enthusiastic antiquarian, and he often called upon Day when he needed a printer to help him indulge his hobby. Parker had commissioned Day to have the first Anglo-Saxon type cast, and with this handsome font Day had printed a sermon by Ælfric that Parker had titled *A testimonie of antiquitie* (1566), a work for which Parker wrote the preface and did the editing, the first Anglo-Saxon book printed in England. Until the archbishop's death Day continued to print limited editions of antiquarian curiosities for Parker — including *The Gospels of the Fower Evangelists* (1571), edited by Foxe in Anglo-Saxon, and Bishop Joannes Asser's *Ælfredi regis res gestae* (1574), a copy of which Parker presented to Elizabeth.

Day had other connections with the ecclesiastical hierarchy that were even more profitable to him than his relationship with Parker — for instance, that which followed the royal patent that Day secured on Alexander Nowell's *Catechismus* (1570). Nowell, the dean of St. Paul's Cathedral, had written his first catechism, later known as *The Large Catechism,* at Cecil's suggestion during the late 1560s. The convocation of English bishops approved Nowell's finished work, which had been reviewed in draft by Cecil. When the first edition in Latin appeared, it was printed by Reginald Wolf, as were the next four editions — two of them in Latin and the other two in Greek. In 1570 Thomas Norton made an English translation of Nowell's *Large Catechism,* and Day published it. Nowell prepared two shorter versions of his catechism, known as *The Middle Catechism* (c. 1570) and *The Short Catechism* (c. 1572), which Norton also translated and Day published as well.

On 12 May 1574 Day was granted a patent for ten years on all of Nowell's works, with *The Large Catechism* and *The Small Catechism* named specifically by their Latin appellations. Thereafter Day published all versions of Nowell's catechisms, whether they were in English, Latin, or Greek. Nowell had been a friend of John Foxe since their college days at Oxford, and Foxe may have recommended Day to Nowell. Day had also been publishing since 1569 the antipapist tracts of Thomas Norton, the English translator of Nowell's catechisms, when Day published *A warnyng agaynst the dangerous practises of papistes.* Norton was also a friend of Foxe and would have known Day in Norton's official capacity as the lawyer for the Stationers' Company. Day clearly enjoyed a reputation for reli-

An initial letter perhaps specially cut for Actes *and* Monuments *and depicting
(from the left) Day, Foxe, and another man at the side of the
enthroned Queen Elizabeth*

ability among the members of England's secular and ecclesiastical hierarchies.

As the production of Day's presses increased during the late 1560s, the variety of subjects covered in his books also increased. Most of Day's books still dealt with religious subjects, but he began to produce many titles that could be classified under the rubric of humanist learning. Norton and Sackville's Senecan tragedy in blank verse, *The Tragedy of Gorboduc* (1565), had been printed in an unauthorized edition by William Griffith. When Norton revised his classically influenced tragedy, Day printed it under the title *The Tragidie of Ferrex and Porrex.*

Day also branched out by printing the first English translation of a work by Euclid: *The elements of geometrie* (1570), translated by Sir Henry Billingsley, was one of Day's deluxe folios. It was lavishly illustrated, and the translator's preface makes it clear that Billingsley bore the cost of printing. Day published the first edition of *The Scholemaster,* a treatise on education by the late Roger Ascham, who had been tutor to Queen

Elizabeth during her youth. Since Ascham had been a friend of both Alexander Nowell and John Foxe, perhaps Day obtained his manuscript from one of these sources. In any event, Day also printed three subsequent editions of *The Scholemaster* in 1571, 1573, and 1579, and for several years after 1570 Day produced a smattering of other texts of scholarly interest – such as Thomas of Walshingham's *Ypodogime Neustriæ* (1574) and *General and rare memorials pertayning to the perfecte arte of nauigation* (1577).

After 1577 the character of Day's output changed again, as on 28 August of that year he received his last royal license. It was a renewal of the license granted in 1567 but with some differences. This grant was not for any fixed term, as those of 1559 and 1567 had been, but for life, and it also named Day's son, Richard, as joint patentee and stipulated that when Day or his son should die, the rights it conferred would reside with the survivor. At about this time Day's production of books began to narrow in scope, and from 1577 until his death he printed almost exclusively his steady sellers – multiple editions of

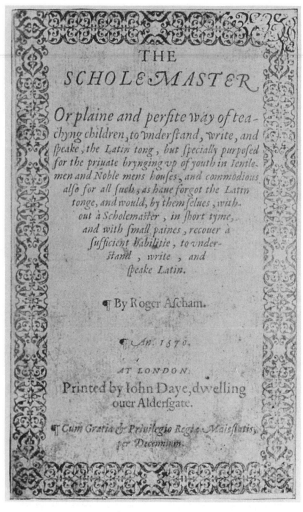

Day's title page for a treatise on education by Roger Ascham,
former tutor to Queen Elizabeth

works such as *The Metrical Psalms* (forty-three editions), Nowell's catechisms (nine editions), Becon's works (eight editions), and a final edition of *The Actes and Monuments* (1583). Thus, as he grew older Day prepared for the future by providing a new patent for his son and more capital for his wife.

Yet in retrospect, while Day might appear to have been one of the more prosperous as well as preeminent stationers, his relations with the Stationers' Company and its members were complicated. In 1558–1559 Day was fined five shillings by the Stationers' Company for printing *An excellent treatise made by Nostredamus*. Day was not above trying to cut costs by avoiding the company's registration charge, although he routinely protected his most important works through royal licenses. That he did routinely enter his copies in the Stationers' Register but still resorted to royal patents even after the advent of the royal charter shows, however, that he did not have complete faith in the company's ability to enforce his copyrights.

Day maintained commercial relationships for most of his career with men such as Abraham Veale, Anthony Kitson, and John Kingston, who made their livings in the book trade despite not being stationers. The Stationers' Company was not fond of having members of other companies working in the book trade, but such coolness apparently did not bother Day. He became a company officer for the first time in 1561, when he served as renter, and by 1563 he had become a master stationer and a member of the court of assistants. Throughout his tenure as an assistant Day participated in the annual audit of company finances and contributed generously to maintenance of the Stationers' Hall. He also served as ju-

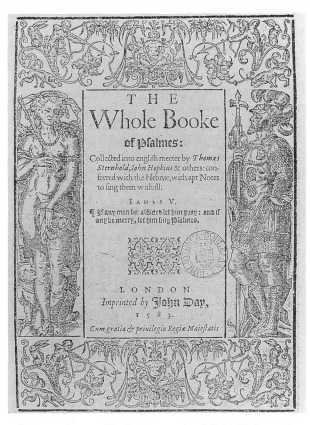

Title page for a psalter that Day employed John Wolfe to print,
using Day's imprint, in 1583

nior warden in 1564 and 1566, as senior warden in 1571 and 1575, and as company master for one term in 1580. As a master stationer Day was in many ways unexceptional and respectable, but he was also apt to work outside the company machinery when it suited his purposes.

Perhaps for that reason Day was not universally popular among stationers. When he built his bookshop in St. Paul's Churchyard at the expense of fifty pounds, rival booksellers hindered him by convincing the aldermen to refuse to let him occupy the shop, and Day was able to occupy these premises only after Archbishop Parker had interceded with Cecil on his behalf. That Day sought government intercession in the dispute rather than attempting arbitration through the Stationers' Company reveals how heavy-handed he could be. Along with four other stationers (including Richard Tottel, another holder of royal patents) he was summoned before the Court of Aldermen on 1 March 1575 "to answer objections." What the specific objections against Day and his fellows were is not known, but the most common objection against Day is easy to see: he was too successful. Most members of the book trade envied Day's exclusive privileges

to print popular and easily produced books such as *The ABC with Little Catechism*. Printers wanted to print such consistent sellers, and booksellers were unhappy at being forced to pay whatever wholesale price a patent holder such as Day demanded. During the last decade of his life his patents were infringed upon frequently, and a movement against monopolies developed.

This movement began sometime during August 1577 when a complaint was lodged with the Privy Council against the granting of royal patents. The complaint named Day and all the other principal patent holders and specifically stated that Day had "the Printinge of *A.B.C:* and *Cathechismes* with the sole selling of them by collour of A Commission These bookes weare the onlie Releif of the porest sort of that Companie." This was the first salvo in a war that was not satisfactorily settled until the next century.

The Privy Council responded by appointing a commission, consisting of John Hammond and Thomas Norton, to study the matter. This commission was weighted in favor of the monopolists, for Norton was lawyer to the Stationers' Company and did little to defuse the situation. One of the principal agitators against the monopolists was Day's former apprentice, John Wolfe, who used his knowledge of Day's business to gain an advantage. In a 1584 complaint to the Star Chamber Wolfe accused Day of overstrenuously pursuing a search of Wolfe's premises for pirated copies of *The Metrical Psalms.* He also accused Day of printing inferior copies of the Psalms, offered to pay a yearly fee of one hundred marks for the privilege of printing *The Metrical Psalms,* and promised to charge but one half of the current retail rate of six pence apiece.

Day answered such threats to his privileges in several ways. In 1582 he had lodged a complaint against Roger Ward, an ally of Wolfe, for illegally printing *The ABC.* He attempted to allay Wolfe's opposition by employing him to print *The Metrical Psalms* in 1583, but Wolfe responded by continuing to print the books without permission thereafter. Finally the Privy Council Commission mediated an agreement that was negotiated between such patentees as Day and the complainants. As part of the agreement designed to appease the poorer printers of the trade, Day ceded his rights to approximately thirty of his copies, including the works of Becon, Tyndale, Calvin, and Peter Martyr. Conspicuously absent from the list were *The ABC, The Metrical Psalms,* Nowell's *Catechisms,* and *The Actes and Monuments.* Yet this strategy did little to alleviate the situation, and John Day did not live to see the dispute resolved. He died on 23 July 1584 while traveling to visit his second wife's family in Suffolk, and he was buried in the parish church at Little Bradley.

Since he was a minister rather than a printer, Richard Day – who, under the terms of his father's 1577 license, had inherited the rights to all of John Day's remaining patents – agreed to allow a group of stationers to produce editions of his privileged books for a fee. Among Richard Day's assigns was Wolfe, who had abandoned antimonopolistic agitation when he received lucrative inducements from the patentees. Richard Day continued to exercise his father's privileges until his own death around 1606, when they became the property of the Stationers' Company. Day's books thereafter became part of the English stock. Day's most famous book, Foxe's *The Actes and Monuments,* continued to be printed by the Stationers' Company well into the seventeenth century.

During his career Day had engaged in almost every activity that a stationer might perform. His printing business must have been enormous, if the number of laborers he employed and presses he owned accurately indicate this. From 1561 through 1583 Day had bound nine apprentices, two of

whom had been freed by him and another of whom, John Wolfe, had been freed by the Fishmongers, the guild of fish sellers. According to the Stationers' Register Day had also redeemed four men who had not been apprenticed to him, and when Day had bound Peter Manfield as an apprentice in 1578, it was stipulated that Manfield would serve the first six years of his apprenticeship under Nicolas LeBlond, a binder. Late in his career Day had therefore been preparing to provide binding services on his premises.

In an inventory that Christopher Barker made of London printing houses and presses for lord Burghley during 1583, Day is listed as having four presses. His print shop had an enormous capacity, as he had printed more than two hundred editions in the 1570s alone. The language of his royal patents furthermore makes it clear that he had served both as a publisher and as a printer, and he had produced many of his most profitable or famous books at his own expense. Yet these publishing activities had not precluded him from working for customers such as Archbishop Parker and the city of London. Day's imprints make it clear that he had maintained a bookshop at his Aldersgate premises, and as his business had expanded during the 1570s he built a shop adjacent to St. Paul's Churchyard. Few if any Elizabethan stationers engaged in a variety of activities as wide as that which Day had pursued.

John Day's career demonstrated the power of the printing press both to shape public opinion and to enrich the holders of copyrights. Day and other holders of patents profoundly influenced the history of publishing, for they helped to establish the concepts of copyright and intellectual property. Without the attempts of such monopolists to protect their livelihoods, the notion of authorial copyright might not have evolved. Day's marketing of Foxe's *The Actes and Monuments* also helped shape the English people's view of their own history, for as a book next to the Bible in English churches, *The Actes and Monuments* helped the English foster a belief in themselves as a chosen people. Without that belief the English might perhaps not have amassed an empire.

References:

H. Anders, "The Elizabethan ABC and the Catechism," *Library,* fourth series 16 (June 1935): 32–48;

William Baldwin, *Beware the Cat,* edited by William A. Ringler and Michael Flachmann (San Marino, Cal.: Huntington Library, 1988);

Cyprian Blagden, *The Stationers' Company: A History, 1403–1959* (Cambridge, Mass.: Harvard University Press, 1960);

Thomas F. Didbin, ed., *Typographical Antiquities,* volume 1 (London: Miller, 1810);

Harry R. Hoppe, "John Wolfe, Printer and Publisher, 1579–1601," *Library,* fourth series 14 (December 1933): 241–288;

John N. King, *English Reformation Literature: The Tudor Origins of the Protestant Tradition* (Princeton: Princeton University Press, 1982);

Sir David Lindsay, *The Tragicall Death of David Beaton Bishope of Sainct Andrews* (London: Day & Seres, 1548);

Henry Machyn, *The Diary of Henry Machyn* (London: Camden Society, 1848);

A. L. N. Munby, "The Gifts of Elizabethan Printers to the Library of King's College, Cambridge," *Library,* fifth series 2 (March 1948): 224–232;

John G. Nichols, "Memoir of John Day the Printer," *Gentleman's Magazine,* 102 (November 1832): 417–421;

Nichols, ed., *Narratives of the Days of the Reformation* (London: Camden Society, 1859);

C. F. Oastler, *John Day, the Elizabethan Printer* (Oxford: Oxford Bibliographical Society, 1975);

Matthew Parker, *The Correspondence of Matthew Parker, Archbishop of Canterbury,* edited by John Bruce and T. T. Perowne (Cambridge: Cambridge University Press, 1853);

Hallett Smith, "English Metrical Psalms in the Sixteenth Century and Their Literary Significance," *Huntington Library Quarterly,* 9 (May 1946): 249–271;

John Stow, *Survey of London* (London: Wolfe, 1598);

J. Strype, *The Annals of the Reformation* (Oxford: Clarendon Press, 1824);

J. C. Tarr, "John Day, Printer of the Reformation," *Black Art,* 1, no. 3 (1962): 73–85;

Ernest J. Worman, *Alien Members of the Book-Trade During the Tudor Period* (London: Bibliographical Society, 1906).

                                                            – Bryan P. Davis

Henry Denham

(London: 1559 – 1590?)

In the introduction to his *Transcript of the Stationers' Registers,* Edward Arber recognizes Henry Denham as one whose place as a printer correlates with those of William Shakespeare or Edmund Spenser as authors, or of Sir Frances Drake or Sir Martin Frobisher as men of action. He apprenticed himself to Richard Tottel on 14 October 1556, and during his apprenticeship his first imprint appeared, *The treasure of gladnesse* (1559), a psalter with marginalia. He took his freedom on 30 August 1560. In 1564 Denham was printing in Whitecross Street, Cripplesgate, but he established his own printing shop in 1565 in Paternoster Row, at the sign of the Star. Early in his career, in 1564, he was fined for printing unlicensed primers, and in 1565 he was again fined for using indecorous language and improper behavior. In 1583 Denham moved to Aldersgate Street, still at the sign of the Star. There, according to a 1583 census of printing presses, Denham had four presses; only six other printers had more than he.

Denham's principal business initially derived from printing works by Protestant reformers, works such as a 1565 sermon of John Knox or Robert Crowley's *An Apologie or Defence, of Those Englishe Writers & Preachers Which Cerberus the Three Headed Dog of Hell, Chargeth wyth False Doctrine, vnder the Name of Predestination* (1566). Denham soon became both a productive and high-quality printer who, according to R. B. McKerrow, "was furnished with a large and varied assortment of letters, his blacks being noticeable for their clearness and beauty, while his nonpareil and other small sizes are remarkable for their regularity."

Denham's press produced some of the most important literary works, including translations of major classical writers, of both the Continental and English Renaissance. Among these were William Painter's *The Palace of Pleasure* (1566), Seneca's *Octavia,* titled *The ninth tragedy of Lucius Anneus Seneca* (1566), Pliny's *The Secrets and Wonders of the World* (1566), George Turbervile's translation of Ovid's *Heroicall Epistles* (1567) and Turbervile's own *Epitaphs, Epigrams, Songs and Sonets* (1570), Desiderius Erasmus's *Colloquia* (1568), T. Wylson's translation

Title page for the first English edition of Thomas Nuce's translation of a work by Seneca, printed by Denham in 1567

of *The three orations of Demosthenes* (1570), and Baldassare Castiglione's *The Courtyer* (1577).

He also printed Nicholas Udall's *Ralph Roister Doister* (1566?), often regarded as the earliest play of the English Renaissance, and many works reflecting the emerging interest of the Renaissance in natural philosophy, the science of the time and its applications. Among these were John Maplet's *A Greene Forest, or An Naturall Historie* (1567); Thomas Hill's *A contemplation of mysteries, effects and signification of comets* (1574?); Konrad von Gesner's *The newe Jewell of Health, wherein Is Contayned the Most Excellent Secretes of Phisicke and Philosophie* (1576); Girolamo Ruscelli's *Secreti . . . Six Hundred Foure Score and Odde Experienced Medicines* (1566); Hill's translation of *The Contemplation of Mankinde, Contayning a Singuler Discourse*

Title page for Thomas Hoby's translation of The Covrtyer,
*one of the central works of humanist philosophy in
sixteenth-century England*

after the *Art of Phisiognomie* (1571); Leonard Mascall's *A Booke of the Art and Maner, Howe to Plante and Graffe All Sortes of Trees* (1572); and Horatius Morus's *Tables of Surgerie* (1585).

McKerrow is uncertain about what time Denham's press achieved its excellence, but after 1583 Denham undoubtedly acquired some of his letters and devices from Henry Bynneman, who had previously acquired them from Reyner Wolfe. The excellence of Denham's printing was distinguished by more than the quality of his letters; he also apparently had a reputation for accuracy, for he printed many dictionaries and books on language. Some of these included William Salesbury's *A playen and familiar introduction teaching how to pronounce the letters of the Brytishe tongue, now commonly called Welshe* (1567); John Hart's *An orthographie, conteyning the due order and reason, howe to write or paint thimage of mannes voice* (1569) and *A methode or comfortable beginning for all unlearned whereby they may be taught to read English* (1570); Thomas Cooper's *Thesaurus linguæ Romanæ & Britannicæ* (1565); William Bullokar's *Bullokars*

Booke at Large, for the Amendment of Orthographie for English Speech . . . (1580); Ledoyen de la Pichonnaye's *A Playne treatise to learne in a short space the French tongue* (1576); and Jean Veron's *Dictionarie in Latine and English* (1584).

Two important sources of business for Denham were from the patents of William Seres and Henry Bynneman. From 1578 Denham was Seres's assignee for printing books of private prayer, psalters, and primers in both Latin and English, a lucrative patent that he used in producing Philipp Melanchthon's *Godly prayers, meete to be vsed in these later times* (1579); Johann Haberman's *The Enimie of Securitie, or a Dailie Exercise of Godly Meditations* (1580); *Psalter or Psalmes . . . from the Great Bible* (1580); *Psalter . . . pointed as it shall be soong in churches* (1580); Abraham Fleming's *An Epitaph . . . vpon the Godlie Life and Death of the Right Worshipfull Maister William Lambe* (1580); Theodore Bèze's *Psalmes of David, Truly Opened and Explained by Paraphrasis* (1581); Saint Augustine's *A pretious booke of heauenlie meditations called a private talke of the soule with God*

(1581), *Augustines praiers & S. Augustines psalter* (1581), and *Augustines Manuel Conteining special and piked meditiatins, and godlie praiers* (1581); Thomas Bentley's three-volume *The Monument of Matrones* (1582); Daniel Tossanus's *The Exercise of the Faithfull Soule: That Is to Say, Praiers and Meditations for One to Comfort Himself in All Maner of Afflictions* (1583); and Anne Wheathill's *A handfull of holesome . . . hearbs, gathered out of the goodlie garden of Gods most holie word . . . collected and dedicate to all religious ladies* (1584).

After Henry Bynneman's death in 1583 Denham and Ralph Newbery served as Bynneman's deputies and, on his behalf, assigned fourteen of his registered titles to the Stationers' Company to be printed by the company's poor for their relief. On 30 December 1584 Newbery and Denham entered in the Stationers' Register their rights to Bynne-man's patent for all dictionaries, chronicles, and histories. Under this patent they printed Caradoc of Llancarvan's *Historie of Cambria* (1584), John Stow's *A Summarie of Englyshe Chronicles* (1587), and the formidable second edition of Raphael Holinshed's *Chronicles of England, Scotland, and Ireland* (1587) in a folio edition of nearly three thousand pages. This edition is remarkable for its variety of fonts and the careful proofreading and correction it received at the hands of Abraham Fleming. Currently in the Huntington Library, the proof sheets from this edition – collected and bound, probably as a presentation copy – attest to the excellence of Denham's printing. After his death Denham's printing materials were passed to Richard Yardley and Peter Short.

– Cyndia Susan Clegg

William Dugard

(London: 1648 – 1662)

William Dugard (also spelled Du-Gard) was a rather unusual figure in the book trade in that he did not serve an apprenticeship as a stationer. Instead, on 10 February 1648, as headmaster of Merchant Taylors' School, he was made a freeman of the Stationers' Company so that he might help correct the company's schoolbooks. The fee ordinarily assigned for such special admission to the company was in his case remitted. Once admitted, Dugard bought the presses of James Young and installed them at his school, where he did not confine himself to such correcting or even to the printing and publishing of pedagogical works. Rather, he ranged well afield, into political and religious works and, in one major instance, to a distinguished work of recent literature.

His forays into politics and religion got him into trouble with state authorities on several different occasions, but Dugard, a colorful and irrepressible figure, somehow always managed to land on his feet. Jailed by Parliament in 1650 for having printed works sympathetic to the cause of King Charles I, he emerged from prison a month later as a convert to republicanism and was soon appointed printer to the state – and then, when Oliver Cromwell assumed total power, printer to the lord protector. Sharing this last position with Henry Hills, Dugard held it through 1654.

Much of his work during 1650–1654 thus necessarily included books, tracts, and proclamations printed at the behest of the government, in addition to a semimonthly news sheet, *Les Nouvelles Ordinaires de Londres,* that Dugard both edited and printed for distribution abroad and for the French-speaking community in London. How he managed to balance his two careers as schoolmaster and printer-publisher is a bit of a mystery, and indeed the governors of Merchant Taylors' School were concerned about this as well. Beginning in 1653 they were demanding that Dugard cease his printing activities. He resisted doing so, although his production decreased somewhat after 1656, and the school court finally succeeded in dismissing him as headmaster on 12 December 1660, ostensibly because he had over a period of several years admitted 275 students and thus violated school statutes limiting enroll-

ment to 250. After protesting his dismissal, Dugard responded by setting up a private school in Coleman Street, London, and taking many of his former students with him. He died on 3 December 1662 while head of this school.

Born 9 January 1606 in Worcestershire, Dugard took a B.A. degree at Sydney Sussex College, Cambridge, in 1626 and an M.A. in 1630. He began teaching as an usher in Oundle School in Northamptonshire, and by 1637 he had become master of the Free School in Colchester, Essex. In May 1644 he was appointed headmaster at London's distinguished Merchant Taylors' School. Although he frequently did not enjoy harmonious relations with those who had hired him, Dugard was apparently a dedicated and successful teacher. At Colchester enrollment under his leadership increased from nine to sixty-nine students, and while at Merchant Taylors' School he developed a new set of texts for use at his own and other schools. His *Rhetorices Elementa,* first published in 1648, proceeded through eleven editions by 1694 and was still being reprinted well into the eighteenth century; his *English Rudiments of the Latin Tongue,* first published in 1656, was similarly still being reprinted in the 1730s.

Leona Rostenberg has counted 171 books that Dugard printed, partly for himself and partly for others. He made some thirty entries in the Stationers' Register, but many of these are for works he printed at the order of the government by virtue of his position as printer to the state, and Dugard is thus best regarded primarily as a printer rather than as a publisher. His work is generally agreed to be of good quality, but it is unclear whether he did his own presswork. His various works were sold by more than thirty different booksellers, most often perhaps by Francis Eglesfield, but no particular pattern is evident in his choice of booksellers – or in their choice of him. Many of the works that he published as well as those that he merely printed for others were, understandably, pedagogical in nature – thirty-three such works, by Rostenberg's count. These include his own six textbooks and an edition of Lucian's *Dialogues* (1649) that he edited and to which he attached a Latin translation. The

Title pages for Greek and Latin grammar textbooks that headmaster William Dugard wrote for use at his Merchant Taylors' School, before he began his career in publishing

term *pedagogical* being widely conceived, many other Dugard books might be included under the same rubric – for instance, an edition of Xenophon's *Cyropaedia* (1648), works of a scientific and medical nature such as William Harvey's *Exercitationes de Generatione Animalium* (1651), and religious or theological works such as John Downame's *Brief Concordance or Table to the Bible* (1652). A high proportion of the books Dugard printed, again quite understandably, were in Greek or Latin.

Dugard is most well known, however, for his political printing and publishing activities. Having set up his presses during the second civil war, he wasted little time before engaging himself in contemporary political controversy, in which he supported the side of Charles I against Parliament. Shortly after the death of King Charles on 30 January 1649 Dugard made his lasting mark in these struggles. Within five days of the king's execution, copies of *Eikon Basilike, The Pourtraicture of His Sacred Majestie in His Solicitudes and Sufferings* were circulating in London streets. This was a work claiming to present the thoughts of Charles while he had

awaited trial and then execution, and the work was purported to be by the king's own hand – although the book is now known to have been primarily the work of Bishop John Gauden.

While plainly of no help to Charles, the *Eikon* proved to be the most effective piece of royalist propaganda to emerge from the English Civil War period, as it went through thirty-five different London editions and twenty-five more in Ireland and abroad within a single year. The first edition was published by Richard Royston and printed by John Grismond and Roger Norton, although other stationers soon produced editions as well. Dugard printed several of the early editions, and his efforts contributed significantly to the text's history with an edition, evidently the twenty-second, published on 15 March 1649.

This edition, printed by Dugard and sold by Eglesfield, was the first to include a body of supplementary material: the *Apophthegmata Aurea, Regia, Carolina,* a collection of sayings derived from the text and compiled by Edward Hooker, corrector or proofreader to Dugard's press; Charles I's own

Εἰκὼν Βασιλικη.

THE
POVRTRAICTVRE
OF

HIS SACRED
MAIESTIE
IN

HIS SOLITVDES
AND

SVFFERINGS.

Rom. 8.
More then Conquerour, &c.

Bona agere, & mala pati, Regium eſt.

M.DC.XLVIII.

Title page of the work that purportedly represents the last reflections of Charles I and for which Dugard, the printer of several editions, was arrested in 1660

"Reasons against the pretended Jurisdiction of the High Court of Justice"; a copy of Prince Charles's letter to his father from The Hague on 23 January 1649; and, most notably, four prayers that the late king was supposed to have offered during the time of his captivity and that he handed over to his attendants the night before his execution. The prayers created an excitement of their own, and they were quickly incorporated into other editions. In presenting this new material Dugard supplied a separate title page for the *Apophthegmata,* on which he declared himself as the printer. This was the first and only edition of the *Eikon* before 1660 to carry a printer's full and real name, and in response to this open act of defiance Parliament on 16 March issued an order for Dugard's arrest. Upon examination Dugard was able to show that the prayers had in fact been licensed (to yet another stationer, John Playford), whereupon Dugard was released from custody and the licenser, James Cranford, dismissed from his position. Upon his release Dugard immediately printed yet another edition of the work that the government had found objectionable.

The prayers have a history of their own, for the first of them, as John Milton soon discovered, had been "stol'n word for word" from the mouth of Pamela, the heroine of Sir Philip Sidney's *Arcadia* (1590). Milton's *Eikonoklastes* (1649), his state-sponsored, chapter-by-chapter reply to the King's Book, proceeded to pillory Charles I for, as Milton put it, "borrowing to a Christian use Prayers offerd to a Heathen God." In the second edition of *A Vindication of King Charles the Martyr* (1697), Thomas Wagstaffe charged that Milton had forced an imprisoned Dugard to insert the fraudulent prayer in the text so that Milton in turn could attack Charles for having uttered it. Wagstaffe's account is untrue – the text of the prayers was obtained by Edward Hooker

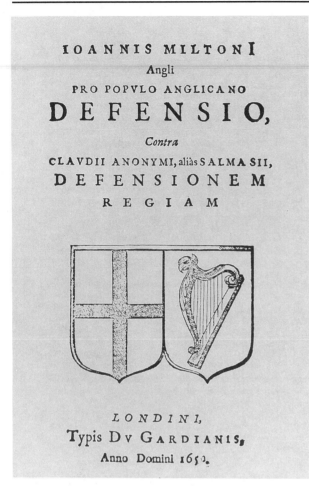

IOANNIS MILTONI
Angli
PRO POPVLO ANGLICANO
DEFENSIO,
Contra
CLAVDII ANONYMI, aliàs SALMASII,
DEFENSIONEM
REGIAM

LONDINI,
Typis DV GARDIANIS,
Anno Domini 1650.

Title page for John Milton's defense of the Commonwealth, the publication of which signaled Dugard's apparent loyalty to the republican government

from Edward Simmons, the same attendant to King Charles who had provided Royston with the initial manuscript of the *Eikon* – and its chronology is confused: Dugard's stint in prison, when he needed help to extricate himself, did not occur until a year later. Yet the story has been slow to die, having been revived in the eighteenth century by William Lauder in *Charles I Vindicated from Plagiarism* (1754) and Samuel Johnson, and again in the twentieth century by William Empson in *Milton's God* (1961).

Within a year Dugard was in trouble again, this time for having prepared an edition of the *Defensio Regia pro Carolo Primo* by Claude de Saumaise. First published in Leiden in November 1649, this work was perhaps subsidized by Charles II (as its title page claims) to present his father's case, and that of the divine right of kingship generally, to a wide European audience. Printing it in England was another act of defiance to the new Commonwealth government, and for attempting to do so Dugard

was imprisoned at Newgate Prison; his presses were seized; and, by order of the council of state, he was dismissed from his position at Merchant Taylors' School.

His stay in Newgate seems to have pacified Dugard, whose wife and six children had been turned out of doors. After James Harrington – either the republican political theorist and author of *The Commonwealth of Oceana* (1656) or his more politically active cousin of the same name – and perhaps Milton had intervened, Dugard emerged from Newgate on 2 April 1650 now evidently loyal to the new government. His presses were returned to him, and after some delay he was on 25 September 1650, again by order of the Council of State, reinstated as headmaster at Merchant Taylors' School. Late in the same year he was, as printer to the state, preparing for publication Milton's *Pro Populo Anglicano Defensio* (1651), the offical government response to the work for which he had been arrested eleven months earlier. In 1652 Dugard was, similarly, engaged in printing John Drury's French translation of Milton's *Eikonoklastes*.

Even his position as printer to the state did not keep Dugard out of danger, however, for he entered in the Stationers' Register on 13 November 1651 and early in 1652 published *Catechesis Ecclesiarum quae in Regno Poloniae,* a translation of the Polish catechism issued at Racow early in the century. This was a Socinian manifesto denying the Trinity and hence was deemed a blasphemous, scandalous book by the English state and religious leaders. On 27 January 1652 all copies of the book were ordered to be seized, and Dugard was once again examined. This time he implicated Milton for having licensed the book, and Milton, too, was called forth to explain his actions. Milton did so, claiming that he had acted according to his conscience, and referred his examiners to his own *Areopagitica* (1644). No action was taken against Milton, presumably because of the service that he had rendered the state in writing *Pro Populo Anglicano Defensio,* but on 2 April 1652 all copies of the *Catechesis Ecclesiarum quae in Regno Poloniae* were ordered to be burnt. Dugard had earlier, on 29 January, requested that his entry for the work in the Stationers' Register be canceled.

Dugard was to have one final brush with state authorities, this time with a new government, in which he again revealed his characteristic combination of stubbornness and opportunism. After the restoration of the Stuart monarchy in 1660 he was caught harboring in his house James Harrington, who had helped him ten years earlier. When summoned in October 1661 to account for his actions,

Dugard explained that he was simply returning the favor Harrington had done him in the past; but he also seems to have taken the opportunity to remind the new powers of the service he had done the Stuart cause in the past, in printing the *Eikon Basilike*, Saumaise's *Defensio Regia*, and George Bate's defense of Charles I's actions in his struggles with Parliament, *Elenchus Motuum Nuperorum in Anglia* (1649).

The important literary work associated with Dugard is the 1655 edition of *The Countess of Pembroke's Arcadia* by Sidney. In his *Dictionary of Booksellers and Printers . . . from 1641 to 1667* Henry Plomer assumes that George Calvert and Thomas Pierrepont, at whose shops the volume was sold, were the publishers of the work and Dugard merely its printer. Yet Dugard had assumed John Leggett's half interest in the work on 20 October 1649, and the other half interest is not mentioned in the Stationers' Register after 22 July 1644, when it had been transferred to the James Young who sold Dugard his presses in 1648. Because Calvert and Pierrepont acquired Dugard's half interest from the executor of his estate only on 18 January 1665, one must presume that Dugard was the driving force behind the 1655 edition.

The volume is somewhat misleadingly titled, as all editions of Sidney's work had been since 1598, for it contains not simply Sidney's great heroic romance but all of Sidney's literary works – *Astrophel and Stella* (1591) and his other sonnets, the *Defence of Poesie* (1595), and his masque, "The Lady of May." The *Arcadia* had been appearing in increasingly elaborate editions since its original publication in quarto in 1590, when it contained only what is now called the "New" *Arcadia,* the two and a half books of the unfinished revision of Sidney's romance. By 1593 (when the last three books of Sidney's first manuscript version were added) and 1598 (when his other literary works were first included) the format of the volume had been altered to folio, and in that format it was republished once more in the sixteenth century and nine times during the seventeenth century.

With Dugard's edition the trend toward compendiousness and magnificence reached its high point in a volume of 686 pages, the subsequent editions of 1662 (also published by Dugard) and 1674 being page-for-page reprints of the 1655 edition. In 1655 the volume included all of Sidney's literary works and the continuations or supplements to the *Arcadia* by William Alexander, Robert Beling, and James Johnstoun that had been attached to the work in the 1620s and 1630s. For the first time it also included a frontispiece portrait, a prefatory life of Sidney, extracts from William Camden's *Annales* on Sidney's death, nine pages of commendatory verse and prose by various hands, and, at the end of the volume, an "Alphabetical Table, or, Clavis whereby the Reader is let in to view the principal Stories contein'd in the *Arcadia,* as they stand in their proper places."

This last item is of particular interest, both because appending such a table to a work of fiction seems odd and because the table appears to be something between an outright index and the first step toward a commonplace book. Many of its entries – for instance, "Eas the nurs of Poetrie" or "Hospitalitie maintain'd by good husbandry" – seem to be devised as starting points for essays by a potential reader. This addition to the volume is especially helpful in suggesting how Sidney's romance was designed by its promoters to be read: the *Arcadia* was a work to be honored and studied carefully, a work from which one might properly draw moral, political, and rhetorical lessons. The table, or clavis, thus may also express Dugard's concerns as a pedagogue and thereby highlight again his unusual route to membership in the Stationers' Company. But this was an index-writing age, and one should not regard Dugard's inclusion of such a table simply as idiosyncratic; in the year following this edition of Sidney, George Herbert's volume of lyric poems, *The Temple,* was reissued with a similar alphabetical table at its back, and this from the house or shop of a totally different stationer, Philemon Stephens.

References:

F[rancis] F. Madan, "Milton, Salmasius, and Dugard," *Library,* fourth series 4 (September 1923): 119–145;

Madan, *A New Bibliography of the Eikon Basilike of King Charles the First* (Oxford: Oxford Bibliographical Society, 1950);

William Riley Parker, *Milton: A Biography,* 2 volumes (Oxford: Clarendon Press, 1968);

Leona Rostenberg, "Republican Credo: William Dugard, Pedagogue and Political Apostate," in her *Literary, Political, Scientific, Religious and Legal Publishing, Printing & Bookselling in England, 1551–1700: Twelve Studies* (New York: Franklin, 1965), I: 131–159.

          – *Peter Lindenbaum*

John Dunton

(London: 1681 – 1711)

John Dunton was an eccentric, sometimes scurrilous, always irrepressible bookseller and publisher whose idiosyncratic autobiography, *The Life and Errors of John Dunton* (1705), is a valuable chronicle of the Augustan book trade. His gossipy life story abundantly details the business of bookselling at the turn of the century and sketches many portraits of his fellow stationers, publishers, printers, and booksellers. Casting a retrospective glance over his career, Dunton recalls that "of six hundred Books I have Printed . . . I know but of seven I am angry at." A prolific publisher, he is best known for his innovative weekly periodical, *The Athenian Gazette, or Casuistical Mercury, Resolving All the Most Nice and Curious Questions Proposed by the Ingenious* (1691).

The anonymity of its learned writers, known as members of the Athenian Society, and the novelty of its question-and-answer format drew its devoted readership from denizens of the popular coffeehouses. The eventual relaxing of publishing restrictions in 1696 and the subsequent flourishing of newspapers and periodicals softened the titillating edge of Dunton's Whiggish venture, which suspended publication in 1697 as his life and career thereafter soured. Unable to compete with the newly formed publishing *congers* (a term Dunton coined to describe those bookselling associations formed to police copyright outlaws), Dunton accumulated enormous debt and, fleeing angry creditors, lived much as a fugitive, estranged even from his second wife. With apparent signs of growing derangement, he turned to writing political invective and became, to Alexander Pope's satiric eye, "a broken Bookseller and abusive scribbler."

Dunton opens his autobiography with an auspicious characterization of his birth: "It was almost a relief to me to cry out with Job, iii. 3. Let the day perish wherein I was born, and the night in which it was said, There is a man-child conceiv'd." He was born at Graffham in Huntingdonshire on 4 May 1659, the only child of Lydia Dunton, daughter of Daniel Carter of Chesham, and Rector John Dunton of Graffham, a third-generation cleric to be so named. Reverend Dunton expected his son to be a fourth-generation clergyman, but the stability of the Dunton household was dashed when Mrs.

John Dunton (engraving after a portrait by Gucht)

Dunton died within a year of her son's birth. She was buried on 3 March 1660, and Reverend Dunton, sorrow-stricken, boarded his young son at William Reading's school at Dunsgrove and withdrew to Ireland.

Returning to England to accept the rectorship of Aston Clinton on 11 May 1663, Reverend Dunton married a daughter of Rev. John Marriat, one Mary Lake, with whom he had four more children – Sarah, Mary, Elizabeth, and Lake Dunton – and set about belatedly training young John for the church. Not an apt student for Reading, Dunton frustrated his father's desires. "My Father tried all the methods with me that could be thought of, in order to reconcile my mind to the love of Learning," he was to recall, "but all of them proved useless and ineffectual." Acknowledging his son's "roving inclinations," Reverend Dunton negotiated a trial apprenticeship for fifteen-year-old Dunton with

Thomas Parkhurst, an eminent Presbyterian bookseller in London.

Whig politics and philandering occupied much of Dunton's seven years with Parkhurst, and Dunton regretfully recounts the tribulations of his early days in London, especially the pains he inflicted on Parkhurst and his father. Dunton ran away from Parkhurst, but upon Reverend Dunton's urging, the bookseller gave the chastened young man a second chance and officially apprenticed him on 7 December 1674. Two noteworthy incidents mark Dunton's apprenticeship: on behalf of several thousand Whig apprentices on 2 September 1681 he presented a petition to the mayor of London, and on the expiration of his apprenticeship Dunton "invited a hundred Apprentices to celebrate a *Funeral* for it, though," as he later reflected, "it was no more than a youthful piece of vanity."

On 5 December 1681 Dunton was admitted to the freedom of the Stationers' Company and, acting on the advice of his late father (who had died on 4 November 1676), decided to lease a shop "'in a convenient place,' but, that I might not run the hazard of too large a rent, . . . I took up with half a shop, a warehouse and a fashionable chamber." Under the sign of the Black Raven, Dunton established his bookstall in 1681, the first of three in the market quarter of London, with the publication of his first book – *The Lord's Last Sufferings* (1682) by the Dissenter Reverend Thomas Doolittle. Following a common practice, Dunton used this book as barter with other book dealers and through such trade furnished his own shop "with all sorts of Books saleable at that Time." Later in 1682 he published a handful of funeral sermons, including those written by his father (*The House of Weeping*), and Stephen Jay's *Daniel in the Den,* a political tract dedicated to Anthony Ashley Cooper, third earl of Shaftesbury. His early publishing ventures, primarily in devotional literature, attracted the attention of hack writers who, as Dunton recalls, "began to ply me with '*Specimens,*' as earnestly, and with as much passion and concern, as the *Watermen* do *Passengers* with *Oars* and *Scullers.*"

A favorite pastime of Dunton's bachelorhood was that of sampling Sunday sermons by dissenting preachers, presumably an acceptable way to become acquainted with the Nonconformist movement as well as with young women. Shortly after joining Dr. Samuel Annesley's congregation, Dunton fell in love with the minister's daughter, Elizabeth. Through the spring and summer of 1682 they courted, exchanging many letters that they signed as "Philaret" (Dunton) and "Iris" (Elizabeth), and on 3 August 1682 they married at the church of Allhallows on the Wall, London. Much of Dunton's early success is attributed to Iris, as Dunton always called his first wife, whose stability and astute business sense appeared to counteract Dunton's penchant for extravagance and "rambling," the latter a characteristic feature of both his life and his writing style.

Early in 1683 Dunton apprenticed Samuel Palmer, who was to be bound to him for eight years. Throughout 1683 and 1684 Dunton continued to publish devotional literature written by leading Nonconformists, and this sympathy for dissenting writers may account for his arrest, in early July 1683, for allegedly having published a "plot sermon." In what has been called the "Rye House Plot" (1682–1683), anti-Catholics, led by the earl of Shaftesbury, championed for succession the duke of Monmouth, who was the Protestant bastard son of Charles II. He denied the charges and, after a hearing before King Charles II and his council, was released. In 1684 the young bookseller printed a sixteen-page catalogue that advertised approximately 170 works, including Bibles and schoolbooks, of his inventory. Dunton fondly reminisces about this early period of his career and marriage to Iris: "We took several journeys together into the country, and made visits to both our Relations; but, look which way we would, the World was always smiling on us."

In 1685 he published *Maggots: or, Poems on Several Subjects,* a small volume of juvenile poems composed by his longtime friend and future partner, Samuel Wesley – the husband of Iris's sister, Susannah Annesley, and later the father of the Methodist founder, John Wesley. "Maggots," as Peter Murray Hill suggests, "had come to have a metaphorical significance about this time, meaning whimsical, odd, a trifle crack-brained." The titles of these poems – "On the grunting of a Hog," "On a Cow's Tail," or "A Dialogue between a Chamber-Pot and a Frying-Pan," to name but a few – seem to confirm this.

From 1685 to 1688 Dunton traveled to New England and the Continent, a trip interrupted about midway by a ten-month stay in London. In his memoirs Dunton recalls this adventurous three-year "ramble":

> When I was thus seated to the best advantage at the Black Raven in Princes-Street, and as happy in my Marriage as I could wish, there came an universal damp upon Trade, occasioned by the defeat of Monmouth in the West; and, at this time, having 500 *l.* owing me in New-England, I began to think it worth my while to make a voyage of it thither.

Dunton may have withdrawn from his London trade at this time because King James II in May 1685 began strenuously to enforce regulations prohibiting treasonable publications, laws that would dampen Dunton's Whiggish, Nonconformist inclinations. The trip to Massachusetts Bay Colony, a haven for English Dissenters, may also have been a convenient dodge from creditors, because Dunton had agreed to serve as surety for a debt of fifty pounds owed by another brother-in-law (the husband of Iris's sister, Bethia Annesley). For this Dunton was duly arrested in Gravesend before he could finally depart from England late in October 1685.

He divided the stock he planned to sell in New England between two ships; one of these, however, was lost, and Dunton suffered an estimated loss of £500 from this. On 27 January 1686 he arrived in Boston, was received by a host of ministers friendly with his father-in-law, and set up a retail bookstore. Boston booksellers attempted to buy him out at wholesale, but Dunton, with the help of his apprentice, Palmer, established a flourishing business. His autobiography and voluminous letters provide colorful portraits of turn-of-the-century Boston and Bostonians, who comprised much of his New England clientele. Dunton recounts in detail his lively social life with fellow publishers, Puritan clergy, women friends, and notables such as Cotton and Increase Mather, one of whose sermons he secured in Cambridge and published in Boston. With Palmer carefully overseeing the shop, Dunton traveled throughout colonial America, where he saw the sights and diligently recorded his impressions for posterity.

One of Dunton's most memorable sidetrips was his Roxbury visit to a "Rev. Mr. *Elliot,* the great Apostle of the Indians." Elliot presented Dunton with "twelve Indian Bibles, and desired [him] to bring one of them over to Dr. Annesley; as also with twelve 'Speeches of converted Indians,' which himself had published." Returning to Boston, Dunton discovered two-thirds of his stock was sold and, fearing a saturated Boston market, set up another warehouse in Salem, where Palmer easily managed to sell the remaining books. It is doubtful, however, that Dunton's New England enterprise was profitable, as he remarks in proverbial tones: "He that trades with the inhabitants of Boston should be well furnished with a Grecian Faith; he may get promises enough, but their payments come late." Dunton set sail for London on 5 July 1686 and arrived one month later.

Yet his reunion with Iris, as he recounts, was quickly spoiled: "At my return, I expected nothing but a golden life of it for the future, though all my satisfactions were soon withered; for, being so deeply entangled for my Sister-in-law, I was not suffered to step over the threshold in ten months." Virtually under house arrest and hoping to avoid confrontation with creditors, Dunton secluded himself at home and even had to disguise himself as a woman in order to venture out: "I got my self shaved, and put on as effeminate a look as my countenance would let me; and being well fitted out with a large scarf, I set forward; but every step I took; the fear was upon me." After nearly a year of living incognito Dunton escaped to the Continent in early summer 1687. He rambled leisurely across the Netherlands and Germany for more than a year before returning to Iris on 15 November 1688, not long before the Glorious Revolution established William, prince of Orange, at Saint James's Palace.

Dunton's career peaked during the reign of William and Mary, especially from 1688 through 1698, as he confesses:

> The humour of *rambling* was now pretty well off with me, and my thoughts began to fix rather upon Business. The Shop I took, with the sign of the Black Raven, stood opposite to the Poultry Compter, where I traded ten years, as all other men must expect, with variety of successes and disappointments. My Shop was opened just upon the Revolution. . . .
> So soon as I enter'd upon Business, I was all over infected with a new itch of *Printing.*

Within six months of his homecoming Dunton had refurbished and restocked his shop and embarked on a gregarious and bold stage of his publishing life. Stephen Parks estimates Dunton's production for this decade at 214 publications, including 11 periodicals and 29 editions of older works, while he was also involved in dozens of projects for which he served as either co-author or publisher. Such sheer volume compares impressively with two leading postrevolutionary publishers, Edmund Curll and Robert Dodsley, for Dunton's business was confined to London alone. Through most of this period Dunton maintained this breakneck pace, slowing dramatically only upon the death of Iris in 1697.

The books Dunton published in 1689 and 1690 share a dissenting piety and Whiggish political vein with those that he had published before the Monmouth Rebellion. In 1689 he attracted a readership preoccupied with the "dying speeches" of Protestant radicals, a literature gaining currency as "the new martyrology" for which Dunton was partially responsible, as Jonathan Swift ironically notes in his *Tale of a Tub* (1704): "that worthy Citizen and Bookseller, Mr. *John Dunton,* hath a faithful and painful Collection, which he shortly designs to publish in Twelve Volumes in Folio, illustrated with Cooper-Plates. A Work Highly useful and curious, and altogether worthy of such a Hand."

Dunton did publish several editions of these miscellanies, among the most popular of which were *The Dying Speeches, Letter and Prayers, &c. of Those Eminent Protestants Who Suffered in the West of England* (1689) and *A New Martyrology: or, The Bloody Assizes: . . . to This Treatise Is Added, the Life and Death of George Lord Jeffryes* (1689). Dunton also specialized in political biographies – such as *The Popish Champion: or, A Compleat History of the Life and Military Actions of Richard Earl of Tyrconnel* (1689) and *The Abdicated Prince: or, The Adventures of Four Years* (1690) – that vilified James II and ennobled William III. Printing news sheets or newsletters with such titles as *A Continuation of News from That Part of His Majesties Fleet That Now Lies at High-Lake near Chester,* he made early forays into periodical literature during these two years. Dunton also forged a healthy partnership with New England friends such as the Mathers, for whom he acted as London publishing agent throughout the 1690s.

Dunton's career began in 1691 a seven-year flowering, a period filled with ebullient self-confidence and emotional stability. He was wholly or partly responsible for two works – *Religio Bibliopolae* (1691), pseudonymously written by a Benjamin Bridgwater, and *A Voyage Round the World* (1691). Benjamin Bridgwater has been linked with Dunton especially since he writes, tongue-in-cheek, in his autobiography that Bridgwater "was, in part, Author of 'Religio Bibliopolae.' But, alas! in the issue, Wine and Love were the ruin of this ingenious Gentleman." As an unmistakable imitation of Sir Thomas Browne's sentimental *Religio Medici* (1642), *Religio Bibliopolae* was probably a collaborative, if not partially plagiarized, project designed to profit by being associated with Browne's memoirs; through five successful editions before 1750, it did so.

The prefatory verses to *A Voyage Round the World* seem calculated to convey surreptitiously Dunton's authorship to readers: "The Author's Name When Anagramatized is Hid unto None," and other lines refer to a "faithful Ulysses, / . . . Casting Anchor i' th' arms of his beautiful Iris." The capricious style of the work would also surely echo in the ears of readers familiar with *A Ramble Round the World,* a periodical published in 1689 by the dissenting bookseller Richard Janeway and sim-

Title page for Dunton's biography, a valuable source of information about the British book trade during the late seventeenth and early eighteenth centuries

ilarly linked with Dunton through its idiomatic vocabulary, as its introductory remarks reveal: "I have been a Rambler ever since I was 14 Years Old, and have Travelled through all Countries in the World; Whether it were a Maggot in my head, or a breeze in my Tail, or Quick-Silver in my Feet, I know not." As a predecessor to *A Ramble Round the World,* the facetiously autobiographical *A Voyage* (the opening chapter of which is titled, "Of my Rambles before I came into my Mother's Belly, and while I was there") chronicles the zany life of "Don Kainophilus" and later caught the attention of Laurence Sterne, whose rambling novel *The Life and Opinions of Tristram Shandy* (1759–1767) is a stylistic heir of *A Voyage.*

These two pseudonymous works did not exhaust Dunton's creativity in 1691, for he also conceived an idea for a periodical with an unusual question-and-answer format: *The Athenian Gazette, or Casuistical Mercury, Resolving All the Most Nice and Curious*

Questions Proposed by the Ingenious. His memoirs describe at length and with self-adulation his rationale in initiating such an endeavor: "I am now to entertain the Reader with the PROJECTS I have engaged upon; for I have been sufficiently convinced that, unless a man can either think or perform something out of the old beaten road, he will find nothing but what his Forefathers have found before him." With this philosophical observation in place, Dunton recounts the moment of his imaginative conception:

> I was one day walking over St. George's Fields, and Mr. Larkin and Mr. Harris were along with me; and on a sudden I made a stop, and said, "Well, Sirs, I have a thought I will not exchange for fifty guineas." They smiled, and were very urgent with me to *discover* it; but they could not get it from me.

With feigned modesty he names his brainchild: "The first rude *hint* of it was no more than a confused idea, of concealing the Querist, and answering his Question." A tremendous success, *The Athenian Gazette* changed its name to *The Athenian Mercury* after the first two numbers and continued, at first weekly then twice weekly, to appear in a nearly unbroken sequence of twenty regularly published volumes from 17 March 1691 to 14 June 1697.

Initially Dunton, Richard Sault (an Oxford-educated mathematician and brother-in-law married to another of Annesley's daughters), and John Norris (an Oxford platonist) anonymously wrote the responses to reader queries, but soon Samuel Wesley replaced Norris to form a self-sworn secret triumvirate. The early numbers of the paper identified Dunton as "our Bookseller" and "P. Smart" as its publisher. On 10 April 1691 the three brothers-in-law signed a contract obliging Dunton to pay ten shillings each to Sault and Wesley for every number printed. Gilbert D. McEwen reports that there was to be a meeting

> every Fryday in the afternoon in some Convenient place betwixt the sd Wesley and Sault to consult of what they have done and to receive new Questions for the next week and the party not coming before 3 of ye Clock is to forfeit one Shilling to be spent and the party that has not finisht his paper by that time excepting Corrections shall forfeit one shilling to be likewise spent.

The signatures of James and Mary Smith were added as witnesses and as commercial beneficiaries of this agreement, because the Smiths' coffeehouse became the "Convenient place" where the three writers met and where, as advertised in the paper,

"*All Persons . . . [should] send their Questions by a Penny Post Letter.*" Correspondence was so great that readers were occasionally asked to halt their queries.

The new "Notes and Queries" format plus the grandeur of the Athenian Society account for much of the immediate success of the periodical. The aura of mystery that Dunton created about the Athenian Society in referring to the three anonymous mavens was a stroke of commercial genius, and McEwen believes that Swift and Charles Gildon heightened this aura about the learned club. Enamored of the gazette's antipedantry but ignorant of Dunton's hand in it, Swift penned a juvenile "Ode to the Athenian Society" and sent it on Valentine's Day to "bookseller" Dunton, who printed it in a supplement to the fifth volume.

Gildon's *History of the Athenian Society* (1692), McEwen continues, built on Swift's admiration and helped to fashion the image of the society by adding a biblical association from Acts 17:21 to the classical erudition of the Athenian Society: "*For all the Athenians and Strangers which were there spent their time in nothing else, but either to tell, or to hear some News.*" On the frontispiece to his *Young Students' Library* (1692) Dunton printed an emblem of the Athenian Society that depicted Athens, Rome, Oxford, and Cambridge in its four corners. Curiosity in newsworthy and learned discourse spawned accolades and commendatory poems from other notables such as Sir William Temple, Daniel Defoe, and Nahum Tate, all of whom were later shocked to discover Dunton's surreptitious role in the project and were dismayed by their having praised it.

The folio half-sheet *Athenian Mercury* was hawked through the streets of London by "Mercury Women," but its devotees were the patrons of Augustan coffeehouses, where the paper's provocative content could be endlessly rehashed. The questions and answers covered a gamut of topics, Wesley largely responding to religious, historical, and literary matters and Sault covering the technical and scientific. Questions on the occult and marvelous, marriage and courtship, or general social behavior was no one's particular bailiwick. Dunton's quirky style linked him with publishing topics, though his primary responsibilities lay in overseeing production.

Occasionally the periodical inflamed political and religious furor with innuendos barely legal to print under strict licensing regulations. More often it drew an amalgam of questions, such as "Whether 'tis Lawful for a Man to beat his Wife?," "How came the spots on the Moon?," and "Where was the Soul of Lazarus for the four days he lay in the

Grave?" To cultivate a female readership – a special interest Dunton maintained – the gazette printed a host of questions about "the feminine," marriage, and courtship. On 27 February 1693 Dunton even launched *The Ladies Mercury,* a journal devoted exclusively to female readers.

Though serious advice on matters of the heart was orthodox, facetious questions elicited humorous responses. Editors once urged spousal blackmail to a disgruntled wife:

> Show him [your husband] this *Mercury,* and tell him if he don't amend, his *Name* shall be printed in't at length the first *Tuesday* of the next Month. But to be graver . . . be as patient as possible, unless the Husband's such a *Brute,* that this manner of behaviour will but make him more *insulting.*

Another time the editor curtly counseled a reluctant bachelor: "Quest. *I've wrote before on the following subject, but cou'd receive no answer. I've been too often prevail'd upon by the allurements, &c. what's your advise in this matter? Answer.* Marry!"

McEwan argues, "No other periodical of the century printed as much verse or made as much over it editorially as the *Athenian Mercury.*" By his count, forty-three numbers contain poetical questions and verse, and a monthly "Poetical Mercury" was inaugurated in January 1692. Wesley, the "Poetical Member" of the club, offered critiques of contemporary poems, composed poetical responses to questions submitted in verse, assembled poetical reading lists, and printed much of his own Miltonic devotional poetry. Elizabeth Singer, known as "the Pindarick Lady" – a female poet laureate of "Athens" – contributed more than two dozen poems to the periodical, amassed an enthusiastic readership with her youthful poetry, and later, as Mrs. Rowe, became a respectable protégée of Isaac Watts. McEwen writes that the Athenian Society was repeatedly asked to name the best poet and best poem of the age, a request to which they cleverly quipped,

> The best *Poem* that ever was *made* is the *Universe,* and he who *made* that, the first and best *Poet.* But for artificial Poems, not to meddle with the Scriptures, a great part whereof, as part of *Job,* several of the *Psalms,* the *Canticles, Isaiah, Lamentations,* &c. is undoubtedly the best and noblest Poetry in the World. It is *Virgils Æneids.*

The success of *The Athenian Mercury* quickly spawned journalistic rivalries, imitators, and parodies. A scandalous battle erupted between Dunton and Tom Brown, a competitor who on 1 February 1692 started a nearly identical "notes and queries"

periodical, the *London Mercury* (later titled *The Lacedemonian Mercury*). Ever ready for a spirited squabble, McEwen reports that Dunton challenged this competitor in print the day following publication of Brown's first number:

> *Yesterday Morning was publisht a Paper interfering with our Athenian Project. . . . [W]e therefore here give publick notice, That those Questions which he pretends to answer shall be answer'd again by us, that so neither our Querists, the Booksellers, nor the* London-Coffeehouses *may be imposed upon by buying Questions twice answer'd, for they shall always find in our Papers the best of his Thoughts, and our own Improvements upon all* Questions *whatever, together with Remarks upon his Errors. We shall now change one of our days of publishing into that of his, and oftener if he gives any further occasion.*

Dunton's incessant badgering drove Brown out of print by 30 May 1692; Parks writes that in the 31 May *Athenian Mercury* Dunton, calling Brown an "impudent lyar," had the final word.

The Athenian Mercury continued twice weekly until 1696, when public interest dwindled and the paper no longer provoked imitators or controversy. The slackening of licensing strictures under William III encouraged the appearance of new periodicals, and the number of these alone apparently blunted the sharp edge of Dunton's original. After making a couple of concerted attempts to reinvigorate his dying project, Dunton at last suspended operations with the tenth number of volume twenty in 1697. Several editions of collected popular numbers were issued as *The Athenian Oracle* in 1703–1728, 1820, and 1893.

Critical historians may consider 1691 to have been Dunton's creative *annus mirabilis,* yet Dunton says in *Life and Errors* that in 1692 "I was put in possession of a considerable Estate upon the decease of my Cousin Carter. And now the Master and Assistants of the Company of Stationers began to think me sufficient to wear a Livery; and in the year 1692 they honoured me with the Cloathing." After musing on the social prestige this rank afforded him, Dunton swells to reverie:

> The World now smiled on me. I sailed with wind and tide, and had humble servants enough among the Stationers, Booksellers, Printers and Binders: but especially my own Relations, on every side, were all upon the very height of love and tenderness; and I was so caressed almost out of my five senses, that I thought there was no such Villain in Christendom as a *Summer-Friend.*

With *The Athenian Mercury* running at full tilt Dunton devised *The Young Students' Library,* a venture ancillary to the periodical, to be published as

Doth not Gods Creation suffice thee but as if thou woldest exceed him thougoest about to mend it Chrisost: Hom. 4. in 1. ad Tim.
At ye Resurrection thy maker will not acknowledge thee   August: Tom 10. ser: 12 4 7
London Printed for I. Dunton at the black Rauen in the Poultery. 1683

Engraving from England's Vanity; or, The Voice of God against the Monstrous Sin of Pride in Dress and Apparel *(1683), one of the many works of Nonconformist devotional literature with which Dunton began his publishing career*

an Athenian supplement that would compile translations from Continental journals and extracts from books published since 1665. Having printed only a few of these supplements, Dunton entered into a second acerbic trade war, this time with Jean Cornand de la Crose.

In the summer of 1691 Cornand de la Crose began a journal, *The Works of the Learned, or an Historical Account and Impartial Judgement of Books Newly Printed, Both Foreign and Domestick,* that furnished both abstracted translations of foreign periodicals and critical reviews of them. Without the protection of copyright, translations were then the property of the shrewdest businessman, and Dunton drew this "interloper" into a quarrel that spilled into the pages of their competing journals – in one of Dunton's familiar battle strategies that eventually drove an exhausted Cornand de la Crose into retirement. Parks reports that on 10 May 1692 Dunton announced: "Having bought of the late Undertaker of the *Works of the Learned* his right to a Monthly Journal of Books, the said Journal will be now carried on by a *London Divine* (under the Title of *the Compleat Library,* or *News for the Ingenious,* &c.) who will continue it monthly." After some delay the first installment of

The Compleat Library appeared, bearing the initials of Richard Wolley, the London divine.

Though he never repented of his charlatanism in the Brown and Cornand de la Crose affairs, Dunton did regret publishing in September 1692 *The Post-Boy Rob'd of His Mail: Or, the Pacquet Broke Open.* In his autobiography a penitent Dunton writes of this, "You know, Reader, Youth are rash and heedless: green heads are very ill judges of the productions of the mind. . . . And this was my case with respect to 'The Second Spira;' 'The Post-boy robbed of his Mail;' 'The Voyage round the World;' " and four others that he names. *The Post-Boy* transformed the club framework of the Athenian Society into a group of learned wits who steal a postman's mail pouch and divulge the contents of the more-intriguing missives. The pretense of prying into private letters obviously appealed to Dunton's audience, for *The Post-Boy* was a commercial success: a second volume was printed in 1693, and both volumes were reprinted in 1706 and 1719.

Dunton's most productive year followed in 1693. Attracting and printing much anti-Quaker literature as well as sundry other genres of devotional literature, The Black Raven served as a lodestone for religious controversy. The works of the Mathers turned a healthy profit for Dunton in 1693, Cotton Mather's *Wonders of the Invisible World* moving through three editions. Parks notes that Dunton's publication of Elia Benoit's *History of the Famous Edict of Nantes* (1693–1694) moved a pleased Queen Mary to grant him sole proprietorship over it: this was Dunton's only royal license and, ironically, a financial albatross.

Another of Dunton's publishing broils transpired in 1693, this time involving Sault's *Second Spira,* one of the seven works Dunton regretted having published: "The World may perhaps expect I shou'd here say something of the SECOND SPIRA. – This *Narrative* was put into my Hands, by Mr. *Richard Sault,* the *Methodizer, December. 26. 1692.* Mr. *Sault* assur'd me, he receiv'd the *Memoires,* out of which he had form'd the *Copy* from a *Divine* of the *Church of England.*" This work claimed to be the dying confession of an atheist and, as its title announces, is the successor to *A Relation of the Fearful Estate of Francis Spira, 1548;* this chronicled the spiritual agonies of the senior Italian "Spira," whose seesawing conversions from Roman Catholicism to Protestantism to Roman Catholicism made for gripping reading, especially for an English Protestant audience fascinated with the reprobate soul. An avowed imitation of Francis Spira's biography, *The Second Spira* was published by Dunton in January 1693, but soon afterward rumors claimed that it was counterfeit. Sault, unable to identify the "Second Spira" or the cleric who purportedly heard the confession and gave his record of it to Sault for publication, withdrew to Cambridge under fire from Dunton; Dunton later claimed that Sault himself was the "Second Spira" and absolved himself of any complicity in the scandal, though *The Second Spira* was one of his leading publications. He sold thirty thousand copies in six weeks and, by 1719, reaped the profits of thirty editions.

In 1694–1695 Dunton's bustling trade saw the first signs of a downward swing with only three dozen new publications in 1694, according to Parks, and about one dozen in 1695. Two of Dunton's new items include a voluminous (more than seven hundred pages) *The Ladies Dictionary; Being A General Entertainment for the Fair-Sex* (1694) – a mediocre collection of pieces pitched for a female audience – and the beginnings of James Tyrrell's *General History of England* (eventually published in 1696). Escaping the noisy commercial district, Dunton moved from the Poultry to Jewen Street in September 1694 to devote more time to his reading. John Harris shared a warehouse with Dunton, whose books were then sold in Edmund Richardson's bookshop.

Early in 1696 Dunton temporarily suspended *The Athenian Mercury* and began two new periodicals: *Pegasus: with news, an observator, and a Jacobite courant,* a thrice-weekly news periodical with feature stories that ran in two volumes from 15 June 1696 to 14 September 1697, and *The Night-Walker: or, evening rambles in search after lewd women, with the conferences held with them &c.,* a monthly repository of salacious accounts of London prostitution. Dunton and a couple of disguised clergymen made nightly excursions into the darker sides of London and exposed this "wickedness" to their readers, as he recounts one such sally in *Life and Errors: "The First Night,* we resolv'd to Ramble, Mr. *T* – and my self, made an Appointment with our *Reverend Knight Errants,* to meet 'em at the *Bull-Head.* . . . [W]e kept to the Assignation very punctually, and had pickt up a *Young piece of Wickedness.*" Cast in the dual role of undercover investigative reporter and moral crusader, Dunton would typically chastise the prostitute, reporting the transaction in urgent detail as he does in this story of his first night, "she began to gather up a little too close with us, whereupon I rose up, and with as Ghostly a Look as I cou'd well affect, I said, 'Madam, *keep off; you think I am Flesh and Blood . . . Reclaim, your Whoredoms, or you are unavoidably lost, your Life is almost run out, and the Time you have to repent is very short.*" A stage for Dunton's self-dramatization, *The Night-Walker* was a short-lived adventure that folded after eight months.

The close of 1696 initiated Dunton's downward spiral with a series of tragic blows. In November Iris fell mortally ill, and in December her father died. Though Dunton received little inheritance from Annesley, whose estate was divided unequally among his twenty-five children, he was doubtless a stabilizing presence for his mercurial son-in-law. On 14 May 1697 *The Athenian Mercury* issued the first number of its final volume. And on 28 May 1697 Iris died. He devotes a section of his autobiography to "*A Comprehensive View of the* LIFE *and* DEATH *of* IRIS," a veritable saint's life, and published portions of her spiritual diary in both his autobiography and his periodical *The Post-Angel* (1701). By all accounts Dunton owed his financial solvency to his wife's management and, in retrospect, his emotional balance as well. Shortly after Iris died, a thirty-eight year-old Dunton retired from active publishing and embarked on another thirty-five years that moved toward gradual destitution and insanity.

In 1698 Dunton published *An Essay, Proving, We shall know Our Friends in Heaven. Writ by a Disconso-*

Numb. 4.

The Athenian Mercury:

Resolving WEEKLY all the most

Nice and Curious Questions

Propos'd by the INGENIOUS.

Saturday, April 4th. 1691.

Quest. 1. HOW Beasts came into Islands? to which may be added, for the Similitude of the Argument another, sent by an ingenious Gentleman from Cambridge —— How some remote Islands came first to be inhabited?

Answ. The latter of the Questions, which appears to me much the less difficult of the two, and on which the other may perhaps have some dependance, shall for these Reasons be first Answered. In order to which it must be remembred, that this being a thing only to be guest at, History therein leaving us in the dark, all we can do, is to advance some probable Hypothesis, which must stand till it appears chargeable with any absurdity.

We say then, that the World was first Peopled from the East, as Holy Writ assures, and History and Reason perswade, Arts and Arms first flourished there, and almost innumerable Armies appearing in early times, whence repeated swarms or inundations still issuing in the same Course with the Sun, thrust on one another from Place to Place, and Island to Island, we mean those less remote from the Continent, and which in clear Weather might be seen from it, and Ships easily get thither; for whatever other Authors say, we are sure there was Shipping as early as Noah; but what's this to those more remote, as America, when the Compass was not invented? first let that be prov'd an Island, and then we'll dispute further on't; in the mean time shall take the liberty to suppose on, that 'twas People from the North-west part of Tartary, which if not a Continent, must yet be much nearer to those parts than our side of the World. For the second Question——Beasts might pass the same way, and perhaps easier than Men; If 'tis all Land through inaccessible Snows and Woods, if only some strait and narrow Sea separates, nothing more common than for Sailers in that part of the World to find great Numbers of living Beasts floating upon the Ice, and this way as well as other wild Beasts might be driven over, or be there without so much trouble, if we admit this following Hypothesis, wherein I can foresee no absurdity. That there were Islands before the Flood can't be prov'd by History or Reason: let's suppose therefore there were none, but some actually made by its Fury and Violence, other parts of the Continent only disposed or prepared for Islands, continuing joyn'd by a very small Isthmus; while that remain'd, there was a Bridge large enough for the Beasts to go over, which being in process of time worn away, whereof Tradition, Observation and History gives us Instances, those Peninsulas were thereby transform'd into compleat Islands.

Quest. 2. Whether a Person Divorc'd by Law, may lawfully Marry another, while those they were first marryed to are yet living?

Answ. The best Casuist that ever was, resolves the Question in a few words, 5th of St. Matth. 32. Whosoever shall Marry her that is Divorced, committeth Adultery; and that's enough to give the importunate Querist satisfaction, if he really either wants or desires it.

Quest. 3. Whether Polygamy were Lawful to the Jews?

Answ. To answer this, we must consider the Term, Lawful, in respect to the Law of Nature writ in the minds of Men. The positive Laws of God, and even the Ceremonial Institutions for the People of the Jews, and those Laws, or Usages and Customs which had the force of Laws, which they established among themselves, as they were a Body Politick. By the last I know not but it might be lawful, at least 'twas certainly customary, and seems tolerated by Moses, who was their sovereign Prince and King in Jesurun; for the same Reason Divorces were, namely for the hardness of their Hearts, and to prevent worse consequences. By the Laws which God himself reveal'd to 'em by Moses, we find not one Syllable like any such Permission, whence it does not appear that by them 'twas ever lawful. By the Laws of Nature I think it absolutely unlawful; and to this our Saviour reduces the Jews, telling 'em —— from the beginning it was not so. Had there been any necessity of more Women than one, more would have been form'd for the first Man —— he that all conduc'd to his happiness, and what does otherwise is unnatural. It seems disagreeable to the Law of Nature, to permit such a practice as draws with it the most fatal inconveniences, and unnatural disturbances in Families and ... Empires, which ... unavoidably follow, as we may ... in the Serraglios of the Eastern World ...

An issue of Dunton's most notable publishing venture, a weekly periodical that enjoyed great financial success because of its appeal to the interests of Augustan coffeehouse patrons late Widower, on the Death of his Wife, and Dedicated to her Dear Memory (dated 10 July 1697), in which he confesses to his dead wife: "my Inclinations are at present wholly adverse from [a second marriage], because I think it utterly impossible for me ever to find such another as thy self." He, nevertheless, soon proposed – first to an unaccepting Elizabeth Singer, the "Pindarick Lady" of *The Athenian Mercury,* and then to Sarah Nicholas, who accepted. They were married in the fall on 23 October 1687. His second marriage to Sarah, whom he called "Valeria," was unfortunate because it appears her future inheritance inspired a debt-ridden Dunton's proposal. Her mother, Mrs. Jane Nicholas of Saint Albans, had recently inherited a good sum of money upon her husband's death but would not squander it on Dunton, whose failed projects, sister-in-law's debt, and outstanding medical bills (from Iris's sickness) were nearly bankrupting him. Mrs. Nicholas stood firm, even in the face of Dunton's published tirades against her, and early in 1698 Valeria returned to her mother's house for the remainder of her life.

At first Dunton sold many of his copyrights in order to pay his creditors, but this failed to meet their demands. In April 1698 he arrived in Dublin with ten tons of his books, valued at £1,500, to be publicly auctioned – still a relatively new way to sell such works. In 1699 he published *The Dublin Scuffle: Being a Challenge Sent BY JOHN DUNTON, Citizen of London, to Patrick Campbel, Bookseller in Dublin. Together with the Small Skirmishes of Bills and Advertisements. To Which Is Added, the Billet Doux, Sent Him by a Citizen's Wife in Dublin, Tempting Him to Lewdness. With His Answers; also Some Account of His Conversation in Ireland, Intermixt with Particular Characters of the Most Eminent Persons He Convers'd with in That Kingdom.*

As this partial title suggests, Dunton describes in three epistolary sections his business affairs, his Irish travels and acquaintances, and his battle with Campbell, an Irish bookseller who had become his latest archenemy. The first section belligerently chronicles his relationship with Campbell, who, according to Dunton, had thrice refused to settle accounts with him: "*The third time I saw him,* he shuffl'd about my Books at that rate, that a Stranger in his Shop (to whom I offer'd to refer my Cause) resented it: *And from that time forward* (only for demanding my own, and telling him how unfairly he dealt by me) he became my Enemy." The second section denies Dunton's involvement in an illicit love affair with an "Irish Dorinda," and in the third section of *The Dublin Scuffle,* as in much of *Life and Errors,* Dunton presents a biographical treasury of

Irish booksellers inseparably mixed with his autobiographical confessions and blatant attempts to purge his spotted reputation. Despite having this "scuffle," Dunton apparently did well by his auctions, and he sailed for London at the end of the year.

There, with Valeria and her mother insistently refusing to pay his standing debt, Dunton again resorted to hiding from angry creditors – this time in the lodgings of sundry female friends and landladies. He relentlessly demanded financial aid from his second wife, and in the early 1700s his friend Anne Baldwin printed his numerous libels against his wife and mother-in-law in publications such as *The Case of John Dunton, Citizen of London: With Respect to His Mother-in-law, Madam Jane Nicholas, of St. Albans; and Her Only Child, Sarah Dunton. With the Just Reasons for Her Husband's Leaving Her* (1700). Airing his family's dirty laundry never shook a penny from them, however: Jane Nicholas died in 1708 and Valeria in March 1721, neither having ever reconciled with Dunton.

Still yearning after 1700 for his early success as founder of the Athenian Society, Dunton inaugurated a few short-lived periodicals with the flavor and format of *The Athenian Mercury.* Written entirely by Dunton under the pseudonyms "Fido" and "Incognitus," *The Post-Angel* (from January 1701 to September 1702) created, among other regular features in the monthly, an angelic messenger service, "for sure a *Post-Angel* is able to *Out-flit a Post-Master, Post-Man, and Post-Boy.*" *The Secret Mercury: Or, the Adventure of Seven Days* (1702) was a weekly that informed its readers of "*the Vanity and secret Lewdness of the Town.*" In 1703 the first of several volumes and reprints of *The Athenian Oracle* appeared, a collection of popular questions and answers from *The Athenian Mercury.* In 1704 Dunton started three periodicals: *The Athenian Spy,* a magazine serially publishing love letters from female readers; *Athenae Redivivae: Or, the new Athenian Oracle,* another question-and-answer periodical that failed, as Dunton believed, because of the competition it faced from the successful *Review* of Daniel Defoe; and *The Athenian Catechism,* a penny paper directed to the "poorer Sort" of reader.

The opening years of the eighteenth century mark Dunton's gradual turn from bookselling and publishing to writing, as he recalls in *Life and Errors:*

This House of mine is filled with a *rambling* Tenant, and, being born to travel, I am ever pursuing my destiny; so that you may call me "a Citizen of London and of the World:" yet, wherever I come, I love to be guessed at, not known, and to see the World unseen; and for this reason I am now learning "The Art of living *Incognito.*" I

Frontispiece to Dunton's Young Students Library *(1692)*

entirely reliable, resource for understanding early modern bookselling and booksellers. Dunton composes hundreds of biographical thumbnail sketches of his colleagues, sketches noting everything from the locations of their shops to their reputations and trading styles. His portrait of Thomas Guy is typical:

> Mr. *Tho. Guy, in Lombard-Street,* he makes an Eminent Figure in the Company of stationers, having been Chosen *Sheriff* of *London,* and paid the Fine, and is now a Member of Parliament, for *Tamworth.* He entertains a very sincere Respect for *English* Liberty. He's a Man of strong Reason, and can talk very much to the Purpose, upon any Subject you'll propose. *He's truly charitable,* of which his ALMESHOUSES for the Poor, are standing Testimonies.

The full title of Dunton's memoirs reveals some of the style of his piously bombastic autobiography: *The Life and Errors of John Dunton late Citizen of* LONDON; *Written by Himself in Solitude. With an Idea of a New Life; Wherein is Shewn How he'd Think, Speak, and Act, might he Live over his Days again: Intermix'd with the NEW DISCOVERIES The Author has made In his Travels Abroad, and in his Private Conversation at Home. Together with the LIVES and Characters of a Thousand Persons now Living in* London, *&c. Digested into* Seven Stages, *with their Respective Ideas.* Dunton divides this autobiography into "stages" and recounts the cupidities of each before he refashions each of the stages into a moral lesson for his reader.

Through the brash egoism, however, shine traces of Dunton's sharp wit and shrewd business know-how. The many pen portraits of authors, booksellers, publishers, printers, and other important figures of the time reveal the wide arc of his social circle, which was indispensable for successful trading during this period of uneven copyright regulation. Parks notes that the extraordinary strength Dunton garnered through these acquaintances enabled him to resist pressures to join wholesale "congers," enough strength to negotiate and enforce publishing contracts on his own. Though he saw the benefits of these trade unions and even advocated separating bookselling from publishing ventures, he changed his opinion later when he fell victim to the piracy of a conger that printed his copyrights.

After 1711 Dunton's standing within the trade fell to that of laughingstock, with the exception of such longtime associates as Anne Baldwin, Elizabeth Mallet, and John Morphew. From freelance writer to political hack, Dunton ranted and raved for the Hanover monarchy and shamelessly de-

must here (to my mortification) reckon myself among the number of *Scribblers,* for my present income would not support me, did not I stoop so low as to turn Author; but I find it was what I was born to, for I am a willing and everlasting Drudge to the Quill, and am now writing "A Farewell to Trade."

The Art of Living Incognito (1700) is the first of many manic, spiteful, and confessional "scribblings" that occupied Dunton for the rest of his life. After 1700 his behavior was pathetically and ironically that of a *"Rambling Tenant"* whose busy quill could neither keep him from debtor's prison nor shelter him from the growing scorn of the book trade.

In 1705 Sarah Malthus published his memoirs, *The Life and Errors of John Dunton,* which presents his life story against a gossipy backdrop of the Augustan bookselling industry. Not a best-seller in the eighteenth century and reprinted with *The Dublin Scuffle* in a bowdlerized edition by John Nichols in 1818, it is now recognized as a critical, though not manded remuneration for doing so. In 1713 T. Warner published Dunton's *Nick or Nothing,* a tract that excoriated "the Pretender, Popery, and Slavery" and that Defoe described as "a continual rhapsody of scandal and raillery." Swift referred to it in his satiric *Publick Spirit of the Whigs:* "Among the present writers on that side, I can recollect but three of any great Distinction, which are the *Flying Post,* Mr. *Dunton,* and the author of the *Crisis.*" *Neck or Nothing* was for ironist Swift "the shrewdest Piece, and written with the most Spirit of any which hath appear'd from that Side." In 1715 King George I rewarded Dunton for his journalistic loyalty, but this was not sufficient, and in 1716 Dunton petitioned the king for further reward in *Mordecai's Memorial: Or, There's Nothing Done for Him. Being a Satyr upon Some-body, But I Name Nobody: (Or, in Plainer English, a Just and Generous Representation of Unrewarded Services, by Which the Protestant Succession Has Been Sav'd out of Danger.*

The last decade and a half of Dunton's life was punctuated with old vendettas: his writings attack former associates, his mother-in-law, the king, and political enemies. Even after the death of his second wife in 1721 and the acquisition of his long-awaited inheritance, he was unable to remain solvent and again petitioned King George from Fleet Prison for money in 1723. His last work, *An Essay on Death-Bed-Charity* (1728), is a harangue against people (such as his mother-in-law) who will their estates to the poor. On 24 November 1732 a forgotten Dunton died in the house of his executor, Richard Nowland.

The history of the Augustan book trade and the history of John Dunton – publisher, bookseller, pamphleteer, entrepreneur – are inevitably and ingeniously bound for us by his encyclopedic autobiography. Written after the height of his career, it chronicles the people and practices of turn-of-the-century publishing from the inside perspective of one of the formative figures of that trade. The ebullient, brash, and original spirit that informs both Dunton's own life and his biography of the publishing world is impossible to ignore.

Letters:

William Henry Whitmore, ed., *Letters Written from New-England A.D. 1686 by John Dunton* (Boston: Prince Society, 1867).

References:

John Dunton, *The Life and Errors of John Dunton, Citizen of London,* 2 volumes (1818; reprinted, New York: Franklin, 1969);

Peter Murray Hill, *Two Augustan Booksellers: John Dunton and Edmund Curll* (Lawrence: University of Kansas Libraries, 1959);

Gilbert D. McEwen, *The Oracle of the Coffee House: John Dunton's Athenian Mercury* (San Marino, Cal.: Huntington Library, 1972);

Stephen Parks, *John Dunton and the English Book Trade: A Study of His Career, with a Checklist of His Publications* (New York: Garland, 1976).

– Tamara A. Goeglein

George Eld

(London: 1603 – 1624)

Among the 428 extant editions published by George Eld, some are of primary significance, including William Shakespeare's *Sonnets* (1609) and *The Historie of Troylus and Cresseida* (1609), John Marston's *The Malcontent* (1604), Cyril Tourneur's *The Revenger's Tragedy* (1607), and the second and third editions of Christopher Marlowe's *The Tragicall History of the Life and Death of Doctor Faustus* (1620, 1624). As a premier printer of play texts, Eld printed thirty titles on his own and shared in the printing of four others. These and the eighty-seven other literary works from his presses establish him as a significant printer of the belles lettres of the period; religious works, otherwise, constitute the bulk of his production.

Little is known of George Eld's life. As the son of John Elde, a carpenter in Scraptin, Derby, Eld was apprenticed to Richard Bolton at Christmastime 1592 and was freed on 13 January 1600. Because apprentices could not be freed until they became twenty-four years old, Eld therefore probably had been born sometime in the mid 1570s. After gaining his freedom he acquired his own printing shop in an usually short period of time. Although nothing is known of his association with the shop's previous two owners, Gabriel Simson and Richard Read, Eld may have worked for them as a journeyman printer. In any event he married the twice-widowed Frances Simson following the death of Read circa 1603. Eld was to be elected to the livery of the Stationers' Company on 6 July 1611 but was never admitted as a master printer.

The lineage of the well-equipped, two-press shop in Fleet Lane, just west of Paul's Churchyard, is well documented. The relationship formed between masters and apprentices during periods of apprenticeship probably explains in part how Read, shortly after Simson had died (sometime before 11 August 1600), had succeeded Simson in acquiring the shop in 1601 – through marriage to the widowed Frances. Read (freed 18 January 1580) and Simson (freed 10 April 1583) had both been apprenticed to Richard Jugge, the queen's printer, from 1558 until his death in 1577. Jugge's son, John, acquired nominal control of his printing materials during the widowhood of Jugge's wife, Joan: John

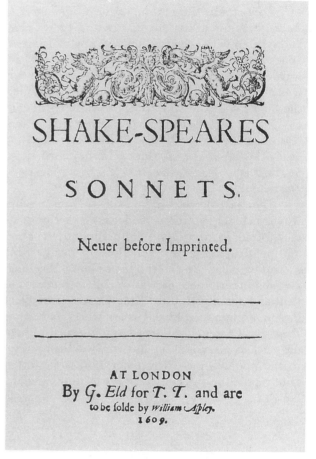

Title page for George Eld's unauthorized first edition of William Shakespeare's Sonnets *(1609)*

Jugge is listed in the 1583 Stationers' census of printing houses as owning two presses. With William White, another apprentice whom Jugge had also freed, Simson in 1585 formed a partnership, using the printing materials of their former master. The Stationers' census of 1586, however, shows the two presses belonging to Richard Watkins, the son-in-law of Richard Jugge.

Simson and White most probably operated the shop and did the actual printing for Watkins, a bookseller. Simson and White moved the Jugge materials to a new location for the shop in Fleet Lane "over against Seacoal Lane" sometime between 1588 and 1591. When their partnership dissolved in 1597, Simson retained the materials and the house,

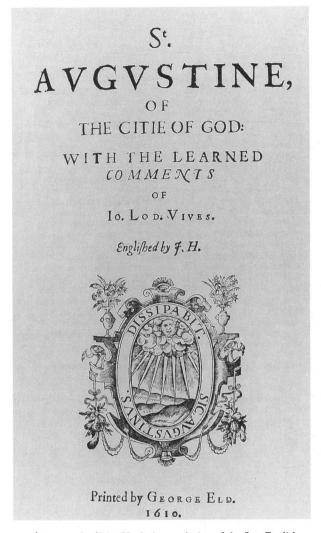

Title page for John Healey's translation of the first English edition of Saint Augustine's vindication of Christianity

and Eld imprints of 1607 and 1615 indicate that the shop remained here, identified by the sign of the Printer's Press, until it was again moved to a location in Little Brittain sometime before 1621. Eld took Miles Flesher as his partner in 1617, and Flesher is identified in imprints with Eld until the latter's death from the plague in 1624.

Although Eld's first imprint appeared early in 1604, a radical shift in the business arrangements and production level of the shop indicates that Eld had begun to manage it early in 1603. During Read's operation of the shop in 1601–1602, his production was limited to about twenty relatively short jobs. The largest projects included Sir William Cornwallis, the Younger's *A Second Part of Essayes* (1601), Ben Jonson's *The Fountaine of Selfe-Love, or Cynthias Revells* (1601), and a portion of Jonson's *Every Man in his Humour* – which Read, for some rea-

son, printed jointly with Simon Stafford. The five publishers (John Brome, Walter Burre, Matthew Law, William Jones, and Edmund Mattes) for whom Read printed in 1601–1602 never returned with further work.

Production at the shop in 1603 rose dramatically, as editions were contracted by twelve new publishers – William Aspley, Cuthburt Burby (two editions), Edmund Blount (three editions), Francis Burton, Geoffrey Chorlton, John Harrison II (two editions), John Harrison IV, Felix Norton, John Norton, Thomas Pavier (two editions), George Potter, and Thomas Thorpe (three editions). Eld was obviously successful in aggressively seeking new sources of work: many of these jobs were of substantial size, and Aspley, Blount, Burton, and Thorpe became regular customers. During 1604–1608 Eld printed six or more editions for each of

A

HISTORIE CON-

tayning the VVarres, Treaties, Mar-

riages, and other occurrents betweene

England and Scotland, from King William the
Conqueror, vntill the happy Vnion of them
both in our gratious King I A M E S.

With a briefe declaration of the first Inhabitants of this
Illand: And what seuerall Nations haue sithence setled them-selues therein one after an other:

INNOCENTER SAPERE

Imprinted at London by G. Eld. 1607.

*Title page for a first edition of one of the two dozen histories
Eld published*

these four publishers, and he shared in printing sections of four additional books for Aspley. In 1604 Eld began printing for John Wright, who was to bring him fourteen books by 1609 (a total of forty-four by 1623), and Thomas Adams, who was to provide him with nine works. This rising production and increase in new clients that date from early 1603 characterize the two decades in which Eld owned the shop.

His sharing of printing responsibilities also began in 1603, as Eld farmed out sections of George Downame's *A Treatise concerning Antichrist* (1603) to Richard Bradock and Thomas Creede, probably because the resources of his shop were overburdened. Many of the production figures are hidden in Eld's contribution (Book 3) to John Florio's translation of Michel de Montaigne's *The Essayes, or Morall, Politike, and Millitarie Discourses* (1603), of which Valentine Simmes shared the printing with Eld. The

thirty folio sheets printed in packed, pica roman prose would have constituted about sixty quarto prose sheets, enough to occupy a press for more than two months. That publisher Edmund Blount, who spared no expense in producing a book of such monumental size and significance, would have entrusted the printing of book 3 to a printer with the record of Richard Read is inconceivable. Nor would Blount have been likely to trust a printer who had produced only one dramatic quarto and half of another in printing Matthew Gwinne's Latin drama *Nero Tragaedia Nova* (1603). Eld apparently had the business acumen necessary to convince publishers to try his shop.

Everything thus indicates that Eld took over the shop in 1603. His favorite printer's mark – a pair of opposed scrolls, or "volutes," that appear frequently on his title pages – was used for the first time early in that year. Perhaps Read had succumbed to the plague of 1603, and his widow, Frances, waited a respectable mourning period (as she had apparently done after George Simson had died) before marrying Eld and passing ownership of the shop to her new husband. In any event Eld's imprint first appeared in 1604.

He printed books covering a wide range of subject matter: medicine, science, mathematics, husbandry, philosophy, government publications, politics, horsemanship, handwriting, legal texts, chronicles, rhetorics, almanacs, commonplace collections, and languages. He concentrated mainly, however, in the fields of literature (87 titles), drama (40 titles, including pageants and masques), religion (111 titles), sermons (46 titles), news books (54 titles), and history (24 titles). His success as a jobbing printer is evident especially in the category of religious and sermon texts. The 157 titles he printed of works in these two categories include editions by a hundred authors and nearly half as many publishers. His competitive success is clear in the fact that only he printed the entire one- or two-text oeuvres of many such authors.

The literary texts printed by Eld include reprints of old prose classics as well as short verse texts. Among the former, Eld printed the first twenty-five sheets of Sir Philip Sidney's *The Countesse of Pembrokes Arcadia* (1605), Barnabe Riche's *Riche His Farewell to Militarie Profession* (1606), John Lyly's *Euphues, the Anatomy of Wit* (1617), and two editions of George Pettie's *A Petite Pallace of Pettie His Pleasure* (1608, 1613). In addition to the first edition of Shakespeare's *Sonnets,* Eld printed sixty-five verse texts, most of little literary significance. Among these are four editions of George Wither's *Abuses*

Stript (1613), Samuel Daniel's *Certaine Small Poems* (1605), Sir Thomas Overbury's *A Wife, Now a Widow* (1614), several works by Nicholas Breton, and six first editions of texts by John Taylor, the now-ridiculed but then quite popular "water poet." The third edition of the anonymous *The Merry Devil of Edmunton* (1617) is among the seven jestbooks printed by Eld. Most of his printing of ballads (nineteen) occurred after 1615 and was done for various publishers.

The printing of William Camden's *Remaines of a Greater Work* (1604), which Eld shared with Simmes, complements other works of literary criticism from the period. Its references to contemporary poets have been largely overlooked: among the "chief of poets" are listed – in addition to Shakespeare – Jonson, Marston, Sidney, Edmund Spenser, George Chapman, Michael Drayton, Thomas Campion, Daniel, and the now unknown Hugh Holland.

Eld was involved in the printing of forty-four dramatic editions (including two closet dramas), and eight of these were joint printing ventures. As primary printer, Eld shared the production of George Chapman's *All Fools* (1605) with William White and Simon Stafford. With Valentine Simmes as primary printer Eld shared in printing the three editions of Marston's *The Malcontent* and two editions of Thomas Dekker's *The Honest Whore* (1604); with William Jaggard as primary printer he shared the printing of Dekker and John Webster's *Westward Hoe* (1607); and with Nicholas Okes as primary printer Eld jointly printed Matthew Gwinne's *Vertumnus* (1607).

By himself Eld printed four titles by Thomas Middleton – *The Puritane, or The Widdow of Watling-Streete* (1607), *Your Five Gallants* (1608), *A Trick to Catch the Old-One* (1608), and *A Faire Quarrell* (1617) – as well as Jonson's *Seianus His Fall* (1605) and *Ben: Jonson His Volpone, or the Foxe* (1607), Chapman's *The Conspiracie, and Tragedie of Charles Duke of Byron* (1608), Dekker's *The Shoemaker's Holiday* (1610), and the third edition of Shakespeare's *The Tragicall Historie of Hamlet* (1611). Chapman's *The Memorable Maske of the Middle Temple, and Lyncolns Inne* (1613) is among the half-dozen masques and pageants printed by Eld.

Of considerable interest to students of drama is John Greene's *A Refutation of the Apology for Actors* (1615), which Eld published and printed in partnership with William White. Aroused by Thomas Heywood's *An Apology for Actors* (1612), this hardcore Puritan attack on the theater reveals attitudes that had not changed from those held in the time of Philip Stubbes. That Eld published it is

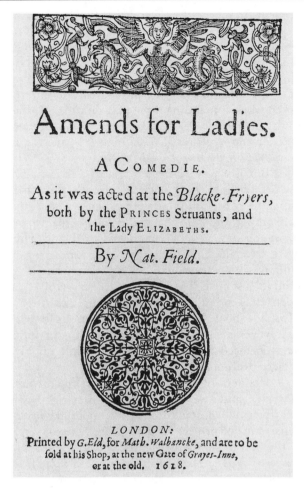

Title page for a play written by a popular member of Shakespeare's company

an irony, one that surely reveals his business acumen: he was one of the chief disseminators of the "Heathenish and Diabolicall institution" of plays and the "abominations" and "filth" that they contained. To successful publishing printers, the marketability of a work was more important than its content.

Of the seven works about exploration that Eld printed, two are of special historical interest to Americanists: Virginia Company of London's *A True and Sincere Declaration of the Purpose and Ends of the Plantation Begun in Virginia* (1610), Edward Waterhouse's *A Declaration of the State of the Colony in Virginia, with a Relation of the Barbarous Massacre,* and Henry Briggs's *A Treatise of the Northwest Passage* (1622).

Eld's success in aggressively seeking new clients apparently created the financial base and confidence he needed to begin publishing on his own shortly after having taken over the shop, and he seems to have been a highly motivated young entrepreneur. In one respect he is rather typical, as many jobbing printers occasionally would buy a relatively short text, enter it in the Stationers' Register to establish a copyright, and publish it themselves. Beginning in 1607 Eld so invested in publishing short books, for in that year he purchased and entered seven works, including three play-quartos: Middleton's *The Puritane, or The Widdow of Watling-Streete,* Dekker and Webster's *North-warde Hoe,* and Tourneur's *The Revenger's Tragedy.*

But Eld was perhaps the most risk taking of the printer-publishers, because the early projects in which he chose to invest were expensive and time-consuming, the kind that could occupy his presses for much of a year. He managed to finance such work by balancing his large publication projects with a regular printing of both ephemera and large folio jobs such as *The Shepherd's Kalendar* (1604; not Spenser's) and Eucharius Roesslin's *The Birth of Mankind* (1604). His record of publications for each year reveals several substantial quartos or folios being printed for other publishers while his own projects were under way.

His debt-free acquisition of the shop through marriage and the success of his first few years clearly provided money for Eld to undertake his expensive major projects. Eld purchased the copyright to the first of such projects, Jean de Serres's *A General Inventorie of the Historie of France* (1607), from William Ponsonby in early 1606. The year between its entry in the Stationers' Register and its imprint date is characteristic of his projects, and *A General Inventorie* clearly was a good choice for such a first effort: Eld reprinted it twice, in 1611 and 1624. It was followed by Simon Goulart's *Admirable and Memorable Histories* in 1607, and Jean Le Petit's *The Low-Country Commonwealth* in 1609. Eld also joined printer Adam Islip in printing Le Petit's *A General History of the Netherlands* in 1608 and Louis de Mayerne Turquet's *The General History of Spain* in 1612.

These were massive printing projects. *A General History of the Netherlands* required more than 750 sheets, enough to occupy a single press for more than two years, and it is easy to understand why Eld and Islip had shared in printing it. These projects were even more expensive because each required the extended services of indefatigable translator Edward Grimeston, whom Eld most likely employed almost continuously from 1606 onward. While Eld, like most printers, printed ephemera in order to sustain his business, his vision of his publishing mission is extraordinary, for such historical works as he completed are among the most substantial reference works published during the period.

Eld entered a total of sixty-two titles in the Stationers' Register, of which forty-five are extant. That he ever printed the remaining seventeen is unclear. The extant titles include twenty-two religious titles, seven literary titles (as well as four other dramatic titles), and seven historical titles.

That Eld distributed his publications at wholesale rather than selling at retail is clear from the canceled title pages of Middleton's *A Trick to Catch the Old-One.* The original imprint specified that this was "Printed by G. Eld, and . . . to be sold at his house in Fleete-lane at the signe of the Printer's Press." Before the edition had been completed, a cancel title page was substituted with the imprint, "to be sold by Henry Rockytt, at the long shop in the Poultrie under the Dyall." Following a common practice, Eld had sold the entire edition to bookseller Rockytt while it was still being printed, and Rockytt had required the replacement title page in order to advertise the location of his shop. As most of Eld's publications do not identify a bookseller, Eld evidently distributed them through the usual wholesale channels.

References:

Peter Blayney, *The Texts of King Lear and Their Origins* (Cambridge: Cambridge University Press, 1982);

Adrian Weiss, "Bibliographical Methods for Identifying Unknown Printers in Elizabethan/ Jacobean Books," *Studies in Bibliography,* 44 (1991): 183–228;

Weiss, "Font Analysis as a Bibliographical Method: The Elizabethan Play-Quarto Printers and Compositors," *Studies in Bibliography,* 43 (1990): 95–164;

Weiss, "Reproductions of Early Dramatic Texts as a Source of Bibliographical Evidence," *TEXT: Transactions of the Society for Textual Scholarship,* 4 (1988): 237–268.

         — Adrian Weiss

Eliot's Court Press

(1584 – 1674)

The printing house in Eliot's Court, a firm responsible for publishing many artistically superior volumes of classical editions from the early 1580s until its cessation around 1674, originated with the death of printer Henry Bynneman of Thames Street, London. Bynneman died intestate in December 1583, but he had appended the following provision to his final entry in the Stationers' Company register: "Always provided that the said Henry Bynneman shall from tyme to tyme according to his good discretion, chose and accept any fyve of this cumpanye to be parteners with him in the imprintinge of these bookes." In partial accordance with Bynneman's twilight proviso four men of varying degrees of experience as printers – Edmund Bollifant, Arnold Hatfield, John Jackson, and Ninian Newton – acquired by transfer the ownership of Bynneman's type factotums, pictorial initials, and ornaments shortly after his death. Bollifant, Hatfield, and Newton had all previously served apprenticeships in the Fleet Street printing house of Henry Denham and Ralph Newberry, associates of Bynneman, while Jackson purportedly provided the foursome with financial means for making their initial foray into the print trade in 1584.

The four originally established their business in Eliot's Court, Old Bailey, although little information remains about the precise nature of their arrangements. Despite their association as proprietors of the press at Eliot's Court, their four names never appeared together in the imprint of any book; only the names of those printers who participated in the actual publication of a particular edition appear in the imprint of that volume. During 1584 the press issued two volumes for John Wight – Edmund Bunny's octavo edition of Robert Parsons's *Booke of Christian Exercise* and Bunny's *Treatise Tending to Pacification,* both published in August of that year and bearing the imprint of Newton and Hatfield as printers. As in future volumes that the firm was to publish, Bynneman's types and factotums are readily identifiable in both editions.

In 1585 Jackson and Bollifant produced a nine-volume octavo edition of Cicero, while Newton and Hatfield compiled editions of Julius Caesar's *Commentaries* and Horace in sextodecimo. Bol-

lifant also published the *Britannica Historia* of Virunus Ponticus for Denham and Newberry, while Jackson produced Franciscus Duarenus's *De sacris ecclesiae ministeriis ac beneficiis librii VIII* for George Bishop, one of the assigns of Christopher Barker's London publishing firm. Bollifant also printed one of the firm's most significant early publishing successes, William Bulloker's edition of *Æsop's Fables.*

Despite such successes, however, the printers at Eliot's Court suffered under the same copyright laws that troubled so many printers of their day. In 1585 Joseph Barnes, an Oxford printer, pirated Wight's copyright of Robert Parsons's *Booke of Christian Exercise* (1582) – a volume that the printers at Eliot's Court described as remarkably "vendible" and from which they had expected to enjoy sizable profits. The printers responded by publishing Bishop Thomas Bilson's *The True Difference betweene Christian Subiection and Vnchristian Rebellion* (1585), a text protected by a copyright that belonged to Barnes, who immediately alerted the authorities. After raiding Eliot's Court, seizing one of the presses, and imprisoning Bollifant, the authorities released him following an urgent petition to the Privy Council from the master and wardens of the company.

In the decade following their participation in the Barnes affair, the printers at Eliot's Court enjoyed strong and abiding support from their colleagues in the print trade. In addition to receiving the loyal patronage of clients such as Bishop, Newberry, and Barker, the printers at Eliot's Court were employed by many important contemporary booksellers, including such publishing luminaries as John Norton, Bonham Norton, John Bill, John Wolfe, and Francis Coldock. The printers also received a coveted contract to print the greater part of the Latin Bible published by the assigns of Barker in various editions in 1592 and 1593.

In the fourth part and in the Apocrypha of that Latin Bible edition H. R. Plomer identifies the caduceus device that distinguished Bynneman's typefaces as well as volumes produced by the various printers at Eliot's Court. Plomer's identification of this feature allows scholars to recognize the number and variety of foreign and domestic volumes

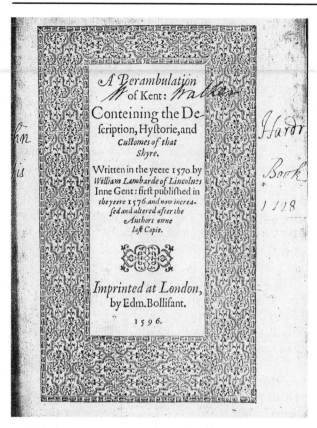

*Title page for one of the local history volumes printed at the
Eliot's Court Press by Edmund Bollifant (courtesy of the
Lilly Library, Indiana University)*

published by the Eliot's Court printers during this
period. Such volumes include Rembert Dodoens's *A
Niewe Herball or Historie of Plantes* (1586), Moses
Pflacher's *Analysis typica omnium cum veteris tum novi
Testamenti Librorum Historicorum* (1587), Livy's
Romanae Historiae (1589), John Twyne's *Joannis
Twini, Bolingdunensis, Angli, de rebus Albionicis Britanni-
cus atque Anglicis* (1590), Guillaume de Saluste du
Bartas's *Babilon* (1596), William Lambard's *Perambu-
lation of Kent* (1596), Christof Wirsung's *Praxis Medi-
cinae universalis,* (1598) and Matthew Sutcliffe's
*Matthæi Sutliuii de vera Christi ecclesia aduersus Rob.
Bellarminum* (1600).

During this era the firm also endured many
significant personnel changes. After printing *A
Niewe Herball* in 1586 Newton left the firm, as did
Jackson nearly a decade later, when he ended his
association with the establishment around 1596.
Bollifant, surely the most creative and productive
of the early printers at Eliot's Court, died in early
1602. Melchisidec Bradwood, formerly an apprentice in John Day's shop and known for his familiarity with the artistry of printing, quickly filled
Bollifant's role with the firm.

On 5 July 1602 a consortium of booksellers
including Bishop, William Ponsonby, Simon
Waterson, John Norton, and George Adams
noted in the Stationers' register their intention to
print an edition of Plutarch's *Works,* a folio editon
that was to require more than fourteen hundred
pages when Hatfield and Bradwood printed it in
1603. In 1606 Bradwood printed a pamphlet, *Copy of
a Letter written by E. D.,* as well as George Thompson's *Vindex Veritatis* and Abraham Ortelius's
Theatrum Orbis Terrarum — this last being a folio
edition with the imprint of John Norton, although
the volume features ornaments and a caduceus
that clearly reveal its Eliot's Court heritage. Norton later commissioned Bradwood to print Sir
Henry Savile's edition of the Greek classics, a
project that required the printer — along with six
apprentices and supplementary type, initials, ornaments, and devices borrowed from the Eliot's
Court printing house — to relocate to Eton. Although Norton assumed full credit for
Bradwood's craftsmanship by placing only his
name in the imprint of such handsome editions as
the *Chrysostom* (1610), Bradwood's artistic excellence in this project earned renown from his peers
in the London printing circle. His exemplary folio
edition of Michel Montaigne's *Essays* (1613) further
confirmed his attention to the artistry that often
marked the finest work produced during that era of
the British trade.

During Bradwood's extended absence in Eton,
Hatfield, the last of the firm's founders, died in January 1611, shortly after publishing his final volume,
Joseph Hall's *Polemice sacra* (1611). In his will Hatfield appointed Bradwood as one of his overseers
and also left money to purchase a ring. At this time
Edward Griffin assumed Hatfield's managerial duties, professional requirements that had increased
dramatically because of Bradwood's protracted absence in Eton, where he died in 1618. In an effort to
maintain the increasingly complex day-to-day operations of the firm, Griffin secured the services of
George Purslowe, a printer who had served his apprenticeship under the tutelage of Richard Bra-
docke. Before accepting a position at the printing
house at Eliot's Court, Purslowe purchased printing
materials — including initial letters, ornaments, devices, and perhaps a press — from Simon Stafford, a
printer from Hosier Lane. Purslowe also deftly secured from the widow of another printer all of the
legal and financial interests in her late husband's
copies; this Purslowe did while also reportedly developing his own romantic interest in the widow,
presumably his future wife, Elizabeth.

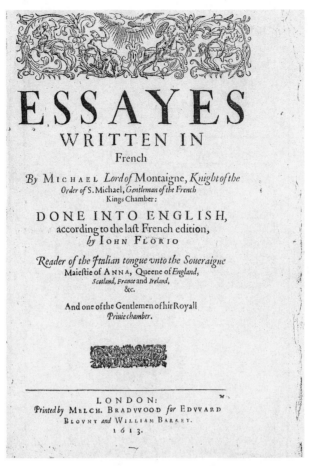

ESSAYES
WRITTEN IN
French

By MICHAEL Lord of Montaigne, Knight of the
Order of S. Michael, Gentleman of the French
Kings Chamber:

DONE INTO ENGLISH,
according to the laſt French edition,
by IOHN FLORIO

Reader of the Italian tongue vnto the Soueraigne
Maieſtie of ANNA, Queene of England,
Scotland, France and Ireland,
&c.

And one of the Gentlemen of hir Royall
Priuie chamber.

LONDON:
Printed by MELCH. BRADVVOOD for EDVVARD
BLOVNT and WILLIAM BARRET.
1613.

*Title page for John Florio's 1613 English translation of
Eyquem de Montaigne's* Essays, *printed at the Eliot's
Court Press by Melchisidec Bradwood (courtesy of the
Lilly Library, Indiana University)*

In this manner Purslowe provided the firm with some valuable professional commodities, in addition to his much-needed services as a printer. In late 1613 or early 1614 Griffin published Purslowe's first edition, Leonard Wright's *A display of dutie.* Following publication of this first volume Purslowe shared with the firm those ornaments and initials he had purchased from Stafford's publishing house, and he later became a full partner in the Eliot's Court printing house.

In 1616 Purslowe printed an edition of Robert Greene's *Mourning Garment,* and the imprint of this volume lists the printer's address as the "East end of Christchurch." Purslowe likely resided during this period near Christ Church, Newgate Street, a location not three minutes' walk from the Eliot's Court printing house, and the printer's proximity to the establishment, as well as his interest in adding his own printing resources to those of the firm, confirms his significant position with the Eliot's Court Press at this time. The publication in 1620 of the

Reverend Elnathan Parr's *A Plaine Exposition upon the Whole Eighth, Ninth, Tenth, Eleventh, Twelfth Chapters of the Epistle to the Romanes* reveals Purslowe's creative combinations of Bynneman's blocks and headpieces, and it suggests that Purslowe's professional presence at the firm was finally filling the artistic lacunae that the deaths of Bradwood and Hatfield had left.

The continuity of the firm suffered another setback, however, with the death of Griffin in 1620. His widow, Ann, subsequently secured the services of John Haviland to replace her husband as a managing partner there. The youngest son in the large family of a Gloucestershire clergyman, Haviland had gone abroad in 1613 to search for Greek type. In the tradition of Bradwood, Haviland was to provide the Eliot's Court firm with many handsome, artistic volumes, particularly in its editions of the writings of Sir Francis Bacon. In 1623, for example, Haviland printed a Latin folio edition of Bacon's *Works,* followed in 1625 by a quarto edition of

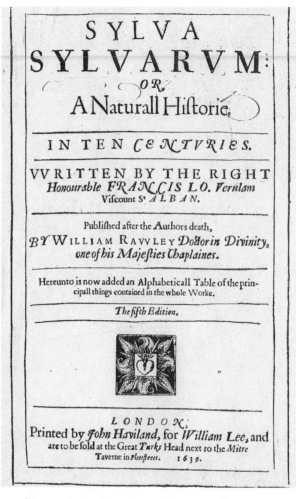

SYLVA
SYLVARVM:
OR,
A Naturall Historie.

IN TEN CENTVRIES.

VVRITTEN BY THE RIGHT
Honourable FRANCIS LO. Verulam
Viscount St. ALBAN.

Published after the Authors death,
BY WILLIAM RAVVLEY Doctor in Divinity,
one of his Majesties Chaplaines.

Hereunto is now added an Alphabeticall Table of the prin-
cipall things contained in the whole Worke.

The fifth Edition.

LONDON;
Printed by John Haviland, for William Lee, and
are to be sold at the Great Turks Head next to the Mitre
Taverne in Fleetstreet. 1639.

Title page for the fifth edition of Francis Bacon's historical
studies of various natural phenomena, printed at the
Eliot's Court Press by John Haviland (courtesy of
the Lilly Library, Indiana University)

Bacon's essays. In 1627 he published Bacon's *Sylva Sylvarum,* between Latin and English editions of the author's *Historia Naturalis* in 1622 and 1638, respectively.

Despite the death in 1632 of Purslowe, whose role in the printing house fell to his widow, Elizabeth, the firm continued to prosper. It possessed three presses at this time, and it began printing many theological volumes, most notably of the Psalms in meter, as well as various legal volumes. According to Plomer, assessing the true production of the Eliot's Court Press from 1601 to 1640 remains difficult, however, because the firm's association with a particular volume can be revealed only by identifying specific initials or ornaments in it, or by examining the publisher's imprint – which, in the case of the Eliot's Court Press, bears only the printer's initials.

Following Haviland's death in 1638 the firm began a new, uncertain era in its management. In his will, approved by the magistrate on 20 November of that year, Haviland bequeathed fifty pounds to Ann Griffin and Elizabeth Purslowe, as well as an additional twenty pounds to Griffin's son, Edward Griffin II, for the purchase of a ring. His will also featured the following proviso that directed the disposition of the materials and ownership of the printing house at Eliot's Court, and the will therefore significantly influenced the nature of the firm's final years of operation:

Item my will and mynde is that my executor John Wright the elder doe not intermeddle with the lettinge, settinge, contracting for or disposing of my printing howse or the materialls thereof, but that he leave it to be disposed of and ordered by my brother Miles Flesher, and my friend Andrew Crooke. And my desire is that they contract with and sett my said printinge howse and materialls thereof to Thomas Broad printer for such yearly reasonable sum of money as the said Miles Flesher and Andrew Crooke shall in their discrecons think fit.

While a printer by the name of Thomas Broad never assumed administration of the printing establishment at Eliot's Court, Haviland's will nevertheless succeeded – if only for a while – in continuing to operate the firm in the manner that it had been run before his death. Edward Griffin II entered into a partnership at the firm that already included Elizabeth Purslowe and, presumably, Ann Griffin. This triumvirate continued to maintain the business through the civil war and Commonwealth eras, during which times the press printed many ecclesiastical books and pamphlets. In 1641, for instance, it printed John Colet's *Daily Devotions* – a duodecimo edition printed by Edward Griffin II for John Benson and also a quarto edition of Jan Sictor's *Epithalamium auraico Britannicum.* On 27 September 1642 Robert Sidney, earl of Leicester's *A Letter from the Lord of Leicester,* printed for John Wight, was published, and in 1643 Griffin printed Joseph Caryl's *The Nature of a Sacred Covenant* for John Rothwell and Giles Calvert. The firm also produced two additional volumes for Wight, a quarto edition of *An Ordinance of the Lords and Commons* (1644) and *The Propositions of the Lords and Commons for a Safe and Well-Grounded Peace,* published from the King's Head printing house in the Old Bailey on 17 July 1646.

Although precise historic details of the firm's final years remain unknown, the deaths of Edward Griffin II in 1652 and of Elizabeth Purslowe in 1656 again altered the management of the printing house. Griffin's widow, Sarah, assumed day-to-day management of the printing house following her husband's death. A 1668 survey of the number of presses and workmen employed in London printing houses reveals the slow decline of the Eliot's Court Press after the deaths of such master printers as Bradwood and Haviland: by that year the firm possessed only two presses, one apprentice, and six workmen. Sarah Griffin maintained the printing house with the assistance of Bennett Griffin, presumably her son, from 1657 until at least 1674, when many printing customs changed: in particular, the old blocks and pictorial initials that the firm had used so prevalently throughout its history were no longer used, and the ultimate fate of the Eliot's Court Press has thus become difficult to ascertain.

References:

H. R. Plomer, "Eliot's Court Press, Decorative Blocks and Initials," *Library: Transactions of the Bibliographical Society,* fourth series 3 (December 1922): 194–209;

Plomer, "The Eliot's Court Printing House, 1584–1674," *Library: Transactions of the Bibliographical Society,* fourth series 2 (December 1921): 175–184.

                                              – Kenneth Womack

Richard Grafton

(London: 1534 – 1573)

Richard Grafton was a man of several careers. As printer to Henry VIII and Edward VI, he published some of the most significant texts of the English Reformation, including the first complete Bible in English and early versions of the *Book of Common Prayer*. As a chronicler he produced compendious historical collections in the medieval tradition, collections that, because of their moralistic views of historical process, were outdated almost from the days of their publication. As a liveryman of the Grocers' Company of London, he participated in the administration of his guild, sat in Parliament, and took part in civic and charitable affairs.

His varied life left many records, but although his character must be assembled from scattered letters, title pages, and prefaces, the picture that survives is consistent. Although he cannot be called a mover and shaker, Grafton was an active man of some influence, one who professionally dealt with several of the more important theologians and politicians of his day. Concerned as much with reputation as with profit, he was an entrepreneur who rose from undistinguished beginnings to make himself, for a time, useful to the powerful.

Born the son of Nicholas Grafton of Shrewsbury, Grafton apparently benefited from some education and enjoyed early success as a merchant. The earliest record about him dates from 1526, when he was apprenticed to London grocer John Blage. By 1534 he had been admitted to the livery of the Grocers' Company, a powerful group of London merchants with strong ties to Protestantism. He maintained his association with the Grocers' Company throughout his life and served the organization as a warden in 1555. Twice married, he had several children – including a daughter, Joan, who later became the wife of Richard Tottel, publisher of the famous *Tottel's Miscellany* (1557). Grafton's son, Nicholas, became a successful barrister and had confirmation of arms made to him in 1584.

About 1534 Grafton and fellow grocer Edward Whitchurch opened a printing shop in London within the precincts of the Greyfriars, a monastic house dissolved by King Henry VIII. Thomas Cromwell, then the vicar general, may have suggested that Grafton and Whitchurch enter the publishing business, for Cromwell needed reliable and well-funded representatives to underwrite and coordinate an important project – a translation of the Scriptures into English. At the time no authorized, vernacular version of the Bible existed, although many translations that were dangerous to own and unlawful to read were circulating. The desire for an English Bible was great, and those in power recognized its usefulness as a political instrument that could theoretically be used to unify the beliefs and practices of the new Anglican Church.

Grafton and Whitchurch set about publishing a translation of the Scriptures produced by Miles Coverdale but based on the work of William Tyndale. Tyndale was considered one of the best authorities on scriptural texts, but he had been condemned as a heretic by Cromwell in 1534, and to associate with him was dangerous. Therefore, instead of using their Greyfriars press, Grafton and Whitchurch had the printing of their Bible done in Antwerp, far from the tensions of Henry VIII's court, and had the loose sheets shipped to London for binding.

As work progressed, Grafton stayed in close touch with his patron. He anticipated resistance to the Bible and also hoped to forestall rival printer James Nicholson of Southwark, who was preparing his own cheaper translation of it. So before publishing it Grafton sent Cromwell six copies of the text and a letter, dated 28 August 1537, asking for a license under the Privy Seal as a "defense at this present and in time to come for all enemies and adversaries." As Grafton explained to Cromwell, he had printed the Bible to his "great and costly labors and charges" – £500 expended on fifteen hundred volumes – and he feared financial ruin if Nicholson were to sell his translation at a cheaper price. Therefore, Grafton bluntly asked Cromwell to guarantee a market by requiring each curate in England to buy one copy and every abbey six, and he added his wish that only "the papistical sort" should be compelled to purchase them. Through the mediations of Cromwell and Archbishop Thomas Cranmer, this Bible was published in 1537 with a license from Henry VIII. It came to be known as the "Matthew" Bible, because the only name on its title page was that of Thomas Matthew, long believed to be a pseudonym for Tyndale or for John Rogers, an editor who later became the first Protestant martyr under Queen Mary I.

The success of the Matthew Bible and the confidence of knowing that he had well-placed protectors encouraged Grafton to attempt other projects. Little more than a year after the Matthew Bible had appeared, he and Whitchurch were in Paris under Cromwell's protection to oversee publication of a Latin-English New Testament, which appeared in November 1538 from the press of François Regnault. Though published separately, this New Testament was part of a more ambitious work in progress, the first complete Bible translated from the original Greek and Hebrew into English. Paris offered the advantage of superior printing facilities, but the venture was extremely risky, as Grafton was well aware: France was Catholic, so the printing was to be done under the eyes of the Inquisition. From the French king Cromwell had secured a license granting permission for his representatives to print the Bible and transport it to England, but the license contained a phrase making their safety contingent upon their success in "avoiding any private or unlawful opinions" – a condition virtually impossible for a Protestant translation to fulfill, and one that rendered the license useless.

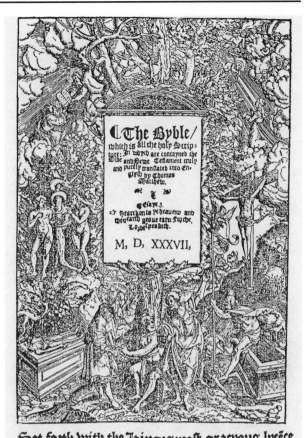

Title page for Richard Grafton's edition of the "Matthew Bible" (1537)

On 17 December 1538 the French inquisitor general issued a citation requiring Regnault and his associates to appear before the Inquisition on the following day. Grafton and Whitchurch escaped to London, leaving Regnault and most of the unbound Bibles behind. Officials of the University of Paris seized some two thousand copies and, according to John Foxe's *Acts and Monumentes* (1563), burned them in Paris's Place Maulbert. Others were sold to a haberdasher who reportedly used them to line hats. As soon as Grafton arrived in London, Cromwell sent him back to France to salvage what he could and, with the aid of Edmund Bonner's ambassadorial negotiations, to arrange for the printers and their equipment to be transported to London. When work was eventually completed in London, the final product was impressive.

Published in 1539 as *The Bible in English*, Grafton's "Great Bible," which sold at a price of ten shillings bound, was a richly illustrated folio. Two vellum copies, possibly presentation texts, survive at St. John's College in Cambridge and at the National Library of Wales. Royal injunctions requir-

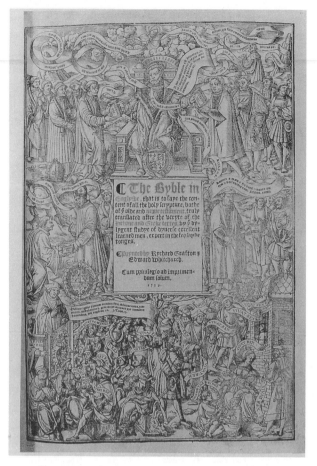

Title page for Grafton's "Great Bible," The Bybie in
Englyshe *(1539), an illustrated folio edition*

ing all churches to purchase copies created sufficient demand to warrant seven editions within two
years. After 1541, however, the atmosphere of tolerance in which the Great Bible had emerged began to
change. Free access to a vernacular Bible inspired
not only faith among the laity but also sufficient ir-
reverence and contention to provoke Parliament, in
1543, to prohibit public reading of Scripture. Thereafter, only males with proof of education could own
or publicly read a Bible.

When Cromwell was executed in June 1540
Grafton lost a patron, but he did not otherwise suf-
fer from the association. In fact, in the same year
Henry VIII made him the exclusive printer to Ed-
ward, the Prince of Wales. During this period
Grafton's printing business produced many service
books, such as *The Gospels and Epistles of All the Sun-
days and Saints Days That Are Read in the Church All the
Whole Year* (1540) and *The Primer Both in English and
Latin* (1540).

Despite the caution with which he characteristically acted, Grafton was arrested in January 1541

and brought before the Privy Council to answer ac-
cusations that he had published ballads defending
the executed Cromwell as well as a translation of
Philipp Melanchthon's attack on the Six Articles
that Parliament had passed in 1539 to establish the
principles of the Anglican Church. While Grafton's
acts may give the impression of a courageous man
with strong beliefs and loyalties, this impression is
marred by the fact that he had published the ballads
under the name of Richard Bankes, a business rival.
If his motive had been prudence, it backfired.
Grafton was sentenced on 6 January to six weeks in
Fleet Prison, although he was released early by
order of the king.

The year continued to offer troubles. In *Acts
and Monumentes* Foxe records that in 1541 Grafton
and Whitchurch were brought before the authorities for "persecution" as a result of their lapse in correct religious practice: they had not been regularly
confessed, as required by the Six Articles. No sentence is recorded for either man, although a term in
prison would not have been unusual. Foxe's brief
account also records Grafton's residence at the time —
St. Owen's Parish, in Newgate Market.

Despite these interruptions the 1540s was a period of great activity for Grafton. He had achieved
recognition for his Bibles and enjoyed some status
at Henry's court. Besides primers and psalters his
printing house issued secular works such as *A Glass
for Householders* (1542); Desiderius Erasmus's *Apoph-
thegms* (1542); *The Precepts of Plutarch for the Preservation of Good Health* (1543), translated by John Hales;
and Erasmus's *A Very Pleasant and Fruitful Dialogue
Called the Epicure* (1545). Several of these works bear
Grafton's motto, *Suscipite incitum verbum Iaco,* and his
device — a visual pun on his name: a grafted fruit
tree appears growing through a tun, or barrel.

In the 1540s Grafton made his first venture
into publishing historical works by printing two
versions of a fifteenth-century chronicle by John
Hardyng. Rendered entirely in verse, *The Chronicle
of John Hardyng* (1543) began with the founding of
Britain by survivors of the Trojan War and progressed to the reign of King Edward IV. Its principal theme, as stated in Hardyng's preface, was that
Scotland belonged to England by rights but had
been "false from the beginning." The focus of this
chronicle on Scotland's rebelliousness made it a
timely publication, for Thomas Howard, fourth
duke of Norfolk, had led an expedition against Scotland in 1542. Hoping to enlist a new patron,
Grafton attached a verse dedication praising Norfolk as God's "sharp scourge and rod" to the recalcitrant Scots.

Grafton also appended a lengthy prose continuation that brought the narrative of events covered by the *Chronicle* into the thirtieth year of the reign of Henry VIII. For this continuation Grafton drew upon the "most credible and authentic writers," chiefly upon Polydore Vergil, but some evidence also suggests that he incorporated an English version of Sir Thomas More's *History of King Richard III* (1543), edited and adapted to chronicle form.

On 28 January 1544 Grafton and Whitchurch's work with divine service books was recognized by a royal license that gave the two an exclusive seven-year patent for printing them. From this year until the accession of Mary Tudor in 1553 Grafton enjoyed a virtual monopoly on printing service books during a period when demand for such works was increasing. Yet he had the privilege of printing only officially approved books, and the limitations governing such approval were constantly debated. Printers moved cautiously to avoid arousing the anger of the Privy Council at publications that transgressed the shifting boundaries of accepted doctrine, and yet Grafton seems occasionally to have overstepped these bounds. On 8 April 1543 Charles C. Butterworth recounts that Grafton and several others were imprisoned briefly for printing "such books as were thought to be unlawful," most likely books containing translations based on "heretical" texts by outlawed authors such as Tyndale, whose work had been expressly forbidden by an act of Parliament that same year.

As the patented printer of service books, Grafton published Henry VIII's authorized *Primer* on 29 May 1545. Its full title stated the book's purpose: *The Primer, Set Forth by the King's Majesty and His Clergy, to Be Taught, Learned, and Read, and None Other to Be Used throughout All His Dominions.* Butterworth writes that in the king's view, stated in a royal injunction published on 6 May 1545, an authoritative, vernacular primer would facilitate the use of English in divine services and educate the young "in the knowledge of their faith, duty and obedience." It was hoped that such a book would decrease those "vain disputations" brought about by the doctrinal "diversity" of many primers then in use. Henry VIII's injunction guaranteed instant demand; within a year Grafton produced thirteen editions in English and Latin.

With the accession of King Edward VI in 1547 Grafton became the king's printer, an appointment that gave him the exclusive privilege to publish royal proclamations and acts of Parliament. Grafton also retained his patent on service books, and he and Whitchurch continued to work together. On 30 November 1547 Grafton published Edward VI's authorized *Primer,* and, although printing for the king kept him busy, he also managed to publish several secular works, such as James Harrison's *Exhortation to the Scots* (1547) and a work that must have accorded with his own developing interest in historical writing – Arthur Kelton's *Chronicle Declaring that the Britons Are Descended from Brute* (1547).

Although Grafton had edited historical works by other authors, he became a chronicler by accident. In 1547 his friend Edward Hall died and willed to Grafton a sizable manuscript history of the Tudor dynasty, which he thereafter edited and published as *The Vnion of the Two Noble and Illustre Famelies of Lancastre and Yorke* (1548). As he had done with Hardyng's *Chronicle,* Grafton edited this work extensively. In addition, he acknowledged that he "diligently" completed the narrative, which had covered events only until the twenty-fourth year of Henry VIII, by compiling Hall's notes, left piecemeal in "diverse and many pamphlets and papers." Grafton justified his continuation of Hall's narrative by stating in a note to his reader that Hall in his last years had been "not so painful and studious as before he had been," but Grafton maintained that the finished work was "utterly without any addition of mine."

In the brief, annalistic format of Grafton's entries, his section does lack the breadth and detail of Hall's earlier narrative. Typical of Grafton's style is the note with which he concludes a section relating the death and burial of Jane Seymour: "The king's majesty kept his Christmas at Greenwich in his mourning apparel, and so was all the Court till the morrow after Candlemas Day and then he and all other changed." As he completed Hall's narrative, Grafton maintained its tone and theme – that in the Tudor line lay the divinely ordered salvation of England. The narrative is thus unquestioningly monarchical and resolutely unanalytical – with no searching for motives and no questioning of the sources of the Tudor myth – and offers only the "great moral drama" of Tudor ascendancy, as May McKisack writes.

Other titles that appeared from Grafton's press during this period included John Caius's *A Boke, or, Counseill against the Disease Commonly Called the Sweate, or Sweatyng Sicknesse* (1552); historical works dealing with the Scottish situation, such as William Patten's *The Expedicion into Scotlāde* (1548); and such influential works as rhetorician Thomas Wilson's *The Rule of Reason* (1551) and *The Arte of Rhetorique* (1553).

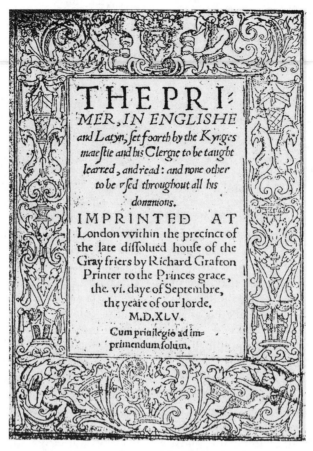

Title page for one of Grafton's primers

Following the death of Edward VI, Grafton, still the exclusive printer to the court, published the proclamation of Lady Jane Grey as queen. With the aim of establishing himself in her court, he signed himself *reginae typographus,* or "the Queen's Typographer." Nine days later, however, Mary Tudor ascended the throne, and Grafton, with some trepidation, found himself publishing her proclamation. For his presumption Mary fired him and on 29 December 1553 appointed John Cawood in his place. Grafton and Whitchurch were jailed for several weeks, and Foxe records that although Mary at her coronation issued a general pardon, this did not include those held in the Tower and in Fleet Prison, where Grafton and Whitchurch had been incarcerated. About this same time Grafton's printing facilities were dismantled and sold, either by the queen or by Grafton. Several engraved plates and borders used previously in his books appear in later publications by associates and rival printers.

With their careers in printing terminated and their connections to the court severed, Grafton and Whitchurch apparently dissolved their long part-nership and turned to new pursuits. Whitchurch left London for his country home, but Grafton remained in the city and prospered despite being a well-known Protestant in a period of Catholic ascendancy. Given his early troubles with Mary Tudor, the cautious Grafton most likely did not press his religious views too strenuously. In fact, he managed to be elected to Parliament during her reign and sat as a member for London in 1554 and 1557, at a time when many of his associates, such as John Rogers and Archbishop Cranmer, reaped the whirlwind of political misfortune and religious persecution.

With the accession of Elizabeth, Grafton turned his attention to civic and charitable affairs. He served as chief master of Christ's Hospital in London and also as one of the first masters of Bridewell Hospital, a former royal residence that John Stow reports had been bequeathed to London by Edward VI as a "workhouse for the poor and idle persons of the City." In 1561 Grafton was one of a group of prominent citizens commissioned to supervise repairs to the recently damaged St. Paul's Cathedral. Yet another term in Parliament followed for Grafton in 1562–1563, when he sat as a member for Coventry.

At this time Grafton also began to write historical narrative under his own name, apparently in reaction to a poor edition of Thomas Lanquet and Thomas Cooper's *An Epitome of Cronicles Conteining the Whole Discourse of the Histories as Well of This Realm of England, as All Other Countreis,* compiled by Robert Crowley and printed in 1559 by Thomas Marshe. E. J. Devereux reports that Grafton found the Crowley edition to contain "little truth and less good order," and Grafton believed that he could do better. On 21 February 1563 his son-in-law, Richard Tottel, published Grafton's *An Abridgement of the Chronicles of England,* a work generally of little value to modern scholars but read widely in its day, if only to catalogue its plentiful errors.

Like many other chronicles of its period, Grafton's *Abridgement* was more a compilation than an original narrative. Grafton lifted whole blocks of material from various Latin, Anglo-Saxon, and contemporary "authorities" such as the Domesday Book and chronicles by Geoffrey of Monmouth, Jean Froissart, and Robert Fabyan. It was also entirely conventional in portraying human history as the transcript of divine action, a history in which political turmoil and personal misfortune were the consequences of heedless and evil lives. As a result, the study of history was to supply examples of godly action rewarded and godlessness brought low. Moral truth rather than strict, factual accuracy was the primary consideration, although the better historians attempted to present accurately the most reliable evidence.

Unfortunately for his reputation, Grafton's *Abridgement* was neither accurate nor reliable. Enraged by Grafton's effrontery in publishing an inaccurate rival to his Crowley volume, Marshe commissioned John Stow to reedit the text Crowley had used. Stow, who had already gained recognition as an editor of Geoffrey Chaucer's works and as a student of antiquities, agreed to do the work and in 1565 published *A Summarie of Englyshe Chronicles.* At its publication Stow visited Grafton and rather tactlessly showed his host a copy of the *Abridgement* that Stow had liberally marked for errors. According to Devereux, Stow claimed that Grafton had missed not only "almost all the years of our Lord God, but also the years of the beginnings and endings of all the kings of this realm." In the preface to a second edition of his *Abridgement* Grafton acknowledged some errors but, in a rather weak attempt to save face, blamed them on "miswriting," "misentering," and "misprinting." Angered by Stow's criticism, he

Title page for Nicholas Udall's translation of Desiderius Erasmus's Apophthegmes

immediately began a campaign to discredit the younger chronicler and to salvage his own reputation.

Grafton quickly published *A Manuell of the Chronicles of Englande: From the Creacion of the Worlde to This Yere of Our Lorde, 1565* (1565), a book that used Stow's more accurate *Summary* as its principal source. Devereux recounts that in the dedication Grafton bequeathed the book to the Stationers' Company, which he asked to use the work "to the commodity and benefit" of the company and to see that it was "cleanly wrought and with diligence corrected" through subsequent editions. However, the real purpose of his dedication was to request that the company use its influence to prohibit publication of any historical works except his own – a direct attack on Stow, whom Grafton mentioned obliquely as "one that [had] counterfeited my volume" and caused "my travail to pass under his name." For Stow's insult of having publicized Grafton's errors, Grafton unsuccess-

¶ An Homelie of the saluacion of mankynde, from synne and death euer-lastyng, by onely Chiste our sauioz.

Ecause all men be synners, and offenders against God, and bieakers of his lawe and comaunde-mentes, therfoze can no man by hys awne actes, wooikes, and dedes, (seme they neuer so good) be iusti-fied, and made righteous befoze God: but euery man of necessitie is constrained to seke foz another righteousnes, oz iustificacion, to be receiued at Gods awne handes, that is to saie, the remission, pardon, and foзgeuenesse of his synnes ₹ trespasses, in suche thynges as he hath offended. And this iustificacion oz righteousnesse, whiche we so receiue by gods mercy, and Chistes merites, em-biaced by faith, is taken, accepted, and allowed of God, foz our perfect and full iustificacion. Foz the moze full vnderstandyng hereof, it is oure partes ₹ ductie, euer to remember the greate mercy of God, how that (all the woзlde beynge wzapped in synne, by bieakyng of the lawe) God sent his onely sonne, our sauioz Chist into this woзlde, to fulfill the lawe foz vs: ₹ by shedyng of his most pzecious bloudde, to make a sacrifice and satiffaccion, oz (as it may be called) amendes, to his father foz our synnes : to af-swage his wzathe ₹ indignacion, conceiued against vs foz thesame. In somuche thₑt infantes, beynge baptised and diyng in their infancie, are by this sa-crifice wasshed from their sinnes, biought to Gods fauoz, and made his childoзen, and inheritoзs of hys kyngdome

The efficacie of Chistes Passion and Oblacion,

Page from The First Book of Homilies *(1547), one of the works for which Grafton acquired an exclusive right to print following his appointment as printer to King Edward VI*

fully attempted to prevent Stow from ever publishing history again.

Grafton spent the next few years compiling another more expansive and ambitious chronicle, published on 31 March 1569 as *A Chronicle at Large, and Meere History of the Affayres of England.* As he stated in his dedication to Sir William Cecil, he wrote to supply the need for a "full, plain, and mere [i.e., pure, unmixed] English history," one that avoided letting English history become too "intermingled" with the affairs of foreign nations while it corrected the "envious constructions" "slanderously" penned by foreign historians. Many contemporary histories, he continued, were either too short, "leaving thereby some necessity of larger explication," or too long, "with many tedious digressions, obscure descriptions, and frivolous dilatations." Against this somewhat overblown general critique Grafton claimed his history to be ideal: "Large enough (I trust) without tediousness, short enough without darkness, merely and only of England." These were claims that the work did not fulfill.

Instead of limiting itself to the "mere" history of England, the two-volume compendium began with Creation and made sluggish progress through biblical and classical prehistory to recent times. Like many others, this chronicle was largely genealogical; it served to establish origins and lines of descent from antiquity to contemporary Britain. Naturally Grafton began with the most important genealogy – that of Jesus Christ – and transcribed it straight from the Old Testament. He divided the narrative into seven sections corresponding to the seven "Ages of the World." Grafton and his contemporaries lived in the Seventh Age, which began with the birth of Christ and would last until the end of the world.

The first section expounded on the origins of the British race. This material, which Grafton admitted having taken straight from Fabyan's *Chronicle* (1516), claimed that Britain, then called Albion, had been originally inhabited by "certain giants" conquered by Brute, a descendant of Aeneas. The idea that a race of giants had once dwelt in Britain was not new to Grafton's generation. Such accounts

THE

Expedicion into Scot-
lande of the most wooxthely fox-
tunate pxince Edward, Duke
of Soomerset, vncle vnto our
most noble souereign loxd ykī-
ges Maiestie Edvvard the. VI.
Goouernour of hys hyghnes
persone, andPxotectour of hys
graces Realmes, dominions ꝃ
and subiectes:made in the
first yere of his Ma-
iesties most pxos-
perous reign,·
and set out
by way
of diarie,by
W.Patten Lon-
doner.

VIVAT VICTOR.

Title page for William Patten's historical study of Edward VI's
expedition into Scotland (1548)

sound inexcusably naive to modern readers, but Grafton's narrative was fully within the bounds of what was then conventional wisdom, although such accounts were beginning to be questioned. He gave due credit to Fabyan for this account, but elsewhere in his narrative he often copied material verbatim without attributing it to the original author. This, plus his general lack of discernment in selecting and using his "sources," left Grafton open to charges of carelessness, plagiarism, and ineptitude as a writer and scholar – charges vigorously put forth by critics such as Stow.

For example, in *A Survay of London* (1598) Stow mocked Grafton for having recorded "fables" about a local curiosity, a stone found in Breadstreet ward that Grafton had personally inspected and reported to be the tooth of a man twenty-eight feet tall. Elsewhere Grafton had recorded as truth the story of a man with a mouth sixteen feet wide. These accounts were dismissed by the more critical Stow as complete fantasies, although he made these charges nearly thirty years after Grafton had written. By the end of the sixteenth century historical research was

taking advantage of both documentary material and professional perspectives unavailable to Grafton's generation. While Grafton did not write reliable historical accounts, neither did he willfully traffic in lies. His limitations as a historian appear to have been unfortunately compounded from his unrealistic opinion of his talents, his carelessness at scholarship, and his failure to recognize methodological innovations that were just beginning to transform English historical writing.

Grafton lost his battle with Stow by default, for he died in 1573 and was buried in Christ Church on 24 May. The record that history leaves of him is uneven. His work with English Bibles and service books was important and has been well documented; his work as an editor of Hardyng and Hall, though questionable, deserves further attention. His original work as a chronicler, though long considered to be of little value to scholars, continues to be read – if only as an example of what F. Smith Fussner calls the "transitional" work that sharply contrasts with the more serious work being done in the period. Both his sense of history and his methodology mark him as vestigially medieval, completely overshadowed by figures such as William Camden, Raphael Holinshed, and Stow. In fact, Grafton's greatest contribution to English historiography may have been indirectly to provoke Stow to take up historical scholarship with much better and more lasting results.

Modern reconstructions of his professional rivalry with Stow cast Grafton as a man concerned more with reputation and the sale of his books than with truth and scholarly accuracy. While this may be partially true, it is important to remember that Stow had the advantage of surviving Grafton and of articulating his version of the quarrel. Unfortunately for Grafton's reputation, Stow's detailed notes tell a story of bitter professional rivalry within the seemingly placid brotherhood of antiquarians, a story nonetheless interesting to modern researchers. And Stow's personal and highly prejudiced accounts have often been the bases for modern impressions of Grafton the historian.

Bibliography:

E. J. Devereux, "Empty Tuns and Unfruitful Grafts: Richard Grafton's Historical Publications," *Sixteenth Century Journal,* 21 (Spring 1990): 33–56.

Biography:

J. A. Kingdon, *Richard Grafton, Citizen and Grocer of London* (London: Privately printed, 1901).

References:

Charles C. Butterworth, *The English Primers, 1529–1545* (New York: Octagon Books, 1971);

John Foxe, *The Acts and Monuments of John Foxe,* 8 volumes (New York: AMS, 1965);

F. Smith Fussner, *Tudor History and the Historians* (New York: Basic Books, 1970);

Edward Hall, *Hall's Chronicle,* edited by Henry Ellis (London: Johnson, 1809);

John Hardyng, *The Chronicle of John Hardyng,* edited by Ellis (London: F., C. & J. Rivington, 1812);

Ronald B. McKerrow, *Printers' and Publishers' Devices in England and Scotland, 1485–1640* (London: Bibliographic Society, 1913);

McKerrow and F. S. Ferguson, *Title-page Borders Used in England and Scotland 1485–1640* (London: Bibliographic Society, 1932);

May McKisack, *Medieval History in the Tudor Age* (Oxford: Clarendon Press, 1971);

J. F. Mozley, *Coverdale and His Bibles* (London: Lutterworth, 1953);

Henry R. Plomer, *A Short History of English Printing, 1476–1900* (London: Kegan Paul, Trench, Trubner, 1915);

Alfred W. Pollard, ed., *Records of the English Bible* (London: Oxford University Press, 1911);

Thomas Rymer, *Foedera,* 3 volumes (London: Hardy, 1873);

H. Maynard Smith, *Henry VIII and the Reformation* (New York: Russell & Russell, 1962);

John Stow, *A Survey of London,* 2 volumes, edited by Charles Lethbridge Kingsford (Oxford: Clarendon Press, 1908);

Herbert A. Summer, *Historical Catalogue of Bibles in English* (London: British and Foreign Bible Society, 1968).

Papers:

The British Museum holds a letter from Grafton to Stow, as well as several Grafton letters (mostly reporting progress on his Bibles) to Cranmer and Cromwell. Other Grafton materials are in the British Public Records Office, among the letters and papers of Henry VIII.

– William Keith Hall

Joseph Hindmarsh

(London: 1678 – 1696)

In a career spanning nearly two decades and consisting of some 150 imprints, Joseph Hindmarsh distinguished himself as a premier bookman of Restoration London. Not only did he enjoy the prestige of being "Bookseller to His Royal Majesty," as Hindmarsh's imprint read, but he also published and sold an appealing variety of mostly English-language works in the fields of literature, state affairs, history, social manners, divinity, classical studies, navigation, and medicine. His engagements with successful contemporary literary authors such as John Oldham, Thomas Durfey, and, to a lesser extent, John Dryden, Nahum Tate, Edward Ravenscroft, and Aphra Behn are inviting case studies in collaborative relations between seventeenth-century bookmen.

Similarly, Hindmarsh's publication of romantic prose narratives by Behn and Marie Desjardins (Mme. de Villedieu) attests to his ability to anticipate consumer markets. His commercial instincts in the vendibility of new writings by women in London and on the Continent were sound. Throughout his career he was a faithful servant of public tastes, a creator of markets for selected writers of his choice, and, finally, an effective conduit between authors and the larger print culture of the seventeenth century. Contemporary published advertisements for his stock serve as a historical record of some of the most volatile moments in English political life as well as many exuberant moments in late-Caroline literature.

Having prestigious connections to the royal court, Hindmarsh published with evidently little serious regard for governmental regulation and controls. On three occasions, in fact, he was called before the courts for blasphemous, libelous, and Jacobite publications. Whether Hindmarsh was motivated by entirely mercantile interests or by the liberal principles of an uncensored English press espoused in John Milton's *Areopagitica* (1644), his shop in Cornhill was a colorful model of the culture of the Restoration bookshop, with its bustle, book talk, and brisk commercial exchange. His apparent willingness to publish manuscripts by ardent royalists and opposition propagandists alike reveals him to be a publisher-bookseller committed to supplying the Crown and the Commonweal with a range of titles to satisfy a variety of reading tastes.

Biographical information on Hindmarsh, by way of his parentage, early education, and apprenticeship, is elusive. Based upon such facts of Hindmarsh's career as his place of business, his career dates, the nature of the material he published or sold, his prestigious court connections, and his many commercial engagements, one can deduce that he was born into an educated family sometime in the 1650s and died sometime after his last publications in the late 1690s. His personal loyalties and allegiances are not entirely clear, for although he published many royalist, antipapal, and Jacobite writings, he also published and disseminated such writings as the Reverend Thomas Ashenden's controversial *The Presbyterian Pater Noster* (1680?) and English-language editions of Catholic writings by Louis Maimbourg and Giovanni Cardinal Bona. Henry R. Plomer's *Library* article records that Hindmarsh's imprint at the Golden Ball in Cornhill was continued after his death by one "H. Hindmarsh," probably a near relation, who published anti-Quaker literature and Jeremy Collier's influential *A Short View of the Immorality and Profaneness of the English Stage* (1698).

Hindmarsh's career in the book trade of Restoration London began in 1678. Setting up at the Black Bull in Cornhill then was a brave decision for any publisher-bookseller, for these were the feverish years of the Popish Plot controversy that inundated the market with papist and antipapist propaganda. In such a hysterical climate Hindmarsh judiciously lent his imprint to two manuscripts that fell well within the strictures of the Licensing Act of 1662 then in force: *Loyalty and Peace* (1678), sermons by the Reverend Samuel Rolls, chaplain to Charles II, and *Les amours des grands hommes* (1679), a harmless English-language edition of romantic narratives by the popular French writer Mme. de Villedieu. (An advertisement in Bona's *Guide to Eternity* [1688] identifies Hindmarsh as the sole publisher of the English version of Villedieu's work, but Donald Wing's *Short-Title Catalogue* and the *National Union Catalogue* list Hindmarsh's successful contemporary, Henry Herringman, as the publisher, and this sug-

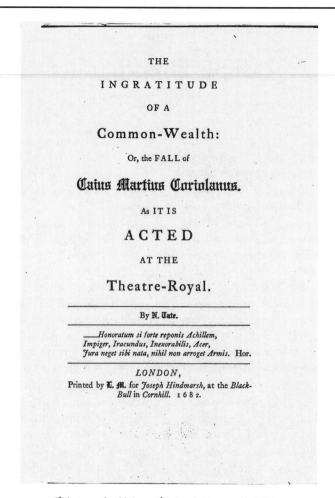

THE

INGRATITUDE

OF A

Common-Wealth:

Or, the FALL of

Caius Martius Coriolanus.

As IT IS

ACTED

AT THE

Theatre-Royal.

By N. Tate.

——*Honoratum si forte reponis Achillem,*
Impiger, Iracundus, Inexorabilis, Acer,
Jura neget sibi nata, nihil non arroget Armis. Hor.

LONDON,

Printed by T. M. for *Joseph Hindmarsh,* at the *Black-*
Bull in Cornhill. 1 6 8 2.

Title page for Nahum Tate's adaptation of William
Shakespeare's Coriolanus *(1682)*

gests either that Hindmarsh shared this copyright with Herringman or that Hindmarsh merely sold the work.)

The 1680s were years that shaped Hindmarsh's career and reputation. During the lapse of the Licensing Act from 1679 to 1684, Hindmarsh was free to publish various writings to supply an increasingly diverse reading public that was agitated by the machinations of Anthony Ashley Cooper, earl of Shaftesbury, and the open rebellion of James Scott, duke of Monmouth. Based on advertisements in his editions of Maimbourg and Bona, Hindmarsh's inventory included predictably loyal writings by Tory propagandists and Stuart royalists, as well as impressive offerings by several of the day's most popular poets and dramatists. Either because Hindmarsh supported Milton's call for an unlicensed press or was prompted by strictly business interests, he also supplied the market with vendible material produced by papists and sectarians. His personal motives aside, Hindmarsh's role as a royal

bookseller was to keep the administration current on all seditious writings that might undermine the security of the Commonweal. Yet he was also an astute businessman in the transaction of his affairs, and his entrepreneurial qualities evidently led him to the courts in the 1680s and 1690s.

From 1679 through 1684 Hindmarsh published a broad range of literature, chiefly poetry and drama. His lists for these years included at least twenty imprints by Durfey, whose works such as *The Progress of Honesty* (1681), *New Operas* (1681), *New Collection of Songs & Poems* (1682), and *Several New Songs* (1684) proved most profitable to Hindmarsh. He also published Ravenscroft's raucous *London Cuckolds* (1682) and Tate's *Ingratitude of the Common-Wealth* (1682), a popular adaptation of William Shakespeare's *Coriolanus*. Hindmarsh's long-standing interest in the works of John Oldham was made known in the 1680s, when he published Oldham's *Poems & Translations* (1684) and then the premier edition of Oldham's collected *Works* (1684).

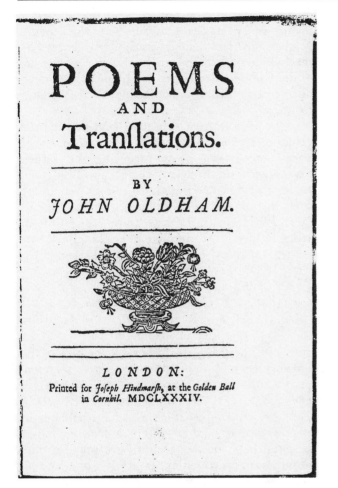

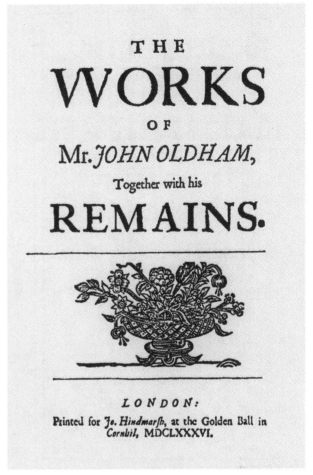

Title pages for two of Joseph Hindmarsh's editions of John Oldham, a translator and satiric poet whose works had earned the publisher's admiration

He also published John Crowne's *City Politicks* (1683), Thomas Southerne's *Disappointment* (1684), and apparently an early edition of the first part of Aphra Behn's *Love-Letters* (1683). This Behn edition is commonly thought to be a bibliographical ghost, but records in the *Term Catalogues,* the Stationers' Register, and Hindmarsh's advertisement in Maimbourg's *Treatise* (1685) suggest that this is not so. Hindmarsh also diversified his inventory by publishing such nonbelletristic fare as Sir Robert Talbor's *English Remedy* (1682), premier English-language editions of Cicero's *De natura deorum* (1682) and Eutropius's *Breviary of Roman History* (1684), David Abercromby's *Whole Art of Converse* (1683), and Capt. Peter Blackborrow's *Navigation Rectified* (1684).

Whether prompted by lofty liberal principles or a desire for quick profits, Hindmarsh published several controversial titles. Some of these pamphlets, satires, and tracts would not have offended the Crown, but some may have contributed to the disaffection and factionalism within the culture, as Hindmarsh added to his stock with several editions of Oldham's popular *Satyrs upon the Jesuits* (1681), Edward Pelling's *Apostate Protestant* (1682), the Reverend Adam Elliot's *Vindication of Titus Oates* (1682), Richard Kingston's *Vivat Rex . . . on the Discovery of the Phanatick Plot* (1683), and John Wilson's *Discourse of Monarchy* (1684).

Although the Licensing Act had lapsed at this time, Hindmarsh nonetheless was held to libel laws, which he violated on two occasions. The more serious of these offenses lay in his publication of Ashenden's four-page Presbyterian tract, *The Presbyterian Pater Noster.* Although this work had been published anonymously by Hindmarsh, it bore the amusing imprint "Printed for *Tom Tell-Truth* at the *Sign of Old King's Head* in *Axe-Yard,* King Street, Westminster," and Hindmarsh was brought to trial at the Old Bailey on the charge of "blasphemous libel" for having published this in February 1681. Narcissus Luttrell's copy is priced, dated,

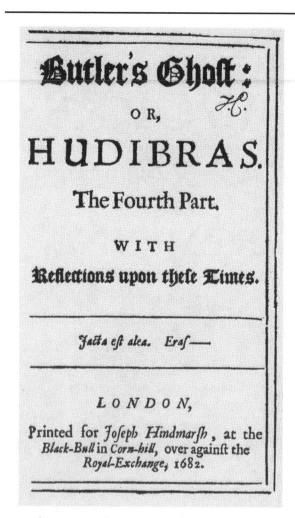

Title page for Thomas Durfey's sequel to the popular satiric narrative Hudibras (1662–1663, 1680) by Samuel Butler

and inscribed in his hand as "2[d]. 17.February.1681/2. A damn'd Atheisticall and blasphemous Thing."

Following the public execution of Charles I in 1649, public sentiment in England was adamantly anti-Presbyterian. Among others, Sir Roger L'Estrange, a royal licenser of the press, had published several ardent Tory pamphlets labeling Presbyterians as "dang'rous Fanatiques" whose doctrines were responsible for the English civil wars and the death of Charles I. Luttrell reports that Nathaniel Thompson, the printer of *The Presbyterian Pater Noster;* publisher Hindmarsh; and Ashenden were all indicted by the grand jury at the sessions at Guildhall. The Hindmarsh-Ashenden case is recounted in a four-page pamphlet of the day, *The Tryal and Condemnation of several Notorious Mal-Factors, at a Sessions of Oyer & Terminer Holden, for the City of London . . . April.13.1681.* In June 1684

Hindmarsh was convicted and sentenced to pay a fine of twenty pounds. Luttrell also reports that in October 1682 Hindmarsh was similarly charged by Lord Grey of Werke and by Lord North, who brought a "*scandalum magnatum*" against Hindmarsh for having published Adam Elliot's *Modest Vindication of Titus Oates* (1682).

A conservative publications list marked the second phase of Hindmarsh's career, covering the years 1685 to 1695, as the Licensing Act of 1662 was revived with the accession of James II in 1685. During this decade Hindmarsh's stock was dominated by literary titles: Behn's *Miscellany* (1685); Tate's *Poems* (1685); the *Essay upon Poetry* (1685) of George Villiers, second duke of Buckingham; several Durfey titles, such as *A Third Collection of New Songs* (1685), *Banditti* (1686), *The Commonwealth of Women* (1686), and *A Complete Collection of Songs & Odes* (1686, 1687); Oldham's *The Remains of . . . Oldham* (1687); and Ravenscroft's *Titus Andronicus* (1687), a Shakespearean adaptation.

With the triumph of liberal principles in the Glorious Revolution of 1688, the Crown's surrender of authority to govern the English press in 1689, and the enactment of the first copyright act in 1709, government censorship and surveillance of the press ceased to inhibit and harass writers, printers, publishers, and booksellers. For the first time authors were protected by statutory rights, and piracy was fined. During this phase of his career Hindmarsh apparently resumed his characteristic habits of publishing and vending whatever he judged would accelerate sales and increase profits.

Four notable successes in his list of literary titles must have pleased him: Dryden's play *Don Sebastian* (1690) and a second edition of his poetry, *Miscellany Poems* (1692); a posthumous reprinting of Behn's *Love-Letters* (1693); and Giovanni Paolo Marana's *The Turkish Spy* (1693), whose copyright was conveyed to Hindmarsh by Robert Midgley, a cleric and royal censor. Hindmarsh's nonliterary stock at this time included John Chalmers's *English Orthography: A New Spelling Book* (1687) and devotional writings by John Kettlewell, a nonjuror and member of George Hickes's circle, who wrote *Of Christian Prudence* (1691) and *Christianity, A Doctrine of the Cross* (1691).

Luttrell found Hindmarsh to be a staunch Jacobite in February 1690 when the latter was brought before the lord mayor for having printed a "scurrilous" (i.e., Jacobitical) pamphlet. Hindmarsh was fined, and he refused to take the oath of allegiance to William III. As a list of his collected imprints reveals, Hindmarsh had implicitly embraced a long-standing support of the principles of heredi-tary succession when he had published Sir George Mackenzie's *Antiquity of the Royal Line of Scotland* (1686), John Curtois's *Sermon On Kings* (1685), and David Tenner's *Prerogative of Primogeniture* (1685). Hindmarsh quietly closed his career in the book trade by publishing two conservative titles, Charles Hoole's *Vocabularium parvus . . . A Little Vocabulary* (1696) and Richard Sare's *Divine Antidote* (1696).

Hindmarsh evidently maintained generally cordial relations with the Restoration book culture. As facts of his career and contemporary accounts suggest, he never was a party to pirated or unautho-rized publication, as was Richard Marriot, his enter-prising contemporary at St. Dunstan's Churchyard in Fleet Street — who in 1663 had published a pi-rated edition of Katherine "Orinda" Philips's po-ems. Hindmarsh evidently respected the rights of his authors, and he maintained a mutually profit-able camaraderie with a small clique of selected writers whose work he favored and published re-peatedly: Durfey, Oldham, and, to a lesser extent, Dryden, Tate, Ravenscroft, and Behn. Hindmarsh's repeated engagements with these figures materially enlarged their status with readers. As Kathleen M. Lynch demonstrates in *Jacob Tonson, Kit-Cat Pub-lisher* (1971), Hindmarsh knew books and markets, and he was willing to outbid other publishers for es-pecially salable manuscripts. Evidently such a modus operandi encouraged John Dryden, who usually published his work with Tonson at the Judge's Head at Chancery Lane, to bring his play *Don Sebastian* to Hindmarsh's shop at the Golden Ball in Cornhill in 1690 and to leave Tonson, the publisher of the first edition of Dryden's *Miscellany,* when a second edition of that latter work was planned.

The proprietor of the imprint "Joseph Hind-marsh, Bookseller to His Royal Majesty . . . in Cornhill" supplied the court and Restoration read-ers with an impressive variety of books, pamphlets, and broadsides. Most of the contemporary book formats are represented in his stock: octavos such as Talbor's *English Remedy,* large octavos such as Oldham's *Works,* quartos such as Ravenscroft's *Lon-don Cuckolds,* and folios such as John Rushman's *Tryal of my Lord Strafford* (1690). Following Tonson's practice, Hindmarsh published prologues and epi-logues on folio half-sheets printed on both sides and with the imprint appearing at the bottom of the sec-ond page, as in the epilogue to Thomas Otway's *Venice Preserved* (1682), the prologue and epilogue to Ravenscroft's *Dame Dobson* (1683), and Durfey's prologue and epilogue to John Lacy's *Sir Hercules Buffoon* (1684).

While his personal political and religious alle-giances were either ambivalent or subordinated to mercantile motives, Joseph Hindmarsh profession-ally met the first obligation of the publisher-bookseller of his day: he was a shrewd but honest middleman between author and reading public, and he endeavored to improve the state of both.

References:

Cyprian Blagden, *The Stationers' Company* (Cambridge, Mass.: Harvard University Press, 1960);

Arthur E. Case, ed., *A Bibliography of English Poetical Miscellanies, 1521–1750* (Oxford: Oxford Uni-versity Press, 1935);

Louis Edward Ingelhart, ed., *Press Freedoms: A Descrip-tive Calendar of Concepts, Interpretations, Events & Court Actions, from 4000 B.C. to the Present* (West-port, Conn.: Greenwood Press, 1987);

Narcissus Luttrell, *A Brief Historical Relation of State Affairs . . . 1678–1714,* 6 volumes (Oxford: Ox-ford University Press, 1857);

Kathleen M. Lynch, *Jacob Tonson, Kit-Cat Publisher* (Knoxville: University of Tennessee Press, 1971);

Ralph Edward McCoy, *Freedom of the Press: A Bibliocyclopedia. Ten-Year Supplement (1967–1977)* (Carbondale: Southern Illinois Univer-sity Press, 1979);

Henry R. Plomer, "S. Paul's Cathedral and Its Book-selling Tenants," *Library,* new series 2 (July 1902): 261–270;

Plomer, *A Short History of English Printing, 1476–1898* (London: Kegan Paul, Trench, Trübner, 1900);

Robert Rea, "Bookseller as Historian," *Indiana Quar-terly for Bookmen,* 5 (1949): 75–95;

Fredrick Seaton Siebert, *Freedom of the Press in En-gland, 1476–1776: The Rise and Decline of Gov-ernment Controls* (Urbana: University of Illinois Press, 1952);

Autrey Nell Wiley, *Rare Prologues and Epilogues of the Restoration, 1642–1700* (London: Allen & Un-win, 1940);

James Winn, *John Dryden and His World* (New Haven: Yale University Press, 1987).

— Maureen E. Mulvihill

William Jaggard
(London: 1591 – 1623)

Isaac Jaggard
(London: 1613 – 1627)

John Jaggard
(London: 1591 – 1623)

Publishing and printing often became family enterprises in the early years of the trade, and two generations of stationers named Jaggard (or Jaggar) were notable in the London book trade from 1591 to 1627. Both flourished as booksellers, publishers, and printers into the early 1600s, but the Jaggard name lives principally because William and his son, Isaac, printed the First Folio of William Shakespeare's plays.

John and William were sons of John Jaggard, a barber-surgeon, and Bridget, who after her husband's death in 1584 married William Morley in January 1586. The family lived in the parish of St. Botolph outside Aldersgate, a suburb of London. On Michaelmas (29 September) 1584 both William and John began their apprenticeships, which Stationers' Company records show were to run for eight- and seven-year periods, respectively. Apprentices were customarily released at age twenty-four, but John, the older brother, was not made a freeman of the company until August 1593, more than nine years after he had been apprenticed to Richard Tottel at The Hand and Star. Tottel was serving his second term as master of the Stationers' Company when John Jaggard began his apprenticeship, and after Tottel's death in 1594 John continued to work for the heirs and successors of his former master. He published and finally printed works bearing his own name and the names of other stationers, including his brother, and he remained to the end of his life at the same address of Tottel's former shop on Fleet Street near the Inns of Court.

In 1594 John Jaggard published Giacoma di Grassi's *True Arte of Defence,* a book on Italian dueling, and was prospering by 1597, when he married Elizabeth Mabbe on 5 June. By March 1599 John Jaggard's shop no longer held its patent for printing law books, but he advanced steadily in the Stationers' Company, which admitted him to its livery in

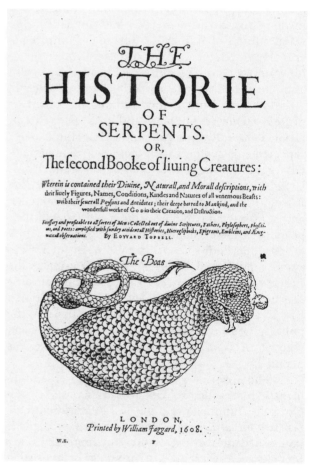

Title page for a work of natural history and mythical "Beasts" that was among the earliest works William Jaggard printed

1602. He later served as renter-warder for the company in 1609–1610 and, with others, represented the Stationers at the lord mayor's dinner in October 1613. In 1619 Jaggard was elected underwarder of the company and served in 1621 on the Stationers' court of assistants.

Although established independently of his brother, John Jaggard until the last years of his life

138

published several books printed by his brother William, notably the 1602, 1612, and 1613 editions of Francis Bacon's *Essays.* Thomas Heywood's translation of *The Two Most Worthy and Notable Histories* by Caius Sallustius Crispus appeared in 1608 with only John's name on the title page, but its registration had been entered at the Stationers' Company by William. Ralph Blore, an early partner of William Jaggard, had been apprenticed to Richard Tottel, and Blore's shop was located near The Hand and Star. Partnerships and working agreements typically formed, changed, and re-formed among stationers, and the Jaggards advanced in the book trade through a network of family and professional connections. John's son was admitted to the Stationers' Company on 4 July 1620, but little of his career has been documented.

William Jaggard and his son Isaac are the most notable members of the family because of their association with the works of Shakespeare, and the printing of the First Folio at their shop has made it the object of more interest than any other printing establishment of the period. William Jaggard was apprenticed in 1584 to London printer Henry Denham, who had served his own apprenticeship under Tottel in the 1550s. Noted for high-quality printing and the fine typeface and decorative initials he used, Denham produced beautiful books and ran a successful business that held patents for the Psalter and all works of private prayer. Like his brother John, William Jaggard was thus apprenticed to a major stationer who greatly influenced his career and provided him with experience in book illustration that would inspire his own ventures in the trade. Admitted to freedom in the Company on 6 December 1591, William served a shorter apprenticeship than had been specified in his original indenture, and by April 1593 he set up as a bookseller in the churchyard of St. Dunstan's in the West — not far from Richard Tottel's shop, where his brother worked in Fleet Street. On 26 August 1594 William married Jayne Urique in St. Bride's parish.

William Jaggard rose in the book trade through both ambition and skill. In 1593 he petitioned the Stationers' court of assistants for the privilege of publishing broadsides to advertise plays, but the rights for playbills passed instead through Alice Charlwood, widow of John Charlwood, to her new husband, James Roberts. William Jaggard's interest in the bills persisted, and in 1602 he leased from Roberts the right to print them. Eventually William Jaggard shared the Robertses' address and later succeeded them in their shop at Aldersgate Street and the Barbican. The first entry

that he made in the Stationers' Register, on 4 March 1595, was for a book whose copyright had become derelict from disuse, *The Booke of Secretes of Albertus Magnus,* a compendium of medicinal uses and occult properties of plants, animals, and minerals. The book proved popular enough for William to reprint it in 1599 and 1617, and his son Isaac again did so in 1626. By 1597 William had taken a second apprentice, Thomas Cotes, and his bookselling was thriving.

Yet another book that William Jaggard published early in his career linked his name with Shakespeare. In 1599 he published *The Passionate Pilgrime,* a slender volume with a title page claiming the work to be "By W. Shakespeare." The book actually contains only four sonnets by Shakespeare — two from *Loves Labours Lost* (1598) — and poems by several other authors such as Sir Walter Ralegh, Christopher Marlowe, and Richard Barnfield. Apparently capitalizing on interest in Shakespeare's previously unpublished sonnet sequence, Jaggard padded *The Passionate Pilgrime* with ornamental borders and blank leaves, and the book sold well enough to be printed a third time in 1612.

Although the first two editions of this work had caused no trouble for the publisher, in 1600 William Jaggard and Blore were found guilty of printing a work that had not been officially registered, Sir Anthony Sherley's *A True Report of Sir Anthony Shierlies Journey Overland to Venice.* The book was printed by Blore for John Jaggard, but John was not charged, and Blore and William Jaggard were fined. Copies of the book were confiscated for political reasons, because Sherley had been in the service of Robert Devereux, the recently fallen earl of Essex. The incident demonstrates the early partnerships that developed between the Jaggard brothers, and William Jaggard's obvious misrepresentation of Shakespeare's authorship earned him the scorn of many later critics: in the nineteenth century A. C. Swinburne called Jaggard an "infamous pirate, liar, and thief," epithets not wholly justified in the context of early trade practices.

William Jaggard was above all a shrewd entrepreneur, as demonstrated by the royal warrant of 1604 that ordered all parish churches to set up copies of the Ten Commandments printed exclusively by William Jaggard. He must have invested significantly to procure this monopoly, and it is clear that the fines assessed Jaggard by Queen Elizabeth's censors did not deter his advancement under James. In fact, he may have been adjusting his political allegiances in 1601 when he published with his friend Thomas Pavier *A View of all the Right Honourable*

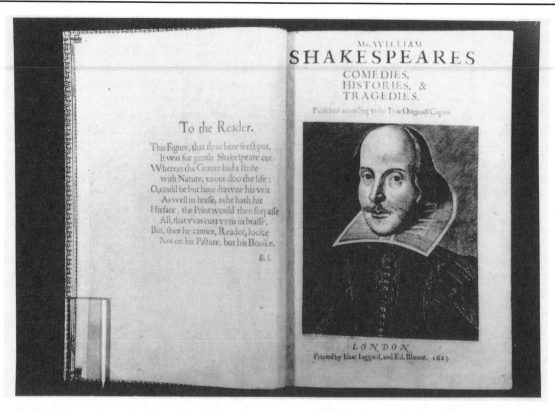

To the Reader.

This Figure, that thou here seest put,
It was for gentle Shakespeare cut,
Wherein the Grauer had a strife
with Nature, to out-doo the life :
O, could he but haue drawne his wit
As well in brasse, as he hath hit
His face ; the Print would then surpasse
All, that vvas euer vvrit in brasse.
But, since he cannot, Reader, looke
Not on his Picture, but his Booke.

B. I.

Mr. WILLIAM
SHAKESPEARES
COMEDIES,
HISTORIES, &
TRAGEDIES.
Published according to the True Originall Copies.

LONDON
Printed by Isaac Jaggard, and Ed. Blount. 1623.

Prefatory note to the reader (by Ben Jonson) and title page for Isaac Jaggard and Edmund Blount's most renowned project, the 1623 Shakespeare First Folio

the Lord Mayors . . . of London, a folio volume chronicling the lord mayors with woodcut borders and portraits and including a dedication written by Jaggard to Sir William Ryder, the current lord mayor, who had helped put down Devereux. Characteristic of William Jaggard's interest in decorative printing, the *View* is an early example of illustrated books that he published and would later print.

By 1604 William Jaggard had advanced from bookselling to the more-lucrative printing, as he moved into the shop at Barbican and Aldersgate Street. In 1607 he printed a large illustrated folio, *The Historie of foure-footed Beastes,* a compilation of animal lore collected by Edward Topsell from Conrad Gesner and other authors. In 1608 this was followed by Topsell's *The Historie of Serpents; or, The second Booke of liuing Creatures,* another large folio depicting mythical and actual "venemous Beasts." Responsible for the written text, Topsell was curate at the church of St. Botolph Without Aldersgate, the family parish.

Jaggard's illustrated books include genealogical and heraldic works as well as works of anatomy and natural history. Notable is Robert Glover's Latin work on the trappings of nobility, *Nobilitas*

Politica et Civilis (1608), a book that Edwin Eliott Willoughby has called "the most sumptuous of Jaggard's productions," with engravings of court costume "among the best examples of this poor period of book-illustration." *Nobilitas* was edited by Glover's nephew Thomas Milles, a former client of James Roberts's press. Milles was to have several works printed by William Jaggard and must have been a respected friend.

William Jaggard's press work, however, was not always well received. In 1609 he printed Thomas Heywood's verse chronicle *Troia Britanica,* with proofreading errors so serious that the author remained annoyed years later. According to Heywood, Jaggard had refused to add an errata slip to the work, and when Jaggard's third edition of *The Passionate Pilgrime* appeared in 1612 with the addition of some poems by Heywood that were attributed to Shakespeare, Heywood blasted Jaggard in a preface to *An Apologie for Actors* (1612), pointing out that publishing Heywood's verse as if it were Shakespeare's would arouse suspicion about Heywood's rightful claims of authorship elsewhere. He also claimed that Jaggard had refused to acknowledge printing errors in order to place "fault upon the necke of the author." For whatever reason, Jaggard canceled the title page of unsold copies of his 1612 *Passionate Pilgrime* to remove Shakespeare's name. Sensitive, perhaps, to charges of error-ridden printing, Jaggard in 1612 and 1614 produced works by Thomas Wilson with that respected Puritan's testimonials to the diligence of the printer, but questions of William Jaggard's skill persisted in part because of his increasing ill health and disability.

By 1613 William Jaggard was beginning to lose his eyesight, a loss probably resulting from a sexually transmitted disease and its treatment. His illness came near the zenith of his career. On 17 December 1610 he had been made printer to the city of London, a position secured by purchase. Although little of his official printing remains and the revenues were probably not high, the position was valuable to the family, and Isaac Jaggard was to succeed his late father in this office. In 1613, at the age of but eighteen, Isaac was admitted to the freedom of the Stationers' Company "by patrimony": as the son of a stationer, he did not have to serve a formal apprenticeship.

Undoubtedly as his father's blindness progressed, Isaac assumed increasing responsibilities in the Barbican shop, where three presses printed for both the Jaggards and other booksellers' shops. In addition to printing for the city of London, the Jaggards produced sermons and Puritan devotions, illustrated books of heraldry and science, and literature, including popular ballads. William continued to serve as a printer for his brother John; their names appear together in the 1611 and 1613 editions of Bacon's *Essays*. In 1613 William's health seems to have prevented completion of *The Treasurie of Ancient and Modern Times,* and antiquarian work edited by Milles. The first volume of the *Treasurie* was published in 1613, but the second did not appear until 1619, printed by and for William Jaggard, whose preface explained that he had been "prevented by sicknesse" from completing the two folio volumes together.

After Isaac entered the profession two notable illustrated books appeared, both "Printed by W. Iaggard dwelling in Barbican, and are there to be sold, 1616." The first – *Mikrokosmographia: A Description of the Body of Man,* a large folio dedicated to the Barber-Surgeons' Company – had been compiled and translated by physician and "Professor in Anatomy and Chirurgery" Helkiah Crooke and had been printed before. The second, *Somatographia Anthropine, or A Description of the Body of Man,* was a much smaller volume composed of figures and tables from the other work "set forth either to plea-

Page from Hamlet *in the First Folio*

sure or to profite those who are addicted to this Study. By W. I. Printer." The *Somatographia* shows how William Jaggard used expensive illustrations while reaching a wider audience. In his preface Jaggard writes that "this small volume . . . being portable" may serve as a handy reference for readers who could not afford to buy the larger work. The Jaggards were prospering as printers of illustrated works, and by 1618 records of real estate transactions show that William was also investing in city property. Far from being debilitated by blindness, he was active in business in the years before the family's most important project, the printing of the First Folio of Shakespeare.

In 1619 William Jaggard had begun printing in quarto Shakespeare's *Henry VI* (Parts 2 and 3) and *Pericles,* parts of a project often considered an unsuccessful attempt to publish a collected edition of plays attributed to Shakespeare. Jaggard printed a total of nine quartos for Thomas Pavier, his fellow

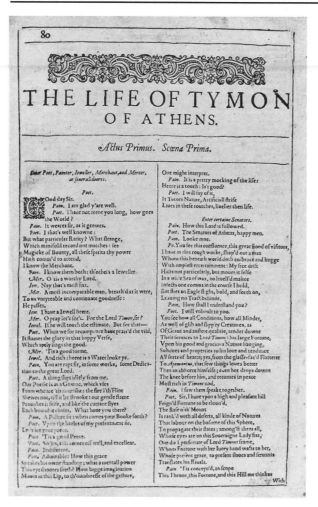

Page from Timon of Athens, *first printed in the First Folio*

stationer and longtime friend who had the rights to four plays; Arthur Johnson and Nathaniel Butter, other stationers owning rights, were probably also involved. Shakespeare's acting company, the King's Men, objected, and in May 1619 the lord chamberlain ordered that approval from the King's Men would be required before any of its plays could be printed. Probably intending to sell them as remainders from old editions, Jaggard continued to print quartos with falsely dated title pages. Sets of nine such quartos were bound if they were not sold together, and all but one of the plays carried a printer's device used by the Jaggards. Yet this unauthorized printing did not seem to inhibit the King's Men from working with the Jaggards when John Heninges and Henry Condell prepared Shakespeare's plays for the press in the early 1620s. In fact, the Jaggards' association with Pavier and accumulation of rights to plays printed earlier became vital to their production of the Folio.

Isaac Jaggard, whose name appears with Edward Blount's on the title page of the First Folio, was probably responsible for printing activity in the family shop by 1620. In March of that year William Jaggard registered the first complete English translation of Giovanni Boccaccio's *Decameron,* and its title page carries Isaac's name as printer. Isaac also became a renter-warder in the Stationers' Company in that month, and he seems to have been active in negotiations for publishing the Folio, *Mr. William Shakespeare's Comedies, Histories and Tragedies,* although his father was far from retired. Probably sometime in 1621 members of the King's Men agreed with a group of stationers to publish the first authorized collection of Shakespeare's plays from manuscript. Although the company was entitled to approve the printing of plays that it owned, individual stationers owned the rights to publish many of Shakespeare's plays. Thus, as Heninges and Condell prepared manuscripts for the press, agreements had to be made with holders of publishing rights recorded with the Stationers' Company.

A partnership was finally formed by stationers William Jaggard, Edward Blount, John Smethwick, and William Aspley, who paid for the edition and among themselves owned rights to several plays. The players, who owned the manuscripts, were probably paid a fixed amount, and the publishers would share the profits made after publication expenses had been met. The plan was complicated by the necessity of paying for rights to still other plays held by stationers outside the cartel, and as a folio devoted entirely to plays, the project was unprecedented, involving economic risk in spite of continued popular interest in the work of Shakespeare, who had died in 1616. The unauthorized quartos of 1619 demonstrated the marketability of his plays, but a folio, carrying only two pages of text on each side of each printed sheet, was more costly to produce: using a maximum amount of paper and requiring a larger binding, a folio had a relatively high price even for an unbound copy that the buyer could be expected to bind at his own expense. Profits for the publishers would be decreased by the cost of rights secured from others, and no folio devoted entirely to plays had before been ventured in English. The Shakespeare First Folio proved successful and was reprinted in a second edition in 1632, but its production was both difficult and risky.

A study of Folger Shakespeare Library copies of the First Folio has shown that the Jaggards' printing of the volume was complicated further by adding plays to the production schedule after printing had begun, by continuing negotiations for rights while the text was being set in type, and by delaying the printing of the First Folio to print other folio volumes concurrently in the Jaggard presses. From Charlton Hinman's meticulous investigation and collation of the First Folio more is known about the Jaggards' printing between 1621 and 1623 than about that of any other press operating in the period. Hinman and subsequent bibliographical analysts agree that at least nine compositors set Shakespeare's text in type.

In reconstructing the work of these compositors from physical evidence and designating their work by letters of the alphabet, scholars have determined that "Compositor B" seems to have been responsible for almost half of the pages in the Folio, and he apparently supervised the work of at least one apprentice pressman, "Compositor E." An inexperienced compositor, this apprentice was probably John Leason, the least-experienced worker in the shop, who was apprenticed 8 November 1622 and is the most likely person responsible for the errors, spelling preferences, and typesetting practices identified in the text. Because all type was hand set and only a limited amount of type had to be reset to print successive sheets, Hinman's intensive study of many copies of the First Folio and his comparison of them with other work printed in the shop from 1621 to 1623 have demonstrated that the First Folio printing of Shakespeare's plays began in 1622, early in the year when the Jaggards were still working on editions of Thomas Wilson's *The Christian Dictionary* and Augustine Vincent's *A Discoverie of Errours*. Both of these had been begun in 1621, a year of notable activity for the Jaggard press, which had also published, for example, an edition of Ralegh's *History of the World*.

Vincent's *Discoverie* was of special interest to William Jaggard, because it responded to Ralph Brooke's *A Catalogue and Succession of the Kings, Princes, Dukes, Marquesses, Earles, and Viscounts of This Realme of England,* a work on heraldry and genealogy that Jaggard had published in 1619. As a member of the College of Arms, Brooke had based his work on that of Jaggard's associate, Milles, and Brooke claimed to be correcting "many errours . . . lately published in Print; to the great wronging of the Nobility." However, Brooke's own work was riddled with errors that he sought to dismiss as faulty printing. For the *Catalogue* in 1619 Jaggard had printed errata, "Faultes escaped in Printing," and Brooke had been sharply criticized by colleagues for remaining errors, such as one that had even misrepresented the genealogy of the head of the College of Arms. Apparently an arrogant and abrasive person,

Brooke maintained his story about printer's errors and arranged almost immediately for a second edition to be printed by one of Jaggard's competitors.

In response, Jaggard agreed to have Vincent, a young herald, produce his own revision and enlargement largely to protect the Jaggards' interest in the work and to defend William's reputation. Printing of the First Folio was temporarily stopped to produce Vincent's work as quickly as possible. Brooke's second edition appeared first, carrying a title that claimed it would correct "divers faultes, committed by the Printer" of the 1619 volume. Adding to the anger William Jaggard must have felt at receiving such public blame for Brooke's oversights and at bearing the loss from unsold copies of a now-superseded edition, Brooke went on to insult Jaggard personally.

Vincent's carefully corrected *Discoverie of Errours in the first Edition of The Catalogue of Nobility* appeared in 1622 with William Jaggard's own preface, in which Jaggard asserted that Brooke had imputed errors not "to his owne *blindnesse* but to the blindnesse of his Printer," and gave examples of factual errors not subject to typographical misconstruction. Jaggard claimed that proof copies had been sent daily to Brooke when he had been unable to come to the press and suggested that Brooke's manuscript would show not only the author's culpability but also the many improvements made by the good sense of the compositors. Defending his professional reputation, Jaggard answered Brooke's ridicule and concluded, "howsoever it hath pleased God to make me, and him to style me a Blinde-Printer, . . . it is no right conclusion in schooles, that because *Homer* was Blinde and a *Poet,* therefore hee was a *Blinde-Poet*. Farewell."

William Jaggard was much more personally involved with his response to Brooke than with delays in printing the Shakespeare First Folio. Another large volume, a translation of André Favyn's *Theater of Honour and Knight-Hood,* also occupied the Jaggard presses while the First Folio was being printed, and William Burton's illustrated *Description of Leicestershire* may have been printed entirely between the beginning of the printing for *Mr. William Shakespeare's Comedies, Histories and Tragedies* and its completion in 1623.

Interrupted though it was, the printing of the First Folio seems to have followed the general order indicated on its title page – the comedies being printed first, followed by the history plays and tragedies. However, textual analysis indicates that difficulties in securing rights caused some deviations from this order. For ex-

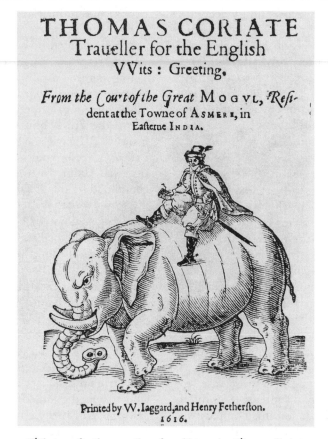

THOMAS CORIATE
Traueller for the English
VVits : Greeting.

From the Court of the Great MOGVL, *Resi-*
dent at the Towne of ASMERE, in
Easterne INDIA.

Printed by W. Iaggard, and Henry Fetherston.
1616.

Title page for the narrative of world traveler Thomas Coriate

ample, the histories were begun before the comedies were completely printed, and before all of the history plays had been set up, the compositors returned to and finished the comedies. Negotiations with Matthew Law for rights to *Richard II, Henry IV* (Parts 1 and 2), and *Richard III* seem to have been prolonged; Henry Walley's rights to *Troilus and Cressida* delayed its printing, ultimately displacing it from the originally planned sequence of tragedies. Substantial evidence shows that the printing of *Troilus* was temporarily given up, and some copies of the Folio were even sold before the play was printed and included in the volume.

By the end of October 1623 the last play, *Cymbeline,* had been printed with the colophon naming "W. Iaggard" as one of the publishers. By early November (the date is not known precisely) William Jaggard had died, and the rights to hitherto-unpublished plays in the Folio were registered by Isaac Jaggard and Edward Blount on 8 November 1623. Soon afterward copies were being sold with the now-famous engraved portrait of Shakespeare by Martin Droeshout on the title page. As Peter W. M. Blayney has explained, the portrait was

printed separately on a rolling press, and it exists in three states showing the engraver's alterations. By 5 December 1623 Sir Edward Dering had purchased two copies in London, and before 17 February 1624 a copy had been deposited at the Bodleian Library, Oxford. Now at the Folger Library, a copy presented to Augustine Vincent in 1623 survives with his notation that it was a gift from William Jaggard, although it was probably transmitted to Vincent by Isaac Jaggard after his father's death.

With Isaac's name on the title page and William's in the colophon, the First Folio preserves not only eighteen of its thirty-six plays that had never been printed before but also the Jaggard family name. William Jaggard's will, proved 17 November 1623, names his wife Jayne executrix, with Thomas Pavier and John Evans as overseers. Four children are named — Isaac, Thomas, Joan (Yardsley), and Alice (Bowles) — and silver plate is bequeathed to the Stationers' Company. Isaac succeeded his father at the shop in the Barbican and as printer to the city of London.

He continued to print Puritan and anti-Catholic religious works, as well as one volume of a second edition of Boccaccio's *Decameron* between 1624 and 1625. In spring 1625 Isaac married Dorothy Weaver, whose father, Edmund, was a stationer. Before the end of that year, in October or November, Jayne Jaggard, Isaac's mother, died. Her will suggests that by 1625 her daughter Joan had died and Alice had married. The will also provided money for a university education for the younger son, Thomas, and to Isaac and his sister, Alice Bowles, went the bulk of the estate. Neither Jayne nor William Jaggard's wills mention William's brother John or his son of the same name. But early in 1626 Isaac gained two apprentices; one had served William Jaggard, and the other had served John Jaggard, who had died in 1623.

In 1626 Isaac printed an edition of Albertus Magnus's *The Secrets of Albertus Magnus* and, for Edmund Weaver, Henry Cockeram's *The English Dictionarie*. Among the items printed in 1627 was a twelfth impression of Sir Thomas Overbury's *Sir T. Overburie his Wife,* published by Robert Swain, and an edition of Lancelot Andrewe's *Seuen Sermons on the Wonderfull Combate . . . between Christ and Sathan.* The *Seuen Sermons* were probably printed after Isaac's death, which occurred sometime between 5 February and 23 March 1627. Dorothy Weaver Jaggard executed her husband's will, and by June 1627 she had transferred the business to Richard and Thomas Cotes, the latter having served his apprenticeship under William Jaggard. The Cotes brothers printed the second edition of *Shakespeare's Comedies, Histories & Tragedies,* to which the young John Milton contributed a commemoration of the author in 1632.

After scarcely three decades the Jaggard family was no longer printing. Although the younger John Jaggard had been admitted to the Stationers' Company in 1620, his name does not appear in later records. Having printed notable works of religion, travel, heraldry, and science, the Jaggards are famous for their printing of the Shakespeare First Folio, a volume that Blayney has called "incomparably the most important work in the English language."

References:

Peter W. M. Blayney, *The First Folio of Shakespeare* (Washington, D.C.: Folger Shakespeare Library, 1991);

Charlton Hinman, *The Printing and Proofreading of the First Folio of Shakespeare,* 2 volumes (Oxford: Clarendon Press, 1963);

Michael Kiernan, "The Order and Dating of the '1613' Editions of Bacon's *Essays,*" *Library,* fifth series 29 (December 1974): 449–454;

Ronald B. McKerrow, *Printers' & Publishers' Devices in England & Scotland, 1485–1640* (London: Bibliographical Society, 1913);

Robin Myers, *The Stationers' Company Archive: An Account of the Records, 1554–1984* (Winchester: St. Paul's Bibliographies / Detroit: Omnigraphics, 1990);

Edwin Eliott Willoughby, *A Printer of Shakespeare: The Books and Times of William Jaggard* (London: Allan, 1934).

– *Steven Max Miller*

Francis Kirkman

(London: 1652 – 1680)

Author, publisher, and bookseller Francis Kirkman was noted for collecting and publishing plays, romances, and drolls (condensed, raucous tales extracted from familiar plays) from the 1650s through the 1670s. With other Restoration writers he experimented in the development of the novel through works such as *The English Rogue Described in the Life of Meriton Latroon, a Witty Extravagant* (1665 and 1668, co-authored with Richard Head) and his own *The Counterfeit Lady Unveiled* (1679). Kirkman demonstrated the financial necessity of combining publishing and bookselling, even resorting to circulating libraries to distribute effectively the literature of the Restoration. He also popularized the technique of illustrating texts in works such as *The English Rogue Described*; his *The Unlucky Citizen Experimentally Described in the Misfortunes of an Unlucky Londoner* (1673); his collection of selected works, *The Wits, or, Sport upon Sport* (1673); and his translation into English of Prince Erastus's *The History of Prince Erastus, Son to the Emperour Dioclesian* (1674). Finally, Kirkman was one of the earliest author-publishers who successfully defied the monopoly of the Stationers' Company in order to get his works into print.

Francis Kirkman was born 23 August 1632 to Francis Kirkman Sr. and his wife, Ellen. Kirkman's father, who later acquired the estate of Benfield Croft in the native Berkshire of the elder Kirkman, moved with two brothers to London, where they became members of the Blacksmiths' Company, in which Francis Kirkman Sr. was elevated to the position of upper warden. Young Kirkman's parents, whom he describes as "severe" in his autobiographical *Unlucky Citizen,* intended that he enter the clergy, but the death of an influential clerical uncle altered those plans. Kirkman adds that while he learned Latin from a "harsh schoolmaster," he developed a keen interest in reading romantic, knight-errant literature. Apprenticed at age fourteen to a London scrivener, Kirkman characterizes the experience as "an absolute bondage under a rigid master." After his mother's death and his father's remarriage, Kirkman left his scrivener apprenticeship for a similar position with a bookseller, whose slipshod administration of the shop increasingly made Kirkman the effective manager of the operation.

During his apprenticeship years Kirkman mastered French and began to collect many French romances. He also translated from French to English the previously unpublished sixth portion of Páez de Ribera's *Amadis de Gaule* (1652), a knight-errant romance originally written in Spanish and widely read during the Elizabethan era. The same year Kirkman published another English translation from the French, Antoine du Périer's *The Loves and Adventures of Clerio and Lozia.* Although he made little or no profit from the sale of these translations, he established a bookshop in an old alehouse near the Tower of London in 1652 and was made a freeman of the city in the following year.

A pattern of running afoul of the magistracy emerged in Kirkman's youth. Kirkman disapproved of the Protectorate government of the 1650s and once befriended a jailed Anglican cleric. By the age of thirty he had been arrested sixty times — for not returning a borrowed book on the first occasion but most often thereafter for unpaid debts. He married Ann Phillips in June 1654 at St. Olave's Church, Hart Street but soon had to sell the wedding clothes to pay debts. A daughter, Elizabeth, was born eleven months after their marriage.

With an inheritance he acquired after the death of his father in 1661, Kirkman established a bookshop at the sign of John Fletcher's Head near St. Clement-without-Temple Bar in the Strand. His business specialized in the sale of plays and romances, and he used a circulating library to reach a wider clientele. While occupying his new quarters, Kirkman published a catalogue of 690 plays purportedly representing the totality of published English plays, most of which he possessed. In 1661 he also published five drolls: John Webster and William Rowley's *A Cure for a Cuckold* and *The Thracian Wonder;* John Cumber's *The Two Merry Milk Maids;* William Wager's *Tom Tyler and His Wife;* and Robert Cox's *The Merry Conceited Humours of Bottom the Weaver.*

From his youth in Berkshire through his early experiences in London, Kirkman's primary hobby

Engraved portrait of Francis Kirkman (courtesy of Providence Public Library)

was that of collecting English plays. One of his advertisements claimed that he had read every English play and was familiar with the careers of the major playwrights. He also arranged to publish for the first time a couple of manuscript plays in his possession, and he even tried his own hand at writing what was to be published in 1661 as *The Presbyterian Lash; or Noctroff's Maid Whipt, a Tragy-Comedy,* a satire based on an account of a well-known contemporary Presbyterian minister, Zachary Crofton, accused of abusing a female servant and imprisoned in the Tower.

No sooner had Kirkman's career begun to prosper than he entered a partnership in 1661 with Henry Marsh, Nathaniel Brook, and printer Thomas Johnson at the Prince's Arms in Chancery Lane. The partners continued to publish picaresque literature, but their reprinting of John Fletcher and Francis Beaumont's popular comedy *The Scornful Lady*

(1616) aroused legal complaints from the copyright holders. In order to save himself from punishment, Marsh charged that Kirkman alone was responsible for pirating of the text. Authorities arrested Kirkman and confiscated the fourteen hundred playbooks that he possessed — and that he was never to recover.

Obviously shaken by the incident, Kirkman retired for the next three years to his family estate at Benfield Croft, Berkshire, which provided him with a comfortable income. There he began writing a work based on Geronimo Fernandez's romantic Spanish tale, *The Famous and Delectable History of Don Bellianis of Greece, or, The Honour of Chivalry,* later published in three parts during 1671–1673. In its preface Kirkman discusses two types of "histories" that were becoming popular reading: late-medieval knight-errant romances, represented by *Don Bellianis;* and Renaissance heroic romances such as

Clerio and Lozia. He also notes that works of the latter type originated not in England but rather in Spain and France.

When Kirkman returned to London in 1665, he arrived in the midst of the Great Plague, during which his father-in-law and brother-in-law died. Having been obliged to support relatives afflicted by the disease, Kirkman in 1666 once served nine days in Bishopsgate Prison for nonpayment of debts. One positive consequence of his return to London, however, was his acquisition of the Prince's Arms shop following the death of Marsh, his former partner, and by 1667 Kirkman was again publishing and selling plays and romances.

He issued Francis Bailey's *The Spightful Sister: A New Comedy* in 1667; the pseudonymous *Poor Robin's Jests, or The Compleat Jester,* to which Kirkman wrote a preface in 1669; an English translation of Pierre Corneille's *Nicomede, A Tragi-Comedy* (1671), to which he attached as an addendum his 1661 catalogue that by then included 806 English plays; and two parts of *The Wits, or Sport upon Sport* (1673), featuring rather well-drawn illustrations in addition to his own preface. *The Wits* consisted of a collection of drolls written mostly by playwrights Beaumont and Fletcher but also from familiar plays of William Shakespeare and masques of Ben Jonson. Actor Richard Cox had created a popular audience for the drolls in London playhouses during the 1650s.

Between 1669 and 1671 Kirkman moved his business from Chancery Lane to Bishopsgate Street, then to the Ship in Thames Street (next to the Customs House), and finally to St. Paul's Churchyard (next to his former establishment, the Prince's Arms). For health and financial reasons he sold his last business and retired to the countryside. During his stay in Berkshire in the early 1670s Kirkman composed the largely autobiographical *Unlucky Citizen.*

Not only does it recount many of the personal difficulties of Kirkman's youth and career, but it also aims to instruct "parents and children, masters and servants, husbands and wives" in correcting vices and nurturing virtues. It includes a portrait of the author, and for most of the chapters Kirkman provides illustrations portraying his unfortunate circumstances. His exaggerations in the preface include a comparison of his plight with those of Job. Michael McKeon sees this work as a rather serious confessional in which Kirkman attributes his misfortune to his own bad character rather than simply a period of bad luck, and he finds that Kirkman's attraction to romances reflects a personal crisis that

his low social status and his quest for authoritative affirmation engendered.

Again returning to London in 1673, Kirkman contracted more debts that resulted in yet another arrest. Having opened a new bookshop in Fenchurch Street near Aldgate, he published *The Counterfeit Lady Unveiled* (1673), probably the best of many versions of the life of the contemporary female rogue Mary Carleton of Canterbury. Criminal biographies were enormously popular in the Restoration era, and Carleton had gained attention in the 1660s by recounting in print her varied misdeeds. Many scholars believe that Kirkman's work, which appeared soon after her execution by hanging at Tyburn, later provided Daniel Defoe with a model for his antiheroine Moll Flanders in *The Fortunes and Misfortunes of the Famous Moll Flanders* (1722).

Kirkman's longest and best-known concern in his writing-publishing career was with a work of experimental fiction, *The English Rogue Described in the Life of Meriton Latroon, a Witty Extravagant.* The first installment of this romance, published in 1665, had been written by Richard Head and may have relied upon Head's own experiences. Soon afterward Kirkman printed some verse to celebrate its publication and republished the work through his own shop. When Head refused to write a second installment, Kirkman himself wrote and published a second part of *The English Rogue* in 1668.

Antiheroic rogue literature had emerged in Spain and France as a result of Renaissance vernacular interests of popular audiences. During Elizabethan times biographies of English rogues had become popularized as supposed means of warning potential victims about the tricks of underworld figures. Yet the English contribution to this genre by Head and Kirkman sensationalizes crime by replacing manners with vulgarity and romance with eroticism. The principal character, Latroon, becomes simply a promiscuous cheat and thief. Despite the poor literary quality of editions of this work by Head and Kirkman, a popular market existed for this genre among the common classes, and the two collaborated on a third and fourth installment published by Kirkman in 1671. Some of Latroon's overseas adventures anticipate the techniques of Daniel Defoe in *The Life and Strange Surprizing Adventures of Robinson Crusoe* (1719). Yet Kirkman's tale digresses into anecdotal asides full of indecent and even violent acts. A promised fifth installment never appeared, but just before his death Kirkman republished the first four parts in 1680, a publishing decision attesting to the continuing profitability of *The English Rogue.*

During the late 1670s Kirkman's publishing activity began to slow and became more varied. In 1674 he printed *A Course of Catechizing,* a summary of Anglican catechisms for each Sunday, and in 1675 he republished with Fleet Street bookseller Thomas Dring the third edition of William Phillips's *Studii legalis ratio, or, Directions for the Study of the Law.* In 1677 Kirkman published Robert Whitcombe's *Janua divorum, or, the Lives and Histories of the Heathen Gods and Goddesses and Demy-gods,* an account of classical deities. When Nicholas Cox republished Kirkman's play catalogue in 1680, it probably signaled that Kirkman had died.

Kirkman was neither a sterling writer nor a publisher of the best English literature. R. C. Bald states that Kirkman's prose is "garrulous and slipshod, but never dull; it has the tang of popular speech." *The English Rogue* and *The Counterfeit Lady Unveiled* were prominent antiheroic contributions to a literary genre that anticipated the great fictional novels of the eighteenth century. Kirkman's use of illustrated texts also helped to attract the widest possible popular reading audience.

Because Kirkman was not a member of the Stationers' Company, the institution established, in part, to maintain monopolistic control of publishing, his ability to publish outside the guild betokened the coming of a new freedom for publishers. It was a given in the Restoration era that publishers must either contract with booksellers to market their products or, as in Kirkman's case, serve the dual functions of publishers and booksellers. That trend would continue for at least a hundred years before independent publishing houses would develop. Kirkman's further use of a circulating library in metropolitan London demonstrated yet another innovative method of circulating published works.

Bibliography:

Strickland Gibson, "A Bibliography of Francis Kirkman," *Oxford Bibliographical Society Publications,* new series 1 (1947): 47–152.

References:

R. C. Bald, "Francis Kirkman, Bookseller and Author," *Modern Philology,* 41 (August 1943): 17–32;

Ernest Bernbaum, *The Mary Carleton Narratives, 1663–1673: A Missing Chapter in the History of the English Novel* (Cambridge, Mass.: Harvard University Press, 1914);

Frank Wadleigh Chandler, *The Literature of Roguery* (Boston: Houghton, Mifflin, 1907);

Francis Kirkman, *The Wits, or Sport upon Sport,* edited by John James Elson (Ithaca, N.Y.: Cornell University Press, 1932);

Michael McKeon, *The Origins of the English Novel, 1600–1740* (Baltimore: Johns Hopkins University Press, 1987).

– Daniel W. Hollis III

Leonard Lichfield I

(Oxford: 1634/1635 – 1657)

Joseph Barnes

(Oxford: 1585 – 1616/1617)

John Lichfield and William Wrench

(Oxford: 1616/1617 – 1618)

John Lichfield and James Short

(Oxford: 1618 – 1624)

John Lichfield and William Turner

(Oxford: 1624 – 1627)

William Turner

(Oxford: 1627 – 1644)

Henry Hall

(Oxford: 1644 – 1679?)

John Lichfield
(Oxford: 1627 – 1634/1635)

Leonard Lichfield II and Anne Lichfield
(Oxford: 1657 – 1671)

Leonard Lichfield II
(Oxford: 1671 – 1685/1686)

Leonard Lichfield III
(Oxford: 1685/1686 – 1744)

Leonard Lichfield IV
(Oxford: 1744? – 1754?)

Falconer Madan pointed out in 1925 that "the third quarter of the seventeenth century was the most interesting and eventful period in the history of the Oxford University Press, until recent times." Anyone compiling a history of the Oxford University Press and writing from the perspective of the university would undoubtedly agree. The first architypographus, or controller of the press, Samuel Clarke, was not appointed until 1658, and the university had no printing house until the completion of the Sheldonian Theatre in 1669. However, Oxford employed university printers long before it owned a press, and if one were to construct a history of printing in seventeenth-century Oxford from the perspective of the men and women actually engaged in the presswork, then the most interesting and eventful period of printing would have to be earlier, in the second quarter of the century, roughly the period when the print shops of John and Leonard Lichfield and of William Turner and Henry Hall flourished in the city of Oxford.

The fortunes of the Lichfield shop in particular first rose and then fell as the university press evolved. The family business, begun by John Lichfield in 1617, lasted through five generations and ended about 1754. It reached its peak early, during the career of Leonard Lichfield I, who ran the business from 1635 to 1657. As his father before him had done, Leonard enjoyed a dual position as both a printer to the university and a semi-independent printer in the city. The profits from privately contracted printing jobs enabled the Lichfields to undertake the printing of learned works for the university, and their primary remuneration from these works came from selling the

books themselves. This arrangement survived the upheaval of the Civil War; after the Restoration the university finally established its press and eventually employed its own printers. This left the Lichfields fully independent as it also left them behind.

Printing at Oxford began in the fifteenth century. From sometime in the late 1460s or more probably the 1470s until 1486 a total of seventeen books appeared. One was the first grammar book written in English, the *Long Parvula* (circa 1481), which has been attributed to John Stanbridge and survives only as a fragment. Another fragmentary piece dating from this period was Cicero's *Pro T. Milone,* the first work by a classical Latin author printed in England. Printing at Oxford was then dormant for about thirty years, until a flurry of activity from 1517 to 1520 produced eight more works – seven of which, according to Harry Carter, were merely "booklets of eight or ten leaves." Another period of no printing followed until 1585, the year in which Joseph Barnes opened his printing shop, the forerunner of the Lichfield family business.

Harry Carter writes that Cambridge, under a charter of 1534, had held the "right to have within its precinct three stationers and printers or vendors of books, who might lawfully print there all manner of books approved." Not until 1583, however, did Cambridge exercise its right, a move that stirred Oxford to a jealous response. In 1584 the Convocation of Oxford University moved to lend Barnes, an Oxford bookseller, £100 in order to set up a press. Apparently Queen Elizabeth I acquiesced to Oxford's step forward:

THE
ANATOMY OF
MELANCHOLY,

VVHAT IT IS.

VVITH ALL THE KINDES,
CAVSES, SYMPTOMES, PROG.
NOSTICKES, AND SEVE-
RALL CVRES OF IT.

IN THREE MAINE PARTITIONS
with their seuerall SECTIONS, MEM-
BERS, and SVBSEC-
TIONS.

PHILOSOPHICALLY, MEDICI-
NALLY, HISTORICALLY, OPE-
NED AND CVT VP.

BY
DEMOCRITVS Iunior.

With a Satyricall PREFACE, conducing to
the following Discourse.

MACROB.
Omne meum, Nihil meum.

AT OXFORD,
Printed by IOHN LICHFIELD and IAMES
SHORT, for HENRY CRIPPS.
Anno Dom. 1621.

Title page for the first edition of Robert Burton's popular satire on human learning and endeavor

a Star Chamber decree of 1586 limited the freemen of the Stationers' Company to practicing in London, but it named Oxford and Cambridge as exceptions and permitted each of them one press and one apprentice, along with as many journeymen as necessary. No number of printers to be allowed was specified, but it may be assumed that each university was to have had one printer.

When Joseph Barnes commenced printing, he was already an established businessman. In 1573 he had been licensed as an Oxford bookseller by the Oxford University vice chancellor, and in 1575 he was licensed to sell wine. Barnes was not a London stationer, and whether or not he had at some time learned the craft of printing, he probably at least employed an experienced journeyman, for the work produced was of an acceptable standard.

Barnes lacked a black letter font, a reflection of humanism at Oxford. Because it was new, his shop was modern and well stocked with the best

type for both letters and flowers that London-based typefounders produced – notably Robert Granjon's big capital letters, italics, and flowers, and Pierre Haultin's roman text typefaces. Producing more than three hundred books, many of which related to Protestant theology, Barnes functioned as the sole university printer until his retirement in 1616–1617. Among his books now considered most important were the first catalogue of the Bodleian Library (1605), Charles Butler's *Feminine Monarchie, or a Treatise concerning Bees* (1609), and Capt. John Smith's *Map of Virginia with a Description of the Countrey* (1612). Although his business was actually a private one, Barnes commenced a practice, continued and augmented by his successors, of using as his devices the arms of the university in varying forms. Barnes died heavily in debt in 1618 at age seventy-two, leaving his wife and daughter virtually destitute. His will included an inventory of goods worth £1,128, but clearly his press had not brought in much money.

Barnes resigned as printer to the university on 12 February 1616–1617 and was succeeded immediately by two printers, John Lichfield and William Wrench – one of whom may have been technically an apprentice. Wrench remained in Oxford for only one year, then dropped out of sight. Lichfield, on the other hand, rapidly became an established printer, working with another partner, James Short, from 1618 to 1624. William Turner succeeded Short and worked with Lichfield from 1624 to 1627. After quarreling, Turner in 1627 left to begin his own shop, and Lichfield ostensibly worked alone until he resigned his position on 7 January 1634–1635 in favor of his son Leonard.

John Lichfield's origins remain obscure, the first mention of him in Oxford annals occurring in January 1604–1605, when he was licensed to sell ale. Where he learned how to print is also buried in obscurity; he was not a London stationer, at least, and no records exist of his having been apprenticed in Oxford through the university. He did have obvious university connections, however, for not only was he appointed as printer, but in late March 1617 he was elevated to the rank of inferior, or yeoman, bedell of law, a university administrative servant whose duties included keeping the matriculation register, collecting fees, conveying official messages, and carrying a mace in processions. A bedell, or beadle, was traditionally underpaid, and the university traditionally compensated for his low wages by granting him a license to sell ale. Of course, Lichfield had already acquired that right.

In assuming his post as university printer, Lichfield purchased most, if not all, of Joseph Barnes's printing stock. Strickland Gibson records that Lichfield was one of three men who on 20 May 1619 "prized" the inventory of goods mentioned in Barnes's will; among other tallies, they determined that the value of the goods "in the Shoppe, and in the warehouse, in bookes, bounde, and vnbounde" totaled £300. The details of the change of ownership remain unknown. As the university did not own any printing type until 1619, when Sir Henry Savile's "silver" Greek type matrices were brought to Oxford, Barnes's type fonts were presumably his own property. Besides his italic and roman types, Barnes had owned a small Greek font at least since 1586 and a limited amount of Hebrew type at least since 1596. These, along with Barnes's devices, ornaments, and perhaps press, soon graced John Lichfield's shop, which Madan located as being in Oxford's "Butcher Row (now Queen Street, the street leading west from Carfax)."

For the first eight years of its operation, from 1617 to 1624, Lichfield's shop produced only about six volumes a year, increasing its output to nine in 1619, diminishing to four in 1623, and returning to six in 1624. The official university business in which Lichfield and his partners appeared to engage most often was the generally hurried printing of occasional volumes of verses by university members. These poems – often in Latin, occasionally in English, and sometimes in obscure learned languages – commemorated births, marriages, safe returns from travels, recoveries from illnesses, and deaths of prominent people, with emphasis on the royal family. A common practice begun with Joseph Barnes was for the last poem in each collection to be presented as though it were the printer's personal contribution. That the printers actually composed these concluding poems is doubtful, but the imagery employed in them evokes the printing house, and the inevitable panegyrics on the royal family truly reflect the political sentiments of the printers. Certainly readers of the poems nominally contributed by John and later Leonard Lichfield I would have rightly perceived the printers to be staunch Royalists.

When not printing to the university's specific order, John Lichfield was free to work for various Oxford stationers and booksellers, several of whom had London ties. In fact, both John and his son apparently conducted most of their business for such others rather than for the university. Not much is known of these men, aside from their names and occasional personal information gleaned from old let-

ters that were later used as wastepaper in the bindings of Oxford books. At any rate, intimate connections appear to have existed between the university printers and Oxford booksellers – particularly in the 1620s and 1630s between the Lichfield shop and Henry Cripps, Edward Forrest, Thomas Huggins, William Webb, Henry Curteyne Francis Bowman, Thomas Allam, and John Wilmot.

A superficial examination of the titles John or Leonard printed for these men reveals no obvious pattern of one bookseller or another specializing in any genre. Possibly some university authors habitually worked with a favorite stationer, a favorite printer, or both. In any event, John Lichfield maintained a constant and seemingly good business, both official and unofficial, with the university community, and the works he printed are generally serious and often learned.

The best-known product of his press is Robert Burton's *The Anatomy of Melancholy,* published by Henry Cripps. John Lichfield printed the first four editions of this work (1621, 1624, 1628, 1632), and Leonard Lichfield printed part of the fifth (1638). As one might expect, sermons penned by Oxford scholars – including, for example, William Pinke's series titled *The Tryall of a Christians Syncere Loue vnto Christ,* printed for Edward Forrest – appear prominently among John Lichfield's titles. The series began in 1630, when William Turner printed in quarto two sermons by the recently deceased Pinke, a fellow of Magdalen College who had been known as an excellent classical scholar, linguist, and "a thorough-going Puritan." In 1631 John Lichfield printed the first edition of four of Pinke's sermons. Like Turner's, this book is a quarto edition, and in fact the second and third sermons are reissues of Turner's sheets; the signatures and pagination are separate for each sermon. In 1634 John Lichfield printed the second edition, this time reduced to duodecimo size, a precedent that subsequent editions followed. The third edition appeared in 1636 under Leonard Lichfield's supervision, and twenty years then elapsed before he printed the fourth edition in 1656. William Hall printed the fifth edition in 1659.

The amount of control that the university could exert over its printers was questionable. In fact, by permitting Lichfield and a partner to work as a team when the Star Chamber decree of 1586 had implied that only one printer would be allowed, the university demonstrated a degree of leniency toward them. They were to print at the university's order and would be remunerated through the sale of the books. Obviously, though, as their list of bookselling associates attests, between university jobs they could print for whomever they pleased — provided, of course, that the endeavor was within the law. In effect, they were quite independent, even appropriating the title of printer to the university and using the university devices as their own on title pages whenever they deemed it advantageous for themselves. Madan noted in 1925 that the university's ultimate power amounted to a right "to turn them out" if dissatisfied with their workmanship.

John Lichfield's third partner, William Turner, was exactly the kind of troublemaker the university would have preferred to disown; I. G. Philip has described him as "the most contentious and litigious Oxford printer of the seventeenth century." Turner took his freedom on 24 May 1622 and in 1624 succeeded James Short as university printer. He seems to have injected new energy into Lichfield's shop, if the increased number of books printed after his arrival has any meaning. From 1624 to 1627, the years of Turner's partnership, Lichfield's production increased dramatically, beginning in 1625 with eighteen books and sermons and ten royal proclamations (the last a result of the court having temporarily abandoned plague-ridden London for Oxford) and then settling down to eleven publications in 1626. Three of the 1625 and three of the 1626 titles were lectures and sermons by John Prideaux, Regius Professor of Divinity at Exeter College. Before separating, Lichfield and Turner jointly printed five books in 1627; then Lichfield completed two and Turner produced four more independently that year.

What caused the two men to quarrel is not actually known, but the repercussions were great, at least for Oxford. In 1626 and again in 1627 and 1628, according to the records of the Chancellor's Court,

> there weare diverse variances controversies and differences betweene the sayd William Turner and the sayd John Litchfeild for and concerninge certaine summe or summes of money, debts, dues, goods, utensills of printinge or other things demaundable.

Turner demanded goods worth £100, and the two men separated, Turner receiving about half the Lichfield ornaments and probably type as well, but not the devices. Turner set up shop elsewhere in Oxford and, like Lichfield, designated himself printer to the university.

This now obvious flouting of the Star Chamber decree that permitted the university only one printer was finally resolved through the exertions of

the influential William Laud, bishop of London and a member of the Privy Council, later archbishop of Canterbury, and from 1629 to 1641 chancellor of the university. The ambitious Laud recognized that Oxford lacked the letters patent for printing that Cambridge enjoyed, and in 1632 he obtained from King Charles I similar letters, amplified in 1633, allowing Oxford three printers, each of whom would be permitted two presses and two apprentices. There continued, however, only two printers, and, according to a complaint made by William Turner's successor circa 1661, each had only one press until 1655 or so.

Chancellor Laud had great plans for expanding the learned press at Oxford: he wished to have printed many of the rare manuscripts — early Christian texts in Greek, Hebrew, Arabic, and Syriac — held by the Bodleian Library. To accomplish his goal, he believed that he needed first to establish a Greek press, and that meant installing as the chief printer a man learned in Greek. Laud had prepared for this change by obtaining the king's permission to have three printers at Oxford, but the chancellor obviously had reservations about elevating either of the two existing printers, Lichfield and Turner, into the leading position. In fact, he had developed a distaste for both men, and having secured the letters patent, Laud wrote to the vice chancellor in 1633:

> [C]onfirm not either of the two Printers which you now have, in any of the Rights of these *Patents* till all Orders concerning them be setled. Secondly, ... name as yet no third *Printer,* but keep the place empty, that you may get an able man, if it be possible for the Printing of *Greek,* when you shall be ready for it. ... Lastly, such Orders, as shall be thought fit to be made for the limiting of your *Printers,* and keeping them in due obedience to the university upon all occasions ... I think, may now very fitly be inserted into a Chapter by themselves among the Statutes, that so they may have the more binding Authority over them.

While the third position remained unfilled, the university negotiated in 1634 with Turner to print the chronicle of Malalas with the Savile Greek types. Turner, not in the least sympathetic to the ideal of a learned press that could not possibly turn a profit, instead took this opportunity to "abstract" the Savile types, which he eventually returned in February 1639–1640. Turner had already established himself as an undesirable: according to Henry R. Plomer, in 1631, along "with Michael Sparke, senr., and other London booksellers, he was tried before the Court of Ecclesiastical Commissioners on the charges of printing unlicensed literature and books that were other men's copies." During the 1630s the Oxford vice chancellor, Dr. Richard Baylie, grew increasingly displeased with Turner's attitudes. In a letter to Laud in January 1636–1637 Baylie complained that Turner had rudely refused to comply with university wishes and preferred to print "Almanakes, and w^t else hee pleaseth, att his owne will." Despite his irritation Baylie was reluctant, however, to pursue his complaint to its logical end, as he explained that

> [Turner] is a man extremelie needie of witt and wealth, vtterlie vnable . . . to manage ye printing either for his owne, or ye Vniversities improvement, and soe necessitous, in regarde of his meanes, that if hee should p^{r}sentlie bee discommuned (as his extraordinarie peevishnes, or extreme sottishnes, hard to say w^{ch}) hath deserved, hee, and his, were vtterlie vndone.

So Turner remained a university printer until his death, circa October 1644. One of his former apprentices, Henry Hall, succeeded Turner as university printer on 21 November 1644 and bought his "presses, letters and utensils," according to Plomer.

Laud, as his 1633 letter attested, had already formulated his own low opinion of the university printers as a class. From 1633 to 1634 he was revising the university statutes, in which he mentioned the role of the eventual chief printer, the architypographus or scholar-printer. Part of his justification for filling the vacancy with a learned man grew from his dissatisfaction with Oxford printing up to that time. One section of the statutes, which in 1637 were printed (ironically, by Turner) in Latin, explains that

> since experience of the trade shows that these mechanic craftsmen for the most part look for profit and saving of labour, caring not at all for beauty of letters or good and seemly workmanship, and bundle out any kind of rough and incorrect productions to the light of day, be it provided by this statute that an Architypographus shall preside over the University's public printing office, which is to be established in a building specially devoted to this purpose. He shall be a man thoroughly acquainted with Greek and Latin literature and deeply learned in philological studies. . . .
>
> To his post, . . . be it provided by this statute that the office of Superior Bedel of Civil Law . . . as soon as it next becomes vacant shall be for ever annexed.

Despite these elaborate plans, Laud's ideal scholar-printer remained only a dream until the latter part of the century. The bedelship did not become vacant until 1656, and the Sheldonian Theatre was not completed until 1669.

Turner's negative attitude toward the learned press and the obvious dissatisfaction such an attitude created in the chancellor and vice chancellor are clear enough, but the roles played by John Lichfield and his son Leonard are not so clear, because the evidence in their cases is far less tangible. After Turner had separated from Lichfield in 1627, John Lichfield continued printing at a fairly regular rate, producing approximately ninety titles from 1628 to 1635. For the most part these books continued to be of a theological nature. Leonard Lichfield during these years was most likely refining a knowledge of printing by assisting in his father's business.

Leonard Lichfield had been born in Oxford in 1604, but no other record of him exists until 12 November 1630, when he was designated "privilegiatus" – that is, admitted as a privileged person to the university precincts. The university differentiated between scholars and certain privileged local tradespeople who, because of the nature of their various businesses, regularly interacted with the school. Perhaps Leonard's new status was akin to that of a London stationer taking up his freedom; he was certainly of a comparable age by 1630 to have completed an unofficial apprenticeship under his father.

In 1632 and 1633 the Lichfield shop produced two books that stand out from the other titles for the light they can shed on the father-and-son printing team. The first, printed in 1632, was a third edition of George Sandys's translation of Ovid's *Metamorphosis,* the cause of a lawsuit for which several members of Lichfield's shop gave depositions in 1635. The second, printed in 1633 before Turner removed the Savile Greek types, was the *Epistola ad Corinthios* of Pope Clement I, recorded in both Latin and, for the first time, the original Greek.

In 1635 George Sandys brought suit against William Stansby, the well-known London printer, whom Sandys believed owed him money after the London printer had done the preliminaries and last sheets of the 1632 edition of the *Metamorphosis,* the main text of which had been printed at Oxford by the Lichfield shop. The case is interesting not for its outcome, but for the depositions made by the Oxford printers.

In August 1635 three employees of the Lichfield shop testified to their involvement in the printing of Sandys's translation. Foremost among them was Leonard Lichfield, who after the retirement of his father that preceding January had been named a university printer and was now running the business. According to his deposition, in 1632 when his father had undertaken the printing of Sandys's book, Leonard "as his servant did helpe to print the same." His self-designation as a servant helps confirm his position under his father's tutelage. The other two deponents from the print shop – William Hall, about twenty-five years old in 1635, and John Luxford, twenty-four years old – were each described as a "printer," a title probably attributable simply to the fact that they worked in a print shop and not meant to imply that there were actually four printers simultaneously in the Lichfield business during 1632. Perhaps they were both apprentices, although no record exists of the university having so appointed them. William Hall was probably the son of Henry Hall, the same William who is known to have been printing in Oxford from 1657 to 1672; in 1662 he was a university printer working with his father. Of John Luxford there is no additional record.

The depositions reveal some things about relations between the Lichfields and London printing. Leonard Lichfield testified that he knew Sandys, the complainant, but did "not very well know" Stansby, and this identified Sandys as an intermediary for the London and Oxford printing establishments. Many lines of communication obviously had existed and would continue to exist between London and the university town; if the Lichfields did not correspond with members of the London printing trade, then certainly the authors of Oxford books and local Oxford booksellers provided means of establishing business relationships between the province and the metropolis. Imprints reveal that as time went on, Leonard Lichfield developed varied ties with London booksellers: in 1640 he printed for both Richard Royston and Samuel Enderby.

Details of the publication of the *Epistola ad Corinthios* can help explain the relations between the Lichfield father-and-son printers and the university. When university administrators complained about their printers in the 1630s, they either described those printers generically as mere craftsmen or, in matters of pointed admonition, directed their ire at Turner alone. The Lichfield shop was never mentioned by name, and this suggests that perhaps John and Leonard may have been contaminated with Turner's reputation more through simple proximity than through any real negligence of their own.

In 1633 John Lichfield was entrusted with printing the *Epistola,* using the Savile types, in Latin and Greek. The completion of this task marked this as perhaps the first book to emerge from the embryonic learned press; certainly it was a nonprofit endeavor. Whether or not the printed epistle met the university's standards of correctness, the apparent

willingness of the Lichfield shop to undertake the order signals an attitude at variance with Turner's toward the ideal of a learned press. Naturally the Lichfields, who were running a private business, needed to turn a profit, but their ambitions apparently did not arise wholly from a desire to make money. No doubt proud of their association with the university, they sought to make themselves fuller members of its elite society, a goal best met by proving themselves worthy of running a learned press.

The approximately ninety titles produced by Leonard Lichfield's press from 1635 to 1641 reflect such a compromise between his responsibility for printing academic books and the practical necessity of maintaining a profitable business. Sermons seem to have been a mainstay of the business: they sold well, and certainly Lichfield was blessed with a concentration of clergymen at the university, many of whom desired to see their sermons in print. The Lichfield shop continued to work for John Prideaux, bringing out four of his sermons in separate editions in 1636 and an edition of twenty collected sermons in 1637. The religious upheavals of the period only added to Lichfield's advantage, as theologians refuted each other in print as well as in the pulpit.

The most significant of the theological works Lichfield printed was *The Religion of Protestants a Safe Way of Salvation; or, An Answer to a Book Entitled Mercy and Truth, or Charity Maintained by Catholiques* (1638), by William Chillingworth, a Trinity College fellow who had converted to Roman Catholicism but who then, in his own words, "upon better consideration became a doubting papist." The book did not attack the Roman Catholic Church or defend the Anglican Church, but rather upheld free inquiry by the individual. Although a second edition was published in London within five months, a third edition did not appear until 1664, and Chillingworth's book bore no real fruit until after 1688. Harry Carter points out that "With its exaltation of conscience, of revelation interpreted by reason and learning, of tolerance, it had, if constant reprinting can be trusted as a sign, a profound effect on religion in England at the end of the century and in the early part of the next." Chillingworth's ideas strongly influenced Gilbert Burnet and John Tillotson, and five editions of *The Religion of Protestants* were to appear between 1704 and 1742.

Many of Leonard Lichfield's books were in Latin and obviously intended for educated, specialized audiences; whether or not he made much profit from them is unknown. One example is *Apparatus ad*

Title page (by Francisco Clein) and engraving (by Salomon Savery) for John Lichfield's complete edition of Ovid's Metamorphosis *(1632), translated by George Sandys*

origines ecclesiasticas, a 1635 folio work by Richard Montague, a bishop who discussed pre-Christian antiquities. Another is the 1636 enlargement of *Elementa ivrisprvdentiae,* a quarto volume by Dr. Richard Zouche of Oxford, and still another well-known work is Francis Bacon's *Of the Advancement and Proficience of Learning* (1639). The care given to the printing of these specialized books contrasts markedly with the apparently more hurried printing of many of the sermons.

Leonard Lichfield also printed poetry and even a few plays. Among the works of poetry, the Oxford commemorative verses appear most often, but he also printed poetic works by Thomas Bushell, Charles Fitz-Geffry, and Thomas Randolph. Members of the Oxford faculty were often versatile authors. Jasper Mayne of Christ Church not only contributed verses to the memorial series and wrote sermons but also wrote plays. In 1639 Lichfield printed a folio edition of his play *The Citye Match. A Comoedy,* which had been planned for presentation before the king in August 1636 at Oxford, but which "was put off." Lichfield printed Thomas

Randolph's *Poems* and two of his plays – *The Mvses Looking-glasse* and *Amyntas* – in a single quarto volume in 1638 (and a second edition in octavo in 1640). Randolph, a fellow of Trinity College, Cambridge, had died in 1635, and his brother, Robert, of Christ Church, Oxford, edited the volume, and this probably explains why it was printed at Oxford rather than Cambridge.

Less easily explained is the late 1639 or 1640 printing of two quarto plays by John Fletcher, who had died in 1625. Lichfield printed *The Tragoedy of Rollo Duke of Normandy,* a second edition, and *Rule a Wife* and *Have a Wife* in separate volumes, but the title pages reveal that the two were meant to be companion pieces. The two ornaments used, a lion and a unicorn, are halves of a standard pair, and, beginning with their fourth lines from the top, both title pages were printed from the same setting of type. Lichfield may have obtained the two plays in manuscript from a troupe of traveling players, for *Rollo* is the second quarto work but was not printed from a copy of the first, which had been printed in London during the previous year. Evidence from

*Title page for Sir Francis Bacon's 1640 survey of
human knowledge and learning, published in its first
complete edition in English*

damaged types and variations in medial comma spacing reveal that the same two compositors worked on both plays and that each had his own type case. They apparently set seriatim, one compositor setting the first four consecutive pages of a sheet while the other worked on the last four pages.

Whether or not Lichfield planned to continue printing more plays, any desire to do so would have been cut short by political unrest and the accompanying demands in Oxford for printing of a different kind. The outbreak of the Civil War in August 1642, with the headquarters for Charles's forces having been established at Oxford, ended normal printing in Oxford for many years. Lichfield, an ardent Royalist, and Henry Hall, Turner's successor as a university printer, were kept busy printing innumerable declarations and proclamations for the king in their shops. Lichfield even accompanied the king into the field and, with his press mounted in a wagon, was present at Edgehill in October

1642. "THE PRINTERS CONCLVSION To Her MAJESTIE," the closing poem in a 1643 collection of verses dedicated to the queen, recorded the actions of his printing press during that battle:

Madam,
That Traytrous and Vnlettered *Crew*
Who fight 'gainst Heaven, *Their* Soveraigne, *and* You,
Have not yet stain'd my Hallowed FOUNTS, *The spring*
Must needs be Cleare that issues from the King.
Presses of Old, as Pens, did but incite
Others to Valour; This It Selfe did fight:
In Ranks and Files these Letters *Marshall'd stood*
On Dismall Edg-Hill-day, *yet 'twas not blood*
They boaded by their Black, for Peace they sought
And Teem'd with Pardons while the Rebells fought.
Yet those that found it on that Boysterous day
Tooke't for some Dread Commission of Array;
And thought each Letter Theta, *every Point*
To give a Period to a Life *or* Joynt;
They Plunder'd, *and so turn'd it ore and ore*
As th' had ne're used their Neck-verse worse before....

Yet now it glories in its foyle, and will
Be throughly reconcil'd even to Edg-Hill. . . .

LEONARD LICHFIELD.

Lichfield's imprint was often forged in books printed in London at that time, and Plomer points out that Puritan tracts stigmatized him as "the malignant printer."

On 6 October 1644 a serious fire in the city damaged the Lichfield print shop and warehouse, but advance warning allowed much equipment and many books to be saved. Consumed in the flames, however, were all the unbound copies of part of the Epistle of Barnabas that had been printed in 1642 in Latin and Greek. By chance, one imperfect copy survived; the printers had discovered that one sheet was wrongly imposed, and either Lichfield or a compositor had taken the copy home. Madan has noted that "the rejected imperfect copy is the sole but sufficient representative of the claim of Oxford to have first printed the Epistle of St. Barnabas in Greek."

Despite the fire Lichfield was printing proclamations within a matter of weeks, but when Charles retreated in 1646 and Oxford fell to the Parliamentary forces, the printers who had so publicly supported the king found themselves with little work to do. Notorious as a Royalist printer, Lichfield seems to have barely subsisted during the Interregnum. Virtually all the printing he managed to carry out was done secretly, mainly for Richard Royston in London. Indeed, from October 1648 through May 1649 apparently no book or pamphlet was published in Oxford. The debt the king eventually owed Lichfield for his printing during the Civil War was a large sum – £1,294 19s. 4d. On 28 November 1661 Lichfield's widow, Anne, petitioned Charles II for payment, and from 1662 to 1665 she received as much as £1,016 11s. on the debt.

In 1654, three years before his death, Lichfield uncharacteristically turned to eulogizing Oliver Cromwell at the end of yet another set of commemorative verses. Perhaps he was simply following the lead of the university. The academics' pusillanimous homage to Cromwell elicited a stinging poetic response from Thomas Ireland, who satirized many of the hypocritical contributors, including Lichfield. Percy Simpson observes that "our only glimpse of this printer" occurs in one brief stanza:

Len. Leichfield too ventures t' flame in the reare,
Yet how he turn'd poet pray hold a blow there,

But he quickly found friends, being Beadle Esquire
Plaudite fat gut.

Leonard Lichfield died in March or April 1657. His successors included his son, Leonard II, and widow Anne, who were named printers to the university on 14 May; thus, two printers replaced one, and the university then had three printers. Madan criticizes the increase, observing that "this compassionate election of a third university Printer, though within the Statute, was unfortunate." Apparently Leonard II was in poor health; from 1659 through 1667 he printed virtually nothing by himself, and the overseeing of the business was left to Anne. Under her guidance the shop slumped further. She seems to have lacked the business sense of her late husband, and Madan, who noted in 1925 that "her first imprint is 'Oxoniæ, excudebat Anne Lichfield Academiæ typographus,' " accused her of knowing "no more Latin than a cat." Equally bad, Anne had little aesthetic judgment: she insisted on exhuming the old typeface flowers that her husband had earlier put away and thereby supposedly weakened the quality of Oxford printing for years.

Despite such apparent aesthetic deficiencies, Leonard II (or Anne, using his name) printed the first newspaper in Oxford. In the fall of 1665 Charles II and the court were in Oxford while the plague continued in London. According to Madan's *Brief Account* (1908), the king at that time "determined to institute an official Gazette, which should contain all appointments, with court and general news." The first number of *The Oxford Gazette,* "Published by Authority," appeared on 15 November bearing the colophon "Oxford, printed by Leonard Lichfield, Printer to the university, 1665." Lichfield printed the newspaper through 22–25 January 1665–1666, twenty-one numbers in all. The king left Oxford on 27 January, and printing of the *Gazette* was moved to London, where, beginning with number 24 for 1–5 February, its title became *The London Gazette*. This newspaper, the official organ of the British government, was to exist for more than three hundred years.

Meanwhile, the university press was finally being established. When the law bedelship became vacant in 1656, the way was clear for the appointment of the first architypographus, Dr. Samuel Clarke, in 1658. Following Laud's original conception of the press, the architypographus supervised the work of the three university printers, but they continued to do the printing with their own fonts and with their own presses in their own shops. In 1666 Dr. John Fell, dean of Christ Church and later bishop of Oxford, became vice chancellor of the university and the driving force behind the university's purchase of type, ornaments, punches, and matrices. He suggested the building of the Sheldonian Theatre; he encouraged papermaking at Wolvercote, near Oxford; he saw that presses were bought and French compositors brought in; and he looked for ways to finance the press. Madan comments on his treatment of the Lichfields and Halls:

> Fell seems to have been wise . . . in his dealings with the existing Printers to the university, though there is no documentary evidence on the point. He appears to have allowed them still a great measure of freedom in their private dealings with authors and publishers, only emphasizing his right to call on their time and work, when the Theatre compositors had too much on their hands, or were unsuitable. But he steadily went on purchasing type and ornaments, so as to be increasingly independent of the private stock of the printers.

For a while the university printers were needed at the Sheldonian Theatre. Anne Lichfield was paid £18 6s. by the university to print five hundred copies of the first book completed there, *Epicedia Universitatis Oxoniensis, in Obitum Augustissimæ Principis Henriettae Mariae Reginæ Matris* (1669), a volume of verses lamenting the death of the queen mother. The book bears the imprint "E Typographia Sheldoniana" and presumably was printed with the Lichfield types – the Lichfields and Halls were occasionally contracted to print on the university's presses from 1670 to 1672.

Anne Lichfield died in 1671, and Leonard II died of a fever on 22 February 1685–1686. His son, Leonard III, continued the family business from 1685–1686 to 1744. Harry Carter notes how the reputation of this third Leonard has suffered because of the presence of the university press: Leonard III was "the only master of the craft in [Oxford] besides the university. If he were not overshadowed by the other, Lichfield might be distinguished among eighteenth-century printers by his substantial production."

Unfortunately, little is known of Leonard Lichfield III. He was apprenticed to his father for seven years in 1681 and presumably succeeded him in 1686–1687, as the Lichfield imprint continues without a break. He was never appointed printer to the university, but he purchased new fonts of type cast in Fell's matrices; he used university devices occasionally; and some of his books bear the vice chancellor's imprimatur, indicating that he had connections with the univer-

sity. In 1700 Lichfield printed Charles Leigh's *Natural History of Lancashire, Cheshire, and the Peak,* and in 1705 he printed the second edition of Robert Plot's *Natural History of Oxfordshire,* but most of the books and pamphlets he produced were sermons, poems, essays, and manuals of instruction. Because Lichfield's printing charges for sermons were cheaper than those of the university press, many clergymen preferred his press. Furthermore, as Carter points out, "there is reason to think that sermons of dubious orthodoxy or tending to make trouble would go to him. He printed seven sermons by [Henry] Sacheverell to the university's one."

Following the death of Leonard Lichfield III, the name of a fourth Leonard Lichfield, who was located in Holywell, occasionally appears in imprints. Carter surmises that he may have gone out of business in 1754 "because there was a sharp rise in the number of sermons issuing from the university Press after that year." Nothing more is known of him or of his press.

Thus, the Lichfield printing business seems to have faded away in the growing presence of the Oxford University Press. It had lasted longer, though, than any other independent press in the city of Oxford. By 1700 Leonard Lichfield III alone had survived what John Johnson and Strickland Gibson describe as "the slow obliteration of the old independent craft printer of Oxford in his own field." At the conclusion of "The Oxford Press, 1650–75," Falconer Madan praises four "great men that built up the Press at Oxford" before 1900. The two seventeenth-century men he names are Archbishop Laud and Dr. Fell, and indeed the Oxford University Press was founded through their efforts. But the contributions of the Lichfields, along with those of Turner and the Halls, deserve recognition, for without their labor the university could not have printed books during much of the seventeenth century, and the press could not have evolved.

References:

Harry Carter, *A History of the Oxford University Press* (Oxford: Clarendon Press, 1975);

Andrew Clark, ed., *Register of the University of Oxford,* volume 2 (Oxford: Oxford Historical Society, 1887);

Richard Beale Davis, "George Sandys *v.* William Stansby: The 1632 Edition of Ovid's *Metamorphosis*," *Library,* fifth series 3 (December 1948): 193–212;

Strickland Gibson, *Abstracts from the Wills and Testamentary Documents of Binders, Printers, and Statio-*

ners of Oxford, from 1493 to 1638 (London: Bibliographical Society, 1907);

W. W. Greg, *A Bibliography of the English Printed Drama to the Restoration,* volume 2 (London: Printed for the Bibliographical Society at the University Press, Oxford, 1951);

John Johnson and Gibson, *Print and Privilege at Oxford to the Year 1700* (London: Oxford University Press, 1946);

John D. Jump, "Introduction" to John Fletcher's *Rollo Duke of Normandy* (London: University Press of Liverpool, 1948), pp. x–xxxiv;

P. L., "A Note on Joseph Barnes, Printer to the University, 1584–1618," *Bodleian Library Record,* 2 (December 1947): 188–190;

Falconer Madan, *A Brief Account of the University Press at Oxford with Illustrations Together with a Chart of Oxford Printing* (Oxford: Clarendon Press, 1908);

Madan, *Oxford Books: A Bibliography of Printed Works Relating to the University and City of Oxford or Printed or Published There,* 3 volumes (Oxford: Clarendon Press, 1895–1931);

Madan, "The Oxford Press, 1650–75: The Struggle for a Place in the Sun," *Library,* fourth series 6 (September 1925): 113–147;

Paul Morgan, "The Oxford Book Trade," in *Studies in the Book Trade,* edited by R. W. Hunt, I. G. Philip, and R. J. Roberts, Oxford Bibliographical Society Publications, new series 18 (Oxford: Oxford Bibliographical Society, 1975), pp. 71–89;

I. G. Philip, "A Seventeenth-Century Agreement Between Author and Printer: *Documents relating to the publication of Nathanael Carpenter's* Geography Delineated, *1625,*" *Bodleian Library Record,* 10 (December 1978): 68–73;

Percy Simpson, *Proof-Reading in the Sixteenth, Seventeenth and Eighteenth Centuries* (London: Oxford University Press, 1935);

George Walton Williams, "Textual Introduction," in John Fletcher's *Rule a Wife and Have a Wife,* volume 6 of *The Dramatic Works in the Beaumont and Fletcher Canon,* edited by Fredson Bowers (Cambridge: Cambridge University Press, 1985), pp. 485–500.

– *Barbara Fitzpatrick*

Barnaby Bernard Lintot

(London: 1699 – 1736)

Barnaby Lintot was one of the most prestigious literary publishers in the early half of the eighteenth century. Both the quality and the quantity of his publication lists came nearer than those of any other bookseller to rivaling the lists of the great Jacob Tonson. While Lintot published the works of many of the greatest writers of the era, his long (though eventually stormy) association with Alexander Pope helped greatly in establishing his standing as a publisher.

Barnaby Bernard Lintot was born on 1 December 1675 in the village of Southwater, Sussex. John Lintott (the father of Barnaby, who would eventually choose to drop the use of his first name as well as the second of the final *t*'s from his surname), was simply a yeoman farmer – although some other family connections to the printing business would eventually develop: Barnaby's uncle, Joshua Lintot, was to be a printer to the House of Commons from 1708 to 1710. Barnaby Lintot served a full apprenticeship in the print trade from 1690 to 1699, first under Thomas Lingard and later under John Harding. Though he was not released from the apprenticeship until 1699, his name appears on the title pages of two 1698 editions of plays: John Crowne's *Caligula* and Sir John Vanbrugh's *The Relapse*. Soon after he obtained his freedom, Lintot set up a shop at the sign of the Cross Keys in Fleet Street. On 13 October 1700 he married, and in 1703 the couple had a son, Henry, who would ultimately inherit Lintot's business.

During the early years of his career Lintot bought copyrights to various literary works, especially plays. One of his notebooks has survived and has been published in volume eight of printer John Nichols's *Literary Anecdotes of the Eighteenth Century* (1814), and it provides much information about financial transactions between bookseller-publishers and writers in the era.

It reveals, for example, that in 1701 Lintot bought one-third of the copyright to Colley Cibber's comedy *Love's Last Shift* (1696), for which he paid £3 4s. 6d. That prices varied considerably is clear from the fact that in 1705 Lintot paid £36 for Cibber's *Perolla and Izadora* (1706), £15 in 1702 for George Farquhar's *The Twin Rivals* (1703), and

£30 in 1706 for the latter's *The Beaux Stratagem* (1707). Nor did price variations always correlate with the value that posterity has placed on the works purchased. In 1703 Lintot paid the forgotten Thomas Baker more than £32 for *Tunbridge-Walks; or, the Yeoman of Kent* (1703), and in 1706 he paid £50 for Edmund Smith's *Phaedra and Hippolytus* (1709). In 1704 Lintot paid £7 3s. for half the copyright of John Dennis's *Liberty Asserted* (1704), and in the next year he paid £21 10s. for all rights to Dennis's *Appius and Virginia* (1709). Susanna Centlivre in 1703 received £10 for her play *Love's Contrivance* (1703) and in 1709 another £10 for her *The Busie Body* (1732). Nicholas Rowe's popularity, by contrast, earned him £50 in 1713 for *The Tragedy of Jane Shore* (1714) and £75 in 1715 for *The Tragedy of Lady Jane Gray* (1715). All this buying of copyrights clearly indicates that Lintot had learned – perhaps from the example of the fast-rising bookseller Jacob Tonson – that his success depended on having a strong backlist and holding exclusive rights, and early in the century he set about compiling a list that would ensure stability and strength for his business.

The pillar of Lintot's business was to be the work of Alexander Pope, whose first publication, "Pastorals," appeared at the end of Tonson's sixth collection of *Poetical Miscellanies*. Published on 2 May 1709, the book announced the advent of the greatest poet of the age. Tonson had actually contracted with Pope to publish the sequence of poems in 1706, but many delays had intervened – delays that did nothing to bond Pope to Tonson. Moreover, the size of the Tonson empire made Pope uneasy and caused him to regard Tonson somewhat apprehensively. He wrote in a letter of 20 May 1709 to his friend and mentor William Wycherley that "Jacob creates poets, as Kings sometimes do Knights, not for their honour, but for money."

Pope seems to have respected Tonson, and in later years the two developed a strong friendship, but the poet seems to have been determined from early days to avoid becoming one of Tonson's stable of authors – even though Tonson had paid him £13 for the *Pastorals,* a fee that by contemporary standards was quite fair. Keeping his options open,

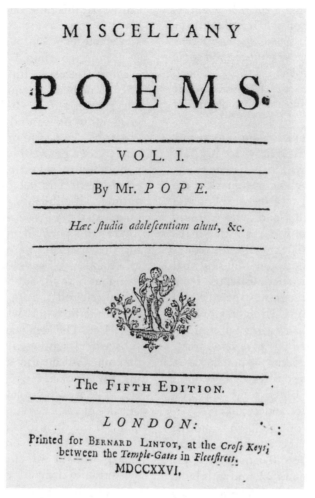

MISCELLANY

POEMS.

VOL. I.

By Mr. *POPE.*

Hæc studia adolescentiam alunt, &c.

The FIFTH EDITION.

LONDON:

Printed for BERNARD LINTOT, at the *Cross Keys,* between the *Temple-Gates* in *Fleetstreet.*
MDCCXXVI.

Title page for the fifth edition of a miscellany edited by Alexander Pope. The first edition of this collection is titled Miscellaneous Poems and Translations, by Several Hands *(1712).*

Pope therefore published his next major work – *Essay on Criticism,* which appeared on 15 May 1711 – with a virtually unknown Catholic bookseller named William Lewis. Yet this was evidently not a happy arrangement either, for Pope soon decided that Lewis was not adequately promoting the poem and, exasperated, took it upon himself to mail out copies to be reviewed.

Meanwhile, Lintot – having continued to observe Tonson's successes – had decided to publish a rival miscellany volume and in 1709 had produced one, *Oxford and Cambridge Miscellany Poems,* edited by Elijah Fenton. The success of this endeavor encouraged Lintot, who approached Pope to propose that the writer contribute to Lintot's next collection. Pope agreed, and he contributed his latest work, "The Rape of the Lock." In March 1712 Lintot paid him £7 for this first, two-canto version, and the publisher gave it pride of place by letting it con-

clude his volume, *Miscellaneous Poems and Translations, by Several Hands* (1712). The collection also included Pope's translation of Publius Papinius Statius and Pope's "To A Young Lady, with the Works of Voiture," along with some shorter poems. Published on 20 May 1712, the volume established Lintot as a publisher able to compete on the same ground as the great Tonson.

In 1713 Lintot, following the first performance of Joseph Addison's *Cato* on 14 April, published Dennis's *Remarks upon Cato,* strictures on this play that had taken London by storm. For the copyright to this work Tonson paid Addison the staggering sum of £107, an investment that paid Tonson huge returns for many years. Had it not been for Pope, Dennis's criticism of the play might have been forgotten as only one among many voices praising or damning *Cato.* Pope quickly produced and printed anonymously a pamphlet, *Narrative of Dr. Robert*

Norris, Concerning the Strange and Deplorable Frenzy of Mr. John Dennis, which went on sale less than three weeks after Dennis's *Remarks upon Cato.* The *Narrative* is of interest not only because it intensified some animosity between Pope and Dennis that had been seething since Pope's treatment of Dennis in the *Essay on Criticism* but also because the figure of Lintot appears in it.

In the *Narrative* Pope depicts Dennis as raving mad and confined to his bedroom, where his publisher, Lintot, attends him. As Lintot listens to the dialogue between Norris (a well-known quack of the day) and Dennis, he begins to grow nervous and mutters, "If [Dennis] be really mad, who will buy the *Remarks?* " Lintot eventually leaves with Norris, and they continue to discuss Dennis. Lintot relates how Dennis had reacted when someone said that Shakespeare's dramatic practice differed from Dennis's critical principles: Dennis "swore the said Shakespear was a *Rascal,* with other defamatory Expressions, which gave Mr. *Lintott* a very ill opinion of the said *Shakespear.*" While Pope's *Narrative* treats Dennis roughly, Lintot generally appears as a rather likable, if simple, person. Knowing Pope's satiric capabilities, the real Lintot might have divined that he could ask for no kinder outcome.

Certainly Lintot bore Pope no ill will, and the two continued their business relationship. In February 1713 he published Pope's *Windsor Forest,* for which he paid a little more than £32, and in July he paid £15 for the *Ode for Musick (on St. Cecilia's Day)* (1713). In 1714 Lintot also published Pope's revised and expanded five-canto *The Rape of the Lock,* for which he paid a mere £15, although Pope would soon be receiving much higher prices from Lintot.

Apart from the works he was publishing, some measure of Lintot's growing stature can be seen in respect he received from the Stationers' Company, to which he was elected in 1708. Being elected to various offices in the company for many years, Lintot finally rose to the level of underwarden in 1729 and 1730. His acceptance among his colleagues, evidenced by collaborations with Tonson and others, is another measure of Lintot's stature. After the fall of the Harley-Bolingbroke ministry the House of Commons commissioned Lintot, Tonson, Timothy Goodwin, and William Taylor to print *A Report from the Committee of Secrecy* (1715), which revealed the Jacobite negotiations that the fallen ministers secretly carried out. Landing such a commission was a stroke of political good fortune that firmly established Lintot's respectability among the ascendant Whigs – a consequence that may have benefited the publisher of Pope, the Catholic Tory

satirist. At this time Lintot was also appointed, with Tonson and Taylor, to print parliamentary votes, an appointment Lintot held until 1727.

Pope continued to provide Lintot with his greatest successes, however. In the last months of 1713 Pope began to make known his plan to translate Homer's *Iliad.* He knew exactly what sort of production he wanted, and he let rival publishers know: he planned to print the poem in six volumes, one volume per year, and he wanted to finance its publication by subscription. Most subscription projects hitherto had been far less ambitious, with the author and publisher producing only a single volume, usually a lush folio. Pope was determined to produce the poem in an oversize quarto, thus reducing the luxuriance somewhat and increasing the affordability of the volumes. He also devised a time-payment plan for subscribers: two guineas paid at the outset, and one due upon receipt of each volume except the final one, which the subscriber would receive free. The idea was a good one not only for the subscribers, who would have to pay less money at one time, but for the publisher as well: by continuing the project for several years, the publisher would be free to cancel later volumes if production or sales of earlier volumes did not go well. Pope demanded the right to choose the type to be used, the textual decorations, and even the paper. He knew exactly what he wanted, and he knew that he was in a position to demand it.

Lintot won the bidding and signed an agreement, dated 23 March 1714, with Pope – an agreement highly favorable to the poet. He was to receive free of charge 750 copies for the subscribers (thus, Pope was to keep all the subscription money) plus two hundred guineas per volume. Lintot was to receive the copyright and the right to republish the poem in other, nonquarto formats one month after its initial publication. He planned to direct his sales toward the top of the market, and he planned a large folio *Iliad* to follow the publication of Pope's quarto.

The first volume of the quarto edition appeared on 6 June 1715, and the final volume in 1720. Pope's *Iliad* is a milestone in publishing history; the beauty of the quarto edition is well known to anyone who has ever seen the clarity and evenness of the print and the unity of typeface, decoration, and text that Pope accomplished. The credit for the edition must go chiefly to Pope, for Lintot was functioning in this venture as little more than an agent. Pope was handsomely rewarded: he is said to have earned between £4,000 and £5,000 on the project, undoubtedly by far the greatest amount

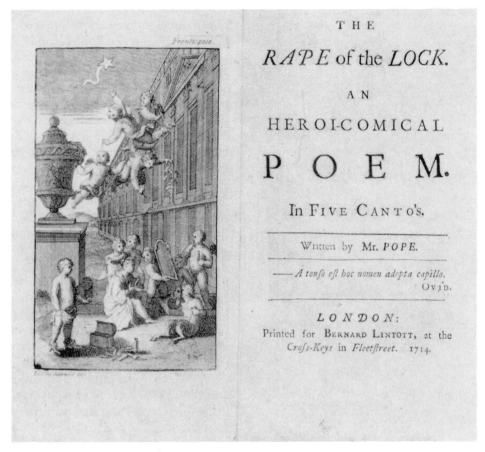

THE

RAPE of the *LOCK.*

AN

HEROI-COMICAL

POEM.

In FIVE CANTO's.

Written by Mr. *POPE.*

——*A tonfo eft hoc nomen adepta capillo.*
OVID.

LONDON:
Printed for BERNARD LINTOTT, at the
Crofs-Keys in *Fleetftreet.* 1714.

Frontispiece and title page for the first edition of Alexander Pope's mock-heroic poem

any author had ever made from sales of a single title. Lintot, however, did not fare as well. He had overestimated the size of the top end of the market, and, although some have estimated that he made profits of more than £700 on it, his folio edition did not sell as well as he had hoped. When a Dutch printer published a pirated duodecimo edition that was clandestinely imported and that sold very well, Lintot had to counter by publishing a duodecimo of his own.

But if Pope deserves credit for his success, he certainly worked hard enough for it: he alone was responsible for securing subscribers and handling any defaulters. Though it was common enough for the marketing of subscription editions to be handed to authors, the effort frequently exhausted and irritated Pope, who relied on the help of many friends, including Jonathan Swift, who worked hard to enroll subscribers for the volume. The subscription list of 575 names included a blend of Tory and Whig interests, as Pope's popularity at last overcame party alignments. Subscribers included Princess Caroline of Wales, 176 aristocratic names, and

eleven Oxford colleges. Many of Pope's Roman Catholic friends subscribed, as did most of the leading literary figures of the day: not only Pope's close friends such as John Gay and Swift, but also Cibber, Richard Steele, Samuel Garth, and Anne Finch, Countess of Winchilsea.

Other successes for Lintot accompanied that of Pope's *Iliad.* In 1713 Lintot had begun working with Gay, whom he paid £25 for *The Wife of Bath* (1713). In 1715 Lintot bought for £43 the poem that would establish Gay's reputation as a writer of urbane Augustan verse, *Trivia; or, the Art of Walking the Streets of London* (1716?), and in 1717 he paid Gay another £43 for *Three Hours After Marriage* (1717), a play ascribed to Gay but in fact a collaboration between Gay, Pope, and John Arbuthnot.

During the winter of 1715–1716 Lintot moved his shop to a location near the Thames, and he began negotiations with Tonson for further collaborative publication of plays. The two signed an agreement of partnership on 6 February 1718 stating that, eighteen months hence, they would own jointly any plays purchased by them. In 1719 Lintot

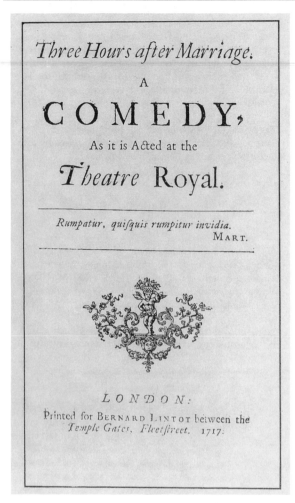

*Title page for Pope's only play, a collaborative effort with
John Gay and John Arbuthnot*

continued to branch out by purchasing one-twentieth
of the first English daily newspaper, *The Daily Courant.*

Lintot also entered into somewhat unusual financial agreements with some writers. He contracted in 1715 with John Urry for an edition of
Geoffrey Chaucer, for which proceeds would be divided three ways: one-third to Lintot, one-third to
Urry, and one-third to Christ Church, Oxford, for the
expenses of building the Peckwater Quadrangle. Urry
died in 1716, but the work was completed with the aid
of others, such as Thomas Ainsworth. Urry had
taken so many liberties with the text, however, that
the edition, which finally appeared in 1721, is renowned as one of the least reliable ever produced.
Lintot also arranged for shared-risk subscription
productions of Durant Breval's *Remarks on Several
Parts of Europe* (1726) and Samuel Jeake's *Charters
of the Cinque Ports* (1728), in which the publisher
and the authors also shared in the proceeds.

On 10 January 1725 Pope issued public proposals for a subscription-financed translation of
Homer's *The Odyssey.* Pope planned this translation
as a collaborative effort and recruited Elijah Fenton
and William Broome to share the task with him. No
copy of the proposals is known to exist, so the details of this collaboration are not clear, although
Pope later quoted from the proposals in *The Dunciad*
(1729), where he refers to two friends helping him.
In any case, some members of the public, and ultimately Lintot as well, seem not to have fully understood or accepted that others would be doing much
of the work. As it turned out, only twelve of the
twenty-four books would be translated by Pope, although he quite actively oversaw and corrected the
work of Fenton and Broome.

This time Lintot was more shrewd than he
had been in the first contract he had signed with
Pope: under the terms of this second agreement
Lintot paid Pope only half as much as he had paid
for *The Iliad,* and the publisher arranged for two
rival subscription editions — one large folio and one
small. Pope's edition was a large quarto in five volumes, which were published between April 1725
and June 1726. This treatment angered Pope, and
difficulties with Broome and Fenton widened the
split between the poet and the publisher. The two
collaborators had also enrolled subscribers, and
Lintot, balking at being expected to provide free
subscription copies for Broome, threatened to take
the three to Chancery Court.

Lintot paid Broome £400 for the eight books
that comprised Broome's share of the translation,
another £100 for the subscriptions that he arranged, and another £100 for the notes. Fenton received a total of £300, and Pope got £600. Pope
also got the money from his subscribers, who numbered more than one thousand, so he again made
handsome profits on the project. Yet other conflicts
occurred between Pope and his two assistants as the
work continued. They agreed to minimize the
amount of translation that Broome and Fenton
would actually be responsible for doing. To make it
appear as though Pope, with his considerable literary reputation, had responsibility for much of the
translation was probably a good business decision
for marketing the book, but the two collaborators
were not pleased with the decision.

Some bitterness grew. Broome in particular
was reported to have publicly criticized Pope and
his command of Greek, and Broome later complained publicly about the amount he had been
paid. All this angered Pope, who was to incorporate
Broome into *The Dunciad.* Following publication of

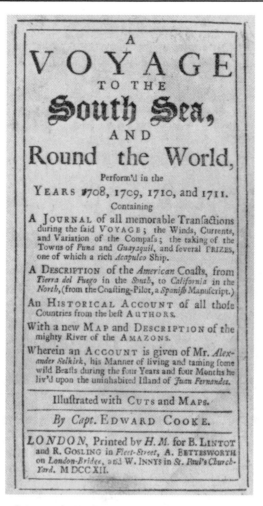

A
VOYAGE
TO THE
South Sea,
AND
Round the World,
Perform'd in the
YEARS 1708, 1709, 1710, and 1711.
Containing
A JOURNAL of all memorable Transactions
during the said VOYAGE; the Winds, Currents,
and Variation of the Compass; the taking of the
Towns of *Puna* and *Guayaquil*, and several PRIZES,
one of which a rich *Acapulco* Ship.

A DESCRIPTION of the *American* Coasts, from
Tierra del Fuego in the *South*, to *California* in the
North, (from the Coasting-Pilot, a *Spanish* Manuscript.)

An HISTORICAL ACCOUNT of all those
Countries from the best AUTHORS.

With a new MAP and DESCRIPTION of the
mighty River of the AMAZONS.

Wherein an ACCOUNT is given of Mr. *Alexander Selkirk*, his Manner of living and taming some
wild Beasts during the four Years and four Months he
liv'd upon the uninhabited Island of *Juan Fernandes.*

Illustrated with CUTS and MAPS.

By *Capt.* EDWARD COOKE.

LONDON, Printed by *H. M.* for B. LINTOT
and R. GOSLING in *Fleet-Street*, A. BETTESWORTH
on *London-Bridge*, and W. INNYS in *St. Paul's Church-
Yard.* M DCC XII.

*Title page for Capt. Edward Cooke's narrative of his
explorations, published by Lintot in 1712*

The Odyssey, Pope broke altogether with Lintot, set up a relationship with bookseller Lawton Gilliver, and dealt directly with printer John Wright: Pope went on to have his work printed by Wright, usually under only a one-year copyright, and then sold to Gilliver. He soon quarreled with Gilliver and moved to yet another young bookseller, Robert Dodsley. As he grew older, Pope seems to have become increasingly aware of the commercial value of his work and determined that men such as Lintot would not profit from it any more than was necessary. Pope did all that he could to wrest control of publishing from the booksellers; to a great degree he was successful in doing so, and his struggles helped insure that authors would enjoy increasingly prominent rights in coming years.

In the 1720s, though, he still had to deal with Bernard Lintot. Pope's letter of November 1716 to Richard Boyle, Lord Burlington, a letter in which Pope wrote humorously and at some length about the printer, characterizes Lintot both personally and professionally. It refers to Lintot as "the enterprizing Mr. *Lintot,* the redoutable rival of Mr. *Tonson,*" and, in recounting a short horseback trip Pope had taken in Lintot's company, the poet represents him as being worried about inferences that would be drawn from his movements. "Now damn them!" Lintot begins one reflection on the press,

> If I should go down into *Sussex,* they would say I was gone to the Speaker [then Sir Spencer Compton]. But what of that? if my son were but big enough to go on with the business, by G—d I would keep as good company as old *Jacob.*

Lintot's reference is to Tonson's powerful political connections; his constant cursing reinforces Pope's suggestion that Lintot is crude, and the presentation of Lintot's reference to Tonson implies that Lintot is small beer by comparison. Throughout the letter Lintot appears as a Philistine, interested in literature only as a commodity he can buy and sell. (Ironically, Pope himself was more aware of the commercial value of poetry than any writer had ever been; toward his aristocratic reader of his letter, however, he plays the role of gentleman author, quite above monetary concerns.) Pope continues, in the letter, by asking Lintot about his opinion of translators, and the bookseller curses them as an especially untrustworthy lot:

> In a hungry fit, they'll swear they understand all the languages in the universe: I have known one of them take down a *Greek* book upon my counter and cry, Ay this is *Hebrew,* I must read it from the latter end. By G–d I can never be sure in these fellows, for I neither understand *Greek, Latin, French,* nor *Italian* my self. But this is my way: I agree with them for ten shillings *per* sheet, with a proviso, that I will have their doings corrected by whom I please; so by one or other they are led at last to the true sense of an author.

When Pope asks how Lintot determines the correctness of the correctors, Lintot responds, "Why I get any civil gentleman (especially any *Scotchman*) that comes into my shop, to read the original to me in *English.*"

Pope's portrait of Lintot is amusing, one to be discounted in some degree because its aim is clearly to entertain Lord Burlington. Yet the entire letter provides an interesting picture of Lintot. He had undertaken many translation projects at this time, perhaps because his rival Tonson was well known for his high-quality translations. Pope does not confine his portraits of Lintot to private letters, however. In *The Dunciad* he includes Lintot in the episode of the booksellers' footrace, in which he describes "huge Lintot" thus:

> As when a dab-chick waddles thro' the copse,
> On feet and wings, and flies, and wades, and hops,
> So lab'ring on, with shoulders, hands, and head,
> Wide as a windmill all his figure spread,
> With arms expanded Bernard rows his state,
> And left-legg'd Jacob seems to emulate.

The reference in the last line is to Jacob Tonson's pronounced limp (a common satiric caricature of him referred to his "two left legs"), but it also characterizes Lintot merely as an imitator of Tonson, a second-rate parvenu. The charge of imitation is to some extent true, as Lintot had always keenly observed Tonson's successes and in many cases learned from them. The remaining criticism of Lintot seems to be purely personal – of his rather large and awkward figure. Lintot escapes lightly compared to many figures in this poem, and he also

appears briefly in *An Epistle from Mr. Pope to Dr. Arbuthnot* (1734), where the importuning Arbuthnot asks Pope to recommend him to the bookseller. And in the 1735 "Prologue to the Satires" Pope includes a couplet on Lintot's bookshop. Lintot had apparently employed an in-house promotion scheme by setting up authors' names in large red letters near their books, and Pope found the practice rather vulgar:

> What though my name stood rubric on the walls,
> On plaistered posts, with clasps, in capitals.

Swift also writes satirically about Lintot in a poem dated 1725. He begins by cataloguing some of the past great men of the book trade – Christophe Plantin, Louis Elzevir, and Manutius Aldus – and says that "Others with Aldus would besot us; / I, for my part, admire *Lintottus.*" The poem goes on to suggest Lintot's immodesty:

> His character's beyond compare,
> Like his own person, large and fair.
> They print their names in letters small,
> But LINTOT stands in capital;
> Author and he with equal grace
> Appear, and stare you in the face.

Swift ends the poem with a joke, standard at least since Dryden's time, about remaindered books being used for toilet paper. He says of other publishers that

> Their books are useful but to few,
> A scholar, or a wit or two:
> Lintot's for general use are fit;
> For some folks read, but all folks ––––.

Around the time of the conflict with Pope over *The Odyssey,* Lintot's thoughts were evidently turning toward his family heritage and toward his retirement. He began improving his father's property in Sussex and began to explore the genealogy of his family. Nichols reported that circa 1726 Lintot approached the custodian of the heraldic manuscripts of the earl of Oxford, Humphrey Wanley, who noted in his diary:

> Young Mr. Lintot [probably Henry] the Bookseller came enquiring after *Arms,* as belonging to his father, mother, and other relations, who now, it seems, want to turn *gentlefolks.* I could find none of their names.

Wanley's implied sneer at the merchant trying to climb above his station may recall Pope's depiction of Lintot in the 1716 letter to Lord Burlington. Both

Wanley and Pope discerned Lintot's ambition to rise in the world, an ambition that one could not acknowledge at that period without inviting satiric response.

Lintot's son, Henry, was approaching manhood at this time and was being gradually worked into the business. Henry was admitted to the Stationers' Company in 1730, and henceforth his name appeared jointly with his father's in company matters. Barnaby Lintot apparently turned the business over to Henry and retired to Sussex soon after this time. He was nominated for the post of high sheriff of Sussex in late November 1735, and he died on 3 February 1736. The post of sheriff, and the publishing business, passed to his son Henry.

Until his death in 1758 Henry carried on the business, but he did not enjoy any triumphs like that of his father's *Iliad*. He continued and expanded his father's interest in legal printing, as he received the official patent of law printer in 1748. He had a daughter, Catherine, who also went into the printing business and entered a partnership with the great novelist and printer Samuel Richardson; she is said to have amassed a considerable fortune.

Though Pope, Swift, and others may have laughed at Barnaby Lintot's social ambition, he certainly reached the forefront of the publishing profession in his time. Many of his publishing decisions may have been made by imitating Jacob Tonson, but, as Pope himself must have allowed, a great model deserves imitation, and Lintot must be given credit for recognizing the worth of what Tonson was doing. If most of the design of the great *Iliad* was the work of Pope rather than of the publisher,

to Lintot also must go the credit for having recognized its value. Lintot's surviving record book reveals him to have been a serious, painstaking businessman, and among all the satiric barbs hurled at booksellers in the era, it is worth emphasizing that Lintot was never accused of treating his authors dishonestly or unfairly. Nichols concludes that "against his benevolence and moral character there is not even an insinuation." In the age of Edmund Curll and of *The Dunciad,* that is a considerable eulogy indeed.

References:

Matthew J. C. Hodgart, "The Subscription List for Pope's *Iliad,* 1715," in *The Dress of Words: Essays on Restoration and Eighteenth Century Literature in Honor of Richmond P. Bond,* edited by Robert B. White Jr. (Lawrence: University of Kansas Libraries Press, 1978), pp. 25–34;

Kathleen M. Lynch, *Jacob Tonson: Kit-Cat Publisher* (Knoxville: University of Tennessee Press, 1971);

Maynard Mack, *Alexander Pope: A Life* (New York: Norton, 1986);

W. A. Speck, "Politicians, Peers, and Publication by Subscription," in *Books and Their Readers in Eighteenth-Century England,* edited by Isabel Rivers (New York: St. Martin's Press, 1982), pp. 47–68;

James A. Winn, "On Pope, Printers, and Publishers," *Eighteenth-Century Life,* 6 (January–May 1981): 93–102.

– *Raymond N. MacKenzie*

Humphrey Lownes

(London: circa 1590 – 1630)

Although the books Humphrey Lownes produced during his career as a London trade printer do not include important first editions of major works, his life reveals much about his profession in the early 1600s. Lownes owed his successful business to his two marriages — first to the daughter of a prosperous and powerful stationer, Thomas Man, and second to the widow of printer Peter Short, whose dowry was her husband's shop. This second marriage enabled Lownes to switch from being a small-time publisher to a larger printer who produced books for his brother, bookseller Mathew Lownes; for his first wife's father; and for a group of London booksellers, some of whom specialized in religious works. By the time of his death in 1630 Lownes was able to leave a thriving business to his partner and former apprentice, Robert Young.

Humphrey and his older brother, Mathew, were sons of Hugh Lownes, a farmer and fletcher in Rode, Cheshire. Mathew was apprenticed to printer Nicholas Ling from 29 September 1582 to 11 October 1596, while Humphrey was apprenticed to a relative, William Lownes, from midsummer 1580 to 26 June 1587. Both Humphrey and Mathew became liveried members of the Stationers' Company — Humphrey on 1 July 1598 and Mathew on 3 July 1602 — and Humphrey was to hold office as master of the company in 1620–1621 and in 1624–1625, indications of some status (or at least longevity) in the trade. During both of Humphrey's terms in office Mathew was to serve as senior warden.

That Mathew was able to marry in 1597, the year after his indenture ended, while Humphrey married the daughter of Thomas Man in a ceremony held in the Stationers' Hall in 1591, four years after he was freed, may indicate their relative financial positions. The only appearance of the name of Humphrey Lownes in the Stationers' Company loan book records that on 20 October 1614 he paid five pounds of the twelve-pound debt of John Asheton, a former apprentice who had been freed on 3 July 1610.

Humphrey Lownes's career began with a quarto translation of *The Oration and Declaration of Henrie the Fourth, to His Armie, before Paris* (1590), which was printed to be sold by Lownes. In 1592 two books were printed for Lownes — Richard Johnson's *The Nine Worthies of London: Explaining the Honourable Exercise of Armes* in verse and prose, and Philip Stubbes's *A Perfect Pathway to Felicitie, Conteining Godly Meditations, and Praiers*. In the following years he published an average of two or three books per year. In 1598 and 1599 Lownes had six works printed by Felix Kingston, a London printer originally apprenticed as a grocer but a printer since 1597. These works were registered to Lownes alone or in partnership with other booksellers, such as Thomas Man. William Perneby's *A Direction to Death: Teaching Man the Way to Die Well* is typical of these works; most were theological. At this time Lownes sold books at a shop near the west door of St. Paul's Churchyard, the usual location for booksellers. When he married the widow of Peter Short, he moved to his wife's shop at the Star on Bread Street Hill, just outside St. Paul's.

Once he became a printer Lownes was no longer as free to decide what works he printed. He was forced to accept or reject the jobs that came to him, but some of his preferences are still apparent in the works he produced. Of the 386 works he printed, reprinted, or shared in printing, 234 are theological. Many are sermons, and some are tracts attacking Roman Catholicism. In addition, each of the four pieces of music he printed were sacred compositions, and many of the works that he and his contemporaries would have regarded as literary were based on current religious conceptions — as in Nicholas Breton's *The Soules Immortall Crowne Consisting of Seaven Glorious Graces* (1605) or the translation of a work by French Huguenot Philippe de Mornay, *Six Excellent Treatises of Life and Death* (1607), an anthology of classical and medieval sources including Marcus Tullius Cicero, Lucius Annaeus Seneca, the Bible, Saint Ambrose, and Saint Cyprian. Lownes also spent much time between 1606 and 1616 printing twelve works (in quarto, octavo, and duodecimo formats) by Bishop Joseph Hall for seven different booksellers, although Samuel Macham was the main investor.

Perhaps the strongest indication of the intersection of Lownes's business and spiritual interests is the fact that he printed four editions of John

Gee's *The Foot Out of the Snare* (1624). This virulently anti-Catholic work had, as an appendix to the third and fourth editions, "The names of such as disperse, print, binde or sell popish bookes." Gee named Catholic clergy and physicians living in London in the first two editions, and the following editions included his rebuttals to those who attacked his veracity. Obviously he could not afford to give his detractors such a weapon as having his work printed or published by men who could be connected in any way to Catholicism.

Although Lownes continued to print sermons and other devotional works throughout his life, the titles that he registered at the end of his life were mainly literary – partly because printing rights were transferred within the Lownes family. When Mathew Lownes died on 3 October 1625, his copyrights, including several well-known and profitable literary works, were left to his son, Thomas, to whom they were transferred on 10 April 1627. But Thomas died in 1627, so on 30 May these rights were transferred to Humphrey Lownes and his former apprentice, now partner, Robert Young. Two of the works had been previously printed by Humphrey for Mathew Lownes: Sir Philip Sidney's *The Arcadia* (the seventh, eighth, and ninth editions in 1605, 1613, and 1622 or 1623) and Edmund Spenser's *The Faerie Queene* (the third edition, 1609–1617). Having acquired these copyrights, Lownes enlisted other printers in joint ventures to print new editions of *The Arcadia* (1628–1629) and Sir Francis Bacon's *Historie of the Raigne of King Henry the Seventh* (1628).

Yet Lownes did not long retain the rights to these important titles, for on 6 November 1628 he assigned many of them to George Latham, a relative, and to George Cole, another member of the Stationers' Company. Like Lownes, Cole had married a stationer's widow and had become an influential member of the company, but he was a professor of civil law, not a bookseller. The circumstances surrounding Lownes's decision to transfer his copyrights are unknown, though they may have been exchanged in lieu of cash. On 6 December 1630, shortly before Lownes's death, many of these rights were returned to Robert Young, who reprinted some of these titles in the following years.

In all, Lownes printed seventy-five literary works, twenty-seven of which were poems or verse translations. He published little drama, being a joint printer for one masque – Thomas Dekker's *The Magnificent Entertainment: Given to King James, upon his Passage through London* (1604) – and only four plays. In 1600 he published jointly the second edition of

Title page for Humphrey Lownes's 1611 folio edition of major works by Edmund Spenser

Thomas Heywood's *The First and Second Partes of King Edward the Fourth* and was the printer of the third through sixth editions (1605, 1613, 1619). The other plays he printed were the first edition of the anonymous *A Pleasant Comedie, Called Wily Beguilde* (1606) and Samuel Rowley's *When You See Me, You Know Me* (1605), which was printed by Lownes and others for Nathaniel Butter. William Shakespeare used this play as a source for his own *Henry VIII*. The only noteworthy literary first editions Lownes printed were by Michael Drayton: *Mortimeriados* (1596) and the folio first edition of *Poly-Olbion* (1612 or 1613), both published by Mathew Lownes.

Lownes's later editions of popular Renaissance works were more important to contemporary readers than to readers today, and the fact that he printed first editions of translations of classical works such as George Chapman's translation of Hesiod's *The Georgicks of Hesiod* (1618) and Thomas May's translation of *Virgil's Georgicks* (1628) was of greater significance to his original customers than to modern scholars. Lownes was both publisher and, later, printer of several editions of the English translation of *Bartas His Devine Weekes and Workes* (1604, 1608, 1611, 1614, and 1620/1621) by Guillaume de Saluste du Bartas. The popularity of this work in England is attested by the influence of du Bartas on the metaphysical poets, by the fact that Lownes reprinted it so often, and by the fact that Young published and printed yet another edition in 1633. The copyright for it, too, was transferred from Lownes to Cole, to Latham, and then to Young.

Lownes printed many educational works, including thirty-eight that were largely secular. Thomas Man published most of the works of educator John Brinsley the elder, and Man hired Lownes to print most of them, including *Ludus Literarius* (1612), a work whose title page explained that it was "Intended for the helping of the younger sort of teachers, and of all schollars." Brinsley's assistance to "the younger sort of teachers" went as far as classical translations, of which Man and Lownes produced five works: Aesop's *Esops [F]ables Translated Grammatically, and in Propriety for the Grammar-Schoole* (1617), Marcus Porcius Cato's *Cato Translated Grammatically; Directing for Understanding, Construing, Pursing, Making, and Prooving the Same Latin* (1612), Cicero's *The First Book of Tullies Offices Translated Gramatically* (1616), Mathurin Cordier's *Cordierius Dialogues Translated Grammatically* (1614), and *Ovids Metamorphosis Translated Grammatically* (1618). These works for teachers are supplemented by an assortment of catechisms, Latin and French grammar books, and a few reference works for students. In divinity these included several publications of English concordances and various catechisms for children to memorize and recite.

On 24 March 1605 in the court of the Stationers' Company Lownes and Kingston pleaded guilty to "disorderly printing" – that is, to having printed more copies than were allowed – of a primer to which the Stationers' Company owned the rights. Rather than paying a fine, the two were sentenced to give proceeds from the sale of the excess copies to the poor of the company.

Lownes printed fifteen Latin titles in his career, enough to make it difficult to infer whether he borrowed or owned the type necessary to print in Latin. The Latin sorts may have been part of Peter Short's stock, because Henry Bynneman, the printer who had worked at the Star on Bread Street Hill until 1583, had held a patent as a royal printer in both Latin and Greek. At Bynneman's death the shop had passed to Henry Denham and finally to Peter Short.

One fact making it unlikely that Lownes may have used Bynneman's type is the ease with which type metal could have been recast into new fonts. An occasional need for type in a foreign language might not have been enough economic incentive to maintain such type in the perpetually cash-short business of printing, where batter and wear were continually degrading some of the most expensive equipment. Rather than maintain a portion of his capital in relatively unprofitable Greek or Latin fonts, any London printer who owned the shop could well have had them recast into English characters. In several of Lownes's works an occasional phrase or line appears in Greek, printed in a size and typeface to match the surrounding text. A nonspecialist printer such as Lownes may well have borrowed, as needed, a handful of sorts from one of the neighboring printers rather than keeping several sets of Greek type.

A survey of some of the works Lownes printed reveals that he was a competent craftsman. As a printer who produced many quality reprints, he often marketed such works by advertising on their title pages that they were "much inlarged," "purged of many grosse faults," and "corrected & much amended." And these copies often do contain added material. But to judge the quality of Lownes's work as fairly high by the standards of his day is not to say that it was without faults. The third edition of Joshua Sylvester's *Lachrimae Lachrimarum* (1613) includes a short doggerel note to the authors of the elegies that Lownes is printing, one couplet of which reads:

> If (which we feare) som-where we miss your Text;
> Better inform'd, wee'l mend it in the next.

One of his most glaring errors appears on the title page of his edition of Aesop's fables, which reads *Esops eables*. Yet certainly Lownes seems to have supplied his pressmen with a fairly high quality of ink that, along with their skill, helps preserve an impressive clarity of his smaller typefaces. He also gained many ornaments from Short, which he used to create some beautiful title pages.

While Lownes printed books for many London booksellers, his largest source of business was from his closest family member, his brother Mathew. From 1605 through 1625, the year of Mathew's death, Humphrey printed or reprinted fifty-four books for his brother, two or more each year. Mathew commissioned Humphrey to print many types of works – theological, literary, and historical – in various formats, including a piece of

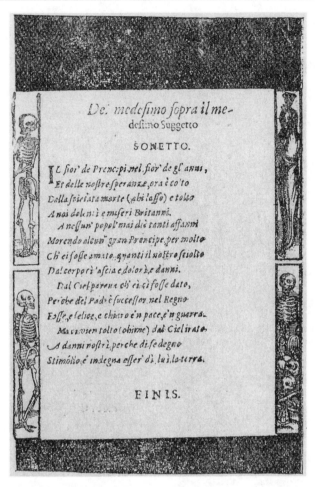

De: medesimo sopra il me-
desimo Suggetto

SONETTO.

IL fior' de Prencipi nel fior' de gl'anni,
Et delle nostre speranze, ora è co'to
Della spietata morte (ahi lasso) e tolto
A noi dolenti e miseri Britanni.
A nessun' popol' mai diè tanti affanni
Morendo alcun' gran Prencipe, per molto
Ch' ei fosse amato, quanti il nostro sciolto
Dal corpo ci'ascia e dolor h,e danni.
Dal Ciel pareua ch' ei ci fosse dato,
Perche del Padre successor nel Regno
Fosse, e felice, e chiaro e'n pace, e'n guerra,
Ma viv'un tolto (ohime) dal Ciel irato,
A danni nostri, perche di se degno
Stimollo, e indegna esser di lui la terra.

FINIS.

Page from Joshua Sylvester's Lachrimae Lachrimarium
*(1612), a collection of elegies printed by Lownes in memory
of Prince Henry, son of King James I*

music, Giovanni Croce's *Musica Sacra: to Six Voyces. Newly Englished* (1611). But printing books for Mathew was not Humphrey's only method for increasing his business. For Richard Redmer, an apprentice freed by Mathew Lownes in 1610, Humphrey printed five books, three of them in the year Redmer was freed. Mathew was also in a position to urge other booksellers to patronize his brother's shop.

Humphrey's business with Man, his prosperous father-in-law, was transacted in the years after the death of Lownes's first wife. Man had five theological works printed by Lownes from 1604 through 1606, perhaps as a way to assist his former son-in-law in starting up a new business, but the bulk of their business together was done from 1612 through 1618. Although Man's publications were mainly theological, he appears to have been interested in and supportive of John Brinsley, because Man asked Lownes to print and reprint his books on pedagogy and his translations for teachers six-

teen times. In all, Lownes printed twenty-nine books for Man.

The other publisher who shared expenses for printing some of Brinsley's work with Lownes was Samuel Macham. Lownes printed a total of thirty works for Macham, who owned several of them in conjunction with other booksellers. Most of these titles were theological, as Macham was one of the principal publishers of the popular Bishop Joseph Hall, who generated a great deal of business for Lownes through his prolific writing of sermons. Unlike Lownes's other major business associates, Macham was not related to Lownes by birth or marriage, but he did make Lownes one of the overseers of his will, which suggests that they were friends. Macham left his business to his wife, Joyce, upon his death in 1615, and Lownes reprinted two works for her – the seventh edition of Brinsley's *The True Watch, and Rule of Life* (1615) and a revised and rewritten second edition of Samuel Ward's sermon *A Coal from the Altar, to Kindle the Holy Fire of Zeale*

Engraved title page (left) for John Parkinson's Paradisi in Sole Paradisus Terrestris *(1629) with an illustration (right) in this popular early English book on gardening*

(1616). Before Macham's death on 22 March 1614 Lownes had lent Macham money against his share of the English Stock, and court records indicate that Joyce Macham repaid the loan.

Among other booksellers with whom Lownes did repeat business were several who published theological works almost exclusively. For example, John Bartlet, a former apprentice of Man, brought Lownes twelve books to be printed between 1626 and 1630. Only one of them, the anonymous *A New Invention for Shooting Fire-Shafts in Long-Bowes* (1628), was not theological. Clement Knight had served his apprenticeship to a draper but later became a bookseller, a career track he shared with several other London tradesmen of the day. Knight also had Lownes print twelve titles for him, about one book per year between 1604 and 1614. All but two of these works were sermons, and such steady business must have greatly helped Lownes keep his shop going. Cambridge

bookseller John Porter also published some of Hall's sermons, and Lownes printed eight titles for him. Because Porter was at the university, he had greater access to scholars who were writing theological works that composed so much of the book trade. Yet Porter arranged for most of his books to be printed in London, and he shared many of his imprints with London booksellers.

George Latham, a son-in-law and former apprentice of Mathew Lownes as well as a possible cousin to the Lowneses, sent Humphrey Lownes nine titles, two of which he reprinted, to print — half of Latham's publications. Other booksellers who had Lownes print many works include James Boler; Robert Milbourne; Nathaniel Newberry, who had a large business; and William Leake, who owned the copyright to both John Lyly's *Euphues: The Anatomy of Wit,* of which Lownes printed three editions (1606, 1607, 1613), and the only work by Shakespeare that Lownes reprinted, the ninth edition of *Venus and Adonis* (1608?). The 219 works that Lownes printed for these stationers represent substantially more than half of his entire business.

Another large source of copy for Lownes's presses was the Stationers' Company. Between 1604 and 1629 Lownes printed forty-one titles from the English Stock, but not at a steady rate. Only eight titles from the Stationers' Company Stock appeared from Lownes's press in the 1620s, perhaps because he was well established and did not need the business. From 1604 through 1610 he produced about two works per year for the Stationers' Company, and the remaining works were printed from 1611 through 1619. Produced in several formats, these works include editions of the popular rhymed translation of the Psalms by Thomas Sternhold and John Hopkins (1605, 1612, and 1628?), the *Pretious Booke of Heauenlie Meditations* ascribed to St. Augustine (1604, 1612, 1621, and 1629), *The Imitation of Christ* (1605, 1609, 1617, and 1629) by Thomas à Kempis, and several catechisms, including the Church of England's *Middle Catechism,* translated by Alexander Nowell (1621 and 1625). Obviously among Lownes's clientele these titles sold very well.

The Stationers' Company attempted to keep its member printers supplied with business even before the establishment of the English Stock, so it is not surprising that Short, the previous owner of Lownes's shop and his wife's first husband, had printed earlier editions of these same popular and profitable books. But the twenty-six reprints of Short editions that Lownes produced included more specialized work that the Stationers' Company and other printers brought him, and in many cases the fact that Lownes was using Short's type and printer's marks simplified the task. For example, Lownes's edition of Thomas Lodge's translation of Flavius Josephus's *The Famous and Memorable Workes of Josephus* (1609) reproduced the printer's marks, initials, and ornaments throughout, exactly as Short had used them in his edition of this work, *The Famous and Memorable Workes of Iosephus* (1602). Having taken over Short's shop brought Lownes business from booksellers who wanted new editions printed.

Lownes's shop was allowed two presses, and he produced an average of about fifteen works (or portions of works) per year. He needed a great deal of help to do that amount of printing, and fourteen apprentices are listed as having been bound or turned over to Lownes during his career. Records show that he freed at least five of them, including

his son, Humphrey, and Young, Lownes's future partner. Indentured for a period of about eight years, the apprentices were signed in shifts so that the shop would not have fewer than two (and usually three) working at a time. One apprentice, Richard Badger, was part of the business that Lownes took over from Short, to whom Badger had been apprenticed in 1602. Following the same procedure, Samuell Tilburye and John Winter, the two apprentices bound to Lownes at the time of his death, were to be freed by Lownes's partner and successor, Young, when their terms were up.

As was the custom, Lownes's son, Humphrey Lownes Jr., was freed by patrimony on 7 July 1612. He entered in the Stationers' Register one book printed by his father – Joshua Sylvester's *Lachrimae Lachrimarum: or the Distillation of Teares Shede for the Death of Prince Panaretus* (1612), a collection of elegies following the death of Henry Frederick, Prince of Wales. That Lownes's son was publishing the elegies for the son of the king may have been a subtle compliment to the royal family; whatever it represented, it was the only work that Humphrey Lownes Jr. registered. If he decided to go into another line of business, his occasional attendance with his father at the Stationers' Court from 1613 to 1625 is hard to explain, but what is known is that on 28 October 1625 the Stationers' Company turned over the younger Lownes's share in the English Stock to his cousin, Thomas Lownes, because Humphrey Jr. had recently died.

Robert Young, who was to be Lownes's successor, had been bound to another printer, Henry Ballard, on 3 September 1604. As sometimes happened, Young was turned over to Lownes before his term of indenture was up, and Lownes freed him on 23 November 1612. From that time forward he worked in Lownes's shop and by 1624 was printing works under his own name. The number of books he printed increased each year, until by 1629 he had printed or had shared in printing nineteen titles. Lownes had made him a partner sometime near the end of 1627, after the deaths of Lownes's own son and of Mathew's son, Thomas, had made it clear that no one from the family would be able to continue the business.

One indication that Lownes left Young a thriving business is that in the ten years after Lownes's death, Young reprinted twenty-five titles that Lownes had previously produced, some more than once – including one piece of music, William Hunnis's dolefully titled *Seven Sobs of a Sorrowfull Soule for Sinne* (1636), Sir Walter Ralegh's *History of the World* (1630), Sidney's *Arcadia* (1633), and du Bartas's *Du Bartas His Diuine Weekes, and Workes* (1633).

Of the 386 books he printed, Lownes produced forty-two folios, a number probably below the average at that time. As were the books printed by his contemporaries, most of Lownes's works appeared in quarto – 185 in all. One hundred and five others were in octavo, eighty-five in duodecimo, and four in the smaller sextodecimo format.

Because he did not print the first editions of any of the immortal Renaissance writers, Humphrey Lownes's shop has never been the subject of intense study that other printers of his time have merited. However, through his web of family connections in the business, through his acquisition of a shop by marriage, and through the pattern of his business as a job printer, his career reveals several contradictory trends in his trade at that time – when the older structures of guild and family businesses coexisted with what was evolving into a more modern, strictly commercial enterprise.

References:

Cyprian Blagden, *The Stationers' Company: A History, 1403–1959* (Cambridge, Mass.: Harvard University Press, 1960);

Douglas Bush, *English Literature in the Earlier Seventeenth Century: 1600–1660* (Oxford: Clarendon Press, 1966);

William A. Jackson, ed., *Records of the Court of the Stationers' Company 1602–1640* (London: Bibliographical Society, 1957);

C. S. Lewis, *English Literature in the Sixteenth Century, Excluding Drama* (Oxford: Clarendon Press, 1954);

D. F. McKenzie, *Stationers' Company Apprentices 1605–1640* (Charlottesville: Bibliographical Society of the University of Virginia, 1961).

– *Rebecca Cline*

Humphrey Moseley

(London: 1627 – 1661)

Humphrey Moseley was the foremost publisher of what David Masson, the great nineteenth-century biographer of John Milton, called the "finer literature" of the period of the English civil war and interregnum. Moseley's years of greatest production and activity (circa 1640–1660) coincided almost exactly with the period in which the parliamentary forces and then Oliver Cromwell were ascendant, and while Moseley was a Royalist who made no secret of his sympathies and in fact announced them openly in various prefaces to works he published, he seems never to have incurred the displeasure of the parliamentary or Cromwellian government. The government appears to have assumed that it had little to fear from the aristocratic, or upper-class, highly literate, and court-oriented audience to which Moseley's volumes were designed to appeal.

His list was made up largely of poetry, plays, long prose romances (mainly translated from the French), histories, and books of humane learning. He did publish religious and political literature as well, but he avoided the fiercely polemical tracts of the time that might have appealed to a more volatile readership. Even though out of sympathy with the government of his time, he rose steadily in the ranks of the Stationers' Company, where he served as junior renter, senior renter, member of the court of assistants, stockkeeper of the English Stock, and finally underwarden, all from 1648 to 1660. He died a relatively wealthy man on 31 January 1661, leaving many small bequests totaling some £130. Among these were twenty-shilling gifts to publishers Nicholas Fussell, Thomas Dring, and Henry Herringman, as well as similar gifts to printers Thomas Newcomb and William Wilson – and ten pounds to the Stationers' Company for silver plate. The major part of his estate he left to his wife and daughter, both named Anne. His wife continued his trade for several years after his death, although in a curtailed manner; she began selling off Moseley's copies in 1664, and the last works to appear with her name on their title pages are dated 1671.

Moseley began his apprenticeship on 29 March 1619 under bookseller Mathew Lownes, who had published the works of Sir Philip Sidney in 1605

and 1613 (and was awarded copies of the Dublin edition of 1621) and of Edmund Spenser in 1609, 1611, and 1617. Moseley was freed in 1627 and went into partnership with bookseller Nicholas Fussell, another young man in the trade who had gained his freedom. The two set up shop at the sign of the Ball in St. Paul's Churchyard. They must have acted primarily as sellers of other stationers' works and built up capital for major publishing ventures to come, for the two entered only four titles in the Stationers' Register, and only eight works have the names of both men on their title pages during what was apparently seven years of partnership.

Moseley's first independent entry in the Stationers' Register was on 17 July 1634 and was for a translation of Giovanni Francesco Biondi's romance *Donzella desterada: Or, The Banish'd Virgin* (1635). This work is the only one extant whose title page names Moseley's shop as the Three Kings in Paul's Churchyard. By 1638 Moseley had moved to the Prince's Arms (a shop appropriately named, in view of Moseley's later political sympathies) in St. Paul's Churchyard, at which shop he remained for the rest of his career.

Only in 1645 did Moseley hit his full stride as a publisher, producing from six to twenty-eight new titles each year from then through 1660. These books were combinations of works Moseley took over from other publishers (most often Richard Marriott and Thomas Walkley) and, much more commonly, titles that appeared first under his own imprint. Among the former were works of John Donne, Francis Quarles, Thomas Carew, and many Jacobean and Caroline playwrights. In a transaction registered on 19 August 1667 many of Moseley's own titles, in turn, were taken over after his death by Henry Herringman, who assumed the publishing rights to works of Donne, Ben Jonson, Sir John Denham, Sir William Davenant, Carew, Sir John Suckling, and Richard Crashaw.

Moseley seems to have published between 250 and 300 separate items in the course of his career, but it is difficult to establish the precise number: Moseley entered and/or advertised many that either were never issued or are no longer extant. In choosing and presenting these works, Moseley displayed

Frontispiece and title page for the first collected edition of the poems of John Milton

a genius for marketing that set him well apart from competitors who published similar literature in his own time and was perhaps matched only by Jacob Tonson, his end-of-the-century successor. Other booksellers before Moseley may have compiled lists or catalogues of the works they published, but Moseley developed this particular technique of advertising and marketing to a high art.

He had catalogues directed to the Courteous Reader printed in duodecimo, octavo, and folio versions and updated them continually so that the number of listed titles increased from the 59 items in the earliest — a list included at the back of a translation of Pierre Corneille's *The Cid* (1650) — to 75 items (also in 1650), 180 items in 1654, 246 items in a 1656 list, and finally 363 items evidently in a 1660 list (since it contains titles published in 1660 and grouped under the heading "Books now in the Press, and about to be Printed"). The earlier lists are usually divided into three categories, which convey the range of Moseley's publishing interests: "Various Histories, with curious Discourses in Humane Learning, &c." (twenty-nine works in the lists of 1650); "Choyce Poems, with Excellent Translations, and Incomparable Comedies and Tragedies,

Written by Several Ingenious Authors" (thirty works on those same early lists); and "Several Sermons with other Excellent Tracts in Divinity, Written by Some Most Eminent and Learned Bishops and Orthodox Divines" (sixteen works).

His 1660 list, a copy of which now appears bound in with a Bodleian Library copy of Edmund Waller's *Poems* (1645), is an octavo catalogue of thirty-two pages with new subdivisions reflecting Moseley's particular emphases toward the end of the 1650s. It presents new, separate categories labeled "Comedies and Tragedies" and "New and Excellent Romances Lately Printed." The final twenty-three items are listed under a heading, "These Books I purpose to Print, Deo Volente." God, alas, was not willing, and none of the books under this heading appeared with Moseley's imprint. The very existence of such a list, though, indicates that Moseley by no means saw his career ending in 1660, something also evident in a series of Stationers' Register entries of 29 June 1660 in which Moseley reregistered some forty-seven titles. He was evidently preparing for whatever new conditions the restoration of the Stuart monarchy was to bring, both in the book trade and in fashions of taste generally. Individual plays or volumes of them composed a high proportion of these items.

Moseley's various prefaces also constitute a form of advertising, and they reveal him to be a figure of some learning and sophistication as well as one of considerable flamboyance. He was not a self-deprecating man, and in his prefaces he is given to praising not only authors and works he is publishing but also himself for having brought the work that follows before the discerning public. In the prefatory epistle to the reader of Suckling's *Last Remains* (1659), for instance, Moseley speaks of how much thirst and general enquiry there have been for the poems he is presenting, an interest the reader will understand once he or she has read the poems and will thereupon believe Moseley – who has "(now for many years) annually published the Productions of the best Wits of our own, and Forein Nations." Moseley also frequently informs readers of how much care he has taken to gather the author's own manuscripts for his texts, as in the case of William Cartwright's *Comedies, Tragi-comedies, with Other Poems* (1651), and indeed his productions are consistently marked by a careful attempt to obtain authoritative texts. Often instead of merely providing an errata page, Moseley draws attention to the printer's errors in a preface and commends his own honesty in doing so (as he does in the case of Madeleine de Scudéry's *Continuation of Artamenes,* 1654).

In these prefaces also he explicitly proclaims his religious and political views, often in the form of laments over the present bad state of English political and religious affairs. In Bishop Arthur Lake's *Ten Sermons upon Severall Occasions* (1640) he refers to "the Maladie of this present Age"; another time he remarks that Oxford was still a university in the days when Cartwright was alive and writing. In dedicating the second part of de Scudéry's *Artamenes* to Lady Anne Lucas in 1654, five years after Charles I was beheaded, Moseley remarks that the previous volume of the romance had left off at the point where the great King Cyrus was on the block, while the present volume "shews what means were us'd to preserve him, a Felicity which all good Princes have not enjoy'd."

Yet Moseley's religious and political views are also everywhere implicit in his whole list of publications, a list constructed to entice a specific clientele into his shop. In the 1650–1651 folio list of Sermons and Tracts in Divinity at the back of Robert Stapylton's translation of Famianus Strada's *De Bello Belgico* (1650), for instance, fifteen authors are listed: one (Nicholas Darnton), a figure of strong

Engraved portrait of John Fletcher by William Marshall, published in Humphrey Moseley's 1647 edition of Comedies and Tragedies *by Francis Beaumont and Fletcher*

Puritan tendencies; another (Richard Sibbes), a moderate, conforming Puritan; and the majority, conservative, High Church figures such as Donne, Lancelot Andrewes, Lake, Josias Shute, Edmund Reeve, and Thomas Reeve.

Amid all his publishing activity are signs that Moseley was not simply capitalizing on current literary taste but helping to shape it as well – in effect, creating a market and leaving his personal stamp upon it. In the preface to one of his more important volumes, *Poems of Mr. John Milton* (1645), he speaks of the "incouragement" that he had "already received from the most ingenious men in their clear and courteous entertainment of Mr. Wallers late choice Peeces" and how this has prompted him to "adventure" once more "into the World, presenting it with these ever-green and not to be blasted Laurels" of Milton, from whom he has solicited them.

That Moseley solicited Milton for the poems may or may not be true (Milton might well have

*Title page for a travel book by James Howell, the
author-translator whose works were most often
published by Moseley*

sought out Moseley), but the two 1645 volumes of poems are designed to be part of a series of contemporary English poets that Moseley was in the process of presenting. From 1645 to 1651 he published not simply the *Poems &c., written by Mr. Ed. Waller* and *The Poems of Mr. John Milton* but also *Poems &c. by James Shirley* (1646), Suckling's *Fragmenta Aurea* (1646), Carew's *Poems, with a Maske* (1651), Thomas Stanley's *Poems* (1651), and Cartwright's *Comedies, Tragi-comedies, with Other Poems* — all volumes bearing physical similarities to one another. The volumes are all printed in octavo and have title pages with similar typeface and layout. The title page of Milton's *Poems* points out that "The Songs [herein] were set in Musick by Mr. Henry Lawes Gentleman of the Kings Chappel, and one of his Maiesties Private Musick," and similar information appears on the title pages of the volumes by Waller, Carew,

and Cartwright as well as on the second title page of Suckling's *Fragmenta Aurea*. The volumes by Milton, Shirley, and Suckling all bear frontispiece portraits of the authors by William Marshall. Three of the volumes — those of Milton, Carew, and Shirley — appear adjacent to one another in Moseley's later catalogues and with virtually the same title, variations upon *Poems, with a Maske*. All this is plainly designed to get the reader to regard the volumes as a group and perhaps to buy the whole set.

The odd man out in this series is the Puritan (and later, republican) John Milton, as all the others are distinctly Royalist poets and directly attached to the court in one way or another. Admittedly, ambiguities abound in Milton's volume. These are a young man's poems, recording his growth as a poet from 1624 (at the age of fifteen) to 1639 and containing a fair degree of poetic experimentation.

Engraved title page by Marshall for Sir Robert
Stapylton's translations of Musaeus (1647)

"Lycidas," which contains a stinging attack on the established clergy of 1637, is followed in the volume by a masque (*Comus* of 1634), which is, after all, an aristocratic and courtly form of entertainment, even if Milton may have been attempting to reform the genre and the attitudes of those who normally attend such performances.

Critics disagree over how strongly or consistently Puritan and radical a figure Milton was before 1640, but his allegiances by 1645 are beyond question. In the 1640s Milton had engaged in extended polemical debate, first in a series of tracts attacking the episcopacy and then in a highly controversial set advocating divorce. Given Milton's recent activity, publication of his poems by Moseley may well have offered Milton a form of renewed respectability. But whatever the case, Moseley's publication of Milton in this particular series, and especially with the title-page reference to Lawes as musician to Charles I, highlights the courtly elements of

the volume and tilts it toward Moseley's distinctly court-oriented readership – precisely the type of audience from which Milton had been distancing himself in the previous five years.

Moseley's most important publication of dramatic works was the 1647 folio edition of Francis Beaumont and John Fletcher's *Comedies and Tragedies*. This was actually a joint venture with Humphrey Robinson, but Robinson, as Moseley informs readers in his elaborate address, helped only to finance the volume, whereas all the "Care & Pains" in gathering the various pieces were Moseley's alone. The volume contains thirty-four plays never before published, and Moseley takes pride in having eliminated any that had appeared before: "I would have none say, they pay twice for the same Booke."

He takes pride as well in the particular texts he has obtained. All were "from such as received them from the Authours themselves," and each presents the whole play, even those passages that were cut in

The VSE of
PASSIONS
Written in French by
J.F. Senault.
And
put into English
by
Henry Earle of
Monmouth
1649.

Passions arraign'd by Reason here you see,
As shee's Advis'd therein by Grace Divine:
(But this, (yowll say)'s but in Effigie !
Peruse this Booke, and you in ev'ry line
Thereof will finde this truth so prov'd, that you
Must, Reason contradict, or grant it Tri:

Engraved title page by Marshall for Jean François Senault's
The Use of Passions *(1649), translated*
by Henry Carey, earl of Monmouth

performance. But the lasting importance of the volume lies in its publication in folio format. Moseley writes that he "would scarce have adventured in these slippery times on such a work as this" if "knowing persons" had not assured him that "these *Authors* were the most unquestionable *Wits* this Kingdome hath afforded." The effect of publishing a considerable collection of plays in folio was to join Beaumont and Fletcher with Shakespeare and Jonson, the only other English playwrights to have been published in that format. Moseley was thereby assuring that Beaumont and Fletcher's high reputation would continue after the playhouses were to reopen with the Restoration.

This desire to keep the dramatic tradition alive during the period of the closing of the theaters seems to underlie much of Moseley's publication of plays. From 1653 he began publishing plays in a new format — octavo rather than the usual quarto —

and he did this, too, as he had for his volumes of poetry from 1645 through 1651, as part of a series. Thus, for authors of lesser stature than Shakespeare, Jonson, and Beaumont and Fletcher, Moseley produced editions of plays with all the volumes bearing similar titles, a highly standardized typographical layout, and an engraved frontispiece portrait of the author: Richard Brome's *Five New Plays* (1653), Shirley's *Six New Plays* (1653), Philip Massinger's *Three New Plays* (1655), Lodowick Carlell's *Two New Plays* (1657), and Thomas Middleton's *Two New Plays* (1657). As their titles suggest, all these volumes contain plays never before published. Moseley also published individually other plays by these playwrights that had been published before but this time in the same octavo format, presumably so that they could be bound in, if the buyer so wished, with the volume containing the newly published plays. What Moseley had done to promote new poetry from 1645 to 1651 he was now systematically doing for the drama as well.

As Moseley indicates in some prefaces, he occasionally seems to have published without the knowledge and consent of the author, for instance, in the cases of Abraham Cowley's *The Mistresse* (1647), Robert Heath's *Clarastella* (1650), and Henry Vaughan's *Olor Iscanus* (1651). Such a practice and a claim look back to a slightly earlier era of manuscript circulation when a gentleman-author might hesitate to submit his work to the stigma of print. But Moseley also participates in practices that foreshadow those of a later century. The single author whose work Moseley published most often was James Howell: at the end of one of Howell's works, a compilation and translation of the second part of Scipione Mazzella's *Parthenopoeia* (1654), is "A Catalogue of Mr. Howells Works in severall Volumes. Printed by Mr. Humphrey Moseley," which lists fifteen different works. This list is in turn followed by another, containing eighteen items and titled "More of Mr. Howels Works Printed by other Men."

Howell, prolific author that he became, had not begun as a writer but rather, having graduated from Oxford, began his adult career as the representative of a glass manufacturer seeking material and workmen on the Continent. There he developed a proficiency for foreign tongues and proceeded to act as agent on several missions for the Caroline court. In 1643, however, he was arrested by order of the Long Parliament, had his papers seized, and was committed to Fleet Prison, where he remained until 1651. His only offense, he claimed, was his loyalty, but Howell's letters and his seventeenth-century biographers refer also to his considerable debts and his insolvency, and it would appear that Howell, particularly during his incarceration, had to rely on his pen in order to live. Moseley was evidently the publisher to whom Howell – with his various political tracts and allegories, familiar letters, travel books, and translations – most frequently turned.

As with Howell, Moseley had many other writers whose translations and other works he regularly published: Robert Gentilis, whose translations of Paolo Sarpi, Virgilio Malvezzi, Biondi, and others appeared under Moseley's imprint in 1639, 1642, 1647, 1650, 1654, and 1655; Stapylton, who translated Juvenal, Musaeus, and Famianus Strada under Moseley's imprint; and Henry [Carey], earl of Monmouth, whose translations of Malvezzi, Jean François Senault, Guido Bentivoglio, Traiano Boccalini, and Paolo Paruta all appeared under Moseley's imprint from 1648 through 1657. From the pen of Thomas Stanley, Moseley published translations of Juan Perez de Montalvan and Girolami Preti (1647), Theocritus (1649), and Anacreon (1651), as well as Stanley's own *Poems* (1651) and his three-volume *History of Philosophy* (1655, 1656, 1660).

There is no way of knowing whether these authors went to Moseley first with each project or he to them, and there are no records revealing whether Moseley actually paid his authors for their work. Someone with a title, especially, would appear not to need to write to make a living, and Stanley was a man of considerable wealth. But Moseley approaches or anticipates the condition scholars associate with eighteenth-century publishers – that of having what amounts to a stable of authors to whom they could turn for desired works. The high number of translations that Moseley published particularly give rise to this impression.

References:

Paulina Kewes, "'Give Me the Sociable Pocket-Books . . .': Humphrey Moseley's Serial Publication of Octavo Play Collections," *Publishing History,* 38 (1995): 5–21;

Peter Lindenbaum, "The Poet in the Marketplace: Milton and Samuel Simmons," in *Of Poetry and Politics: New Essays on Milton and His World,* edited by P. G. Stanwood (Binghamton, N.Y.: Medieval and Renaissance Texts and Studies, 1995), pp. 249–262;

David Masson, *The Life of John Milton* (Cambridge & London: Macmillan, 1859–1894), III: 448–459; VI: 398–405;

Lois Potter, *Secret Rites and Secret Writings: Royalist Literature, 1641–1660* (Cambridge: Cambridge University Press, 1989);

John Curtis Reed, "Humphrey Moseley, Publisher," *Oxford Bibliographical Society Proceedings and Papers,* 2, part 2 (1928): 55–122.

– *Peter Lindenbaum*

Joseph Moxon

(London: 1647 – 1684)

Joseph Moxon is best known as the author of the first printer's manual in English, *Mechanick Exercises: Or, the Doctrine of Handy-Works. Applied to the Art of Printing* (1683). To his contemporaries he was the owner of a bookshop that sold maps and globes. He was also a printer, a self-taught typefounder, the author of popular handbooks on mathematics, a member of the Royal Society, and hydrographer to King Charles II. (In this last capacity Moxon was responsible for making hydrographic surveys and constructing charts of sea depths, currents, and general topography. In an age of increasing sea power, navigational charts for sailors were even more important than maps of land.) Although he printed or published seventy-three books, maps, and other works, Moxon never became a member of the Stationers' Company. Yet in seventeenth-century London he was an important, if unconventional, man.

Moxon probably learned the trade of printing from his father, James, who was printing books in Holland for illegal export to England from 1637 through 1643. A radical Puritan, to judge by his production, James Moxon was one of three English printers in Holland whom Archbishop William Laud tried to prosecute for having printed libelous tracts against the English church and government under the name of John Bastwick. A spy passed information to the English government when James Moxon moved from Delft to Rotterdam in 1638. His son was then twelve years old, a good age to begin learning his father's trade. By 1646 James and Joseph Moxon were back in England and openly printing in London at a shop at the upper end of Houndsditch, near Bishopsgate.

Joseph Moxon's working life, like that of some of his more well-known contemporaries, followed a series of stages as he pursued trades and avocations that interested him. From 1647 through 1649 he worked with his father as a trade printer, and the two printed ten titles, two for theological bookseller Henry Overton and five for Puritan bookseller William Larnear. As James Moxon's previous work would lead one to expect, these tracts and broadsides are all related to rapidly unfolding current events and are religious and political in nature: a typical example is *The Sacramental Stumbling-Block Re-*

Engraved portrait of Joseph Moxon, in his A Tutor to Astronomie and Geographie *(fourth edition, 1686)*

moved (1648), a pamphlet by an author who is identified only as "W. L." and who argues that the episcopacy was a violation of biblical tenets.

Joseph Moxon must have felt safe from political persecution and secure in his ability to earn a living, because on 17 February 1648 he married Susan Marson; on 16 June 1650 their daughter, Susan, was baptized. By 1650 Moxon apparently had grown tired of trade printing. His father continued to print, but Joseph's name does not appear in a book again until 1654. In the preface to his *Mathematicks Made Easie; or a Mathematical Dictionary* (1679) Moxon refers to a time "About thirty years ago when I first began to apply myself to Mathematical Learning." During this time Moxon set

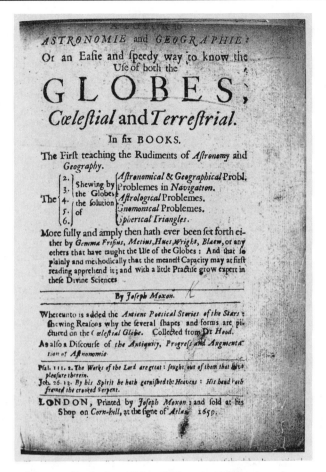

Title page for the first edition of Moxon's 1659 book on the use of globes

himself to learn how to make maps, globes, spheres, and the mathematical instruments for which he would become known. This new direction of his work proved to be a shrewd step in his career, because after the outbreak of the Civil War no one else in London was making globes. Moxon probably went to Holland for this training, because a reference in his later writing indicates that he was in Amsterdam in the summer of 1652.

In 1653 Moxon was back in London with a new shop "at the signe of Atlas, in Cornhill; where you may also have Globes of all sizes." In 1654 he published *A Tutor to Astronomie and Geographie, or an Easie and Speedy Way to Know the Use of Both the Globes, Caelestial and Terrestrial,* a translation of a work by Willem Janszoon Blaeu. Moxon's opening remarks in the 1654 book indicate that one aim of this work was to promote the sale of his globes:

> I indeed desire particularly to inform you; they being the latest done of any, and to the accomplishing of which, I have not only had the help of all; or most of the

best of other *Globes, Maps, Plats,* and *Sea-Draughts* of New Discoveries, both of our Authors and other mens, that were then extant, for the Terrestrial Globe; but also the Advice and Directions of divers learned and able Mathematicians, both in *England* and *Holland,* for Tables and Calculations both of Lines and Stars for the Celestial.

Another publication in 1654, John Dansie's *A Mathematical Manual: Wherein Is Handled Arithmetick, Planimetry, Stereometry, and the Embatteling of Armies. Whereby Any Man Can Learn to Multiply and Divide in Two Hours by Radologie* [rhabdology], *without Any Trouble at All to the Memory,* aimed to promote the sale of an early version of the slide rule – known, after its inventor, as "Napier's Bones."

In 1655 Moxon translated and printed Giacomo da Vignola's *Vignola: Or the Compleat Architect,* a work that proved to be extremely popular. He engraved the title page and other illustrations himself, and the book was in fact the first publication that Moxon had completed on his own. He published two more editions of this work, in 1665 and in 1673, and his son, James, printed two more edi-

Engraved title page by Moxon for Vignola, or the
Compleat Architect *(1655), a work that Moxon
translated and printed*

tions following Moxon's death. (Because Moxon's
father and son were both named James, scholars
have long confused the work of the two men and
mistakenly assumed that James was either a brother
or another relative of approximately the same age
as Joseph Moxon.)

Moxon also published in 1655 a map titled *A
Plat of All the World,* and perhaps on the strength of
its sales he took a twenty-one-year lease on a shop
in Cornhill near St. Michael's Church. Dated 23
March 1655, this lease describes him as a "Citizen
and Weaver of London," for although Moxon made
his living as a printer, he had completed no apprenticeship in the Stationers' Company and had never
become a member. By law, the number of printers
was restricted to twenty, so small printers such as
Moxon were candidates for prosecution. Other
guilds, most notably the drapers, offered guild status and some legal protection to printer members.
With his radical Puritan connections, Moxon must

have become anxious at the Restoration, and in
1664 he became a full member and "was called to
the livery," of the Weavers' Company. Moxon arranged that he could be translated into another
company of his choice when he desired, but for
some reason he never joined the Stationers' Company and remained a member of the Weavers' for
the rest of his life. Perhaps he was counting merely
on his status as a citizen of London to prevent the
company from interfering with his business in producing maps, globes, and technical books. His only
other known association with the Weavers' Company was through the publication in 1677 of *Minerva,
or, the Art of Weaving,* a book of verse by "R.C."

Moxon did not entirely give up printing religious polemic, such as he had printed with his father, on current events. In the late 1650s he printed
three such pamphlets: John Plasse's *Grace and Mercy
to a Sinner, in a Time of Afflictions, or the Serious Meditations of M. Tho. Ford of Rochester: During the Time of his
Imprisonment, before His Execution* (1657), W. B.'s *The
Trappan Trapt* (1657), and Henry Denne's *A Contention for Truth in Two Several Publique Disputations . . .
betweene Mr. Gunning and Mr. Denne. Concerning the
Baptisme of Infants, Whether Lawful or Unlawful* (1658).
Moxon printed this last work for Francis "Ele-
phant" Smith, an Anabaptist and later the subject of
government persecution under Charles II.

During the final years of the 1650s Moxon
was also doing the type of printing at which he ex-
celled – intricate mathematical tables. In 1657 he
printed John Newton's *A Help to Calculation,* a book
of 126 pages, all but ten of which are logarithmic tables, well-set and printed without errata. That same
year he printed the tables for *Trigonometria,* a work
by the eminent mathematician William Oughtred.
The fact that Moxon was asked to set the tables indicates that he was recognized as the best printer in
London for the task. During this period Moxon also
printed William Eland's *A Tutor to Astrologie* (1657);
John Palmer's *The Catholique Planisphaer* (1658), another text on a mathematical instrument; Isaac de
Caus's *New and Rare Inventions of Water-Works*
(1659); and an edition of Edward Wright's *Certain
Errors in Navigation* (1657), as well as more maps.

In 1659 Moxon published a work he had written himself, one that proved quite popular and that
he reprinted three times – *A Tutor to Astronomie and
Geographie, or an Easie and Speedy Way to Know the Use
of Both the Globes, Caelestial and Terrestrial* (a distinct
work from the 1654 book of the same title). But
then, from about the time of the Restoration,
Moxon seems to have stopped printing for nine
years and to have taken up other interests.

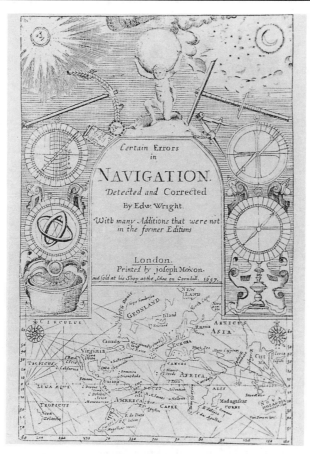

Title page for Edward Wright's Certain Errors in
Navigation *(1657), a revised edition of one of the
most important treatises on navigation published
in Elizabethan England*

Events in his personal life, as well as in his political situation, may have influenced his decision to cease printing. In 1659 his wife died. Moxon may also have grown concerned that his political affiliations or some of his previous printing would make him an easy target for prosecution by the Stationers' Company. Laws passed in 1649, 1653, and 1662 were designed to restore governmental control of the press, but at the time of the Restoration sixty printers were operating in London. Moxon could avoid prosecution for illegal printing by specializing in globes, maps, and technical printing, which no one else in London was qualified to do. Another indication that the Stationers' Company no longer maintained the power it once had is the fact that Moxon's *A Tutor to Astrology* (1658) included *An Ephemeris for the Year 1657,* as it proclaimed on the title page, a violation of what would earlier have been regarded as the monopoly on almanac publication that the company claimed.

Instead of publishing and printing in the first years of the reign of Charles II, Moxon appears to have turned to making globes, maps, and what he called "plats" (charts). On 10 January 1662 Moxon's petition to the king for permission to make globes, maps, and sea plats was granted, and he was appointed hydrographer to the king, a position he retained for the rest of his life. He was also further secured from unpleasant scrutiny by the Stationers' Company, because his royal license superseded the founding charter of that organization. In 1663 the second edition of *Vignola* indicated that Moxon's shop had moved in Ludgate Hill near Fleet Bridge, still at the Sign of Atlas. Moxon was remarried on 8 June 1663 to Hannah Cooke of St. Lawrence Jewry, an eighteen-year-old woman whose parents were deceased. When asked to give his occupation at this time, he listed himself as a printer.

In the fall of 1663 Moxon made the acquaintance of Samuel Pepys, the famous diarist, who wrote on 8 September that he had been

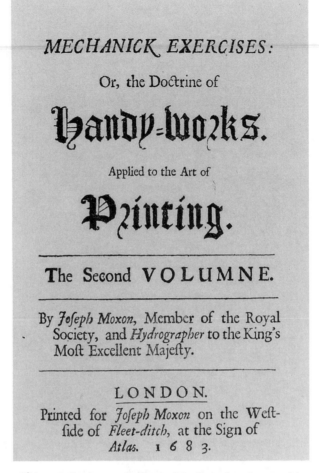

MECHANICK EXERCISES:

Or, the Doctrine of

Handy-works.

Applied to the Art of

Printing.

The Second VOLUMNE.

By *Joseph Moxon*, Member of the Royal Society, and *Hydrographer* to the King's Most Excellent Majesty.

LONDON.

Printed for *Joseph Moxon* on the West-side of *Fleet-ditch*, at the Sign of *Atlas.* 1 6 8 3.

Title page for the second volume of the first printer's manual in English, written and printed by Moxon

among other places to Moxon's and there bought a payre of globes cost me £3 10s. – with which I am well pleased, I buying them principally for my wife, who has a mind to understand them – and I shall take pleasure to teach her.

Pepys may even have bought a copy of Moxon's *A Tutor to Astronomy and Geography,* as Moxon was to dedicate his third edition of it to Pepys in 1674. In 1664 Pepys bought globes for the Admiralty Office, where he worked, and he wrote that on 14 March 1664 he went "to Mr. Moxons, and there saw our office globes in doing, which will be very handsome – but cost money."

In 1665 Moxon published *A Tutor to Astronomy and Geography, or the Use of the Copernican Spheres,* his very freely translated and adapted second part of Willem Janszoon Blaeu's *Institutio Astronomica,* dedicated to Viscount William Brouncker, the president of the Royal Society. This publication was followed by another hiatus in Moxon's career, during which

he suffered disaster and trained himself for a new profession: his shop in Ludgate Hill near Fleet Bridge was destroyed by the Great Fire that devastated London in September 1666. No record remains of the extent of his losses, but most of his stock of globes, books, maps, and instruments – as well as his printing equipment – was most likely lost. Most London printers, centered as they were in St. Paul's Churchyard, suffered similar losses of materials, equipment, and printed stock.

Moxon's new trade was to be that of a type cutter. In 1667 he cut punches for the symbols used to print Bishop John Wilkins's *Essay toward a Real Character and a Philosophical Language* (1668). By 1668 his contemporaries knew that he was designing roman and italic alphabets, and in 1669 he printed *Proves of Several Sorts of Letters Cast by Joseph Moxon,* a folio sheet with samples of his product – seven roman and four italic types. It was an astute move to study typefounding when most of the printers remaining in business needed to replace type stocks lost in the fire, but it was a difficult trade to learn quickly.

Using his own type, he printed and published in 1670 another folio book of his own, *Practical Perspective*. In *Mechanick Exercises* he later explained his belief that the design of a letter should involve mathematical principles of proportion, not just the instincts of an artisan's eye. In his history of English typography Talbot Baines Reed notes that Moxon made the claim for "Typography equally with Architecture to be regarded as a Mathematical Science." Herbert Davis and Harry Carter, editors of a modern edition of *Mechanick Exercises*, comment that the type used to print the *Practical Perspective* has "some dignity, though the individual letters are of a rather rustic cut and badly justified, inasmuch as they do not stand true in line and slope unevenly." But in 1842 Charles Henry Timperley, chronicling the industry of printing, judged Moxon's type more candidly by comparing it to the Elzevir types, several of which were reviled for heavy lines and stubby serifs: Moxon's "science does not seem to have led him to any improvement in shape, for the characters which he formed are like the ugly Elzevirs." Reed wrote of Moxon's efforts, "His theories, as put into practice by himself, were eminently unsuccessful; and though the signboards of the day may have profited by his rules, it is doubtful if typography did."

The fifty years following the Great Fire were perhaps the nadir of English typefounding, as the better types were being imported from Holland or were often decades out of date rather than designed domestically. Carter and Christopher Ricks point out that "books relied on copperplates to avoid the commonplace," and an examination of Moxon's books bears this out. Whether they concern astronomy, the use of globes, or architecture, the copious illustrations of Moxon's work afford the main visual pleasure for readers; in an era of bad printing Moxon is distinguished by neither the high nor the poor quality of his printing. By 1680 Moxon and Peter de Walpergen in Oxford were the only punch cutters in England who could work in steel. Moxon was not doing innovative work, and he often selected Dutch designs as his models.

Another alteration in Moxon's pattern of doing business at this time perhaps reflects his fear of legal conflicts with the Stationers' Company: on the title pages of books he published after 1671 he no longer specified whether or not he had printed them as well, although he apparently did continue printing until 1680. After the fire he had been work-

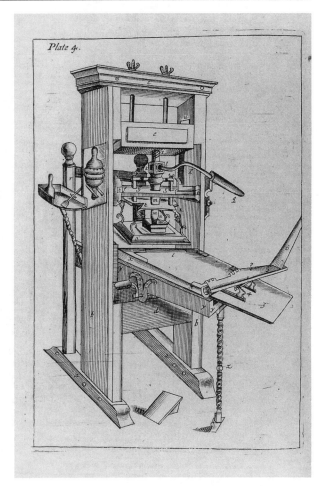

Illustration of a seventeenth-century printing press, from volume two of Moxon's Mechanick Exercises

ing from 1667 to 1671 at a shop in Russell Street in Westminster, again at the sign of Atlas. Apparently he wanted to return to the site at which he had worked before the fire, because on 20 April 1670 he signed a new lease for the property in Ludgate Hill, where he promised to pay ten pounds a year and to build a house. He was not able to fulfill this contract, however, and on 2 April 1673 his landlord secured a judgment against him for his failures to pay his rent and to rebuild on this property. Assessment records show that by May 1673 he was living in a house on Ludgate Hill near Fleet Ditch, and by 1675 his finances were so improved that he tried to regain possession of the land he had leased.

In 1673 Moxon published *A Description of the Seven United Provinces of Netherland*, a quarto pamphlet containing the first known map engraved by his son, James, who was beginning his career as an engraver, a publisher, and vendor of globes. Joseph Moxon was moving into more distinguished social circles through his professional contacts. Before

Illustration of a typefounder, from Mechanick Exercises

1672 he had met Edmond Halley, still a student but already interested in astronomy. In 1674 the edition of *A Tutor to Astronomy and Geography* that Moxon had written appeared with a dedication to Pepys, and Moxon appeared in a discussion of scientific and technical topics in the diary of physicist and inventor Robert Hooke.

Moxon's writing and publications in 1676 and 1677 reveal some of his interests. He published *Regulae Trium Ordinum Literarum Typographicarum: Or, the Rules of the Three Orders of Print Letters* (1676), a small quarto book on lettering for sign painters and carvers, and his preface to this announced that he intended to publish a manual for printers. His study of type design in 1668 would thus be connected to what would become his two-volume publication of *Mechanick Exercises* in 1683. In 1676 and 1677 he and James printed a series of playing cards based, perhaps, on the fashion for politically satiric cards. The two Moxons printed and sold "Astronomical Playing-Cards," geographical and geometrical cards, and, most curious, "The Gentile House-Keeper's Pas-

time, or the mode of Carving at the Table, represented in a pack of Playing Cards . . . set forth by the best Masters in that faculty." The first set sold for 1 shilling plain, 1s. 6d. colored, and 5 shillings colored with gilt stars, according to the *Term Catalogue,* which listed contemporary publications. In 1677 the first reference is made, in R. C.'s *Minerva,* to James Moxon's shop, "in the Strand, near Charing Cross, right over against King Harry the Eighth's Inn."

By the time of the 1678 poll tax Moxon's financial difficulties were apparently resolved, as he was sharing the house on Ludgate Hill with a family wealthy enough to afford two servants. At that time Moxon's family, including his wife and his son, also employed a servant, who earned a wage of £2 10s. per annum.

In January 1678 Moxon was elected to fellowship in the Royal Society, and he issued the first installment of the *Mechanick Exercises: Or, the Doctrin of Handy-Works* on smithing. The first monthly number of this series sold for sixpence, but publishing delays followed in this ambitious scheme, and in 1680 the entire first volume of fourteen installments was offered for sale at seven shillings. It described the trades of smithing, joinery, carpentry, turning, and bricklaying, and it represented only part of Moxon's interest in writing popular handbooks.

In 1679 he published another book he had written, *Mathematicks Made Easie; or a Mathematical Dictionary*. Moxon's preface explains that he is not a mathematician himself and has been able to complete this work only after much time and with the help of a friend, whom he identifies only as H. C. He also capitalized on the interest in such how-to books by republishing the fifth book of his *A Tutor to Astronomie and Geographie* with the title *Mechanick Dyalling: Teaching Any Man, Though of Ordinary Capacity and Unlearned in the Mathematicks, to Draw a True Sun-Dyal on Any Given Plane,* a work so popular that his son was to reprint it twice. Moxon had not finished designing type, and in 1679 he also cut a set of punches for an Irish type used by Robert Boyle to reprint the Bible in Irish in 1681 and 1685. He also published a work by Roger Palmer, earl of Castlemaine, whose wife had left him to become one of Charles II's most powerful mistresses. Palmer wrote *The English Globe* (1679), explaining the advantages of a globe design that he had created and that Moxon was selling.

Moxon was apparently inactive as a publisher from 1679 through 1683. When he resumed by publishing *Mechanick Exercises* in 1682 Carter and Davis point out that he offered a puzzling explanation for the delay when he advertised the work:

> The continuation of my setting forth *Mechanick Exercises* having been obstructed by the breaking out of the Plot, which took off the minds of my few Customers from buying them, as formerly; And being of late much importun'd by many worthy Persons to continue them; I have promised to go on again.

Low sales, rather than the excitement aroused by the Popish Plot, may have caused the delay, but whatever the reason, Moxon issued all the installments, though at irregular intervals, and was advertising the second volume of the *Mechanick Exercises* in summer 1684. The first issue of the second volume contains an interesting glimpse of Moxon's involvement in trade politics, because he dedicates the work to Bishop John Fell, Sir Leoline Jenkins, and Sir Joseph Williamson. In addition to holding various political and ecclesiastical offices, these men were the surviving partners of four others who had arranged to do the printing for the university press

at Oxford. At this time the university press and the Stationers' Company were engaged in a dispute about whether the university had been granted the right to print books, and Dr. John Wallis of Oxford had published a paper explaining how printing had first been practiced in England at Oxford in 1468. Without referring to the quarrel, Moxon adopts Wallis's account of the origin of printing and quotes from it in his preface. Clearly he wishes to take a stand on the side of the university press.

As the first printer's manual in English, *Mechanick Exercises* has been heavily relied upon for information about practices in the book trade in Moxon's time and before. As a written treatise, it reveals much about Moxon himself. Davis and Carter comment that Moxon "writes as though the printers' technique of his day, with all its shortcomings, were so precious that he must commit it to paper for fear it might be lost." In the middle of a three-page chapter explaining how to tie up a page of type so that it can be removed from the galley and later replaced, Moxon writes a passage like this:

> Having whipt the *Cord* twice about the *Page,* he holding two of his Left Hand Fingers against the *Direction*-corner upon the *Cord,* that it slip not, with the Ball of his Thumb of his right Hand, and the Balls of his Fingers to assist, thrusts against the opposite diagonal corner of the *Page,* and removes it a little from the *Ledges* of the *Galley,* that he may with the Nail of the Thumb of his Right Hand have room to thrust the *Cord* whipt about the *Page,* lower down upon the *Shank* of the *Letter,* (to make room for succeeding whippings of the Cord, and then thrusts or draws the *Page* close to the *Ledges* of the *Galley* again: then whips the *Cord* again about the *Page* (as before) till he had whipt it four or five times about the *Page,* taking care that the several whippings lye parallel to each other, not lapping over any of the former whippings.

The precise (sometimes tedious or confusing) language of these directions made it possible for Reed to write of *Mechanick Exercises* in 1887 that "to this day it is quoted and referred to, not only by the antiquary who desires to learn what the art once was, but by the practical printer, who may still on many subjects gather from it much advice and information as to what it should still be." Perhaps one reason that Moxon felt he had to be so exact is that, not having been a member of the Stationers' Company in daily contact with other printers, he had nonetheless worked for many years on the fringe of the trade.

Whether or not another, more typical printer might have produced a more concise *Mechanick Exercises,* relying upon the reader's knowledge of the practices of the craft, it is clear from Moxon's other publications, especially through the dictionaries of mathematical and architectural terms in *Mathematicks Made Easie* and *Vignola,* is that he was very interested in the terminology of the trades and sciences he studied. One of the most useful portions of the *Mechanick Exercises* is its short "Dictionary Alphabetically Explaining the Abstruse Words and Phrases That Are Used in Typography," which defines some of the unique jargon of printing as Moxon knew it.

As well as appreciating the language of his trade, Moxon also respected the manual dexterity required by all the trades he wrote about. In the preface to volume one of *Mechanick Exercises* he explains why he decided not to use the subtitle of his work, *The Doctrine of Handy-crafts,* as the main title:

> I found the Doctrine would not bear it, because *Handy-craft* signifies *Cunning* or *Sleight,* or *Craft* of the Hand, which cannot be taught by Words, but is only gain'd by Practice and Exercise: therefore I shall not undertake that with the bare reading of these *Exercises* any shall be able to perform these Handy-works; but I may safely tell you that these are the Rules that every one that will endeavour to perform them must follow, and that by the true observing them, he may, according to his stock of Ingenuity and Zeal in diligence, sooner or later inure his hand to the *Cunning* or *Craft* of working like a *Handy-craft,* and consequently be able to perform them in time.

The *Mechanick Exercises* was Moxon's last book. Tax records show that he was not living at Ludgate Hill by August 1688, and he may have left by 1686, the year in which he published his final edition of his *A Tutor to Astronomie and Geographie.* In February 1691 he died at his son's house in Warwick Lane and was buried on 15 February. He died intestate, and on 10 October 1691 his son was granted his effects, which did not exceed thirty-nine pounds. His typefounding equipment had gone to master typefounder Robert Andrews some years before, perhaps as early as 1683. James Moxon continued to work as an engraver and printer, and occasionally as a publisher and author, until his death, when his widow succeeded him as a vendor of globes.

References:

Harry Carter and Christopher Ricks, "Foreword to the Dissertation," in *A Dissertation upon English Typographical Founders and Foundries,* by Edward Rowe Mores (London: Oxford University Press, 1961), pp. lix–lxxix;

Joseph Moxon, *Mechanick Exercises on the Whole Art of Printing (1683–4),* edited by Herbert Davis and Carter (London: Oxford University Press, 1962);

Talbot Baines Reed, *A History of the Old English Letter Foundries* (London: Stock, 1887);

Charles Henry Timperley, *Encyclopaedia of Literary and Typographical Anecdote* (London: Bohn, 1842).

– Rebecca Cline

Nicholas Okes

(London: 1607 – 1645)

Nicholas Okes and John Norton

(London: 1628 – 1629)

Nicholas Okes began to specialize in printing small, topical, and occasionally controversial works early in his career. Into this category fall many plays, masques, entertainments, books, and pamphlets of literary and historical interest, most of which his contemporaries would have dismissed as inconsequential ephemera. Yet readers have since come to regard such works as among the foremost imaginative achievements of the age. Okes's unusually long career of more than thirty years embraces an unmatched range and quantity of works of literary and theatrical distinction.

Okes's father, John Okes, was a horner, a maker of goods from horn. Various properties and monetary bequests specified in his will suggest that he was fairly prosperous. The name of Okes's mother is unknown, and the year of his birth is also uncertain but is most likely 1579. He was apprenticed to a stationer, William King, on 25 March 1596 as a substitute for his probably elder brother, Peter, who had been bound to King at Christmas 1595 but who had presumably quickly determined that the stationer's trade was not for him. A bequest conditional upon his return to England in John Okes's will of 1614 raises the possibility that Peter may have set sail for distant parts, perhaps during the early days of his apprenticeship.

Printer Richard Field openly granted Nicholas Okes his freedom on 5 December 1603, so a transfer of his apprenticeship from King to Field probably occurred after Okes had been bound. Three days after being freed, Okes applied for a license to marry Elizabeth Beswick. The date of his first wife's death is unknown, but it possibly occurred before 1614, for she is curiously not mentioned in John Okes's will. If this omission signifies that Mary had died, Nicholas Okes's fourth child, born in 1619, was the daughter of a second wife of whom no record survives; but if the missing reference carries no implications relating to Mary's demise, the child was Mary's daughter. His second, or possibly third, wife was Mary Pursett, the widow of bookseller-publisher Christopher Pursett, who had been one of Okes's first customers in 1607. Okes and Mary applied for a marriage license in the last week of February 1624, but the marriage was brief: she died no later than early January 1628.

Nothing is known of where Okes worked between the completion of his apprenticeship and his acquiring the printing business of George and Lionel Snowdon in 1607. The fact that Field was not one of the dozen or so printers with whom Okes shared in the printing of books during his early years as a master printer renders unlikely the possibility that he had served as a journeyman in Field's shop. Okes may have worked for the Snowdons in this capacity, however, before he arranged to purchase their establishment in 1607. Okes's son, John, who eventually took up his father's trade, was born during these years, probably in 1605.

Okes procured Lionel Snowdon's share of the Snowdon partnership on 29 January 1607, and on 13 April he followed up by assuming control of George Snowdon's share. Printing materials and equipment that this partnership used had belonged to Thomas Judson in 1598, and some of the Snowdon ornaments have been traced back even further. From Judson many of these materials and equipment had been passed to John Harrison III and from him to the Snowdons. The stages through which Okes acquired the Snowdons' business and achieved the status of a master printer appear to have followed a carefully orchestrated plan. In restricting Okes's share to Lionel Snowdon's junior position in the partnership, the Stationers' Company appears to have been reluctant to confer the title of master printer on a twenty-seven-year-old journeyman with barely three years of experience beyond his apprenticeship. If so, Okes seems to have succeeded in circumventing the company's apprehensions by following a two-stage procedure in finally taking over the business. In imprints from October 1607 to 1615 Okes gave his address as "nere Holborne bridge," to which he occasionally added, "at the signe of the Hand."

AN
ADVICE HOVV
TO PLANT TO-
BACCO IN
ENGLAND:

AND

How to bring it to colour and
perfection, to whom it may be profita-
ble, and to whom harmfull.

The vertues of the Hearbe in gene-
rall, as well in the outward application
as taken in FVME.

WITH

THE DANGER OF THE SPANISH
TOBACCO.

Written by C. T.

LONDON,
Printed by NICHOLAS OKES, and are to
bee sold by WALTER BVRRE.
1615.

*Title page for one of many informational manuals printed
by Okes*

Almost immediately upon taking charge of the shop Okes radically changed the focus of its print work and, as a consequence, the nature of its printing procedure. He seems to have aimed particularly to cater to a market driven by topical interests, and to serve these interests he established connections with publishers and booksellers such as Nathaniel Butter and Thomas Archer, who dealt in such fare. Most of his books are therefore in smaller formats and relatively brief. Most of his surviving work is in quarto format, a smaller proportion in octavo, and still smaller in duodecimo. Occasionally he produced books in even smaller formats. Folios, which were reserved for more serious and substantial publications, are relatively rare among his books. Because successful sales of topical or sensitive works are likely to have depended, then as now, on comparatively swift production, both printer and publisher would have sought to achieve a fast turnaround

time from manuscript form to finished, printed copy.

Okes's books cover a broad spectrum of subject matter. They include sensational tabloid accounts such as *News from Italy, or a Prodigious Accident concerning the City of Pleurs* (1618) and *A True Relation of a Barbarous Murder Committed by Enoch ap Evan, Who Cut off His Own Natural Mother's Head and His Brother's* (1633); reports of various recent European and Asian political upheavals such as Henry Brereton's *News of the Present Miseries of Russia Occasioned by the Late Wars* (1614); and a profusion of various manuals such as C. T.'s *How to Plant Tobacco in England* (1615) and medical commentaries such as Angelo Sala's *Opiologia, or a Treatise concerning the Nature, Properties, True Preparation, and Safe Use of Opium* (1618).

His titles for most years also included recent sermons and other devotional literature. The best-sellers among these, such as Samuel Smith's *David's Blessed Man* (1614) and *David's Repentance* (1614), went through ten or more editions during twenty-four years. National events such as the death of Henry, prince of Wales, in 1612; the marriage of Princess Elizabeth to Frederick, elector of the Palatinate, and their departure to Bohemia in 1613; and the deaths of Queen Anne in 1619 and King James in 1625 are all well represented in elegies, encomia, and commemorative publications from Okes's shop. In addition to such items, lists of his books are sprinkled with scientific studies, almanacs or parts thereof, travel accounts, political commentaries, treatises on witchcraft, geographical and historical works, and anti-Catholic tracts.

Interest in Okes, however, rests most firmly on his printing of various works of popular literature – jestbooks, collections of epigrams, underworld exposés, satiric pamphlets (both verse and prose), lord mayors' shows, civic entertainments, and, especially, plays. His first printing of dramatic literature is represented by the "Pied Bull" quarto of William Shakespeare's *M. William Shak-speare: His True Chronicle Historie of the Life and Death of King Lear and His Three Daughters* (1608), various problematic and anomalous features of which almost certainly reflect his inexperience with play texts. During his career Okes printed the earliest and, in some instances, the only contemporary editions of many of the period's most highly regarded dramatic works, including Ben Jonson's *Ben: Jonson, His Case Is Altered* and *The Masque of Queenes Celebrated from the House of Fame* (both 1609); Thomas Middleton and Thomas Dekker's *The Roaring Girle, or Moll Cut-Purse* (1611); John Webster's *The White Divel* (1612) and

The Tragedy of the Dutchesse of Malfy (1623); Shakespeare's *The Tragedy of Othello, the Moore of Venice* (1619); various plays in the Francis Beaumont and John Fletcher canon – *The Knight of the Burning Pestle* (1613), *The Maides Tragedy* (1619), *Phylaster, or Love Lyes a Bleeding* (1620), and *The Tragedy of Thierry King of France and His Brother Theodoret* (1621) – James Shirley's *The Wedding* (1629); and John Ford's *'Tis Pitty Shee's a Whore* (1633).

Okes's printing in other dramatic genres includes a long list of lord mayors' shows by various authors and many civic entertainments written by Middleton to commemorate notable events in the city of London. His shop also printed important nondramatic works by many of the same authors and others such as Robert Daborne, Samuel Daniel, John Donne, William Lithgow, and Anthony Munday. The rich veins of drama and other literature represent only a small proportion of Okes's production in any given year, however – a circumstance that helps place in context the relatively mediocre workmanship found in the printing of many of these works. The status of plays as inconsequential and ephemeral entertainments in those times was reflected both in the kind of printing establishment that handled them and in the less-than-conscientious treatment they were accorded by printers who specialized in topical material – most of which was probably more straightforward and easy to print than theatrical texts. The average quality of work produced by Okes's house was considerably poorer than that of the best houses of the time, but the quality of his work was not the worst.

A succession of fines incurred for various printing infractions suggests that Okes was something of a risktaker. The record of his printing house soon after he became a master printer includes a series of offenses and fines logged in documents of the court of the Stationers' Company and other authorities. On various occasions he contravened regulations by printing unlicensed and/or unentered books, by "pirating" works (printing without authority books to which others owned the copyrights), and maintaining too many apprentices (many of whom were not properly indentured through the Stationers' Company), and by using and training men who were not members of the company – these last practices presumably intended to cut Okes's labor costs.

In some instances testimony relating to his breaking of company rules provides interesting and valuable sidelights on the printing trade of his time. In 1621, for example, he incurred a four-pound fine

for printing two pirate editions of George Wither's *Wither's Motto*. A deposition connected with this offense claimed that each of Okes's editions was of three thousand copies, a figure matched by an edition of Arthur Hopton's *A Concordancy of Yeares* that Okes had printed in 1615, apparently with company approval. He also merited fines for two offenses of disorderly printing in 1624, and the second of these, dated 6 November, added the warning that he was "not to print any booke hereafter without license vpon payne to have his presse taken downe." Despite being threatened with severe penalties, Okes persisted in breaking regulations. He paid only a fraction of the fines imposed, and his printing house remained in operation throughout his lifetime – despite a continuing record of infractions that must comprise only a small proportion of his offenses.

For example, Okes has recently been identified as the printer probably in 1624 or 1625 of Thomas Middleton's inflammatory political allegory, *A Game at Chæss*. His decision to print this work may have followed his involvement in other risky ventures, particularly his printing of Thomas Scott's *The Second Part of Vox Populi* (1624), which had served as one of Middleton's sources. The Privy Council's swift and stern reaction to the presentation of Middleton's play by the King's Men – cessation of performances by the company, suppression of the play, closure of the Globe Theatre, and a warrant for the playwright's arrest – would likely have meant a severe penalty for the printer, had he been known. In such cases involving controversial material Okes would presumably have received some form of compensatory payment, but his professed inability to settle fines on several occasions together with other instances of financially straitened circumstances falls well short of prosperity.

Standing against Okes's printing of controversial work and his substantial record of ignoring Stationers' Company regulations is Thomas Heywood's early fulsome praise "To my approued good Friend, M^r· *Nicholas Okes,*" appended to his *Apology for Actors* (1612):

> The infinite faults escaped in my booke of *Britaines Troy,* by the negligence of the Printer, as the misquotations, mistaking of sillables, misplacing halfe lines, coining of strange and neuer heard of words. These being without number, when I would haue taken a particular account of the *Errata,* the Printer answered me, hee would not publish his owne disworkemanship, but rather let his owne fault lye vpon the necke of the Author: and being fearefull that others of his quality, had beene of the same nature, and condition, and finding you on the contrary, so carefull, and industrious, so serious and laborious to

doe the Author all the rights of the presse, I could not choose but gratulate your honest indeauours with this short remembrance. Here likewise, I must necessarily insert a manifest iniury done me in that worke, by taking the two Epistles of *Paris* to *Helen,* and *Helen* to *Paris,* and printing them in a lesse volume, vnder the name of another, which may put the world in opinion I might steale them from him; and hee to doe himselfe right, hath since published them in his owne name: but as I must acknowledge my lines not worthy his patronage, vnder whom he hath publisht them, so the Author I know much offended with M. *Iaggard* (that altogether vnknowne to him) presumed to make so bold with his name. These, and the like dishonesties I know you to bee cleere of; and I could wish but to bee the happy Author of so worthy a worke as I could willingly commit to your care and workmanship.

Yours euer
Thomas Heywood.

Heywood clearly aims in part to castigate publicly another printer, William Jaggard, for various faults, but he also goes out of his way to commend Okes's care and industry. Apparently as a further expression of his appreciation Heywood entrusted four more books to Okes in 1613: *The Brazen Age; The Silver Age; A Funerall Elegie, upon the Death of Henry, Prince of Wales;* and *A Marriage Triumphe.* Yet after 1615 a puzzling gap of sixteen years intervened before he returned to Okes and his son with a stream of new works.

In 1615 and 1623 Okes was limited to one press, but from his early days he is likely to have had a second, or "proofing," press that, when deadline pressures mounted, was probably put into full service. When he was unable to fulfill commitments single-handedly, Okes farmed out parts of his books to other printers; at least eighteen others shared in printing various books with him. When the tide of topical material ebbed during slack periods early in Okes's career, he worked on books that were less urgent but still fairly short (to preclude tying up his press if urgent new work should appear) and for which an established or anticipated demand existed. Such material constituted the stock work of his shop, and this pattern of printing set in his early years seems borne out by later practice.

Many older titles appear in his reprint editions: these include the anonymous *A Comedie of Mucedorus* (1615) and other oft-reprinted and perennially popular works such as Robert Greene's *Greenes Groatsworth of Witte* (1621) and Christopher Marlowe's *Hero and Leander* (1637). Among more-recent books treated to numerous editions in Okes's hands that likely served a similar purpose were

Gervase Markham's *Markhams Maister-peece,* printed originally in 1610 and reprinted in four subsequent editions between 1615 and 1636, and several religious works by Samuel Smith. For the latter and many other frequently reprinted books Okes held the copyrights.

When more urgent work would appear, Okes would interrupt the stock work, which he would set aside in order to concentrate his efforts on the priority item. The scheduling of work in Okes's shop was probably subject to constant review and adjustment in accordance with the relative urgency of projects in hand. Such a system of discontinuous but "concurrent" printing within a single establishment and shared printing between two or more houses provided a flexibility and adaptability that allowed a maximum rate of production for a printing house of Okes's size.

By 1618 Okes had moved his shop to Foster Lane, a move possibly effected by the expiry of the lease inherited from his father. Okes's own son, John, was freed by patrimony at the age of twenty-one on 14 January 1627. Despite the absence of any record of a formal partnership between father and son, John was apparently being groomed from his early years to assume control of the business. His initials appear in an imprint as early as 1625, and he was placed in charge of the shop while his father was imprisoned in the Counter for an unknown misdemeanor in early 1627, a circumstance that may have advanced the date at which he gained his freedom. In 1630 Nicholas transferred to his son a collection of his copyrights, and he began sharing imprints with him about 1635. From then on their imprints name father, son, or both, but in accordance with no apparent principle of determination. By 1636 John was, in effect, running the house.

His involvement in the business proved particularly beneficial in 1627, when Nicholas Okes, one of the printers of Sir Robert Bruce Cotton's *Short View of the Long Life and Reign of Henry the Third,* which appeared without the author's knowledge and without licence, again fell foul of the authorities. On this occasion John Okes took the blame, presumably to take the heat off his father and possibly thereby, in light of the 6 November 1624 warning, to protect the business. John Okes's complicity is unlikely to have been more than incidental, however.

In 1628 Okes entered into what became an acrimonious partnership with stationer John Norton, with whom Okes shared imprints only in 1628 and 1629. Okes's series of discomfiting debts and failures to pay during several years may be linked to

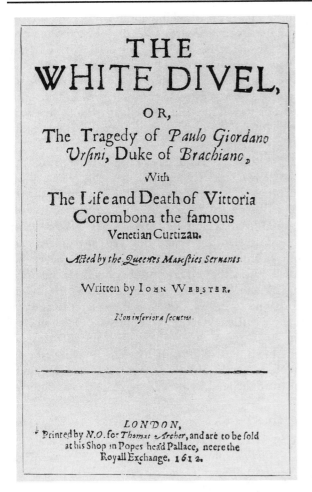

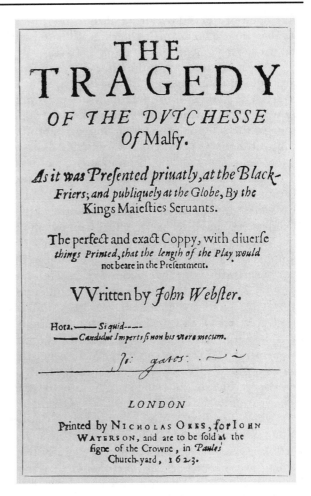

Title pages for the two major tragedies on which John Webster's reputation is based

his alliance with Norton. Norton removed equipment and printing materials from the Foster Lane premises in 1633 to set up a clandestine, illegal press in association with what Okes called "a Company of disorderlie & factious persons," the former printer Robert Raworth and Richard Hodgkinson. When the press was discovered, the Stationers' Company impounded it and melted and defaced type, to what Okes called his "great disgrace and losse."

The latter years of the partnership with Norton coincided with investigations into the printing trade initiated in 1634. These culminated in the Star Chamber decree of 11 July 1637 that reduced and limited to twenty the authorized number of printing houses in London. Although most cautious printers would have been on their best behaviors during this inquiry by Sir John Lambe, Okes and Norton were found to be the most serious violators of several ordinances – including those of keeping too many apprentices and training and employing workers who

were not members of the Stationers' Company. Such discoveries undoubtedly stood against them when the Court of Star Chamber finally drew up its list of twenty sanctioned printers.

By mid 1636 John Okes had moved to the wellyard of the parish of St. Bartholomew the Less, possibly while his father continued to operate from the house in Foster Lane. Removal of the business to St. Bartholomew's wellyard may have been delayed until Nicholas's projected retirement, probably later the same year.

Okes's involvement in printing part of a new edition of St. Francis of Sales's *Introduction to a Devout Life* in 1637 dealt a possibly decisive blow to his prospects for securing a place among the twenty ordained London printers. Inclusion of "passages . . . tending to popery" in the printed work, passages that had been excised from the licensed copy, generated a stir aggravated, no doubt, by political attitudes attuned to the coming Puritan revolution. Various accounts of circumstances involving Okes have been preserved by virtue of their relation to the 1640 impeachment of Archbishop William Laud and his subsequent trial for treason in 1644.

At issue concerning the 1637 St. Francis of Sales edition is the question of whether Nicholas or John was to blame for printing the Okes portion of the work. Discrepancies between various accounts point to the likelihood that respondents modified their testimony to protect specific individuals or interests. John Okes's bid to be numbered among the authorized printers and his father's wish to ensure thereby the succession and continuity of the business were among their chief interests; and this time Nicholas may have deliberately taken responsibility for the printing in order to draw the court's fire from his son and thus leave him free of taint in the eyes of the print trade investigation. In a petition to Laud on 28 June 1637 Okes expressed his intention to pass his business immediately to his son. This move spurred Okes's partner, Norton, to make a final desperate attempt to assert his own claim to the printing house. He countered with a petition protesting that Okes's plan threatened his and his family's livelihood and made no allowance for their eight-year-old partnership.

Since the Okes-Norton printing house was not among those permitted by the Star Chamber decree, Nicholas Okes was prevented, upon his death, from turning over his business to John, though he was allowed to continue to print for the remainder of his own life. A petition by John's sister Mary a year or so after the decree pleaded that her brother be allowed the next vacant printer's place. The details of events are lost, but John Okes was admitted to the livery of the Stationers' Company on 1 June 1640. This fact, along with the subsequent uncontested passage of Okes's business to successive heirs, indicates that he was granted the place left by the death of John Haviland in 1639, probably prior to John Okes's admission to the livery. Norton never obtained a place and died in debt in 1640. Events overtook the Okeses' plans, however. John ran the printing house in the wellyard of Little St. Bartholomew's until late 1643, but he probably died near the end of this year. In accordance with John Okes's will, Nicholas assisted his son's widow in managing the business until his own death, most likely in early April 1645 at the age of sixty-six. He was buried on 11 April.

Although Nicholas Okes may be censured for flawed workmanship in the printing of many important works, he deserves at least qualified thanks for ensuring their survival. In addition to having printed frustratingly defective books, Okes was responsible also for others that reveal signs of care and attention. Heywood's tribute may be exceptional, but, although few authors oversaw the printing of their works as scrupulously as Heywood leads one to believe, there is no reason to suspect that his commendation was unmerited. Such neglect on the parts of both an author and a printer — whether Okes or one of his fellows — may be lamented but should be recognized as in no small measure dictated by prevailing cultural conditions.

References:

Peter W. M. Blayney, *Nicholas Okes and the First Quarto,* volume 1 of *The Texts of "King Lear" and Their Origins* (Cambridge: Cambridge University Press, 1982);

C. William Miller, "A London Ornament Stock: 1598–1683," *Studies in Bibliography,* 7 (1955): 125–151;

Adrian Weiss, "Textual Introduction to *A Game at Chess,*" in *Textual Companion to the Collected Works of Thomas Middleton,* edited by Gary Taylor (Oxford: Oxford University Press, forthcoming, 1997).

— Paul A. Mulholland

John Playford

(London: 1647 – 1684)

Henry Playford

(London: 1684 – 1703)

A well-known publisher and bookseller in Samuel Pepys's London, John Playford dominated the English music publishing trade for a thirty-six-year period through the turbulent Commonwealth and Restoration periods. In the early years of the Commonwealth he rejuvenated a music publishing market with his celebrated *The English Dancing-Master* (1651), a collection of popular country dances set to folk-music tunes that might otherwise have been forgotten. A friend of such musicians as Henry Purcell, Henry Lawes, Thomas Campion, and John Hilton, Playford published a series of songbooks that anthologized hundreds of their aires, dialogues (*Select Musicall Ayres, and Dialogues,* 1652), and catches (*Catch That Catch Can,* 1652).

Thinking that his clientele might be more inclined to purchase songbooks had they a rudimentary knowledge of instrumental music and theory, he edited several versions of a methodical textbook, *Introduction to the Skill of Musick* (1654). He was equally eminent in the field of sacred music, where, with the requisite consent of the Stationers' Company, he not only revised the authorized Elizabethan Psalter of Thomas Sternhold and John Hopkins but eventually published his innovative *The Whole Book of Psalms with the Usual Hymns* (1677) with tunes harmonized in three parts. Playford's only surviving son, Henry, inherited his father's prodigious business and continued publishing into the eighteenth century.

Playford was born in Norwich, where a monument at St. Michael-at-Plea attests to his family's prominence. Entitled to bear arms with Scottish collaterals pictured in Playford's portraits, his family was large, and local records show that many of them were scriveners or stationers. While no existing documents record the history of Playford's early schooling, he is assumed to have attended the Norwich Cathedral School (Almonry), where he evidently cultivated a passion for the divine service. Shortly after his father's death, Stationers' Company records show that "John Playford, son of John Playford of the Cittie of Norwich, Mercer" appren-

ticed himself on 23 March 1640 to John Benson, a London publisher of St. Dunstan's Churchyard, Fleet Street, and on 5 April 1647 he was freed from his apprenticeship.

His freedom entitled him to trade as a publisher, and the new bookseller quickly set up shop in the porch of the Temple Church, as his imprint indicates, "Near the Church door" or "In the Inner Temple," where he lived for a time and conducted business for most of his life. In 1653 he was admitted as clerk to the Temple Church, an office he held with distinction until the end of his life, and soon after this appointment he married Hannah Allen, daughter of Cornhill publisher Benjamin Allen. Except for Henry, who was probably their second son, little else is known about their children. Having received an inheritance from Hannah's father, the Playfords moved in 1655 to rural Islington, where she conducted a school "over against the church where young gentlewomen might be instructed in all manner of curious work, as also reading, writing, musick, dancing, and the French tongue," so advertised in a 1659 edition of Playford's *Select Ayres and Dialogues.* When Hannah died in 1679, Playford sold this house and purchased another in Arundel Street, "near the Thames side, the lower end, against the George," as his imprint announced, where he lived for the remainder of his life.

The contours of Playford's career reveal his lifelong Royalist leanings. During the civil war many booksellers, including Playford, published and sold news stories in the form of tracts and pamphlets. Though these publications gradually became a greater political risk, Playford and his current associates, Francis Tyton and Peter Cole of Cornhill, nonetheless entered in the Stationers' Register on 22 February 1649 *King Charls His Tryal* (1649), a pamphlet bearing no publisher's imprint and narrating the king's prosecution and scaffold speeches. For this, and most likely for young Playford's other Royalist pamphlets, a warrant was issued for his arrest. Nothing more is known about this affair until after the Restoration, when Playford published the

Engraved portrait of John Playford in his textbook, An
Introduction to the Skill of Music *(seventh
edition, 1674)*

compilation *England's Black Tribunal* (1660), an enlarged edition of the Commonwealth trials and executions. Playford's promotion to the livery in the
Stationers' Company the next year may constitute a
royal reward for his loyalty to the Crown.

With the establishment of Cromwell's government, Playford turned exclusively to publishing and
selling music literature. On 7 November 1650 Playford registered *The English Dancing-Master* (1651),
whose title page was to promise "Plaine and Easie
Rules for the Dancing of Country Dances, with the
Tune to Each Dance" and to feature an engraving
by the renowned Bohemian Václov Hollar, a design
of Cupid playing the lute and instructing a gentleman and women in dance. The tunes and diagram-
matic directions for the various "rounds,"
"squares," and "longways" dances carefully correspond to the text throughout. Several features of
this early piece illustrate publishing patterns that
were to become common among most of Playford's
projects: it was reprinted in many editions (eighteen

or twenty by 1726); its printing format was altered
(from quarto to duodecimo); and its title was
changed (subsequent editions beginning with that of
1652 deleted the term *English* and instead bore the
title *The Dancing Master*). Such frequent slight modi-
fications considerably confuse music historians and
bibliographers interested in establishing Playford's
inventory. The preface to *The Dancing Master* also inaugurated a practice that became a trademark: Playford addressed his readers, "the Gentlemen of the
Inns of Court." This astute marketing technique of
Playford, who was arguably one of the first publishers to do this, cultivated a commercial readership.

In 1651 Playford also published *The Musicall
Banquet,* the three parts of which included lyra viol
music, dancing tunes, and catches. It was the kernel
of the songbook and instrumental industry that
Playford developed in the early years of the 1650s.
"Musick and Mirth," the last part of *The Musicall
Banquet,* was the prototype for his series of catches
that began in 1652 with 143 songs edited by Hilton
and known successively as *Catch That Catch Can, The
Pleasant Companion* (1672), and *The Musical Companion*
(1673). Pepys, an avid musical amateur, writes that
on 15 April 1667 he purchased a copy of "Playfords
new ketch-book, that hath a great many new fooler-
ies in it," and he records three days later that he
"tried two or three three-parts in Playford's new
book; my wife pleasing me in singing her part of the
things she knew, which is a comfort to my very
heart." A modest composer in his own right, Playford contributed more than thirty songs appearing
mainly in later editions of *The Musical Companion,*
songs with titles such as "Hail, Happy Day! Now
Dorus Sit Thee Down" and "Comely Swain, Why
Sitt'st Thou So." The miscellany had grown to 225
songs by 1673 and was reprinted until the middle of
the eighteenth century.

In 1652 Playford also inaugurated another
songbook series known initially as *Select Musicall
Ayres, and Dialogues;* in its second and third enlarged editions as *Select Ayres and Dialogues* (1653,
1659); and in its fourth edition as the first volume
of *The Treasury of Music* (1669). These "treasuries"
contained poems by Cavalier poets Richard Love-
lace and Robert Herrick and vocal compositions by
the likes of John Wilson and Henry Lawes. The
preface by Lawes to his own *Ayres and Dialogues*
(published by Playford in various editions of 1653,
1655, and 1658 and reissued as the third part of *The
Treasury of Music* in 1669) reveals much about the
plight of the professional musician during the Commonwealth and about Playford's role in supplying
the public with tunes from those formerly employed

as court musicians: "[Playford] made bold to print in one book [*Select Musicall Ayres, and Dialogues,* 1652], above twenty of my songs whereof I had no knowledge till the booke was in the presse, and it seems he found those so acceptable that he is ready for more."

One of Playford's last publishing schemes, begun in 1673 after Charles II reestablished the monarchy, was the songbook series *Choyce Songs and Ayres* (1673; later titled *Choice Ayres, Songs and Dialogues,* 1675) whose title page is directed to the tastes of king and court: "Most of the Newest Songs Sung at Court, and at the Publick Theatres, Composed by Several Gentlemen of His Majesties Musick." Playford managed to publish his secular songbooks during both Puritan and Royalist governments.

In 1653 Playford apparently sought to become England's foremost music publisher by issuing a comprehensive *Catalogue of All the Musick-Bookes That Have Been Printed in England, Either for Voyce or Instruments,* a broadside bibliography not simply for his own business records but for announcing the likely scope of his future marketing ventures. Another key to Playford's success may also have been in his habit of working primarily with a single printer at any one time: first with Thomas Harper until his death in 1656; next with William Godbid until his death in 1679; then with Godbid's widow, Anne, and her business partner, John Playford the younger (Playford's nephew); and finally with his nephew alone.

In 1654 Playford built upon the incipient interest in instrumental music he had shown earlier in *The Musicall Banquet.* He began to invest in instrumental and music theory textbooks by publishing his *Breefe Introduction to the Skill of Musick, for Song and Viall* (1654). This manual contained rudimentary lessons for several instruments and voice as well as theoretical essays written by Campion, Purcell, and Playford himself (although scholars conjecture that Playford may have cleverly plagiarized portions of his discourse). This tutor was a great success, underwent many alterations, and was reprinted in many editions until 1730, although the exact number is uncertain because printing mistakes were made in numbering the editions. Pepys wrote on 22 March 1667 of having walked from Greenwich to Woolwich "all the way reading Playfords *Introduction to Musique,* wherein are some things very pretty."

The prefatory letters to *Breefe Introduction* reveal Playford's sense of shifting public sentiments. Addressed "To all Lovers and Practitioners of Musick," the preface to the first edition suggests that he is giving his customers what they want: "I was desired by some Masters to print the Scale of Musick, or Gamut." Yet by the second edition of 1655 Playford has adjusted his tone, zealously cajoling "Those who are Lovers hereof, [to] allow Musick to be the Gift of God." With his 1662 edition Playford began to call himself *Philo-Musicae,* the lover of music, and extended the coverage of this work to instrumental literature as well. Throughout his career he published and sold a wide selection of this stock, including Matthew Locke's *Little Consort* (1656) for viol and violins, *Musick's Hand Maide* for harpsichord (1663), *Musick's Delight on the Cithern* (1666), *Apollo's Banquet for the Treble Violin* (1669), and *The Pleasant Companion* (1672) for the flageolet (recorder).

On 20 April 1661 Playford was admitted to the livery of the Stationers' Company. Although it was not extraordinary for yeomen to wait to be granted the privileges of the livery (the right to bind apprentices and purchase common stock in the guild), the fourteen-year reluctance of the company to accord such recognition to Playford may have resulted from his dangerous Royalist sympathies during the Interregnum. On 20 June 1681 the court heard and obeyed a mandate from Charles II declaring, "Our will & pleasure is, That you forthwith admitt and receive the said John Playford . . . to . . . yoᵣ Court of Assistants. . . ." Royal approval and status in the Stationers' Company were essential prerequisites to Playford's publication of sacred music, because in 1603 James I had granted the guild exclusive privilege to print metrical psalms, a patent confirmed by subsequent charters.

The company had been regularly exercising this monopoly by reprinting the 1562 psalter arranged by Sternhold and Hopkins. Yet in 1661 the company deemed it time for a revised edition and bestowed this honor on Playford, who conservatively reformed the Elizabethan psalmody. While not a grand financial success during its publication from 1661 to 1688, *The Booke of Psalmes* was for Playford a stepping-stone to his next book of metrical psalms, *Psalms & Hymns in Solemn Musick* (1671), which provided innovative four-part harmonizations of selected psalms. Playford's final Psalter, *Whole Booke of Psalms . . . Compos'd in Three Parts* (1677), was a spectacular best-seller. With the growth of voluntary parish choirs toward the close of the century, *Whole Booke of Psalms* was adopted for use in England and in America and was reprinted in twenty editions until 1757.

In the 1684 preface to *Choice Ayres* Playford announced his intention to retire officially and turn

Title page for the fifth edition of Playford's collection of popular country dances and folk tunes

over his business to his son, Henry, who had been apprenticed to his father in 1674 and freed in 1681. Financial records of the Stationers' Company indicate that Playford died between 24 December 1686 and 7 February 1687. As a tribute to their publishing friend, Nahum Tate and Purcell composed a "Pastoral Elegy on the Death of Mr. John Playford" (1687), beginning:

> Gentle shepherds you that know
> The charms of tuneful breath,
> That Harmony in Grief can show
> Lament for pious Theron's death!

Playford's death marked the beginning of the end for his publishing empire. Whether or not his father's hold on the English music publishing market was understandably losing its grip by 1684, Henry was able to match neither his father's market dominance nor his eminence in the Stationers' Company. Henry initially emulated his father's practices and reissued many of his best books, including *The Dancing Master* (1690 and 1703), *An Introduction to the Skill of Musick* (1687 and 1703), and *Apollo's Banquet* (1687, 1690, and 1691). To counter the introduction of new typographical technologies that bode ill for his music publishing techniques, he initiated various schemes that proved unsuccessful: publishing *Wit and Mirth: Or Pills to purge Melancholy*

(1699), a cheap collection of popular songs, and *Mercurius Musicus: Or, The Monthly Collection of New Teaching Songs* (1699–1702), a musical periodical; encouraging music clubs; and arranging for auctions of music books and artworks. Friends of his father did not, however, wholly abandon Henry, whose own crowning achievement is his handsome publication of Purcell's *Orpheus Britannicus* in 1698.

John Playford has been historically cloaked in the grand patriarchal mantle of being "the father of music publishing." This is unfortunate, because such an epithet oddly diminishes Playford's business acumen for having recognized in 1650 a lull in the English music trade and having cultivated lucrative markets for his publications during both the Commonwealth and the Restoration periods. Though this seventeenth-century bookseller left no memoirs, his dedication to the Crown seems to have been driven by lifelong personal loyalties rather than commercial whim. His political commitments were ultimately repaid, as the restored Charles II granted Playford a monopoly on the patented Psalter, a copyright that Playford made yet more profitable through his metrical innovations. Playford characteristically built his fortune with careful speculation and, perhaps, an uncanny intuition about trends in public taste. He likewise brought his ingenuity to bear on the flourishing world of secular music, in which he built markets for songbooks and instrumental music as well as supplied audiences with a basic manual for appreciating the rudiments of music theory and practice.

Bibliography:
Peter A. Munstedt, "John Playford, Music Publisher: A Bibliographic Catalogue," dissertation, University of Kentucky, 1983.

References:
Cyrus Lawrence Day and Eleanore Boswell Murrie, "English Song-Books, 1651–1702, and Their Publishers," *Library,* 16 (March 1636): 355–401;

Margaret Dean-Smith, ed., "Introduction," in her *Playford's English Dancing Master, 1651* (London: Schott, 1957), pp. ix–xx;

Frank Kidson, "John Playford, and 17th-Century Music Publishing," *Musical Quarterly,* 4 (October 1918): 516–534;

Donald William Krummel, "Song Books," in his *English Music Printing, 1553–1700* (London: Bibliographical Society, 1975), pp. 113–123;

Krummel and Stanley Sadie, eds., *Music Printing and Publishing* (New York: Norton, 1990);

Robert Latham and William Matthews, eds., *The Diary of Samuel Pepys,* 11 volumes (Berkeley: University of California Press, 1979);

Lillian M. Ruff, "A Survey of John Playford's 'Introduction to the Skill of Musick,'" *Consort,* 22 (Summer 1965): 36–49;

Nicholas Temperley, "John Playford and the Metrical Psalms," *Journal of the American Musicological Society,* 25 (Fall 1972): 331–378;

Temperley, "John Playford and the Stationers' Company," *Music and Letters,* 54 (April 1973): 203–212.

— Tamara Goeglein

William Ponsonby

(London: 1577? – 1604)

William Ponsonby – Elizabethan bookseller, publisher, and prominent member of the London Stationers' Company from 1571 to 1604 – appears in this volume primarily because he published most of the works of Sir Philip Sidney and Edmund Spenser, a praiseworthy endeavor that partly explains Ronald B. McKerrow's pronouncement in *A Dictionary of Printers and Booksellers* (1910) that Ponsonby "may be described as the most important publisher of the Elizabethan age." As a figure of cultural history Ponsonby also helped to fashion the legal and commercial machinery of modern English printing by challenging the power of the printers, the authority of royal patents, and the nascent privileges of authors. McKerrow knew in 1910 essentially what some contemporary literary historians find themselves rediscovering: that Ponsonby and his fellow publishers, while edging the printers from the center of power in the Stationers' Company, encouraged the development of an English print culture and secured moderate economic and political power over what would become a communications industry. While the importance of printers diminished to the point that it reflected merely their mechanical skills, Ponsonby prepared himself to maintain a more influential position among an elite group of publishers, tradesmen, and entrepreneurial intellectuals.

Ponsonby's enterprising spirit, business acumen, and personal circumstances shaped his esteem for intellectual property long before the concept attained legal status. Moreover, his prominence among his fellow publishers reflected the consistency of his sympathies and of his reluctance to allow mere commercial interest to dictate what he produced: he opposed the monopolizing effects of royal patents and privileges, by which designated printers and publishers secured exclusive rights to certain kinds of texts, and except for one occasion of piracy he never published the almanacs, schoolbooks, and prototabloid broadsides of sensational news and science that helped keep many in business. With the assistance of seventeen reputable printers between 1577 and 1604 Ponsonby produced at least seventy-four handsome and well-edited volumes, a selective library of Elizabethan literary, historical, and religious works for which he has not been forgotten.

Although records of the Stationers' Company offer much information about Ponsonby's life in the trade, his publications must compensate for the scarcity of other biographical data in reconstructing his life. Ponsonby's productions display his sympathy with the political and religious positions sponsored by Robert Dudley, earl of Leicester, and generally with the political and literary circles surrounding Leicester and his nephew, Sidney. Following the deaths of Sidney and Leicester in 1586 and 1588, respectively, Ponsonby built his career on their legacy. He engaged in publishing ventures with Sidney's agents and sister, the countess of Pembroke; he immortalized Spenser's works; and in 1589, 1590, and 1598 he published three texts dedicated to Robert Devereux, earl of Essex – Leicester's rival, antagonist, stepson, and chief ideological heir. For Ponsonby this orientation drew him toward Protestant politics that sought, unsuccessfully, a strong and sustained English military and diplomatic aggression against Spain and the papacy. It also interested him in study and exploration of every discipline and of some of the most sophisticated, inspired literature of the English Renaissance.

Ponsonby's achievements deviate from the norm, at least from that established by H. S. Bennett, whose general estimates of the numbers of Elizabethan books categorize these different kinds of books by the subject matters implicit in their titles: religion (40 percent); literature (25 percent); geography, history, and news (10 percent); law (10 percent); arithmetic, astronomy, and popular science (8 percent); commerce, economics, education, and conduct (5 percent); and miscellaneous (2 percent). Ponsonby's publications fall largely among Bennett's first three categories, as much of the rest comprises schoolbooks and government publications, mostly privileged texts controlled by royal patents.

Ponsonby's deviations from Bennett's norms reflect the intellectual predilections of an elite, increasingly secular body of readers. Of sixty-six titles, including two published in partnership and ex-

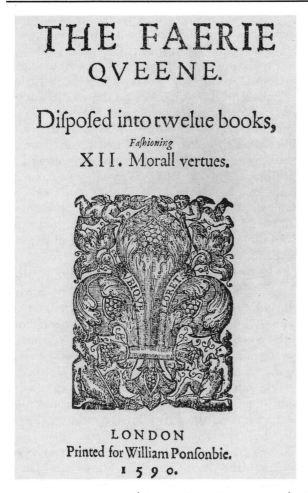

Title pages for the first two parts (books 1–6) of Edmund Spenser's allegorical epic

cluding nine reprinted editions, Ponsonby published twenty-seven literary volumes (41 percent); twenty-two volumes on subjects of history, military science, and political philosophy (34 percent); fourteen volumes on religion (21 percent); and three volumes on practical science (4 percent). Compared with Bennett's figures, Ponsonby published almost twice as many literary, three times as many historical, and half as many religious texts. Although he published works on all these subjects throughout his career, religious works marked his early years (1579–1589), literature his prolific midcareer (1590–1596), and history and military science his later years (1596–1604). As his success and reputation grew, so did the format size of his books: he started out publishing octavos, graduated to quartos by 1589, and published nine folios during his later years. His production affords a revealing profile of his life in the Elizabethan book trade.

Yet Ponsonby has received sustained attention only in Michael Brennan's 1983 article, which includes a chronological list of Ponsonby's publica-

tions. Focusing on Ponsonby's relations with the Leicester and Sidney circles and concluding that he made politic and high-minded commercial choices in publishing most of his books, Brennan asserts that Ponsonby's "preeminence in the book trade from 1590–1600 was largely if not totally due to his allegiance to the political and religious views of the Leicester faction" and to Sidney's relations and friends, who allowed him to publish Sidney's works. While this assessment is perhaps essentially true, Brennan's rather absolute and reductive statement may oversimplify the structures of power in Elizabethan publishing, subtly suggest that Ponsonby's commercial interests were banal, and limit too severely his independence from these social and commercial influences. Whatever the truth of the matter, Ponsonby apparently courted those whose views he favored, but he also apparently published just about what he wished.

He certainly led a full life in the trade, beginning on 25 December 1560, when William Norton, future master of the Stationers' Company, apprenticed him. On 11 January 1571 Ponsonby paid for and attained his freedom from the company, a status accorded only about half of those who began apprenticeships. Because a statute of the London Common Council in 1556 had set the age of twenty-four as the earliest at which apprentices could be freed, Ponsonby probably was that age when he gained his freedom, and his date of birth would thus have been in 1546 or very early in 1547. Sometime before 25 March 1577, when Paul Lindley became his first apprentice, he opened a shop in large quarters opposite the great north door in St. Paul's Churchyard, the center of the book trade. On 24 June 1578 Ponsonby engaged his second apprentice, Edward Blount, who would become one of the partners in publishing William Shakespeare's First Folio (1623). During the late 1570s Ponsonby courted and married Joan Coldock, daughter of Francis Coldock, master of the Stationers' Company in 1591–1592 and 1595–1596. The culture of the print trade encouraged members to form and develop such relationships, as career aspirations motivated members to keep family ties within the company. No documents record the birth or death of any Ponsonby children, but his commercial offspring – his books – provide a vivid and fascinating biographical portrait.

While he was establishing his shop and beginning to secure his place in the company, Ponsonby made his first entry in the Stationers' Register on 17 June 1577, although he did not publish John Allday's anthology *The Praise and Dispraise of Women: Gathered out of Sundry Authors,* until 1579. This octavo volume is a selected anthology of pieces on issues concerning the midcentury feminist controversy that John Knox's inopportune publication of *The First Blast of the Trumpet against the Monstrous Regiment of Women,* an incendiary diatribe against female rule, had aroused in 1558. This work had been aimed at Queen Mary I, whose death a few months after its publication left Queen Elizabeth I to contend with Knox's unintended smear on her reign. Despite his earnest endeavors to secure Elizabeth's goodwill, she never forgave the famed Scottish Calvinist, and her enmity colored English religion and politics during much of her reign. Ponsonby's volume was thus resurrecting the memory of Knox to defeat him with varied and open-minded inquiry, an approach that demands the broad intellectual perspective that was to characterize all Ponsonby's work, including his religious publications.

Of the sixteen volumes Ponsonby published between 1577 and 1586, ten are resolute but moderate Protestant texts endorsing the views of those Continental reformers favored by Elizabeth and the earl of Leicester. For instance, Ponsonby published three translations (from Latin and French) of works by Heinrich Bullinger, who had succeeded Ulrich Zwingli as head of the reformed community in Zurich. Unlike his predecessor, Bullinger made some conciliatory gestures toward Martin Luther and John Calvin and generally espoused a moderate theology that attracted strong sympathy among English Protestants. In 1570 Elizabeth had commissioned Bullinger to write a rebuttal of her excommunication by Pope Pius V. John Day, one of Leicester's protégés in the print trade, had published Bullinger's Latin text in 1571 and an English translation by Arthur Golding the next year.

Bullinger's theology – moderate Protestantism with a Continental radical edge – runs deep in Ponsonby's output. In 1582, for example, just before publishing his final work by Bullinger, Ponsonby produced a substantial translated edition of *The Homilies or Familiar Sermons of M. Rodolph Gualther Tigurine upon the Prophet Joel* by Rudolph Walther, a notable Zurich preacher. In the same year Ponsonby published a translation of an influential commentary on the Council of Trent by Martin Chemnitz, the practical, moderate German theologian who helped unite the Lutherans. The next year, with the diversity of his publications increasing, Ponsonby reinforced his commercial prospects by bringing out two popular books of Protestant religious instruction.

In 1585 and 1586 he published what might have been mildly controversial works by John Tomkis, the translator of the Bullinger texts. The first work is a lively exposition of the Lord's Prayer in a question-and-answer format; the second – *A Sermon Preached on the 26 Day of May 1584 in Saint Mary's Church in Shrewsbury: Before the Right Honorable the Earl of Leicester* (1586) – opens with an effusive dedication to Leicester outlining his kindly attention to and general theological sympathy with Tomkis. Ponsonby would have sympathized with Bullinger's views, as promulgated in the Second Helvetic Confession of 1566 and accepted as doctrine in Scotland, France, and Hungary, and in this context Ponsonby's implicit ties to Bullinger deserve mention. Spenser's first publication – translations from Petrarch and Joachim du Bellay – appeared in Jan van der Noot's *A Theatre for Worldlings* (1569), a work heavily influenced by Bullinger's commentary on Revelation. Moreover, Bullinger championed as lyric poetry the Psalms of David, which Sidney was to transform into English poetry.

In addition to his various Protestant texts, Ponsonby published during his early years a translation (from French) of the duke of Anjou's journey from London to Antwerp following the first round of marriage negotiations with Elizabeth; a pleasing text of Cicero's *Consolatio* (1583), printed in small italic; and his first excursions into imaginative literature, beginning with Henry Middleton's beautiful printing of *Sacrosancta bucolica* (1583), a Latin pastoral poem in honor of Elizabeth by Ogerius Bellehachius. In 1584 Ponsonby innocently but presciently published the pastoral romance *Gwydonius, or Greene's Card of Fancy,* one of the first works by the notorious Robert Greene, after whose dissolute death in December 1592 Ponsonby published a third edition of the *Card* and part II of Greene's *Mamillia,* which Ponsonby had entered in the Stationers' Register in 1583.

Between 1583 and 1589 Ponsonby published only four volumes, two editions of Greene's *Card of Fancy* and Tomkis's two pieces, and this small number of publications suggests that these were relatively lean years for independent publishers. Ponsonby responded to the situation by actively involving himself in the most widespread and revolutionary episode in an ongoing conflict between the privileged and unprivileged stationers – between those few who held lucrative royal patents for exclusive publication of certain books or kinds of books and those many who held no patents. Ponsonby and many others entered the fray when it finally seemed relatively safe to do so, following the death of the powerful, exceptionally privileged John Day on 23 July 1584.

In the years preceding Day's death, the dangerous protest against such privilege that Day and others held had been sustained by the piratical publication of those privileged works by, among others, John Wolfe – one of the most colorful and controversial Elizabethan printer-publishers, who, his reputation restored, would later print Spenser's *The Faerie Queene* for Ponsonby in 1590. Wolfe had been apprenticed to John Day in 1564, but he gave up his apprenticeship to pursue publishing in Florence and perhaps in Venice before he returned to England in the early 1580s to begin prodigious publication of unlicensed works.

By 1583 Wolfe had been twice imprisoned, and his radical, unrepentant position is evident in words and actions ascribed to him by the wardens of the Stationers' Company, who submitted on behalf of the patentees in spring 1583 a "Supplication to the Privy Council . . . against John Wolfe and His Associates." Amid many scandalous charges in this document and in a separate enclosure, "Notes or Articles of the Insolent and Contemptuous Behavior of John Wolfe and His Confederates," appears an exposition of Wolfe's presumptuous attitude, with which Ponsonby may well have been sympathetic at the time. Edward Arber has summarily recounted part of this confrontation in his *A Transcript of the Registers of the Company of Stationers* (1875):

> Wolfe being admonished that he being one so mean a man should not presume to contrary her Highness's government: "Tush," said he, "Luther was but one man, and reformed all the world for religion, and I am that one man that must and will reform the government in this trade, meaning printing and bookselling."

During the next few years, dense with further protest and punctuated by the Star Chamber decree of 1586, the stationers' trade and, indeed, Wolfe himself, were reformed in ways that few could have imagined.

Meanwhile, following the death of John Day in 1584, Ponsonby and others imposed on the privilege of Richard Day, who had inherited his father's patents, by producing for sale within a year or so more than twenty-five thousand copies of *The ABC with Little Catechism,* a book that appeared in every schoolroom and most literate households of the realm. In two actions brought before the Star Chamber in 1585 – one directed at fifteen stationers alleged to have produced ten thousand copies and the other focused on Ponsonby and two other reputable stationers, each of whom had bought five thousand copies of *The ABC* – Richard Day sued the challengers of his patrimonial privilege.

Ponsonby's answer to the charges probably represented the opinions of most unprivileged members of the company. He admitted that he had bought the printed texts with "ready money," as any member of the company might have, but he denied that he was guilty. Claiming not to know that Day had inherited his father's patent, Ponsonby added that he did not know who had printed the books he bought and implied that they might have been legally printed by one of Day's assigns. Implying also that no such inherited privilege should have been legal anyway, Ponsonby expressed his main point: the effects of privilege on the poorer members of the company were devastating.

His argument, forthright but ingenious, insisted that Elizabeth would restrain her grants of privilege if she knew the extent to which they "enrich a few and by that means . . . take away the trade of living of a great multitude, which were a

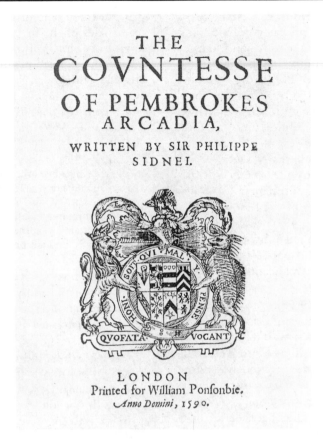

THE
COVNTESSE
OF PEMBROKES
ARCADIA,
WRITTEN BY SIR PHILIPPE
SIDNEI.

LONDON
Printed for William Ponſonbie.
Anno Domini, 1590.

*Title page for the "New Arcadia," which Sir Philip Sidney had
been revising but had failed to complete before his death*

decay to her Highness's commonwealth and to their utter undoing." Ponsonby urged the court to allow the commonalty of the company to print and sell at least *The ABC,* and he objected indignantly to the charge that he had "encouraged . . . lewd and evilly disposed persons, in contempt of . . . her highness's royal prerogative to imprint any of the said book." If Day remained convinced that his charge was just, Ponsonby suggested, Day should pursue the case at common law.

In addition to his pointed reply, Ponsonby, citing the same legal loophole as the other seventeen accused, entered a demurrer to Day's complaint: that the bill was void because Richard Grafton, who had signed it, had never been sergeant-at-law or reader in court. Judge suggests that Grafton "was being put in his place by an authorized member of the legal fraternity," Christopher Yelverton, the lawyer who was defending the obviously guilty on a technicality and thereby effectively undermining the power of royal patent. Shrewdly, high-handedly, and smugly rescinding no patents, the Star Chamber reacted to this noise from disgruntled stationers and bickering lawyers by throwing the whole mat-

ter into the hands of the power elite in the Stationers' Company.

On 23 June 1586 the Star Chamber enacted the most influential legislation on printing to appear during the reigns of Elizabeth and James I. Its decree regulated the numbers of printers and presses and made the company more responsible than ever for regulating production and enforcing the law. In essence, the new regulations and responsibilities made the powerful and privileged members of the company even more so, and they responded to various acts of piracy against patents as if they had shaped their attitudes from the Star Chamber: they fined some pirates, threatened others, and, as a gesture of good will, may have turned over a few patents to common production, as they had done in similar circumstances in 1584.

They also made John Wolfe – who would know the haunts and methods of his former cohorts in piracy – head enforcer, or beadle, of the company. He embraced energetically his new duties and grew increasingly powerful in the trade before his death in 1601. The company's new independence and apparent power made it more than ever a complicit arm of government regulation. At the same time, however, stricter regulation of copy within the company encouraged stationers to enter publications in the register, thereby strengthening the rights of all stationers to control their copy.

In November 1586, five months after the Star Chamber decree and a month after Sidney's death, Ponsonby made the most crucial decision of his career by informing on a fellow stationer who had submitted for licensing a manuscript of what is now known as Sidney's *Old Arcadia* (a manuscript version rediscovered only in 1907). Ponsonby conveyed this intelligence to Sidney's friend Fulke Greville, first lord Brooke, who on the same day wrote to Francis Walsingham, Sidney's father-in-law, to recount the episode and endorse the course of action suggested by "one Ponsonby, a bookbinder" – that is, to halt its publication by contacting the licensers of the press, Archbishop John Whitgift or Richard Cosin, who held the copy. Greville suggested that the family print the copy of *The Arcadia* (1590) that Sidney had been revising, the manuscript that Greville had sent to Walsingham's daughter Frances, Sidney's widow, at her request. Greville also argued that other works of Sidney should be printed, works that "require the care of his friends" to save them from the "common errors of mercenary printing."

At the time of his contact with Greville, Ponsonby's action might have seemed purely mercenary to some members of the company, for a dead author's unpublished works conventionally were fair game. Ponsonby could probably have sufficiently justified his conduct by invoking the inviolable memory of Sidney, but the fact remains that he used the influence of powerful people outside the company to gain advantage over a fellow stationer. The motivations and the implications of Ponsonby's action offer insights into the history of English publishing, particularly into the evolving concepts of copyright, intellectual property, and authorship. Following in the footsteps of bibliographers and legal historians, Brennan and Joseph F. Loewenstein, two recent investigators of these issues, reach complementary conclusions about how these issues impinge on Ponsonby's career.

Brennan outlines the means by which Ponsonby became the official publisher of Sidney and the Sidney circle, including his sister, the countess of Pembroke: Ponsonby established an innovative right to copy based on an understanding of mutual trust and common aims between the publisher and, in this case, the agents of the author. This author-publisher relationship was not new in the European

Initial letter from William Ponsonby's 1590 edition of Sidney's The Covntesse of Pembrokes Arcadia

print trade, but it became increasingly common in England during the 1590s, a fact that makes Ponsonby's example significant.

By advising Greville to contact the governmental licensers of the press, Ponsonby may merely have been directing him to the holders of copy. Yet, as Loewenstein argues, Ponsonby might also have held other motives. His action pitted his own still-imminent right to copy, garnered through independent negotiation, against the company's right to regulate publication of such copy by entry in the Stationers' Register. That is, if someone as powerful as Walsingham had not intervened, the company would have accepted as the absolute right to copy – despite any objection of author, heirs, or agents – that license and entry of the stationer whom Ponsonby exposed.

Thus, while initially circumventing and then relying on the regulatory power of the company, Ponsonby established the right to copy in an implicit agreement that whoever maintained such an understanding with the consent of the author's agents would hold the right to copy on future publications of the author's works. The fact that Sidney was dead, combined with the power of Sidney's heirs, limited the hopes that Ponsonby had for holding independently rights to copy, for he clearly had sought publishing power beyond both royal privilege and company regulation. As Loewenstein points out, Ponsonby more than once in his career – in his challenge to Day

Title page for Ponsonby's edition of Spenser's collected minor poems and partly rewritten juvenilia, published soon after the success of The Faerie Qyeene (1590)

and in his litigation against the pirated *Arcadia* of 1599 – demanded a ruling on rights to copy from the courts of common law. Ponsonby's innovation in copyright practice worked well with Spenser, who was still living while Ponsonby was publishing the poet's work; from Spenser he apparently secured conditional rights to copy on works unpublished and not yet produced. Whatever Ponsonby's aims beyond commercial success might have been, his interview with Greville assured his success.

On 29 June 1588 Ponsonby was clothed in the livery of the company, an honor accorded only about 16 percent of freedmen and one that opened the way for him to hold positions of responsibility in the company. Surely more significant to Ponsonby, whose success transcended company power, were his entries in the Stationers' Register on 23 August 1588: not only Greville's revised edition of

Sidney's *Arcadia*, but also Sidney's translation of the first *Semaine* of Sallust du Bartas's *Divine Weeks*, which encompassed 7,696 lines in Joshua Sylvester's 1605 version. For some reason Ponsonby apparently never published Sidney's du Bartas, for no known copy survives. Ponsonby, his influence established, stood poised to fashion his future, as he secured copy on the first three books of Spenser's *The Faerie Queene*, which he entered on 1 December 1589 and then published in 1590.

Between 1590 and 1596 he published thirty-five volumes – twenty-one of imaginative literature, almost all connected to the cultural legacy of Sidney. Having earned the favor and trust of Sidney's family and friends, Ponsonby cornered the market on publications related to Sidney. Beginning with the 1590 *New Arcadia,* with its apparent errors perhaps attributable to Greville's insistence on control of the text and the corrections of such errors made by the countess of Pembroke for the second edition in 1593, Ponsonby published virtually all of Sidney's literary work except the *Old Arcadia.* Beginning with the 1590 *Faerie Queene,* he published all of Spenser's poetry except *The Shepheardes Calender* (1579).

Then in 1591 he published two of Abraham Fraunce's experiments in English hexameters that recall those of the circle of literati (including Spenser, Greville, Gabriel Harvey, Daniel Rogers, Thomas Drant, and Edward Dyer) that had formed around Sidney in the late 1570s and early 1580s. These were followed by two translations from French – Philippe de Mornay's *Discourse of Life and Death* (1592) and Robert Garnier's *Antonius, a Tragedie* – both done by the countess of Pembroke and printed in a single volume (1592), and *Six Books of Politics or Civil Doctrine* (1594) by Justus Lipsius, Sidney's friend. Tied in spirit to Sidney and Spenser and reflecting Ponsonby's own aesthetic, political, and religious sympathies, other publications of this period include two editions of Walter Bigges's account of Sir Francis Drake's voyage to the West Indies (published in 1589 and 1596, each endorsing the aspirations of the second earl of Essex and his son); Richard Harvey's *A Theological Discourse of the Lamb of God and His Enemies* (1590), which both reconciled some animosities raised in the Martin Marprelate controversy and significantly instigated the war of words between Gabriel Harvey and Thomas Nashe; Sir Walter Ralegh's *A Report of the Truth of the Fight about the Iles of Azores This Last Summer, betwixt the Revenge, One of Her Majesties Shippes, and an Armada of the King of Spaine* (1591); Thomas Bedingfeld's translation of Niccolò Machiavelli's

The Florentine Historie (1595), Ponsonby's second folio volume; Adam Hill's Puritan *The Defence of the Article* (1592); Francesco Guicciardini's controversial *Two Discourses of Master F. G.* (1595), not included in the Florentine edition and printed, in columns of various type, in French, English, Latin, and Italian; Zachary Jones's translation of Jacques de Lavardin's *The Historie of George Castriot* (1596), a five-hundred-page folio including Spenser's commendatory sonnet; and George Chapman's enigmatic *The Shadow of Night: Containing Two Poeticall Hymnes* (1594).

During this time of multitudinous and no doubt often frenzied publication Ponsonby became acquainted with Spenser, as he published eight volumes of the poet's work – nearly 40 percent of Ponsonby's literary productions between 1590 and 1596. Unlike his formal and submissive relations with Sidney's family, Ponsonby's work with Spenser probably involved sincere friendship. The two men likely met in late 1589, drawn together by contacts in the Sidney circle or by Ralegh, Harvey, or even Wolfe, the last of whom was now a powerful legitimate stationer. Spenser and Ponsonby must have worked closely as *The Faerie Queene* proceeded through the press and may have begun soon after its publication to put together Spenser's *Complaints,* which appeared in 1591.

Ponsonby's preface to *Complaints* asserts the publisher's control of authorship, in a statement to which Spenser apparently acquiesced. At least, Ponsonby as publisher claims responsibility for putting together the volume in order to shield Spenser from possible controversy or embarrassment caused by the publication of these works. This preface distances the new epic poet from his disparate and potentially controversial volume and at the same time seeks to build an audience for his works, as parts of Ponsonby's preface reveal in this excerpt from *The Yale Edition of the Shorter Poems of Edmund Spenser* (1989):

> Since my late setting forth of the *Faerie Queene,* finding that it hath found a favorable passage amongst you, I have sithence endeavored by all good means (for the better increase and accomplishment of your delights) to get into my hands such small poems of the same author's as I had heard were dispersed abroad in sundry hands, and not easy to come by, by himself; some of them having been diversely embezzled and purloined from him, since his departure overseas. Of the which I have by good means gathered together these few parcels present, which I have caused to be imprinted altogether, for that they all seem to contain like matter of argument in them: being all complaints and meditations of the world's vanity, very grave and profitable.

Ponsonby promotes Spenser's volume by narrating a dramatic publishing event and goes on to advertise several of Spenser's lost works, which he hopes to publish soon. He closes by asking readers to "gently ... accept" the poems while they "graciously ... entertain" the new poet. Although Ponsonby and Spenser seldom saw each other during the six years of their commercial engagement, they seem to have understood and respected each other, and from their relationship remains Spenser's incomparable work.

While publishing Spenser, Ponsonby also spent much time protecting his exclusive right to Sidney's work, a privilege endorsed and defended by Sidney's heirs but challenged several times by unauthorized printings. After 1596 his reputation was firmly established, and his responsibilities with the Stationers' Company increasingly demanded his time. He served on the Stationers' Court of assistants from 6 May 1597 to 6 September 1602, and his duties increased when he served as an under warden from 1598 through 1599. Apparently these demands on his time did not suit him, for he paid a five-pound fine for declining to serve a second consecutive term as upper warden.

Between 1597 and 1604 he published only nineteen volumes, partly because of his company duties and partly because more than half of those volumes are lengthy, elaborate, expensive, and sometimes folio books, such as his 1598 edition of Sidney's works. These publications – most of them political, religious, philosophical, and martial works – attest to Ponsonby's consistent ideological sympathies and sustain his reputation for commercial and intellectual sophistication. Moreover, their dedications, as much as their authors and titles, reflect Ponsonby's prestige in the late-Elizabethan book trade. Richard Barckley, for example, dedicated to the queen his six-hundred-page *Discourse of the Felicity of Man* (1598). Robert Barret, in an elaborate tribute to the Herbert family, dedicated his handsome folio, *Theory and Practices of Modern War* (1598), to young William, lord Herbert. Richard Crompton dedicated his *Mansion of Magnanimitie* (1599) to the second earl of Essex, and amid complex prefatory matter, the translator of de Mornay's *Fowre Bookes, of the Institution, Use and Doctrine of the Holy Sacrament of the Eucharist in the Old Church* (1600) dedicated his nearly five-hundred-page folio to the lords of the Privy Council. For his impressive *An Historical Collection of the Continuall Factions, Tumults, and Massacres of the Romans and Italians* (1601) William Fulbecke composed a Latin dedication to Thomas Sackville. Philemon Holland's translation of Plutarch's *The Philosophie, Commonlie Called, the Morals* (1603) — an enormous, fourteen-hundred-page folio produced by a partnership of ten — was dedicated to King James I. Ponsonby's last and most elegant volume, with an engraved compartment title page, was Sir Clement Edmondes's *Observations upon Caesars Comentaries* (1604), dedicated to Prince Henry.

Ponsonby died soon afterward, for in September 1604 his rights to *Arcadia, The Faerie Queene,* and Edmondes's *Observations* were transferred to Simon Waterson, Ponsonby's brother-in-law. Ponsonby left an impressive legacy of publication, an achievement of remarkable historical significance not only because many of his books remain in print but also because his body of work provides an authoritative record of late-Elizabethan reading habits. As twentieth-century scholars continue to investigate the production of Ponsonby's fellow stationers, students of the period will be offered a more accurate and comprehensive picture of the Elizabethan age than any list of canonical texts can furnish.

Biography:

Michael Brennan, "William Ponsonby: Elizabethan Stationer," *Analytical and Enumerative Bibliography,* 7, no. 3 (1983): 91–110.

References:

H. S. Bennett, *English Books and Readers 1558–1603: Being a Study in the History of the Book Trade in the Reign of Elizabeth I* (Cambridge: Cambridge University Press, 1965);

Cyprian Blagden, *The Stationers' Company: A History, 1403–1959* (London: Allen & Unwin, 1960);

Victor Bonham-Carter, *Authors by Profession: From the Introduction of Printing until the Copyright Act of 1911* (London: Society of Authors, 1978);

Michael Brennan, *Literary Patronage in the English Renaissance: The Pembroke Family* (London: Routledge, 1988);

G. W. Bromiley, ed. and trans., *Zwingli and Bullinger* (Philadelphia: Westminster, 1953);

Elizabeth L. Eisenstein, *The Printing Press as an Agent of Change: Communications and Cultural Transformations in Early-Modern Europe,* 2 volumes (Cambridge: Cambridge University Press, 1979);

W. Craig Ferguson, *Pica Roman Type in Elizabethan England* (Aldershot: Scolar, 1989);

Philip Gaskell, *A New Introduction to Bibliography* (Oxford: Oxford University Press, 1972);

P. M. Handover, *Printing in London: From 1476 to Modern Times* (London: Allen & Unwin, 1960);

Clifford Chalmers Huffman, *Elizabethan Impressions: John Wolfe and His Press* (New York: AMS, 1988);

Alfred Forbes Johnson, *A Catalogue of Engraved and Etched Title-Pages Down to the Death of William Faithorne in 1691* (London: Bibliographical Society, 1934);

Cyril Bathurst Judge, *Elizabethan Book-Pirates* (Cambridge, Mass.: Harvard University Press, 1934);

John N. King, *English Reformation Literature: The Tudor Origins of the Protestant Tradition* (Princeton: Princeton University Press, 1982);

Joseph Loewenstein, "For a History of Literary Property: John Wolfe's Reformation," *English Literary Renaissance,* 18 (Autumn 1988): 389–412;

Ronald B. McKerrow, *Printers' and Publishers' Devices in England and Scotland, 1485–1640* (London: Bibliographical Society, 1913);

McKerrow and F. S. Ferguson, *Title-Page Borders Used in England and Scotland, 1485–1640* (London: Bibliographical Society, 1932);

Edwin Haviland Miller, *The Professional Writer in Elizabethan England: A Study of Nondramatic Literature* (Cambridge, Mass.: Harvard University Press, 1959);

Harry Ransom, *The First Copyright Statute: An Essay on* An Act for the Encouragement of Learning, *1710* (Austin: University of Texas Press, 1956);

Phoebe Sheavyn, *The Literary Profession in the Elizabethan Age,* second edition, revised by J. W. Saunders (Manchester: Manchester University Press, 1967).

— Wayne Erickson

John Rastell

(London: 1509? – 1536?)

William Rastell

(London: 1529 – 1534)

See also the John Rastell entry in *DLB 136: Sixteenth-Century British Nondramatic Writers, Second Series*.

John Rastell belongs to the circle of humanists who flourished during the first decades of the reign of Henry VIII. Although he is primarily known today as the author of dramatic interludes as well as two prose works, *The Pastyme of People* (1529) and *A new boke of Purgatory* (1530), he also participated in religious controversies, served as a government lawyer, helped design the Field of the Cloth of Gold and other political spectacles, tried to be the first Englishman to colonize the New World, and designed the first permanent theater in England.

Born probably in 1475 into a politically prominent family in Coventry, Rastell's early years are obscure, although he may have studied at Oxford. He spent several years in London reading law as a member of the Middle Temple, and probably during this period he met Sir Thomas More, who was also then studying law at Lincoln's Inn.

After completing his legal studies, Rastell returned home to take up a practice established by his father and grandfather. He married Elizabeth More, sister of Thomas More; fathered three children (William, John, and Joan); took part in local politics; and generally prospered. In 1509–1510, for reasons that remain unclear but probably involved a decline in the economy of Coventry, his increasing ambitions, and his increasing involvement with More and his circle, Rastell and his family moved to London. He

found a patron in the privy councillor to both Henry VII and Henry VIII, Sir Edward Belknap, who employed him as an overseer for various building projects. This may seem to have been an odd endeavor for a lawyer, but Rastell was versatile. Shortly after his move Rastell took up a second vocation: he established a publishing house, which contributed significantly to the development of printing – especially the printing of music.

Rastell served in the French war of 1512–1514, in which he was responsible for transporting artillery. He probably learned the printer's trade during this period, and he returned to France during 1515–1516 to procure the font of secretary type that he used in printing his law books. Why Rastell chose to add publishing to his many occupations remains something of a mystery. If he foresaw possible opportunities for enjoying great financial returns, he may have wanted to establish himself before others did. If he were fired by humanist notions that education would solve everyone's problems, he might have considered publishing useful books to be a means of enriching both the commonwealth and himself. In any event Rastell clearly considered publishing sufficiently important to include one "Thomas Bercula, printer," among the group that he organized in his attempt to colonize the New World, an adventure that ended in a debacle in 1517: the crew mutinied, leaving Rastell stranded in Ireland.

In *The Pastyme of People* Rastell's comments on the consequences of the invention of printing suggest that, after a lifetime in the trade, he still viewed publishing as an instrument of both learning and social change. "[T]he craft of printing of books," he wrote there, "began in the city of Almaign named Magonce which is now marvelously increased which hath been cause of great learning and knowledge and hath been the cause of many things and great changes & is like to be the cause of many strange things hereafter to come."

Perhaps because of Rastell's initial training and livelihood, the first two books he printed were aimed at lawyers: an edition of John Stanbridge's *Accidence* (1509) and a yearbook of statutes for Edward V and Richard III (1509). Rastell's interest in publishing legal texts continued throughout his career, and although legal publishing seems aimed at a specialized audience with particular interests, Rastell intended his texts for a broader audience and for broader purposes. He was the first to publish an abridgment of the statutes in English, and he did so as a public service. As he writes in *The Statutes Prohemium* (1519),

> Because that the laws of the realm of England as well as the statutes as other judgements and decress, be made and written most commonly in the French ton[g]ue: divers men thereof muse and have oftentimes communicacion and argument: considering that in reason every law whereto any people should be bounden ought and should be written in such manner and so openly published and declared that the people might soon without great difficulty have the knowledge of the same laws.

Consequently, Rastell published many translations of statutes and legal terminology from French into English, and they remained in print well into the seventeenth century.

The beginning dates and the sites of his publishing enterprise are not certain. The last page of one of his first books states that the work was "Imprinted by John Rastell dwelling at the Fleet Bird at the abbot of Winchcombe his place." Sometime between 1510 and 1519 Rastell established his publishing house at the south side of St. Paul's Cathedral, where he produced most of the books that historians and bibliographers attribute to his press.

Rastell's publishing venture began modestly. In the revised edition of Alfred W. Pollard and Gilbert R. Redgrave's *A Short-Title Catalogue of Books Printed in England, Scotland and Ireland* (1986), W. A. Jackson, F. S. Ferguson, and Katherine F. Pantzer indicate that between 1509 and 1525 Rastell published between one and three books a year. Perhaps the most notable of his early productions was More's translation of Gianfrancesco Pico's *Here Is Conteyned the Lyfe of Iohan Picus Erle of Myrandula . . . with Dyuere Epistles & Other Warkis of the Seyd Johan*

Picus (1510?). Although Rastell specialized in printing legal texts – such as Sir Anthony Fitzherbert's *Tabula prime(–tertie) partis magni abbreviameti libroru legu angloru* (1517), *An Abridgement of Statutes* (1519), and *The exposicions of the termys of ye law of England* (1526) – he also published an array of other books on topics such as grammar, medicine, literature, music, and marriage: Thomas Linacre's *Linacri progymnasmata Grammatices vulgaria* (1525?), Henry Medwall's *Here is coteyned a godely interlude of Fulgens cenatoure of Rome, Lucres his doughter* (1520?), William Harrington's *In this boke are conteyned the comendacions of matrymony* (1528), Aelius Donatus's *de octo partiubus orationis* (1515), and his own *A new interlude and a mery of the nature of the iii elements* (1520?).

Beginning in 1525 production at Rastell's press increased significantly. That year he published eight books; in 1529, nine books; and in 1530, clearly a banner year, twelve books – again, a diverse range of works. In addition to legal texts these included such anonymous works as *The Seeing of Urine* (1526); *One Hundred Merry Tales* (1526); the verse romance, *Sir Eglamour* (1528); various books by John Skelton, including *Divers Ballads and Ditties Solacious* (1528) and *Magnyfycence* (1533); and More's opening salvo against Lutheranism, *A Dyaloge of Syr Thomas More Knyghte* (1529). Rastell also published his own prose works – *A new boke of Purgatory* and a world history, *The Pastyme of People* – as well as his dramatic interlude, *A New Comedy on Beauty and Good Property of Women* (1525). Rastell also published Lucian's dialogue, *Necromantia* (circa 1525); Walter Smyth's jestbook on the More circle, *The Widow Edith* (1525); Geoffrey Chaucer's *The Parliament of Fowls* (1525; the first installment of an edition that Rastell never completed); and Miles Coverdale's *Ghostly Psalmses and Spiritual Songs* (1535).

In addition to missing colophons and the fragmentary condition of some texts, Rastell's habits of leaving his press for months at a time and allowing others to use both his press and his printing sign, The Mermaid, have confused bibliographers and historians seeking to ascertain exactly which texts he published. Rastell seems to have had printing relationships with Richard Bankes, Peter Tereveris, and John Gough, but as Pollard and Redgrave write, the nature of their relationships "has been largely unexplored, and how much he was involved in later items using his type and even his devices is unclear."

Consequently, bibliographers have had to rely on other means for determining the facts of his production. For example, Pollard and Redgrave assign Stanbridge's *Accidence* to Rastell's press because the colophon states that the book was printed at the sign of the "meare mayde," but this fact does not necessarily signify the same as a colophon statement of "Rastell me fecit." And there are other problems. *The Book of the New Cards* (1530), which showed how to use playing cards to learn how to read, identifies no publisher but has been assigned to Rastell's press because he was interested in education and because the type used in the book is the same as that used for Rastell's printing of the government document *Liber Assisarum* (1530), in which he urges readers to "read truely the numbers of algorisme." Similarly, because Rastell published *One Hundred Merry Tales* and Smyth's *The Widow Edith*, *The Book of One Hundred Riddles* (1526) has been assigned to Rastell's press on the basis of his interest in jestbooks and the similarity of the type used in it and in other Mermaid productions.

Rastell's publication of Chaucer's *Parliament of Fowls* is of little significance to Chaucer scholars, but it does reflect the interest in Chaucer among humanists. Rastell prefaced his edition with his own verses in rhyme-royal, his only attempt at writing nondramatic verse. In the fourth stanza of this preface Rastell suggests that he is the first to print the poem ("I have it achieved / And it published and made to be printed"), which implies that Rastell was unaware of William Caxton's earlier edition. Perhaps Rastell worked from a corrupt manuscript, but one reason that his text has been ignored by Chaucer's editors is that, for the sake of propriety, Rastell completely rewrote stanza 38 in order to remove the indelicate discovery of Venus disporting with her porter Richesse.

Although Rastell published only two pieces of music – a fragmentary broadside ballad, *Away, Morning* (1525), and a short, three-part song included in an edition of his play *The Four Elements* (1520?) – his achievements – as printer of the earliest broadside with music, the earliest song printed in an English dramatic work, and the first musical score – merit places of honor in publishing history. Previously the printer had to make two or three impressions, and this procedure made books very beautiful but very expensive. Rastell's technical achievement was to discover a process by which text, staves, notes, clefs, lines for bars, and time signatures were printed at the same time, an achievement all the more notable because no one knows where Rastell had acquired his music type. Although some of his workmen probably knew how to set music, A. Hyatt King finds it unlikely that any had the technical skill actually to create the type. Yet, as King writes, from neither France nor England "does any music survive in this type, nor does it resemble any other extant face used [in Rouen] or elsewhere."

Rastell's interest in typographical experimentation also appears in his *The Pastyme of People,* which recounts the history of Europe, although his primary focus is clearly on England – from its mythological origins through the Roman and Anglo-Saxon periods, up to the death of Richard III. As an added attraction, he includes some fairly crude woodcuts of English monarchs. Rather than separating the various histories into discrete chapters, Rastell devised a novel typographical arrangement. By setting out his history in horizontal columns on each page, he thus intertwines the history of England with other narratives. As his narrative frequently breaks off in midsentence to begin another narrative, Rastell enables his reader to discern at a glance the state of Europe in any given year.

When T. F. Didbin published his edition of *Pastyme* in 1811, he rearranged the entire book "in regular order," for he felt that Rastell had succeeded only in befuddling the reader:

> Rastell's impression [is so] confusedly arranged, that the Reader find [*sic*] himself at Rome, Paris, and London, in the same page, and mixing foreigners and Englishmen, before he knows where he is, or can remember preceding events.

However, this work, along with *A new boke of Purgatory,* is now available in a modern edition that restores Rastell's original typographical arrangement.

Rastell's son William who was born circa 1508, joined his father's publishing house around 1526 and worked there until 1529, when he established his own business. As his father had done, William trained as a lawyer, maintained a successful practice, and published legal texts such as abridgments of contemporary statutes. The younger Rastell shared some of his father's other publishing interests as well, such as humanism, travel literature, history, jestbooks, and drama. He printed translations of Julius Caesar's *Commentaries* (1530) and Cicero's *Tullius de amicicia, in Englysh* (1530?), for example, and Damião de Goes's *The Legacy or Embassy of Prester John unto Emanuel King of Portugal* (1533). He also printed Robert Fabyan's *Fabyan's Cronycle newly printed* (1533), which John Rastell would use as a major source for his *The Pastyme of People,* and jestbooks such as *The Book of a Hundred Riddles* (1530). Among his dramatic publications were Henry Medwall's *Nature: A goodly interlude of Nature* (1530) and John Heywood's *A mery playe, be-*

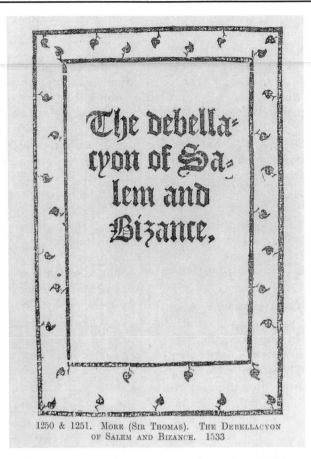

The debella-
cyon of Sa-
lem and
Bizance.

1250 & 1251. MORE (SIR THOMAS). THE DEBELLACYON
OF SALEM AND BIZANCE. 1533

Title page for one of four books by Sir Thomas More, William Rastell's uncle, that appeared with the Rastell imprint in 1533

tween Johan Johan, the husband, Tyb, his wife, and Syr Jhan, the preest (1533), *A mery playe betwene the pardoner and the frere, the curate and neybour Pratte* (1533), and *The Play of the Weather* (1533).

The two Rastells differed radically, however, in religious matters, and their differences influenced their contributions to publishing. John initially had opposed the Protestant reformers and intended his *A new boke of Purgatory* to rebut the heresies of reformers such as John Frith of Cambridge. No doubt to Rastell's dismay, his work received little notice until Frith refuted it, along with the views of More and Bishop John Fisher, in *A disputacion of Purgatorye* (1533?). More and Fisher ignored Frith's attack, but Rastell responded to it with a further book on purgatory that has been lost, and he may have spoken personally with his antagonist. Frith, by then imprisoned in the Tower of London, answered with *An other boke against Rastel named the subsedye or bulwark to his fyrst boke made by Jhon Frithe, presoñer in the Tower* (1533?). As John Foxe reports in his *Actes and Monuments* (1563), this quarrel proved to be unlike most others, for Frith actually succeeded in convinc-

ing his opponent of the error of his ways: John Rastell converted to Protestantism.

At first his new religion was advantageous, for it followed the government's drift. Rastell found a patron in Thomas Cromwell, who regularly commissioned him to do administrative work, and by 1534 Rastell reached the height of his success when Cromwell appointed him and Roland Lee, bishop of Lichfield and Coventry, to crush a rebellion in Wales. The same year, however, Rastell suffered another financial crisis, lost his house in Monken Hadley, and became embroiled in a series of lawsuits. Perhaps thinking that returning to printing would relieve his financial problems, he proposed many schemes – including one book on how religious laws affected the courts and another book of prayers in English – but neither project went beyond the planning stages. Having become a radical reformer, Rastell in 1535 attempted to convert the monks of London's Charterhouse, much to their derisive laughter.

Rastell's Protestantism unfortunately led to his downfall. Shortly after Henry VIII had executed

More for refusing to grant the supremacy of the king in religious affairs, the government threw Rastell into the Tower for refusing to pay tithes and for arguing that the clerisy should live on free offerings, not tithes – a position dangerously more radical than that of the government. A defeated man and a prisoner, Rastell died of natural causes in 1536.

William Rastell, on the other hand, remained firmly on the side of Catholicism. His antireformist attitudes are evident throughout his publishing of works such as William Barlow's *A Dialogue Describing the Original Ground of the Lutheran Factions* (1531), John Fisher's *Here after ensueth two fruytfull Sermons* (1532), Germen Gardynare's *A letter of a yong gentylman . . . wherein men may se the demeanour and heresy of Johñ Fryth* (1534), and Fridericus Nausea's *A Sermon of the Sacrament of the Alter* (1533). This last work was translated by John More, and it indicates the closeness of William Rastell's ties to the More family. Indeed, Rastell's significance in the history of publishing stems from his devotion to his uncle, Sir Thomas More. Perhaps having sensed John Rastell's shifting religious allegiances, Thomas More had begun to transfer much of his publishing work to William Rastell's house. In 1529 Rastell published More's *The Supplication of Souls;* in 1533 he printed four of More's polemical works – *The apologye of syr Thomas More knyght, The second parte of the cofutacion of Tyndals answere, The debellacyon of Salem and Bizance,* and *A letter of syr Tho. More knyght impugnynge the erronyouse wrytyng of John Fryth.* In 1534, William Rastell's last year as an independent publisher, he produced More's *The answere to the fyrst parte of the poysened booke.*

This last publication put him into a potentially lethal situation. By 1534 More's refusal to countenance Henry VIII's divorce of Catharine of Aragon had become intolerable to the government, which was looking for an excuse to charge More with treason. The king's council that year had compiled a book accusing Pope Clement VII of bastardy, heresy, and other offenses, and someone had published a book attacking this volume. Cromwell, secretary to Henry VIII, summoned William Rastell to charge him with having published this work, and although the matter did not proceed further, Rastell was not convinced that Cromwell altogether believed him, and he asked More to write to the lord chancellor to clear his name. Taking this opportunity to clear his own name as well, More wrote the letter. As the year 1534 marks the end of William Rastell's imprint, though, it is hard not to speculate that William's brush with the law at this time con-

vinced him to abandon the publishing trade as too dangerous.

No record exists of how John and William Rastell got along during this period, but John's irascibility and the fact that William was publishing works by those whom John was seeking to rebut suggest that relations were strained, at best. One can only guess how the father reacted when Cromwell, his patron, accused Rastell's son of heresy. Whatever the relations were within the Rastell family, William certainly fared better in life than his father did, even if the authorities were ultimately no more enamored of the Catholic son than they were of the radical Protestant father. No doubt seeking to avoid further religious controversy, William was to thrive as a lawyer. He was called to the bar in 1539 and made an autumn reader at Lincoln's Inn in 1547, the same year that Henry VIII died. The change in monarchs, however, brought a more rigorously Protestant kingdom, and this England became intolerable for such a devoted Catholic. Soon after the accession of Edward VI in 1547, William left England to live in Louvain, and he returned to resume his legal and political career only when the Catholic Mary Tudor became queen.

In 1557 William edited *The workes of Sir Thomas More Knyght, sometyme Lorde Chauncellour of England, wrytten by him in the Englysh tonge,* which Dale B. Billingsley calls a "painstaking treatment of his uncle's works." About 157 copies of this beautiful book survive today, and because Rastell worked as much from More's papers as from his publications, this text is so dependable that it forms the basis for much of the Yale edition of More's collected works. The book was more than a personal testimonial; it was intended, and was understood, as a highly politicized declaration of Catholic supremacy, a memorial to one of the church's most visible martyrs, and a celebration of Mary's vision of an England restored to the true church. As Rastell wrote in dedicating it to the queen, More's writings "forward your Majesty's most godly purpose, in purging this your realm of all wicked heresies" – such as Protestantism. Rastell's editorial intention to fashion More as a Catholic martyr is especially evident in the last three hundred pages, in which Dale B. Billingsley finds that Rastell designed the volume in order to "accent More's spiritual development and to minimize the immediate political circumstances of his death."

It is interesting that although John and William Rastell used their printing presses to support opposite sides in the English Reformation, both shared an interest in promoting the use of the English language. William's edition of More's works quite deliberately excludes the Latin books of his uncle – even the work for which More is best known today, *Utopia* (1516) – partly because Rastell was interested in promoting the "eloquence and property of the English tongue," as Billingsley concludes. John Rastell had maintained the same purpose in his publishing of Chaucer.

In 1558 Mary I advanced William to a puisne judgeship, and until he retired in 1563 he continued in that position under Elizabeth I, who evidently did not hold his religion against him. William Rastell then moved back to Louvain, where he died on 27 August 1565 and was buried beside his wife.

Bibliography:
Albert J. Geritz, "Recent Studies in John Rastell," *English Literary Renaissance,* 8 (Winter 1978): 341–350.

References:
Joseph Ames, *Typographical Antiquities, or The History of Printing in England, Scotland, and Ireland,* edited by T. F. Didbin (Hildesheim, Germany: Olms, 1969);

Dale B. Billingsley, "The Editorial Design of the 1557 *English Works,*" *Moreana,* 23, no. 89 (1986): 39–48;

E. J. Devereaux, "John Rastell's Press in the English Reformation," *Moreana,* 13, no. 49 (1976): 29–47;

Devereaux, "John Rastell's Text of *The Parliament of Fowls,*" *Moreana,* 7, no. 27 (1970): 115–120;

A. G. Dickens, *The English Reformation* (London: Batsford, 1964);

Albert J. Geritz and Amos Lee Lane, *John Rastell* (Boston: G. K. Hall, 1983);

Peter C. Herman, "Early English Protestantism and Renaissance Poetics: The Charge Is Committing Fiction in the Matter of Rastell v. Frith," *Renaissance and Reformation,* 18 (Winter 1994): 5–18;

A. Hyatt King, "The Significance of John Rastell in Early Music Printing," *Library,* fifth series 26 (September 1971): 197–214;

Richard Marius, *Thomas More* (New York: Knopf, 1984);

Thomas More, *St. Thomas More: Selected Letters,* edited by Elizabeth Frances Rogers (New Haven & London: Yale University Press, 1961);

H. L. Plomer, "John Rastell and His Contemporaries," *Bibliographica,* 2 (Fall 1896): 437–451;

A. W. Reed, *Early Tudor Drama: Medwall, the Rastells, Heywood, and the More Circle* (London: Methuen, 1926);

Reed, "The Editor of Sir Thomas More's English Works: William Rastell," *Library,* 4 (June 1924): 25–49.

– Peter C. Herman

Richard Royston

(London: 1628 – 1686)

Richard Royston – the future Royalist publisher; stationer to Charles I, Charles II, and James II; and master of the Stationers' Company – was baptized on either 14 or 15 October 1601 in St. Peter in the East, Oxford. If the usual three-day interval between birth and baptism was maintained in his case, Royston – the eldest child of a prosperous Oxford tradesman – was thus born on either 11 or 12 October. His father, also named Richard, was a tailor and an important civic figure in Oxford, particularly in the parish of St. Peter in the East. The family members of Royston's mother, the Tidemans (or Titemans), were also tailors who were influential in civic and parish affairs. Although the location of the Roystons' house is unknown, if they lived within the parish bounds of St. Peter in the East, they would have lived in the heart of academic Oxford, with Queen's, Merton, Magdalen, and New Colleges; Oxford University; and St. Edmund Hall as neighbors. The Bodleian Library was in its first stage of development and was opened in the year after Royston's birth, and the whole quadrangle was completed four years after he had gone off to London as an apprentice stationer.

On 3 February 1617 Royston was bound for a nine-year apprenticeship to Josias Harrison. However, the court book of the Stationers' Company on 7 February 1619 records that

> whereas John Piper hath kept disorderly in his house Richard Reston [Royston], which was bound to Josias Harrison and not turned ou' to him, and for [that] the father of the said Richard Reston did desire to haue him away and the said John Piper was willing likewise to parte wth the said appr', the matter was referred to the Table, and it is order that the said John Piper shall pay vnto the mr Reston xvij *li* of the xx *li* that he had with him.

It is hard to explain how Royston, apprenticed to one stationer, could have been kept in the house of another, but Harrison entered only four books in his entire career, all in 1615 and 1616. He disposed of all these copyrights in April and May 1619, and after 1 May 1619 his name vanishes from the records of the book trade. Apparently Harrison was never really in business on his own and was in no

position to train an apprentice, while Piper was a moderately active stationer until the mid 1620s. On 28 June 1619 the whole matter was rectified: the original apprenticeship entry of 1617 was crossed out, and Royston was bound for seven years to John Grismond.

After this shaky start with Harrison and Piper, a start that at least taught Royston some problems of marginal publishing and bookselling operations, his seven years with John Grismond taught him to be a successful man of business. Grismond had begun his freedom in the company on 2 December 1616 and by 1618 had established himself in a shop called The Gun, near the Little North Door of St. Paul's Cathedral, before he moved to another shop, also The Gun, in St. Paul's Alley in 1621.

What made Grismond successful, and what appears to have made nearly all stationers successful during the seventeenth century, was being a member of trade associations with other printers and publishers, a practice Royston was to follow in his career. One of Grismond's closest associates was John Marriott, who had been freed the same year as Grismond and who was the publisher of Nicholas Breton, John Donne, Michael Drayton, Philip Massinger, Francis Quarles, George Wither, and many others. Grismond was both a typefounder and a printer, although his name appears in no known imprint as a printer, so Royston must have been broadly trained in the printing and selling of books. Many of the authors and stationers associated with Grismond were also to be associated with Royston during his career. Grismond and Marriott traded particularly in religious literature, but Grismond, often in association with other stationers, entered and/or published the works of Lancelot Andrewes, Donne, and Wither and the second part of Drayton's *Poly-Olbion* (1622).

Although some kinds of literature and book trade operations in which Royston would have been trained are known, little is known about daily life in the trade. Grismond is recorded as having only one other apprentice during Royston's apprenticeship, and Royston must therefore have performed the full range of apprentice duties: minding the shop and serving customers; running errands; fetching stock

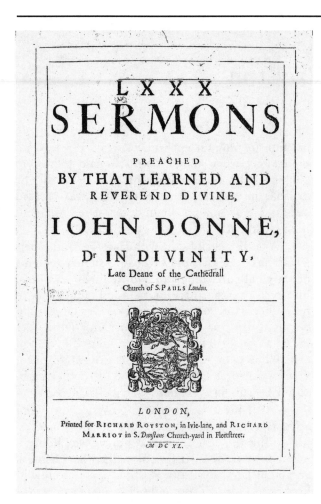

Title page for a collection of John Donne's sermons, as well as the first publication of Isaac Walton's "The Life and Death of Dr Donne" (courtesy of the Lilly Library, Indiana University)

and store in the warehouse; perhaps assisting the master when books were taken to Stationers' Hall for entry; and even, in this particular shop, helping to cast the type. The apprenticeship system of the Stationers' Company had been separated into printing and nonprinting responsibilities, but Grismond, being both a typefounder and a bookseller-publisher, would have provided Royston with a wider and more technical knowledge than that gained by nonprinting apprentices.

The close geographical bounds of the London book trade at this time no doubt also shaped Royston's orientation to the trade. When Grismond moved his shop from the Little North Door of St. Paul's to Paul's Alley, he moved no more than 200 feet, and when Royston set up shop in Ivy Lane after gaining his freedom, he moved no more than 150 feet from the shop where he had been apprenticed. Peter W. M. Blayney gives a clear understanding of how members of the trade were crowded together, and a bright and alert young apprentice must have intensely observed and absorbed the intricacies of the trade in such a setting.

On 6 August 1627 Royston was sworn and admitted as a freeman of the Stationers' Company, and during the next year he set up shop in Ivy Lane at the sign of the Angel. This remained his business address until he was burned out by the Great Fire in 1666, and imprints of three works describe this address as "next the Exchequer Office," which would mean that it was just a little more than halfway along Ivy Lane. It is impossible to tell how a twenty-five-year-old stationer such as Royston got his business started, but the influence of members of the Royston family, still prominent in Oxford municipal and parish records during the first half of the century, may have helped.

The first appearance of Royston's name in a printed book is also revealing. In three copies of John Grent's *The burthen of Tyre: A sermon preach'd at Paul's Crosse* (1627) a variant imprint "for R. Royston" appears, but the main imprint for this book is "for John Grismand." Thus, Royston's master, who had freed him in this year, may also have assisted him in setting up his business.

Whatever the case, in 1629 Royston began his publishing career alone when on 26 January he entered "An Elegie upon the Death of the most hopefull Prince HENRY Eldest sonne to his Maiestie of Bohemia." This sixteen-stanza poem by R. Abbey was published later in the year as a single-sheet broadside with the imprint in the lower right corner: "*LONDON,* | Printed for *Richard* | *Roystore* [*sic*]." This was not an auspicious beginning, but it foreshadowed much about Royston's career: Henry was the eldest son of Elizabeth of Bohemia, the daughter of James I and sister of Charles I, and Royston was to remain loyal to the Stuart cause and the Church of England – frequently at his considerable financial and personal cost.

Often dealing with two or three generations of the same family, Royston quickly built relationships with several stationers, such as Roger Norton I and Roger Norton II, and John Grismond I and John Grismond II. On 6 September 1629 he bound his first apprentice, a James Weaver, and on 1 October 1629 he made his first joint entry – of John Evans's *The Sacrifice of a contrite heart* – with Francis Coules. This work was published in 1630 but with neither Royston nor Coules identified in the imprint.

From 1630 to 1640 Royston built up an interesting and considerable list of publications and copyrights of important authors. Many of these publications were religious works, most notably

Donne's *LXXX Sermons* (1640), which Royston owned and published jointly with Miles Flesher and Richard Marriott; Royston was also later to be involved in publishing Donne's *Fifty Sermons. The Second Volume* (1649). In 1638 he acted as the seller of the fifth edition of Donne's *Devotions on Emergent Occasions,* although he did not own the copyright. Royston also seems to have taken some interest in the drama, for he eventually owned, though he did not publish, William Berkeley's *The Lost Lady* (1638), and he owned and published the two parts of Thomas Heywood's *The Fair Maid of the West* (1631). Along with his old master Grismond and four other stationers, he also owned and published one of the most important emblem books of the century, George Wither's *Emblems Ancient and Modern* (1635).

His first best-seller appeared in 1630, when he entered and published *A Banquet of Jeasts. Or Change of Cheare. Being a Collection of Moderne Jests. Witty Jeeres. Pleasant Taunts. Merry Tales.* No author of this collection of 195 jests is identified, and the preface is signed "Anonimos," but this book, which is usually attributed to an A. Armstrong, eventually became known as part 1. Subsequent editions or "impressions" of it, with widely varying contents, followed in 1632, 1634, 1636, and 1639. In 1633 a second part, containing 200 jests, was published, and this may also have appeared in a second edition in 1636. The two parts were then published in a combined edition in 1640 with their contents much rearranged. *A Banquet* demonstrates another characteristic of Royston's career – his tendency to work with one printer through multiple printings of a given title, if it were at all possible to do so: except for the 1639 edition, Miles Flesher was the printer for all of these editions for which a printer is listed.

By 1640 Royston appears to have become an established stationer with sound connections in the trade. However, with the outbreak of the Civil War in 1642 Royston was presented with several difficulties. First, the English book trade was centered almost entirely in London, which early became the parliamentary capital. For a man of Royston's strong Royalist and Anglican opinions, life and business might have grown difficult: besides the threat that the government posed for him, strong parliamentary sympathies existed within the Stationers' Company. Second, because Oxford had become the Royalist capital, getting bundles of printed materials from Oxford to London and thereby across what was the only front line of this war might be dangerous.

In any case, Royston continued to print as he had intended. Charles I declared war on 22 August 1642, and on 14 September George Thomason notes in his *Catalogue of the Pamphlets, Books, Newspapers, and Manuscripts Relating to the Civil War, the Commonwealth, and Restoration, . . . 1640–1661* that *Proquiritatio,* an anti-Parliament pamphlet, "was scattered up and down London the 14 & 15, & suppressed by an order 16th Sept." Royston's name alone appeared boldly in the imprint, yet the confused state of affairs brought no repercussions for him at this time. During the next few years he began to acquire copyrights for and to publish the works of a few high-Anglican divines, particularly Jeremy Taylor and Henry Hammond, for whom he would become virtually the sole publisher. They had much to recommend themselves to Royston, to the circle of Royalist stationers to which he belonged, and presumably to his customers. Both Taylor and Hammond were chaplains to Charles I; both were apparently with the king's armies in the field; and both were prolific writers, although Taylor became a much more popular author than Hammond.

But in a few years Royston pushed his luck too far, as this entry from the House of Lords calendar for 31 July 1645 makes clear:

> Petition of John Wright, printer to the House. About two years ago he printed a small book called the Soldier's Catechism [1644, by Robert Ram], composed for the Parliament army, but some mischievous person [Henry Hall, an Oxford stationer] has published under the same title a book charging the Houses of Parliament with rebellion, treason, and the like. [This book was Thomas Swadlin's *Souldier's Catechism* (1645), which Hall had published.] Petitioner prays that Richard Royston may be sent for, to give an account of the printing of the book, as he is the vendor of it, and the constant factor for all other scandalous books and papers against the proceeding of Parliament.

The outcome was predictable. Two weeks later, on 15 August, the following is recorded in the same calendar:

> Petition of Richard Royston, now a prisoner in the Fleet. Acknowledges the justice of his sentence, and will be very careful not to offend in like kind again. Has no one to follow his trade and support his wife and children but himself, and therefore prays their Lordships in their clemency to discharge him of his imprisonment.

Apparently his petition was granted, for on 15 October 1645 he entered Henry Hammond's *Of Conscience* (1645) in the Stationers' Register. He was to fail in keeping his vows of good conduct, yet troubles for Royston developed even more quickly with his fellow stationers.

On 17 March 1646 he entered Sir Christopher Hatton and Jeremy Taylor's *The Psalter of David* (1646), a devotional manual with prayers, collects, and devotions as well as the official translation of the Psalms. Leonard Lichfield had originally published this work (without having made a copyright entry) at Oxford in 1644, and Royston's publication of it caused problems because the text incorporated some of the Authorized Version of the Bible – the copyright to which was held, in part, by the Stationers' Company. On 14 December 1646 at a meeting of the company's court Royston was to be summoned before the court concerning "the printing of our Psalms."

On 18 January 1647 Royston appeared before the court and submitted himself to the will of the court. There it was

> put to the voate whether hee should pay either these three Sumes, vizt 20£. 30£. or 40£. a thousand bookes, for the said impression already printed. It was by the maior part voated he should pay [£30] a thousand for this impression, and vpon leave first obteyned of this Co[u]rt after the same rate for another Impression of the same booke if he shall desire it.

On 5 February Royston returned to the court, declared that he had printed 1,250 copies of *The Psalter of David,* paid a fine of £30. 7s. 6d., and asked leave to print another edition. The court agreed that he could do so at the same rate, if he would first indicate how many copies he would print and who the printer would be.

There is no evidence that he did either of these things. He certainly did print another edition in 1647, but perhaps the tumult of the close of the Civil War during 1647–1649 kept the company from taking any action. Binding one apprentice in 1647 and two apprentices in 1648 (indications that his business was not a small one), he appears to have continued his normal business activities. He continued to enter and publish books, although if they were too controversial he often omitted his name from the imprints.

Despite such discretion, however, political events began to ensnare him toward the end of 1648. The king, a prisoner of the Parliament, was moved from castle to castle until he arrived at Windsor on 23 December 1648. *Eikon Basilike,* a work supposedly written by Charles I during his imprisonment, appeared shortly thereafter, although John Nichols in *Literary Anecdotes* (1812) reports that Royston had been involved with publica-

tion of this work months earlier, according to manuscripts once owned by eighteenth-century publisher William Bowyer:

> Mr. Royston, who first printed the book, informed Sir William Dugdale that, about the beginning of October 1648, he was sent to by the King, to prepare all things ready for the printing some papers, which he purposed shortly after to convey to him; and which was this very copy, brought to him the 23d of December next following by Mr. Edward Symmons. Mr. Edward Symmons, who conveyed both copies (viz. that written by Mr. Odart and that by the King) to the press, declared upon his death-bed, that it was the King's work.

By the end of the year Royston had contrived to print *Eikon* by using a series of printers, and he began distributing it. The involvements of many others in this affair offended authorities, but Royston's action brought a punishment that was not too severe and seems to have been long delayed. Following the execution of Charles I on 30 January 1649 each of forty stationers in October of that year was bound through a bond of £300 and two sureties of £300 "not to print any seditious or unlicensed books, pamphlets, or pictures, nor suffer his presses to be used for any such purposes." Among those bound were William Duggard; Roger Norton; John Grismond, the younger; Lichfield of Oxford; and Richard Coates – all of whom were printers that Royston had employed in producing *Eikon.*

On 24 October Royston himself was called before the Council of State, which sought "for suppressing scandalous pamphlets to examine Rich. Royston, stationer, and Jno. Grismond, printer, as to printing a virulent and scandalous pamphlet [probably *Eikon*]; likewise to inquire after the printers and publishers of a book entitled Anarchi Anglicana [a work that Royston later published openly in 1660 and 1661]." Following this inquiry Royston on 31 October was bound through a bond of £500 with two sureties of £500 each, on conditions that he was thereafter to appear "when required and that he was not to print or sell any unlicensed books or pamphlets in the meantime."

The size of these fines must have compelled Royston to keep his head below the parapet for some years. His publication of Taylor's *The Great Exemplar* (1649) and *Holy Living* (1650) indicates that he was taking precautions. On 26 October 1648 *The Great Exemplar* was entered in the name of Francis Ash, and on 7 March 1650 a similar entry occurred for *Holy Living.* These were the only works of Tay-

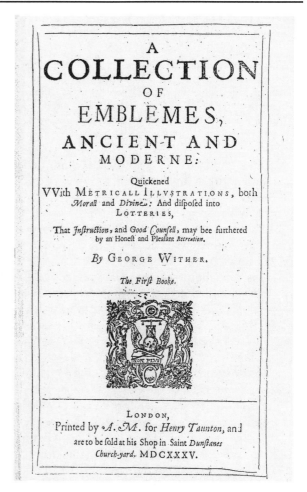

Frontispiece and title page for one of the most important emblem books of the seventeenth century, an edition Royston published with five other stationers

lor that Royston did not enter during this time, and one must ask why.

Francis Ash was a bookseller and bookbinder in Worcester and was reputed to be a man of Papist, or at least High Church, inclinations. In Michael Sparke's *A Second Beacon Fired by Scintilla* (1652), for instance, Ash was accused of being a trader in papist pictures and of binding them in copies of the English Bible. He had the great advantage of being in Worcester, a Royalist stronghold during the Civil Wars, and therefore of being safe from the immediate oversight of both the government and the Stationers' Company, but his location makes it more likely that someone such as Royston might have entered the books under Ash's name rather than that Ash himself had done so.

Both books might have caused Royston trouble, and he was in enough trouble during 1648–1651. The title page of *The Great Exemplar* proclaimed its author to be "*Jer. Taylor,* D.D. Chaplain in Ordinary to His MAJESTY," and one of its two dedications was to Mary, countess dowager of Northampton, the widow of Spencer Compton, second earl of Northampton and a famous Royalist commander who had been killed at the battle of Hopton Heath in 1643. In the case of *Holy Living,* which would become Taylor's most popular work, the author's name does not appear on the title pages of its first, second, or third editions (1651–1652), but the first prayer in the appendix of prayers is "For the King &c.," which Royston – in a rare concession to political exigencies – cautiously retitled "For the Ruler &c." in the second edition.

But what is interesting is that copies of the first editions of both books exist with Ash's name in the imprints, as one might expect, and copies also exist with Royston's name in the imprints. From the number of copies that survive, it is impossible to determine which of the imprints was more numerous. Ash died either during the siege of Worcester in September 1651 or shortly thereafter, and on 24 November 1651 the Stationers' Register records that these works were

> Assigned over unto him [Royston] by vertue of a noate under the hands and seals of Wm. Ash and Alexander Ash, executors of Fran. Ash, and by order of the Co[u]rt beareing date this 21th of Novemb[e]r 1651, these two copies vizt: *The greate exemplar, or, the Life of Christ,* and *The rule and exercise of holy liveing.*

During the early 1650s Royston continued to enter and publish books (mainly those of Hammond and Taylor) and to bind apprentices, but he was clearly a man trying to keep his nose clean. Yet he also continued to innovate. Thomas Hearne reports that in April 1651 Royston had become the first stationer to pay a royalty, or copy money, to one of his contributors: Henry Hammond, "the first man in England that had copy money[,] . . . was paid such a sum of money (I know not how much) by Mr. Royston, the King's printer, for his Annotations on the Testament [*Annotations on the New Testament,* 1653]."

Yet Royston could not withdraw from dangerous causes. He had earlier been involved in publishing the pseudonymous Theodorus Verax's *Relations and Observations, Historical and Politick, upon the Parliament Begun Anno Dom. 1640* (1648, by Clement Walker), and a second part, *Anarchia Anglicana or, The History of Independency,* was published in 1649. Walker, a leader of the Presbyterian faction in Parliament, was not an author whose works one might think Royston would have published, but until his death in 1651 Walker opposed the independent faction and had been imprisoned both in Bristol in 1643 and in the Tower in 1649 – and his *History of Independency* violently attacked Oliver Cromwell and the current ruling faction.

What appeared to become another problem for Royston began on 16 August 1652, when much of the first sheet of the *History of Independency* was seized at the printing house of Peter Cole. On 6 September Cole told the court he would help in the search for the other printed sheets, and finally, a year later, the Council of State issued a warrant for the arrest of Royston and Edward Dod, a bookseller also in Ivy Lane. On 7 October 1653 a committee examined Royston, Dod, and Richard Thomlins (another printer) before deciding on 10 October that all three, "apprehended on suspicion of having printed scandalous papers, [were] to be set at liberty, on good bail to appear on summons." Again Royston apparently escaped.

In the 1650s Royston developed two interesting professional approaches, the first of which

might serve to disarm some offense that his publications might arouse: he developed a standard disclaimer that was to appear in many of his books published during this decade. An early example appears in Taylor's *Eniautos* (1653):

> The *Printer* to the *Reader.*

> The absence of the Author, and his inconvenient distance from *London,* hath occasioned some lesser escapes in the impression of these Sermons, and the Discourse annexed. The Printer thinks it the best instance of pardon if his Escapes be not layd upon the Author, and he hopes they are no greater then an ordinary understanding may amend, and a little charity forgive.

Royston repeated this formula, with varying degrees of quaintness, into the 1680s. Hammond's *A Vindication* (1654) uses an identical disclaimer, as do the second editions of Taylor's *Eniautos* and Bishop Laurence Womock's *The Examination of Tilenus* (1658). Even after the 1650s this disclaimer appears in such works as Edward Fowler's *Dirt Wip't Off* (1672), which says:

> These and other Faults have been occasioned through the Authors absence, and by the hasty Printing of this Treatise, which thou art desired both for thy own sake and for his, to correct with thy Pen, before thou settest thy self to the serious reading thereof.

A full amplification of the formula appears in Jean Claude's *The Catholic Doctrine of the Eucharist* (1684):

> The Printer to the Reader

> The absence of the Translator, and his inconvenient distance from *London* hath occasioned some lesser Escapes in the Impression of this Book; The Printer thinks it the best instance of Pardon if his Escapes be not laid on the Translator, and he hopes they are no greater than an ordinary Understanding may amend, and a little Charity may forgive. *R. Royston.*

His second professional change, one which signals Royston's confidence in his position in the book trade, appears on the spare leaves of his various editions, where he began to publish catalogues of titles for sale. This practice was a normal advertising technique found in books by the same writers or by authors who shared political or theological positions, and Royston's use of it was extensive. In William Lyford's *The Plain Mans Senses Exercised* (1655) the catalogue encompasses ten closely printed quarto pages.

Despite such a display of confidence in his trade status, through the early 1650s Royston otherwise kept his head well down. Yet on 3 November 1656 he was again called before the court of the Stationers' Company for his printing of the Psalter, and he promised to pay four pounds that he agreed he still owed the company – a considerable reduction on his earlier promise of thirty pounds per thousand and a promise that indicates either a small print run or Royston's obstreperousness. He continued to bind and free apprentices as well as to enter and publish books, among them Blaise Pascal's *Additionals to the Mystery of Jesuitism* (1658) and many works by Taylor and Hammond.

In the late 1650s he also began to publish the works of Peter Heylyn, an apologist for Charles I and Archbishop William Laud, and was soon in trouble with the Stationers' Company again, as court records of the company show:

28 June 1658[.] Dr Heylyns Booke to be burnt. Mr Royston & Richard Marriott being sum[m]oned & present the Table acq[uain]ted them that an Order was brought to them from the Councell [of State] for the seizing and sending to Whitehall to be burnt Dr Heylyns late Booke agt the Sabbath lately printed by them or their order And required them forthw[i]th to bring to the Warden what bookes were remaining in their hands who instead therefof averred that they had disposed of them all.

Clearly Royston was not impressed by these threats, for he entered two more books by Heylyn on 20 August, and on 3 September Cromwell died and the Interregnum began to crumble. For the book trade this change in the political milieu is probably best signaled by Royston's entering the first part of Walker's *History of Independency* on 25 February 1660, as well as the anonymous *The Faithfull, Yet Imperfect Character of . . . Charles I* (1660) and "The Regal Intruder" (never published) on 5 March.

Having been proclaimed king in London on 26 May 1660, Charles II landed at Dover on that date and entered London on 29 May. On 4 June the court of the Stationers' Company, being a little slow to recognize changed circumstances, again questioned Royston for not yet having fulfilled his promise to pay the company thirty pounds for every thousand of Hatton and Taylor's *Psalms of David* that he had printed, but Royston would not take this request seriously. On 29 November 1660 Charles II granted him a monopoly on printing the works of Charles I, and Edward Almack writes that the king called *Eikon,* which Royston had risked his life and career to print and publish, "the most excellent discourses and soliloquies of our blessed father."

The Stationers' Company should have realized that its continued pursuit of the fine that Royston had promised to pay was fruitless, but since the company did not, Royston sought to drive the point home. On 22 June 1662 the court again summoned him about having published the Psalter, but its records show that this time his response was quite different:

Mr Royston being now and formerly demanded to pay what he owes to the Company for Leave to print the Booke called Hattons Psalter (he having promised £40 [his promise had really been £30 per thousand] on every Impression) returnes that it is not the same Translation w[i]th theirs, and therefore presumes nothing due; Adding, That he will obteine Authority for his so doing.

Having established that the king was on his side, Royston the next day was provisionally admitted to the livery of the company and had several of his fines dismissed, but a letter from Charles II on 6 May 1663 was required to force the company to grant him membership and to have him admitted to the position of assistant. On 11 May the company complied and elected him as an assistant. From this day until his death Royston was hardly ever absent from a meeting of the court of the Stationers' Company, and by 23 October Royston was also performing his work as a stationer to the court of Charles II.

By the spring of 1666 Royston was a warden of the company and was in a position to direct the workings of that system that had directed him. But 1666 brought the worst, and last, outbreak of the bubonic plague that had infected London, and England, since the Black Death of 1348. Then in the first week of September a fire, helped by a long dry spell and a strong easterly wind, started near London Bridge and spread, during four days, to burn out most of central London. The fire destroyed St. Paul's Cathedral as well as the printing and publishing industry that surrounded it.

Royston, as both a stationer and a member of the government of the company, was doubly concerned. The *Calendar of State Papers Domestic* records that in late September he petitioned the king and his council "for pardon for buying some books which though unlicensed, have been freely sold for years past. Abhors all thoughts of disloyalty and is reduced to great extremity by the late fire." And on 29 September another entry notes "The King in compassion to the losses sustained by his stationer, Rich. Royston, in the late fire, wishes an order to

Frontispiece by Faithorne for the 1663 edition of Jeremy Taylor's The Rule and Exercises of Holy Living

the treasurer of the chamber to pay him 300 *l.* out of the first moneys that come in."

From October through December the court book of the Stationers' Company records the work of the master and wardens to get the printing and publishing business back in order. Royston's own catalogues were to reflect the consequences of the fire: one of their headings from Joseph Mede's *Works* (1672) reads, "*A Catalogue of some Books Reprinted, and of other New Books Printed since the Fire, and sold by* Richard Royston," and another, from Thomas Pierce's *The Signal Diagnostick* (1670), enumerates "Books Printed since the Fire for *R. Royston*."

In late 1666 and much of 1667 Royston was one of the stationers involved in apprehending the irrepressible John Darby, a printer almost never on the right side of the law. Entries from the Stationers' Company court book reveal much about Darby's style. On 5 February 1667 Royston was charged with examining Darby's poaching from books in the English Stock, and on 4 June an "indictment against Darby [was] to be drawn up by the Clerk and given to Robinson on behalf of Warden Royston." The court no doubt acted on the indictment, perhaps by defacing Darby's type and

taking away his press, for on 22 August 1667 the court book notes that "This day Mr Warden Tyler gaue notice to ye Table, that one Norman A Joyner Informed him, that he was now making a Printing Presse, bespoken by John Darby; Wherevppon ordered, that the Warden doe speedily waite vppon Mr Secretary Morrice, And Acquaint him therewith."

From 1668 onward Royston became concerned more with the business of the company than with his own. He entered fewer titles in the Stationers' Register, and though he continued to publish those that he already owned, he added few to his list. On 3 July 1669 Royston stood for election to the office of upper warden of the company, but he lost both this election and that of the following year, in which he was again a candidate for this same office. Yet his trade with the court of Charles II continued, as he was paid £500 for stationery wares delivered to the king. Royston finally was elected upper warden of the company on 1 July 1671, and he spent the balance of that year conducting company business. At this time he virtually ceased to enter books in the register, although he continued to bind apprentices.

On 5 July 1673, following one of a continuing series of inquiries into old differences that continued to fester between the company and Royston, he was nominated for and elected to the position of master of the company. His first year as master was almost entirely occupied with company business; as a printer, he entered only a few books and bound two apprentices during this time. On 4 July 1674 he was renominated as master and was reelected.

However, Royston could not clear his reputation among many of his stationer colleagues. Between 20 March and 6 April 1676 Royston and others were called before Sir Roger L'Estrange (the censor for the press and stage) and the lords for having printed and sold libelous works. When Royston was called, records of the Royal Commission on Historical Manuscripts report that

> Rich. Royston said he never had any copies of the *Appeal,* or other libels mentioned. He had seen the *Packet of Advice,* and his servant paid one Jonathan Edwin for them. Could say nothing of *Smirk,* or the others.

This inquiry may have been a witch-hunt, and in any event Royston was still appreciated at the court of Charles II, which on 9 April 1677 made the following grant to him:

> Richard Royston, Bookseller in ordinary to the King, of a licence and privilege for the sole printing and publishing for fourteen years *The History of the Church of Scotland, beginning A.D. 203 and continued to the end of the reign of King James VI* by John Spotswood, late Archbishop of St. Andrews, of which he is the sole owner and proprietor [having entered this title on 9 November 1653], and which he is now about to set out in a fair volume in *folio,* being the fourth edition, with a prohibition of printing or selling the said work without the said Royston's knowledge and consent and of importing the same from abroad during the said term.

One finds it hard to understand Royston's need for such a grant. He had published Spottiswood's work in 1655, 1666, and 1668, and this grant seems unnecessary unless he expected surreptitious publication from Scotland or elsewhere.

Perhaps he sought such protection because he thought that other stationers might act as he had acted on earlier occasions. On 23 September 1678 he entered Henry Dolling's *Totum hominis sive summa humani* (1678). The author's name is almost certainly pseudonymous, and the translated title is *The Whole Duty of Man,* the title of a work by Richard Allestree that had been one of the most popular books of the century since its first appearance in 1659. Members of the Pawlett family (Robert, then George, then Edward) were the sole publishers of this work in English from 1671 to 1700, and Royston had published a Welsh translation of the work in 1672 – so with this entry Royston was trying to assert his rights in a Latin translation as well.

On 4 November 1678 Robert Pawlet complained to the Stationers' court that Royston "was printing of [Pawlet's] Coppy Entituled totum hominis It was ordered that Mr Pawlett be at his Liberty to take his Course at Law agt ye said Mr Royston if he thinke fitt." Whether Pawlet thought fit or not, he published a Latin version in 1680 as *Officium hominis,* with the imprint "*pro Roberto Pawlet,*" and a second edition was published in 1690 by Edward Pawlet. But if the present was a problem for Royston, it was also true that the past would not leave him alone. On 8 July 1679 he paid two pounds for permission to print *The Psalter of David* again, although no one knows how many copies he printed or how grudgingly he paid for them. Paying such a sum surely was not difficult, for on March 1680 he was assigned £232. 4s. 5d. for "stationary wares" that he had supplied to the court of Charles II.

The remainder of 1681 and 1682 passed rather peacefully for Royston; he entered a few books in the Stationers' Register and kept occupied with company business. At the company elections on 30 June 1683 he acted in a particularly magnanimous fashion when he was nominated, along with several others, for the post of master: they all withdrew in favor of Roger Norton, who had been the printer of many Royston books. Royston bound his last apprentice – Edward Pepys, the son of Samuel Pepys of Clifton, Buckinghamshire – on 6 August 1683.

A new and serious threat to the whole company of stationers appeared in 1684. Charles II, determined to increase his support in the House of Commons, demanded the surrender of all borough charters and later the charters of the livery companies of London. He intended to issue new charters that would demand greater loyalty of newly elected members of Parliament, and the liverymen of London formed the electorate of the city. On 26 March the Stationers' court received a subpoena to the King's Bench, and, with Royston's name heading the list of the signers, all the assistants resigned their places to the master and wardens.

At a general court the next day a draft petition to the king was unanimously agreed to by the company court. On 7 April Royston was included in a list of assistants "acceptable" to the king. A new charter was issued in ten days; a version of it in En-

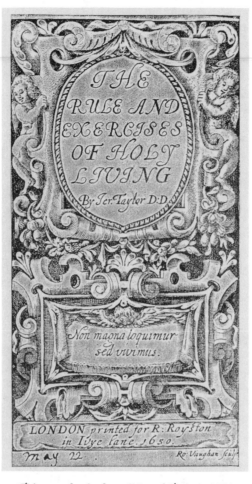

*Title page for the first edition of Taylor's 1650
religious exhortation*

glish was read to the company on 27 May; and the assistants were resworn on 2 June 1684.

Nathaniel Thompson's *A Choice Collection of 120 Loyal Songs* (1684) celebrates this occasion in "A new song, in praise of the loyal company of Stationers, who, for their singular loyalty, obtained the first charter of London, 1684." The second stanza of this begins with an allusion to a figure whom Cyprian Blagden has identified as Royston: "With limping *Dick* the *Zealous,* / went doting *Yea,* and *Nay.*" Royston's loyalty and zealousness paid well, for on 24 September he was paid £316 for having supplied stationery materials to the court of Charles II.

As loyal as he may have been on behalf of the company and its new charter, Royston encountered troubles with the company two more times in the last years of his life. On 2 November 1685 Robert Scott, George Wells, and Richard Bentley complained to the Stationers' Court about Royston having printed their text of John Fell's biography of Henry Hammond, and at a court meeting on 7 December Wells and Bentley formally accused Royston of this violation. Royston and the three stationers failing there to agree on some resolution, Royston returned to a subsequent court meeting on 1 February 1686 and requested "further to consider" the matter, and his request was granted.

Having published folio collections of Hammond's works in 1674 and 1684, Royston had a large interest in these works, and certainly he must have been tempted to include John Fell's life of Hammond in these folios. Unfortunately he did not own the copyright to it: John Martin, James Allestry, and Thomas Dicas had entered this work on 6 June 1661, and John Martin's widow had transferred this copyright to Robert Scott on 21 August 1683. How Wells and Bentley became involved in the controversy is not known, for there appears to be no transfer of copyright to them and their names appear in no imprints of it. The court book records no subsequent resolution of this dispute, which may

Engraved frontispiece, with a portrait of Thomas Hobbes by
Robert Vaughn, for Hobbes's Philosophical Rudiments
concerning Government and Civill Society *(1651)*

have been settled by the death of Royston later that year.

But death could not stop one last occurrence of the contentiousness that characterized Royston's life. On 3 May 1686 a question was again raised about his infringement of the rights of the English Stock, and the source of this problem may have again been *The Psalter of David,* for Royston paid twenty pounds for having printed it and two other books on 2 June 1681. Whatever may have constituted the basis for this last offense, the court record provides a remarkable picture of Royston in his final appearance on 7 June:

> Report concerning R Royston's Printing Stock Books The Mast[e]r and Wardens made report That pursuant to an order of the last Court [3 May] they had treated w[i]th Richard Royston for Satisfaction for the damage Susteined by the Company by his comprinting severall

of their Coppies belong[in]g to the English Stock w[hi]ch damage they computed to 54 *l* 9s, but vpon Mr Roystons allegacon of his Meritts for services formerly don for the Company the same was moderated to 20 *l* w[hi]ch 20 *l* he had since paid in, but because he expected that ye 20 *l* likewise should have been alsoe allowed him he presented a paper to the Court Setting forth some service he did the Company soone after the dreadfull ffire of London ab[ou]t their renewing of their Pattent for Schoole Bookes, w[hi]ch being read the Court were well satisfied w[i]th what the Mast[e]r & Wardens had don in the whole affaire And Ordered That ye Paper be retorned him by the Clerke w[i]th this notice That ye Court were of opinion, that the Mast[e]r & Ward[e]ns had considered the whole matter & had been very kind to him in takeing but 20 *l* for the Damage he had don the Company in printing their Coppies.

This portrait of Richard Royston, now eighty-five years old and pleading for a remission of twenty pounds for his most recent appropriation of the

English Stock of the company in which he had been a lower warden, an upper warden, a master (twice), an assistant (almost perpetually since the Restoration), and an active agent in promoting company interests (so long as they did not conflict with his) is a memorable one. On 3 July this stationer was somehow again nominated to serve as master of the company, although Henry Herringman was elected at this court meeting, the last that Royston attended. Sometime between court meetings on 6 December and 20 December 1686 Royston died, for his gift of five pounds to the poor is recorded on the latter date.

Royston was buried in Christ Church, Newgate Street. His tomb at that site (which was destroyed during World War II) bore the following inscription:

Richard Royston, bookseller to three kings, died 1686, in the 86th year of his age. Elizabeth, wife of Luke Meredith, grand-daughter of the above Richard, 1689 Mary Chiswell, late wife of Richard Chiswell, bookseller, another daughter of the above Richard Royston, 1689.

Of Royston's wife, Margaret, there appears to be no record, but the Royston children and grandchildren continued to be active and irascible in the book trade. In 1714, for example, Jacob Tonson published *The Ladies Library,* "Written by a Lady" (believed to be Lady Mary Wray, Jeremy Taylor's granddaughter) and "Published by Mr. Steele." The work is a collection of works by various seventeenth-century divines, with huge chunks drawn from Taylor, particularly from *Holy Living.* Royston Meredith and Elizabeth Meredith, Royston's grandchildren and heirs, complained to Richard Steele that by publishing *The Ladies Library* he was robbing them — "two poor orphans who have very little else to subsist on" — of their literary property.

Steele retorted that he intended to do "all good offices [he could] to the reverend author's grandchild now in town." Royston Meredith thought this to be "a blind excuse for his notorious plagiarisms" and published the correspondence in *Mr. Steele detected: Or, the Poor and Oppressed Orphan's Letters to the Great and Arbitrary Mr. Steele* (1714). What more could one expect from the descendants of a man who specified in his will that his copyrights could be held only by persons who were members of the Church of England? Royston was, as John Dunton called him, "orthodox Roystone" — a man who brazenly conducted himself through any dispute of his rights or the rights of his beloved Stationers' Company.

References:

Edward Almack, *A Bibliography of the King's Book or Eikon Basilike* (London: Blades, East & Blades, 1896);

Cyprian Blagden, *The Stationers' Company: A History, 1403–1959* (London: Allen & Unwin, 1960);

Peter W. M. Blayney, *The Bookshops in Paul's Cross Churchyard* (London: Bibliographical Society, 1990);

John Dunton, *The Life and Errors of John Dunton,* 2 volumes (London: Nichols, 1818);

G. K. Fortescue, ed., *Catalogue of the Pamphlets, Books, Newspapers, and Manuscripts Relating to the Civil War, the Commonwealth, and Restoration, Collected by George Thomason, 1640–1661,* 2 volumes (London: British Museum, 1908);

Thomas Hearne, *Reliquiae Hearnianae: The Remains of Thomas Hearne,* edited by Philip Bliss (Oxford: Printed for the editor, 1857);

D. F. McKenzie, *Stationers' Company Apprentices, 1605–1640* (Charlottesville: University of Virginia Press, 1961);

McKenzie, *Stationers' Company Apprentices, 1641–1700* (Oxford: Oxford Bibliographical Society, 1974);

John Nichols, *Literary Anecdotes,* 6 volumes (London: Nichols, 1812);

William Proctor Williams, "The First Edition of *Holy Living:* An Episode in the Seventeenth-Century Book Trade," *Library,* fifth series 28 (June 1973): 99–107.

— William Proctor Williams

William Seres

(London: 1546? – 1579?)

As a result of the lucrative patents he held on private prayer books and Psalters, William Seres was one of the more wealthy and influential of Elizabethan stationers. As a young man during the reign of Edward VI, he was a religious reformer involved in the book trade, a proselytizer as much as a businessman. He associated with older printers such as Edward Whitchurch and Anthony Scoloker, who shared his reforming ardor, and he worked for a time in partnership with John Day, who also supported religious change. By the end of Edward's reign Seres had obtained exclusive royal licenses to print all books of private prayer (primers) and all Psalters. He received this privilege through the good offices of his former master, William Cecil, the future Lord Burghley and treasurer.

The reign of the Catholic Queen Mary I interrupted the progress of Seres's career, but although he lost his privileges after her accession, his setback seems to have been only temporary. By 1557 Seres had recovered enough influence within the book trade to be included among the original court of assistants when the Stationers' Company received its royal charter. After Elizabeth I had been crowned, Seres's religious inclinations were once again legitimate, and by July 1559 his royal license to print primers and Psalters had been reinstated. The foundation of Seres's future had been laid, as with his earlier patent, through the intercession of William Cecil.

Seres's connections with Cecil and his support of the Elizabethan religious compromise between radical and orthodox reformers are evident in the books that Seres printed. In 1563, for instance, he published the official interpretation of the fire at St. Paul's Cathedral in Bishop James Pilkington's *The burnynge of Paules church in London,* a work that assigns that fire to papist machinations. Some of Seres's books served Cecil's ends, and Seres also published books prepared by Elizabethan courtiers patronized by Cecil, works such as Thomas Hoby's translation of Baldassare Castiglione's *The Courtyer* (1561) in a quarto edition and Arthur Golding's translation of Ovid's *The Fyrst Fower Bookes of P. Ouidius Nasos worke, Metamorphosis* (1565, the complete edition appearing in 1567), works that first appeared in English under Seres's imprint.

After the accession of Elizabeth I, Seres was more concerned with maintaining the status quo than with changing it: he and his fellow monopolists dominated the hierarchy of the Stationers' Company and used its bylaws to maintain their privileges. Seres served as master of the Stationers' Company five times, and as one of the holders of privileges, he fought against a coming generation to preserve such privileges. The rights that the monopolists established to intellectual property were the bases that led eventually to authorial copyrights a century and a half later. Seres's wealth and power put him and his son, William II, at the center of changes in the book trade that extended far beyond the late 1570s.

Seres's early life is so obscure that most of his biographers ignore it entirely. In his monograph on John Day, C. F. Oastler follows Seres's eighteenth- and nineteenth-century biographers by asserting that Seres was a native of Suffolk, although no evidence supports this assertion. Some have speculated that because Seres used the sign of the Hedgehog on his commercial premises, he had once been the servant of Sir Philip Sidney, whose badge was that of the hedgehog. Cecil's sponsorship of Seres's patents on primers and Psalters in 1553 more strongly indicates that the printer had once been in Cecil's service. Yet while Cecil certainly exerted his influence on Seres's behalf, that Seres ever served him personally cannot be certain. The earliest fact known about Seres's life is that he became a free citizen of London as a member of the Stationers' Company in 1548. During his first four years as a stationer Seres worked exclusively in partnerships with Scoloker, Whitchurch, Day, and William Hill.

Each of Seres's early partnerships published books that espoused reformist religious beliefs during the reign of Edward VI. Scoloker, one of Seres's early partners, had been an exile on the Continent when Henry VIII was a defender of the Catholic faith. With Scoloker, Seres published the work of reformers such as John Bale; William Tyndale; John Frith; Pierre Viret; and Herman V, archbishop of Cologne. The most important book they pub-

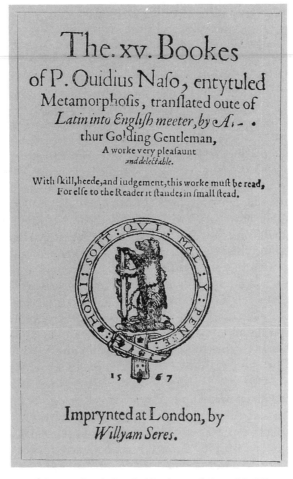

The. xv. Bookes
of P. Ouidius Naſo, entytuled
Metamorphoſis, tranſlated oute of
Latin into Engliſh meeter, by Arthur Golding Gentleman,
A worke very pleaſaunt
and delectable.

With ſkill, heede, and iudgement, this worke muſt be read,
For elſe to the Reader it ſtandes in ſmall ſtead.

Imprynted at London, by
Willyam Seres.

*Title page for Arthur Golding's translation of Ovid's
complete works, the first English-language edition*

lished was Bale's *A brefe Chronycle concernyng the Ex-aminacyon and death of the blessed martyr of Christ syr John Oldecastell* (1544), which co-opted the genre of the saint's legend for Protestant purposes. Another interesting book that Scoloker and Seres published together was Hans Brinkelow's *The Complaint of Roderyck Mors* (1548). The book's false imprint, "Geneve in Savoye, M boys," illustrates that even in 1548 a printer did not necessarily want his name attached to every book he printed. Since Geneva is hardly in Savoy and Scoloker was living in the Savoy Rents at this time, Scoloker and Seres shared a sense of humor that complemented their religious zeal. Their work together also included *A goodly dysputacion betwene a Christen Shomaker, and a Popysshe Parson* (1548), which Scoloker translated from the German. Dialogues between an uneducated laborer and an educated representative of the Catholic hierarchy composed an extremely popular genre during the early English Reformation. All of Seres's and

Scoloker's books that can be firmly dated were printed by 1548, and their partnership could not have lasted beyond then, as Scoloker moved to Ipswich before 1549.

Whitchurch, another of Seres's early partners, was also well known for his Protestantism. He and Richard Grafton had collaborated to publish the first complete edition of the Bible in English, and Whitchurch had been committed to Fleet Prison in 1540 for continuing to print Protestant books after Henry VIII had condemned and beheaded Thomas Cromwell. Seres joined Whitchurch in publishing an edition of Proverbs rendered in English meter by Thomas Sternhold. If this attribution is correct, perhaps Seres's association with Cecil recommended him to Sternhold. In any event, Seres's association with Whitchurch acquainted him with most of the leading English religious reformers.

Seres's most lasting and productive partnership was with John Day, another member of the younger generation of Protestants who gained prominence during the reign of Edward VI. Day and Seres may have begun printing together as early as 1546, but they most actively collaborated during the period 1548–1550. Their imprints indicate that they occupied joint business quarters at the sign of the Resurrection near Holborn conduit during 1548. During 1549 the partners sold books under the same sign in Cheapside near the Little Conduit, although they maintained separate quarters by then.

Seres moved to a shop in Peter's College at the west end of St. Paul's Cathedral sometime during that year, and from that time his premises were always under the sign of the Hedgehog. While Seres and Day published many books similar to those produced through Seres's other partnerships, they also published a few books on subjects that were not religious. William Turner's *The names of herbes in Greke, Latin, Englishe, Duche & Frenche* (1548) and Sir John Cheke's *The hurt of sedicion howe greueous it is to a Commune welth* (1549) are two notable examples. Because Turner was most often a religious writer and Cheke was Cecil's brother-in-law, the publication of their nonreligious books by Seres and Day is not really surprising.

Between 1548 and 1550 Seres and Day printed a complete edition of the Bible, including the Apocrypha, in a series of five octavo volumes. The last of these volumes to appear, the Pentateuch, was actually printed by Day alone. They also printed a five-part folio edition of the Bible, an edition that partially revised the series of Bibles printed by Whitchurch and Grafton between 1537 and 1540. As one of the few large folios on which Seres ever worked, it was an elaborate volume printed in both black and red and containing many woodcuts and illustrated initials.

Seres and Day offered various inexpensive products to readers who shared their religious beliefs; most of the books they published were either devotional works or anti-Catholic propaganda. Their publication of Luke Shepherd's *Ion Bon and Mast parson* (1548), a satiric treatment of orthodox eucharistic beliefs, so offended the Catholic constituency among London aldermen that Day was nearly jailed. Seres and Day also printed other satiric poems, as well as works by Robert Crowley, another Protestant propagandist. Among the devotional works they printed was Hugh Latimer's *Sermon of the Plow* (1548) and, in 1549, two sermons he preached before King Edward; individual sermons by Thomas Lever and a collection of fourteen others by Bernardo Ochino; and an edition of William

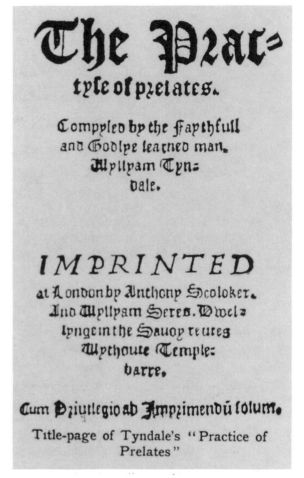

Title-page of Tyndale's "Practice of Prelates"

Title page for reformist William Tyndale's treatise The Practyse of Prelates *(1548)*

Tyndale's controversial New Testament translation with his commentary on the gospel of Matthew. Among the other commentaries in their catalogue were Philipp Melanchthon's on Daniel and John Hooper's on Jonah.

They also published Bale's *Image of Both Churches* (circa 1550) and at least two confutations of Anabaptist opinions. It is probably no coincidence that Seres and Day published these latter works at the same time that William Cecil was serving with Archbishop Thomas Cranmer, Bishop Nicholas Ridley, and Bishop Thomas Goodrich on a commission that tried and censured Anabaptists. *The recantation of Jacke lent vicare generall to the mooste cruell Antichriste of Rome* (1548) and *The copie of a letter sente to one maister Crispyne chanon of Exceter for that he denied ye scripture to be the touche stone of all doctrines* (1548) are representative of the anonymous propaganda they printed. Most of these books were inexpensive octavo editions of no great technical merit. During most of the rest of his career Seres published the

Title page for John Bale's chronicle of Sir John Oldcastle, the Wycliffite martyr who seems to have served as one of the models for William Shakespeare's Falstaff

same sort of books: inexpensive octavos and an occasional more expensive quarto.

The exact arrangement of Seres and Day's partnership is not known. Since Seres worked with other partners and Day issued books under his own imprint, it would seem that Seres was primarily a publisher who provided capital. In his joint imprints Seres was habitually listed second, a probable indication that he served as a retailer. During his early years as a stationer Seres seems to have been a procurer of manuscripts and a source of capital, but he was probably not a printer. The fact that no books appeared under Seres's imprint in the year immediately following the dissolution of his partnership with Day supports a notion that he was not actively printing until after 1551. The same division of responsibilities probably characterized Seres's other partnerships.

When Seres and Day relocated to separate business quarters in 1549, Seres set up shop under the sign of the Hedgehog in Peter's College near the southwest corner of St. Paul's Cathedral. The college was under the control of William May, the dean of St. Paul's, with whom Seres had some personal relationship, for he paid no rent to the deanery for his shop. During 1549–1550 the Seres-Day partnership was flourishing, as their maintaining of three workshops and their production of books demonstrated. But their moves into separate business quarters signaled an end of their partnership: by 1551 the two no longer published books under a joint imprint, and in that year Seres published the first book under his own imprint, Thomas Ruddoke's *A remembraunce for the maintenaunce of the liuynge ministers*. By 1553, three years after having dissolved their partnership, Seres and Day possessed the royal patents that were to create their respective fortunes.

On 11 March 1553 Seres received a royal patent on the printing of all Psalters and on primers or private prayer books, except for the *Book of Common Prayer,* and he published one Psalter and three primers that year. Seres quickly used his privileges, which did not last long, for with the accession of Mary I on 6 July 1553 his days as a patent holder were numbered. As an entry in the *Calendar of the Patent Rolls* for 3 July 1559 notes, Seres "had a license from Edward VI to print primers agreeable to the Book of Common Prayer, but under Queen Mary was 'defeated' thereof and imprisoned and was deprived of great numbers of books to his utter undoing." While it is true that Seres lost his monopoly on primers and may have been imprisoned for a time, this report of his "utter undoing" is an overstatement. He probably printed no books during 1554, which was clearly not his best year commercially, but Seres's setback was merely temporary.

Seres's actions during Mary's reign were not those of a man completely dispossessed, as the 1559 patent roll entry suggests. In 1554, the first full year of Mary's reign, the Stationers' Company moved its hall from Milk Street to Peter's College, and Seres, who was becoming important in the government of the company, was therefore obliged to move his place of business next door. Perhaps this change of quarters partially explains why Seres did not publish during 1554, but from this new site he was to publish books under the sign of the Hedgehog at the west end of St. Paul's Cathedral toward the Ludgate for the rest of his career. Seres had in fact probably taken part in negotiating with his friend May for relocating the Stationers' Company at Peter's College. In the years after May had been deprived of his deanery by Edmund Bonner, Mary's Catholic bishop of London, Seres paid rent of four shillings for a basement room in the Stationers' Hall on May's behalf. Furthermore, the Stationers' Register for 1554–1557 records a donation of twenty shillings by Seres for a new glass window and wainscoting in the new company hall. While these sums of money were not great, such gestures are not those of a man who had been utterly undone. They are the acts of a man on the move in the hierarchy of his trade.

Seres's publishing activity from 1554 to 1557 was not comparable to that before Mary's accession, but his books were not totally out of circulation. He began to reestablish himself by publishing works of a more neutral content than those earlier works of stridently Protestant propaganda. In 1555

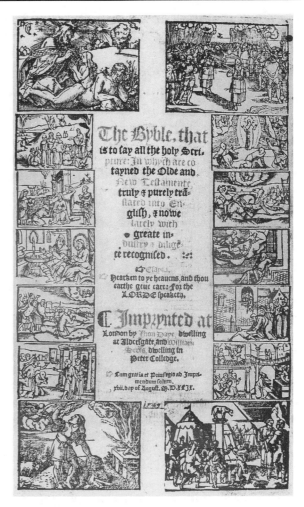

Woodcut title page for the 1549 edition of the "Matthew Bible" reprinted by Seres and John Day

Seres had enough capital to invest in a joint venture with Richard Jugge, Henry Sutton, and Robert Toy, and they paid William Powell to print Peter Martyr's *The decades of the newe worlde or west India,* surviving copies of which bear the imprints of all four investors. Powell also printed Walter Wedlocke's *A lyttle treatise called the Image of idlenesse* for Seres that same year. He continued to sell books from his shop at the west end of St. Paul's, and his consistently high standing in the Stationers' Company shows that as a bookseller he remained relatively successful.

The Worshipful Stationers' Company was granted a royal charter in 1557, a document in which the stationers promised to pursue self-censorship practices if the government were to acknowledge their copyright to any books that they registered with the company. Seres, whose name appeared twenty-first on the charter's list of stationers, was already a liveried member of the company, and he became an original member of the company's court of assistants, that group of master printers from which the stationers' principal officeholders were selected. He had already served as a renter prior to the royal charter, and his rise through the company's principal offices continued steadily upward after 1557. The assistants set the official policies of the company – policies that for the next quarter century favored the interests of monopolists, patent holders such as Seres had once been and would be again. From 1557 to 1577 Seres either was a member of the court of assistants or held a company office every year. He served as the upper warden of the Stationers' Company twice, in 1561 and 1565, and as master of the company five times – in 1570, 1571, 1575, 1576, and 1577. Five times during years when he did not hold office, he consigned the wardens' accounts in the Stationers' Register. From the time of its beginning as a royally chartered guild until his death, Seres was an important figure in the internal politics of the Stationers' Company.

Intimations of Seres's importance are reinforced by the alacrity with which his royal patent was restored after the accession of Elizabeth I. In one of the earliest actions to reinstate printing privileges that had been reapportioned under Mary's government, a patent granted during Elizabeth's first regnal year (1558–1559) restored Seres's exclusive right to print primers and Psalters for the rest of his life. Many others who had their printing privileges restored had them reinstated for only a fixed number of years, so Seres's patent was one of the most generous. In 1571 another patent superseding this one was granted, and it extended the monopoly on printing Psalters and primers to both Seres and his son, William II, for the lifetime of the survivor.

Seres immediately printed one Psalter and one primer in 1559 and continued to produce both works throughout the rest of his career. While he occasionally published quarto-sized Psalters, he generally issued his primers and Psalters in octavo and smaller formats. He also wasted little time in asserting the rights of his privileges. On 25 May 1560 the high commission issued to the Stationers' Company an order signed by Edmund Grindal, the bishop of London, and four others – an order requiring the master, the wardens, and the queen's printers to punish anyone responsible for infringing Seres's privileges. Seres's willingness and need to defend his privileges reflect how lucrative they were.

Although he was never as radical in religious matters as he had been prior to Mary's reign, Seres continued to print devotional works and began to

print more moderate religious propaganda after 1560. In that year he published John Calvin's *Two Godly and Notable Sermons preached . . . in the yere 1555* and Pilkington's *Aggeus the Prophet declared by a large commentary.* Seres also printed a series of pamphlets that evaluated the religious conflict in France from the Huguenot perspective. The common feature of all these works is that they accorded with Church of England policy. During Elizabeth's reign Seres was in a position to capitalize on his associations within the church and government.

One way in which Seres did so was by printing official documents for the Church of England, a cash-paying customer. He began such printing for the church in 1560, when he produced the anonymous *Interrogatories For the doctrine and maners of mynisters, and for other orders in the churche.* He continued to fulfill church commissions for many years, as he did in arranging to print the anonymous *Forms for Visitation by Metropolitan* (1575) and various other official documents for the sees of Canterbury, London, Durham, and York at one time or another.

Another way in which Seres took advantage of his connections was by publishing the works of royal courtiers. Cecil was a patron of the arts, and Seres printed works by courtiers whom Cecil patronized or knew well. In 1565 Seres published Golding's translation of *The eyght bookes of Caius Iulius Caesar conteyning his martiall exploytes,* with a dedicatory epistle addressed to Cecil. Seres also reprinted *The hurt of Sedition* by Cheke, Cecil's brother-in-law, in 1569, a work that he had originally published with Day, and he published Thomas Blundeville's *The fower chiefyst offices belongyng to Horsemanshippe* (1565–1566) in a four-part quarto edition. Seres produced the greater portion of his high-quality quarto editions for royal courtiers.

Occasionally Seres's presses spoke on the behalf of the government, whether his motives were those of gratitude or of invitation. Signed with the initials W. S., *An Aunswere to the Proclamation of the Rebels in the North* (1569) is a poem that has been attributed to Seres himself. Whether or not he actually wrote it, the poem certainly voices the official attitude toward the northern rebellion that had been precipitated by the arrest of Mary Stuart. His series of pamphlets conveying Huguenot views of the French religious wars were also as congenial to the government as they were to the Anglican Church. In many of his professional activities Seres supported the interests to which he owed much for his wealth.

The pattern of Seres's activities that emerges from the Stationers' Register shows him to have

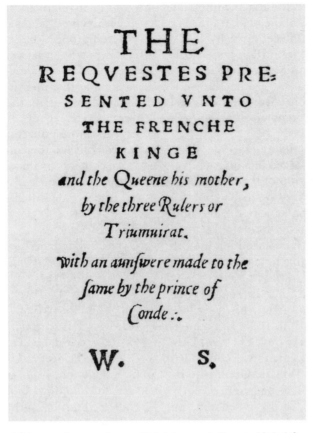

*Title page for one of many official documents Seres published for
the government, this one circa 1562*

been an adept businessman and an enthusiastic member of the company. From the time that stationers' copyrights had been confirmed by royal charter, he consistently registered his books with the company. During the period 1556–1569 he officially bound ten apprentices for terms varying from seven to ten years, and his business must have been formidable to have required so many apprentices. The fact that none of these apprentices were freed casts some doubt on Seres's efficacy as a master, although he was clearly acting as a full-service printer and publisher through these years.

As a member of the court of assistants, Seres participated directly in regulating the book trade. In 1576 he and Thomas Purfoote were named as the first pair on the company's roster of searchers, whose duties were to conduct weekly inspections into the operation of print shops in order to find what works and how many books various printers were producing. Because most of the searchers on the roster were also patent holders, they could make sure that their rights were not being infringed at the same time. Another aim was to discover printers who were employing either illegal apprentices or journeymen, ones for whom the company had not been paid the proper fees.

By 1570 Seres had built a highly successful publishing business; he foresaw, however, that his son, William II, would not carry on that business, and he therefore moved to provide for his son. As early as 1571 Seres had begun assigning a portion of his printing to Henry Denham, a younger stationer. By 1575 Denham was actually printing most of the works that were published under Seres's imprint, including his patent properties, and Denham continued to print Psalters and primers for Seres's assignees well into the 1580s. Giving or selling the bulk of his printing tools to Denham, Seres eventually divested himself completely from his printing business – although he maintained control of his privileges as a means of providing for his son.

During the last year that Seres served as master of the company a militant group of junior stationers lodged a formal complaint with the Privy Council against monopolies in the book trade. Being joined in their petition by members of the glass sellers and cutlers, these stationers alleged that patents granted to private individuals would ruin many of the poorer members of the book trade. The petition specified those privileges held by Seres, John Jugge, Richard Tottel, John Day, James Roberts, Richard Watkins, Thomas Marshe, Thomas Vautroller, William Byrde, and Francis Flowers, and it was undersigned by thirty-five stationers and ten men who, free of other companies, made their livings by bookselling.

From the time of this petition until 1584, Seres and his son were closely involved in a dispute over the contemporary organization of the book trade. To study the problem, the Privy Council appointed a commission that was sympathetic to the monopolists, but the dispute continued into the reign of James I, and Seres did not live to see it end. With some difficulty his son was able to maintain control over the patent on primers and Psalters until they became part of the English Stock in 1603. When young Seres attempted to assert his privilege through a Privy Council suit in 1582, some question arose about the legitimacy of his claim. Ultimately the legitimacy of his patent was confirmed through the intervention of William Cecil, who intervened on behalf of the son as he had previously done on behalf of the father: Cecil's signed notation appears on the report sent to the queen. The absence of the elder Seres's name on this suit confirms that he was no longer alive by 1582; in all probability he had died before the end of 1579.

That relatively few copies of Seres's Psalters have survived seems odd, because they were such coveted properties. For a wealthy, important printer, Seres left a relatively small legacy of books. Perhaps the only explanation is that those books were so popular that their failure to survive ironically betokens how widely they were read or "consumed." Seres's real legacy, and that of all the sixteenth-century monopolists in the book trade, lies in having established the concept of intellectual property. If the contents of a book had not been established as a property, the concept of copyright might never have been established as well.

References:

Cyprian Blagden, *The Stationers' Company: A History, 1403–1959* (Cambridge, Mass.: Harvard University Press, 1960);

Thomas F. Didbin, ed., *Typographical Antiquities* (London: Miller, 1810);

John N. King, *English Reformation Literature: The Tudor Origins of the Protestant Tradition* (Princeton: Princeton University Press, 1982);

C. F. Oastler, *John Day, the Elizabethan Printer* (Oxford: Oxford Bibliographical Society, 1975);

Hallett Smith, "English Metrical Psalms in the Sixteenth Century and Their Literary Significance," *Huntington Library Quarterly,* 9 (May 1946): 249–271.

– Bryan P. Davis

Peter Short

(London: 1589 – 1603)

During the last fourteen years of the reign of Queen Elizabeth I, Peter Short printed many noted literary works: the second edition of Ben Jonson's *The Comicall Satyre of Every Man out of His Humour* (1600), the third edition of Christopher Marlowe's *Hero and Leander* (1600), the first edition of Francis Meres's *Palladis Tamia* (1598), the first edition of Edmund Spenser's *Amoretti and Epithalamion* (1595), and the first edition of William Shakespeare's *The True Tragedie of Richard Duke of Yorke, and the Death of Good King Henrie the Sixt* – that is, *Henry VI, Part 3* (1595). Other Shakespearean works that Short printed include the first edition of *The Tragedy of King Richard the Third* (1597, the printing of which Short shared with Valentine Simmes), the first two editions of *The History of Henrie the Fourth* [Part I] (1598), the second edition of *The Rape of Lucrece* (1598), and the fifth edition of *Venus and Adonis* (1599). Of some particular interest to Shakespearean scholars is that on 2 May 1594 Short entered as his own copy *A Pleasant Conceited Historie, Called the Taming of a Shrew* and printed the first two editions of it in 1594 and 1596.

Short's significance lies also in the many famous music books that he produced, for perhaps only such contemporaries as Thomas East and John Windet were competitors as printers in this field. The music books that Short printed include the first edition of Michael Cavendish's *14 Ayres in Tabletorie* (1598); the first two editions of John Dowland's *The First Booke of Songes or Ayres of Fowre Partes* (1597) and the first edition of his *The Third and Last Booke of Songs or Aires* (1603); the first edition of Giles Farnaby's *Canzonets to Fowre Voyces* (1598); the first edition of Anthony Holbourne's *The Cittharn Schoole* (1597); the first edition of William Hunnis's *Hunnies Recreations* (1595) and the fifth through the eighth editions of his popular *Seuen Sobs of a Sorrowfull Soule* (1592); the first editions of Robert Jones's *The First Booke of Songes and Ayres* (1600) and *The Second Booke of Songes and Ayres* (1601); the first editions of Thomas Morley's *Canzonets; or, Little Short Songs to Fovre Voyces* (1597), *Canzonets or Little Short Aers to Five and Six Voices* (1597), and *A Plaine and Easie Introduction to Practicall Musicke* (1597); and the first edition of Philip Rosseter's *A Booke of Ayres* (1601).

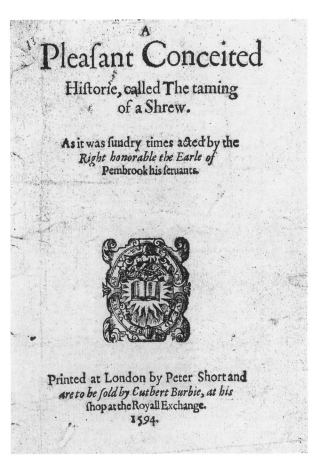

A Pleasant Conceited Historie, called The taming of a Shrew.

As it was sundry times acted by the Right honorable the Earle of Pembrook his seruants.

Printed at London by Peter Short and are to be sold by Cutbert Burbie, at his shop at the Royall Exchange. 1594.

Title page for the first quarto edition of what is generally believed to be a corrupt text of William Shakespeare's The Taming of the Shrew

Details of Short's early life have been rather obscure. Information yet to be published indicates that he was by discipline a grocer and was admitted as a freeman of the Stationers' Company in 1589 by translation, a privilege by which a member of one company was granted membership in another through special arrangements between the two. According to records of his freedom in the wardens' accounts of the grocers of London, Short was freed by grocer John Kingston on 14 June 1585, and on 18 February 1589 other records of the court of aldermen in the London Records Office show that "Shorte [was] translated from the Grocers to the Stationers." So a record of the Stationers' Register B showing that Short was "admitted A freman of this

Title page for the first edition of John Dowland's collection of music

company *per Redempcione[m]*" on 1 March 1589 is not in fact accurate.

Neither Short's birthplace nor the date of his birth is known, but the date is most likely not in or after 1562: he was freed in 1585, and apprentices were usually admitted as freeman at the age of twenty-four, after seven or eight years of service to their masters. Short is known to have married, but details about the marriage and family are uncertain. His son, Henry, was trained presumably in his father's profession and freed "by patrimony" on 3 March 1617, too late to succeed his father in the paternal business, because Short by then had long been dead. Little is known about this son's fortune, but the Poor Book of the Stationers' Company indicates that he received benefactions from the company during the first three quarters of 1625. Also rather puzzling is the Christian name of Short's widow. A. W. Pollard and G. R. Redgrave's *A Short-Title Catalogue* (1991) identifies "Elizabeth Short" as Short's wife and "Short, Emma" as his widow. The initial *E.* appears as her name in the im-

print of all the books that she printed after her husband's death – as, for example, in the third edition of Dowland's *The First Book of Songes or Aires of Foure Parts* (1603). She had been engaged to Humphrey Lownes Sr. for some time before 3 November 1603, but the actual date of their marriage is unknown. In any case, after his death in 1630 she appears to have received benefactions from the Stationers' Company until the first quarter of 1634.

Short, who eventually took over the business of Henry Denham, was associated with Richard Yardley in 1589, the year of Short's translation to the Stationers' Company, but he and Yardley produced no books until 1590. In that year Saluste du Bartas's *A Canticle of the Victorie Obteined by the French King, Henrie the Fourth* appeared with Yardley's imprint, and it was reissued in 1592 as the second part of *The Triumph of Faith* with the joint imprint of Yardley and Short. The imprint of the books they produced suggests that their printing house stood on Bread Street Hill at the sign of the Star, but their joint work, for whatever reason, appears to have become impractical early in 1592, with their last joint entry in the Stationers' Register on 17 February and their last joint publication of the seventh edition of Thomas Rogers's translation of Thomas à Kempis's *Of the Imitation of Christ* both appearing in that year.

On 5 May 1592 Short made his own first entry in the register – for Thomas Tymme's *A Plaine Discouerie of Ten English Lepers* (1592) – and his subsequent entries were generally for works that he alone was to publish. Even the few jointly registered entries that he made do not carry Yardley's name alongside Short's but rather the names of other partners, as does his 26 June 1598 entry for the first edition of Thomas Lodge's translation of Flavius Josephus's *The Famovs and Memorable Workes of Iosephvs* (1602). By the time of his first independent entry in 1592, Short must have had confidence in his ability to run his business without Yardley, as the flourishing production of books at his printing house during the next several years attests.

Short and his widow are known to have printed, either in whole or in part, at least 225 books, including 28 subsequent editions of works he had printed earlier. Throughout the whole period he ran his house both as a trade printer and as a printer-publisher, although during 1595–1596 he appears to have been much more interested in his work as a trade printer. By 1594 he had relationships with more than a dozen stationers – such as Edward Blount, Cuthbert Burbie, Thomas Butter's widow, John Flasket, John Harrison the younger, William Jaggard, Richard Jones, William Leake,

Woodcut portrait of Elizabeth I in A Booke of Christian
Prayers *(1590), one of the earliest books that Short
printed with Richard Yardley*

Thomas Man, William Mattes, Thomas Millington, and William Ponsonby – and most of these stationers continued their business with Short at least for a few years. About forty booksellers employed Short, but those who can be regarded as his longstanding customers are few: Burbie and Leake, in addition to the assigns of William Seres and Richard Day. Some apparent disagreements – between Short and John Wolfe on 13 July 1598 and Short and Burbie on 7 September 1600 – limited the amount of work that Short performed for such customers.

Short was accustomed to the common practice of shared printing, as he worked with at least 16 different colleagues in printing a minimum of 34 books, including 11 subsequent editions of works that he had previously printed. Such printers with whom Short worked jointly included Edward Allde, Richard Bradock, Thomas East, George Eld, Richard Field, John Harrison the youngest, Abel Jeffes,

Richard Jones, Felix Kingston, Joan Orwin, Thomas Purfoot, Richard Read, James Roberts, Valentine Simmes, Richard Tottell's successor, and Charles Yetsweirt's printer. Short's affinity for shared printing may be compared to that of Valentine Simmes, who shared in printing at least 16 of a total of 155 books, or to that of Thomas Creede, who jointly printed at least 33 of a total of 381 books.

Short had an enormous stock of decorative initials, blocks, and borders, a stock probably comprising the richest variety of his time and making his prints the most attractive of his time. Most of his ornament stock is presumed to have been inherited from Henry Denham, and the best examples of it probably include the title page of, and the illustrations in, John Foxe's *The Actes and Monuments* (1597). Short owned several sets of decorative initials of various sizes and families. Particularly notable among them are fairly large woodcut initials

1 5 9 9.

¶ *AT LONDON*
Printed by Peter Short, dwelling on Bred-
ſtreete hill at the ſigne of
the Starre.

Imprint in John Dee's Course of the Philosophical Studies
(1599), identifying the site of Short's printing house

generally known as the A S series and attributed to engraver Aston Sylvius of Antwerp: Short possessed complete sets of two different families. He appears also to have owned a pair of the most popular alphabet of foliage design without a square encircling the foliage.

Early in April 1596 Short was employed to finish what Denham had left of Foxe's *The Actes and Monuments,* and he was able not only to complete this two-volume work but also to produce a variant edition of the second volume. The title page of this variant bears the new date of 1597, and this means that in 1596 Short was in all probability fully occupied with this mammoth work from 7 April to the end of the year. It is not surprising, therefore, that his total production that year was most remarkable: 494 sheets. This figure seems unexpectedly large from a shop with one press, and Short may have used a second press that he was not officially allowed to keep.

His next most productive years were those of 1599 and 1602, when he printed 347.5 and 349 sheets, and 1600, in which he printed 313 sheets. His average production of 336.5 sheets per year for these three years may thus represent a practical maximum limit of Short's productivity with one press: about 1.12 sheets per day, or about 8.9

quarto pages a day, calculated on the basis of a year of 300 working days. The busiest years of contemporary printer Thomas Creede render slightly larger but similar figures: Creede printed 359.5 sheets in 1596, 369.75 in 1597, 369.5 in 1598, and 386.5 in 1606. These figures from the shops of both Short and Creede are much higher than the one sheet per day figure given by R. B. McKerrow as a compositor's norm. This suggests that Short's business was generally successful – perhaps with the exception of the single year of 1601, when some unknown circumstances suddenly reduced his production to a total of only 84 sheets.

Despite this remarkable productivity, records about Short's apprentices are scarce. On 2 February 1592, only a fortnight before his last entry for a book to be printed with Yardley, Short received James Ridley as his first apprentice, but no record of Ridley's freedom remains. More than three years before the scheduled date of Ridley's freedom Richard Stretton also joined Short to begin an eight-year apprenticeship like that of Ridley. Then on 12 April 1602, two and a half years before the scheduled date of Stretton's freedom, Short took his third apprentice, Richard Badger, to serve for another eight years from 25 March 1602.

But Short died before the end of Stretton's eight-year term, and again no record of his freedom is found in the registers, although Badger is known to have been freed on 7 May 1610 by Humphrey Lownes, the second husband of Short's widow and successor to his business. Despite this absence of records regarding the freedom of Short's first and second apprentices, the record of productivity achieved by Short's printing house during the years 1594–1600 and 1602 makes their absence hard to believe. No master could possibly have run his house economically without his apprentice or apprentices, and if one ever gave up his service in the middle of his term, his master would have to fill the opening and thereby make a rather irregular pattern of taking apprentices.

Short's pattern appears remarkably regular, however, and despite the missing documentation of their freedom, their presence in his printing house seems beyond doubt. In fact, Edward Arber's *Transcript of the Registers of the Company of Stationers of London* records that Short was once fined one shilling for having neglected his duties to present his apprentice to the court of the Stationers' Company promptly at the beginning of his apprenticeship. This apprentice may have been Badger, for the date of this record, 12 April 1602, matches that of the date on which Short presented Badger, as his apprentice, to the Stationers' court.

Short faced other, more potentially serious, professional problems with his colleagues. Having been admitted into the livery of the Stationers' Company on 1 July 1598, he was among fourteen printers accused of having printed forbidden books less than a year later, on 4 June 1599. The archbishop of Canterbury and the bishop of London publicly announced this offense in the Stationers' Hall, to the disgrace of Short and his colleagues, but apparently none of the books Short had printed were actually burnt in the hall. In spite of having suffered this disgrace, Short managed to improve his professional image in the company and was elected on 17 March 1600 as one of the four stockkeepers of the privileges of William Seres Jr., a partnership that he had shared with some other stationers since 18 March 1594. More than eighteen months later, on 19 October 1601, the court also decided that he and William Leake would receive fifty-five pounds a year "for mr Seres ãnuytie," and only ten days afterward Short, Thomas Dawson, and Simon Waterson represented the company at a banquet held by the lord mayor of London.

Following a most productive year Short died sometime after 31 December 1602, when he made his last entry of a book that was to appear in the following year with his name still appearing in its imprint: Sir Hugh Platt's *A New, Cheape and Delicate Fire of Cole-Balles* (1603). The exact date of his death is not known, but it was likely to have been prior to 12 July 1603, when Felix Kingston entered as his copy a book that Short's widow printed with her name in the imprint: Thomas Thayre's *A Treatise of the Pestilence* (1603). Or, at the latest, his death may have occurred before 9 August 1603, the date printed as part of a new title given to a second edition of John Dee's work, *A Letter, Nine Yeeres Since: Containing a Most Briefe Discourse Apologetical* (1603), the printing of which was shared by Short's widow and Valentine Simmes.

Short apparently died without having made a lawful will. By either an oral or a written promise, however, he must have decided to offer forty shillings a year for twenty-six years from Christmas 1603, "to th[e] use of the poore of this [Stationers'] Company yssuing out of a rent in mugwell streete that he held of St Barthnes hospitall." The execution of his promise, which appears to have remained incomplete in July 1631, was left in the hands of both the company and his widow's second husband, Humphrey Lownes Sr., who pledged among other items Short's "Rac'd boule" for the loan of £22 8s. from the company on 10 July 1629.

References:

Alan E. Craven, "The Compositor of the Shakespeare Quartos Printed by Peter Short," *Papers of the Bibliographical Society of America,* 65 (December 1971): 393–397;

W. Craig Ferguson, "The Stationers' Company Poor Book, 1608–1700," *Library,* 31 (March 1976): 37–51;

D. F. McKenzie, *Stationers' Company Apprentices, 1605–1640* (Charlottesville, Va.: Bibliographical Society of the University of Virginia, 1961);

R. B. McKerrow, "Edward Allde as a Typical Trade Printer," *Library,* 10 (September 1929): 121–162;

Silvanus P. Thompson, "Peter Short, Printer, and His Marks," *Transactions of the Bibliographical Society* (London) 4, part 1 (1896–1898): 103–128;

Akihiro Yamada, *Peter Short: An Elizabethan Printer* (Tokyo: College of Humanities, Meisei University, 1989);

Yamada, *Thomas Creede Printer to Shakespeare and His Contemporaries* (Tokyo: Meisei University Press, 1994);

Susan Zimmerman, "The Use of Headlines: Peter Short's Shakespearean Quartos, *1 Henry IV* and *Richard III*," *Library,* 7 (September 1985): 218–255.

– Akihiro Yamada

Valentine Simmes

(London: 1589? – 1623?)

Valentine Simmes (also spelled Symmes, Sims, and Sems) was a rather disreputable printer, but he is important as the printer of several first editions of William Shakespeare. The only record of his birth is in the Stationers' Company record of his apprenticeship, where his birthplace is given as Adderbury in Oxfordshire, and his father, Richard, is identified as a shearman, one who "shears the nap from cloth in its final stages of preparation."

Simmes was apprenticed for eight years beginning at Christmas 1576 to printer and bookseller Henry Sutton, from whom he was freed on 8 March 1585. As Simmes had to be at least twenty-four years old to be presented, he must have been born in or before 1561. Sutton had ceased printing in 1562 and was a bookseller by the time Simmes was apprenticed to him. A stationers' court book entry for 1 March 1596 indicates that Simmes had been the "servant" of Henry Bynneman, but as Bynneman had died in 1583, that service must have been during Simmes's apprenticeship. He must have acquitted himself well, for by 1596 Bynneman's widow was willing to transfer all of her late husband's copies to him.

Johane Sutton, widow of the master to whom Simmes had been apprenticed, presented Simmes to the Stationers' Company to receive his freedom on 8 March 1585. What he did for the next four years is not known, but in July 1589 he was approached by John Hodgkins and offered a job ostensibly printing pirated copies of the privileged school grammars, but really printing what proved to be the famous Martin Marprelate tracts, scurrilous pieces attacking the Anglican establishment as well as the Crown. Simmes was offered twenty pounds a year and his keep, and these were not bad terms. With his companions Simmes went to Wolston Priory, near Coventry, and printed two pamphlets before moving, one step ahead of their pursuers, to Newton Lane near Manchester. There, by an unlucky accident (a case of type falling to the ground in front of interested spectators), they were discovered and apprehended.

Having been questioned by the earl of Derby, Simmes and the others were sent to London to be interrogated by the Privy Council. Records of this interrogation still exist. Simmes's deposition suggests that he was a recalcitrant witness, qualifying some of his testimony with phrases such as "he thinketh" instead of directly responding to queries. This disposition may have been intentional, but in light of his rather shady future, this behavior may have constituted his naturally evasive manner. Following the interrogation, which probably involved torture, Simmes was able to sign the deposition, but his fellow compositor, Arthur Thomlyn, was able only to make a mark, possibly because he was in no condition to sign. As this deposition was taken on 10 December 1589, the entire escapade lasted about five months; the date of Simmes's subsequent release from prison is not known.

The next four or five years of Simmes's life are blank. However, by 1594 he was legitimately in business and took one apprentice, John Bodley, on 30 September. He may earlier have taken Richard Cowper also as an apprentice in March, but there is some uncertainty about the dates, and only a marginal note assigns the entry to 1594.

Various twentieth-century scholarly catalogues and indexes assign about 230 titles or editions to Simmes's printing operation. None of these dates before 1594, however, so this year most likely marked the beginning of his business. He began with a black-letter pica type and used some roman and occasional italic. During a three-year period he came to use the roman pica as his principal font. He started with one factotum of two naked youths, right hands joined in a circle of leaves at the top and left hands on a compartment in the middle. This thirty-two-millimeter square factotum appears in

*Simmes's earliest factotum, which he used in one-third of
his books*

one-third of his books. By 1597 he had another of two naked boys holding a coronet, a twenty-one-millimeter square design popular among other printers such as Thomas Creede. By 1598 he had acquired a third, of a leaf design within a double border and measuring forty-four millimeters by forty-five millimeters. These factotums are unique to Simmes and useful, if not conclusive, in identifying his books.

From William How, Simmes acquired printing equipment, including several of How's ornamental initials and one device – a flattened circle measuring forty-four millimeters by fifty-four millimeters and containing a boy with a weight holding him down. According to Ronald B. McKerrow, this device signifies talent kept from rising by the burden of poverty. Simmes's other distinctive device, used from the late 1590s, is that of a popular mask of a grotesque face with a curled mustache. The device can be recognized by its damaged state: a gouge on the right side, a nick on the left, and a broken line in the right mustache.

Simmes's place of business appears in books printed in 1595, and he remained in the same place for most of his career. The shop was on Addle (or Addling) hill at the White Swan near Baynard's Castle. He was probably there from the beginning in 1594, the year during which he printed five or six books – all but one a reprint. Of the five publishers who came to Simmes in 1594, only one, Thomas Adams, became a fairly steady customer. Ralph Newbery, who had once been associated with Byn-

neman, returned to Simmes only once, in 1600. The others – Widow Newman, William Jaggard, and Gregory Seton – never returned.

This first year set some patterns for Simmes's later printing. It appears to have been fairly normal for publishers to shop around for a printer and to use several who could give customers the best deal in the shortest time. Simmes printed books for sixty-three different publishers, half of whom never returned to him. His most regular publisher was Nicholas Ling, who had been apprenticed to Bynneman during Simmes's time in service there. Ling brought twenty-one books that Simmes was to print alone and another six that he was to print in partnership. Eight other publishers (Thomas Adams, William Aspley, Joseph Barnes, Edmund Blount, John Busby, Thomas Bushell, Clement Knight, and Thomas Pavier) each brought Simmes between five and twelve books. Sixty titles list Simmes alone on the imprint.

In contrast, between 1594 and 1607 thirty-nine different publishers employed Thomas Creede – seventeen coming only once, and ten more than five times. James Roberts printed for forty-eight different publishers, of whom only seven brought five books or more, and almost half (twenty-one) came only once. Ling, Simmes's most frequent customer, during this period relied on a total of eleven different printers to publish his seventy-nine books, but he gave the bulk of the work to only two – Roberts (twenty-

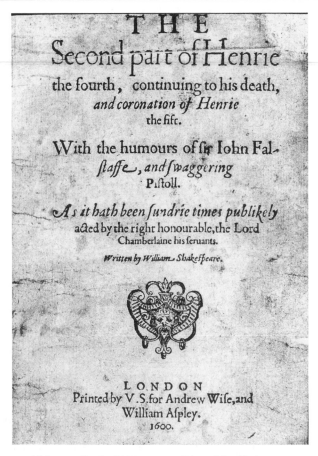

*Title page for the 1600 quarto edition of the Shakespeare
history play in which the popular character Falstaff
makes his second appearance*

nine works) and Simmes (twenty-seven titles) — although he gave most of the others more than a single book.

Almost from the beginning Simmes was in trouble with the Stationers' Company. In 1595 he engaged in the sporting activity of printing a privileged school grammar, the rights to which belonged to Francis Flower, a gentleman who usually allowed his patented work to be printed for a considerable fee. As a result of this violation of Flower's patent, Simmes's press — along with twenty reams of completed sheets — was seized and carted off to Stationers' Hall. Then on 8 September, as Walter W. Greg and Elizabeth Boswell report, Simmes was punished by having his type melted down and redelivered to him along with his other "printing stuff."

Simmes's next clash, whatever it was, resulted in the Stationers' Company ordering his apprentices to be set over to Roberts on 7 June 1596 and ordering Simmes not to take any more until the terms of these reassigned apprentices were over. Yet this in-

junction appears not to have been rigidly enforced, as Simmes took another apprentice in 1601 before he presented John Bodley in 1602.

Simmes was also reprimanded for the usual infractions in the following years: a fine for disorderly printing in 1598, a warning (also issued to thirteen other printers) in 1599 against printing unlicensed satires (as well as anything by Thomas Nashe), a fine in 1601 for having printed a proclamation without permission and a query in the same year about Simmes's warrant for having printed a particular book. The assistants were apparently keeping their eyes on him. Twice in 1603 he was in trouble for unlicensed printing, and he was warned not to meddle in such activities again.

Simmes's surreptitious printing of Catholic books constituted yet another offense to the authorities. Scholars have identified at least five such books that he is believed to have produced between 1596 and 1604. These attributions give added weight to an unsigned, undated letter to the king reprinted in *Valentine Simmes* (1968), a letter that reads, in part:

> Most gracious Sovereign. Valentine Symmes who was now taken printing seditious books, has done the like seven times before this; first he printed the things of Martin Marprelate, after has been meddling in Popish books, he by forbearing has become worse.

William Pierce conveys the frustration and distress of authorities toward Simmes in repeating Bishop Richard Bancroft's comment on him: "I could have hanged the fellow long ere this if I had listed." For unknown reasons Simmes was quietly replaced as a master printer, and the only information about this action appears in a short note in the stationers' court book, dated 2 March 1607: "Willm Hall ys admitted to be a printer in the place of Valentine Symmes."

Although he was down, Simmes was not yet out. Five books were printed by or for him between 1610 and 1612, and in 1619 he assigned some books to others. Early in 1622 he petitioned the archbishop of Canterbury to be reinstated as a master printer, but this was denied. Following this denial of his petition, the stationers' court on 13 December 1622 confirmed the denial but agreed to increase his pension from four pounds to six pounds a year. He had been a regular pensioner from the second quarter of 1618, and the last entry of his name in the list of pensioners is that for the third quarter of 1623 — after which, presumably, he died.

Simmes is significant for having printed several Shakespeare quartos that, incidentally, have proved to be rich resources for compositor studies. He began printing these in 1597 with the first edition of *The Tragedie of King Richard the second,* which he reprinted the next year, and *The Tragedy of King Richard the Third,* which he printed in collaboration with Peter Short. In 1600 he printed the first edition of *The Second part of Henrie the fourth,* which he reprinted in 1604, and of *Much adoe about Nothing.* His last Shakespeare quarto was the 1603 edition of *The Tragicall Historie of Hamlet Prince of Denmark,* which has received considerable attention.

Beginning in 1599 with George Chapman's *A Pleasant Comedy Entituled: An Humerous Dayes Myrth,* other dramatic texts also came from Simmes's shop. In 1600 he printed the first edition of Thomas Dekker's *The Shoemakers Holiday* and Anthony Munday and his collaborators' *The first part of the true and honorable historie, of the life of Sir John Old-castle.* In 1604 came three more publications, all shared in

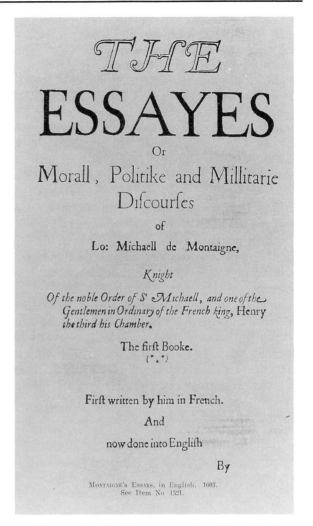

Title page for John Florio's translation of Montaigne's Essayes *(1603)*

some measure with other printers: William Alexander's *The Monarchick Tragedies,* which he was to reprint in 1607; Dekker's *The Honest Whore;* and three printings of John Marston's *The Malcontent.* The last plays he published were the first editions of George Chapman's *The Gentleman Usher* (1606) and Thomas Heywood's *The Fayre Mayde of the Exchange* (1607), together with the third edition of the anonymous *The Taming of a Shrew* (1607).

Simmes's press published three major nondramatic books. The first, a large folio of almost 200 leaves, was Samuel Daniel's *The Works of Samuel Daniel newly augmented* (1602), a work for which Simmes shared the printing. This was followed by an even more sumptuous production, John Florio's translation of Michel de Montaigne's *Essayes* (1603), a folio of 340 leaves that also was jointly printed. In 1605 he printed Michael Drayton's *Poems,* a smaller octavo of 250 leaves.

Several shorter individual works by major authors also came from Simmes's shop. Michael Drayton's *Matilda* (1594) appeared in Simmes's first year, along with Barnabe Riche's *Riche his Farewell to Militarie profession,* and in 1595 a reprint of Robert Greene's *Pandosto.* Thomas Lodge's *Rosalynde* followed in 1598 and both Greene's *Menaphon* and Thomas Nashe's *Nashes Lenten Stuff* in 1599. Another book by Lodge, *Paradoxes against Common Opinions,* was printed in 1602, as was a reprint of Greene's *Greenes Never Too Late,* a work that Simmes reprinted again in 1607. In 1606 he printed Ben Jonson's *Hymenaei* and Riche's *Faults, faults, and nothing else but Faults,* and with two others Simmes shared in printing Dekker's *Newes from Hell.* The rest of Simmes's output is varied: several books of sermons, history, polemics, and literary works now forgotten.

All these books, together with his dramatic publications, show that Simmes was a competent printer. With a good eye for design and layout, he generally used good paper and careful inking to avoid the show-through that makes many books of the period appear unreadable. He was thus a printer whose work was certainly at or above the standard of the day.

References:

Craig W. Ferguson, "The Stationers' Company Poor Book, 1608–1700," *Library,* 31 (March 1976): 37–51;

Ferguson, *Valentine Simmes* (Charlottesville, Va.: Bibliographical Society of the University of Virginia, 1968);

Walter W. Greg and Elizabeth Boswell, *Records of the Court of the Stationers' Company 1576–1602 – from Register B* (London: Bibliographical Society, 1930);

William A. Jackson, *Records of the Court of the Stationers' Company 1602–1640* (London: Bibliographical Society, 1957);

Ronald B. McKerrow, *Printers' and Publishers' Devices in England & Scotland 1485–1640* (London: Bibliographical Society, 1949);

William Pierce, *An Historical Introduction to the Marprelate Tracts* (London: Constable, 1908).

– W. Craig Ferguson

Tace Sowle

(London: 1691 – 1749)

Andrew Sowle

(London: circa 1660 – circa 1690)

Tace Sowle succeeded to the business of her father, Andrew Sowle, in 1691 and became the leading Quaker printer of her generation. Immediately after taking over the Sowle press, she expanded its production, with her name appearing in more than two hundred imprints during the first fifteen years of her career. Her press was the primary channel through which the Friends' work was published, and she printed the major works of the founders of Quakerism, such as George Fox, Margaret Askew Fell Fox, Robert Barclay, James Naylor, William Penn, George Whitehead, and Isaac Penington. Quakers relied on their printers to organize the local, national, and international distribution of their books, and the Sowle press was an important exception to the rule that printing houses generally did not retail their own products. For more than half a century Tace Sowle served the largest Nonconformist sect in England not only as the primary printer but also as the primary publisher, warehouser, collecting agent, and adviser on market demands. From the time that Andrew Sowle set up a secret press some time before the Restoration until 1829, when the business can no longer be traced, this unique publishing operation flourished both in London and, through family connections, in America.

As the Quakers' sobriquet – "Publishers of Truth" – suggests, early Friends used extensively the power of the printed word to shape public opinion and foment sociopolitical change. Quaker commitment to the use of the press may be inferred from the fact that in 1659 and 1660 this illegal Nonconformist sect, despite comprising less than 1 percent of the population, published about 10 percent of all the titles printed in England. Between the beginnings of the movement in the early 1650s and the appearance of the first Quaker bibliography in 1708, 440 Quaker authors produced 2,678 different publications. At this time of harsh persecution and strict press licensing, this sect published no fewer than 2.25 million books and tracts. Products of the Sowle press not only influenced the internal devel-

opment of the movement but also mediated relationships among the Friends, the government, and the public at large.

Early Quakers were perceived as posing a serious threat to the social order, and in general Friends' books could not even be submitted for licensing with any hope of approval. From the passing of the Licensing Act in 1662 until its lapse in 1679, Friends' books rarely show printers' names in imprints. Because of the risks involved, Quaker works were generally published only by those in sympathy with the Friends. Other early printers and publishers of Quaker works include Giles Calvert, Thomas Simmonds, Robert Wilson, Mary Westwood, Benjamin Clark, and Thomas Northcott. Yet by the time Tace Sowle succeeded to her father's business in 1691, Andrew Sowle had established a virtual monopoly over Quaker printing, and after the lapse of the Licensing Act the worst persecution was over.

Andrew Sowle served his apprenticeship with Ruth Raworth, one of the many Nonconformist women printers and publishers of her generation. During the third year of Sowle's apprenticeship Raworth married Thomas Newcomb, an important radical (Puritan) publisher. After this apprenticeship in illegal printing and publishing, Sowle was freed in 1653. While he began to print for the fledgling Quaker movement almost immediately, the location of his first press remains a secret. Sometime after the Restoration he openly set up shop in Holloway Lane, Shoreditch, "at the sign of the Crooked Billet." This location served as his printing house, shop, and personal residence, and he lived there about thirty years.

John Tomkins's important collection of early Quaker biographies, *Piety Promoted, in a Collection of Dying Sayings of Many of the People Called Quakers* (1701), tells of Andrew Sowle's repeated losses at the hands of government authorities for having printed unauthorized materials. William Penn records that Sowle's printing house was "often searched, and his materials, as presses, letter, &c. as

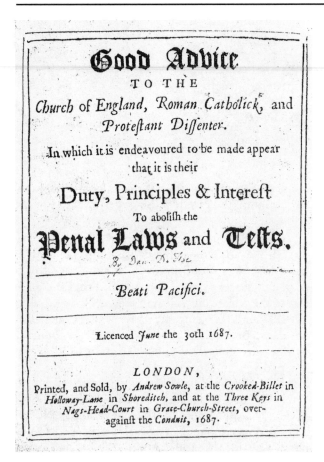

Title page for one of the more that eighty Quaker works, printed by Andrew Sowle, who — as his imprint specifies — had a shop off Grace Church Street, near the main Quaker meetinghouse (courtesy of the Lilly Library, Indiana University)

often broke to pieces, and taken away, as any Friends' books were found printing by him." Penn states that this government harassment of the Sowle press went on "for many years together: during which time . . . [Sowle] met with great losses, and had, at one time by his adversaries, about a thousand reams of printed books taken from him." Given this hostile climate, it is not surprising that Sowle's name does not appear in imprints before 1680. The first imprint showing his name gives his address as "Devonshire New Buildings" near Bishopsgate Street, the site of the first public Quaker meetings in London. In 1687 imprints indicate that his books were sold at the Three Keys in Nag's Head Court off Gracechurch Street, across from the main meetinghouse.

Sometime near the Restoration, Andrew Sowle married a woman named Jane, and the couple had two daughters, both of whom were trained in the family business. Elizabeth, the youngest, married her parents' apprentice, William Bradford, in

the early 1680s, and she later immigrated with him to Pennsylvania, where the two became the first Quaker printers in the American colonies. (William Bradford later defected from the Friends and became the first government printer for the province of New York.) Tace Sowle, the elder daughter, was freed of the Stationers' Company by patrimony in 1695 and became her father's legal successor. By 1690 Andrew Sowle was described as "an old man" and nearly blind, and after this date his name no longer appears in imprints. In actuality Tace Sowle succeeded her father in 1691, and she had probably assumed management of the printing house sometime earlier. Andrew Sowle died at his house in Shoreditch in 1695, attended by his friend William Penn. During the eleven years that his name had appeared in imprints, Andrew Sowle published far more than eighty items for the Friends.

Immediately after Andrew Sowle's death, Tace and Jane Sowle gave up the Shoreditch address and combined printing house, shop, and residence at White-Hart Court in Gracechurch Street, across from their old shop at Nag's Head Court. They also acquired a shop in Leadenhall Street at the sign of the Bible. The fact that Tace Sowle bound two new apprentices within the first two years of her own freedom may attest to her ambition. She immediately increased the production of the Sowle press — from an average of seven works per year for the years 1687–1690 to an average of twenty-three works per year one decade later. The eleven-year period between her formal, legal takeover in 1695 and her marriage in 1706 was the busiest of her career, and in fact the busiest in the 150-year history of the Sowle press. In her first fifteen years as a printer for the Friends, Tace Sowle published more than three hundred works.

In 1705 bookseller John Dunton described Tace Sowle as

> both a Printer as well as a bookseller, and the Daughter of one; and understands her Trade very well, being a good Compositor herself. Her love and piety to her aged Mother is eminently remarkable; even to that degree, that she keeps herself unmarried for this very reason . . . that it may not be out of her power to let her Mother have always the chief command in her house.

Sowle did in fact marry the following year (1706), but she nevertheless ensured that her mother would remain the primary power in the house. Seventy-five-year-old Jane Sowle became the nominal head of the family press the same year that her daughter was married. Imprints after this date read "J.

Sowle," and for the next thirty years Tace Sowle's own name disappears.

Tace Sowle never gave up her name for that of her husband, Thomas Raylton, but instead used the compound "Tace Sowle Raylton." Thomas Raylton was not a member of the Stationers' Company, and he apparently never actively participated in the production of printed works. Unlike his wife and mother-in-law, he had no training or experience as a printer. His apprenticeship was as a blacksmith, but at the time of his marriage into the Sowle business he was working as a hosier. Records show that he did help in warehousing and distributing books (customarily the wife's job in male-headed printing households) and in negotiating with the Friends. But records also show that Tace Sowle Raylton continued to oversee the production of publications – as she had done for sixteen years before she was married, and as she would do for another twenty-six years after she was widowed.

R. S. Mortimer indicates that from 1706 through 1738 "the Sowle press continued as the main Quaker publisher, issuing upwards of three hundred works in just over thirty years." When Jane Sowle died in 1711 at the age of eighty, imprints began showing "assigns of J. Sowle" – that is, Tace Sowle Raylton. After 1715 the Leadenhall Street outlet was abandoned for a new shop in George Yard in Lombard Street, also at the sign of the Bible. After 1716, when Tace moved her printing house to the George Yard site as well, this would remain the location of the Sowle press and its successors for the next century.

After the death of Thomas Raylton in 1723, Tace Sowle Raylton continued to manage her printing house. In 1736 she employed a foreman – Luke Hinde, a relative. Thirty years after her name had disappeared from imprints, it suddenly reappeared, beginning with an edition of Robert Barclay's *An Apology for the True Christian Divinity* (1736), printed by "T. Sowle Raylton and Luke Hinde." In 1739, when Tace Sowle Raylton was seventy-three years old, Luke Hinde became her partner, and from 1739 until her death in 1749 the two published about seventy works for the Friends – "a much smaller output than the two hundred issued during the years 1690–1706," Mortimer writes, "but none the less including the main Quaker authors of their period."

In November 1749 Tace Sowle Raylton, a wealthy, independent businesswoman with two houses and additional real estate in Blackfriars, died at eighty-three years of age. Her will left fifty pounds to her "nephew William Bradford of New York in America printer" and thirty pounds to the London Women's Meeting, which was to distribute this to the poor. Her printing house and the bulk of her estate went to Luke Hinde, who succeeded her. Hinde continued to publish for the Friends until his own death in 1766, whereupon he was succeeded by his second wife, Mary Phillips Hinde.

Without employing a foreman or remarrying, Mary Phillips Hinde continued as the Friends' printer and publisher for nearly a decade, during which time the press imprints began to show "No. 2 George Yard" instead of "the Bible." In 1775 she turned the business over to James Phillips, a relation, and twenty-two years later Phillips took his son, William Phillips, as a partner, and the firm became "James Phillips and Son." William Phillips succeeded his father in 1800 and continued to publish Quaker literature for nearly thirty years, although not at the rate of his predecessors. During 1805 and 1806 William Phillips appears to have had a partner named Fardon, but from 1807 until his death in 1828 he again worked alone. The "C. Phillips" whose name appears in one imprint in 1829 was his second wife, Christiana Walduck Phillips, who spent several months trying to settle outstanding accounts with the Friends following the death of her husband. After 1829 the Sowle-Hinde-Phillips dynasty disappeared, marking the end of an era for the Quaker press. In 1828 the Meeting for Sufferings (which had overseen details of production since the 1670s) established a printing committee to take care of publishing matters and turned its attention to other affairs.

To understand the operation of the Sowle press, one must first understand the workings of Quaker central organization, for this body acted in the capacity of the modern publisher (financing production, supplying printers with copies, and overseeing national and international distribution). After the intensified persecution of Quakers in the early years of the Restoration, George Fox and other leading Friends designed a program to give the movement organizational strength. Monthly and quarterly meetings were established in the various districts and counties throughout England, with national business meetings to be attended by representatives of these groups. Many organizational bodies that met in London – particularly the Yearly Meeting, the Second Day's Morning Meeting, and the Meeting for Sufferings – shared central control of the society. From the beginning, one of the primary purposes of Quaker central organization was to supervise and control the Quaker press.

During the Restoration the Quakers were the most heavily prosecuted Nonconformist sect in England, and after more than fifteen thousand Friends had been imprisoned, it is easy to see why Quaker leaders sought to ensure that their authors would avoid unnecessarily provoking the authorities. George Fox had been concerned with such matters from the earliest days of the movement, and by 1672 a complex system of internal review was established. The problems with this internal censorship are obvious – in the marginalizing or silencing of dissenting voices and in the decline of a movement with the potential to effect radical social change into the respectable quietism of the eighteenth century. On a more positive note, however, Thomas O'Malley notes that "by employing caution and political sensitivity" and by attempting to speak with something approaching a collective voice, this persecuted minority managed to survive. Unlike many other women printers and publishers of her day, Tace Sowle managed to stay out of jail.

The three bodies of central organization that controlled the Quaker press were the Yearly Meeting, the Morning Meeting, and the Meeting for Sufferings. Each of these bodies had its own duties, yet each closely cooperated with the others. The Yearly Meeting met annually in London in late May or early June and was composed of representatives from major cities and the counties. On the second day of the meeting a committee of ten Friends met to review the year's distribution of books, and later in the day the proposals of these Friends were reviewed by the group. At the first Yearly Meeting in 1672, the committee of ten established a set of policies that was to stand throughout the eighteenth century. One such policy specified that no books or editions were to be produced without their approval. The committee was to decide the number of books that were to be sent to each county and to whom they were to be sent. A printer was to send books abroad only when he or she was instructed to do so, and in the quantities ordered.

The official board overseeing the censorship of Quaker publications was the Morning Meeting, which gathered weekly in London starting in September 1673 and included about a dozen "antient men Friends." Because its primary task was to approve manuscripts before they were printed, the Morning Meeting spent most of its time reading books aloud, debating them line by line with meticulous care, and deciding which specific passages were to be altered or omitted. Pamela M. Ambrose observes that "no author or subject [was] beyond the scrutiny of the committee, and no one, whatever

their status, [was] guaranteed publication." Books not passed for printing immediately were either sent back to the author with detailed suggestions for revision or rejected outright as untimely, unsuitable, or too dangerous. Even books to be reprinted had to be reedited, for the political climate of Restoration England (and hence the conditions of publication) shifted from decade to decade. Orders to print or reprint had to be recorded in the minute book of the meeting by the official secretary. Approved books were then passed to the Meeting for Sufferings, which met weekly in London beginning in 1675 and coordinated the details of production and distribution.

By Tace Sowle's day the major sources of financing for Quaker publishing were general collections and moneys that Quarterly Meetings paid directly to printers for books. At the first Yearly Meeting in 1672 a general stock was created to cover the expenses of publishing, and from this stock (and sometimes from the loans of individual Friends for particular projects) Tace Sowle would be advanced sums of up to £300. Books were frequently printed in editions of one thousand copies, and while the Friends were constantly concerned about costs, they clearly could pay for such numbers with ease. This central organization also supplied Sowle with copies to print from, although they did not necessarily own those copies.

Central organization allowed the early Friends to distribute their books with an efficiency unparalleled in their time. It is a paradox of early Quakerism that the Friends' modes of publication were at once innovatively underground and blatantly open. They devised complex strategies to minimize detection and prosecution, yet they kept printed tracts and books flowing into the hands of those in power. In *The Beginnings of Quakerism* (1955) William C. Braithwaite quotes from a letter to George Fox in 1660, for instance, recounting how some copies of one work "is [sic] given abroad in Whitehall, and others of them is sold in divers shops, and some of the women cries them about the streets."

As early as the 1650s Quaker books reached continental Europe and the American colonies and spread throughout England, Ireland, and Wales as traveling preachers carried printed materials with them. Works from the Sowle press were delivered to Monthly Meetings throughout Great Britain and Ireland (in 1691, to 151 meetings in England and Wales alone) and to booksellers willing to vend them in "Cityes and Great Townes." Books were also shipped to continental Europe – especially to Holland, Germany, France, and Spain – and to the

"Czar of Muscovy" in a special delivery. Sowle's books were distributed throughout the American colonies, including Pennsylvania, Rhode Island, New York, Maryland, and North and South Carolina. In 1722 a special delivery was made to her nephew, printer Andrew Bradford, who found it easier to import seven hundred copies of the first Quaker history, Willem Sewel's *The History of the Rise, Increase and Progress of the Christian People Called Quakers* (1722), from his aunt Tace in London than to print them himself. Regular shipments of Sowle's books also reached the West Indies, including Antigua, Barbados, and Jamaica.

Sowle's methods of local distribution were equally thorough. Books were sold at her own retail outlets, distributed by women wholesalers to other retailers who would sell them, and delivered to coffeehouses and other public places such as Turners' Hall, where between 1696 and 1700 apostate Quaker George Keith was holding his anti-Quaker rallies. Tracts were hand-delivered by Friends to the king and his council, to members of Parliament, and to magistrates, clergymen, and other religious and political authorities both locally and throughout the nation – as well as to those "in foreign partes beyond the seas." Sowle's books, for instance, are known to have reached the governors of New York and New England colonies.

A great advantage of serving as primary publisher to the Friends was the Quaker quota system of distribution, whereby each district automatically received an allotment of every Quaker book produced. In the early days of central organization, individual counties were responsible for paying printers for any number of books automatically sent to them, but this system quickly proved unworkable, and policies were revised. From 1680 through 1690 printers sent only those books that different localities had requested by title and quantity – a practice that led to a much smaller total distribution and caused policies to be reevaluated again.

From 1691 each Monthly Meeting was required to take two copies of every work priced under sixpence and one copy of more expensive works, and printers once again sent all books automatically as soon as they were printed. In 1695 the Yearly Meeting confirmed the success of this policy and raised the quota to two copies of every work priced under two shillings and sixpence, and one copy of more expensive works. This collective agreement that all Friends throughout the country were to maintain a standing subscription to all officially authorized books was an innovative and suc-

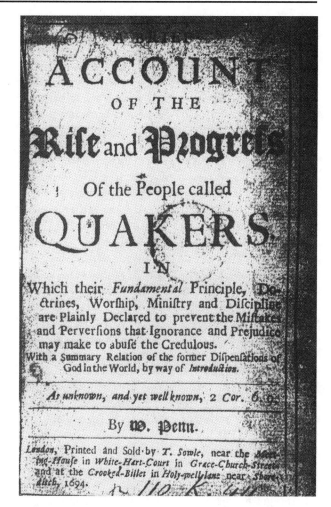

Title page for A Brief Account of the Rise and Progress of the People Called Quakers *(1694) by William Penn, the prolific Quaker author whose* Works *Tace Sowle printed in 1726*

cessful form of mass subscription publishing – the first of its kind on such a scale in England.

In the *Yearly Meeting Epistle* of 1695 the Friends explained that they had implemented the quota system not only to further missionary aims but also to ensure material ones of immediate concern to Sowle: to provide "for some Ease to Friends concerned in the Printing." Tace Sowle was guaranteed a large volume of work as long as she printed officially approved books in the manner that the Friends required. Friends in the counties could also order Quaker books in addition to those works automatically sent to them. To stimulate their interest Sowle customarily bound lengthy trade lists into the backs of the works that she printed, and in 1708 she printed the first Quaker bibliography, John Whiting's *A Catalogue of Friends Books; Written by Many of the People, Called Quakers.*

In addition to having a guaranteed market, loans of capital, and assistance with distribution, other advantages of serving as a publisher for the Friends included help in collecting bills and even some protection against piracy. Because Sowle was producing and distributing huge international consignments, she sometimes had to extend large sums of credit for years at a time, and in particularly difficult collection cases she appealed to Quaker leaders for assistance. When she first took over her family press in 1691, for instance, one of the first things that she did was to attempt to settle her father's outstanding accounts. The minutes of the 13 April 1691 Morning Meeting record that at the age of twenty-five she attended in order to show this august body of Quaker leaders "severall Accounts of Books sent to Barbados and Bristoll some Years since and not paid for." Four Friends were appointed to write Barbados and Bristol, but a year later the debts were still outstanding. On 29 January 1683 disputes about one printer's having reprinted the books of another led the Morning Meeting to rule that Friends' printers were not to reprint or distribute another printer's books without explicit permission — a method for stabilizing book trade practices that was also ahead of its time.

Of course, serving as the Friends' primary printer and publisher also imposed considerable disadvantages as well. Whether Sowle was performing as printer, publisher, warehouser, accountant, or consultant on market demands, Sowle was always "on call," and central organization expected her services at the same price charged by tradespeople "of the world." At the same time, however, from her earliest years in the trade Sowle was making recommendations to central organization about what should be published, and the Friends' leadership listened to her advice. Minutes of the 13 July 1691 meeting record that Sowle's first recommendation was for the works of Elizabeth Bathurst – including her "Sayings of Women" – to be printed in a collected edition (*Truth Vindicated by the Faithful Testimony and Writings of . . . Elizabeth Bathurst,* 1705), and the Morning Meeting consented, "she first Acquainting Charles Bathurst and his wife of it." At this time of strict internal control the occasional willingness of the Friends to leave publishing matters to Tace Sowle's judgment is remarkable. In response to a particular crisis in 1698, for instance, records of a 27 November meeting show that the Morning Meeting ordered her to print one thousand copies of one work and one thousand copies of

another, "and also to Print what more she sees meet."

To the Quakers, by far her most important contribution was that of publishing the first folio edition of the works of Fox, the founder of their sect. In 1691, the year of Fox's death, a committee of Friends met "to consider the fittest method to divide his Writings into." While historians such as Braithwaite single out the publication of Fox's *Journal* (1694) as "beyond question the most important literary event in the history of the Friends," early Friends saw Fox's journal, epistles, and doctrinal books as one coherent publishing project and the writings themselves as a unit. This is reflected on the title pages of the first edition, where the *Journal* is identified as "The First Volume" and the *Epistles* (1698) as "The Second Volume," while the *Gospel-Truth Demonstrated, in a Collection of Doctrinal Books* (1706), although not so marked, forms the third volume. When Tace Sowle was entrusted with the first volume of this major publishing project, she had just taken over her family press. The publication of Fox's folio works kept her busy for more than a decade.

Editing, printing, and correcting the first volume of these works took three years, and in 1694 the Friends finally announced their plans for distributing this volume "throughout the World." By the following year the task of editing the materials for the second volume was nearly completed, and the Yearly Meeting began looking ahead to the third volume, the doctrinal books. In 1695, five years *after* she had taken over the management of the Sowle press and four years after she had undertaken this major publishing project for the Friends, Sowle was freed by the Stationers' Company. Either that year or the next, the Friends awarded her the job of printing the 420 works comprising Fox's *Epistles.*

In 1697 the Friends met her request for an advance of £100 to cover initial printing costs, and in March of the following year the committee in charge reported that they had "treated with Tace Sowle about printing ['G. ff's Epistles'] but not having agreed with her." By the end of the month an agreement had been reached on such details of publication as edition size, format, font, and paper, but significantly, Sowle had been unwilling to budge concerning the price. She had promised to do the job only "at a price not exceeding one penny per sheet," "and if she can afford them lower . . . she will."

By the end of November 1698 the *Epistles* were finally printed – more than four years after the edit-

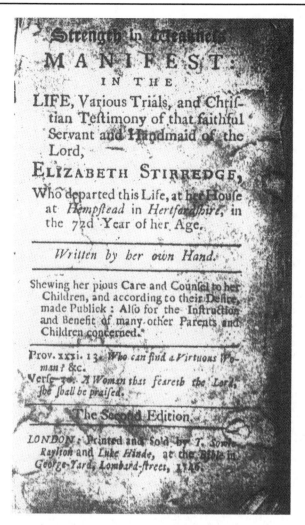

*Title page for the second edition (1746) of Elizabeth
Stirredge's frequently reprinted journal*

ing of this complex volume had begun. While Sowle
had been able to print about ten sheets a week, the
process had been frequently delayed by the inability
of the committee to keep her supplied with edited
copy. The following spring the Yearly Meeting of
1699 "enquire[d] of Tace Sowle, why the Collection
of G. ff's Epistles are [*sic*] so dear." Not surprisingly,
they were soon satisfied that "she [could] afford it
no Cheaper."

The Friends turned to the doctrinal books and
immediately agreed to advance Sowle money for expenses. By 1704 the committee was especially eager
to settle publication details, as subscribers had already been found for 939 copies of this final volume. Sowle originally estimated the size of the job
to be "200 sheets at least" and estimated a fair price
to be fourteen shillings per book, bound in calves'
leather. The volume would eventually require
about seventy sheets more than she had estimated,

and the price would be raised to eighteen shillings.
The Yearly Meeting guaranteed that it would purchase one thousand copies and authorized the Meeting for Sufferings to lend her, "for Incouragement
of printing G. F's Doctrinal Books," "any sume . . .
not exceeding 300 pounds."

By 1706 the doctrinal books were finally
printed as *Gospel-Truth Demonstrated in a Collection of
Doctrinal Books*. Less than one year after this volume
was completed, the Friends were told that "Tace
upon her Examination is now fully satisfyed" that
the Friends had taken the allotment of one thousand
copies for which they had initially subscribed. The
Meeting then agreed to write to Ireland, Scotland,
Holland, Pennsylvania, "and all other places in
America that Correspond with Friends" to inform
booksellers that "they may take off such Quantityes
as they shall please to write for." Thirteen years
after this massive publishing project had begun, the

publication and initial distribution of George Fox's works in folio was complete.

In addition to the works of George Fox, Sowle also published the major works of theologian Robert Barclay, whose *Apology for the True Christian Divinity* was a staple of the Sowle press. First published in Latin in 1676 and in English in 1678, the *Apology* systematized the principles of Quakerism and became a virtual handbook for the Friends. Sowle published Barclay's *Apology* at least five times in English (1701, 1702, 1703, 1733, and 1736) as well as in French (1702), Spanish (1710), Latin (1729), and Danish (1738). She also published Barclay's *A Catechism and Confession of Faith,* which had been first published in 1673 and which Sowle published at least three times — in English (1716 and 1740) and in Latin (1727). In 1717 she published an edition of Barclay's *Anarchy of the Ranters and Other Libertines* (first published in 1676), and in the following year she reprinted a collection of Barclay's writings that had been first published in 1682 as *Truth Triumphant.*

William Penn had been a close friend of Andrew Sowle, and the Sowle press published nearly all of this prolific author's works. Tace Sowle published editions of Penn's major works such as *No Cross, No Crown* (first published by Andrew Sowle in 1669), *A Key Opening a Way to Every Common Understanding* (first published in 1692 and reprinted in English, French, and Danish), and *A Brief Account of the . . . People Called Quakers* (first published in 1694). Tace Sowle also published at least one edition of Penn's *Primitive Christianity Revived* (first published in 1696), *The Christian-Quaker* (first published in 1673), the related *Discourse of the General Rule of Faith* (first published in 1699), *Some Fruits of Solitude* (first published in 1693), *More Fruits of Solitude* (first published in 1702), and many other books by Penn. She also published separately Penn's *Preface to [George Fox's] Journal* (1694), a work widely considered to be Penn's finest writing, and in 1726 she produced an edition of his *Works.*

Between 1701 and 1740 Sowle printed the first seven parts of *Piety Promoted, in a Collection of Dying Sayings of Many of the People Called Quakers,* a collection of biographical accounts of early Friends (including Andrew Sowle and Thomas Raylton, but not Tace Sowle). She also published the aforementioned *History of the . . . Christian People Called Quakers,* Sewel's history of the sect that was widely read by Quakers throughout the eighteenth century and brought to the attention of an even wider audience in the nineteenth century by the praise of Charles

Lamb. It remains an important source for historians of Quakerism today.

Sowle routinely published basic works intended to maintain movement cohesion: she was printing the annual *Yearly Meeting Epistle,* in quantities of six hundred to one thousand copies, for example, from the time that she was twenty-five years old. While her publication of the first Quaker bibliography, the aforementioned *Catalogue of Friends Books* by John Whiting, was initially intended for advertising purposes, that work has served as the basis for bibliographies of Quaker writings ever since.

From the earliest days of her career Tace Sowle was a major printer and publisher of seventeenth- and early-eighteenth-century Nonconformist women writers. For seventeenth-century women writers in particular, the importance of having access to the Quaker publishing "support system" may be surmised from the fact that Quaker women produced twice as many printed editions as any other female group. The Sowle press printed more than one hundred works by at least fourteen different women writers. These women include Bathurst; Sarah Cheevers; Elizabeth Chester; Anne Docwra; Mary Edwards; Alice Ellis; Katharine Evans; Jane Fearon; Alice Hayes; Elizabeth Jacob; Mary Mollineaux; Elizabeth Stirredge; Jane Truswell; Margaret Fell Fox, the "mother of Quakerism"; and Jane Lead, the prolific theosophical visionary.

Several works of these women were published many times, particularly the works of Bathurst, Hayes, Mollineaux, and Stirredge. Sowle printed at least three of the six eighteenth-century editions of Bathurst's *Truth Vindicated by the Faithful Testimony and Writings of . . . Elizabeth Bathurst* (1695, first published in 1679 as *Truth's Vindication*). In 1749 Sowle and Hinde printed Hayes's *A Legacy, or Widow's Mite* (1723), a work that was published five times before the end of the eighteenth century. Mollineaux's *Fruits of Retirement,* first published by Sowle in 1702, was published at least eight times before 1800 — four times in England and an additional four times in Pennsylvania. Stirredge's journal, *Strength in Weakness Manifest: In the Life, Various Trials, and Christian Testimony of . . . Elizabeth Stirredge* (published by the Sowle press in 1711 and 1746), was published at least four times in the eighteenth century.

In 1710 Sowle published Fell Fox's autobiographical *A Brief Collection of Remarkable Passages and Occurrences Relating to the Birth, Education, Life, Conversion, Travels, Services, and Deep Sufferings of . . . Margaret Fell; but by her Second Marriage, Margaret Fell Fox.* In 1715 she published an edition of Katharine

Evans and Sarah Cheevers's *A Brief History of the Voyage . . . to the Island of Malta,* an account of their three-year imprisonment by the Inquisition that had been first published in 1662 as *This Is a Short Relation.*

The half century spanned by Tace Sowle's career was one of the most formative periods in the history of the British press, as well as a decisive period in Quaker history. As the primary printer and publisher for the largest Nonconformist sect in England, Tace Sowle published nearly six hundred items during her fifty-eight-year career. By the end of its 150-year history the Sowle-Hinde-Phillips firm was one of the longest-running printing houses in England, and the house had seen its greatest development under Tace Sowle's management. Her role as one of the most important Nonconformist publishers of her generation has yet-unrealized implications for the history of the British book trade, for the history of religious Nonconformity, and for the economic and political history of women.

References:

Pamela M. Ambrose, "The Power of the Quaker Press," M.A. dissertation, University of London, 1981;

Charles M. Andrews, "The Quakers in London and Their Printers There," in *Byways in Quaker History: A Collection of Historical Essays by Colleagues and Friends of William I. Hull,* edited by Howard H. Brinton (Wallingford, Pa.: Pendle Hill, 1944), pp. 191–208;

William C. Braithwaite, *The Beginnings of Quakerism* (London: Macmillan, 1912); revised by Henry J. Cadbury (Cambridge: Cambridge University Press, 1955);

Braithwaite, *The Second Period of Quakerism* (London: Macmillan, 1919); second edition prepared by Cadbury (Cambridge: Cambridge University Press, 1961);

Patricia Crawford, "Women's Published Writings 1600–1700," in *Women in English Society 1500–1800,* edited by Mary Prior (New York: Methuen, 1985), pp. 211–282;

John Dunton, *The Life and Errors of John Dunton Citizen of London* (London, 1705; 2 volumes, New York: Franklin, 1969);

Nathan Kite, *Antiquarian Researches among the Early Printers and Publishers of Friends' Books* (Manchester, 1844);

Anna Littleboy, "Friends' Reference Library," *Journal of the Friends' Historical Society,* 18, no. 1 (1921): 1–16;

Littleboy, "Friends' Reference Library," *Journal of the Friends' Historical Society,* 18, no. 3 (1921): 66–80;

D. F. McKenzie, "The London Book Trade in the Later Seventeenth Century" (Cambridge: Privately published, 1976);

R. S. Mortimer, "Biographical Notices of Printers and Publishers of Friends' Books up to 1750," *Journal of Documentation,* 3 (September 1947): 107–125;

Mortimer, "The First Century of Quaker Printers," *Journal of the Friends' Historical Society,* 40 (1948): 37–49;

Percy H. Muir, "English Imprints after 1640," *Library,* fourth series 14 (March 1934): 157–177;

Thomas O'Malley, "'Defying the Powers and Tempering the Spirit.' A Review of Quaker Control over Their Publications 1672–1689," *Journal of Ecclesiastical History,* 33 (January 1982): 72–88;

Michael Treadwell, "London Printers and Printing-Houses in 1705," *Publishing History,* 7 (1980): 5–44;

Luella M. Wright, *The Literary Life of the Early Friends 1650–1725* (New York: Columbia University Press, 1932).

– Paula J. McDowell

Michael Sparke

(London: 1607 – 1653)

Publisher Michael Sparke may be hailed as the mouthpiece of extremist Puritan dogma. He was closely associated with Puritan high priest William Prynne, whose many fulminations Sparke published, and with leading Presbyterian divines whose sermons bear his imprint. For his convictions Sparke suffered the ignominy of the pillory and imprisonment. In disseminating some 150 books and tracts and in writing books Sparke reveals an absolute belief in principles of Puritanism that assailed the depravity of man and espoused the redemption of the elect.

Michael Sparke, the son of Thomas Sparke, a husbandman, was born circa 1588 in the village of Eynsham at the angle of the Upper Thames and the Evenlode. On 3 June 1607 he was apprenticed to London stationer Simon Pauley, an indentureship that, in light of the Sparke family's support of Presbyterianism, appears most puzzling. Sparke later referred to his former master as "one who dealt much in Popish books ... [and] spent his time in Staffordshire at Worley Hall, binding, vending and putting to sale Popish Books, Pictures, Beads and such Trash." Pauley's association with "Popish Trash" no doubt further incited his apprentice's abhorrence of Catholicism at "seeing the gross ignorance of many among them."

From 1623 to 1628 Sparke apparently traveled about the country as an itinerant bookseller and Puritan crusader. As an author who would regenerate mankind, he entered in the books of the Stationers' Company on 3 October 1623 his earliest known work, *The Crums of Comfort; with Godly Prayers* (1628). Designed to aid the spiritual needs of the faithful, the book consists of various prayers, meditations, and scriptural passages selected for appropriate occasions: "prayers for days of the week, prayers for women, prayer[s] for all in distress at Sea, by Storm or Tempest."

Sparke combined piety with patriotic zeal. In *To The Glory of God in Thankefull Remembrance of Our Three Great Deliverances With Eternal Memory,* a broadside that he wrote and published in 1627, he refers to the English defeat of the Spanish Armada, detection of the Gunpowder Plot, and delivery of England from recent pestilence. In 1625 such visitations were naturally attributed to man's depravity

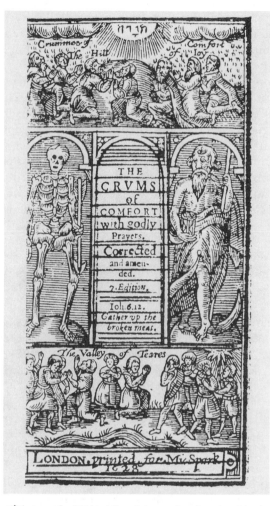

Title page for Michael Sparke's popular devotional book, his earliest known work (1628)

and disregard for moral law evident in "our contempt of thy threatnings, our abuse of thy mercies, our neglect of thy judgments."

Although Sparke was greatly concerned with the wrath of an angry God, he was also disturbed by the terrestrial trials of poor and much neglected children. In his *Greevous Grones for the Poore* (1621) he reflects on the condition of the destitute and on possibilities for improving their fortunes. Despite the success of the Elizabethan Poor Law of 1601, many suffered from a poor harvest and from a depression in the English cloth trade. Sparke viewed with alarm the existence of a large class of unemployed:

Title page for Capt. John Smith's narrative of the early colonial settlement in America

The number of the poore do dailie increase, all things yet worketh for the worst in their behalfe. For there hath been no collection for them, no not these seuen yeares, in many Parishes of this Land, . . . [and] many of these Parishes turne forth their poore . . . Labourers that will not work . . . to begge, filtch and steale for their maintenance.

Despite its moral overtones this treatise by Sparke remains a significant sociological study of economic conditions during the early seventeenth century.

Yet Sparke's pen was not his only weapon for scourging the soul and effecting social improvement. By 1616 he had established premises at the Blue Bible, Green Arbour Court in the Old Bailey, where, until his death some thirty-seven years later, he published the writings of Puritan exegetes, significant Americana, and even lighthearted texts. In January 1617 he registered at Stationers' Hall his first known publication, *The protature [sic] with the armes of Marcus Antonius de Dominis Archiepiscopus Spalatensis,* an account of the conversion to Anglicanism of the wily archbishop of Spalato, a friend of

King James I. Sparke was to publish from 1617 to 1630 approximately fifty books, the majority of which reflected Puritan ideology.

In 1626 Sparke published the first book by William Prynne, *The Perpetuitie of a Regenerate Man's Estate.* Sparke's name was to be closely associated with that of the zealot Prynne, as Sparke was to become the publisher of Prynne's shattering *Histriomastix* (1633) and to suffer the indignity of the pillory and a jail term along with Prynne. His friendship for "Marginal Prynne" is manifest by his bequest of his "seale ring of gold" as a token of affection to his "dear friend."

Although most of Sparke's publications emphasize man's spiritual person and heavenly good, a few are preoccupied with his terrestrial journeys. Among Sparke's most significant publications is the 1624 second edition of Capt. John Smith's *The Generall Historie of Virginia.* Sparke no doubt anticipated a large readership for the adventures of the doughty Smith stalking danger in encounters with savage Native Americans. Yet Sparke may have

Woodcut from Charles Fitz-Geffrey's The Curse of Corne-horders *(1631), one of many collections of
Puritan sermons published by Sparke*

published four editions of the *Historie of Virginia* for
another reason: he deeply admired the Virginia
Company. He had dedicated his *Greevous Grones for
the Poore* to "The Right Honourable Company of the
Virginian and Sommer Island Plantations," and his
brother, Thomas, had sailed on the *Susan* and settled in the Bermudas. During his lifetime Sparke remained interested in the Virginia colony and lent
money to several of the settlers in Jamestown and
Yorktown. Whatever his motives for publishing
Smith's great work may have been, Sparke issued a
best-seller that was reprinted in 1615, 1626, 1627,
and 1631.

Perhaps less alluring to the patriotic Englishman but nonetheless of paramount importance is
the Sparke publication of Peter Martyr, *Famous History of the Indies* (1628). Sparke's association with this
work indicates his business ruthlessness. In 1612
Martyr's *Decades* had been published by London stationer Thomas Adams as *De Novo Orbe, or the Historie
of the West Indies.* Upon Adams's death in 1625 his
copyright passed to Andrew Hebb of the Bell, and,
in order to activate and substantiate his copyright,
Hebb published another edition titled *The Historie of*

the West Indies. Although Hebb claimed his version
was the second edition, Sparke nonetheless also described his publication as the second edition and, to
clear his name from any taint of piracy, registered
his edition as *The Famous Historie of the Indies,* "set
forth first by Mr. Hackluyt and now published by
L. M. Gent."

In addition to such prime Americana, Sparke
offered his readers various selections: Robert
Burton's *The Anatomy of Melancholy* (1624) and
Gervase Markham's *Methode or Epitome* (1628) as
well as his *Faithful Farrier* (1629). Of popular interest were *A speciall remidie for the plague* (1625?), designed to combat the contagion of 1625; Charles
Robson's *News from Aleppo* (1628) by the Hebrew
scholar Abenezrah Kimchi; and the anonymously
written *Booke of Meery Riddles* (1629).

These texts were published by Sparke before
his first encounter with the authorities. On 2 April
1629 a warrant for his arrest was delivered to the
warden of Fleet Prison to take Sparke in custody
"and to keep him safe prisoner until further order,
the cause of his commitment being for printing and
publishing offensive books without license or war-

rant." According to a statement of the ecclesiastical commissioners, Sparke and others had printed and published "various books without the same being licensed by the Archbishop of Canterbury or Bishop of London." Sparke was specifically charged with publishing *Babel No Bethel* (1629), by the Puritan divine Henry Burton, and *The Antithesis of the Church of England* (1629), by Prynne. In his defense Sparke insisted on his rights as a native Englishman: he denied

> the present binding authority of the decree in Star Chamber for regulating printing as directly intrenching on the hereditary liberty of the subjects' persons and goods, and being contrary to Magna Charta, the Petition of Right and other statutes.

He considered Prynne's work "to be a just and necessary defense of the Church of England against the Arminians and thinks that [Prynne] has done all to the glory of God, the honor of the King."

Despite his eloquent appeal Sparke was jailed for some time, and he was reapprehended in April 1631 for having published without license two other books by Prynne – a second edition of *The Antithesis of the Church of England* (1630) and *Lame Giles His Haultings* (1630) – and other works. The state prosecutor directed his severest castigation at Sparke, who had been "within 10 years past several times committed in prison and admonished, and although he promised to submit to his governors as other moderate men do, has as yet been more refractory and offensive than ever." Sparke confessed his role in publishing *The Antithesis of the Church of England*, an offense for which he had already been punished, and he added that he had only two copies of *Lame Giles His Haultings*, both of which he had given to the author.

Apparently official threats and even imprisonment did not intimidate Sparke, for after 1630 his trade list emphasizes books by Puritan spokesmen rather than works such as *The Booke of Meery Riddles*. From 1630 to 1640 Sparke published approximately eighty books, almost half of which are theological: sermons of the brilliant John Preston; the devotional tracts of John Vicars; *The Theatre of Gods Judgements* (1631), by Thomas Beard, Cromwell's schoolmaster; and the writings of William Attersoll, Robert Bolton, and others.

Sparke's most significant publication of this decade was the offensive *Histrio-mastix, The Players Scourge* (1633), by William Prynne. This work marked the apex of antidramatic literature written by Puritan apologists and appeared eight years after

Title page for radical Puritan William Prynne's treatise on the evils of theatrical entertainment

the brief anonymous tract *A Shorte Treatise Against Stage-Playes* (1625), which outlined the reform party's principal criticism of the drama. Prynne's voluminous text repeats the arguments of *A Shorte Treatise Against Stage-Playes* to such an extent that some believe he may have written both works. A dogmatic Puritan fanatic, Prynne little tolerated the "licentious . . . riotous and deboist [debauched]," among whom he included the mimes, puppeteers, and actors of the Stuart stage. To Prynne, a life that deflected from the "waies and workes" of God must be destroyed, and to this end he devoted six years of writing *Histrio-mastix,* a gigantic volume of more than eleven hundred pages with marginal notes and references to long-forgotten authorities. Archbishop William Laud declared that reading Prynne's text and notes would take six years of a man's life. In a mass of arguments and invectives Prynne strove to prove that plays were unlawful incentives to immorality and were condemned by Holy Writ.

The printing of the work was concluded at a most inopportune time, as Henrietta Maria, queen of England, and her ladies were engaged at Whitehall in rehearsing a pastoral play that was not presented until Prynne's book was in circulation. Earlier a troupe of French actresses had attempted to perform at Blackfriars and had been "hissed, hooted and pippen-pelted from the stage." The self-righteous Prynne, who referred to the female actors as "notorious whores," deeply offended the French-born queen of England, and he was charged with libel against the Crown, the state, and the people of England.

Proceedings against Prynne were instituted in the court of Star Chamber during February 1634, with Attorney General William Noy as prosecutor for the Crown. The case was directed not only against "Mr. Pryn, a mover of the people to dis-content and sedition," but also against Sparke, his publisher, as well as the printers William Jones, Augustine Matthewes, and Edward Allde and the ecclesiastical licenser William Buckner. In his defense Prynne declared that he had brought the complete manuscript to Sparke, who in turn had shown it to Buckner. The distraught Buckner stated that he had seen only sixty-four pages of the text "att the request of Sparckes to bee entered unto the Stationers Hall, to intitle Sparke to the sale of it that he advised the booke should not bee published and said to Sparcke he would loose his eares yf he published it." He added that he was unaware of its authorship and that he had great difficulty in reading the manuscript since it had been written in "an illegible hand." He remarked that about six weeks later Sparke had shown him a "few printed leaves of a book entitled 'Histriomastix' affirming he had lost the original written copy and . . . the printed sheets agreed with the written ones which [Buckner] had perused." The unhappy Buckner insisted that he had never granted any license to the text after the first sixty-four pages, and he added that "Whilst the book was printing . . . having casually some notice thereof, [I] endeauoured to stay the same, but it was afterwards imprinted by several printers secretly." He concluded that as soon as he heard that the book had been printed, he delivered a warrant for its restraint and seizure.

Further testimony indicates that Sparke had "much abused" the licenser of the press, had realized that *Histrio-mastix* might be "called in," and had therefore urged customers to purchase it immediately. Prynne was sentenced to life imprisonment, was to lose his ears on the pillory, and was expelled from Lincoln's Inn, where he had served as barrister. Sparke, "the pryme publisher of his booke [and one who] hath divers times offended in lyke nature," was denounced as "the first broacher of the booke." He had "sollicited the printing . . . publish[ed] it, [and] dispersed the whole volume with a desire of gayne knowing the same to contayne most seditious matters. . . ." He was therefore fined £500 and sentenced to stand in the pillory "with papers and imprisonment at the kings pleasure."

Copies of *Histrio-mastix* were to be ferreted out and burned at Cheapside or St. Paul's Churchyard. Messengers of the press were dispatched to Sparke's premises to seize all available copies and to discover the names of purchasers. Examination of Sparke's records indicated that far more than fifty people had purchased copies of the odious text – forty London stationers, nine Oxford dealers, and booksellers in Salisbury, Exeter, Manchester, Ludlow, and Norwich. On 10 May 1634 Prynne and Sparke stood in the pillory while "copies of the book were burnt under [their] nose[s]." On the same day the court of the Stationers' Company deliberated the fate of Sparke, its most subversive member, whom it decided to suspend from its membership rolls for his offenses and to ensure that "no scandall may come or accrue to the Society here[by]."

On 10 March 1640 Sparke's petition for redress was considered, and he was ultimately vindicated by the Long Parliament of 1640. Many of its members admired him, and they voted that "the sentence given against him in the Starre-Chamber was against the law, that soe much of his fine yet unpaied should be discharged, and that hee should have reparation of his damages from those who gave him that iniust sentence." Readmitted to his company and exonerated by his government, the reinvigorated Sparke continued to publish and prosper. He described himself as a "wholesaleman" enjoying extensive contacts at home and abroad. He retained agents in many English towns, and his business ventures extended to Edinburgh, where he dealt with stationer John Wreittoun, who dispatched copies of popular literary works to him. Sparke mentions among his travels a journey to Leiden, Holland, where he probably met members of the great firm of Elzevier and other Dutch dealers. In all likelihood during this trip he arranged to import Bibles and liturgies to be sold in London at far cheaper rates than those offered by Robert Barker, king's printer and Bible patentee.

The lugubrious *Histrio-mastix* is the high spot of Sparke's trade list from 1630 to 1640. During this decade Sparke turned to printing many far-lighter and more-popular books than that characterized by the turgid prose of William Prynne: *The Merry Tales of the Mad Men of Gotham* (1630), ascribed to A.

Engraved title page, by William Marshall, for Richard Braithwait's 1631 book on the appearance and behavior of women

Borde; Richard Brathwait's *The English Gentlewoman* (1631); and Ralph Knevet's *Rhodon and Iris: A Pastorall* (1631). His trade list represents the budding English interest in science: Tycho Brahe's *The Learned Ticho Brahe His Astronomical Conjecture of the New * [Star]* (1632), Bishop John Wilkins's *The Discovery of a World in the Moone* (1638), Danish physician Levinus Lemnius's *Touchstone of Complexions* (1633), and others.

Sparke maintained his interest in the circulation of Americana. In 1639 he issued three editions of Francis Higginson's *New-Englands Plantation,* which he recommended to readers as a work not full of bombast but actually an "Epitomy of . . . proceedings in the Plantations." Three editions of *Europae Speculum,* by Edwin Sandys, former treasurer of the Virginia Company, bear the Sparke imprint. Of greater interest is Sparke's joint publication of Gerard Mercator's great *Atlas.* Sparke registered the work in partnership with Samuel Cartwright on 8 November 1632, but its printing was delayed for two years before it was reentered and the work fi-

nally published in large folio in 1635, the first English edition of *Mercator's Atlas.*

Although its maps were designed essentially for the explorer and traveler, they were also of use to the schoolboy – if he could afford the book. The Puritan considered education an essential step toward godliness, for reading was the means to study of the Bible and to good works. Sparke espoused not only the study and sale of appropriate texts but also the building of more English schoolhouses. In his will he provided an endowment for the construction of a schoolhouse in Eynsham, the town of his birth, and his interest in education is also evident in his publication of *Porta Linguarum* (1631), by the distinguished Czech educator Jan Amos Comenius, whom the Puritan Parliament invited to be a consultant on pedagogical matters.

Comenius's work, appearing in four Sparke editions, provided a shortcut to the study of foreign languages. Its text was later expanded by John Anchoran as *The Gate of the Tongves Vnlocked and Opened* (1639). As editor, he promised the stu-

SCINTILLA,
OR
A LIGHT BROKEN INTO
darke Warehoufes.

With
OBSERVATIONS VPON THE
Monopolifts of Seaven feverall Patents,
and Two Charters.

Practifed and performed, By a Miftery of
fome Printers, Sleeping Stationers, and
Combining Book-fellers.

Anatomifed
And layd open in a Breviat, in which is only a
touch of their foreftaking and ingroffing of
Books in Patents, and Rayfing them
to exceffive prifes.

Left to the Confideration of the High and Honou-
nourable Houfe of Parliament now affembled.

Let not one Brothor oppreffe another.

Doe as you would be done unto.

AT LONDON,
Printed, not for profit, but for the Common Weles
good: and no where to be fold, but fome where
to be given.   1641.

*Title page for Sparke's polemic attack on the practices of
monopolists and other print-trade abuses*

dent "a short way of teaching and thorowly learning within a yeere and half at the farthest the Latin, English, French, and any other language." Other educational treatises published by Sparke include the *New Dialogues or Colloquies or a little Dictionary of Eight Languages* (1639) by Noel Barlement and the *Pathway to the Gate of Tongues* (1635) by Jean de Grave.

By 1640 Sparke was more than fifty years old, and he must have applauded the downfall of the Stuart monarchy and the establishment of the Puritan regime. In July 1641 the courts of Star Chamber and High Commission were abolished, and the printing trade, freed from former governmental restraints, was now subject to the control of Parliament and of various committees. Old resentments within the Stationers' Company, like those within the state, were publicly aired. The royal patentees, the monopolists, and those dealers who had controlled the company's policies be-

came targets of the firebrand — notably of Michael Sparke, who seized the opportunity to attack wealthier dealers and become the defender of underprivileged publishers and booksellers.

Scintilla, or a Light Broken into Darke Warehouses, with Observations Vpon the Monopolists of Seaven Severall Patents, authored and published by Sparke in 1641, bears the imprint, "Printed, not for *profit,* but for the Common Weles good: and no where to be *sold,* but some where to be given." *Scintilla* excoriates the former patentees of the Bible, prayer books, law books, and textbooks. Sparke most severely castigates his old enemy Robert Barker, the former king's printer, for his business methods and control of Bible stock. Despite its invective the work is an extremely important document in the history of printing, as it illuminates topics such as the sizes of editions, paper, and prices of the period. Two years after its publication Sparke issued another work of bibliographical interest, *A Catalogue of Printed Books Written by VVilliam Prynne, Esquire.*

The Puritanism advocated by Sparke was less extreme than that of his "dear friend" William Prynne. Although Sparke championed Puritan control of the state, he rejected control of the state by a radical left wing consisting of John Lilburne, William Walwyn, and Henry Robinson, all of whom preached complete emancipation of the press. As a supporter of middle-class Presbyterian conservatism, Sparke in 1652 wrote and published *A Second Beacon Fired by Scintilla* — a work that assailed, among various wrongs, the lethargy of the current Parliament that had not curtailed the circulation of what it termed "Popish Trash" and books offensive to Presbyterianism. To Sparke the entire book trade was in a state of disarray, having been ruined by sectarian hawkers and writers of papist newsletters:

> Look into Pauls Churchyard how many have lived bravely, . . . entertained . . . men of learning[,] . . . and now, now, now poore honest stationer, . . . where's thy fame? where's thy plenty? . . . I have heard it, and from honest Stationers, . . . that they have not taken 20*s.* a week and their Rent to be paid.

In this *Second Beacon* Sparke attacked those "poysonous Popish books" and the overwhelming demands of the monopolists for the last time. He died in 1653, and his will specified that he was to be interred in the parish church of St. Sepulchre. To his wife he left plate, money, and his house at Hampstead. To family members and business associates he left bequests totaling approximately £286. To fifty apprentices of the Old Bailey he bequeathed copies of Lewis Bayly's *Practice of Pietie* (1613) and his own *Crums of Comfort.*

In abetting Puritanism Michael Sparke hoped to establish a society free of sin, a brotherhood of the elect. He was above all a true Englishman, aware of his rights enunciated by the Magna Carta and the Petition of Right. He epitomizes the Puritan creed of social reform and spiritual regeneration. A zealous spokesman of his own brand of religion, Sparke remembered his family and business associates, his friend Prynne, and other reformers at whose disposal he had placed his press.

References:

William Haller, *The Rise of Puritanism* (New York: Columbia University Press, 1938);

Henry R. Plomer, "Michael Sparke, Puritan Bookseller," *Bibliographer,* 1, no. 9 (December 1902): 410–412;

Leona Rostenberg, *Literary, Political, Scientific, Religious & Legal Publishing, Printing & Bookselling in England, 1551–1700: Twelve Studies,* 2 volumes (New York: Franklin, 1965);

Michael Sparke, *Scintilla, or a Light Broken into Darke Warehouses* (London: Sparke, 1641);

Sparke, *A Second Beacon Fired by Scintilla* (London: Sparke, 1652).

— *Leona Rostenberg*

William Stansby

(London: 1597, 1609 – 1636)

As a first-rank figure in the Jacobean and Caroline printing trade, William Stansby was a craftsman who produced many fine volumes demonstrating a blend of technical proficiency and aesthetic ability. During his twenty-five years as master of the shop at Cross Keys near Paul's Wharf, Stansby printed works by the leading theologians, philosophers, antiquarians, and poets of his time: William Camden, Richard Hooker, John Selden, Francis Bacon, Samuel Purchas, Sir Walter Ralegh, William Shakespeare, Ben Jonson, John Donne, and Michael Drayton, to name but a few. At the same time that Stansby was publishing these authors he also pursued a flourishing trade in chapbooks, sermons, plays, romances, almanacs, and other popular works, most of which show the same attention to quality as the larger, more prominent volumes. The broad subject matter and high quality of the works he published in addition to the length of his career place Stansby in the forefront of early-seventeenth-century printers.

Like so many whose efforts contributed to the vibrancy of early modern London, Stansby began life elsewhere. The parish register of St. Mary Major, Exeter, records the baptism on 8 July 1572 of William, son of Richard Stansby, the third child in the family to be named William but the only one to survive into adulthood. Evidently the wool trade that dominated Exeter's economy did not suit young Stansby's temperament, for unlike his siblings he looked beyond Devonshire when the time came for him to select a vocation. On 12 January 1591 the Register of the Stationers' Company of London shows that "**william Stansby** son of RICHARD STANSBY of EXON cutler hath put him self Apprentice to **John wyndet** citizen and Stacioner of London for vij yeres begynnynge at Christmas *Anno XXXIJ*^{do} *Regine Elizabeth*." Christmas of the thirty-second year of Elizabeth's reign would have occurred in the winter of 1589–1590, and it is not clear why Windet, also originally from Exeter, waited a full year before he registered his binding of Stansby (a delay for which he was fined). Nonetheless, the young apprentice served his term satisfactorily and on 7 January 1597 was admitted as a freeman of the Stationers' Company.

Government and trade regulations, as well as the difficulty that an apprentice would encounter in raising sufficient capital, made it unlikely that a newly freed journeyman could set up his own establishment or purchase an existing one. In most cases the former apprentice would continue working for his old master or hire out at a different shop. Stansby's experience seems typical, for he remained with Windet and worked at the busy shop until the death of his former master thirteen years later. Perhaps to mark his change in professional status, on 28 April 1597 Stansby exercised the right of a freeman by registering with the Stationers' Company the anonymous *The Policy of the Turkish Empire*. When published later that year, this quarto bore the imprint "Printed by Iohn Windet for W. S.," indicating that Stansby began his career by working with his master in a rudimentary partnership, the older printer producing the work and the young journeyman acting as publisher by arranging for the registration, financing, and distribution of the book.

During his years as a journeyman printer Stansby's name appeared occasionally in imprints as a publisher, but generally the public record lacked this information. Then in 1609 his name started to occur regularly as a printer on titles coming from the shop, and this suggests that he had acquired more responsibilities in the business. John Windet's will, attested 21 November 1610, shows that at some time he and Stansby had some understanding about the ownership of the shop, for it identifies "William Stansbie Cittizen and Stacioner of London whoe is nowe Copartner with me in printinge as by certaine Covenauntes made betweene us both touchinge the same at large appeareth." In an unpublished dissertation Mark Bland has argued that Stansby bought his way into this partnership by purchasing a large font of type cast on an English body, substantial amounts of which first appear in books printed by Windet and Stansby in 1609. Whatever the details of the arrangement, within a month of making his will Windet died and left Stansby half of the assets of the business, as well as the right to purchase the remaining half from Windet's two sisters.

By the time Stansby became master of the Cross Keys printing shop he had already begun exercising the prerogatives of a master. On 21 June 1610 he bound in apprenticeship for a period of eight years one Robert Lighteburne, the son of a London sadler named John Lighteburne and the first of sixteen apprentices whom Stansby would bind during his career. Once Windet had died Stansby resumed registering titles with the stationers; on 11 September 1611 he transferred forty-six titles that had previously belonged to Windet, including Hooker's prestigious *Of the Lawes of Ecclesiasticall Politie* (1593) as well as the profitable *Assize of Bread* and mathematical treatises by Thomas Blundeville. One thing Stansby did not officially license, however, was his mastership of the printing house. Stationers' Company records for 8 October 1634 contain a list compiled by Sir John Lambe, dean of the Arches Court of Canterbury, who had been appointed to oversee the stationers' affairs. Stansby's name was among the sixteen "Master Printers now liueing not found registered in the hall Booke" — that is, Stansby was among those who had not received archiepiscopal sanction. That so many licensing lapses could have extended so long without having punitive consequences may indicate that the guild members cared little for outside regulation of this sort, or that Stansby's infraction may have resulted from mere oversight rather than conscious exclusion.

Having become master of his own shop, Stansby's work distinguished the Cross Keys as one of the leading printing houses in early modern London. He produced his share of smaller, popular works such as almanacs, sermons, chapbooks, news books, plays, and political-religious propaganda. Yet while he churned out these titles for the voracious London market, Stansby also began printing prestigious folios of history, theology, and literature. He produced large volumes such as a new edition of Hooker's *Laws* (1611); a translation of Thomas de Fougasses's *The General History of the Magnificent State of Venice* (1612, jointly printed with George Eld); Purchas's survey of religions and cultures, *Purchas his Pilgrimage* (1613); Ralegh's monumental *History of the World* (1614); the first volume of Camden's important *Annales rerum anglicarum, et hibernicarum, regnante Elizabetha* (1615); and the groundbreaking edition of Jonson's *Workes of Benjamin Jonson* (1616). In printing and publishing these books Stansby raised the quality of his craftsmanship to that of the text. The folios feature either engraved or majestically typeset title pages and are set in a clear, open type of English body with ruled

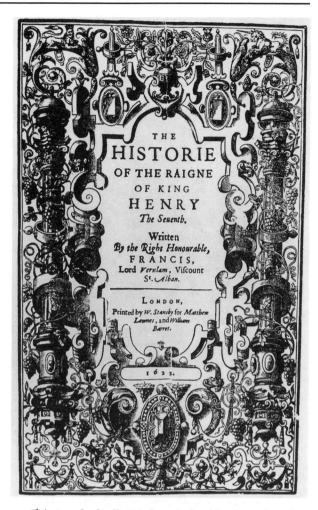

Title page for Sir Francis Bacon's chronicle of the reign of Henry VII

headlines and, in the case of Camden's volume, boxed text. Many of these publications Stansby printed on two different types of paper — regular quality for the retail trade and larger, high-quality paper for special presentation copies.

Such energetic activity typifies the print trade of early modern London, a trade that periodically attracted the regulatory attention of court and city. One official proclamation that attempted to limit the proliferation of printing technology and to protect the investments of the masters indicates that Windet owned at least three presses in 1586. A Star Chamber decree of 1615, "UPON Complaint made to this Court (by the Master printers) of the Multitude of presses that are erected among them," listed nineteen master printers and the maximum number of presses allowed to each. Through such edicts state and commercial authorities aimed to reign in an expanding trade and perhaps diminish the number of printing presses in use. The 1615 decree

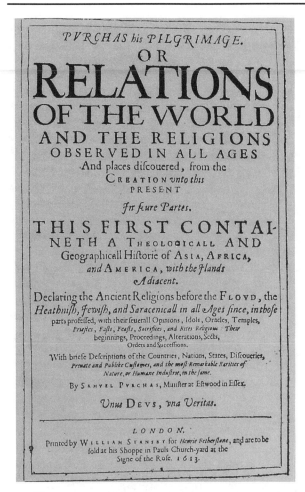

Title page of Samuel Purchas's survey of world religions and cultures

grants two presses to Stansby's establishment, although he may actually have still owned the three that had belonged to Windet twenty-nine years earlier. With only a few changes in the names, on 5 July 1623 the same list of masters and presses appears in the records of the court of the stationers and notes that the printers "according to a former order haue reformed themselues for the number of presses that euery one is to haue and accordingly haue brought in their barres to shewe their Conformitie therevnto." As in 1615, records show that Stansby still possessed two presses.

Guild court documents reveal much about the business practices of printers and their ambitious attempts to circumvent guidelines for their own profit. Stansby's name appears repeatedly in the records and fine books of the stationers, who penalized him for various offenses. Within six months of having taken over the print shop he was fined five shillings for printing an unregistered book, and he incurred similar penalties in

1614 and 1620. On 21 June 1616 the court assessed him £6 13s. "for bynding of Randall Booth an appntice at a scriueno[rs]." On many occasions he was warned for employing foreigners and was ordered to avoid them. Twice the court fined him thirty shillings and forty shillings, respectively, for unfit speech to a fellow stationer, and on a third occasion he was deprived of the benefit of printing from the common English Stock for "iniurious and reproachfull" words in the stationers' hall.

Stansby's most frequent appearances in the official records, however, concern disputes over ownership and over rights to print various properties. The first such conflict involved the printing of a new edition of Hooker's *Laws,* one of the valuable properties that Stansby had inherited from Windet. When Hooker had first begun looking for someone to print his five-volume defense of the Anglican Church against Puritan radicals, he had difficulty finding a publisher who would assume the full risk of such a venture. Finally in 1593 Edwin Sandys bought the book from Hooker and arranged with Windet to print the work; Sandys was to shoulder the risk and take most of the profits. The agreement between Windet and Sandys expired with the death of the former, and in 1611 Stansby immediately produced a new edition, which thereby undercut the value of any copies still owned by Sandys. Although Sandys complained to the stationers, as a nonstationer he technically could not profit from the printing of any book. Stansby eventually retained the right freely to print this popular work, as he did four more times.

Stansby's disagreement with Sandys over ownership signaled the beginning of a trend that would continue throughout his career. In Stansby's first ten years as master at Cross Keys his name appeared in court records concerning such disputes no less than six times, and on three occasions he incurred fines for printing all or part of a book owned by another stationer. He also quarreled with John Barnes over the ownership of Sir Dudley Digges's *The Defence of Trade* (1615) as well as with Sir John Hayward, who claimed that Stansby had printed his *Sanctuary of a Troubled Soul* (1610) "w[th][out] his priuitie." Later in his career Stansby lost the right to publish various translations of Latin works by having failed to print them according to an agreement with Thomas Farnsby.

Yet Stansby's business and legal entanglements were by no means restricted to the Stationers' court. Almost from the beginning of his career as a master he offended various civil and ecclesiastical authorities. The first of these troubles involved him peripherally with a conflict touching the highest reaches of British government. Prompted in part by a desire to please James I, who had imprisoned Ralegh for high treason, and later in part by his growing friendship with Henry, Prince of Wales, Ralegh probably commenced work on his *History of the World* shortly after his incarceration in 1603. Walter Burre licensed the work on 15 April 1611, and Stansby printed it, completing the more than fifteen-hundred-page volume in March 1614.

Shortly thereafter response to Ralegh's work turned sour, and on royal command George Abbot, archbishop of Canterbury, ordered all copies seized and delivered to either him or the lord mayor of London. The clearest reason for this suppression appears in a letter of 5 January 1615 by John Chamberlain, who states that "Sir Walter Raleighs booke is called in by the Kinges commaundment, for divers exceptions, but specially for beeing too sawcie in censuring princes. I heare he takes yt much to hart." Burre also must have taken it to heart, for the suppression of such a large investment must have cost him dearly. According to a letter dated 18 September 1616 by James I, all confiscated copies of Ralegh's *History* were turned over to John Ramsey, one of James's agents who was to dispose of them.

Burre seems to have attempted to redress his losses by suing Stansby. The Stationers' court records on 21 August 1615 note that the bookseller "hath license also to take course by lawe against the said Stansbye," an indication that Burre wished to take the matter outside the guild and file a civil action. Yet the records do not state the subject of the suit, and Bland has argued that Burre's suit concerned not Stansby's printing of Ralegh's *History* but his printing of Jonson's *Workes,* to which Burre held some of the rights. According to Bland, Stansby had begun printing the Jonson folio early in 1615 without first securing rights for those works that he did not own. In time Burre sued, and the settlement came when, in return for rights to print the Jonson folio, Stansby agreed to make up the losses that Burre had incurred from Ralegh's book by printing for him a new edition of it, which he produced in 1617.

That same year William Jaggard undertook to print an edition of the *History,* a move that apparently sparked further disputes over ownership. The resolution seems finally to have occurred on 16 May 1621, when an entry in the Stationers' court records indicates that Stansby agreed to turn over "all the paper that he hath received for the printing

thereof, as well that which is printed as that which is vnprinted and also all tables & other things." A third partner, named Pollard, agreed to reimburse Stansby ten pounds in damages. Shortly afterward Burre transferred by note to Stansby the rights to Jonson's *Workes.*

After the initial difficulties surrounding Ralegh's volume subsided, Stansby resumed his trade with characteristic vigor. He printed another edition of Hooker's *Laws,* an enlarged edition of Purchas's *Pilgrimage,* and Jonson's collected *Workes.* With this last volume Stansby made an important contribution to the future of English literature. Plays, playwrights, and players were not highly esteemed by English society at this time. Public theaters were forbidden within the boundaries of London, and players sought the patronage of nobility in order to escape the penalties of vagrancy laws. Although printed plays held prominent places in London bookstalls, they generally appeared as often poorly edited texts in small, inexpensive quarto editions. Jonson's folio *Workes* marked the first time that the popular literature of the stage received a printed treatment usually accorded only works of the highest status. While contemporaries mocked Jonson's efforts, the impressive volume established a publishing precedent later followed by the Shakespeare Folio of 1623 and Francis Beaumont and John Fletcher's 1647 collected *Comedies and Tragedies.*

Another book Stansby printed during the last years of this decade caught the eye of ecclesiastical authorities, and the ensuing difficulties seriously disrupted his business. John Selden – the lawyer, historian, and antiquary – had first brought to Stansby's print shop works such as Selden's *Titles of Honor* (1614), a history of the various titles in the British Isles, and his orientalist treatise *De Dis Syris Syntagmata* (1617). Evidently happy with Stansby's workmanship, Selden also took his next volume, *The Historie of Tithes* (1618), to Stansby for printing. However, Selden's discussion of church history proved unacceptable to authorities, who suppressed the work. In a letter Selden wrote to a colleague in Paris, the author described a raid on Stansby's shop late in 1617, when agents of the bishop of London confiscated the paper and type used for *The Historie of Tithes.* This trouble over Selden's work significantly hurt Stansby's trade: from 1611 through 1617 Stansby's production had averaged more than eight hundred edition sheets per year, but in 1618 he printed only a little more than five hundred such sheets. His association with Selden caused his production for that year to decrease by almost 40 per-

Engraved title page for William Stansby's edition of Ben Jonson's Workes *(1616). This copy was inscribed by Jonson (Pierpont Morgan Library).*

cent, a significant decline for a usually prosperous printing shop.

Stansby responded to the setback by pushing his business volume upward, although his average output for the next four years still fell short of that achieved during 1611–1617 by more than one hundred edition sheets per annum. As he did throughout his career, Stansby printed a large range of works, from public declarations of burials and christenings to large folio editions of the poems of Drayton and the collected works of theologian Samuel Hieron.

Then, near the end of his first decade as master of Cross Keys, Stansby made another publishing miscalculation, this time one that nearly cost him his business. The reigning emperor of Bohemia had dictated that his successor was to be his cousin, the Catholic Ferdinand of Styria, a choice supported by the Hapsburg Empire but one that Bohemian Prot-

estants rejected. In the spring of 1618 the Bohemian estates revolted against Ferdinand. After attempts at mediation collapsed, Ferdinand was elected emperor, but the Bohemians deposed him and instead selected Frederick, the elector of the palatinate, as king.

A major conflict loomed in central Europe, as the Hapsburgs threatened to invade in order to restore Ferdinand to the throne. In England, James I found himself in an unenviable situation: on one hand he needed to support Ferdinand, for he wished to remain on good terms with the Hapsburgs in order to secure a Spanish match for Charles, Prince of Wales; on the other hand Frederick was his son-in-law and a popular Protestant figure, the focus of fervent anti-Catholic and anti-Spanish frenzy in England.

In the midst of this largest crisis in James's reign, Stansby printed a series of anonymous pamphlets denouncing Ferdinand and supporting Frederick as king of Bohemia. Most of these small quartos claimed to have been printed in Middleburg or The Hague in 1620 and bore titles such as *A Declaration of the Causes, for which, we Frederick, have Accepted the Crown of Bohemia.* One pamphlet, *A Plain Demonstration of the Unlawful Succession of Ferdinand the Second, Because of the Incestuous Marriage of His Parents,* was particularly vehement in its denunciation. At some time James or his agents decided that the anti-Ferdinand campaign had gotten out of hand, and they clamped down on those involved – including Stansby and Nathaniel Butter, the bookseller who had contracted with him to publish the titles.

Butter seems to have been the first to suffer. W. W. Greg writes that in late spring 1622 Butter addressed two petitions to Sir George Calvert, the secretary of state, whom he asked to release him from custody that would otherwise cause an imminent "undoing" of himself, his three children, and his "poore wief great with Childe." Greg adds that, as printer of the offending pamphlets, Stansby soon suffered a punishment similar to Butter's. A petition that Stansby sent to Calvert claimed that, under a warrant from the state, the wardens of the Stationers' Company had "nayled vp & sealed the dores of the Peticõners warehouses & Printing house & haue broken downe his presses to his vtter vndoeing if he be not speedilie restored thereunto being a very poore man."

Stansby later sent Calvert a second petition that attempted to explain why the printer had decided to print the offending pamphlets. This petition reveals the dire straits of someone who had incurred the displeasure of the state. Stansby begins by placing blame for the "smale treatise" on the "earnest p[er]swacõn & instigacõn of Nathaniel Butter Bookeseller." He adds that "Butter not onlie assured the Peticõner that there could be no danger . . . but also promised to saue him harmles from all trouble thereby to arise" and notes that many other pamphlets on the same subject were being "publiquely sold w^(th)out contradicõn."

Having defended his innocence by impugning Butter, Stansby then appeals to Calvert by reminding him that "the Peticõner (by yor Hono^rs Comaund) hath byn a long tyme debarred from the vse of his printing presses by wch meanes being vnable to releiue himselfe & his famelie he wilbe vtterlie vndone." Stansby closes by reminding Calvert that he has committed no further offenses, by asking to be forgiven and to have his presses restored, and by offering "willinglie to suffer all manner of punishment wch shalbe inflicted vpon him . . . yf euer here-

Engraved title page, by Elstrack, for the first edition of Walter Ralegh's monumental History of the World *(1614), which was suppressed by James I*

after he shall offend againe in the like nature." Stansby may have overstated the extent of his financial distress, but these petitions underline his concern for the fate of his shop.

During this period of forced leave Stansby took some steps to recover his business. He made two appearances as a churchwarden in his local church, as the registers of St. Peter, Paul's Wharf, show on 13 February 1624 and again on 1 March 1625 – the only times his name appears in such records until his death in 1638. Perhaps he wished to demonstrate his loyalty to church and state as part of his efforts to regain access to his shop.

Calvert did eventually restore Stansby's presses and warehouses, but not before the printer had lost a volume of trade similar to that five years earlier during the suppression of Selden's *Historie of Tithes.* An examination of Stansby's production in edition sheet totals throughout his career demonstrates how much damage these two incidents caused. When Stansby had begun acting as a partner in Windet's shop sometime in 1609, he almost immediately began to print a large volume of materials. During his most prosperous years of 1610 through 1626 he produced between roughly 500 and 850 edition sheets per year, an impressive pace by contemporary standards. The two years in which his average production was lowest, however, correlate to those years in which Stansby had brushes with civil and ecclesiastical authority – in 1618, when the bishop of London had confiscated Selden's *Historie*, and in 1623, when the stationers secured a court warrant to lock up his presses and warehouses after he had printed the Bohemian pamphlets. These two lean years must have caused serious financial difficulties not only for Stansby and his family but also for his many employees (Bland estimates that at peak times fifteen to seventeen people worked in Stansby's shop).

Butter and Stansby were again to be entangled with the authorities. On 20 April 1629 the ecclesiastical commissioners issued articles charging that Butter had published Joseph Hall's troublesome book *The Reconciler* (1629) and that he had

> delivered the copie thereof to one m^r Stansby the printer and assured him that it was all lawfully Licensed as yo^w. deliu^{r}d it vnto him and soe m^r. Stansby takinge yor. word went forward with the impression and printed 'of that sort' fyfteene hundred or a thousand at the least.

This charge that Butter falsely assured Stansby that the book had been legally licensed lends credence to what Stansby had claimed about the bookseller in that second petition to Calvert years earlier. Another noteworthy fact is that the size of the press run – "fyfteene hundred or a thousand at the least" – reveals interesting details about the number of copies that a successful printer such as Stansby would produce for a typical edition during this period.

Stansby's business rebounded in 1624 and 1625, and the volume of his production approached that which he had achieved during earlier, more prosperous times. He also published a folio edition of Ovid's *Metamorphoses* (1626) translated by George Sandys, a publication that eventually led Stansby once more into court and a fight over publishing agreements. As treasurer of the Virginia Company, Sandys was in America when the first edition of his translation appeared, and he had most likely negotiated with Stansby by letter or agent. When Sandys decided to print another edition of *Metamorphoses* in

1631 he was residing in Oxford, and he contracted to have the work done locally by John Lichfield of Oxford, printer to the university. Remembering the fine work that Stansby had done on the first edition of this work, Sandys also made an agreement with Stansby, who was to act as the London agent for sales of the book.

At some time, however, Sandys determined that Stansby had not remitted a sufficient return from sales of the book, and the translator moved to recover funds that he felt Stansby owed him. As Sandys in 1626 had received a royal patent granting him exclusive rights to publish the work for twenty-one years, he sought redress not from the stationers or from a civil court but rather from the court of exchequer. According to a bill of complaint that Sandys filed with the court in 1635, Stansby had received 820 copies of the translation, including 50 copies on fine paper, and had agreed to pay a royalty of ten shillings per copy. Sandys claimed that at the time of the suit, 126 copies remained unsold – and that Stansby owed him £17 7s. 2d. and was now refusing to acknowledge the copies, the debt, or the agreement to distribute the work.

Stansby responded to Sandys's charges on 16 April 1635. Stansby claimed that Sandys had agreed to cover all shipping and storage costs for the books, that Sandys was to pay for 1,550 copies of the last sheet and preliminaries for the volume, and that Stansby was to pay Sandys a royalty of ten shillings per copy only on those copies that Stansby had sold and received the full price for. Stansby added that Sandys had delivered only 709 perfect and eight imperfect copies for sale, all of which had been sold or delivered except for the eight imperfect copies, and, after deducting his expenses, Stansby admitted owing Sandys £2 17s. 11d. Stansby filed a countersuit later that year with the court of exchequer, to which he stated essentially the same facts and asked that Sandys answer his charges. On 9 May 1636 the court found for Sandys: it accepted his total of 820 copies as correct and ordered Stansby to account for them as well as any of the remaining sheets that he had printed. The court also referred both parties to a Mr. Pevey, an auditor who was to decide what damages Stansby owed Sandys.

During the time Stansby was contesting the details of his business arrangements with Sandys, the printer also faced disciplinary action from his guild. In September of 1635 the Stationers' Company penalized Stansby for poor workmanship on an Anglican Psalter and a Psalter for the Church of Scotland, works that the company claimed were

Engraved title page, by William Hole, for Stansby's 1619
folio edition of the collected poetry of Michael Drayton

"very badly done insomuch that they are vnfitt for sale." For a printer whose career was distinguished by high standards of workmanship and taste, this punishment from his guild indicates that, although he still retained the rights and privileges of a stationer, by this time he had little to do with the actual printing of the work that he owned.

The legal dispute and the penalties for poor workmanship that the stationers imposed roughly coincided with Stansby's decision to sell his print shop to Richard Bishop. Whether these problems with the guild and the court prompted Stansby's decision or whether they were merely coincidental, notes in the Stationers' Register indicate that sometime in 1635 Stansby "sold his Right to Richard Bishop for 700[li] . . . and is cleane out." A list of master printers compiled the next year adds the note, "if Stansby come in it is but to Bishoppes vse: who is a young man and hath not had it aboue 6 or 7 monethes." On 11 April 1636 Stansby sold his interest in the English Stock to Adam Islip for £100, and this marked his withdrawal from the main business of the stationers.

In 1638 he appeared as the publisher in the imprint of one more work, a collection of duets for bass viol by Michael East, but for the most part Stansby no longer participated actively in the printing trade. In 1638 a rudimentary census of London inhabitants lists a Mr. Stansby living on Thames Street with a rent of eight pounds. This address corresponds to one found in the imprint of a 1620 translation of Seneca that Stansby had printed and that had identified him as "dwelling in Thames-streete, by Pauls-wharfe, next to St. Peters Church."

Sometime in mid September 1638 Stansby died. The will of "Stansby, William, of p. St. Peter, Paul's Wharf, Lond. (cit. and stationer)" was made 9 September 1638 and probated 14 September 1638 by his wife, Elizabeth. It contains bequests to relatives and friends, including forty shillings to "my loving frend" John Smithwicke (who had acted as publisher of many books for Stansby) "to make him a ring." The will does not mention offspring, as the Stansbys were childless.

On 17 September 1638 Stansby was buried in St. Peter's chancel, having directed that twenty shillings be given to the poor of the parish at his funeral. The service included an official delegation from the stationers, as an entry in their records two and one-half weeks later notes that Elizabeth Stansby sent five pounds to the company "for the Liueries attendance at her husbands buriall." She died in 1649 and was buried in the chancel with her husband. The church of St. Peter's, Paul's Wharf, was burned to the ground during the Great Fire of 1660 and was never rebuilt. No trace remains of the chancel or of the Stansbys' monuments.

From early in William Stansby's career various circles recognized his work. Travel writer Thomas Coryate, author of two books that Stansby printed, listed the stationer among the "louers of vertue, and literature" in his *Travailer, For the English wits, and the good of this Kingdom* (1616) and placed the printer in the company of Robert Cotton, Inigo Jones, Donne, and Jonson. In later centuries antiquarians and booksellers noted the technical and artistic mastery shown in such books as Jonson's *Workes* and the many editions of Camden, Hooker, and Purchas. Literary editors, scholars, and historians of books consistently rank Stansby among the leading printers of his day. Despite his frequent clashes with state bureaucrats, guild officials, and dissatisfied authors, printer and publisher William Stansby managed to create a body of work that has borne the scrutiny of centuries and emerged untarnished.

References:
M. B. Bland, "Jonson, Stansby and English Typography 1579–1623," D.Phil. dissertation, Oxford University, 1995;

James K. Bracken, "Books from William Stansby's Printing House, and Jonson's Folio of 1616," *Library,* sixth series 10 (March 1988): 18–29;

Bracken, "William Stansby's Early Career," *Studies in Bibliography,* 38 (1985): 214-216;

Bracken, "William Stansby's Early Career and the Publication of Ben Jonson's Folio in 1616," dissertation, University of South Carolina, 1983;

T. N. Brushfield, "Sir Walter Ralegh and his 'History of the World,'" *Transactions of the Devonshire Association,* 19 (1887): 389–418;

Richard Beale Davis, "George Sandys *v.* William Stansby: The 1632 Edition of Ovid's *Metamorphosis,*" *Library,* fifth series 3 (December 1948): 193–212;

Davis, "*In Re* George Sandys' Ovid," *Studies in Bibliography,* 8 (1956): 226–230;

W. W. Greg, *A Companion to Arber, Being a Calendar of Documents in Edward Arber's* Transcript of the Registers of the Company of Stationers of London 1554–1640 *with Text and Calendar of Supplementary Documents* (Oxford: Clarendon Press, 1967);

Cecil Hill, "William Stansby and Music-Printing," *Fontes Artis Musicae,* 19 (1972): 7–13;

John Racin Jr., "The Early Editions of Sir Walter Ralegh's *The History of the World,*" *Studies in Bibliography,* 17 (1964): 199–209;

Racin, *Sir Walter Ralegh as Historian: An Analysis of* The History of the World (Salzburg, Austria: Institut für Englische Sprache und Literatur, Universität Salzburg, 1974);

C. J. Sisson, *The Judicious Marriage of Mr. Hooker and the Birth of the Laws of Ecclesiastical Politie* (Cambridge: Cambridge University Press, 1940).

– *David L. Gants*

The Stationers' Company of London

(London: 1557 – 1710)

The Stationers' Company of London consisted of members of the London book trade — printers, publishers, booksellers, and bookbinders — and served as the organization ordering trade practices in printing houses and bookseller stalls. While a trade in books and book production (and a guild governing the practitioners) had existed in London since the early fifteenth century, the advent of printing led to the establishment of English printing houses and the growth of wholesale book sales. The growth of London printing during the reign of Henry VIII and competition from Continental books led London printers, booksellers, and bookbinders to organize their trade both to increase their competitiveness and to restrict competition from outsiders — those outside England as well as outside London.

As a result of this growth, the Crown granted the Stationers' Company a royal charter in 1557. The history of the company between this date and the introduction of statutory copyright in 1710 is essentially a history of English printing, with the company records revealing not only trade practices developed in a new industry but also the relationships that evolved between the trade and the government, as well as a record of the origins of copyright — that is, the exclusive right of an individual to the economic benefits of a printed text.

The Stationers' Company appeared quite late among London guilds, many of which were declining by the mid sixteenth century. Although its formal incorporation came late, printers, booksellers, and bookbinders had practiced their crafts in London since the late fifteenth century, and by the early sixteenth century they were enjoying guild status. On 24 October 1525, for instance, the London court of aldermen agreed to the translation of a Richard Nele from the craft of stationers to that of ironmongers. In a 12 September 1538 letter to Thomas Cromwell two English printers, Miles Coverdale and Richard Grafton, indicate that the company of London booksellers was preventing their French host, Frances Reynold, from selling his wares in England. This letter indicates that the company could act to restrict participants in the trade, particularly in the interest of controlling "inferior" products.

Cyprian Blagden indicates that, although royal privileges would afford some printers valuable protection for their copy, among the early articles by which the stationers regulated themselves was an ordinance securing the right of a printer to the work that he printed — an early form of copyright — by recording the title with his name in a register book. Evidently an ordinance also required that the copy be presented to the wardens before it was printed, for an entry in the Stationers' Register records that in 1555 a master Wallye was fined twenty shillings "for conselying of the pryntynge of a breafe Cronacle contrary to our ordenances before he Ded presente the Copye to the wardyns." Having the ability both to restrict foreigners and to regulate their craft, the stationers formally requested the grant of a charter through the court of aldermen in London on 3 June 1557, and the grant of their charter conferred on them a status comparable to that of other companies and guilds in London.

Historians such as Glynne Wickham, E. K. Chambers, and Blagden have seen the chartering of the Stationers' Company variously as a draconian measure by the Tudors to control the printed word, as a means by which the authorities might control sedition and heresy, and as a triumph for stationers who "obtained their Charter on their own terms," albeit "at a time when it suited the Crown to make use of their organization for other purposes." By 1557, one year before martial law was instituted on books declared illegal, the failure of Queen Mary's attempts to suppress Protestant texts through government licensing measures was clear. Instead of stepping up licensing by church officials or privy councillors, she turned to the London printers, who had been seeking a company charter since 1552. Mary granted the 1557 charter to the Stationers' Company as a "suitable remedy" to seditious and heretical printing, and she included among the rights by which the company was to enforce its regulations the powers "to seize, take, hold, burn . . . all and several those books and things which are or shall be printed con-

275

Engraved title page for The Whole Book of Psalms *(1614), a frequently reprinted psalter that the Stationers' Company had acquired the rights to print in perpetuity from James I in 1603*

trary to the form of any statute, act, or proclamation."

That the company was formed at the height of Mary's censorship campaign, after its 1542 effort to secure a charter failed, discredits the view that the granting of a charter represented a stationers' victory. Placing the company's efforts to secure a charter in the context of historical events clarifies the company's status. Blagden speculates that Henry VIII may have rejected the company's bid for a charter in 1542 because the powers that the stationers had sought were too wide, and the king may also have feared reform sentiments held by many of the printers. By 1542 Thomas Cromwell had fallen, and Henry VIII was withdrawing from the Protestant religious reforms that Cromwell had initiated. To surrender any control of the printed word would be to risk empowering the voices that the king needed to silence.

Yet if 1542 was too late for the printers to gain their charter, it is less clear why Edward VI was to

set aside their efforts to obtain a charter. In Edward's time printers flourished; then during Mary's regime their numbers diminished by nearly half, as many fled to the Continent. Those who remained in London may have felt it necessary to appeal to the Crown to protect their trade, and to accomplish this, they created a compromise document in the 1557 charter. That Thomas Dockwray, the master of the company at the time of the charter, was neither a printer nor a bookseller but an ecclesiastical lawyer – and probably a Catholic, according to Edward Arber – certainly suggests that the company was employing some bargaining tactics. Whatever the stationers may have conceded in the preamble to their charter and in their choice of a master acceptable to the Crown, they gained in the privileged status that their charter conferred.

Considering the legal ramifications of the charter as a grant of privilege extended through a patent under the Privy Seal reveals the degree to which the company operated independently from the government. Tudor governments used the Privy Seal as part of their regular administrative machinery, and patents issued thereby were in a sense routine business, confirmations of previously arbitrated documents. Furthermore, because such grants and privileges were related to feudal property rights (in which the Crown was transferring its property interests to one of its subjects), the stationers' charter must be seen in terms of what it transferred. Not only did the charter grant the Stationers' Company a corporate right to exist and assign to the company the power to govern itself and its trade, but it also conferred on the company's members in perpetuity the sole economic benefits of printing. Except for the right reserved to the Crown to issue patents (privileges) for works to be printed, the Stationers' Company charter transferred authority over printing from the Crown to the company. The principal relationship, then, between the Crown and the stationers, as between the Crown and the recipients of patent privileges, was a relationship of property – one that derived from the feudal relationship between the Crown and the subject, in which the Crown bestowed economic benefit in return for the subject's loyalty.

With regard to the book trade this feudal legacy meant that stationers, as privileged printers, could enjoy the economic benefits conferred on them by the Crown as long as they did not print works that the laws defined as treasonous or seditious. Beyond that, the charter did not impose substantial controls. Mary's end, which understandably was incorporated into the language of the stationers' charter, was quite clear: that of suppressing "detestable heresies against the faith and sound catholic doctrine of Holy Mother Church." Only one year after the company had received its charter, however, Elizabeth's accession returned England to Protestantism, and her subsequent confirmation of the company's charter in November 1559 was a rather perfunctory document. It neither repudiated the aims of Philip and Mary to use the stationers to eradicate anti-Catholic doctrine in England nor advanced her own interests in a reformed English church. The charter appears in the patent roll followed by Elizabeth's statement of confirmation:

> We have inspected the letters patent of Lord Philip King, and Lady Mary, late Queen of England ... holding firm and agreeable the foresaid letters and all and several the contents of the same, for ourselves, our heirs and successors, as far as in us lies accept and approve of them, and ratify and confirm them to our beloved Reginald Wolfe, now Mastr of the Mistery.

"As far as in us lies" appears as an extraordinary qualification in such a confirmation, but it was probably a useful one. Elizabeth justifiably found the charter legal ("firm and agreeable"), but she must have felt some equivocation at confirming her approval of those parts of the "all and several" contents upholding "Holy Mother Church." Elizabeth's confirmation is dated 10 November 1559, and by 19 July 1560 she had already appointed the first ecclesiastical commission, authorized by the 1559 Act of Uniformity, to "put in execution" the provision of that act for reforming the Church of England.

The 1557 charter conferred on the Stationers' Company privileges and practices common among the older guilds: rights of owning property, regulating conduct of the trade, keeping apprentices, and engaging in searches to protect the trade from "foreigners" (nonmembers) and from poor workmanship. While names of printers, bookbinders, and booksellers predominated among those initial ninety-seven listed in the 1557 charter, the membership also included suppliers of parchment, paper, and stationery; illuminators; notaries; and the ecclesiastical lawyer serving as warden. Once they had received their charter, the stationers could petition the city for the right to have a livery – which would assure the company voting rights in London and in parliamentary elections, participation in London governance, and status among London livery companies – and the stationers became a livery company in 1560.

The charter also specified that the company would be governed by a master and two wardens: it appointed men to the offices and provided for subsequent annual elections for these positions. In these respects the stationers were no different from other city companies. One benefit procured by the stationers in their 1557 charter, however, assured them of a privilege beyond those held by other companies. While the custom of the city allowed men free of one company to engage in the trade of another – a bricklayer, if he chose, could sell fish – the 1557 charter of the Stationers' Company reserved to members of the company the exclusive practice of the trade of printing. This exclusivity, however, did not extend to the booksellers and bookbinders. And though in 1559 the Stationers' Company sought to require that booksellers, regardless of their company, should post a bond to observe rules made by the stationers, the Stationers' Company did not gain such authority over booksellers who were members of other companies until the end of Elizabeth's reign.

Besides the master and wardens appointed in the charter, the Stationers' Company was governed by its court of assistants, who within a few years of the charter assumed control of the company and elected the master and wardens. This master and two wardens, sitting together with the assistants, met traditionally on the first Tuesday of the month. According to Bladgen, by 1562 the Stationers' Company had assumed the structure it was to maintain for years to come. Under the master and wardens were two renter wardens, who collected quarterage fees (dues) from all the members (commonality). In addition, the company appointed a beadle, a clerk, and a cook. As caretaker of company property, the beadle also linked the various constituencies of the company. He oversaw the status of members; noted the deaths of members; summoned members to meetings, feasts, and funerals; and helped collect quarterage. Furthermore, he let the stationers' hall and provided for its cleaning.

The first clerk was appointed in 1571, and he assumed full responsibility for the company's books, particularly for the Register, or entry book, that kept a record of stationers' rights to copy. The yeomanry – those members who had served their apprenticeships to the company, had gained membership by patrimony, or had been "translated" (transferred) from another company – comprised the regular membership, although this group included both young masters and journeymen. Apprentices, who generally served seven years, could be bound at fourteen years of age, but they could not be freed until they reached the age of twenty-four.

The livery was open to those members who could afford the cost of the company's gown (in scarlet and navy) and the admission fees, and only livery members could run for offices and vote in company and city elections. By 1562 the company had drafted ordinances to consolidate the court of assistants' power to order the regular life of the guild by deciding and ratifying policy, binding apprentices, extending freedom, electing the livery, administering charitable obligations, electing new court members, appointing company officers, ensuring attendance at quarter sessions, and supervising members' conduct. While no copy of these ordinances remains, records of the court of assistants indicate that besides matters of guild life, the principal business of the company was that of protecting members' rights to copy. This was accomplished first by requiring company licenses and then by bringing those who violated license restrictions before the court of assistants, which would decide a case and, where warranted, impose fines.

With so much invested in assuring and protecting its members' rights to their copy, the integrity of the company license was central to the stationers' authority, and regulations requiring licensing and recording licenses were important early ordinances. Since these ordinances no longer exist, understanding company licensing has through the years posed considerable difficulties for scholars. Some confusion has derived from identifying company licensing with efforts of Tudor monarchs before 1557 to control heresy and sedition by imposing government licensing contingent upon official authorization.

Henry VIII, Edward VI, and Mary I required that printers obtain licenses from the Crown to print any book, but that license was contingent upon the approval of specified officials. A license could have been required without approval or authorization, as it was for importing wines. The Crown could also have granted a wine import license with a condition – for example, that the wines were not sold above a certain price, or that they be of certain varieties. Having been granted the privilege to exist by letters patent, the Stationers' Company assumed the position of the Crown in requiring licensing. In essence, it extended to its members the privilege to print, and then required that members obtain the company's permission or license for each book that they wished to print. The company clerk recorded the license in the company Register,

in which each entry records the title of the copy, the name of the stationer holding the license, the entry date, and the entrance fee.

The company's license was like a printing "privilege" that granted a holder the sole right to print, rather than a license granted upon the premise of official approval. In situations where a work also received "authorization," or approval, by a government or ecclesiastical official, the entry usually specifies this. While the Stationers' Register is accurate, it offers an incomplete record of everything printed. The company license, in establishing copy ownership, was required only for first editions; subsequent issues and editions, unless their changes were substantial, went unentered. Furthermore, because the royal printing privilege assured copy ownership, Crown printers almost never entered their titles in the Register, and patentees rarely did so. Only works printed by company members are entered, and some works that were apparently licensed were not entered.

In the early years entry of a work in the company Register simply records the license to print and the fee paid to obtain it: "John Judson ys lycensed to prynte the Compendious treates or manvall of prayers . . . iiij^d" or "Lycensed to William Seris to prynte the Image of idelnes and psalmes in mytre noted and proverbis in mytre . . . xii^d." Between 1576 and 1578 most Register entries indicate payment of a fee and add "and a copie," an addendum noting enforcement of the ordinance that the company has been provided with a copy of any book it has licensed. After 1578 mention of such a copy appears less frequently, although entries begin to note the approval of the warden or wardens. For example, a 13 February 1578 entry reads:

> master Norton. Lycenced vnto him vnderth[e h]andes of the wardens. A booke intituled. *An easie entrance into the principal pointes of christian Religion verie short and plaine for the simpler sorte . . .* vi^d.

It may be that the license holder could either obtain the warden's permission to print or submit a copy once the text was printed. Once the licensee had gained permission, the record of the license was entered in the company Register.

Before 1582 the entrance fee was one pence for every three sheets of the book when printed, with a minimum fee of four pence; after 26 March 1582 the fee was standardized at sixpence for a book and fourpence for a pamphlet or a ballad. That the company license is distinct from a license

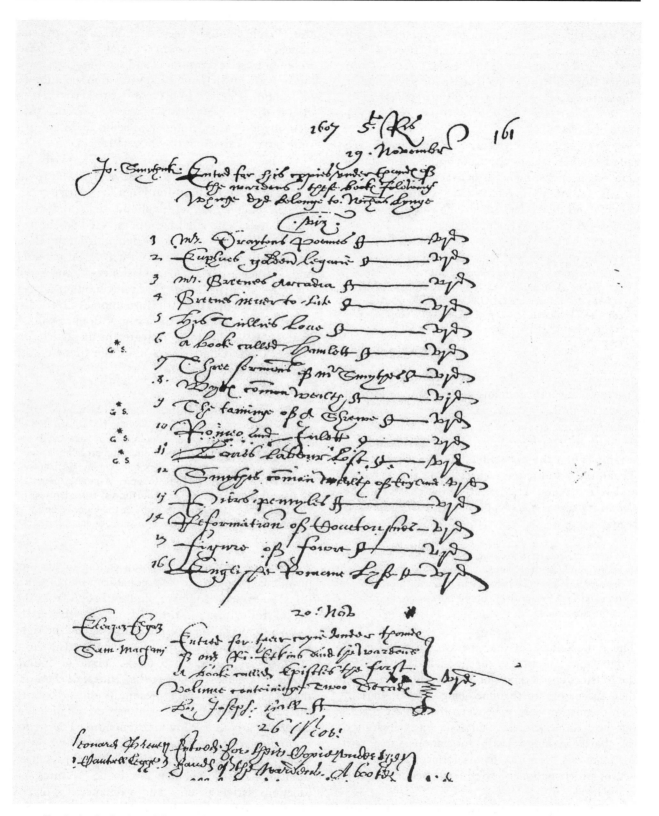

Entries in the Stationers' Register for 29 November 1607, licensing John Smethwick to print sixteen plays, including four by Shakespeare – Hamlet, The Taming of the Shrew, Romeo and Juliet, *and* Love's Labour's Lost *(Register C, f. 161; Stationers' Hall)*

contingent upon official approval is made clear in the Register, which identifies any outside authorizer. For example, one entry dated between 4 September and 27 October 1565 reads: "Receaved of Henry Rocheforth for his lycense for pryntinge *an almanacke and a prognostication* of his own makynge *for the yere of our lorde god 1565* auctorysshed by my lorde of LONDON . . . viii[d]."

Even after 1586, when a Star Chamber decree called for ecclesiastical authorization, the Stationers' Register distinguishes between the company's license (sometimes referred to simply as "his Copie") and the ecclesiastical "allowance." Such an entry for 8 February 1589 reads:

> William Wright Entered for his Copie *a farewell entituled to the famous and [fortunate] generall[s] of our Engishe forces, Sir JOHN NORREYS and Sir FRAUNCIS DRAKE knightes &c.* donne by GEORGE PEELE, And aucthorised Vnder the Bishop of LONDONS hand, and master Coldockes [Warden] hande beinge to the Copies . . . vi[d].

One aspect of the charter that has probably generated misunderstanding is the grant of the right to search and seize materials printed "illegally." Some have understood such a grant to indicate that the stationers served as agents of government censorship when the government ruled works to be illegal; the stationers searched for the illegal works and seized them. The record of the charter in the *Calendar of Patent Rolls* supports such a distinction. It reads:

> The master and wardens shall make search in any place, shop or building of any printer, binder or seller of books for any books printed contrary to statute or proclamation and shall size, burn or convert the same to the uses of the commonalty.

The full patent says that the Crown will "grant, ordain, and appoint . . . that it shall be lawfull for the Masters and Keepers or Wardens aforesaid and their successors for the time being to make search." The distinction here is between the charter requiring the stationers to serve government interests and the charter making it lawful for stationers to search for materials "contrary to the form of any statute, act, or proclamation." Search is not required but is made legal.

Furthermore, any searches may be made only of printers, binders, and booksellers – not of the general citizenry. To the degree that stationers' officers searched to confiscate printed materials that had been declared illegal by statute, act, or procla-

mation, they participated in government censorship. While company records indicate that the stationers did conduct searches, the majority of these were not to seize treasonous and seditious literature but rather texts that had been printed in violation of one stationer's right to his copy or to seize presses operated by noncompany printers. Searches that were made for treasonous and seditious literature were largely carried out by nonstationers.

One striking exception, however, exists. In 1566, consistent with the charge in the 1559 royal patent creating the London High Commission "to inquire touching all heretical opinions, [and] seditious books," the commissioners acted to control the flow of illegal books into England from the Continent and to define illegality for English printers and booksellers. At the commissioners' request, the Privy Council sitting in the Star Chamber issued "Ordinaunces decreed for reformation of divers disorders in pryntyng and utteryng of Bookes" on 24 June 1566. As Blagden indicates in his article on "Book Trade Control in 1566," the first item of these ordinances prescribes

> That no person shall prynt, or cause to be imprynted, nor shall bring, or cause, or procure to be brought into this Realme imprynted, any Booke or copye agaynst the fourme and meanyng of any ordinaunce, prohibition, or commaundement, conteyned, or to be conteyned in any the statutes or lawes of this Realme, or in any Injunctions, Letters patentes, or ordinaunces, passed or set forth, or to be passed or set forth by the Queenes most excellent Majesties graunt, commission, or aucthoritie.

The ensuing provisions prohibit selling or binding prohibited books, provide penalties (book forfeitures, fines, imprisonment, and exclusion from the trade) for violating the ordinances, designate Crown shares in fine revenues, and extend the right of the Stationers' Company to search also those locations where imported books might be found. These ordinances, issued at the request of the London High Commission, represent its effort to clarify the relationship between printing and English law by defining both legality and sanctions. The stationers' charter had maintained the law of the land as the standard for legal printing; these ordinances defined the source of that law to be "statutes, injunctions, letters patents, and ordinances." This, of course, prevented printing against the Act of Supremacy, the Act of Uniformity, and treason laws, but it also prevented printing against the royal privileges granted to the Stationers' Company and to patentees.

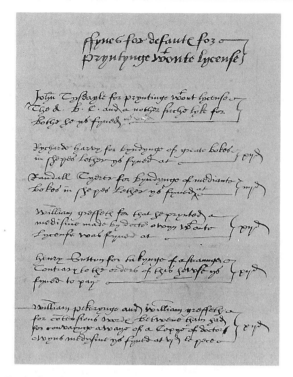

FYNES FOR DEFAUTIS FOR PRYNTYNGE WITHOUTE LYCENSE

Johnne Tysdayle for pryntinge without lycense The A.B.C. and a nother suche lyk for bothe he ys fyned   iiijs viijd

Rycharde harvy for byndynge of greate bokes in shepes Lether ys fyned at   xijd

Randall Tyerer for byndynge of mediante bokes in shepes Lether ys fyned at   iiijd

Williame greffeth for that he prynted a medisine made by doctour owyn withoute Lycense was fyned at   xijd

Henry Sutton for takynge of a straunger Contrary to the orders of this howse ys fyned to paye   xijd

Williame pekerynge and Williame greffeth for contensious wordis betwene thame had for convaynge awaye of a Copye of doctor owyns medysine ys fyned at vjd le pece   xijd

Page of the Wardens' Accounts listing fines imposed on several members by the Stationers' Company in 1558–1559 (Stationers' Hall), with a transcription from Marjorie Plant, The English Book Trade *(1939)*

Furthermore, it protected the Stationers' Company against foreign copyright violations – something that its charter had not done – both by preventing the import and sale of "illegal" works and by extending the stationers' right to search to include venues where such works might be kept. While this clarification extended the stationers' privileges, it also created a means by which Elizabeth's regime could respond to Continental literature opposing the queen and her church. In 1566 this was a serious problem: Catholic presses on the Continent had mounted a formidable campaign against the Church of England and had aroused the concern of Elizabeth's government. One of the High Commission's principal interests in instituting the 1566 ordinances was in creating means by which it could suppress these texts. The stationers' implementation of the searches authorized by those ordinances, however, reveals that the stationers served their own interests as much if not more than they expedited the High Commission's campaign.

Sometime between July 1569 and 1570 Hugh Singleton, one of the searchers appointed by the Stationers' Company, was paid two shillings for "taken up bokes at the Water syde." This lone event, however, was not as significant as the major search in which company searchers had been employed during 1566–1567, immediately after the

1566 ordinances had been issued. Records relating to that search demonstrate that to the Stationers' Company searchers, protecting the company's privilege was as important as confiscating Catholic imprints.

Between July 1566 and July 1567 Thomas Purfoot and Hugh Singleton "rode abroad" as company-appointed searchers, and the transcript of the Stationers' Register indicates that the five pounds they received reflected a "long search." The payment to Purfoot and Singleton actually was made at the end of 1567, after the company account had already closed in payment for their search of booksellers in York early in 1567. According to Robert Davies, the two searchers had inquired first after Latin primers, portasses, missals, or ABCs in Latin and then after works by Thomas Harding, Thomas Dornan, Thomas Stapleton, William Allen, Nicholas Sanders, and John Rastell. All of these writers had contributed to the controversy begun by Bishop John Jewel, and their books had been printed abroad in 1565.

On 8 May 1567 Purfoot and Singleton presented to the ecclesiastical commissioners at York this inventory of unlawful books that the two had found in the possession of York stationers. While their list included a mass book and a portass, many of the works that the booksellers acknowledged having received and sold were those most frequently printed against privilege during Elizabeth's reign. This included primers in Latin and English, copies of William Lily's *Introduction of the eyght partes of speche* (commonly called "the Accidence"), Latin grammars, and Psalters. The York booksellers implicated London stationers Thomas Marshe, Gerard Dewes, and John Wight both as sources of the books seized by the searchers and as sources of illegal books that they had previously received. None of the York booksellers possessed any of the controversial books on the searchers' second list. The only penalty the York booksellers incurred for trading in "illegal" texts was that of forfeiting those copies still in their possession; Marshe, Dewes, and Wight incurred heavy fines from the company for having violated privileges.

The 1566–1567 search indicates that, at least before 1576, Stationers' Company searches were unusual events requiring special authority. Because both the charter and the 1566 ordinances gave the stationers the legal right to search, some have too frequently assumed that the stationers served as agents of government censorship on a regular, continuous basis. This does not appear to have been so. The Purfoot-Singleton search was a singular event for which the two men received special papers; the Stationers' Company paid two shillings sixpence for the "wrytinge of Acctorytye." No records exist of subsequent zealous searches such as that of 1567. In 1576 the Stationers' Company appointed twenty-four searchers (including the master, William Seres, and three other privilege holders) to conduct weekly searches, but the object of their interest was apparently company business rather than heretical and seditious texts. Those 1576 regular searches were most likely instituted in response to a challenge to both the authority of the company and the rights of privileged printers, a challenge that emerged in the late 1570s and early 1580s.

Between 1577 and 1586 challenges to the authority of the Stationers' Company and to royal printing privileges appeared from several sources and finally led the court of the Star Chamber to issue the 1586 "Decrees for order in printing." On one side, journeymen printers and noncompany printers challenged the exclusive printing rights guaranteed to company members and royal privilege holders. The confrontation began in 1577 when journeymen printers filed a complaint against abuses by privilege holders. In 1582 they presented two further petitions complaining to the

Privy Council that their grievances had not been addressed and that the commission which had been formed to hear their concerns was inattentive to their pleas. In 1583 the Privy Council appointed an extended commission to address the concerns of these printers, and the Privy Council's letter establishing the commission makes it clear that members of the printing trade were concerned about "the proliferation of printers, incompetent printing, inconsistent book pricing, and abuses of printing privileges," as well as the effect of privileges on printers of the "poorer sort."

Besides the protests voiced in the journeymen's petition, John Wolfe, a member of the Fishmongers' Company, led an attack against printing patents and the privileges of the Stationers' Company. Wolfe had served as an apprentice to John Day, a Stationers' Company member, between 1562 and 1572, though Wolfe had not completed his apprenticeship. After setting up his printing business in London, probably in 1581, Wolfe apparently applied for a privilege, which was denied because of its general nature, and he then proceeded to print works belonging to other printers – particularly Christopher Barker, the queen's printer. Barker attempted to dissuade Wolfe from printing privileged copies by offering to provide him with business and to translate his freedom from the Fishmongers' Company to the Stationers' Company.

But Wolfe did not then translate his freedom, and he continued to print privileged books, including Latin grammars belonging to Francis Flower's privilege, a violation that ultimately brought him before the Privy Council. Wolfe later made further demands of Barker, from whom he solicited work, a loan, and an allowance of apprentices beyond the usual allotment of one to three granted by the Stationers' Company. While Barker agreed to help Wolfe, the two still reached no agreement, and by 1582 Wolfe was identified as the leader of the whole movement against privileges. With others, he was summoned to appear before the Privy Council but apparently refused to do so and was imprisoned.

Once released, Wolfe and his cohorts appealed first to the Stationers' Company and later to the Privy Council for a redress of grievances against printing the works of patent holders. The members of the Stationers' Company brought before the Privy Council and the court of the Star Chamber the opposing side of the trade issues raised by Wolfe and the printing workmen. Beginning in 1577 Barker had complained that other members of the company were infringing on his printing rights conferred by his patent, and the Privy Council reiterated Barker's privilege to the masters and wardens of the company. Between 7 and 10 February 1582 Day brought a complaint against Roger Ward and William Holmes for their failure to comply with the 29 June decrees that had affirmed both the authority of the Stationers' Company and the printers' privileges "sett forth by the Quenes most Excellent maiestie[s] graunte."

Between 1583 and 1586 several further violations of printing privileges were brought before the court of the Star Chamber. (Ironically, by this time even Wolfe, who had finally received a patent as an assign of Day, brought legal action when someone had violated his privilege.) All of these cases appealed to the precedent established by the 1566 Star Chamber ordinances in designating the venue of the court of the Star Chamber in matters relating to the regulation of the printing trade and to privilege violations, and any or all of these cases may have finally occasioned the 1586 Decrees for Orders in Printing by that court.

In an entirely different yet related matter in 1582 and 1583, a dispute arose between the London stationers and Cambridge University. The university proposed to establish a printing press there under a license issued by Henry VIII, and it appointed Thomas Thomas as printer to the university. Stationers' Company wardens petitioned Bishop John Aylmer on behalf of the company to move William Cecil, Lord Burghley, and John Bell, the vice chancellor of the university to stay the proceedings. The stationers regarded Thomas's appointment as invalid in London, and in June 1583 company wardens seized Thomas's press, which had been set up in London, in an action that both the university and Thomas regarded as an effort by the stationers to eliminate printing at the university. The vice chancellor appealed to Burghley to resolve the matter on Thomas's behalf, and Burghley appears to have supported the university's aims.

Also in 1583 the expanded commission on printing presented its report to the Privy Council. The commission recommended restricting the number of presses, requiring licensing of new presses by either the stationers' wardens or the High Commission, restricting the number of apprentices, punishing incompetent printing, controlling book prices, upholding royal privileges and company licenses, and providing for the poor of the Stationers' Company by having patentees turn over some of their privileges to the company. According to W. W. Greg, "the report throughout envisages a prospec-

tive decree of the Star Chamber." Such a decree, however, was not immediately forthcoming, and pressures mounted. In 1585 and 1586 three cases, all concerning privilege violations, came before the Star Chamber. In May 1586 the Privy Council ordered Roger Ward's presses to be seized for a violation of such privilege, and the queen's patentees also petitioned the Privy Council for reformation of disorders and punishment of those who infringed on privileges.

On 23 June 1586 the court of the Star Chamber issued its Decrees for Orders in Printing. According to Geoffrey Elton, this "so-called order concerning printers arose out of a judgment in a case based on a breach of the proclamation of 1566." The particular breach that forced the decrees is uncertain, but most of the cases currently before the Star Chamber were resolved by upholding royal privileges, company authority, and the 1566 ordinances. The decrees were clearly framed to respond to all the disruptions in the printing trade, not just to the matters before the court of the Star Chamber: the decrees incorporated many of the recommendations that the commission had made on printing in 1583 and upheld the rights of Oxford and Cambridge to have printing presses.

A genuine triumph for the Stationers' Company and the privileged printers, the 1586 Decrees was extraordinarily conservative, for it reaffirmed old practices. Only stationers and privileged printers could print; restrictions were placed on the numbers of printers and apprentices allowed; applications for new presses had to be made to the archbishop of Canterbury; printing was confined to London and the two universities; search and seizure was affirmed as the means of enforcing the decrees; and the approval of outside authority (ecclesiastical officials) "accordinge to the order appoytned by the Queenes majesties Injunctyons" was required before the company could license the printing of a work.

The Decrees unequivocally upheld the rights and prerogatives of the company and the privileged printers in the face of the recent challenges and sought to ensure both adequate work and adequate employment within the company. Measures to restrict the proliferation of presses were expected to provide adequate work for the existing presses, and limiting the number of apprentices was intended to restrict the number of future journeymen printers and create fuller employment. Finally, as an alternative to the court of the Star Chamber, the Decrees gave to the commissioners for causes ecclesiastical (one of whom was to be either the archbishop of

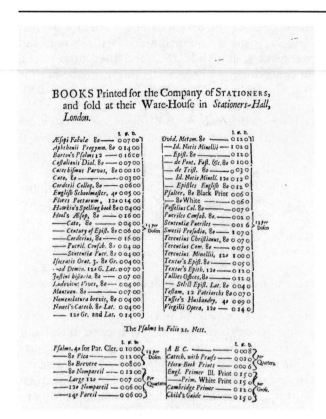

Broadside catalogue of English Stock publications, circa 1695

Canterbury or the bishop of London) jurisdiction to resolve those disorders that involved nonstationers in the printing trade and thereby lay beyond the venue of the stationers' court of assistants.

The Star Chamber Decrees, with their clearly specified provisions for ordering the printing trade, should have affected trade practices more greatly than either the 1559 injunctions or the 1566 ordinances. Indeed, in the years immediately following the Decrees (1586–1602), the Stationers' Company Court Book records twelve searches for presses that were printing illegally by violating patent or copyright. The company also acted five times against printers who operated illegal presses: once against Robert Waldegrave for having printed the anonymous *Diotrephes* (1588), twice against Catholic presses, and twice against nonstationer Roger Ward for having printed privileged books. Stays were also issued against printers to compel them to apply to the archbishop for the right to operate a press.

According to Sheila Lambert, the 1586 Decrees were not altogether effective in regulating labor practices within the Stationers' Company. Despite the restrictions imposed by the Decrees, the number of presses continued to grow until 1615, when the master printers, this time among themselves, agreed to limit the number of presses and printing houses. Furthermore, the numbers of both journeymen and apprentices in the Stationers' Company increased, and these developments led to widespread dissatisfaction at underemployment.

Although the 1586 Decrees may not have been entirely effective in restricting the numbers of presses, apprentices, and journeymen, it apparently served the company well in suppressing a challenge presented from certain members of the Drapers' Company who were engaged in publishing and bookselling. The stationers had insisted that printers (such as John Wolfe) who were free of other companies had to be transferred to the Stationers' Company. Following the custom of the city, freemen from other companies, many of whom in the late sixteenth and early seventeenth century were drapers, had been allowed to engage in publishing and bookselling. According to Gerald D. Johnson, relations between the stationers and drapers deteriorated in the 1580s and 1590s.

> Of major concern to the stationers was the increasing number of drapers engaging in the book-trade during these years. Some new names, such as Yarath James and his apprentice William Barley, appeared in the 1580's, but the alarming increase occurred as the early bookselling drapers indentured apprentices, trained them as stationers, and then freed them as drapers.... If this growth were not checked, the Stationers would soon be rivalled by a de facto "stationers" company inside the Drapers' Guild. Emboldened by the [1586] Star Chamber decree, the Stationers reacted to this threat by pressuring the book-selling drapers. They interfered in the apprenticeship system, restricted the right to enter copies, and hindered the drapers in getting their copies printed.

Initially the "interference" came when the court of the Stationers' Company ordered that a bookselling draper's apprentice should be transferred as a freeman to the stationers and later the court restricted only to stationers the right to enter works in the Register.

Printer Simon Stafford and publisher William Barley, both drapers, brought the conflict between the two companies to a crisis in 1598. The stationers sued the two men in the stationers' court for having printed privileged books (copies of the *Accidence*), and Barley and Stafford responded to this suit by countersuing Thomas Dawson and Cuthburt Burby for unlawful seizure. The affair was brought before the court of the Star Chamber, where the drapers based their argument on the "custom of the city" and the stationers based their position on an argument that the provision for lawful presses in the 1586 Decrees had been violated. In a judgment calling upon the 1586 Decrees as precedent, the court found in favor of the Stationers' Company. This case, followed by the appeal of the Privy Council to the lord mayor to resolve Stafford's claims regarding his trade and the city's custom, led ultimately not only to Stafford's translation to the stationers, but also to the decision of the drapers' court to allow "that the Stationers of this Company should be sett over to the Company of Stationers."

The effect that the Decrees had on practices in the printing trade through its requirement that printers receive outside approval of works they planned to print is a bit more difficult to assess. The real change that occurred was that prior to the 1586 order, stationers could apparently take works to whomever they perceived as having sufficient authority. Shortly after the 1586 order was issued, John Whitgift, the archbishop of Canterbury, established a panel of clerics to whom stationers could appeal for authority. An entry on 3 June 1588 in the Stationers' Court Book identifies

> The names of certen Preachers [and others] whome the Archbishop of Canterbury hathe made Choyse of to haue the pusinge and alowing of Copies. Any one of these settinge his hand to copie, to be suffycient Warrant for thalowance of the same to entringe into the hall books & so to be proceded with all to printinge.

Those named were John Cosin, Thomas Stallard, Richard Wood, Abraham Hartwell, William Gravett, Robert Crowley, W. Cotten, William Hutchinson, and George Dickens.

Such an administrative change should have affected authorization practices, and it did. On one hand, the number of works entered in the Stationers' Register and carrying outside authority throughout each successive decade from 1586 through 1629 increased: 44 percent were so authorized through the 1590s; 68 percent in the first decade of the seventeenth century; 79 percent in the second decade; and 84 percent in the third. On the other hand, the actual percentage of published works that were entered in the Register generally decreased – from 60 percent in 1590–1599 to 50 percent in 1600–1609, 42 percent in 1610–1619, and 49 percent in 1620–1629. While several authorizers served at any particular time, certain ones were called on more frequently than others, but the data is somewhat misleading.

For example, looking at the frequency of Abraham Hartwell's authorizations, Greg concludes that on the panel of correctors "he was the most active and long-abiding member." This evidence might lead one to conclude that Hartwell, as the archbishop's secretary, was inordinately interested in reviewing. Yet Hartwell apparently had a close working relationship with John Wolfe, who was to become one of London's most prolific printers after his translation to the Stationers' Company. Of the 279 works that Wolfe entered in the Register with outside authorization, Hartwell authorized 155.

As the names of new reviewers replaced those on the original panel, another pattern appears in the seventeenth century. In addition to patterns of particular printers and publishers seeking out particular authorizers, the authorizers seem to have been specializing. Between 1612 and 1621 John Taverner, professor of music at Gresham College and Bishop King's secretary, regularly authorized literary and a few political works. George Cottington regularly authorized news books. John Sanford, a poet and grammarian who accompanied John Digby on his embassy to Spain to arrange the marriage of Charles I (in 1623) to the Infanta Maria (of Spain), authorized notable literary and some political works. The religious works that Sanford authorized were uncontroversial, and the religious and political works to which both Richard Cluet and Richard Etkins set their hands similarly represented established views.

It is not surprising, however, that Richard Mocket, whose own *Doctrina et politia ecclesiae anglicanae* (1616) was burned in 1617 for what Greg reports was its "offensive Calvinism," authorized works by outspoken Calvinists such as Stephen Dennison, George Downham, or Peter Du Moulin. Daniel Featly and Thomas Goad, who together gave their imprimatur to 539 works between November 1615 and January 1625, included among their approvals the posthumous works of outspoken Puritans such as Paul Baynes and Daniel Dyke, as well as the works of such well-known Calvinists as George Carleton, Thomas Gataker, and Edmund Elton. Both Goad and Featly authorized works that received official censure – Goad authorized Mocket's *Doctrina et politia ecclesiae anglicanae,* and Featly approved William Crompton's *Saint Austins Religion* (1624) as well as Edward Elton's *Gods Holy Mind* (1625).

While the 1586 Decrees responded to agitation against royal patents in the printing trade, the wider issue of abusive monopolies escalated in the late 1590s when the matter came before the House of Commons. Since patents and monopolies were issued by the Crown and were thereby protected by the royal prerogative, patent matters were not actionable in the common law courts. Furthermore, the sheer number of patents granted by the Crown, particularly to members of the nobility, interfered with trade practices. According to John Guy,

> When faced by pungent criticism and [parliamentary] demands for a committee of investigation in November and December 1597, Elizabeth . . . neutralized the attack by promising to scrutinize existing monopolies and not to allow prerogative machinery to prevent dishonest patentees from being sued in the common-law courts. . . . But the promised reforms failed to materialize. After Parliament was dissolved in February 1598, more new monopolies were granted than old ones rescinded.

The House of Commons again protested abusive monopolies in 1601, and Elizabeth conceded by issuing a proclamation rescinding twelve monopolies and authorizing subjects grieved over patents to seek redress at common law. When James I came to the throne in 1603, he rescinded all Elizabethan patents through a royal proclamation on 7 May 1603. While this ended private patentees in the printing trade, it laid the groundwork for perhaps the most significant change in the Stationers' Company during the seventeenth century – the emergence of the company as a capitalist venture.

Although James's 1603 proclamation had spoken against monopolies and patents, it ended only those extended by Elizabeth; it enabled James to continue to extend privilege – but to his patentees. On 29 October 1603 James issued letters patent in favor of the Stationers' Company, which was thereby granted privilege in perpetuity to print primers, Psalters, Psalms in meter, the *ABC with the little Catechism,* almanacs, and prognostications. This action constituted a regranting of three of the most lucrative of the Elizabethan patents of James Roberts, William and Richard Seres, and John Day. Among these patented titles were Thomas à Kempis's *Imitation of Christ* (1580), Saint Augustine's supposed work *Saint Austens Manuell* (1574), and Alexander Nowell's *Catechismus* (1570). James's letters patent provided that the license was granted to the master, wardens, and commonalty of the Stationers' Company, that the court of assistants was empowered to make rules for executing the patent and imposing "paynes, punyshments and penaltys" to those infringing it, and that its management should remain entirely in the hands of the master, wardens, and assistants.

In 1584 the company had acquired from privileged printers various patents to certain titles that were to be printed by the company's poor, and these titles, along with those included under this 1603 grant, became the basis of what was to be known as the English Stock – a collection of titles that put the Stationers' Company into the business of publishing. The initial holdings were expanded to include law books – including Edward Coke's *Reports* (1609–1619), Richard Crompton's enlarged edition of Anthony Fitzherbert's *Loffice et aucthoritee de justices de peace* (1583), William Lambard's *Loffice et aucthoritee de Justices de peace* (1584), and yearbooks from the reigns of Edward IV, Henry IV, Henry V, Henry VI, Henry VII, and Henry VIII – and some schoolbooks such as Marcus Tullius Cicero's *Offices, Epistolae, and Sententiae;* Aesop's *Fables;* Desiderius Erasmus's *Epitome;* and the works of Publius Vergilius Maro and Publius Terentius Afer as well as John Foxe's *Actes and Monuments* (1563) and Samuel Daniel's *The Historie of England* (1613). For a time during the seventeenth century the English Stock partners engaged in subsidiary enterprises, including a ballad stock, a Bible stock, an Irish stock, and a Latin stock (consisting of books printed on the Continent).

In administering its ownership of Stock copies, the company sold shares to its members, who drew dividends from the shares they purchased. The initial division consisted of fifteen shares for assistants at £200 each, thirty shares for liverymen at £100 each, and sixty shares for members of the yeomanry at £50 each. Shares in the Stock could not be assigned, but a partner's widow might inherit her husband's share or part in a share. When she died or remarried, her shares were reassigned by the court of assistants, and the heirs were repaid the amount of the original purchase.

The Stock initially paid a quarterly dividend and, later, an annual one. The dividend paid on 4 July 1606 was 10 percent, and in December 1619 it was 6½ percent. Blagden estimates that dividends averaged 20 to 25 percent annually and notes that in the second half of the century investors were disgruntled when dividends fell below 12½ percent. A treasurer, who was elected by the partners and stockkeepers and quite literally kept the keys to the warehouses, managed the Stock. The full committee assumed responsibilities for publishing – for deciding what printers would print various titles, ordering and delivering paper, receiving printed sheets into the warehouses, and authorizing payments. The treasurer maintained lists provided by the stockkeepers and committee, filled orders, kept accounts, and made all payments. Despite this structure, according to Blagden, "the business of the English Stock and the business of the Company were difficult if not impossible to keep separate," particularly since, after 1603, the court of assistants often withheld dividends from disobedient company members.

The stationers ostensibly sought the 1603 patent that formed the English Stock to enable the company to employ its poorer printers. Instead, although the Stock did create some employment, economic conditions perpetuated demands for measures to restrict trade facilities and membership. According to Lambert, the central problem facing stationers in the early seventeenth century was a condition of "over-capacity in a period of economic recession." In response to this, "leading printers strove hard to obtain a reduction in the number of presses, [and] the journeymen sought to restrict entry to the trade and to insist on restrictive practices to spread the available work." To protect their claims to available work, printers and publishers, both independently and through the Stock, also sought new monopolies.

While the printers were fairly effective at restraining the number of presses, at least until 1628 monopolies continued to create problems in the trade. While the Stock may have provided work for a few printers, large printing syndicates were often the major beneficiaries. Unemployed printers resorted to piracy of the company's popular and lucrative Stock titles. Even prominent printers resorted to Continental printing of Stock and other privileged titles.

Problems even appeared in the king's printing house, as Bonham Norton, the king's printer, was convicted of libeling Lord Keeper, Thomas Coventry. The 1631 edition of the Bible was tampered with to discredit another king's printer, Robert Barker, and Archbishop William Laud and Bishop George Abbot condemned the quality of workmanship in the king's printing house, where they claimed that quality was being sacrificed for "gain, gain, gain, nothing else." With such abuses rampant it is not surprising that between autumn 1634 and January 1636 the government had Sir John Lambe investigate Stationers' Company affairs extensively.

Lambe made two important findings. First, in compiling a list of master printers (those operating presses), he discovered that most of the old master printers had never been formally admitted to the company as printers, according to the provisions of the 1586 Decrees. As a result, in November 1635 masters were required to present petitions showing by what title they held their printing houses, and twenty-four houses subsequently remained in business with Laud's consent. The second important finding concerned the demands made by journey-

men printers, who had petitioned Archbishop Laud about the masters' breaches of the 1586 Decrees. In response to this petition the masters arranged a meeting between six representatives of the journeymen and six assistants and there drafted a series of articles providing for the employment of journeymen and the restriction of apprentices. Yet this agreement was effectively nullified when a proviso allowing the court to set aside any part of the plan was added during the entry of the agreement in the court books. When the journeymen learned of this, they renewed their appeals to Laud.

In 1637 the Star Chamber issued new decrees to govern printing and to remedy the abuses in the trade and the complaints of journeymen printers. According to Blagden, "the 1637 Decree, like that of 1586 and like the grant of the Charter in 1557, was promoted by the Company for the benefit of Stationers and obtained the sanction of the Government because it promised more effective safeguards than those already in existence" against illegal printing. Lambert concurs with Blagden that "There is no doubt that the bookselling, copyright-owning, and English Stock-shareholding element among the Stationers had achieved all that it dared hope for in the way of officially sponsored control" by the Star Chamber Decree of 1637. But, Lambert adds, "Not only the booksellers, but the journeymen printers too, got almost everything they had been asking for while the master printers at least got official recognition of their need to limit their number."

The 1637 Star Chamber Decree was directed mainly at printers. Twelve of its clauses prohibited illegal printing and provided serious penalties for printers who maintained unauthorized presses, printed unlicensed texts, or printed texts privileged by patent or entry in the company's Register. The decree restricted the number of master printers to twenty, and it reiterated requirements for licensing all books, including reprints, and specified that two copies of each manuscript were to be provided for licensers (one approved copy was to be kept for reference). It restated the company's right to search printing houses for unlicensed printing and for books suspected of criticizing the church or state. It prohibited the printing or importing of books protected by letters patent or by entry in the Register. It restricted bookselling to those tradesmen who had served a seven-year apprenticeship to the trade of bookselling, printing, or bookbinding. It specified that no books wholly or mainly in English were to be printed abroad for importation, that all books from overseas were to be landed at the port of London, and that no stranger or foreigner could sell in

England books that had been printed abroad. The stipulations concerning employees responded to the journeymen's grievances: apprentices were limited to the number of presses maintained; master printers could not employ anyone who was not a freeman of the company; and every printing house had to provide work for at least one journeyman.

The 1637 Star Chamber Decree appears to have been no more successful than the 1586 Decrees in resolving conflicts in the printing trade. Booksellers were among the first to complain about the controls. In his *Scintilla* (1641) Michael Sparke objected heartily to the restrictions imposed against selling imported texts and complained both about the quality of domestic products and about extravagant prices created by monopolistic practices that encouraged shortages of products while locked warehouses stored salable stock. As a remedy to the company's authority, Sparke proposed to increase the size of the court of assistants and decrease the company's hold on monopolies.

Despite its restrictions on printing and presses, the 1637 Decree was relatively ineffective in controlling the monopoly created by Robert Young, Miles Flesher, and John Haviland, who took over several printing houses, bought copyrights, and acquired several profitable privileges. Donald W. Rude and Lloyd E. Berry reprint the complaint of an anonymous author cataloguing abuses in the printing trade sometime between 1638 and 1640. The writer describes the effects of the new monopoly that these three printers formed:

> they ingrosse all worke here in London, that the poorer sort can get little worke, because these ingrossers can forbeare their money, but the poorer sort must have it p^d them weekly what they doe earne, thereby to pay their workmen for so ye report of these men. . . . A Question may be demaunded, whether any Mr Printer or Printers, keeping of printing houses of their owne, and haue so many letters Patents in their hands may be partners with others in their Printing houses. As Mr Young, and M^r ffletcher haue In being p[ar]tner in Mr Barkers printing house. I am sure by divinity, it is condemned, and I am sure it is against the Lords of the Councell Letters to the Contrary.

Rude and Berry suggest that this document may represent an effort from within the Stationers' Company to remedy those trade problems unresolved by the 1637 Decree. Even with company efforts to control abuses, problems had continued after that 1637 Decree, for, as Lambert observes, "it was not easy to get observance of any of the provisions of the decree for no new machinery of enforcement could be provided." The decree threatened those operating illegal presses with the pillory and whipping, but, according to Lambert, "even the threat of whipping was not enough to deter those who sought to turn a dishonest penny in pirating Stock books." Only one case was ever heard in the Star Chamber for illegal printing – a case against John Hammond for having printed Psalms at Henley – and Lambert concludes that "no one was ever whipped through the streets of London for breach of the decree of 1637."

One of the reasons Blagden cites for the continuing agitation over company authority was the changing political milieu. On 5 July 1641 the Long Parliament abolished the courts of the Star Chamber and High Commission. According to Blagden,

> the powerful psychological effect of such a successful attack on royal and High Church power, created conditions in which the Company was challenged from within on two sides and in which the Company not only struggled to replace the lost basis for its authority (particularly as the guardian of copyright) but even made inroads in the interests of the English Stock, on other monopolistic empires.

Lambert is probably right when she says that Blagden overstated the effect of this change, but challenges to the English Stock and dissatisfaction about the number of printers continued through the early 1640s. In 1641 the Long Parliament set up a committee to address specific complaints about printing and on 14 July 1643 passed an "Ordinance for the Regulating of Printing."

According to this legislation, all books were to be officially licensed and entered in the Register; no book belonging to the English Stock could be printed without the company's authority; and the company retained the rights of search and seizure. Evidently these ordinances had no more authority than the 1637 Star Chamber Decree, and in January 1649 the company petitioned Parliament to ensure compliance. On 20 September Parliament, then controlled by the army, passed another act for the "better regulating of Printing," an act that largely reiterated the 1643 ordinances except that it allowed Bibles and Psalms to be printed at Finsbury and removed the limits on the number of printers.

According to Blagden, conflicts between the army and Parliament precluded the effectiveness of the act. Both pirated English Stock books and criticism of the government continued to be printed, and on 7 January 1653 Parliament passed another act – this one restating former restrictions on unlicensed printing and placing authority for printing

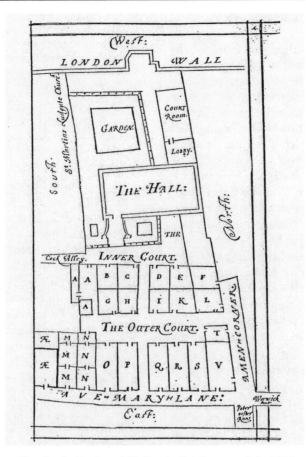

Plan for the Stationers' Hall and adjoining grounds in 1674
(Leybourn's Survey)

and for the behavior of printers in the hands of the council of state. These controls simply denigrated the authority of the company until the Restoration. Unrestricted printing – that is, the proliferation of presses – led to excessive binding of apprentices and employing journeymen outside the company. The company continued to license copy, but the printing of unlicensed texts escalated.

With the restoration of the monarchy, the stationers' sought to reaffirm their authority. In 1662 Parliament passed "An Act for preventing the frequent Abuses in printing seditious . . . Books . . . and for regulating of Printing and Printing Presses," legislation known as the Licensing Act because it required that an official license be printed in each book. Beyond this requirement the 1662 act closely resembled the 1637 Star Chamber Decree, except that this new act no longer required licensing works that were being reprinted; it relaxed control of imported works; and it eliminated earlier harsh penalties. In 1678 the court issued new bylaws that presumably resembled these ordinances passed in 1562.

These 1678 laws established the orderly procedures of company business. They established company court meeting times and procedures; procedures for nominating and electing court members, officers, and the livery; and procedures involving quarterage payments. They also dictated general behavior. According to Blagden, all these bylaws governing procedural and behavioral matters "might have been designated for almost any other City company," but the remaining ten provisions shaped the company's authority as keeper of copyright from 1662 to 1710. According to these, all book trade disputes – including those involving copyright – must come first to the court for settlement. No freeman could establish a press without giving notice to the company's master or wardens, and no one could establish or permit secret presses, or employ anyone who had worked in an unlicensed house. The number of master printers would be reduced to twenty before any new printing houses would be permitted. No master or printer could allow printing of works prohibited by the 1662 Licensing Act, and anyone performing such illegal printing would forfeit his and his widow's claims to a company pension.

These ordinances specified practices for the company to follow as the keeper of copyright, but in 1684 royal actions forced the stationers to seek a new charter. In a move to ensure support for himself and loyalty to the Church of England, Charles II instituted proceedings against London companies to demand surrender of their charters – so that new ones requiring loyalty oaths could be issued. On 22 May 1684 the stationers obtained their new charter, which, according to Blagden, was the first issued. This new charter of the Stationers' Company essentially recapitulated the 1557 charter but added provisions that assistants were to be practicing members of the Church of England and were to take a loyalty oath. The company also secured greater authority for itself, as the charter required company membership for letter founders, press builders, and London booksellers. Furthermore, the charter affirmed the right to copy for titles entered in the company's Register.

Despite the charter's provisions, the company found little success in enjoining company membership on all book trade participants. City fees impeded translations of members from other companies, and earlier licenses issued by the bishop of London to itinerant booksellers prevented the company from controlling the distribution of books. The loyalty tests enabled the king to dismiss assistants, and the implicit threat of this destabilized company authority for a time. The company did pass a resolution to affirm loyalty – only for printers, booksellers, and bookbinders at the time of their election to the court.

According to Blagden, the company remained unsuccessful in restricting illegal printing following the restoration of the monarchy. The 1662 Licensing Act assigned government press control to the office of the surveyor of the press, Sir Roger L'Estrange. Company officials did not work well with L'Estrange, and *Domestic State Papers* contains L'Estrange's repeated reports of unsatisfactory company behavior. Furthermore, the court regarded as inadequate its authority to act against illegal printers or to supervise extensive printing house operations. Blagden writes that

> No printer who had set up in contravention of the Act was prosecuted by the Company unless he printed almanacks ... or psalters.... Urged on by L'Estrange, the Wardens seized Quaker pamphlets and Catholic books and had them burned in the garden at Stationers' Hall or damasked; and in the Michaelmas Term 1681 no fewer than twelve cases were pending, seven insti-

tuted by the Crown and only five by the Wardens who were known to send warning of impending searches to such members of the Company as were foolish enough to be caught dealing in unlicensed books yet not knavish enough to handle counterfeit primers.

Clearly the company's interest, as in the past, lay chiefly in protecting its own copyrights and privileges – and by the late seventeenth century its principal interest lay more in overseeing the English Stock than in serving the government.

It is not surprising that the Licensing Act lapsed in 1679, although it was renewed for seven years with little enthusiasm upon the accession of James II. The lapse of the printing act by April 1695 marked the end of the authority of the Stationers' Company over the English book trade. In 1710 Parliament passed "An Act for the Encouragment of Learning by Vesting the Copies of Printed Books in the Authors or Purchasers of such Copies," which gave authors copyright for titles registered with the stationers and reserved to stationers their rights in English Stock titles. Blagden best articulates the paradoxical loss of the company's power:

> It is strange that within a dozen years toward the end of the Stuart period the Stationers' Company should both achieve the maximum of theoretical authority and experience the minimum of practical power. In May 1684 it received its augmented Charter and by the summer of 1695 it had lost not only this augmentation but the support of the revived Printing Act; it was back where it had been in 1557 and the additional strength which might be derived from the new Ordinances was more than offset by the changes which had taken place in England during the century and a half between the reign of Queen Mary and the reign of Queen Anne.... The Company lost a great opportunity, in the second half of the seventeenth century, of becoming, through a rethinking of the copyright problem, a central and essential rallying point for all members of the book trade throughout the country; that it retained some importance in the eighteenth century was due, paradoxically, to the pull of its most parochial interest – the English Stock.

References:

Edward Arber, *A Transcript of the Registers of the Company of Stationers of London, 1554–1640,* 5 volumes (London, 1875–1894);

Cyprian Blagden, "Book Trade Control in 1566," *Library,* fifth series 13 (December 1958): 287–292;

Blagden, "The English Stock of the Stationers' Company," *Library,* fifth series 12 (September 1957): 167–187;

Blagden, *The Stationers' Company: A History, 1403–1959* (London: Allen & Unwin, 1960);

E. K. Chambers, *The Elizabethan Stage,* 4 volumes (Oxford: Clarendon Press, 1923);

Robert Davies, *A Memoir of the York Press* (Westminster: Nichols, 1868);

Geoffrey Elton, *The Tudor Constitution* (Cambridge: Cambridge University Press, 1960);

George E. Briscoe Eyre, Henry R. Plomer, and C. R. Rivington, *A Transcript of the Registers of the Worshipful Company of Stationers; from 1640–1708 A.D.,* 3 volumes (London: Roxburghe Club, 1913–1914);

W. W. Greg, *A Companion to Arber; Being a Calendar of Documents in Edward Arber's Transcript of the Registers of the Company of Stationers* (Oxford: Bibliographical Society, 1967);

Greg, *Collected Papers,* edited by J. C. Maxwell (Oxford: Clarendon Press, 1966);

Greg, *Licensers for the Press to 1640* (Oxford: Bibliographical Society, 1962);

Greg and E. Boswell, eds., *Records of the Court of the Stationers' Company, 1576 to 1602, from Register B* (London: Bibliographical Society, 1930);

John Guy, *Tudor England* (Oxford: Oxford University Press, 1988);

Gerald D. Johnson, "The Stationers Versus the Drapers: Control of the Press in the Late Sixteenth Century," *Library,* sixth series 10 (March 1988): 1–29;

Sheila Lambert, "The Printers and the Government, 1604–1637," in *Aspects of Printing from 1600,* edited by Robin Myers and Michael Harris (Oxford: Polytechnic Press, 1987), pp. 1–29;

Myers, *The Stationers' Company Archive: An Account of the Records, 1554–1984* (Wincester: St. Paul's Bibliographies, 1990);

Donald W. Rude & Lloyd E. Berry, "Tanner Manuscript No. 33: New Light on the Stationers' Company in the Early Seventeenth Century," *Papers of the Bibliographical Society of America,* 66 (Second Quarter 1972): 105–134;

Glynne Wickham, *Early English Stages,* 3 volumes (London & New York: Routledge, 1959–1981).

– Cyndia Susan Clegg

Jacob Tonson the Elder
(London: 1677 – 1718)

Jacob Tonson
(London: 1718 – 1735)

Of the many Tonsons involved in publishing during the Restoration and eighteenth century, the two most renowned were Jacob Tonson the Elder and his nephew, Jacob Tonson the Younger. The elder Tonson is rightly credited with many innovations in publishing and printing; he also helped establish and then solidify the reputations of John Milton and William Shakespeare by regularizing their texts and printing editions designed to appeal to a wider range of readers than both poets had ever reached. The house of Tonson also printed a wide range of contemporary authors and for nearly fifty years was the premier publishing house in England.

The elder Tonson was born in London (probably in 1656, although the date is uncertain), the son of a barber-surgeon also named Jacob and his wife Elizabeth, whose brother was bookseller Matthew Walbanck. Records are scanty, but it seems likely – given the financial status of his father and the later abilities of the boy – that Jacob received a good classical education. Richard Tonson, a son two years older than Jacob, was apprenticed to the Walbanck firm in 1668, and Jacob was apprenticed in 1670 to stationer Thomas Basset, who specialized in law books, as did the Walbanck firm. To the Tonson family publishing and bookselling would have appeared to be a promising profession not only because the family was connected with the Walbancks but because the Great Fire of 1666 had destroyed many bookshops and printers' establishments. The fire sweeping through the St. Paul's region had destroyed a crypt in which many thousands of books had been placed for protection.

During his eight-year apprenticeship with Basset, Tonson learned the trade of printing well. Though little of his youth is known, he recalls in one letter an incident that suggests he developed an enthusiasm for reading literature, as opposed to merely printing books, during this time. He and a friend eagerly went on a Sunday – the only day that apprentices had free – to the home of the recently deceased Milton in hopes of buying some of the books from his library. Nobody was home when

Jacob Tonson the Elder, from the painting in the Kit-Cat series of portraits by Sir Godfrey Kneller (National Portrait Gallery, London)

they arrived, but their visit nonetheless left a strong impression. Milton had already become something of a literary hero to the young Tonson, whose passionate interest in the poet's works, especially *Paradise Lost* (1667), was to grow in the years to come.

When Tonson was admitted to the Stationers' Company in 1677, his brother Richard was already becoming established and, in addition to printing law books, was producing poems and plays by Aphra Behn, Thomas Rymer, and many of the most famous writers of the period. For some time Jacob published some books jointly with his brother, and he also entered into partnerships with other printers and publishers, arrangements that were perhaps forced upon him by a lack of capital. Jacob's business was not especially distinguished at first; his first publication, in partnership with printer Abel Swalle, was *God's Revenge against the Abominable Sin of Adultery,* an anonymous piece of prose fiction. Yet in 1679 his fortunes dramatically improved when he began a publishing association with the most celebrated writer of the era, John Dryden.

For a time Dryden had lodged with his publisher, Henry Herringman, and had evidently maintained a close relationship with him since 1660, but for unknown reasons the association ceased. One plausible speculation is that after the well-publicized attack on Dryden in Rose Alley on 18 December 1679, Herringman began to fear for his own safety. On that night Dryden had been walking home through the narrow Rose Alley passageway, where he was set upon and beaten unconscious by three thugs. Rewards were offered during the next months, but neither the guilty parties nor their motives were ever discovered.

The literary world assumed (as Dryden seems also to have assumed) that the attackers were employed by some titled personages who had been offended by one of Dryden's satires, and much speculation about the identity of the offended party has continued. John Wilmot, Lord Rochester, has been one suspect, and Louise Renée de Kéroualle, duchess of Portsmouth and former mistress of Charles II, has been another. (Of course, the attack may also have been a simple mugging with no literary or political implications.) The event was reported widely in newspapers, and in this period of political turmoil, when the voices of literary men such as Dryden were increasingly important, writers and printers — any of whom might be next to suffer such fates — felt a certain degree of fear. Herringman might have felt such fears, but this is only speculation; the relationship between Dryden and his publisher seems to have been strained even before the attack, because Dryden was discussing business with other publishers, including Tonson, before the Rose Alley incident.

In any case, Tonson seems to have approached Dryden in the right way at the right time. In that year Tonson brought out Dryden's play *Troilus and Cressida, or, Truth Found too Late,* and before long he was Dryden's exclusive publisher. In 1681 Tonson published Dryden's *Absalom and Achitophel,* the first truly celebrated work to bear Tonson's imprint and the one that firmly established his reputation. On the title page of the first

edition he prudently identified himself only as J. T., but in the second part of *Absalom and Achitophel* (1682) — a work that was probably Tonson's idea, although Dryden contributed only around two hundred lines to this sequel by Nahum Tate — Tonson used his full name.

During the 1680s he gradually bought Herringman's rights to Dryden's earlier works, and he began to establish his press as an important literary firm by printing works of most of the contemporary major writers — Behn, Tate, and Nathaniel Lee. He began to develop a sense of the value of image and publicity, and he was one of the first publishers to use the newspapers to advertise. Such publicity helped not only Tonson but the poets as well: Tonson's enterprising methods and his high-quality printing helped turn Dryden's works into commodities of permanent value. By becoming Dryden's exclusive publisher and by collecting and reprinting his works, Tonson helped Dryden stay highly visible to the public and helped him become not just a contemporary best-seller but an author for the ages.

An important hallmark of the Dryden-Tonson partnership was the series of anthologies and compilations of translations on which they collaborated. The first of these was *Ovid's Epistles* (1680), which featured translations by seventeen different figures. Scholars today differ about whether the idea for the book was Dryden's or Tonson's, but certainly both benefited from it: the book, going through three editions in the decade and more afterward, had a success far beyond that of most classical translations. In 1683 the two began an even more ambitious undertaking: a five-volume edition of *Plutarchs Lives* (1683–1686). Dryden wrote a biography of Plutarch for the first volume and was no doubt instrumental in organizing the whole endeavor, which ultimately involved the work of forty-two translators. Again, the set was successful, and further editions appeared in 1702 and 1716. For a time Tonson was becoming a specialist in translation: in 1684 translations comprised about half of his publication list, and the other half included Wentworth Dillon Roscommon's *Essay on Translated Verse.* Clearly, Dryden and Tonson were creating a market as much as they were tapping one.

The pair were also jointly responsible for an even greater innovation: the poetic anthology, or miscellany. The first of such works, *Miscellany Poems,* appeared in 1684. It included more than a hundred pages of Dryden's work — including "Mac Flecknoe" (which had previously been printed in an unauthorized edition), *Absalom and Achitophel,* and *The Medall* (1682) — together with many dramatic pro-

Jacob Tonson Jr., circa 1720, portrait by Kneller (National Portrait Gallery, London)

logues and epilogues and some translations, including two of Virgil's eclogues. The volume also featured the work of many other contributors, including Tate, Thomas Otway, Sir Charles Sedley, and Rymer. Both the concept and the book were immediate successes, and Tonson and Dryden began planning a second one.

One letter from Dryden to Tonson implies that Dryden had wished in this second miscellany to include some of his previously published work, such as *Religio Laici or a Laymans Faith* (1682), but Tonson pressed him to make this a volume of entirely new material. This new volume, *Sylvae: or, The Second Part of Poetical Miscellanies,* appeared in May 1685; Dryden wrote an extensive preface for it and contributed about a third of the contents, which were dominated by poetic translations. Both volumes were reprinted later that year and offered as a set, and two later miscellanies followed during Dryden's lifetime. Thanks to the efforts of Dryden and Tonson, the anthology became a major new publishing genre — one that was to remain important for many years and that no doubt helped to create both a market and an outlet for shorter poetic work. Alexander Pope's first publications, for exam-

ple, appeared in Tonson's sixth miscellany (1709), and by placing them there the young poet was guaranteed a wider audience than any other method of publishing would have given him.

While Tonson was working closely with Dryden in these endeavors, he was also pursuing his long-standing enthusiasm for the works of Milton. In 1683 he was able to purchase half the rights to *Paradise Lost,* and he bought the other half in 1690. Before Tonson became involved with Milton's epic, it had been neither greatly successful nor ignored, having gone through three editions between 1667 and 1678. Because an edition normally comprised one thousand copies, as many as three thousand copies of the poem existed at that time. Some readers, such as Dryden, recognized at once the greatness of the work, but many did not: for example, Rymer — a critic almost as influential as he was wrongheaded — sneered at *Paradise Lost* as a piece "which some are pleased to call a poem." As the Augustan taste was developing, with its criteria of elegance, metrical smoothness, and Horatian urbanity of tone, Milton's epic was in danger of being seen as a huge, awkward Gothic relic of an age best forgotten. But after Tonson began to publish the poem, it quickly began to achieve the respect it has held ever since: some modern scholars credit Tonson with having created an audience for Milton's great poem and, in effect, with having rescued his reputation from what might have been oblivion.

Tonson approached the text with great care. In purchasing the rights to it, he also insisted on obtaining the corrected manuscript of the first edition, an action that reveals he was approaching the poem as something of great literary value, though its monetary value was dubious. He did not print an edition of the poem until 1688, and some speculate that politics may explain that particular date. Tonson's politics were becoming increasingly Whiggish, and in the mid 1680s, having made friends with men such as John Somers and Charles Sackville, sixth earl of Dorset, he was beginning to move in rather rarefied Whig circles. In the revolutionary atmosphere of 1687–1688 *Paradise Lost* may have seemed to be a document that could advance the anti-Stuart cause.

But even if party politics motivated Tonson to print the poem at that particular time, the 1688 edition was the most luxurious project he had yet attempted. Publishing the folio volume by subscription, he had carefully planned its typography and overall look with impressive illustrations by artist John Baptist Medina. Many of Medina's illustrations provided interesting in-

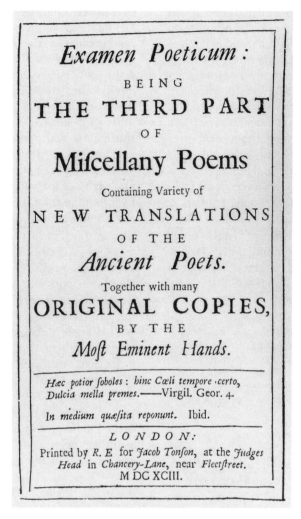

*Title page for the third volume in the series of poetry
anthologies begun by the elder Tonson and
John Dryden in 1684*

terpretations of the text and performed an important service in helping the 1688 public appreciate what many readers before had found to be an obscure, difficult poem. The frontispiece to the volume was the engraving of Milton by Robert White. Below it Tonson printed Dryden's six-line tribute to Milton:

> Three Poets, in three distant Ages born,
> Greece, Italy, and England did adorn.
> The first in loftiness of thought surpass'd
> The next in Majesty; in both the Last.
> The force of Nature cou'd no farther goe:
> To make a third she joynd the former two.

As a puff for Milton, the lines operate on two levels: not only is he lauded as a synthesis of Homer and Virgil, but his Englishness is emphasized in an appeal to both neoclassicist and nationalist strains. As for the text of the epic, Tonson followed the most recent edition (the third, from 1678), but he also consulted earlier printings as well as Milton's own corrected manuscript, and in doing so he made some important emendations to the text. Tonson was to remain in some manner closely involved with the text of *Paradise Lost* for the rest of his life: in the 1730s he wrote letters in the *Grub-Street Journal* on Richard Bentley's 1732 edition of the poem, letters that reveal his close familiarity with the text and its history. These letters convincingly point out major errors in Bentley's edition, which scholars have continued to condemn, so Tonson was still, near the end of his life, defending Milton's literary reputation. In an angry letter to his nephew Jacob about the Bentley edition that the younger Jacob had published, Tonson referred to Bentley in no flattering terms: "I am indeed at present (it cannot last long) not a little concerned at this Vultures falling upon a Poet that is the admiration of England, and its greatest credit abroad."

The whole story of Tonson's interest in Milton emphasizes several points about the publisher. He was an enterprising and foresightful businessman, for *Paradise Lost* was to provide much profit for him through the years: in his later years when he was asked what poet had made the most money for him, Tonson answered, "Milton." He also was a publisher who held some beliefs usually regarded as modern, beliefs in the integrity of the text and in its relation to the worth of the literary artifact. And he cared deeply about literature; it was not just a commodity to him. His own attitude toward the poem and his pride in having helped popularize it are implicit in a prefatory letter that he printed in a 1711 pocket edition. The letter, addressed to John Somers, reads in part as follows:

> It was Your Lordship's Opinion and Encouragement that occasion'd the first appearing of this Poem in the Folio Edition, which from thence has been so well receiv'd, that notwithstanding the Price of it was Four times greater than before, the Sale encreas'd double the Number every Year. The Work is now generally known and esteem'd. . . .

That Joseph Addison first taught the public to appreciate *Paradise Lost* with his fine series of *Spectator* essays is a modern misconception: six separate Tonson editions of the poem had appeared before Addison began his series, and an audience had already been well established. Furthermore, since Tonson published *The Spectator,* he may well have encouraged Addison to pursue the subject of Milton. In 1695 Tonson published an edition of the poem with scholarly annotations by Patrick Hume; this, along with the beautiful 1688 edition, went a long way toward establishing Milton's place in the pantheon of English authors. He went on to print a less expensive quarto edition, and when the Copyright Act of 1709 ensured that he would hold exclusive rights to Milton for another twenty-one years, Tonson published another wave of editions and encouraged further critical discussions (such as Addison's) to solidify Milton's reputation.

But it was not only Milton who gained from Tonson's enterprising approach to publishing. Dryden, a living writer who was something of an outcast as a Catholic Tory in the post-1688 climate, also benefited enormously from his association with Tonson. The *Miscellanies* and the early translations helped establish Dryden as one of England's authorities in classical scholarship and put him at the head of the avant-garde. After the fall of James II, Dryden's Catholicism and politics weakened his hold on such positions, but Tonson's fidelity to his old friend and chief author did not slacken, and as a result Dryden retained more of an audience than he might otherwise have expected. Some Dryden letters from the 1690s complain about money matters involving Tonson, and some scholars have used those letters to argue that Tonson was a hardhearted taskmaster who cared little for Dryden beyond getting his pound of copy from the writer. But although author and publisher had their arguments from time to time, Dryden would have had little serious complaint about Tonson's behavior – quite the contrary, in fact.

By the 1690s Tonson was a fully established, successful publisher who did not urgently need Dryden's work; Tonson's own political views had developed in directions opposed to those of Dryden; and Tonson was increasingly closely involved with Whig leaders. Pressure on him to drop Dryden must have been strong, and yet no evidence suggests that Tonson ever considered doing so. Many of Dryden's letters and some prefaces speak warmly of Tonson as a good friend, and the evidence suggests that the two did share a friendship beyond a mere business relationship, a friendship that transcended their political and social differences and speaks well for the characters of both men.

To be sure, there was occasional animosity – especially during the years before their great edition of Virgil. No doubt fully intending that his lampoon would be made public, Dryden wrote a triplet describing Tonson and enclosed it in a letter to him:

> With leering look, bull-faced and freckled fair
> With frowsy pores poisoning the ambient air,
> With two left legs, and Judas-coloured hair.

This description was widely circulated, but one should not make more of it than the evidence warrants: for a man of Dryden's verbal brilliance, this may be letting off steam. Tonson had trouble with his feet all his life, and the "two left legs" refers to Tonson's odd gait. Dryden's description stuck, and many later satirists would apply the image to Tonson; one anonymous poem, for example, obliquely refers to an unnamed poet's politics by saying that his works can be bought at the shop with the sign of two left feet. The image also occurs in Pope's *The Dunciad* (1728), in which Tonson fares much better at Pope's hands than does any other publisher. In any case, some scholars have wanted to see Dryden as abused by his publisher, but to see things that way one needs to overlook much about the long and fruitful relationship between the two men.

In 1693 Tonson and Dryden produced a luxurious translation of Juvenal and Persius – again, the translations being made by various hands, but with Dryden doing much of the work. This book includes some of Dryden's finest translation work – or, as he refers to it, not translation exactly but something "betwixt a Paraphrase and Imitation." Dryden speaks of his intention to create a Restoration Juvenal: the author, he declares, will be made "to speak that kind of English, which he wou'd have spoken had he liv'd in England, and had Written to this Age." Dryden was clearly developing here a theory of translation as a contemporizing, as the translator's imitating of the author.

This was the sort of imitation that was to dominate English verse for many years – to result in some of the best work of Pope, for example, and in the great "Vanity of Human Wishes" by Samuel Johnson. To say that the whole Augustan theory of imitation was ushered in by the Dryden-Tonson Juvenal would be an overstatement, but certainly the wide appeal of the work helped educate and form the public taste for it. Dryden's brilliant opening essay, "A Discourse Concerning the Original and Progress of Satire," contributed greatly to the imitation movement and to the reading public's understanding of it. The essay also manages gently to introduce nonscholarly readers to Horace, Juvenal, and Persius, and Dryden's distinctions among the three remain widely used today. A second edition, this time with newly commissioned engravings, appeared in 1697, and Tonson produced several reprints during the next two decades.

Sometime in 1694 Dryden and Tonson decided to proceed with a project that had evidently been dear to Dryden for some time: a translation of Virgil's works. They decided to publish it by the subscription method, which at that time was no guarantor of success. Subscription publishing dated from the early seventeenth century, but it was coming to be used more frequently: Tonson had used it with his 1688 *Paradise Lost* and had published a limited edition of Dryden's opera *Albion and Albanius* by subscription in 1687. Tonson did not invent subscription publishing, but *The Works of Virgil* (1697) by Dryden and Tonson became the most influential single volume in popularizing that mode of publication. Subscription publishing, of course, could minimize the publisher's risks, could guarantee a certain base of sales, and – what must have especially appealed to the shrewd Tonson – could, if properly managed, whip up public anticipation for the work

to be published and hence provide a kind of cost-free advertising.

Public interest in Dryden's Virgil quickly became enormous, publication of the book ultimately becoming the literary event of the decade. Tonson agreed to enlist one hundred subscribers at five guineas each (three to be paid in advance), of which Dryden would ultimately get about three, and to pay Dryden in installments: £50 when he first delivered the *Georgics* and *Eclogues*, another £50 for the first four books of the *Aeneid*, £50 when he delivered the eighth, and a final £50 when he delivered the twelfth. For the second printing the price would be two guineas, Dryden and Tonson each getting one. The volume was to have one hundred illustrations that were to be taken from John Ogilby's earlier (1654) translation of Virgil. In the short term the contract seems to have been more favorable to Dryden than to Tonson, although the publisher gained much in prestige and publicity from the project.

The work finally appeared in June 1697, and many consider it one of the great milestones in British publishing. The typography is unusually crisp and clear, with generous, wide margins and beautifully reproduced illustrations. Every fifth line is numbered for ease of reference, and italics introduce each speaker's name. The book is further enhanced by extensive dedications, a listing of subscribers for both the first and the second impressions (though only the first-impression subscribers are numbered), an essay on Virgil by Dryden, and prose arguments written by Addison for each section.

While politics did not destroy the friendship of Tonson and Dryden, this is not to say that politics never strained it. As the nation awaited the publication of *The Works of Virgil*, King William III let it be known that he would welcome its being dedicated to him. Such news must have thrilled Tonson, but Dryden would have none of it. So Tonson resorted to subterfuge, working silently to gratify William despite Dryden: he had his workers alter some of the illustrations so that Aeneas would resemble the king. But Dryden fought back by circulating a set of verses on the comparison, verses pointing out that Aeneas "took his father pick-a-pack, / And [William] sent his packing."

During the last years of Dryden's life he published two more major works with Tonson. The first was the beautiful *Alexander's Feast: Or, the Power of Musique,* published in December 1697; it had been performed with music by Jeremiah Clarke in the previous month. A great popular success, the work

*Illustration by John Baptist Medina from Book One of the
fourth edition (1688) of John Milton's* Paradise Lost,
the first illustrated edition of Milton's epic

went through nine more editions during the next
two decades, and George Frideric Handel wrote
music for it in 1736. In March 1700 Tonson printed
Dryden's *Fables, Ancient and Modern,* a work that did
not sell as well as some earlier pieces had, but it has
steadily gained prestige among Dryden scholars.
Certainly one of the most intriguing selections of it
is the translation of book 1 of Homer's *Iliad,* a work
that Dryden had in fact wanted to translate entirely,
but he died on 1 May 1700 before he could begin.

After Dryden's death Tonson zealously guarded and advanced the artist's reputation. In 1701
Tonson published a fine folio set of Dryden's
works, and he continued steadily to publish various
editions, reprints, and collections of his works. He
worked for Dryden in other ways as well, though
some ways may have been badly planned: for example, he became concerned that some were setting up
Pope as a better poet, and so he spoke about this to
the critic, poet, and playwright John Dennis, in a
conversation that aroused one of Dennis's many attacks on the younger poet. In a more positive action
Tonson approached the retired William Congreve

to write a preface to a 1717 edition of Dryden's
plays, and Congreve's assessments helped strength-
en Dryden's waning reputation as a playwright.

Tonson's solicitude for Dryden even after the
artist's death shows the depth of the printer's regard
for him, despite their political differences. Tonson's
Whig affiliations had begun in the 1680s, when his
involvement with the Kit-Cat Club soon made
Whig politics a serious interest. Clubs had been
gradually becoming important to English literary
and political life, and the growth and development
of coffeehouse society paralleled the growth of
clubs. The form taken by seventeenth-century clubs
ranged from societies holding open public gatherings to those holding closed and secretive meetings;
most were between such extremes, with the more
powerful groups being also the hardest in which to
gain membership. The Kit-Cat Club was one of the
most powerful of all, virtually all its members being
drawn from the top of the Whig hierarchy after
1688; its exclusivity and prestige made it a powerful
source of gossip material, and many books and
pamphlets about the Kit-Cats were printed for the
curious public in the eighteenth century.

Much has been written about the Kit-Cat
Club, but some facts of its origin remain in dispute.
One version holds that the club was named for one
Christopher Cat, a tavern keeper at whose establishment the group began meeting; another version
(that of Addison) says that kit-cats were in fact a
particular sort of pastry, mutton pies, that Cat had
created and served to the group. Yet another version (that of John Arbuthnot) holds that the name
came from the club's admitting both "old Cats and
young Kits." Even more disputed is the date of the
club's origin. Many place it around the turn of the
century, but much evidence indicates that the prin-
cipals, including Jacob Tonson, were meeting regularly in the early 1690s. All agree that Tonson was
involved from the outset, however; indeed,
Tonson's name in the early eighteenth century became identified with the increasingly famous club.

The club may have had its origin in a toasting
club, something of a fad in the latter part of the seventeenth century: a group would meet to drink, to
socialize, and to write and proclaim elaborate toasts
to the current beauties of the day. Lady Mary
Wortley Montagu later told the story of having
been taken to the Kit-Cat Club when she was but
eight years old (around 1697) and of having been
made the toast of the evening, a celebration she
warmly remembered in her later years. In some of
the toasting clubs it became a practice to engrave
the toast on a drinking glass with a diamond; Addi-

son describes such a toasting club meeting in number seventeen of his *Tatler*. Tory satirists, as might be expected, depicted these gatherings in their worst possible light. One anonymous poem, "Faction Display'd" (1704), presents Tonson speaking thus:

> I am the founder of your lov'd Kit-Cat
> A club that gave direction to the State.
> 'Twas there we first instructed all our Youth
> To talk Profane and Laugh at Sacred Truth;
> We taught them how to Toast, and Rhime and Bite
> To sleep away the Day, and Drink the Night.

Such attacks were quite common, and Tonson, perceived as the leader of the club, received much abuse from Tory satirists. He was sometimes given a thinly veiled name such as Bibliopolo; often his first name was given backwards as Bocaj or Bocai, and this name stuck, appearing even in many poems friendly to the club.

A purely social men's club atmosphere – if not quite the drunken dissipation of the satirists – probably describes what was to distinguish the early meetings of the Kit-Cats. References appear in the 1680s to men "clubbing with Ovid" in gatherings of the writers who worked on the translations with Tonson, and it is likely that some informal groupings such as these were forerunners of the actual Kit-Cats and that Tonson's literary connections naturally led to aristocratic and political ones. Tonson seems early to have developed the reputation of being a boon companion, and the combination of social attractions and literary ones may have helped draw members of the Whig elite into his gatherings, for they were naturally interested in strengthening their connections with the great writers of the day in an era when the pen of a great writer wielded enormous power to sway the minds of the public. The presence of Dryden, with his Stuart sympathies, at Kit-Cat meetings in the 1690s would of course have altered the tone of some of these meetings; the Kit-Cats probably grew more overtly political and more exclusively Whig as time went on.

As the membership grew, quarters larger than those Christopher Cat could provide at the Cat and Fiddle were needed, and Tonson used his subscription method to raise funds for a new place in Hampstead Heath, where the group moved in 1703. But in the same year Tonson had a special club room added to his new residence at Barn Elms, where the club met thereafter. Exact membership numbers are somewhat uncertain, but the best estimate is that there were between forty and fifty committed members, with an average meeting consisting of a somewhat smaller group. Tonson commissioned Sir

Godfrey Kneller to create portraits of some forty-eight Kit-Cats, and the entire series – including his portrait of Dryden, probably completed shortly before the poet's death – was hung in the room at Barn Elms. Kneller, who had enjoyed the patronage of Charles II, James II, and William and Mary and who apparently was never really a member of the club, painted the portraits in an unusual size, 36 inches by 28 inches. The portraits include the dukes of Newcastle (Thomas Pelham-Holles), Somerset (Charles Seymour), Devonshire (William Cavendish), Richmond (Charles Lennox), and Grafton (Charles Fitzroy); the earls of Dorset (Charles Sackville), Essex (Algernon Capell), Carlisle (Charles Howard), and Halifax (Charles Montague); as well as a host of lords. Robert Walpole, untitled but soon to be one of the most powerful ministers of the eighteenth century, was also among the group. Besides Dryden, literary men painted by Kneller include William Walsh (Pope's mentor), Sir John Vanbrugh, William Congreve, Addison, and Richard Steele. Also included was the physician-poet Samuel Garth, author of the popular comic piece *The Dispensary* (1699), which Tonson published. Kneller's portrait of Tonson shows the publisher holding his folio edition of *Paradise Lost*.

Tonson generally served as club secretary and organizer; many references from the other members indicate they considered him the central member. The club provided a common meeting ground for the men who were to lead Britain during the Hanoverian era: because of their important role in establishing the Hanoverian succession, Walpole was to refer to the Kit-Cats as the men who saved the kingdom.

The political endeavors of the club resulted in some mysterious events, some of them involving Tonson. For instance, in the summer of 1703 he went to the Continent ostensibly on printing business, a trip he had made before. His stated aims were to get engravings done for his forthcoming edition of *Caesar's Commentaries* (1712) and to purchase paper, as Dutch type and paper were then considered the finest in the world – but some speculated that he may also have had some shadowy political purpose, an assignment from the Kit-Cats. Vanbrugh wrote him a letter describing the rumors:

> The Duke of Somerset had had severall letters from you; but do you know that the Tories (even the wisest of 'em) have been very grave upon your going to Holland; they often say (with a nod) that Caesars Cmts. [commentaries] might have been carry'd through without a voyage to Holland; there are meanings in that subscription, and that list of names may serve for farther

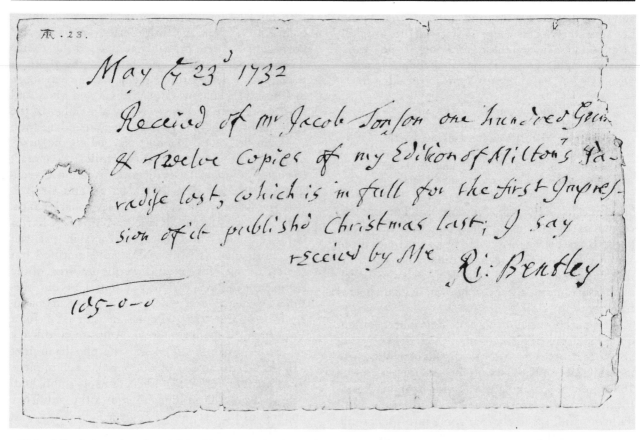

Richard Bentley's receipt acknowledging his compensation for the flawed 1732 edition of Paradise Lost *that he edited for the younger Tonson (Pierpont Morgan Library, New York)*

engagements than paying three guineas a piece for a book; in short I could win a hundred pounds, if I were sure you had not made a trip to Hanover, which you may possibly hear sworn when you come home again; so I'd advise you to bring a very exact journal, well attested.

Similar speculation in a letter to René Louis de Voyer de Palmy, Marquis d'Argenson, from Nathaniel Hooke, a Jacobite, also surrounded a trip Tonson made in 1714, the year of George I's accession. Hooke refers to Tonson's presence in Paris as a mission to spy on the doings of poet Matthew Prior, who was in fact there to carry on negotiations between the Tory administration of Robert Harley, Earl of Oxford; Henry St. John, Viscount Bolingbroke; and the exiled Stuarts, an action for which Prior (along with Harley) would later be imprisoned. Using Tonson for such espionage makes some sense: having published Prior's work, Tonson knew him from his former days as a member of the Kit-Cats, before he had defected to the Tory cause. Furthermore, not being a politician, Tonson might have aroused less suspicion of being a spy than other choices might. But there is no proof that

Tonson's trip was anything other than what it seemed to be — that is, another in a long line of printing-related trips. In fact, when Prior was released from prison in 1718, Tonson published a sumptuous edition of his poems — a fact that might argue there was no strong political ill will between the two.

The Kit-Cats were avid theater patrons as well, and they often attended plays together as members of a large group. As a result, references to them appear in some of the dramatic literature of the time, as in the prologue to William Burnaby's *The Reform'd Wife* (1700): "Thus tho' the Town all delicates afford, / A Kit-Cat is a Supper for a Lord." They were a group whose approval a dramatist would seek. Politics and literature were inextricably related in this period and were strongly intertwined in the theater: the most popular play of the era, Addison's *Cato* (1713), was a powerful piece of Whig propaganda — so powerful, in fact, that the Tories published alternate "keys" to the text and proved that it in fact supported their side. Tonson published *Cato,* for which he paid Addison the huge sum of £107 for the copy-

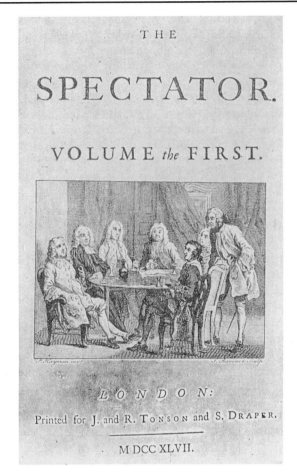

The first number of Tonson's The Spectator *and the title page for the 1747 collected edition of the periodical*

right (by comparison, Milton had sold the copyright to *Paradise Lost* for £20 in 1667). The Kit-Cats were also heavily involved with the subscription effort to build the new Queen's Theatre in Haymarket in 1705, and Tonson was in charge of collecting the subscriptions.

The group also developed many other theater-related schemes, such as a four-hundred-guinea subscription to encourage the production of better dramas. Colley Cibber writes about the outcome in *An Apology for the Life of Mr. Colley Cibber, Comedian* (1740), in which he notes that the plays performed were Shakespeare's *Julius Caesar* (1623), John Fletcher's *A King and No King* (1619), and a combination of comic scenes from Dryden's *Secret-Love, or The Maiden Queen* (1668) and *Marriage A-la-Mode* (1673). Cibber reports that the project was a success, with actors and managers alike profiting.

As Queen Anne's reign progressed, the Kit-Cats became solidly devoted to party politics. The Whigs' greatest successes in the period derive in some measure from the solidarity of the Kit-Cat Club, from which anyone suspected of dealing with

the Tory government was expelled. This happened to Prior, and he remained bitter about it for many years. Yet Tonson's membership must have involved him in some of the most far-reaching developments of the era, such as passing the Act of Settlement with the Regency (1706), providing the legal basis for the Hanoverian succession, and passing the Act of Union with Scotland (1707). Party politics once ironically dictated an accommodation between the club and the powerful Jacobite John Churchill, duke of Marlborough, who was admitted to the club in 1709 in an alliance that helped Churchill finance the vast debts arising from the War of the Spanish Succession. The Kit-Cats were also involved in some ill-fated political projects, most notably the impeachment trial in 1710 of the Tory clergyman Henry Sacheverell, whose defense was so impassioned that he won over the hearts of the populace; riots ensued, and the Whig ministry soon fell.

After Anne's death in 1714, George I took the throne with little serious opposition, a result largely of the work of the Kit-Cats. Such work had included Steele's brilliant anti-Stuart pamphlet *The Crisis*

(1713), which reached a circulation of more than forty thousand. George rewarded the Kit-Cat members generously, but the enthusiasm that had kept the club going was finally waning, and it gradually ceased to be as powerful as it had been. Meetings continued, though less regularly, for some time, but Tonson's presence was always essential, and after he made an extended trip to Paris from the fall of 1718 to the spring of 1720, the club soon ceased altogether.

Yet during his active membership in the Kit-Cats, Tonson continued to strengthen his claim to being England's premier publisher. In 1703 he began an edition – in Latin – of Julius Caesar's works. He engaged scholar Samuel Clarke to edit the collection, and he also contracted with John Watts, who would henceforth print many of Tonson's classical texts, to print the volumes. After nine years of production the works of Caesar, *C. Julii Caesaris quae extant* (1712), was finally published in an enormous folio edition; many scholars feel that British publishing had never seen so magnificent a work. Many maps were included along with eighty-seven engravings, most of them exquisitely detailed landscapes by several Dutch artists illustrating scenes in the *Commentaries*. Dedicated to the duke of Marlborough and including Kneller's portrait of him as a frontispiece, the work was published by subscription, and Tonson printed each subscriber's coat of arms on each double-page plate.

Through the next decade Tonson and Watts were involved in publishing many classical texts. With Michael Mattaire, a schoolmaster and scholar who had acquired a great reputation in the classical works, Tonson published a series known as Mattaire's Classics. The series was printed in a uniform set of gilt-edged duodecimo volumes that included lengthy and thorough indexes. In 1713 alone Tonson published editions of Terence, Lucretius, Saint Justin, Phaedrus, Aesop, Sallust, and Pompey. He published the Greek New Testament the following year and went on to produce editions of many poets such as Ovid, Catullus, and Horace before the series finally concluded with an edition of Lucan in 1719.

Wishing to produce another more ambitious classical text, Tonson settled on Ovid's *Metamorphoses,* again using the method of employing a group of translators whom Samuel Garth this time organized. Many existing Tonson translations of Ovid, including those by Dryden, were to be incorporated, but Garth was in charge of adding some new ones as well. In "Sandys' Ghost," the title of which alludes to George Sandys, the great 1626 translator of Ovid, Pope satirizes the widely publicized project. He shows Garth misled by the mischievous ghost to try to produce a new translation and induced to seek from second-rate minds whatever help he needs:

> Ho! *Master Sam,* quoth Sandys' sprite
>   Write on, nor let me scare ye;
> Forsooth, if Rhymes fall in not right,
>   To Budgel seek, or Carey.
>
> I hear the beat of Jacob's Drums,
>   Poor Ovid finds no quarter!
> See first the merry P[elham] comes
>   In haste without his garter.
>
> Then Lords and Lordings, 'Squires and Knights,
>   Wits, Witlings, Prigs and Peers;
> *Garth* at *St. James's,* and at *White's,*
>   Beats up for volunteers.

After a roll call of the good authors who would not write for such a shoddy enterprise, Pope goes on to list those second-rate writers who will, including Lady Mary Wortley Montagu, and he concludes:

> Now, *Tonson,* list thy Forces all,
>   Review them, and tell Noses;
> For to poor *Ovid* shall befal
>   A strange *Metamorphosis.*
>
> A *Metamorphosis* more strange
>   Than all his Books can vapour;
> To what, (quoth 'Squire) shall *Ovid* change?
>   Quoth *Sandys: To Waste-Paper.*

Despite Pope's ridicule, the edition appeared in 1717 and was successful, being reprinted well into the nineteenth century. Dedicated to Princess Caroline, whose portrait (again by Kneller) appeared as a frontispiece, the series was printed in quarto and included many illustrations. Each of the fifteen books of the *Metamorphoses* was dedicated to a different noblewoman.

Tonson's nephew, the younger Jacob Tonson, had begun to work with him sometime around 1700. He was the son of Richard Tonson, Jacob's elder brother; the elder Jacob Tonson never had any children, and his taking his nephew, the younger Jacob, into the business was almost like an adoption. The younger Tonson increasingly came to run the day-to-day operations of the business while the elder was busy with other pursuits – traveling in Europe, working with the Kit-Cats, or investing in various stock schemes at the time. Yet the elder Jacob was a powerful personality, and publishing was always his first interest; until his retirement after 1718, he never really relinquished control of the business.

The younger Tonson did not have the influence of his uncle, nor was he equally innovative, but from the start he was worthy of his name. In 1707 he negotiated the purchase of copyrights to more than one hundred titles, including three of Shakespeare's plays, owned by publisher Henry Herringman. Prior to this time the elder Jacob had also been actively seeking copyrights to Shakespeare, although the names of the vendors are not always clear — nor is it clear that those vendors actually owned the rights that they were selling. Indeed, the Tonsons' claims to the copyrights were to be frequently and vigorously challenged in the future.

In any case, the elder Jacob had decided to publish Shakespeare's works, and he engaged poet and playwright Nicholas Rowe to edit them. Rowe's edition, a landmark in many ways, appeared in six octavo volumes in 1709. As he had done with Milton, Tonson did not approach Shakespeare as a commodity: from the start, he intended to produce reliable texts with sensible and useful apparatuses, and in Rowe he found an editor who shared his aims. Whereas Patrick Hume (Tonson's editor of Milton) had worked primarily for the scholar, Rowe worked with the general reader in mind. He did not add extensive annotations and notes, but he provided materials that made Shakespeare more clear and readable than any previous edition had been. He provided a lengthy essay on Shakespeare, which was the first extensive biographical study of him and was often reprinted in later editions throughout the century. And in an attempt to regain respect for Shakespeare in an age with markedly different aesthetics, Rowe defended the dramatist against many of the strict neoclassical criticisms of Rymer. Many of Rowe's added stage directions and scene divisions are still accepted today, as are many of his textual emendations. Shakespeare scholars consider this edition to mark the origin of the movement to popularize Shakespeare, and indeed Tonson's and Rowe's labors gained Shakespeare a wider audience of readers than he had ever enjoyed before; many affluent families, for example, purchased multiple copies and distributed them to those in servants' quarters. Tonson's edition was a great financial success, as evidenced by its many reprintings in the ensuing years.

Tonson also set out to reclaim the reputation of another poet whose stock had sunk greatly since the Restoration: Edmund Spenser. He hired poet

Frontispiece, by Michael Van Der Gucht, for Dryden's edition of The Works of Virgil *(1697)*

and musician John Hughes as editor, and, like his earlier choices of Hume and Rowe, this was an excellent decision. Comparing editions and emending for clarity while maintaining Spenser's language and spelling as much as possible, Hughes worked carefully and diligently with the text. He added many essays to introduce the poet and explain the allegory to a public bound to find it extremely obscure. Published in 1715, the edition included all of Spenser's poems plus the prose work "A View of the State of Ireland." It also incorporated illustrations by the French artist Louis du Guernier, who had previously worked for Tonson on the Mattaire classics and was again to do so on the 1717 edition of Ovid's *Metamorphoses*.

Spenser's language, his stanza, his allegory, and his diffused plot lines were simply too alien for Augustan readers, and it was to be several generations before he would be recognized as one of England's greatest poets. Yet the edition had some success, and the modern Spenser reader will still

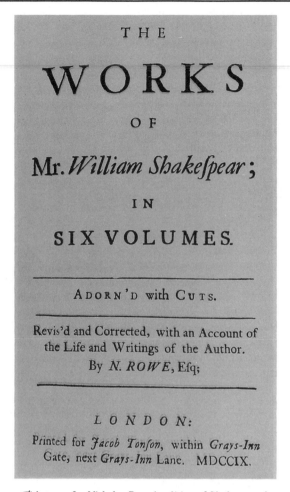

THE

WORKS

OF

Mr. *William Shakefpear*;

IN

SIX VOLUMES.

ADORN'D with CUTS.

Revis'd and Corrected, with an Account of
the Life and Writings of the Author.
By *N. ROWE*, Efq;

LONDON:

Printed for *Jacob Tonfon*, within *Grays-Inn*
Gate, next *Grays-Inn* Lane. MDCCIX.

Title page for Nicholas Rowe's edition of Shakespeare's
Works

find that Hughes's work is of more than mere historical interest. By making Spenser available, Tonson may have contributed to the occasional Spenserian works that appeared in the eighteenth century, especially such works as William Shenstone's *The Schoolmistress* (1737) and James Thomson's *The Castle of Indolence* (1748). The edition may have kept Spenser's reputation alive until the time of Thomas Warton.

Although the public was not willing to take *The Faerie Queene* to heart, the market for Shakespeare remained brisk. The younger Tonson in 1721 conceived an idea for a new edition to be compiled by Pope, who had become the most popular writer of the era. Having enjoyed phenomenal success with his own poetry, his translations of Homer, and works such as the early *Essay on Criticism* (1711), Pope seemed a natural choice to edit and annotate the works of England's greatest poet. The elder Tonson was also enthusiastic about the idea: purchasing a copy of the 1623 First Folio, he again re-

vealed his commitment to textual integrity and promised a more correct edition than Rowe's had been. Pope's edition was published in two parts, volumes one–five appearing in 1723 and the sixth in 1725.

Unfortunately Pope's talents were not those of an editor, and the edition had serious problems – some resulting from Pope's negligence, some from a misguided urge to "correct" the text. Pope's neoclassicism resulted in Shakespeare's diction often being "improved" for greater metrical smoothness, and in the quiet dropping of many scenes and soliloquies because they seemed to violate the artistic unity of the plays. In 1726 the poet and playwright Lewis Theobald published "Shakespeare Restored," an attack on Pope's edition, and while Theobald was no match for Pope as a creative artist, he had far better editorial abilities, and his attack was fully justified. Pope, however, was enraged at the man whose name he had always contemptuously spelled "Tibbald," and he lost little time in incorporating

"The Faerie Queene," Louis DuGuernier's frontispiece for John Hughes's edition of The Works of Mr. Edmund Spenser *(1715)*

into *The Dunciad* (1728) the man he saw as an upstart editor and critic.

The Tonsons, however, looked on the affair with cooler heads, and before long they had managed to join a group of publishers who were going to publish Theobald's corrected edition of Shakespeare. (The Copyright Act of 1709 dictated that the Tonsons' rights to the works of Shakespeare would expire in 1731, and this prospect induced them to cooperate with the other publishers.) Pope was further infuriated by this apparent treachery of his publishers, but the elder Tonson was an adept diplomat and was able to remain on good terms with him: Tonson delayed publishing Theobald's edition for some years (until 1733), and he made sure that Pope's edition remained on the market as long as possible. It is probably pointless to assign blame or praise in the whole affair, but Tonson's motives seem to have been good ones: he

seems to have been concerned ultimately with producing the most accurate edition rather than with showing blind loyalty to Pope. In restoring many readings based on the early quartos, Theobald's edition was to prove far more accurate than Pope's, and it was more scholarly than Rowe's.

The Tonsons continued to publish ambitious editions of earlier English authors: a good edition of Edmund Waller's works in 1729 and a seventeen-volume set of Rymer's *Foedera* (1735) were completed. The two continued to produce entire or partial reprints of collections of Milton, Dryden, and Addison as well as contemporary works by Rowe, Ambrose Philips, George Berkeley, and many others.

Before leaving for his 1718 trip to Paris, the elder Tonson signed over to his nephew all his copyrights for the sum of £2,597 16s. 8d. The copyrights included works by twenty-three authors as well as all the *Miscellanies*. The younger Tonson hoped to become the heir to his uncle's fortune, and in an interesting exchange of letters between him and one Robert Clarke, a servant of the elder Tonson in 1719, young Tonson received information on his uncle's leanings as well as advice on how to maintain his affections (in particular, Clarke recommended sending Tonson gifts of food). The elder Tonson became ill during the 1718–1720 trip to Paris, and a newspaper even printed a rumor of his death as if it were fact, but eventually he did return home in good health.

After that return the elder Tonson gave the Barn Elms estate to his nephew and moved to Ledbury to live alone on the Hazels, an estate that the younger Tonson had helped find and helped resolve problems in purchasing (some outstanding suits against the property complicated the legal paperwork). The elder Tonson remained active in his retirement, visiting and being visited by many of his old friends from the Kit-Cats. He also maintained a vigorous correspondence, much of which survives; the letters from this period between him and Vanbrugh illuminate both their friendship and the character of the elder Tonson. He developed a stronger friendship with Pope during this period as well, as Pope made several visits to the Hazels, once in the distinguished company of Edward Harley, second earl of Oxford, Allen Bathurst, and John Gay.

In arranging one such visit, Pope wrote to Harley in February 1731:

> To entertain you, I will show you a Phenomenon worth seeing & hearing, old Jacob Tonson, who is the perfect Image and Likeness of Bayle's Dictionary; so full of Matter, Secret History, & Wit and Spirit; at almost four-score.

Later in 1731 Pope solicited the elder Tonson to gather information for him about the "Man of Ross," a semilegendary philanthropist of Tonson's neighborhood, and the material was later incorporated into Pope's *Of the Use of Riches, an Epistle to the Right Honourable Allen Lord Bathurst* (1732). Tonson was also busy with nonliterary endeavors – in particular, with the stock market – during the last decades of his life: he invested in many stock schemes of the day, including the ill-fated South Sea project, but he wisely sold out at a profit before the stock failed.

Meanwhile, the younger Tonson's health had weakened, and he died at Barn Elms on 25 November 1735. On 4 December, Pope wrote the elder Tonson a letter of condolence, expressing his affection for both of the Tonsons. The elder Tonson did not live much longer, dying on 18 March 1736 at his Ledbury estate.

The heirs proved to be the younger of Tonson's children, Jacob and Richard. Their inheritances were enormous, and while they maintained the business, they soon withdrew from the retail trade altogether and published only for the wholesale market. They hired scholars to produce new editions of the works of many authors whom the elder Tonsons had published – Milton, George Buckingham, Thomas Otway, Congreve – and reprints of the *Spectator* and the *Guardian*. Samuel Johnson's 1765 edition of Shakespeare was to be a Tonson publication, as was William Warburton's nine-volume 1751 edition of Pope. But the new generation of Tonsons did not have the influence that the forbears had enjoyed. When Jacob Tonson III died on 31 March 1767 and his brother Richard died on 9 October 1772, their copyrights passed to the Rivington firm.

The contributions that the Tonsons made to publishing and to English literature are great indeed. They published little by Pope, only one minor title by Jonathan Swift, and nothing at all by Daniel Defoe; their political orientation no doubt influenced these major omissions. But apart from these names, few of the great authors of the era published works that did not bear the Tonson imprint. Perhaps even more important, though, was the painstaking work that the Tonsons did for past authors: not only great classical writers, but Spenser, Shakespeare, and Milton were kept alive and made accessible for new generations through the efforts of the Tonsons. Did Dryden, with his respect for pre-Restoration authors, "the gyant race before the flood," infuse his enthusiasm into Jacob Tonson? It seems quite possible, but Tonson must also be credited for his ability to learn Dryden's lessons. The Tonson house became far more than that of a mere bookseller: it was an institution seriously committed not only to profit but to the best possible presentation of the best literature. Jacob Tonson and his nephew made profits – huge profits – but they also advanced the state of British publishing.

References:

Stuart Bennet, "Jacob Tonson: An Early Editor of *Paradise Lost?*," *Library*, 10 (September 1988): 247–252;

Sarah Lewis Carol Clapp, *Jacob Tonson in Ten Letters by and about Him* (Austin: University of Texas Press, 1948);

Helen Gardner, "Milton's First Illustrator," *Essays and Studies,* new series 9 (1956): 27–38;

Harry M. Geduld, *Prince of Publishers: A Study of the Work and Career of Jacob Tonson* (Bloomington: Indiana University Press, 1969);

Stuart Gillespie, "The Early Years of the Dryden-Tonson Partnership: The Background to Their Composite Translations and Miscellanies of the 1680s," *Restoration: Studies in English Literary Culture, 1660–1700,* 12 (January 1988): 10–19;

Kathleen M. Lynch, *Jacob Tonson: Kit-Cat Publisher* (Knoxville: University of Tennessee Press, 1971);

G. F. Papali, *Jacob Tonson, Publisher: His Life and Work (1656–1736)* (Auckland, N.Z.: Tonson Publishing House, 1968);

H. B. Wheatley, "Dryden's Publishers," *Transactions of the Bibliographical Society,* 11 (1912): 17–38.

– Raymond N. MacKenzie

Richard Tottell

(London: circa 1550 – 1593)

Although little is known of Richard Tottell's early life, he was apparently the son of William Tothill (as the family name was more commonly spelled) and Elizabeth, daughter of Geoffrey Matthew. William, a prosperous citizen of Exeter, held various public offices such as those of bailiff, sheriff, and eventually mayor. Elizabeth and William had eleven children, four sons and seven daughters. Richard, the third son, married Joan, a daughter of printer Richard Grafton by his first marriage. William, the son of Richard and Joan Tottell, was born in 1560, after which the two had several daughters. Buying houses and shops in London as well as land in outlying areas, Tottell grew steadily more prosperous, and by the time of his death he had become well connected to the London legal establishment and an affluent, influential senior member of the Stationers' Company. Tottell is best known as a printer of law books, but several of the few literary, religious, and historical titles he published are also of enduring importance.

Tottell was apparently apprenticed to one William Middleton, a London printer of law books, circa 1540. His term of indenture was nearing its end when Middleton died in 1547. Elizabeth, Middleton's widow, married another law printer, William Powell, within several months, and she and Powell evidently fulfilled Middleton's wishes and freed Tottell and the other apprentices soon afterward. Tottell, already part of a circle of influential lawyers and law printers, took over the printing house of Henry Smithe at the sign of the Hand and Star after Smithe's death in 1550.

Tottell's career as a printer and a publisher contributed much to the early years of the Worshipful Company of Stationers. When the company received its royal charter in 1556, Tottell was named one of the brothers and listed sixty-seventh of the ninety-four; he had clearly been a member of the unincorporated group of stationers in the years before the granting of the charter. By 1556 Tottell was already one of the more prosperous stationers. Early records of the company list him as having provided ten shillings toward expenses, and later records of the company reflect Tottell's position as one of the most successful printers of his day. He regularly contributed more than all but a few of his fellow members, as he paid high annual assessments and occasionally met expenses for goods and services – a window or gilt spoons for the guild hall – on behalf of the company. Although he was fined small amounts for minor infractions of company rules from time to time, he quickly rose to a position of power and influence among the brethren. He held many offices in the company, which he served as warden four times and as master twice.

In April 1553 Tottell was granted an exclusive right to print all books pertaining to the common law for a period of seven years. No records remain that explain the circumstances of the initial granting of the license, but correspondence from later decades suggests that Tottell's license had resulted from his friendship with several important lawyers and judges. During the term of Tottell's grant the king's printer retained the license to print statutes, although Tottell later challenged this exclusivity. Tottell's license was extended for another seven years and then finally for his lifetime, after which it was to revert to Nicasius Yetsweirt, a Frenchman residing in London and for many years the queen's official secretary for the French language.

The dislocation of Protestant stationers in the early years of Mary's reign aided Tottell's early prosperity. Those printers who had been forced out of business – Grafton, John Day, and Edward Whitechurch among others – had left a regular trade in English Bibles and other theological literature, and Tottell and John Wayland soon took over production of these standard titles. Wayland was a fierce Catholic, and although Tottell was less fierce, his faith was by no means a political or economic expedient. Evidence of this can be found in his 1554 publication of one part of Richard Smith's *A Bouclier of the Catholic Fayth,* dedicated to Mary I. During this period Tottell printed, for example, John Lydgate's translation of Giovanni Boccaccio's *The Fall of Princes* (1555) and Stephen Hawes's *The Pastime of Pleasure* (1555), books previously printed by Protestants whose religion made them temporarily unable to work.

Some have argued that Tottell's monopoly on the printing of law books was one of the least pernicious of the sixteenth-century licenses granted by the Crown. Although Christopher Barker and other printers were later to complain bitterly about Tottell's license, the production of law books during this period was a task for a specialist. Many complications attended the printing of Year Books, treatises, and collections of cases. Most legal works of this period were written in Latin or French and were notoriously difficult to interpret. In addition, manuscripts usually were filled with marginalia, corrections, and interlining and were rife with obscure legal contractions that made them hard copy from which to work. Editorial help, usually from an established lawyer or scholar, was necessary before the compositor could begin, and this added to the difficulty and expense of printing and publishing law books. Tottell refers to this difficulty in more than one preface: in that to a 1556 edition of *The Great Charter,* for example, he complains, "For the exact truth thereof, my copies I might wel folow as thei were, but I could not myself correct them as they ought to be. Therfore in some workes where I could, with my entreatie or cost, procure learneder helpe, ye have them not smally amended."

Those printers opposed to Tottell's monopoly appealed to William Cecil, Lord Burghley, in 1577. The license system that the Stationers' Company and the government mutually enforced considerably handicapped the less prosperous members of the company, whom it effectively excluded from publishing the more profitable categories of works. The rights to print Bibles, catechisms, most schoolbooks, statutes, common law, and other steadily selling titles were concentrated in a few hands and jealously guarded. Typically a license was granted to a stationer for a period of years or often for his lifetime, after which the license would pass to his heirs, his assigns, or some other predetermined printer. Thus, prospects for those stationers outside this circle of privilege were slight.

Engraved title page for one of the few historical works published by Richard Tottell

In their appeal to Cecil these aggrieved printers complained that before the common-law printing license had been granted to Tottell any printer had been free to print these books, and this lack of restriction had helped limit the prices that poor students had to pay. Through the twenty years that Tottell had held his exclusive patent, the prices of these books had risen excessively, they argued. Law books had been important staples for marginally successful printers. These works sold steadily and predictably, and they could be printed to shore up finances or keep workers busy during otherwise slack times. Furthermore, because Tottell held exclusive rights to publish these books and could not be compelled to publish anything against his wishes, he held a kind of intellectual monopoly as well. Tottell could single-handedly prevent any specific work of law, for instance, from being published. Cecil appears not to have acted on the appeal.

Barker, another prominent London printer, also objected to the monopoly. Barker and Tottell were rivals throughout their careers, and their com-

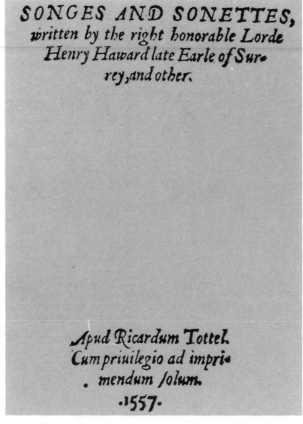

Title page for the highly successful and often-reprinted collection of Elizabethan poetry popularly known as Tottell's Miscellany (1557)

mon business interests occasionally led to open conflict. Barker wrote to Cecil in 1582 that Tottell's law patent had in its time been beneficial, but its value had diminished and would continue to do so unless Tottell or another man were to publish legal works in a different manner, according to the changing needs of the times. While this was probably a fair assessment of the situation, Barker's words hint at the enmity, which lasted many years, between the two men.

One episode in their dispute came in 1577, after the death of John Jugge, who had held the patent for printing statutes. Tottell is said to have claimed the right to the patent and even to have printed several statutes. The matter was settled, however, when Barker was appointed as queen's printer later in that same year. In subsequent years Tottell and Barker found themselves on the same side, as objects of the hostility that non-patent holders of the company developed for the patent holders. In 1586 the two men joined other senior members of the company to finance passage of the infamous Star Chamber Decree, which effectively pre-

served the monopoly rights of the most powerful members of the company.

During his career Tottell printed or published more than a hundred books on common law, many in multiple editions. This constant production of titles in regular, if unspectacular, demand made him rich through his four decades as a printer. As early as 1557 Tottell's business was so good that he could afford to keep at least four apprentices working for him. Surviving records indicate that he employed twenty-four apprentices during a period of roughly thirty years. Although the 1583 survey of London printers conducted for the bishop of London indicated that Tottell owned three presses, only one was in use at this time, at the end of what was Tottell's most productive period. For some time Tottell, one of the few London printers in a financial position to do so, even employed his own binder, a Frenchman named Peter Horsan or Harsaunte.

Tottell's law printing comprised the bulk of his production, which can be divided into three major categories: statutes, treatises, and case re-

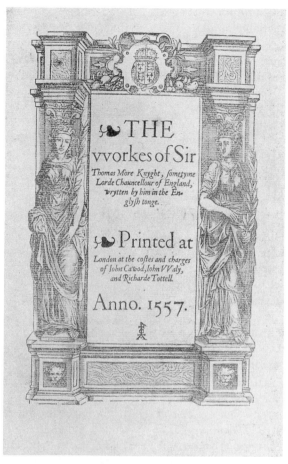

*Title page for the 1557 edition of the works of Sir Thomas
More, published by Tottell, John Cawood, and John
Waly and printed by William Rastell*

ports. While it is true that the queen's printer held the patent to publish statutes, nothing in the grant of Tottell's patent appeared to prohibit him from printing collections or abridgments of older statutes. This fact eventually became the basis of Barker's appeal to the Privy Council in 1578, when he complained that his rights as the queen's printer were being infringed by Tottell's printing of John Rastell's abridged collection of statutes. Ultimately Tottell seems to have been permitted to print the first part and Barker the second.

Statute printing, however, represented only a modest portion of Tottell's production, unlike treatises and case reports. Law treatises are scholarly, authoritative expositions on specific legal topics and were as important to sixteenth-century students and lawyers as they are to students and lawyers today. Tottell printed or reprinted dozens of these. Some — such as Thomas Littleton's *Tenures,* Anthony Fitzherbert's *Natura Brevium,* and William Stanford's *Les Plees del Coron* — were reprinted so many times and issued in so many variant states that accurate dating of any particular volume is extremely difficult, if not impossible. Far more than half of the titles printed and published by Tottell are reports of cases; some are scholarly collections of cases arranged by subject. Volumes in the Year Book series, on the other hand, are arranged chronologically by regnal year. Having Year Books published was a great boon to students, lawyers, and judges, for it made much material generally available for the first time, and this development profoundly affected the practice of English common law. Tottell's Year Books covered the years from the reign of Edward III through the early years of Elizabeth I, an impressive span.

As Tottell's career progressed, his law patent became increasingly valuable, and as a result, he grew less willing to risk capital on other types of publishing. Most of the publishing of literary and other nonlegal works for which Tottell is remembered dates from the first years of his career. These volumes include some of his most important work as well as some of his most forgettable publications.

In November 1553 Tottell published a book by Sir Thomas More, *A Dialogue of Comfort against Tribulations, Made by Sir Thomas More, Knight.* William Rastell – chief justice of the queen's bench, son of printer John Rastell, and also More's nephew – had taken this previously unprinted work to Belgium during his self-imposed exile in the Protestant reign of Edward VI. Upon his return to England, Rastell sought out Tottell, who printed the work. Four years later Tottell printed More's complete *Works* (1557) in a massive folio, an edition jointly financed by Tottell, John Walley, and John Cawood, the queen's printer. Cawood supplied the woodcut initials and perhaps some of the type, but Tottell apparently was responsible for the rest of the production. Such a large undertaking emphasizes Tottell's position as a prosperous printer and an influential publisher, for only a few men in London could have helped finance and execute the printing of this nearly fifteen-hundred-page folio.

In June 1557 Tottell printed the first edition of the work for which he is perhaps best remembered, a small volume of poems called *Songes and Sonnettes, written by the Ryght Honorable Lorde Henry Hawarde, late Earl of Surrey and others* but popularly known as *Tottell's Miscellany.* The book featured 271 poems by Sir Henry Howard, earl of Surrey; Sir Thomas Wyatt; Thomas Churchyard; Thomas, Lord Vaux; John Heywood; and Nicholas Grimald, who was also the editor. In the preface to his first edition Tottell eagerly points out that this collection proves that the English could write poetry as well as the Italians. The work was an instant hit, and a second edition, with a slightly altered collection of verses, was printed before the end of the following month. Tottell produced several more editions, and others published yet more editions after his death. In all, eight editions appeared before the end of the century.

Tottell was also among those early printers who anticipated the role that the press would assume in disseminating news. Within a week of the coronation of Queen Elizabeth I in 1558, Tottell had printed two separate editions of *The Passage of our Most Drad Soueraigne Lady Quene Elyzabeth Through the Citie of London to Westminster the Day Before Her Coronation.* These little volumes were quickly printed with an ornamental border once owned by Richard Grafton, with Grafton's monogram and mark. The text is printed in mixed black letter Roman and italic type.

The rest of Tottell's production of texts other than law works was extremely varied, ranging from classical works to books on animal husbandry. The latter, *A Hundreth Good Points of Husbandry* (1557), included a collection of poems on rural life by Thomas Tusser. This book of poems by the Suffolk farmer was so popular that it was revised and expanded to encompass *Five hundreth points of good husbandry united to as many of good huswiferie,* as the titles of Tottell's later editions of 1573 and afterward promised. He printed books on heraldry, military science, medicine, and various other subjects as well as reprints of standard works such as compiler William Painter's *The Palace of Pleasure* (1566–1567) and William Baldwin's *A Treatise of Morall Phylosophye Contaynyng the Sayinges of the Wise* (1547). Yet as time passed, Tottell's production of books other than law books slowed and then ceased altogether.

Sometime around 1585 Tottell sought a government license to build a paper mill in England. In his petition to Cecil, whose patronage Tottell sought, his ongoing frustration at the inconvenience and expense of having to depend on the work of French papermakers signals his interest in efforts to begin paper production in England. The letter mentions a failed attempt that Tottell and several others had made in the early 1570s. Failures of even earlier English attempts and threats of reprisals from French suppliers of paper had eventually doomed that first effort. Acting without partners when he wrote to Cecil, Tottell offered to provide capital for the construction of the mill, in exchange for which the government would provide the site, ban the export of rags from England, and grant Tottell an exclusive thirty-five-year license for the manufacture of paper. No record of any response to his letter exists, and no evidence of action taken by either the government or Tottell remains.

His health failing, Tottell printed and published few titles after 1586. He seems to have spent most of his time at his estate in Wiston, Pembrokeshire. In 1589 the court of assistants of the Stationers' Company, stating that the affairs of the company were often hindered by his continual absence, moved to censure him. Tottell was discharged from his assistantship in the company and removed from the rolls. However, in the same entry in the Stationers' Company Register he was restored to the rolls and to full membership and allowed to sit at the meetings of the assistants whenever he was in London. This exception was made because Tottell had "bene always a lovinge & orderly brother in the cūpany, and nowe absent [not] for any cause savinge his infyrmytie, & farre dwelling from the cyty."

Tottell died in the beginning of July 1593. His son petitioned the Privy Council to restrain Christopher Barker and his partners from reprinting law books, the patents for which had belonged to Tottell. Charles Yetsweirt, son of Nicasius, who had held the reversionary interest in the patent, also petitioned to enjoin any infringement, and when Charles soon died, his wife, Jane, continued the legal battle and ultimately prevailed. After her subsequent remarriage, she gave up her right to the license, which was passed on to others. As late as 1640, poor printers of London complained of the oppressive nature of the patent that had been originally granted to Tottell, and the patent was eventually dissolved.

Tottell's legacy, however, remained influential. At its best, his work was carefully edited and relatively well printed in a time when craftsmanship was not a universal feature. He was a shrewd businessman — ambitious, entrepreneurial, and able to weather political and religious change — and he was also willing to exploit the advantages of the monopolist, by virtue of which he became a wealthy man. Yet he was capable of turning out truly shoddy work: his printing of Jasper Heywood's translation of Lucius Annaeus Seneca's *Troas* (1559) was so careless that Heywood's next book, printed by Thomas Berthelet, contained an excoriating preface condemning Tottell's treatment of that earlier work. Tottell was a complex figure who loomed large in the Elizabethan print trade and in the early history of the Stationers' Company.

References:

Joseph H. Beale, *A Bibliography of Early English Law Books* (Cambridge, Mass.: Harvard University Press, 1926);

H. J. Byrom, "Richard Tottell — His Life and Work," *Library,* fourth series 8 (September 1927): 199–232;

W. W. Greg and E. Boswell, eds., *Records of the Court of the Stationers' Company: 1576 to 1602 – from Register B* (London: Bibliographical Society, 1930);

Henry R. Plomer, "Richard Tottell," *Bibliographica,* 3, part 11 (1897): 378–384;

Plomer, *A Short History of English Printing, 1476–1898* (London: Kegan Paul, Trübner, 1900).

                                                    – Christopher A. Knott

Robert Waldegrave

(London: 1578 – 1589; New Rochelle: 1589; Edinburgh: 1589 – 1603; London: 1603)

Robert Waldegrave, the son of yeoman Richard Waldegrave, or Walgrave, of Blacklay, Worcester, began his career in the book trade on 24 June 1568 as an apprentice to William Griffith, a London stationer. Waldegrave made his first entry, that for *A castle for the soule, conteining many godly prayers, and diuine meditations, tending to the comfort and consolation of all faythful Christians, against the wicked assaults of Satan* in the Stationers' Register on 17 June 1578. Serving as both a printer-publisher and a trade printer who maintained a shop near Somerset House between 1580 and 1585, Waldegrave frequently printed for Thomas Man the younger and Thomas Woodcock, both of whom published Puritan writers. He apparently maintained operations there intermittently, for in 1583 he also printed in Foster Lane, near Goldsmiths' Hall. His imprints after 1585 suggest that he may have been a bookseller at the White Horse in Canon Lane during 1585–1586, although his imprints do not call this site his shop.

Between 1587 and 1588 he had a print shop in St. Paul's Churchyard at the Crane, and in 1588 his printing materials were seized and destroyed because he had illegally printed John Udall's *The state of the Church of Englande, laide open in a conference betweene Diotrephes, a Byshop, Tertullus, a Papist, Demetrius an usurer, Pandocheus an Inne-keeper, and Paule, a preacher of the word of God* (1588). In 1588 and 1589 he was illegally printing the Martin Marprelate tracts in East Molesey, at Coventry, and at Wolston, although in the fall of 1588 he also appears to have been printing in London, for he printed the anonymous *A true report of the inditement, arraignment, conuiction, condemnation, and execution of John Weldon, William Hartley, and Robert Sutton: who suffred for high treason* for Richard Jones. These executions were on 5 October 1588, and Jones entered the title in the Stationers' Register on 18 October 1588.

Waldegrave also printed briefly at New Rochelle in 1589 before going to Edinburgh, where he was appointed royal printer to James VI. Waldegrave appears to have been in London circa 1601, for Andrew Willet, in the preface to his *An antilogie or counterplea to an apologeticall epistle* (1603), speaks of having sent a copy of a 1600 edition of his *Synopsis*

Papismi to James VI "by your Maiesties Printer." In any event, Waldegrave returned to London not long before his death in 1603, and his wife, Mary Waldegrave, subsequently printed one title in 1604 at Edinburgh.

In the overview of Waldegrave's life in *A Dictionary of Printers and Booksellers in England, Scotland and Ireland* (1910), Ronald B. McKerrow states that "from the outset of his career [Waldegrave] appears to have attached himself to the Puritan party." Martin Marprelate's *An Epistle* (1588), the first of the Marprelate pamphlets printed by Waldegrave, implies that Waldegrave's Puritan press was the object of relentless investigation and suppression by the high commissioners: "Walde-graue dares not shew his face for the blood-thirstie desire you haue for his life," Martin tells the bishops. The bibliographic record and the details of Waldegrave's relations with the Stationers' Company, however, offer a different picture. Although some of the works Waldegrave printed – such as Udall's *The state of the Church of Englande* and the Martin Marprelate pamphlets – certainly provoked the high commissioners, much of Waldegrave's career reflects the degree to which the Stationers' Company protected Puritan printing.

Waldegrave enjoyed membership in the London Stationers' Company when nonstationers were agitating against the authority of the company. Although Waldegrave was neither a liveried member nor a company officer, records from May 1583 show that Waldegrave had two presses. He signed a petition against company abuses of "the poorer sort of printers" and may well have opposed company licensing fees, since he was careless about registering his titles with the company. (Forty-six of the titles he printed were not entered in the register, although the published texts were signed by Waldegrave.)

Between 1580 and 1589 Waldegrave printed ninety-eight titles, eighty of which were in some respect Puritan works – in either their Calvinist theology or their interests in church reform. Waldegrave printed twenty of the eighty, including the Marprelate tracts, without placing his name or the location of his press on either the title pages or colophons, and this procedure made more than 20 percent of

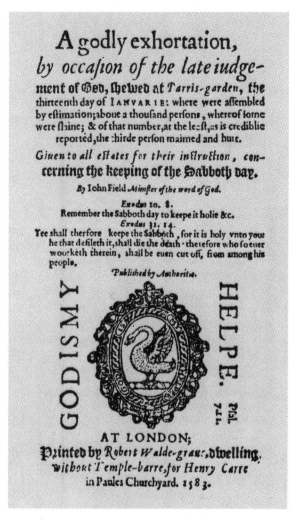

Title page for John Field's pamphlet promoting the observance of the Sabbath, one of many religious reform works that Robert Waldegrave printed at his London address in the 1580s

all of his printing "illegal" during this period. (His unsigned printing is unmistakable, however, because he characteristically used arabic – rather than the more common roman – numerals in his signatures.) Waldegrave's printing of some of these illegal books did get him in trouble with his own company: sometime during 1583–1584, for example, he alienated his fellow stationers for having infringed on William Seres's privilege to print private prayer books. But Waldegrave suffered no disapproval from his peers for having printed, from his "secret" press, works that were in other ways illegal.

Waldegrave's troubles for having printed objectionable religious texts came not from the Stationers' Company but in 1584 from the archbishop of Canterbury, if what Martin Marprelate says in *Hay any worke for cooper* (1589) is to be be-

lieved: "his grace kept him 20. weekes together in the white lyon for printing the Complaint of the comminaltie, the Practize of prelats, A learned mans iudgment." The works to which Martin refers include *A lamentable complaint to the commonalty, by way of supplication to Parliament, for a learned ministery* (1585), *The unlawful practises of prelates against godly ministers* (1584?), and *The iudgement of a most reuerent and learned man from beyond the seas, concerning a threefold order of bishops* (circa 1585), all written by Theodore Beza, translated by John Field, and published anonymously.

The Dictionary of National Biography erroneously reports that Waldegrave was imprisoned for twenty weeks in autumn 1588 after having published of the initial Marprelate tracts. McKerrow says that in 1584 Waldegrave had been imprisoned at the

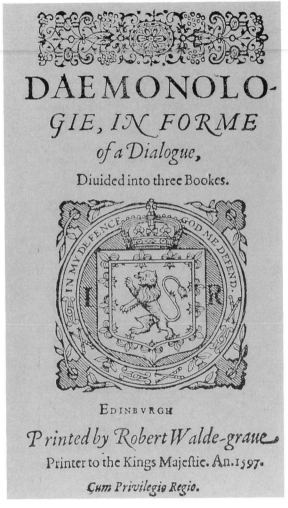

DAEMONOLO-
GIE, IN FORME
of a Dialogue,
Diuided into three Bookes.

EDINBVRGH
Printed by Robert Walde-graue
Printer to the Kings Maiestie. An.1597.
Cum Privilegio Regio.

Title page for the future King James I's dialogue on
demonology, published at Edinburgh by Waldegrave

White Lyon, probably for having printed *A brief declaration concerning the desires of all those faithfull ministers, A dialogue concerning the strife of our Church* (1584), and *A declaration of some such monstrous abuses as our Bishops have not been ashamed to foster.* McKerrow is also relying on *Hay any worke for cooper,* which says that the archbishop of Canterbury

> violated his promise, in that he told the wardens of the stacioners, that if Walde-graue would come quietly to him, and cease printing of seditious bookes, he would pardon what was past, and the wardens promised his wife, that if he were committed, they would lye at his graces gate til he ware released, and for al this, yet he was committed to the white Lyon, where he laye six weekes.

Probably because McKerrow found a 1584 warrant for Waldegrave in the Stationers' Company records, McKerrow places these events in 1584 and assigns the dates of the troublesome works based upon the date of this warrant. The only 1584 record involving Waldegrave that appears in the Stationers' Register and court book concerns his offense of having violated Seres's patent.

Waldegrave did, however, print another pirated text. In 1584 he printed Alexander Nowell's middle Latin *Catechismus,* to which he signed John Day's name, and so Waldegrave was perhaps temporarily imprisoned for printing against privilege, for in a similar case of patent violation Roger Ward had been imprisoned. Yet the high commission may also have imprisoned Waldegrave in order to examine him and discover the identities of the nonconforming authors whose works he was printing, for this is the way in which the London high commission was using imprisonment in the 1570s and 1580s. In 1584–1585 Waldegrave's press and its products were clearly thorns in the side of the arch-

Engraved title page for an interpretation of the Revelation of
Saint John by John Napier, the inventor of logarithms

bishop of Canterbury – sources of distress that the high commission seemed unable to remove, for whatever measures the commissioners took, Waldegrave remained undeterred.

The crisis came in 1588, when agents of the Stationers' Company seized and defaced Waldegrave's press for having printed illegally – that is, without identifying the author, printer, press location, publication date, or ecclesiastical authorization – Udall's *The state of the Church of Englande, laide open in a conference betweene Diotrephes, a Byshop, Tertullus, a Papist, Demetrius an usurer, Pandocheus an Innekeeper, and Paule, a preacher of the word of God.* Udall had already provoked the high commission, and this work was unusually provocative. The high commission had summoned him to appear in 1586, but he had been restored to his ministry through the efforts of some influential friends. His *Diotrephes,* printed in April, received considerable attention in vehemently denouncing the established church, and

the high commission, finding the work seditious, ordered Waldegrave's press seized.

Waldegrave was brought before the Stationers' Company Court of Assistants for having printed the book "without auchtority" and for having disregarded the 1586 Star Chamber Decrees for Order in Printing. According to Walter Wilson Greg and E. Boswell, on 13 May 1588 the court, finding the charges valid, recorded its order "by force of the said decrees & according to the same . . . that the said books shalbe burnte and the said presse letters and printinge stuffe defaced and made vnserviceable according to the said Decrees." Yet three months later Waldegrave was at work printing the Marprelate tracts – this time outside London, and at a press both secret and portable.

The Marprelate tracts offer the only extant record of the ongoing confrontation between Waldegrave and the bishops, but Marprelate's accounts ignore several important details. By printing against

Seres's patent, Waldegrave immersed himself in disputes about both privileged printing and the authority of the Stationers' Company within the print trade of the 1580s. Despite Waldegrave's unwillingness to conform, the stationers appear to have been surprisingly sympathetic to him. They ignored his long history of having printed unregistered or probably unlicensed work. When his printing violated Seres's privilege, rather than destroying his press the company either fined him forty pounds (which he did not pay) or required him to post a forty-pound bond in that amount "to the Companie Concerninge not printinge of any thinge in master Seres pryvyledge."

The company also loaned him money and promised to protest his imprisonment. Twice in 1584 the licensed works of fellow stationers, as entered in the register, required that Waldegrave be the printer: for Timothie Rider's *Widowes Treasorer* on 6 April and for John Harrison's *The Coat armorer of a Christian* on 22 September. The company gave to Waldegrave the printing of Thomas Hill's *Book of Gardening* (1586) – one of the most often reprinted of Henry Bynneman's titles given to the company in 1584 for relief of the company's poor. Some of Waldegrave's fellow stationers may even have forewarned him of their impending search for *Diotrephes*, for Waldegrave was able to spirit away one case of type. In many respects Waldegrave's status as a company member appears to have allowed him protection that he otherwise might not have enjoyed.

Yet regardless of such peer support, Waldegrave's printing of the Marprelate pamphlets placed him beyond company protection. The tracts were censored by royal proclamation, and the high commissioners investigated relentlessly, though unsuccessfully, to discover the printer. According to McKerrow, by March 1589 Waldegrave "had had enough of the dangerous work" and his health was being affected. As the satiric methods of the Marprelate tracts lost favor among even the most dedicated Puritans, Waldegrave left for New Rochelle. There he printed two Puritan tracts in 1589 before moving on to Edinburgh later that year. On 13 March 1590 the Scottish Privy Council granted him a license to print *Confessions of Faith*, and on 9 October he was appointed king's printer. According to McKerrow, more than one hundred titles have been identified with Waldegrave's Edinburgh imprint, although none of these bears an address.

While he was in Edinburgh, Waldegrave printed one more work that raised legal problems for him in England – a 1599 edition of Sir Philip Sidney's *Arcadia*, the English rights to which were held by William Ponsonby. According to Cyril Judge, in 1598 Ponsonby had printed the third edition of *Arcadia* – revised by the countess of Pembroke and enlarged to include Sidney's *The Defence of Poesie* (1595), "Astrophel and Stella," "The May Day Masque," and certain other sonnets – in a high-quality folio edition that sold for nine shillings. Waldegrave's folio edition of the same texts, bearing the imprint "Edinburgh. Printed by Robert Waldegrave. Printer to the Kings Majestie, Cum Privilegio Regio, 1599," appeared in London bookstalls for six shillings. Because the rights to copy protected by the Stationers' Company did not extend outside England, technically this was a legal copy, and despite Judge's claims, this publication did not constitute piracy.

Ponsonby, however, pressed charges in the Court of the Star Chamber against booksellers William Scarlett, Richard Backworth, John Flaskett, Paul Lynley, and John Harrison II and, according to Judge, seized their remaining unsold copies. Ponsonby's writ charged the men with having printed the edition illegally "either in Cambridge or in yo[r] highnes Citie of London or in some other place w[th]in yo[r] highnes realme of England," and to escape detection "they have in the first page & title of the booke sett downe the same booke to be printed in Edenbourough w[th]in the realme of Scotland w[th] the King[s] priveledge there Where indeed it was printed by them or by their procurem[t] here in England."

Begun on 23 November 1599 in the Star Chamber, proceedings were deferred to the Stationers' Court of Assistants, where the matter was finally resolved 8 May 1602. Ponsonby succeeded in stopping the importation of the book from Scotland, and Bankworth and Flaskett paid some damages to Ponsonby. Waldegrave suffered no sanctions, however, and was apparently free to return to print in England once James became the English king in 1603.

References:

Walter Wilson Greg and E. Boswell, eds., *Records of the Court of the Stationers' Company (Register B)* (London: Bibliographical Society, 1957);

Cyril Judge, *Elizabethan Book-Pirates* (Cambridge, Mass.: Harvard University Press, 1934);

Ronald B. McKerrow, ed., *A Dictionary of Printers and Booksellers in England, Scotland and Ireland, and of Foreign Printers of English Books 1557–1640* (London: Bibliographical Society, 1910).

– *Cyndia Susan Clegg*

John Windet

(London: 1554 – 1610)

John Windet was one of the more important printers in London at the turn of the seventeenth century. Nevertheless, little has been written about him. He was primarily a printer of religious pocketbooks and psalm-books, but he also printed mathematics, music, and literary texts. He is most well known as the first printer of Sir Philip Sidney's *Arcadia* (1590), Richard Hooker's *Of the lawes of ecclesiasticall politie* (1593, 1597), Francis Bacon's *Essayes* (1597), and John Dowland's *Lachrimæ* (1604). His production was surprisingly diverse, although he printed few plays. In his relationships with ecclesiastical authorities and with other members of the book trade he provides an interesting example of an early modern printer at work.

Windet was born in the parish of St. Mary Major, Exeter, the son of David Windet. Although the parish records survive only from 1561, the custom of freeing apprentices close to their twenty-fifth birthdays indicates that he was probably born in 1554. His father had married Anne Vowell, alias Hooker, the sister of Roger Hooker, who was in turn the father of the theologian Richard Hooker. William Stansby, who also came from St. Mary Major, Exeter, and who was Windet's successor to the printing house, identified Windet and Richard Hooker as cousins. Windet apparently shared Hooker's godliness and perhaps something of his equanimity: he was active in church affairs, serving as parish constable between December 1591 and December 1593; as a member of the wardmote inquests for 1593–1594, 1598–1599, and 1603–1604; and as an assessor of fifteenths regularly between 1588 and 1604.

The Stationers' Company records of Windet's indenture as an apprentice do not survive, but Windet was apparently apprenticed to John Allde in 1572; Allde freed him on 13 April 1579. It is unclear whether Windet remained with Allde after he gained his freedom. Allde had a son, Edward, whom he freed by patrimony and who succeeded his father as master printer early in 1584, about the same time that Windet established his own business in conjunction with Thomas Judson.

This opportunity to become a master printer arose following the death of Henry Bynneman on 15 April 1583, when Windet and Judson acquired at least some of Bynneman's material and two of his apprentices. Windet and Judson's relationship was formalized by the court of the Stationers' Company on 15 January 1584, which ordered that Judson remain in partnership with Windet for five years. It is unclear whether they remained together in practice, for although both names appear in the majority of colophons throughout 1584, the names do not appear together thereafter. Judson probably returned to his family's business and practiced as a stationer.

Windet appears to have acquired not only some of Bynneman's type, equipment, apprentices, and copies, but also some of Bynneman's business relationships. Windet set up his first shop near Bynneman's former premises on the corner of Thames and Adling Streets, "nigh Baynard's Castle." His first house was The White Bear. It may be the same premises as those occupied by Valentine Simmes between 1592 and 1605. Early in 1588 he moved a short distance down Thames Street to a large building on the east side of St. Peter's Church. He remained at the Cross-Keys for the rest of his life; the building and the business passed to William Stansby, who subdivided the property when he later sold it to Richard Bishop in 1636.

Evidence for the scale of the business that Windet established is fragmentary. In 1586 he is recorded as having three presses. In the same year John Bridges mentioned a corrector. Many of Windet's books have errata lists, and it is clear both from these and the comments of authors that proof correcting was an important printing house activity. Windet appears to have set around two hundred sheets per annum during the 1580s. Presswork was evidently more important to the business than composition. Windet's characteristic method of balancing his composition and presswork was to work on one substantial volume concurrently with smaller items. Long production runs of religious pocketbooks provided him with the income and flexibility required to print the larger, high-quality items that would consolidate his reputation. The larger books also provided the printing house with a stable flow

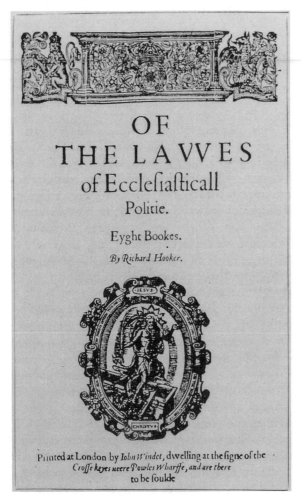

OF
THE LAVVES
of Ecclefiafticall
Politie.

Eyght Bookes.

By Richard Hooker.

Printed at London by Iohn Windet, dwelling at the figne of the
Croffe keyes neere Powles Wharffe, and are there
to be foulde

*Title page for the first part of Richard Hooker's defense of
the Church of England (1593)*

of work that allowed him to withstand the temporary shortages of work that occurred.

His most important output during the 1580s included the third edition of Arthur Golding's translation of Ovid's *The xv. Bookes of P. Ouidius Naso, entitled metamorphosis* (1585), the shared printing of Abraham Fleming's translation of Adrian Junius's *The nomenclator* (1585), Edward Hoby's translation of Matthieu Coignet's *Politiqve discovrses vpon trveth and lying* (1586), Bridges's *A defence of the government established in the Chvrch of Englande* (1587) that provoked the Martin Marprelate controversy, a reprint of Thomas Bright's *A treatise of melancholy* (1586), Hugh Oldcastle's *A briefe instruction and maner how to keepe bookes of accompts* (1588), Nicolaus Clenardus's *Græcæ lingvæ institvtiones* (1588), Jacobus Ceporinus's *Compendium grammaticæ Græcæ* (1585), and Bright's *An abridgement of the booke of acts and monvmentes* (1589) taken from John Fox. To these might be added a religious duo-

decimo that was to become a staple of the business: Saint Augustine's *The glasse of vaine-glorie,* which appeared in multiple editions from 1585 to 1612.

The diversity of the list reflects both the conditions of the trade and Windet's ability as a printer. His principal type for composition was a large-bodied pica, though he also used double pica, long primer, and brevier at this time. His first use of english roman was for one of the most typographically important and culturally influential books of the period, Sidney's *Arcadia.* The Pembroke family lived only a few yards from the printing house. Given their shared West Country origins and Windet's probity within the parish as well as the convenience of the printing house, the choice of the printer seems likely to have come from the Pembroke family.

The appearance of the new type with this volume also suggests that special arrangements, including the purchase of the english roman, had been made. The volume was carefully printed and was produced concurrently with all of Windet's other output during 1589. As with his previous large publications, the format of *Arcadia* was that of the quarto in eights rather than the folio. Its appearance coincided with publication of Edmund Spenser's *The Faerie Qveene:* both books are typographically similar and appear to have encouraged a shift in the typography of literary publications. Indicatively, all seven plays printed in London in 1590 were set in black letter; seventeen of the eighteen printed in 1591 were set in roman.

The printing of Sidney's *Arcadia* coincided with two important events in the history of Windet's business. On 25 December 1589 Windet took on as his apprentice William Stansby, who was eventually to be his successor. It is possible that they were distantly related. Windet and his wife, Alice, had no children (a common occurrence in the early printing trade, when the toxicity of the lead must have affected fertility). Windet, however, did not register Stansby as an apprentice until January 1591, and he was accordingly fined for not presenting him. Stansby's fellow apprentice during much of his indenture was William Jones, who also went on to establish his own business.

A second development in the printing house was the association between Windet and John Wolfe. Though each remained independent of the other, their cooperation and close association date from 1589. Typographical evidence indicates that Windet was responsible for printing some of the material that has been attributed to Wolfe; consequently, a thorough investigation of all of Wolfe's output is necessary so that the material he had printed by others can be identified. Wolfe, in fact, ceased printing early in 1591, about the time that Windet acquired his psalm-book privilege as well as some of his types and ornaments: for instance, the small-bodied pica that appears in the fourth edition of Spenser's *The Shepheardes Calender* (1591). That Wolfe so readily turned over to Windet a privilege that he had fought so bitterly to obtain suggests that the two must have established some agreement – a conclusion reinforced by Windet's acquisition of Wolfe's type and materials and by the printing of material for the city of London that Windet did on Wolfe's behalf.

With the acquisition of the psalm-book business and the printing of other works, Windet's production rose to an average of 320 sheets per annum between 1592 and 1601. The psalm-book material provided an important source of continuous work that was produced in large runs of two thousand copies. Although some psalm-books were set in folio, most were in smaller formats, and these books were invariably set in the very small type sizes of brevier and non-pareil. The raw figures for Windet's composition, therefore, disguise the quantity of type set.

The printing house in which Stansby began his apprenticeship was therefore a stable, sizable business. The years between 1588 and 1592 were prosperous, and the agreement with Wolfe clearly provided Windet with greater security. In 1592 he replaced his pica type, while the following year his arrangement with Wolfe proved fortunate, for the psalm-book production protected Windet from the economic downturn that followed the plague of 1593 and the subsequent harvest failures that occurred between 1594 and 1597. Despite such economic conditions, Windet sustained his production throughout the period. In 1592 he acquired the rights to *The assise of bread,* a six-and-a-half-sheet pamphlet concerned with price regulation that he, and subsequently Stansby, was to print annually, although not all editions have survived. The other book that occupied the press during much of that year was the second edition of Sidney's *Arcadia* (1593). At the same time, Windet also printed the countess of Pembroke's translations of Philippe de Mornay's *A discourse of life and death* and Robert Garnier's *Antonius* (1592).

The second edition of *Arcadia* was Windet's first substantial folio publication and only the third non-psalm-book from his press set with an engraved title-page border. That the book was reprinted so rapidly, albeit with an emended text, suggests the popularity and influence that *Arcadia* had with its Elizabethan audience. As with the first edition, the second must have played an important role in regulating the production flows of Windet's shop. Its role as the major work in progress was subsequently taken by a book that Windet entered in January 1593: Hooker's *Of the lawes of ecclesiasticall politie.*

Hooker's book was also a folio publication and one to which Windet gave considerable care. William Norton had declined to print the work, and Hooker, who could not afford to bear the charges, turned to his cousin and to Edwin Sandys, son of the former archbishop of Canterbury, for assistance. Sandys bought the manuscript for the considerable sum of thirty pounds and free copies for the author. The care that Windet took in producing it is reflected in the typography of the volume. The title page is unusual for its simplicity and for its lack of both scriptural quotation and a summary of the argument (common features of title pages of the period). The title page of the *Lawes* instead presents only the title (with its emphasis on "THE LAVVES"), the name of the author, and the imprint. At the top is an ornament of an altar, and in the center is the device of Christ resurrected, one commonly used by Windet for his psalm-books. The page is set to a shortened depth of forty-six rather than forty-eight lines, allowing ample marginal space around the text, even after Hooker's sometimes extensive notes. According to witnesses in a bitter dispute between Stansby and Sandys in 1613, copies of books 1–4 (1593) sold for 2s. 6d. each, while copies of book 5 (1597) sold for 3s.

Windet's family relationship with Hooker helps explain the closeness of the links between the Cross-Keys and Lambeth Palace. Hooker's association with Archbishop John Whitgift and the Sandys family dated from the 1570s. At the time that the *Lawes* was published Richard Bancroft was personal chaplain to Whitgift. Bancroft's *Davngerous positions and proceedings* (1593), which went through two editions, is another of the connections between the printing house and Lambeth Palace other than the formal mechanisms of licensing. Richard Cosin, Whitgift's protégé and a friend from Whitgift's days as a fellow at Trinity College, Cambridge, was the first to employ Windet as his printer in 1584. John Bridges had also been at Pembroke Hall, Cambridge, with Whitgift during the 1550s. Abraham Hartwell, Whitgift's private secretary from the early 1580s, was regularly associated with Windet's press not only as a licenser but also as a translator of travel literature. William Barlow, who was to succeed Bancroft as Whitgift's chaplain in 1597, also had sermons printed by Windet during the 1600s.

While Windet was printing Hooker's *Lawes,* he was also busy printing for Wolfe many pamphlets mentioned by Thomas Nashe in his attack on Gabriel Harvey. Although Nashe did not mention Windet, the bibliographical evidence connects Harvey's *A new letter of notable contents* (1593) to Barnabe Barnes's *Parthenophil and Parthenophe* (1593), Anthony Chute's *Beawtie dishonoured* (1593), and the anonymous *A true discourse* (1593), referred to by Harvey as "a new-new Pamflet." Nashe records that Chute, Barnes, Harvey, and John Thorius were all "*at* Wolfes, *where altogether at one time they lodged and boorded.*"

In addition to the few items printed for Harvey's associates, Windet printed a range of literature but, prior to 1606, only one play: Thomas Heywood's *Edward the fourth* (1599). In 1594 he printed his most popular book of poetry, Henry Willoby's *Willobie his avisa,* a book in the same literary tradition as the later work of Sir Thomas Overbury *A wife, now a widowe* (1614), being "The true Picture of a modest Maid, and of a chast and constant wife." Both the 1605 and 1609 editions claim to be "The fourth time corrected and Augmented," indicating that at least two other editions had appeared between 1594 and 1605. As the added apology (the augmentation) is dated 30 June 1596, the second edition seems likely to have appeared in that year; whilst the third was probably the edition that on 4 June 1599 was among the books "staid" but not burned by the Stationers' Company.

Other literary works printed during the 1590s included Richard Carew's translation of Torquato Tasso's *Godfrey of Bvlloigne* (1594), a reprint for John Wolfe (with false imprint) of Pietro Aretino's *Ragionamenti* (1594), Barnes's *A divine centvrie of spirituall sonnets* (1595), two editions (one lost) of Thomas Edwards's *Cephalus & Procris* (1595), two editions of Robert Southwell's *Saint Peters complaint* (both 1595), and George Chapman's translations of Homer's *Seauen bookes of the Iliades* (1598) and *Achilles shield* (1598). The typography was varied but broadly reflected a mixture of Continental (Aretino and Chapman) and English tastes.

The first mathematical book set at Windet's press had been the accounting examples in Oldcastle's *A briefe instruction and maner how to keepe bookes of accompts.* This was followed in 1590 by Laurentius Codomannus's *Chronographia* and two works by Thomas Hood: *The vse of the celestial globe in plano,* paid for by the dedicatee, John Lumley; and Hood's translation of Pierre de la Ramée's *The elementes of*

geometrie, to be sold "at the house of Francis Cook." Cooke's translation of *The principles of geometrie* by Georg Henisch followed in 1591. These were all slight volumes, but Windet's next mathematical book was far more substantial. On 23 July 1593 he entered for his copy Thomas Blundevile's *M. Blundeuile His Exercises* (1594), the first edition of which is a ninety-one-sheet quarto set in black letter with woodcut illustrations, foldout insertions, and movable parts. A bound copy in 1595 cost 4s. 6d. It was clearly intended for a different audience from that of the twopence and threepence translations of those works by Codomannus, de la Ramée, and Henisch. It was subsequently expanded to one hundred sheets and reprinted in 1597 and 1605 as well as in further editions by Stansby and Richard Bishop.

The Exercises provides a useful comparison with George Hartgyll's *Calendaria* entered by Windet on 30 August 1594 and printed with the text reset in English and Latin and with the numeric type reimposed. The *Calendaria* is a twenty-six-sheet folio consisting almost entirely of numeric tables. The scale of the tables seems likely to have dictated Windet's choice of format for the volume. Although a section of the *Exercises* is concerned with astronomy, the *Calendaria* is the only book printed by Windet to deal entirely with the positions of "the notablest fixed Starres." Its primary use was for navigation.

As well as the *Calendaria,* Windet printed two substantial historical works during 1594–1595: Giovanni Tommaso Minadoi's *The history of the warres betweene the Turks and the Persians* (translated by Abraham Hartwell) and Lancelot Voisin's *The historie of France,* translated by Sir Edward Hoby. The latter, like Blundeville's *Exercises,* confirms that Windet was not simply a trade printer but someone who printed fairly substantial volumes on his own behalf. Excluding the jobbing work, by the mid 1590s Windet was printing approximately one-third of his output (by title) for himself, a third for Wolfe, and the rest for other publishers.

The octavo or duo-decimo book of religious meditations was an important part of Windet's business. Such a work could vary in length from a few sheets to thirty and represented, together with the Bible and the psalm-book, one of the most popular forms of reading matter. Many of the devotional books that Windet printed went through numerous editions, although not all have survived. Many of them were printed or reprinted during 1596 and 1597, a fact that is suggestive of the economic and social conditions created by the failed harvests,

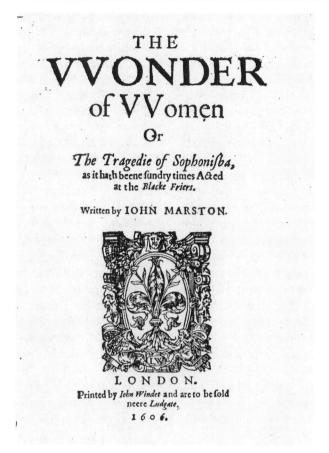

THE
VVONDER
of VVomen
Or
The Tragedie of Sophonisba,
as it hath beene sundry times Acted
at the *Blacke Friers.*

Written by IOHN MARSTON.

LONDON.
Printed by *Iohn Windet* and are to be sold
neere *Ludgate.*
1 6 0 6.

Title page for the 1606 quarto edition of a tragedy by
John Marston

plagues, and price inflation of those years. Such books were frequently read to pieces. For instance, only a proof of the dedication leaf to R. M.'s *The harbour of heavenly harts-ease,* dated 22 January 1597, survives. In the dedication the author asks his wife to "reade it, turn it, teare it with turning. . . ." Although the leaf is a quarto, the text is clearly set as a duo-decimo.

The popularity of the godly pocket-books at this time coincided with an attempt by Richard Sergier to pirate Bacon's *Essayes,* which Sergier entered on 23 January 1597. Bacon intervened at the Stationers' court to prevent its publication, and his *Essayes* was subsequently entered to Humphrey Hooper on 5 February. Windet was the printer. The *Essayes* adopted the format of the godly pocket-book, set as a seven-sheet octavo in pica roman and english italic. Windet was careful to design a volume that was typographically attractive. He frequently used the octavo format for books of this size, partly for ease of composition and binding but also for the intimacy that the format afforded the reader.

The first edition of Bacon's *Essayes* was typographically the most important book to emerge from Windet's press since Sidney's *Arcadia* and Hooker's *Lawes.* Its title page was unusual in being set to the left, rather than being centered. Within the text paragraph marks were used to separate the sententiae. These details seem to have been authorial features that Windet did not later feel constrained to follow: both the duo-decimo second and third editions have centered title pages, while the text of the third edition lacks the paragraph marks. The shift to a duo-decimo format also reduced the quantity of paper used. If Windet printed any further editions for Hooper, none appear to have survived.

Between 1597 and 1600 nearly forty percent of Windet's composition was concerned with five books; these, together with the psalm-books, provided a secure workload. The books concerned were the fifth book of Hooker's *Lawes,* the second edition of Blundevile's *Exercises,* Jan Huygen von Linschoten's *His discours of Voyages into ye Easte & West Indies* (1598), John Stow's *A survay of London*

(1598), and a translation of Philippe de Mornay's *Fowre bookes, of the institution, use and doctrine of the sacrament* (1600). Both the *Voyages* and de Mornay's *Fowre bookes* are substantial folios. There is also considerable evidence of shared printing at this time including *The policy of the Turkish empire* (1597), possibly by Giles Fletcher the elder, that Stansby had printed for him upon taking up his freedom. Valentine Simmes was the other printer, with Windet responsible for seven sheets.

By the end of the 1590s the Cross-Keys had become a substantial business, particularly owing to the income generated by psalm-books. So important was this to Windet that, on 27 February 1599, he entered into a bond of £500 with the partners of the privilege to retain "the woorkmanship . . . belonginge to y^t p'uilege." Every year he printed at least one quarto and one octavo edition; most years he printed the Psalms in folio, while the variety of small editors down to tricemo-duo emphasized his expertise in pocket-book material.

As well as printing another edition of St. Augustine's *The glasse of vaine-glorie* in 1600, Windet added several important new titles to his list of godly pocket-books. The first to appear was Christopher Sutton's *Disce mori,* entered to Wolfe on 21 August 1600. Sutton's *Godly meditations* followed on 13 January 1601. Six days later Wolfe assigned to Cuthbert Burby parts of his rights to these two books, as well as a part of his right to Sir John Hayward's *The sanctuarie of a troubled soule* (1601). It was the last entry in the Stationers' Register that Wolfe was to make. Sutton's *Disce vivere* (1602) did not appear until a year later, and it was entered in the Register on 7 November 1601 only to Cuthbert Burby. During the 1600s Windet acted as Burby's printer for these books; following Burby's death, however, Burby's widow married outside the company, and the copies passed into other hands.

For the years 1601 and 1602 Windet's output rate apparently declined to little more than 220 sheets, his lowest in a decade. Wolfe died sometime between 19 January and 26 March 1601, and Windet was appointed as executor of his considerable estate on 22 April 1601. As executor, Windet was in an advantageous position to acquire assets and privileges, if the Stationers' Company agreed. He used his influence in particular to continue serving as printer to the city of London, the position he had exercised in a de facto manner during Wolfe's lifetime.

Between 1603 and 1608 Windet's rate of composition returned to an average of approximately 280 sheets per annum. It is difficult, however, to give precise figures for these years, because the arrangements for printing psalm-books changed. With the issue of letters patent from King James I on 29 October 1603 and the acquisition of Richard Day's privileges by the Stationers' Company, the English Stock of the Company was formed. Although Windet continued to print psalm-books, his virtual monopoly was ended, and the printing of such work was shared with many others, particularly Richard Field. In addition to Field, other printers with whom Windet worked included Humphrey Lownes, William Jaggard, and Felix Kingston. These arrangements for psalm-book printing emphasize the extent to which standardized conventions could be and were adopted within the trade.

The most important development in Windet's business at this time appears to have resulted from the creation of the English Stock and the changes in the psalm-book privilege. On 2 April 1604 the first two music part books to be printed by Windet were entered in the Stationers' Register: Thomas Greaves's *Songes of sundrie kindes* (1604) and John Dowland's *Lachrimæ* (1604). Windet had, of course, set some music type in his psalm-books for many years, but this was the first time he had printed part-books.

Windet apparently did not print any elegies on the death of Elizabeth; only Radford Mavericke's *Three treatises religiously handled* (1603) addressed the death of the queen and the succession of James. Windet did, however, print several books on the succession, as well as James's own *A meditation upon . . . the first booke of the Chronicles of Kinges* (1603). For Matthew Law he shared the printing of Henry Petowe's *England's Caesar* (1603), and for Walter Burre he printed two editions of Robert Pricket's *A souldiours resolution* (1603). Belatedly in 1604 he also printed a collection of *Northerne poems* and Stephen Harrison's book of engravings, *The archs of triumph.*

Between 1604 and 1608 Windet printed or reprinted many small literary works, of which the most important were John Marston's *Sophonisba* (1606) and a reprint of William Shakespeare's *The history of Henry the fourth* (1608). During 1607 Windet also printed Samuel Daniel's *Certaine small workes,* a volume initially published without its dedications, which were later printed and inserted as a separate sheet. As this volume is a much-expanded and reorganized version of Daniel's *Certain small poems* (1605), the missing dedications may have been sent as a separate parcel to Windet, who overlooked it owing to other problems. Daniel, who had retired to the country, was in poor health and unable to see the volume through the press. In June 1607 Windet's house was affected by the plague, and within two weeks he lost his apprentice George Vokes, two other workmen (one possibly a nephew), and his wife.

By the end of 1608 Windet had been a master printer for twenty-five years. The death of his wife in 1607 had meant that his business could not continue within the family after his death. Stansby had worked for Windet for nineteen years, and the family connections were more ancient. The future of the business was consequently secured when Stansby became Windet's partner; this was done through Stansby's purchase of a large quantity of english roman type for the printing house.

As a consequence, the volume of composition produced by the printing house more than doubled in 1609–1610 and later tripled. The history of the printing house at this time therefore becomes the history of the early career of William Stansby as a master printer, for although Windet's name appeared in some of the imprints, many do not state the name of the printer at all. It seems likely that Stansby had primary responsibility for day-to-day operations of the business.

Windet made his will on 21 November 1610, and it was proved on 8 January 1611, although he had died before 17 December, for records on that day show that William Jaggard was chosen to be printer to the city of London in "steed of John Windett lately deceased." Under the terms of Windet's will, Stansby was given right of first refusal over the printing house, and Windet's sisters were the principal beneficiaries of the estate.

Windet was a printer of some integrity, and the quality of his work was consistently good. As an industrious printer, a faithful and active member of his parish, and a senior member of the Stationers' Company, he built the Cross-Keys into a prosperous and stable business. His successor was to bring to the Cross-Keys a new energy and sense of purpose, as Stansby's ambitions transformed the business into one of the most important printing houses in London of that time.

References:

M. B. Bland, "Jonson, Stansby and English Typography 1579–1623," 2 volumes, dissertation, Oxford University, 1995;

James K. Bracken, "William Stansby's Early Career," *Studies in Bibliography,* 38 (1985): 214–216;

D. W. Krummel, *English Music Printing 1553–1700* (London: Bibliographical Society, 1975).

— *Mark Bland*

John Wolfe

(Florence: circa 1576 – 1579; London: circa 1579 – 1600)

An early belief that John Wolfe was the son of printer Reyner Wolfe has been abandoned; Harry Sellers and Harry R. Hoppe believe that Wolfe, the son of fishmonger Thomas Wolfe, was born in London circa 1547. Because Wolfe was a common surname, other possible details about his birth have been proposed. One account, for instance, is that Wolfe may have sprung from a Continental family, perhaps one that had recently immigrated to England. Such a possibility would explain his predilection for publishing works often in foreign languages, works written by and for Continental Europeans.

John Wolfe's name first appears in the Stationers' Register under the date of 25 March 1562, when he was apprenticed for ten years to stationer John Day, with whom Wolfe said later that he had served only seven of those contracted years. In any case the next record of Wolfe's being in London is in 1579, when two anonymous books, *Sapientissimi regis Salomonis in Latinam* and *Clinton, Purser and Arnold: To Their Countrymen,* were printed for him. At this time he was probably a partner of the established stationer Henry Kirkham, whose shop was located at the Black Boy, opposite the middle door of St. Paul's Cathedral.

Between the end of his apprenticeship and this reappearance in London, Wolfe spent time in Italy, as the 1576 colophons of two short anonymous religious poems in Italian – *La historia e oratione di Santo Stefano Protomartire* and *Historia et vita di Santo Bernardino* – attest. Details about the nature of his involvement in their printing at Florence, the dates of his residence there, and his activities in that city are all unknown.

Back in London in 1582, Wolfe set up his shop in Distaff Lane, near the sign of the Castle, where he began to print works copyrighted to other men and to operate secret presses that had been hidden around London. Hoppe quotes at length Wolfe's narrative of one famous dispute with the Stationers' Company that "became a common talke in Alehouses tavernes and such like places." This dispute about Wolfe's printing of works copyrighted to other men resulted in formal action in 1583, when agents of the Stationers' Company

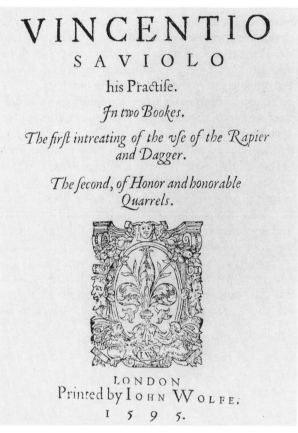

Title page for a manual on fencing and codes of gallantry, subjects of great interest to readers in Elizabethan England

raided his premises on 27 May. There they discovered three printing presses in operation and two more hidden elsewhere. Wolfe was jailed several times – on one occasion, he claimed, for "the space of twentie weekes together wythout bayle or mayneprise."

On 11 June 1583 Wolfe transferred from the Fishmongers' to the Stationers' Company, an event that was formalized on 1 July. Gaining official membership did not deter Wolfe from continuing to print pirated editions for another year, however. His old master, John Day, ordered a search to be made of Wolfe's print shop in May 1584, but Day died in July, and his son Richard made peace with Wolfe and his confederates. This agreement allowed Wolfe to print all the editions of the *Psalms in Metre* from 1585 to 1591. As

Woodcut from Abraham Hartwell's translation of Edward Lopez's A Report of the Kingdome of Congo *(1597),
one of many works on foreign travel and exploration that John Wolfe printed*

a member of the Stationers' Company, Wolfe became more respectable: on 9 April 1587 he became substitute beadle, and on 23 July he was confirmed in that position. He was to hold this position, and an office in Stationers' Hall, until 1598. In 1591 his place of business moved "over against the Great South Door" of St. Paul's Cathedral, and the following year it was located at St. Paul's Chain.

It is not possible to estimate the number of pamphlets and books that Wolfe produced, but annual numbers of his published titles – which range from lows of zero in 1580, two in 1579, and four in 1601, to a peak of fifty-four in 1590 – can provide a rough idea of the range of his yearly volume. Most of his works are typical of late-Elizabethan publishing, but some atypical ones stand out. His contribution to *l'arte dello stampare* (the art of printing) suggests that he followed the Italian Renaissance tradition of humanist printing.

The most startling group of his texts comprises books of Italian authorship that he printed in Italian, often with fictitious places of publication identified on the title pages. He offered these surreptitious books for sale both in London and abroad, notably at the Frankfurt book fair. The writing of introductory matter for these texts as well

as selecting, editing, proofreading, and translating them comprised the collaborative efforts of Wolfe and various Italian émigrés living in London. At times Wolfe contributed prefaces and received, in other prefaces, the grateful praise of editors.

These Italian texts include titles by notorious writers such as Pietro Aretino and Niccolò Machiavelli. Wolfe was the first to print works by the latter in England, as he issued *I discorsi* and *Il prencipe* in Italian in 1584, *Historie fiorentine* and *Dell'arte della guerra* in 1587, and *Lasino d'oro* in 1588. Wolfe's Italian titles also included essays addressing religious toleration: Jacobus Acontius's *Vna essortatione al timor di Dio* (1580); Francesco Betti's *Lettera,* which Wolfe reprinted in 1589; Giovanni Battista Aurelio's *Esamine di varii giudici* (1587); and Thomas Erastus's *Explicatio gravissimæ quæstionis, utrum excommunicatio* (1589). Other important texts that Wolfe printed in Italian include a collection of writings by Albericus Gentilis, the theorist of international law: *De juris interpretibus dialogi sex* (1582); *Lectionum & epistolarum quæ ad ius ciuile pertinent* (1583–1584), a four-book series; *Disputationum decas prima* (1587); and *De iure belli commentationes duæ* (1589). Wolfe also published Continental texts on foreign travel and exploration – for instance, Italian and English translations of Juan

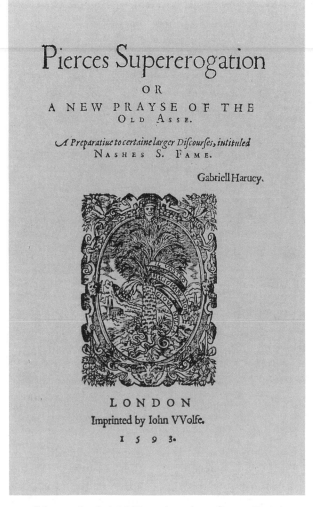

Title page for Gabriel Harvey's reply to Thomas Nashe's
Strange Newes, of the Intercepting certaine
Letters *(1592) in a pamphlet war that*
developed between the two writers

Gonzalez de Mendoza's history of China (*Dell' historia della China* in 1586 and *The Historie of the Great and Mightie Kingdome of China* in 1588) and Giovanni Tommaso Minadoi's *The History of the Warres betweene the Turkes and the Persians* (1595).

Wolfe's printing of works in foreign languages also included French texts, another important group he produced in the late 1580s and early 1590s. He published about 25 percent of all the news from France that appeared before 1600, and some of his simple pamphlets – which appeared in French or in both French and English and could thus be used in learning the French language – simply recounted exciting battlefield news. Important French texts in English also included Michel Hurault's *A Discourse upon the Present State of France* (1588), *An Excellent Discourse vpon the Now Present Estate of France* (1592), and *Antisixtus* (1590). The measured essays of other titles

involve reasoned assessment and espouse moderate positions on religious toleration. These essays reflect and encourage English hopes for the success of Henry of Navarre, who hoped to become, as Henry IV of France, a Protestant king. In 1593, however, he became a Catholic, and Wolfe no longer published French material after that year.

Another group of titles addresses religious, political, and literary moderation in England. As the respectable beadle of the Stationers' Company, Wolfe assisted the Elizabethan government in searching for the hidden press of the Puritan pamphleteer known as Martin Marprelate. Elizabeth's government had encouraged writers to answer Marprelate in his own intemperate style, but Wolfe printed a corrective to both sides in Gabriel Harvey's "An Advertisement for Pap-hatchet, and Martin Marprelate" (dated 1589 but extant only in

Pierces Supererogation, or a New Prayse of the Old Asse, 1593). Harvey apparently worked with Wolfe and helped, perhaps as an editor, not only in accurately printing timely texts but also in promoting what he regarded as significant literature. Wolfe printed books by Harvey on literary topics, and he printed Harvey's side of the stichomythic exchange with Thomas Nashe (1592–1596) as well as works of authors whom Harvey praised: the first three books of Edmund Spenser's *The Faerie Queene* (1590), Barnabe Barnes's *Parthenophil and Parthenophe* (1593), Thomas Churchyard's *Churchyards Challenge* (1593), Anthony Chute's *Beawtie Dishonoured* (1593), and Robert Southwell's *Saint Peters Complaynt* (1595).

John Wolfe printed his own work probably only until 1591. That year his printing materials apparently were passed to Robert Bourne, who actually printed the 1591–1593 titles usually credited to Wolfe's press. Wolfe continued to hold the title of printer to the city of London from 1593 to 1601, but in 1593 his printing materials were dispersed to Adam Islip and John Windet, the latter of whom printed most of Wolfe's publications thereafter. His last business addresses for the period 1598–1599 include Pope's Head Alley, Lombard Street, and near the Royal Exchange. The last record of his business activities is a document dated 1 April 1600 – a recognizance requiring Wolfe, who had already "begun to erecte and builde a Playhowse in Nightingale Lane near East Smithefeilde aforesaid contrary to her Majesties proclamacion and orders," to "procure sufficient warrant from the . . . Privye Councill."

John Windet was appointed executor of Wolfe's estate on 22 April 1601. At the time of his death, Wolfe and his wife, Alice, were living in the parish of St. Benet's, Paul's Wharf. On 5 October 1601, 14 April 1603, 27 April 1612, and 22 June 1612 Mrs. Wolfe transferred many of her husband's copyrights, many of which are for books no longer extant, to other stationers.

References:

H. S. Bennett, *English Books and Readers: 1558–1603* (Cambridge: Cambridge University Press, 1965);

E. K. Chambers, *The Elizabethan Stage* (Oxford: Clarendon Press, 1923);

Harry R. Hoppe, "John Wolfe, Printer and Stationer, 1579–1601," *Library,* fourth series 14 (December 1933): 241–288;

Clifford Chalmers Huffman, *Elizabethan Impressions: John Wolfe and His Press* (New York: AMS, 1988);

Harry Sellers, "Italian Books Printed in England Before 1640," *Library,* fourth series 5 (September 1924): 102–128;

M. A. Shaaber, *Some Forerunners of the Newspaper in England: 1476–1622* (Philadelphia: University of Pennsylvania Press, 1929);

Denis Woodfield, *Surreptitious Printing in England 1550–1640* (New York: Bibliographical Society of America, 1973);

Louis B. Wright, *Middle-Class Culture in Elizabethan England* (Ithaca, N.Y.: Cornell University Press, 1958).

– *Clifford Chalmers Huffman*

Reyner (Reginald) Wolfe

(London: circa 1543 – 1573)

Reyner (Reginald) Wolfe, royal printer to Edward VI for books in Latin, Greek, and Hebrew, was listed seventh among Philip and Mary's "Beloved and faithful lieges" in the charter of the Stationers' Company and was the first master of the company under Elizabeth I. He probably joined the livery of the Stationers' Company when it formed in 1560, and he served repeated terms as master of the company in 1560, 1564, 1567, and 1572. The *Dictionary of National Biography* describes Wolfe, a native of Strasbourg, as "a man of learning and a devoted Protestant" who "settled in England, apparently at Archbishop [Thomas] Cranmer's invitation."

During a presumed trip to the Frankfurt book market in 1530, Wolfe served as a courier between Thomas Tebold and Thomas Boleyn, earl of Wiltshire and a reputed patron of religious reform. Wolfe subsequently established his printing house, identified by the sign of the Brazen Serpent, in Paul's Cross Churchyard on land he purchased from Henry VIII following the demise of the monasteries. The first title Wolfe printed there was antiquarian John Leland's Latin poem on Thomas Wyatt, *Naeniae in mortem Thomae Viati equitis incomparabilis* (1542), and in 1549, after the bones had been removed from the adjoining grounds, Wolfe reportedly expanded his operation into the former charnel house. Peter Blayney writes that

> By 1543 he had set up the first (and only) printing house known to have existed in the Cross Yard, and was printing, publishing and selling books in a large property rented from the Bishop of London. By the time he died in 1573, Wolfe not only owned the shops on the site of the charnel chapel, but also held leases for (at least) all the properties between those shops and the Bishop's Head. All told, his known holdings formed a continuous stretch of more than 120 feet of the best bookselling frontage in England.

Wolfe and his business flourished during the reigns of four Tudor monarchs. During the rule of Henry VIII, Wolfe's house established a reputation for printing works in classical languages – works such as Saint John Chrysostom's *Contra eos qui novilunia observant* (1543), which he printed in both Greek and Latin. Shortly after Edward VI had ascended the throne in 1547, an entry in the *Calendar of the Patent Rolls* records that Wolfe received from him a patent for the "office of the kings typographer and bookseller in Latin, Greek and Hebrew." This position entitled him to print not only all books in these languages but also "charts and maps useful or necessary to the king and his countries in those tongues."

In his official capacity he also printed for the Church of England *Articles to be inquired of in the visitation to be had in the byshopricke of Norwyche, now vacant, in the fourth yere of our most drad souerayn lorde Edwarde the sixte . . . by the moste Reuerend father in God, Thomas Archebyshop of Cantorbery* (1549) as well as Bishop Nicholas Ridley's *Iniunctions geven in the visitation of the reverende father in God, Nycolas byshoppe of London* (1550). The most lucrative of the titles conferred by this patent was that for William Lily's *A short introduction of grammar generally to be used in the Kynges Maiesties dominions* (1548), which was to appear in twelve editions between 1558 and 1570. During Elizabeth's reign this patent also gave Wolfe the right to print Alexander Nowell's *Catechismus* in Latin (1570) and also in Greek (1573). In granting the reversion of this patent to John Cawood upon Wolfe's death, Mary I upheld the patent for Wolfe on 17 July 1558, when she granted to Wolfe and his deputies the right "to search the shops and houses of booksellers, typographers or others in the city and suburbs of London or elsewhere within the realm and to seize all such books as they shall find printed or put to sale without his license."

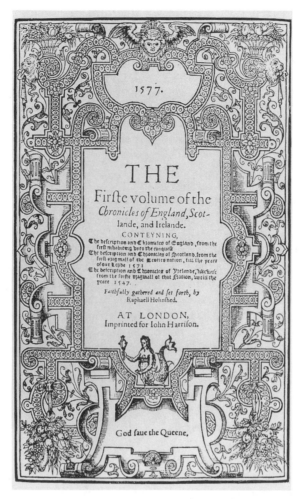

Title page for the first volume of Raphael Holinshed's
Chronicles *(1577). Wolfe's work on compiling*
materials for this project was cut short by his
death in 1573. It was completed by Holinshed
and printed by Henry Bynneman.

Wolfe also obtained another grant from Mary for the assignment to himself and John Gawyn of "the king and queen's estate and interest" in the "manor or sit of the dissolved monastery of Kyrstall alias Kyrkestall and Arthington and of land belonging thereto." This was a property that had been seized from Wolfe's former patron, Cranmer, "before he was attainted of high treason and afterwards burned for heresy." While it might be tempting to suspect that Wolfe found favor with Mary by subscribing to her Catholic agenda, this is most unlikely. A year after she became queen, Elizabeth granted to Thomas Cranmer, son of the former archbishop, rent from the "crown interest in the manor of Kyrstall" that had been "reserved under a grant to John Gawin and Reginald Woulfe" during the reign of Philip and Mary.

Wolfe is most often remembered for the publishing venture cut short by his death in 1573 – Raphael Holinshed's *Chronicles of England Scotland and Ireland* (1577). According to Holinshed's dedication to William Cecil, Lord Burghley, in the first edition of the *Chronicles,* Wolfe had been collecting materials, including maps, for a "Universal Cosmographie" that had proceeded so far that "little wanted to the accomplishment of that long promised worke" when "it pleased God to call him to his mercie after xxv yeares trauell spent therein." Undoubtedly Wolfe's project had been prompted by his exclusive right to print maps and charts, although the *Chronicles,* as completed by Holinshed and printed by Henry Bynneman, focused solely on the British Isles and omitted maps.

Wolfe's press also produced other works related to antiquarian interests. Leland, appointed as the king's antiquary in 1533 by Henry VIII, wrote several poems in honor of the king and his family, and Wolfe printed these as well as *Assertio inclytissimi Arturij Regis Britanniae* (1544) and *KUKVELOV* αϭμα: *Cygnea cantio* (1545). Wolfe also printed Archbishop Cranmer's *A defence of the true and catholike doctrine of the sacrament of the body and bloud of our sauiour Christ* (1550) and *An answer of the Most Reuerend Father in God Thomas Archebyshop of Canterburye, primate of all Englande and metropolitane vnto a crafty and sophisticall cauillation deuised by Stephen Gardiner doctour of law* (1551). After Elizabeth had become queen, Wolfe was to print for the Church of England *Aduertisments, partly for due order in the publique administration of common prayers and usinge the holy Sacramentes, and partly for the apparrell of all persons ecclesiasticall* (1565?) – the official position in the vestiarian controversy – and Matthew Parker's *An admonition to all such as shall intende hereafter to enter the state of matrimony godly, and agreeably to lawes* (1571) as well as Parker's *Articles to be enquired of within the dioces of Canterbury, in the metropoliticall and ordinary visitation of the moste Reuerend father in God, Matthew* (1573).

When Wolfe died in 1573, he left his entire operation to his wife, Johanne or Jone, who published one book before her death a year later. Her will, dated 1 July 1574 and proved 20 July, reveals much about Wolfe's printing house, interests, and heirs. The estate Johanne bequeathed included all the buildings "knowen by the signe of the Brasen Sarpent" as well as other "Tenements yardes and Romes with their appurtenances scituate in Pawles church yarde" in addition to the "presse, letters, furniture coppies and other necessarie instruments and tooles being with in my prynting howse or belong-ing vnto the same for concerning or belonging to the arte of prynting." Substantial assets existed to supply annuities for a son, Henry, two daughters (Susan Hun and Elizabeth Nevenson), and a sister. Her principal heirs and executors were her son, Robert Wolfe, and son-in-law, John Hun, a haberdasher by trade. Another daughter, Mary, the wife of stationer John Harrison, received household goods, and her two children, Reginald and Johan, received plate.

Besides providing for her own family, Johanne's will included the extended family of printers associated with her husband. John Shepperd was given the right of first refusal to lease the Brazen Serpent, a right that he apparently exercised. Lucas Harrison received a life estate in "that tenement, shoppe rowmes and partes and parcells of the saide Chappell" that Wolfe had bought from Henry VIII. Francis Coldocke received a twenty-year lease on the rooms he occupied in the chapel. Henry Bynneman, Wolfe's former apprentice, acquired much of the stock of Wolfe's letters and devices; after Wolfe had died, Shepperd, Harrison, and Bynneman were often to work together.

References:

Peter Blayney, *The Bookshops in Paul's Cross Churchyard* (London: Bibliographical Society, 1990);

E. W. Ives, *Anne Boleyn* (Oxford: Blackwell, 1986);

Henry R. Plomer, *Abstracts of the Wills of English Printers and Stationers from 1492 to 1630* (London: Blades, East & Blades for the Bibliographical Society, 1903).

– Cyndia Susan Clegg

Wynkyn de Worde

(Westminster and London: circa 1491 – 1535)

Wynkyn de Worde's huge production of more than eight hundred separate editions covering almost four hundred titles surpasses that of any other English printer before 1600. Too often dismissed simply as the foreman who had the good fortune to inherit William Caxton's business, de Worde was in his own right an influential figure in the establishment and development of printing technology and of the commercial infrastructures likely to sustain a profitable metropolitan printing business in England. Through his efforts and the example he set for rival printers, the growing reading public of the early sixteenth century had easy and increasingly cheap access to a range of texts, some of proven appeal and others especially sought out or commissioned in response to market demand: English poetry by Geoffrey Chaucer, John Lydgate, and contemporary writers such as John Skelton and Stephen Hawes; religious manuals and devotional prose and verse; grammar books and treatises on education; romances; encyclopedias and shorter informative works of a more practical kind; and plays, satires, and comic stories.

Little is known of de Worde's early life. A native either of Woerden (south of Amsterdam) or of Wörth (then in the duchy of Lorraine), he apparently learned the printing trade and became associated with Caxton in Cologne or in Bruges, where Caxton's first English books were printed. Caxton moved his business to Westminster around 1476, and de Worde seems to have come with him, for he appears in Westminster records from 1479, when his English wife Elizabeth is named as the lessee of property in the sanctuary of the abbey. His name is recorded variously as Winandus van Worden, Johannes or Jan Wynkyn, and Wynkyn de Worde, the last of which was to appear most frequently in the colophons to the books he printed.

Although he is never mentioned in Caxton's writings, de Worde clearly had an important position in Caxton's business. At the time of Caxton's death in 1491 or 1492, de Worde was able to continue production in the shop that Caxton had rented near the Chapter House at Westminster and gradually, after some apparent litigation over Caxton's will was settled, to expand the range of titles printed at the shop and to develop the technical and commercial expertise to ensure the success of the enterprise. In 1496 he signed papers of denization enabling him to hold property in his own name, and in 1500 he moved his premises to a location on the main route between Westminster and London, at the sign of the Sun in Fleet Street, near St. Bride's church. His wife Elizabeth had died in 1498, and a Juliane de Worde, probably a second wife, was dead by July 1500.

De Worde's move seems to have brought commercial and civic prosperity. By 1509 he was also selling his books from a shop at the sign of Our Lady of Pity in St. Paul's churchyard, the center of the London book trade, and by 1524 a tax assessment that had calculated his worth at £201 11s. 1d. marked him among the wealthier inhabitants of St. Bride's parish. His will, dated 5 June 1534 and proved 19 January 1535, described him as a "citizen and stationer" and provided for a circle of interconnected household, business, and parish acquaintances. Civic records document the existence of a William Wynkyn, stationer, and a Richard Wynkyn, of St. Bride's parish – both of whom may have been members of his family.

In terms of the authors and works he favored, certain patterns emerge throughout de Worde's ca-

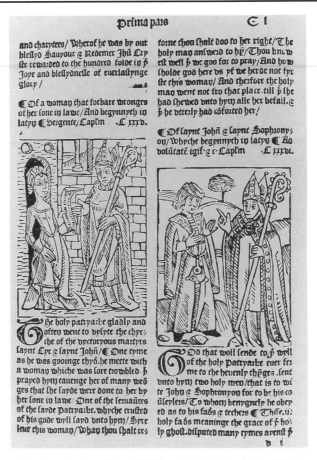

*Page from the first edition of William Caxton's translation of Saint
Jerome's* Vitas Patrum *(1495), illustrated and printed
by de Worde*

reer. During the 1490s he fulfilled responsibilities to the memory of his former master, as he printed Caxton's translation of Saint Jerome's *Vitas Patrum* (Lives of the Fathers, 1495) and produced new editions of well-known texts such as Chaucer's *The Canterbury Tales* (1498) and Sir Thomas Malory's *Morte Darthur* (1498), both of which Caxton had printed. At the same time de Worde established his credentials by printing new pieces such as John Trevisa's English translation of Bartholomaeus Anglicus's encyclopedic *De Proprietatibus Rerum* (The Properties of Things, 1495), a work that had circulated widely in manuscript form.

His move to Fleet Street reflected de Worde's keen sense of the location of his best market. He developed new areas of interest – particularly in grammar books, with reprints of established favorites such as John of Garland's *Equivoca* (1499) and *Synonyma* (1510) and new handbooks by schoolmasters such as John Stanbridge. Another new interest lay in the printing of contemporary religious writing, sometimes in the form of translations – such as Andrew Chertsey's versions of the anonymous *The*

crafte to lyue well and to dye well (1505) that de Worde may have commissioned. Romances such as the anonymous *Appolonius of Tyre* (1510) and satiric and antifeminist texts such as the translation of Antoine de la Sale's *The Fifteen Joys of Marriage* (circa 1507), works of a kind not found among Caxton's production, comprised other new interests.

As he produced more of such work at his shop, de Worde abandoned the production of texts on subjects that represented special interests of others – interests such as indulgences and law books, which were favored by Richard Pynson. De Worde also gradually shifted from the printing of large folio volumes to the production of smaller quarto books, and he seems to have instituted a program for reprinting successful titles. Schoolbooks, particularly the grammars of John Stanbridge and Robert Whittinton, became staples, and they represented almost one-third of his production. Yet there was time for innovation, as de Worde printed the anonymous *Hyckescorner* (circa 1515), among the earliest of printed English plays to survive. He went on to print further in-

334

Page from Robert Wakefield's Oratio de Laudibus Trium
Linguarum *(1528), the first book printed in England to
use italic type and Hebrew and Arabic characters*

terludes and in the early 1530s began to print new
and cheaper octavo editions of schoolbooks.

In the design and production of his books
de Worde diplomatically combined conservatism and experimentation. His first printer's device came from Caxton, and later ones, although of a new design, deliberately retained
Caxton's initials to remind readers of de Worde's
early connection with him. In the 1490s he used
types inherited from Caxton, but as they gradually wore out, he replaced them with new ones
of distinctive French design. Following his move
from Westminster to Fleet Street, some of de
Worde's materials were discarded and came into
the hands of other printers in London and the
provinces, but until his death he continued to use
one of the textura types that he retained, and it
appeared with great frequency in all of the kinds
of work he printed. De Worde may have maintained a foundry on his premises. He was using
roman type by 1520 and italic type by 1528, and
he also printed words from Arabic, Hebrew, and
Greek alphabets in characters cut from wood. The
first surviving example of musical notes printed in
an English book appeared in his 1495 edition of
John Trevisa's translation of Ranulphus
Higden's *Polychronicon*.

In supplying illustrations for his books, de
Worde again used materials that he had inherited
from Caxton to initiate what would become a
more innovative practice. He used some of
Caxton's woodcuts into the early sixteenth century, but he soon accumulated more extensive series of these woodcuts, some of which — such as
those for the *Vitas Patrum* and *De Proprietatibus
Rerum* — he commissioned from a cutter who was
to work for him for many years. Eventually de
Worde's estimated stock of one thousand blocks
that he used was sufficiently varied to meet most
needs, and he only rarely ordered new cuts. He
clearly understood the appeal of illustration, and
he supplied even his shorter books with title-page
woodcuts. He was among the first English printers to supply typographic ornament as well as to
experiment with the design of title pages and with
illustrations from metal blocks. Some of his books
were printed on vellum, and he seems to have
maintained, perhaps on the business premises, the

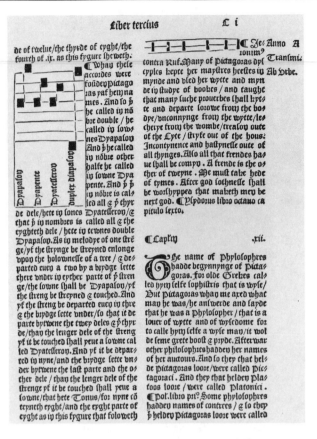

Page from the second edition of Ranulph Higden's
Policronicon *(1495), which includes the first
musical notes printed in England*

services of a skilled binder who had worked for Caxton.

De Worde's relations with other English and Continental printers were complex. To some extent he competed with Pynson: he printed rival editions of popular works such as *The Kalendar of Shepherds* (1508), but he collaborated with Pynson in 1507 on the *Royal Book* and the *Golden Legend* and seems to have shared his own and Caxton's woodcuts with Pynson. De Worde's dispersal of unwanted type and woodcuts to Julian Notary and to the York printer Hugo Goes reveals a collegiality that also distinguished his collaborations in the 1520s and 1530s with younger printers such as John Skot, John Butler, and John Bydell. De Worde's joint ventures with Parisian printers at various times provided service books and other works for the English market, and such efforts were probably connected with his activities as an importer of Continental books. Such business interests necessitated his connections with metropolitan booksellers such as Michael Morin and with more vaguely discernible networks for marketing books in provincial centers

such as Oxford and Bristol, where de Worde seems to have maintained retailing contacts among stationers.

De Worde's circle of acquaintances helped him to acquire texts to be printed and perhaps to underwrite individual ventures or promising markets. Among those who acted as patrons were Roger Thorney, the London mercer named in the epilogues to *Polychronicon* and *De Proprietatibus Rerum,* and the mother of Henry VII, Lady Margaret Beaufort, who in 1494 asked de Worde to print Walter Hylton's *Scala perfeccōnis* (Scale of Perfection, 1494). Perhaps in emulation of Pynson, who occasionally claimed that he had been directed by Henry VII or by Lady Margaret, de Worde styled himself as printer to Lady Margaret in certain books printed in 1509, just before her death, and her name is also invoked in prefatory material in some of his other productions. The connections of poet Stephen Hawes with the court of Henry VII and with Lady Margaret may explain de Worde's monopoly on the publication of his works.

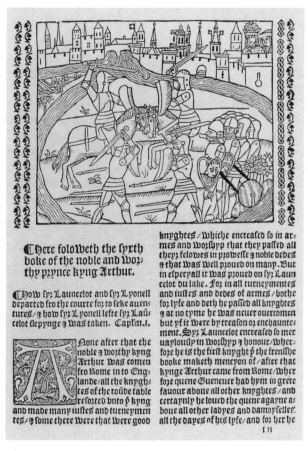

Page from de Worde's 1529 edition of Sir Thomas Malory's
Morte Darthur

Other patrons came from the nobility or from the church and religious orders. At times de Worde worked, as Pynson had, for Syon Abbey: he printed the 1519 edition of *The Orchard of Syon* at the "great cost" of Richard Sutton, its steward, and in 1525 de Worde provided for the Bridgetine nuns sixty copies of *The Image of Love,* attributed to John Ryckes, a work later recalled because of its supposed heretical content. The printing of works by bishops John Fisher, Richard Foxe, Richard Fitzjames, and John Alcock is further evidence of de Worde's reliance on an interconnected circle of patrons, customers, and suppliers of texts. Many of his books were prepared, edited, or translated by individuals such as Chertsey, Robert Copland, and Henry Watson, freelance writers and also (in some cases) printers who maintained their relations with him for many years. Chertsey seems to have specialized in translations of popular French devotional works, whereas Copland, who sometimes furnished prologues with the material he supplied, covered a more comprehensive range – from his translation

of Pierre Gringore's antifeminist *The Complaynte of them that ben to late maryed* (1505?) to the romance of *Helyas Knyght of the Swanne* (1512).

A little evidence has survived to illuminate the detail of de Worde's procedures in acquiring copy and preparing it for print. Many of his books were new editions of works first printed by Caxton or by contemporaries in London, Paris, or Antwerp. Among these is de Worde's 1496 edition of *The Book of St. Albans,* a compendium of information on heraldry, hunting, and hawking, which had been printed by an anonymous Saint Albans printer. The copy that de Worde used to set his own edition is now held by the British Library; he added to it a treatise on angling. In printing other works, de Worde was making available texts that had established circulations as manuscripts or, in some cases (as with contemporary religious writings and poetry, or with certain grammar books), was publishing entirely new texts. In reprinting *The Canterbury Tales* in 1498 de Worde, or the editor he employed, used Caxton's second edition of the work, but he also consulted at least one manuscript copy (now lost), which provided better readings.

Surviving copy from which some of his books were set came from metropolitan contacts such as Thorney, who provided a manuscript of Lydgate's *Storye of Thebes* (1496?) and probably also one of Lydgate's *Le Assemble de Dyeus* (The Assembly of Gods, 1498), and mercer John Colyns, who supplied the romance *Ipomydon* (circa 1522). De Worde did not restrict himself solely to works of London provenance or circulation, however; his text of *De Proprietatibus Rerum* (now in Columbia University Library) came from the midlands, and he also printed the northern alliterative poem *The Quatrefoil of Love* (1510?) and the writings of certain northern mystics.

Although often criticized for thoughtlessly reproducing errors in or making omissions from his setting copy, de Worde at times seriously attended to the modernizing of archaic texts. His 1498 edition of *The Canterbury Tales,* for example, modernizes the spelling and vocabulary of Caxton's edition and translates Latin rubrics into English. The explanatory or hortatory material supplied with some of his texts – such as in an epilogue to Chaucer's *Troilus and Criseyde* (1517), which affirms that "There is no woman, I think, heaven under / That can be true, and that is wonder" – is mainly anonymous and was probably provided by freelance writers such as Copland and Watson. Unlike Caxton, de Worde does not seem to have been interested in writing his own prologues and epilogues.

After his death in 1535 de Worde's business was continued by his former apprentices, James Gaver and John Byddell. Many of the works de Worde had published remained in print in various forms throughout the sixteenth century, and they continued to appeal to markets that he had cultivated. Critical opinion – resting on scholarship that is in pressing need of revision – has tended to condemn him for having pursued commercial success rather than literary ideals and has interpreted the range of his production as a sign of his disinterest in the quality of the material he printed. Yet his enterprise and his innovations were of great significance to the English book trade and, in their contribution to the spread of literacy, to the development of British culture.

References:

H. S. Bennett, *English Books and Readers, 1475–1557* (Cambridge: Cambridge University Press, 1969);

N. F. Blake, "Wynkyn de Worde: The Early Years," *Gutenberg Jahrbuch,* 46 (1971): 62–66;

Blake, "Wynkyn de Worde: The Later Years," *Gutenberg Jahrbuch,* 47 (1972): 128–138;

Mary C. Erler, "Wynkyn de Worde's Will: Legatees and Bequests," *Library,* sixth series 10 (June 1988): 107–121;

Edward Hodnett, *English Woodcuts, 1480–1535* (Oxford: Oxford University Press, 1973);

James Moran, *Wynkyn de Worde: Father of Fleet Street* (London: Wynkyn de Worde Society, 1976);

Henry R. Plomer, *Wynkyn de Worde and His Contemporaries from the Death of Caxton to 1535* (London: Grafton, 1925).

– Julia Boffey

Checklist of Further Readings

Albright, Evelyn May. *Dramatic Publication in England, 1580–1640: A Study of Conditions Affecting Content and Form of Drama*. New York: Modern Language Association of America, 1927.

Ames, Joseph, William Herbert, and Thomas Frognall Dibdin. *Typographical Antiquities; or, the History of Printing in England, Scotland, and Ireland: Containing Memoirs of Our Ancient Printers, and a Register of the Books Printed by Them*. 1810–1819. Reprint, Hildesheim, Germany: Olms, 1969.

Bennett, H. S. *English Books & Readers, 1475 to 1557: Being a Study in the History of the Book Trade from Caxton to the Incorporation of the Stationers' Company*. Cambridge: Cambridge University Press, 1952.

Bennett. *English Books & Readers, 1558 to 1603: Being a Study in the History of the Book Trade in the Reign of Elizabeth I*. Cambridge: Cambridge University Press, 1965.

Bennett. *English Books & Readers 1603–1640: Being a Study in the History of the Book Trade in the Reigns of James I and Charles I*. Cambridge: Cambridge University Press, 1970.

Blagden, Cyprian. *The Stationers' Company, 1403–1959*. Cambridge, Mass.: Harvard University Press, 1960.

Blayney, Peter W. M. *The Bookshops in Paul's Cross Churchyard*. London: Bibliographical Society, 1990.

Blayney. *The First Folio of Shakespeare*. Washington, D.C.: Folger Library Publications, 1991.

Blayney. *The Texts of King Lear and Their Origins, Volume I: Nicholas Okes and the First Quarto*. Cambridge: Cambridge University Press, 1982.

Clair, Colin. *A History of Printing in Britain*. New York: Oxford University Press, 1966.

Darton, F. J. Harvey, and Brian Alderson. *Children's Books in England: Five Centuries of Social Life*. Cambridge: Cambridge University Press, 1982.

Duff, E. Gordon. *A Century of the English Book Trade: Short Notices of All Printers, Stationers, Book-binders, and Others Connected with It from the Issue of the First Dated Book in 1457 to the Incorporation of the Company of Stationers in 1557*. London: Bibliographical Society, 1905.

Feather, John. *A Dictionary of Book History*. London: Croom Helm, 1986.

Feather. *A History of British Publishing*. London: Croom Helm, 1988.

Feather. *Publishing, Piracy and Politics: An Historical Study of Copyright in Britain*. London & New York: Mansell, 1994.

Ferguson, W. Craig. *Pica Roman Type in Elizabethan England*. Aldershot, U.K.: Scolar, 1989; Brookfield, Vt.: Gower, 1989.

Gaskell, Philip. *A New Introduction to Bibliography*. Oxford: Clarendon Press, 1972.

Glaister, Geoffrey A. *Glaister's Glossary of the Book: Terms Used in Papermaking, Printing, Bookbinding, and Publishing with Notes on Illuminated Manuscripts and Private Presses*. 1960. Revised, Berkeley: University of California Press, 1979.

Greg, W. W. *A Bibliography of the English Printed Drama to the Restoration*. London: Bibliographical Society at the Oxford University Press, 1970.

Greg. *Some Aspects and Problems of London Publishing between 1550 and 1650*. Oxford: Clarendon Press, 1956.

Handover, P. M. *Printing in London from 1476 to Modern Times: Competitive Practice and Technical Invention in the Trade of Book and Bible Printing, Periodical Production, Jobbing, Etc*. Cambridge, Mass.: Harvard University Press, 1960.

Hills, Richard L. *Papermaking in Britain, 1488–1988: A Short History*. London & Atlantic Highlands, N.J.: Athlone Press, 1988.

Hinman, Charlton. *The Printing and Proof-reading of the First Folio of Shakespeare*. Oxford: Clarendon Press, 1963.

Judge, Cyril Bathurst. *Elizabethan Book-pirates*. Cambridge, Mass.: Harvard University Press, 1934.

Kidson, Frank. *British Music Publishers, Printers and Engravers; London, Provincial, Scottish, and Irish: From Queen Elizabeth's Reign to George the Fourth's, with Select Bibliographical Lists of Musical Works Printed and Published within That Period*. New York: Blom, 1967.

Krummel, Donald William. *English Music Printing, 1553–1700*. London: Bibliographical Society, 1975.

McCoy, Ralph E. *Freedom of the Press: An Annotated Bibliography*. Carbondale: Southern Illinois University Press, 1968.

McCoy. *Freedom of the Press: An Annotated Bibliography: Second Supplement, 1978–1992*. Carbondale: Southern Illinois University Press, 1993.

McCoy. *Freedom of the Press: A Bibliocyclopedia: Ten-year Supplement (1967–1977)*. Carbondale: Southern Illinois University Press, 1979.

McKenzie, D. F. *The Cambridge University Press, 1696–1712: A Bibliographical Study*. Cambridge: Cambridge University Press, 1966.

McKenzie. "Printers of the Mind: Some Notes on Bibliographical Theories and Printing-house Practices," *Studies in Bibliography*, 22 (1969): 1–75.

McKerrow, Ronald B. *A Dictionary of Printers and Booksellers in England, Scotland and Ireland, and of Foreign Printers of English Books 1557–1640*. London: Bibliographical Society, 1910.

McKerrow. *An Introduction to Bibliography for Literary Students*. 1927. Reprint, Oxford: Clarendon Press, 1967.

Miller, Edwin Haviland. *The Professional Writer in Elizabethan England: A Study of Nondramatic Literature*. Cambridge, Mass.: Harvard University Press, 1959.

Mumby, Frank Arthur, and Ian Norrie. *Publishing and Bookselling*. 1930. Revised, London: Cape, 1974.

Myers, Robin. *The British Book Trade from Caxton to the Present Day: A Bibliographical Guide Based on the Libraries of the National Book League and St. Bride Institute*. London: Deutsch, in association with the National Book League, 1973.

Myers. *The Stationer's Company Archive: An Account of the Records 1554–1984*. Winchester: St. Paul's Bibliographies, 1990.

Myers and Michael Harris. *Aspects of Printing from 1600*. Oxford: Oxford Polytechnic Press, 1987.

Myers and Harris. *Author/Publisher Relations during the Eighteenth and Nineteenth Centuries*. Oxford: Oxford Polytechnic Press, 1983.

Myers and Harris. *Censorship & the Control of Print in England and France 1600–1910*. Winchester: St. Paul's Bibliographies, 1992.

Myers and Harris. *Economics of the British Booktrade, 1605–1939*. Alexandria, Va.: Chadwyck-Healey, 1985.

Myers and Harris. *Spreading the Word: The Distribution Networks of Print 1550–1850*. Winchester: St. Paul's Bibliographies, 1990.

Plant, Marjorie. *The English Book Trade: An Economic History of the Making and Sale of Books*. London: Allen & Unwin, 1939.

Plomer, Henry R. *A Dictionary of the Booksellers and Printers Who Were at Work in England, Scotland and Ireland from 1641 to 1667*. London: Bibliographical Society, 1907.

Plomer. *A Dictionary of the Printers and Booksellers Who Were at Work in England, Scotland and Ireland from 1668 to 1725*. Oxford: Bibliographical Society, 1922.

Plomer. *A Short History of English Printing, 1476–1898*. London: Kegan, Paul, Trench, Trubner, 1900.

Pollard, Alfred W., and Gilbert R. Redgrave. *A Short-Title Catalogue of Books Printed in England, Scotland, & Ireland and of English Books Printed Abroad, 1475–1640*. 1926, Revised and enlarged by W. A. Jackson, F. S. Ferguson, and Katharine F. Pantzer. 3 volumes. London: Bibliographical Society, 1976–1991.

Reed, Talbot Baines. *A History of the Old English Letter Foundries*. London: Stock, 1887. Revised and enlarged by A. F. Johnson. London: Faber & Faber, 1952.

Rostenberg, Leona. *Literary, Political, Scientific, Religious & Legal Publishing; Printing and Publishing in England, 1551–1700: Twelve Studies*. New York: Franklin, 1965.

Simpson, Percy. *Proof-reading in the Sixteenth, Seventeenth and Eighteenth Centuries*. London: Oxford University Press, 1935.

Spufford. Margaret. *Small Books and Pleasant Histories: Popular Fiction and Its Readership in Seventeenth-century England*. Athens: University of Georgia Press, 1981.

Watt, Tessa. *Cheap Print and Popular Piety, 1550–1640*. Cambridge: Cambridge University Press, 1991.

Woodfield, Denis B. *Surreptitious Printing in England, 1550–1640*. New York: Bibliographical Society of America, 1973.

Wright, Louis B. *Middle-class Culture in Elizabethan England*. Chapel Hill: University of North Carolina Press, 1935.

Contributors

Cumulative Index

Dictionary of Literary Biography, Volumes 1-170
Dictionary of Literary Biography Yearbook, 1980-1995
Dictionary of Literary Biography Documentary Series, Volumes 1-14

Cumulative Index

DLB before number: *Dictionary of Literary Biography,* Volumes 1-170
Y before number: *Dictionary of Literary Biography Yearbook,* 1980-1995
DS before number: *Dictionary of Literary Biography Documentary Series,* Volumes 1-14

A

B

Cumulative Index

Cumulative Index

M

Q

R

W

ISBN 0-8103-9933-4